T0324138

This book, as a multidisciplinary compendium, tells the story of creating and delivering distinct value in emerging economies. It offers insightful lessons to businesses, students, and the general public through its intriguing and comprehensive chapters. Enjoy your reading. You are assured of an enriching learning experience as you surf through the pages of this compelling book.

Professor Justice Nyigmah Bawole
Professor of Public Administration and Management
Dean, University of Ghana Business School

Delivering Distinctive Value in Emerging Economies: Efficient and Sustainably Responsible Perspectives from Management Researchers and Practitioners is a comprehensive text that explores a diverse range of theoretical as well as practical viewpoints for the future of emerging economies. Written in a style that is accessible to readers of all proficiencies and expertise, I trust that this book will substantially benefit students, academics, practitioners, and even casual readers.

Dr. Calvin W. H. Cheong
Senior Lecturer in Finance
Programme Chair, Sunway University, Malaysia

Emerging economies have become an opportune interest of practitioners, entrepreneurs and policy makers worldwide. Hence, a contemporary text which explores how to create and deliver distinct value in these economies is a must a read. I am hopeful the contributions would spur the necessary debates and discussions in the spaces which can engineer a positive change in emerging economies. Let this book inspire you to do more for emerging economies.

Bryan Acheampong MP
Honorable Member of Parliament for Abetifi Constituency
Chairman, Foreign Affairs Committee
Member, Defence and Interior Committee
Republic of Ghana

Delivering Distinctive Value in Emerging Economies

Efficient and Sustainably Responsible Perspectives from Management Researchers and Practitioners

EDITORS

Richard Boateng
University of Ghana, Accra, Ghana

Sheena Lovia Boateng
University of Ghana, Accra, Ghana

Thomas Anning-Dorson
University of the Witwatersrand, South Africa

FOREWORDS BY

Professor Justice Nyigmah Bawole
University of Ghana Business School

Dr. Calvin W.H. Cheong
Sunway University, Malaysia

Bryan Acheampong MP,
Honorable Member of Parliament for Abetifi Constituency

Routledge
Taylor & Francis Group
A PRODUCTIVITY PRESS BOOK

First published 2022
by Routledge
605 Third Avenue, New York, NY 10158

and by Routledge
2 Park Square, Milton Park, Abingdon, Oxon, OX14 4RN

Routledge is an imprint of the Taylor & Francis Group, an informa business

Library of Congress Cataloging-in-Publication Data
A catalog record for this book has been requested

ISBN: 978-0-367-71471-0 (hbk)
ISBN: 978-0-367-71473-4 (pbk)
ISBN: 978-1-003-15221-7 (ebk)

DOI: 10.4324/9781003152217

Typeset in Garamond
by Apex CoVantage, LLC

To the current and next generation of practitioners, policy makers and students in emerging economies and beyond.

Contents

PART VI MAKING HIGHER EDUCATION MORE RESPONSIVE

Foreword

This book, as a multidisciplinary compendium, tells the story of creating and delivering distinct value in emerging economies. Its six enriching parts are Beyond COVID-19, Doing Business in Emerging Economies, Managing Consumer Expectations and Behavior, Developing Resilient Economies and Institutions, Innovation and Healthcare, and Making Higher Education More Responsive. This book will be invaluable to everyone—academics, business executives, entrepreneurs, public sector officials, healthcare practitioners, social workers, and higher education administrators interested in emerging economies.

The book draws on the deep insight and experience of management researchers and practitioners across different countries and disciplines to create a nexus of knowledge. It journeys through the new strategies, best practices, and lessons learned from their successes and failures in addressing or circumventing institutional challenges in emerging economies. It highlights the need for institutions and businesses to understand the dynamics in their contextual environment and adopt strategies that embrace the new normal. Further, it calls for inclusivity, recognition of traditions, and the adoption of digitalization in new business models of government, public and private sectors, and enterprises. Leaders in emerging economies are also encouraged to be bold and dynamic in innovating, adapting, and growing their enterprises and institutions. In effect, this comprehensive book offers insightful lessons to businesses, students, and the general public through its intriguing and comprehensive chapters.

Enjoy your reading. You are assured of an enriching learning experience as you surf through the pages of this compelling book.

Professor Justice Nyigmah Bawole
Professor of Public Administration and Management
Dean, University of Ghana Business School

Delivering Distinctive Value in Emerging Economies: Efficient and Sustainably Responsible Perspectives from Management Researchers and Practitioners is a comprehensive text that explores a diverse range of theoretical as well as practical viewpoints for the future of emerging economies. Organized according to six themes pertinent to developing a resilient economy, *Delivering Distinctive Value in Emerging Economies* provides insightful commentary and research that enlightens readers on the trajectory of current and future trends in various areas of economic importance, including digitalization healthcare and education.

Diversity, in recent years, has become a recurring theme in many areas of socioeconomic development. However, despite the term's popularity, much of the related literature is still constrained by a Euro- or Anglo-centric view of development, processes and practices. *Delivering Distinctive Value in Emerging Economies* is a solid effort by the editors to bring together a diverse range of authors from various emerging economies to provide first-hand narratives, and in some cases, inside information on the issues explored within this book. The contributions by the authors highlight the importance of contextualizing theory and practice to suit local norms and practices, respect distinct values and beliefs, and manage cultural expectations. Institutional challenges are identified, and suggestions for policy reform toward greater inclusivity—locally and abroad—are provided.

Written in a style that is accessible to readers of all proficiencies and expertise, I trust that this book will substantially benefit students, academics, practitioners, and even casual readers.

Dr. Calvin W. H. Cheong
Senior Lecturer in Finance
Programme Chair, Sunway University, Malaysia

Emerging economies have become an opportune interest of practitioners, entrepreneurs, and policymakers worldwide. Hence, a contemporary text which explores how to create and deliver distinct value in these economies is a must a read. The notions of a scientific approach to leadership styles, incorporation of cultural artifacts into corporate branding, social influencers and COVID-19 advocacy, and guidelines for embracing the new normal are just the selection of the contributions which provide new directions worth considering. The contributions also passionately encourages the leadership of government, companies, and institutions in emerging economies to be bold and dynamic in establishing new partnerships, appreciating the traditions and dynamics of their context, and adapting institutional structures in a manner that enhances their survival and sustainability.

Written by management researchers and practitioners, I envisage this book will be an invaluable and the indispensable reference to practitioners and students of marketing, human resource, information technology, project management, economics, and emerging economies. I am hopeful the contributions would spur the necessary debates and discussions in the spaces which can engineer a positive change in emerging economies. Let this book inspire you to do more for emerging economies.

Bryan Acheampong MP
Honorable Member of Parliament for Abetifi Constituency
Chairman, Foreign Affairs Committee
Member, Defence and Interior Committee
Republic of Ghana

sustainability. Contextual issues to be addressed include commitment of the political leadership, nonpartisan politicization of the innovation process, and the reduction of corruption.

In summary, Part V shares multidimensional perspectives on developing resilient and sustainable healthcare systems. The perspectives include embracing digitalization, leveraging data mining, resourcing, and effective management of social-cultural and sociopolitical influences.

Finally, Part VI includes four contributions related to making higher educational institutions more responsive and resilient. Three of the contributions examine the use of technology in teaching and administration in higher education. These contributions argue that iterative digitalization approaches for higher educational institutions are recommended, since this approach requires extensive user-involvement. Further, digitalization should not wipe away the established cultures, values, principles, and procedures of an institution. Critical consideration should be carefully directed toward system quality and service quality during implementation and maintenance of the system to facilitate continuous system usage and user satisfaction.

The fourth contribution examines organizational resilience in relation to social engineering among higher education institution professionals. Results reveal personnel knowledge of the threat to be the most important behavioral element for building resilience against social engineering attacks. Similarly, knowledge of password management, information handling, and email security literacy emerged as the most important aspects at the implementation level of building resilience. The chapter concludes by proposing a resilience framework for social engineering schemes in the higher education (HEI) setting.

In summary, Part VI shares that digitalization strategy in higher education institutions should be iterative in deployment, user-focused, and responsive to burgeoning security threats while being open to new and emerging innovations to sustain user satisfaction and continuous usage.

We want to thank the contributors for supporting this book's compilation and the tremendous time and effort dedicated to aiding the double-blind review process. These contributors span more than ten universities, public and private sector institutions across Cyprus, Finland, France, Ghana, Hungary, Malaysia, Nicaragua, Nigeria, South Africa, and Turkey. We can confidently say that this book demonstrates how European, Asian, and African academics and practitioners can effectively collaborate for the good of emerging economies. There are at least five contributions that feature collaborations between authors from two to five different countries across Africa, Asia, and beyond. This is laudable and we are proud that this book has created a platform for such a nexus of knowledge.

Finally, and most importantly, we thank Kristine Rynne Mednansky, *Senior Editor, Taylor and Francis Group*, for continuously supporting us and managing the overall book project from the publisher's side.

We hope you will enjoy reading the book and applying the directions and perspectives communicated by these diverse contributions. We invite you to contact us for questions, feedback, and discussions.

Richard Boateng
University of Ghana, Accra, Ghana

Sheena Lovia Boateng
University of Ghana, Accra, Ghana

Thomas Anning-Dorson
University of the Witwatersrand, South Africa

Editorial Advisory Board

Calvin W. H. Cheong
Sunway University, Malaysia

Divine Quase Agozie
Cyprus International University, Haspolat, Cyprus

Godfred Matthew Yaw Owusu
University of Ghana Business School, Ghana

Roger A. Atinga
University of Ghana Business School, Ghana

Editors

Richard Boateng is a professor of information systems at the University of Ghana Business School. He is the convenor of the BRIGHT Network and lead of the Fairwork Ghana Project. Richard's experience covers the digital economy, cloud computing, e-learning, information and communication technologies (ICT) for development, electronic governance, social media, electronic business, gender and technology, mobile commerce, and mobile health at the national, industrial, organizational and community levels. His papers have been published in in the *International Journal of Information Management, Internet Research, Qualitative Market Research: An International Journal*, and many others. Richard can be reached at richboateng@ug.edu.gh.

Dr. Sheena Lovia Boateng is a lecturer at the Department of Marketing and Entrepreneurship at the University of Ghana Business School. She is a fellow of the Academy of Marketing Science. She also served as a member of the Editorial Advisory Board for the Emerald Emerging Markets Case Study Journal, Emerald Publishing Limited, UK, from 2018 to 2020. She has published seven journal publications, five books, six book chapters, four published conference papers, and one industry report. Her academic work has been published in the *International Journal of Bank Marketing, Journal of Financial Services Marketing*, and the *Journal of Educational Technology Systems*. Her research interests include online relationship marketing, fashion and beauty marketing, entrepreneurship, online branding and advertising, social media marketing, and structural equational modeling in marketing. She can be reached at slboateng@ug.edu.gh.

Thomas Anning-Dorson (PhD) is an associate professor at the Wits Business School, University of the Witwatersrand, Johannesburg, South Africa. He also serves a researcher with The Fairwork Foundation, Oxford Internet Institute, University of Oxford, and a fellow at McGill University, Canada, on the QES Program. His research interest spans the digital economy, innovation, marketing, strategy, value, and emerging markets. He can be reached at thomas.dorson.anning@wits.ac.za.

Contributors

Francis Aboagye-Otchere
University of Ghana Business School
Accra, Ghana

Bryan Acheampong
Honorable Member of Parliament for Abetifi
    Constituency and Chairman
Foreign Affairs Committee
Ghana

Richard Osei Adjei
University of Central Nicaragua Medical
    Center
Nicaragua

Divine Quase Agozie
Cyprus International University
Haspolat, Cyprus

Thomas Anning-Dorson
University of the Witwatersrand
Johannesburg, South Africa

Eric Ansong
Wisconsin International University
    College
Accra, Ghana

Roger A. Atinga
University of Ghana Business School
Ghana

Donald Douglas Atsa'am
University of the Free State
South Africa

Anita Asiwome Adzo Baku
University of Ghana Business School
Ghana

Oluwafemi Samson Balogun
University of Eastern Finland
Finland

Vathana Bathmanathan
Universiti Tenaga Nasional
Malaysia

Kofi Agyenim Boateng
Kwame Nkrumah University of Science and
    Technology
Ghana

Richard Boateng
University of Ghana Business School
Accra, Ghana

Sheena Lovia Boateng
University of Ghana Business School
Accra, Ghana

Nana Akua Boateng-Amartey
University of Health and Allied Sciences
Ghana

Calvin W. H. Cheong
Sunway University
Malaysia

Oluwaseun Alexander Dada
University of Helsinki
Helsinki, Finland

Kwasi Dartey-Baah
University of Ghana Business School
Accra, Ghana

Samuel Nii Odoi Devine
Presbyterian University College
Abetifi-Kwahu, Ghana

Burak Erkut
Institute for Research in Economic and Fiscal
    Issues
Paris, France

Nurudeen Issaka Idrisu
University of Health and Allied Sciences
Ghana

Qudiratu Ngmenensoa Ishak
University of Ghana Business School
Accra, Ghana

Amar Hisham Jaaffar
Universiti Tenaga Nasional
Malaysia

Ricardo Kettledas
University of the Witwatersrand
South Africa

Emmanuel Awuni Kolog
University of Ghana Business School
Accra, Ghana

Theodora Aba Abekah Koomson
University of Ghana Business School
Ghana

Gabriel Korankye
University of Professional Studies
Ghana

Philip Afeti Korto
University of Health and Allied
    Sciences
Ghana

John Amoah Kusi
Chartered Accountant
Ghana

Yvonne Ayerki Lamptey
University of Ghana Business School
Accra, Ghana

Godlove Asirifi Lartey
Professional Tax Consultant
Ghana

Symeon Mandrinos
Swinburne University of Technology Sarawak
Malaysia

Muesser Nat
Cyprus International University
Haspolat, Cyprus

Saviour Ayertey Nubuor
University of Ghana Business School
Accra, Ghana

Temidayo Oluwatosin Omotehinwa
Centre for Multidisciplinary Research and
    Innovation Abuja
Nigeria

Acheampong Owusu
University of Ghana Business School
Accra, Ghana

Godfred Matthew Yaw Owusu
University of Ghana Business School
Accra, Ghana

Akua Peprah-Yeboah
Kwame Nkrumah University of Science and
    Technology
Ghana

Fred Pobee
University of Pécs
Hungary

Jegatheesan Rajadurai
Universiti Tenaga Nasional
Malaysia

Revin Rajan
Asia Centre for Leadership and Civilization
Malaysia

Burcu Toker
Bahçeşehir Cyprus University
Turkey

Edem Emerald Sabah Welbeck
University of Ghana Business School
Accra, Ghana

BEYOND COVID-19

I

Chapter 1

Embracing the New Normal: Guidelines for Small Businesses in Emerging Economies

Richard Boateng and Bryan Acheampong

Contents

Introduction

COVID-19 has not only impacted people's lives. The business environment has also been dramatically affected, which is a statement that resonates deeply with small- and medium-sized enterprise (SME) owners. As the OECD (2020) indicated, "there are several ways the coronavirus pandemic affects the economy, especially SMEs, on both the supply and demand sides".

SMEs, including micro-sized companies, comprise "more than 90 per cent of all firms worldwide, provide 70 per cent of all employment, and constitute roughly half of the global economy" (Dasewicz et al., 2020). This information leaves no doubt that the business environment has been permanently affected by the COVID-19 pandemic. That is, particularly true in the emerging economies where SMEs are even more prevalent. For example, as Dasewicz et al. (2020) reported,

DOI: 10.4324/9781003152217-2

these companies constitute "nearly 90 per cent of all businesses operating in Africa, and they are responsible for 80 per cent of the continent's employment".

However, the experience obtained during the first year of the pandemic revealed to business owners some valuable lessons and gave us an indication of what should be expected beyond COVID-19. Specifically, the SMEs that become adaptable at their core and invest in digitalization would be the best prepared for the new normal.

We argue that companies should embrace the new workplace instead of returning to the old one. In the same way, SMEs with a business culture with flexibility and adaptability as core values have the greatest chance of success, and one key asset in that effort is the use of digital tools. Finally, the different challenges of the new business environment provide the groundwork for collaboration and new partnerships.

The Effect of COVID-19 on SMEs in Emerging Economies

COVID-19 created major challenges no one could expect, and its effects spread throughout our personal lives and businesses. Regarding the latter, as the OECD (2020) expressed, the pandemic affected both companies (supply) and customers (demand).

On the one hand, companies had to learn to deal with fewer persons fully available to work, "as workers are unwell or need to look after children or other dependents while schools are closed and movements of people are restricted" (OECD, 2020). Furthermore, "around 68 per cent of the world's total workforce, including 81 per cent of employers, are currently living in countries with recommended or required workplace closures" (ILO, 2020), which created the necessity to change the way many of these businesses used to work. Additionally, as the OECD (2020) indicated, "supply chains are interrupted leading to shortages of parts and intermediate goods".

On the other hand, customers had to sustain "loss of income, fear of contagion and heightened uncertainty, which in turn reduces spending and consumption" (OECD, 2020). These problems have created a reduction in demand and revenue for companies, which also compounded into layoffs as firms were unable to pay salaries, according to OECD (2020). Furthermore, while this affected both larger and smaller firms, "the effect on SMEs is especially severe, particularly because of higher levels of vulnerability and lower resilience related to their size" (OECD, 2020).

In developing countries, the challenges that were brought by the pandemic were even bigger as these economies largely depend on commodities and international commerce, and SMEs drive the vast majority of the business environment (Shipalana & O'Riordan, 2020). These challenges have impacted access to funds due to a lower capacity to pay, which is, for example, the case for many African countries. In that regard, seven of the 19 rated sub-Saharan countries had their credit ratings downgraded, including some of Africa's biggest economies, at the same time as main commodities, such as oil, suffered price drops (Shipalana et al., 2020). Similarly, Latin American and Caribbean countries, as López and Zaizar (2020) indicated, have also been affected by the pandemic.

Nevertheless, the challenges that SMEs in emerging countries have faced since the start of the pandemic reveal what can be done to accelerate growth beyond COVID-19. In that regard, companies should account for a world that has changed and would hardly return to its pre-pandemic normality, as "the health crisis caused by the COVID-19 pandemic will produce a deep lethargic spell in economies worldwide that will be felt for years to come" (López & Zaizar, 2020). Strategic planning should be more flexible than ever, and, as López and Zaizar (2020) concluded, surviving and competing in the post-COVID-19 normality requires "leaders to take bold and wide-ranging decisions; seek innovative, intuitive, and far-reaching solutions; and quickly adapt and evolve".

As the world evolves to become more digitalized, transforming the workplace, the ways in which old and new clients are approached, and even how collaborations and partnerships are made, flexibility is essential. As López and Zaizar (2020) expressed, "in a more digitalized future, SMEs may enjoy unprecedented global reach through online platforms, from the comfort of their office, factory, or company".

The New Workplace beyond COVID-19

As previously stated, the workplace saw significant changes motivated by health and safety measures to combat COVID-19. According to ILO (2020), the COVID-19 pandemic was a massive experiment in working-from-home arrangements. While some jobs cannot be done at home, the trend is likely to continue to develop teleworking capacities, possibly for the long term (ILO, 2020). Both employees and employers already prefer this way of working. Thus, "with the spread of the COVID-19 pandemic in 2020, large portions of the world's workforce shifted to homeworking, joining hundreds of millions of other workers who had already been working from home for decades" (ILO, 2021a).

On the employee side, working from home has its advantages. Flexibility in working hours is its main benefit (ILO, 2021a). Conversely, it also presents its risks. The main concern of homeworkers "is the blurring between working time and personal and family time" (ILO, 2021a). In addition, less access to training, organizing, occupational safety and health, as well as social security are some of the risks that homeworkers face, while lack of formality is also widespread (ILO, 2021a).

On the employer side, the challenges to adapt a business to the new type of workplace may be relatively higher for SMEs due to their smaller size, low level of digitalization, and difficulties in accessing and adopting technologies (OECD, 2020). Furthermore, reducing production makes the costs of underutilized labor and capital great on SMEs than larger firms. However, many SMEs were required to adopt homeworking or temporarily pause operations due to mobility restrictions and lockdowns imposed by the governments, risking closure.

There is still work to be done to adapt home and remote workers to SMEs' workplaces. Nonetheless, as ILO (2020) indicated, employers and workers are likely to adapt and become more comfortable with the expanded workplace, using information and communication technology (ICT), and understanding the benefits of working from home. As aforementioned, flexibility is the main benefit for homeworkers, alongside other benefits that include the reduction in commuting times, greater autonomy, a better work-life balance, and increased motivation (ILO, 2020). For the employer, the benefits include reduced turnover, enhanced productivity, and greater efficiency, as ILO (2020) expressed. For society as a whole, reduced travel results in a reduction in carbon emissions (ILO, 2020).

ILO (2021a) estimates that, in 2019, 7.9% of global employment was represented by homeworkers, as it grew to 17% by the second quarter of 2020 (ILO, 2021b). Despite the growth that remote working has experienced, the arrangements implemented by the employers in response to challenges posed by COVID-19 may be temporary and workers "will normally be obliged to resume normal working arrangements when the situation permits and as directed by employers" (ILO, 2020).

Nevertheless, it may be of interest to many SMEs to let their employees and management experience the advantages provided by working from home, which should be evaluated case by case. However, adaptability at a company level and digital information and communication tools are the key to being successful in the new workplace. In that regard, companies should keep focusing on making working from home possible and beneficial for their workers (ILO, 2021a). In this sense, companies should adapt and embrace the newly expanded workplace.

On the other hand, even when COVID-19 is no longer a threat, it is advisable for companies to keep health-related practices in the workplace, include them in their processes, and inform the employees. As the World Health Organization (2020) recommends, implementing and maintaining prevention measures would help prevent the spread of other illnesses, such as common cold, flu, and stomach bugs, and help the company stay productive.

The Importance of Adaptability in the New Normal

As López and Zaizar (2020) pointed out, "among many other new opportunities that may arise in a post-COVID-19 future is digital trade. More international commercial transactions will happen electronically through new and existing platforms". SMEs experience greater difficulties when implementing new technologies compared to larger companies or even start-ups (OECD, 2020). These difficulties are related to SMEs' ability to adapt. On that matter, OECD (2021a) comments, saying that "established small firms often struggle to adapt their business operations to the current situation, compared to large firms (and start-ups) and face more operational skills constraints".

The challenges that SMEs have to face to adapt to new technologies and market requirements are linked to the lack of managerial capabilities to embrace changes. For example, during COVID-19, the SMEs were less likely to have the "managerial capability to comply with new regulatory frameworks to guarantee customers and employees safety" (OECD, 2021a). In the same vein, "SMEs are less likely to innovate both in processes and in goods and services, compared to their larger counterparts and to start-ups" (OECD, 2021a).

While COVID-19 has brought many different challenges to SMEs, as described earlier, it has also generated new opportunities for these companies to compete on a larger scale and reduce the gap between them and larger companies. Beyond COVID-19, the level of digitalization would be what differentiates companies in the eyes of their clients, which will be even more significant than their size. As López and Zaizar (2020) stated, "in the next few years, e-commerce growth will likely exceed that of traditional brick-and-mortar retail around the world, both in volume and value terms".

SMEs that embrace change as part of their company culture and develop the capabilities to adapt to new market trends and requirements will be better prepared to deal with the new normality.

Digitalization as the Bridge and the Norm

Companies could make precisely the product that their potential customers want, but if they cannot reach those clients, the products will not sell. Similarly, if their suppliers cannot serve them, they will not be able to create their products. The COVID-19 crisis has heightened the importance of the digitalization of SMEs. Online platforms play an instrumental role in connecting users to new markets, suppliers, or resources, especially as firms have moved operations online and implemented smart working solutions (OECD, 2021b).

As mentioned earlier, SMEs are faced with challenges regarding the adoption of new technologies, as they tend to lag in digital adoption. However, in response to COVID-19, up to 70%

of SMEs have intensified their use of digital technologies (OECD, 2021b). With minimal costs, companies adopted different digital tools, such as social media and other online channels to reach current and new clients and promote their brands. Potential clients expect to communicate with companies through those channels. Hence, some of these new digitally driven strategies and investments are irreversible, and the efficiency gains have now been demonstrated.

Nevertheless, the effort should not end there. SMEs tend to digitalize some business functions first, including the general administration and marketing operations. While "the digital gap is smaller between SMEs and large firms in their business-to-government interactions, in using electronic invoicing or social media, or in selling online" (OECD, 2021), the implementation should continue, as there are other opportunities to take and risks to mitigate.

For example, the "COVID-19 context has also provided an opportunity for hackers to intensify attacks, exploiting SME lack of preparedness and ability to face increasingly sophisticated threats" (OECD, 2021b). Per their limited resources and access to diverse managerial expertise, SMEs stand to lose more when exposed to such crises. As compared to large companies, it may take more resources and time for SMEs to recover from digital security breaches. Going digital has both opportunities and risks, and SMEs' managers and leaders need to be bold and continuously learn the dynamics of the digital transformation.

In this sense, SMEs should keep increasing their digital efforts to facilitate the development of relationships with current and new customers, maintain partnerships with suppliers, and communicate with them. Yet, on the other hand, they should also implement the necessary digital security mechanisms and policies to mitigate unintended consequences which could occur.

New Relationships through Digital Finance Platforms

Digitalization has also helped SMEs take advantage of partnership and collaboration opportunities. In many cases, this has been motivated by the reduction of traditional financing sources. As Dasewicz et al. (2020) suggested, the most significant obstacle that SMEs face in their growth is the financing gap, which "in the developing world stands at US$ 4.8 trillion, with a substantial part of this gap constraining firms at the mid-late growth stage of innovation".

In response to the pandemic, governments deployed large-scale support mainly in the form of debt finance to ease SME liquidity constraints. However, "while this support was necessary for tackling the liquidity crisis of SMEs, a large number of firms will likely struggle to repay their debts, especially those that continue to take on debt to survive the reintroduction of confinement measures" (OECD, 2021a). As the COVID-19 pandemic has made it difficult for many SMEs to pay salaries, it has also diminished their capacity to pay the debt, resulting in "further reduced confidence and a reduction of credit" (OECD, 2020).

Nevertheless, SMEs that transformed their financial processes to include nontraditional sources can take advantage of collaborative finance through digital platforms, such as crowdfunding. Crowdfunding is a "financing mechanism whereby the firm relies on a large pool of individual contributors for funding instead of a smaller pool of traditional high-value investors such as banks" (Dasewicz et al., 2020). In Ghana, for example, the United Nations Capital Development Fund launched two innovative partnerships in the late 2020 to test crowdfunding platforms that will channel remittances into productive investments and offer alternative financing to young entrepreneurs. These financial inclusion and digital financial services are complementary tools to support the initial response and economic recovery of emerging and developing economies affected by the pandemic (UNCDF, 2020).

The investors could also be clients who become part of the process, leading to the formation of new relationships. For SMEs, the crowdfunding platform offers partnerships to access new resources and an opportunity to become more economically resilient.

New kinds of relationships and partnerships such as those mentioned earlier are significant in the new normality beyond COVID-19. As stated by the OECD (2020), "over the longer term, it may be difficult for many SMEs to re-build connections with former networks, once supply chains are disrupted and former partners have set up new alliances and business contracts". The keywords are, yet again, adaptability and digitalization.

Conclusion

This chapter discussed how SMEs in developing countries were affected by the coronavirus pandemic and the actions to increase the chances of being successful in the new normal beyond COVID-19.

SMEs in emerging countries were particularly affected due to their relatively smaller size and dependency on commodities and international commerce of their economies. However, COVID-19 also brought some new opportunities for these companies to reduce the gap between them and larger companies as well as reach new clients and new markets. Adaptability and digitalization are required to take advantage of those opportunities. One example lies in how the workplace has expanded to the employees' homes. However, even after the pandemic, SMEs and their employees could still benefit from adapting their work policies to embrace the expanded workplace as well as use digital ICTs. Moreover, adaptability should be a core value in their company culture.

In that regard, established SMEs had struggled more to adapt themselves to the new normal compared to larger companies and start-ups due to a lack of managerial capabilities to embrace changes. However, SMEs that embrace change as part of their company culture and develop the capabilities to adapt to new market trends and requirements will be better prepared to deal with the business environment beyond COVID-19.

One of the main aspects that shape the new normal is the increased reliance on the aforementioned digital communication tools to build relationships with clients, suppliers, employees, and partners. For example, the use of social media has been on the rise and now presents an opportunity for SMEs to reach their existing clients and new ones.

In addition, digitalization has helped SMEs take advantage of partnership and collaboration opportunities. For example, companies that adapted their finance processes to include new collaborative finance, such as crowdfunding through digital platforms, established new partnerships. This has blurred the line between clients and investors and fostered an opportunity for intimacy with SMEs.

Finally, other technologies are starting to become more prominent in business, mainly green technologies, and SMEs should be flexible enough to evaluate the implementation of those developments. E3G (2020) stated that the road to recovery post pandemic would be significantly facilitated by green technologies. For example, "efficient, climate-friendly cooling could also help many struggling businesses get back on the road to profitability through significant energy cost savings" (E3G, 2020).

References

Dasewicz, A., Simon, J., & Ramanujam, S. (2020). *Financing Small Business is Critical for a Strong Post-COVID Recovery*. Center for Strategic and International Studies (CSIS). www.jstor.org/stable/resrep26410

E3G. (2020). *Building Back Better: How Climate-Friendly Cooling Can Support a Clean, Resilient COVID-19 Recovery*. www.jstor.org/stable/resrep24950

International Labour Organization. (2020). *An Employers' Guide on Working from Home in Response to the Outbreak of COVID-19*. www.ilo.org/actemp/publications/WCMS_745024/lang-en/index.htm

International Labour Organization. (2021a). *Working from Home: From Invisibility to Decent Work*. www.ilo.org/global/publications/books/WCMS_765806/lang-en/index.htm

International Labour Organization. (2021b). *World Employment and Social Outlook: Trends 2021*. www.ilo.org/global/research/global-reports/weso/2021/WCMS_795453/lang-en/index.htm

López, S., & Zaizar, S. (2020). *Dealmaking with China amid Global Economic Uncertainty: Opportunities, Risks, and Recommendations for Latin America and the Caribbean*. Atlantic Council. www.jstor.org/stable/resrep29467.4

Organization for Economic Co-operation and Development. (2020). *Coronavirus (COVID-19): SME Policy Responses*. www.oecd.org/coronavirus/policy-responses/coronavirus-covid-19-sme-policy-responses-04440101/

Organization for Economic Co-operation and Development. (2021a). *One Year of SME and Entrepreneurship Policy Responses to COVID-19: Lessons Learned to "Build Back Better"*. www.oecd.org/coronavirus/policy-responses/one-year-of-sme-and-entrepreneurship-policy-responses-to-covid-19-lessons-learned-to-build-back-better-9a230220/

Organization for Economic Co-operation and Development. (2021b). *The Digital Transformation of SMEs, OECD Studies on SMEs and Entrepreneurship*. Paris: OECD Publishing. https://doi.org/10.1787/bdb9256a-en

Shipalana, P., & O'Riordan, A. (2020). *Impact of COVID-19 on Financial Stability in Africa*. South African Institute of International Affairs. www.jstor.org/stable/resrep27018

Shipalana, P., O'Riordan, A., & Prinsloo, C. (2020). *The Macroeconomic Impact of COVID-19 on Africa*. South African Institute of International Affairs. www.jstor.org/stable/resrep28262

United Nations Capital Development Fund (UNCDF). (2020). *On International Day of Family Remittances UNCDF Launches Two Crowdfunding Platforms Under the GrEEn Project in Ghana*. www.uncdf.org/article/5733/on-international-day-of-family-remittances-uncdf-launches-a-crowdfunding-platform-under-the-green-project-in-ghana

World Health Organization. (2020). *Getting Your Workplace Ready for COVID-19: How COVID-19 Spreads*. www.who.int/publications/m/item/getting-your-workplace-ready-for-covid-19-how-covid-19-spreads

Authors' Profile

Richard Boateng is a professor of information systems at the University of Ghana Business School. Richard's experience covers the digital economy; cloud computing; e-learning; ICTs for development; electronic governance; social media; electronic business; gender and technology; mobile commerce; and mobile health at the national, industrial, organizational, and community levels. His papers have been published in the *International Journal of Information Management, Internet Research, Qualitative Market Research: An International Journal*, and many others. Richard can be reached at richboateng@ug.edu.gh.

Bryan Acheampong is Member of Parliament and the Chair of the Parliamentary Committee for Foreign Affairs, Ghana. He has served in leadership positions in business and politics over the past 20 years. His experience spans security analysis, project and team management, strategic planning, and budget management. He is also an avid entrepreneur who is currently building a hotel which is set to be one of the largest in Africa. Bryan is a doctoral researcher whose research examines mutual understanding in technology projects.

Chapter 2

Vaccinating the World: Social Influencers and COVID-19 Advocacy

Sheena Lovia Boateng

Contents

Overview

Influencer marketing, a type of social media marketing that uses endorsements from individuals with a large and dedicated social following, has recently surged. These influencers can be found on platforms like Facebook, Twitter, Instagram, and TikTok where their influence is harnessed by global organizations for myriad purposes, including the fight against COVID-19. At the onset of the COVID-19 pandemic, in the early months of 2020, the future of social media influencers seemed to be in question. New pandemic-related guidelines and regulations, as well as shifting consumer sentiments and behaviors, forced brands to cut costs, adjust logistics, and retool brand messaging that seemed to be out of touch at the time. Consequently, sponsored posts on platforms like Instagram, for instance, fell from representing 35% of influencer content in mid-February 2020 to representing just 4% of influencer content in mid-April 2020 (Perelli & Whateley, 2020). Suspended or canceled online campaigns began to cast uncertainty on the role

DOI: 10.4324/9781003152217-3

of influencers in the future, leading many to seek alternative sources of income. However, as the crisis wore on, it became evident that social media influencers did, indeed, have a role to play—a critical one that has resulted in a shift in their content, patterns of use of platforms, and partnerships. Recent trends point to a significant opportunity for governments, public health agencies, and other organizations to leverage influencers to shape the global discourse and human behaviors related to COVID-19; particularly amidst the current COVID vaccine hesitance gaining prominence in several parts of the world.

The Rise of Social Media Influencers

Still a relatively new concept, social media influencers have emerged as a highly effective force in helping organizations connect with audiences and consumers on a more authentic level. The use of social media influencers became a core marketing strategy for many organizations as they realized that consumers generally perceive information and recommendations from their peers to be more trustworthy compared to traditional marketing. Consumers relate to influencers on a personal level, in part, due to the interactivity of social media. Influencers build a bond with their followers by posting content regularly and communicating with their audiences directly, helping those audiences feel personally connected. Over the past decade, social media influencers have been frequently tapped, as organizations sought to leverage this sense of authenticity and personal connection to elevate awareness of their brands and increase sales. Now, however, a new goal has emerged among influencers and the organizations they partner with. In a shift from their earlier focus on pushing consumption and peddling commodities, influencers are now making use of their status to drive positive change. In our current global dispensation, it has become more apparent than ever that audiences expect—and often demand—that social media influencers take a stand on social issues. The barrage of divisive events that occurred in 2020, from the COVID-19 pandemic to the Black Lives Matter movement as well as other cases of political and social unrest in various parts of the world, has demonstrated that audiences require influencers to become a part of the solution. Globally, governments, public health agencies, and other organizations are taking note.

The Role of Social Media Influencers during COVID-19

As the COVID-19 pandemic endures, more social media influencers have begun producing and posting coronavirus-related content, often at the request of their governments and public health officials. In the United Kingdom, for example, the government took bold steps to work with influencers to help prevent the spread of COVID-19. In response to previously fruitless attempts to encourage the public's use of the National Health Service test and trace service, the government enlisted the support of social media influencers like Shaughna Phillips. Phillips, who is a star of the reality television program Love Island and has more than 1.5 million followers on Instagram, posted a photo with a caption telling her fans that "the best way for us all to get back to doing the things we love" is by getting tested (Bolat, 2020). Similar scenarios have occurred in the United States, where Surgeon General Jerome Adams encouraged social media influencers to reach out to their audiences with coronavirus-related messages. Adams urged influencers like Kylie Jenner and others to explain the seriousness of COVID-19 and emphasize the importance of practicing preventive measures such as social distancing and self-quarantining (Pagones, 2020). Even the World Health Organization (WHO) has used influencer strategies in its coronavirus messages. Since April 2020, the WHO has relied on a computer-generated imagery influencer called Knox Frost to deliver accurate and trustworthy information about COVID-19 to Millennials and Gen Z (Bolat, 2020).

However, with the introduction of the COVID vaccine, came a new set of challenges that made the opportunity to leverage social media influencers even more apparent. There have been significant challenges in the quest to achieve herd immunity against COVID-19 globally, with millions of adults around the world remaining unvaccinated. For herd immunity to be achieved, 75%–80% of the global population must be protected either through vaccination or having had the illness (Goudie et al., 2021). Still, this may not be achieved unless the fears of those who are vaccine-hesitant are assuaged, and they agree to get the shot. In response to this, various influencers have been posting vaccine-related content, with some sharing video evidence of their own vaccination experiences on social media to encourage their followers to do the same. In the United States, for instance, the Oregon Health Authority partnered with influencers to encourage people to get the vaccine shot. Using the hashtag #MyVaccineReason, the influencers share their reasons for getting the shot on their various platforms to contribute to the positive discussion and share their genuine feelings, as well as facts, about the vaccine (Kelly, 2021). Similarly, in May 2021, the city of San Jose reached out to social media influencers like Johnny Tran, for help in getting young people vaccinated. Tran, an Instagram influencer with more than 64,000 followers, indicated that "it does help to see more of a familiar face sort of advocate for the vaccine, especially when your peers are in support of it" (Budman, 2021).

More so, in emerging economy contexts like Ghana, government agencies, including the Ministry of Information, The Ghana Health Service (GHS), and the Ministry of Health, have partnered with influencers to encourage eligible citizens to get the shot. Ghana was the first African country to receive vaccines through the COVAX facility, having vaccinated over 60% of its first phase target population and around 90% of all health workers (Lemango, 2021). Influencers like Nana Ama McBrown, who has over four million followers on Instagram, in partnership with the governmental agencies mentioned earlier, have consistently encouraged her followers to continue to follow the COVID-19 protocols. She has been featured in several adverts funded by the government of Ghana encouraging citizens to wear a mask, with the hashtag #maskupGH (see Figure 2.1). These adverts have been posted on all her social media handles. Additionally, she has shared her vaccination experience, stating that "if you get the opportunity and wish to take the jab, please do; and let's continue to observe the protocols because that is the way to go" (Tali, 2021).

Although several economies are slowly opening back up, people are still largely practicing social distancing, with many choosing to stay and work from home. This has led to a surge in the consumption of online content, especially social media. The good news, however, is that this content is not all as lighthearted as #QuarantineAndChill or #MyPandemicSurvivalPlan. Recent research on influencer activity online has revealed that 466,175 posts on #coronavirus have resulted in well over 1 billion engagements, with hashtags like #coronavirus, #covid19, #covid, #pandemic, and #coronavirusoutbreak from 800,000 influencer posts resulting in 2.9 million engagements globally (Choi, 2020). Social good campaigns and COVID-19-related information from just 480,000 posts online have been shared over 1.5 billion times. Furthermore, several people, including all classes of influencers, have turned to social media to report their vaccination experiences, using hashtags like #VaccinesSaveLives, #TrustScience, and #Vaccinated. Although peoples' perceptions of the COVID-19 vaccine remain somewhat polarized, getting vaccinated is to date one of the most popular topics online. Hashtags like #IGotMyShot and #Vaccine are connecting thousands of social media users around the world through the posts made by influencers after they have gotten the COVID-19 vaccine (Bolton, 2021). This clearly points to the impact that social media influencers can have when they engage in COVID-19 advocacy, reaching their audiences with critical messages about the pandemic.

Figure 2.1   An example of state agencies partnering with a Ghanaian influencer.

Key Conclusions

As governments, public health agencies, and other organizations consider how to shape the global discourse around crucial issues such as the COVID-19 pandemic and achieving herd immunity through COVID-19 vaccination campaigns, there is clearly an opportunity to leverage social media influencers.

Use Influencers to Achieve the Appropriate Tone

Social media influencers have long been relied upon to deliver authentic and relatable content. Something as simple as an Instagram post with a relatable caption or an informative YouTube video focused on coronavirus prevention or vaccination can make a meaningful impression. In some cases, even lighthearted content can make an important impact. More and more influencers have turned to "edutainment" during the COVID-19 pandemic, posting entertaining content that is also informative and encourages compliance with the rules. One example is 52-year-old multiple-award-winning singer Mariah Carey, who posted a video of herself belting out a high note as she received her first COVID-19 vaccination shot (Ahlgrim, 2021). She said in the video posted to her social media that she felt "excited and nervous" to get the vaccine and encouraged all her followers to get vaccinated as well, saying: "We're all in this together".

Enlist Influencers as Advocates of Accurate Information

An important part of the fight against COVID-19 is delivering information to the public about guidelines and regulations—as well as encouraging adherence to those guidelines. Consumers around the world have been inundated with coronavirus-related information that does not always come from trustworthy sources, and anxiety has left people susceptible to this misinformation. Organizations have the opportunity to enlist social media influencers to provide reliable, accurate information from reputable sources. Influencers can be effective in fighting the spread of baseless, dangerous theories, particularly to the audiences less likely to consume news through traditional sources.

Leverage Influencers to Reach Critical Audiences

Since the start of the COVID-19 pandemic, more people are spending more time at home. This has led to a rapid increase in online content and, especially, social media consumption. According to research conducted by Fullscreen, 34% of 18- to 34-year-olds say they are watching more social media influencer content during the pandemic and because of it (Choi, 2020). With certain audiences engaging less with traditional news sources and spending more time on alternative platforms, now is the time to leverage influencers to encourage these demographics to comply with government guidelines, such as social distancing measures and participating in vaccination exercises. Influencers can play a particularly significant role in reaching young people with coronavirus-related information on their platforms.

References

Ahlgrim, C. (2021, April 5). Mariah Carey Hits a High Note and Jokes She's 'Actually a Vampire' in a Video of Her Getting the COVID Vaccine. *Insider*. https://bit.ly/3z8hYGb

Bolat, E. (2020, September 9). Why the UK Government is Paying Social Media Influencers to Post about Coronavirus. *The Conversation*. https://bit.ly/3fTmWiK

Bolton, F. (2021, January 3). COVID-19 Vaccine Hashtags Connect People through Social Media. *NewsNation*. https://bit.ly/2TCS4tY

Budman, S. (2021, May 24). San Jose Hopes Social Media Influencers Will Encourage More Teens to Get Vaccinated. *NBC Bay Area*. https://bit.ly/2SdqPWF

Choi, S. (2020, September 9). COVID-19 Implications for Influencer Marketing. *Mention*. https://bit.ly/34SzLn1

Goudie, C., Markoff, B., Tressel, C., Weidner, R., & Fagg, J. (2021, May 11). *ABC7 Eyewitness News*. https://abc7.ws/3ghJkRG

Kelly, B. (2021, March 30). OHA Partners with Social Media Influencers to Encourage People to Get COVID-19 Vaccine. *Fox12Oregon*. https://bit.ly/2TCXoxu

Lemango, E. T. (2021, April 27). *Emerging Lessons from Africa's COVID-19 Vaccine Rollout*. World Health Organization. https://bit.ly/3w0IFuB

Pagones, S. (2020, March 20). Kylie Jenner Delivers Coronavirus-Related Social Media Messages. *Fox Business*. https://fxn.ws/3uSj19X

Perelli, A., & Whateley, D. (2020, March 12). How the Coronavirus is Changing the Influencer Business, According to Marketers and Top Instagram and YouTube Stars. *Business Insider Australia*, 22. https://bit.ly/3gfV5bk

Tali, S. (2021, March 10). *Nana Ama McBrown Shares Experience after Taking COVID-19 Vaccine*. https://bit.ly/3fYYKeW

Author's Profile

Dr. Sheena Lovia Boateng is a lecturer at the Department of Marketing and Entrepreneurship at the University of Ghana Business School. She is a fellow of the Academy of Marketing Science. She also served as a member of the Editorial Advisory Board for the Emerald Emerging Markets Case Study Journal, Emerald Publishing Limited, UK, from 2018 to 2020. She has published seven journal publications, five books, six book chapters, four published conference papers, and one industry report. Her academic work has been published in the *International Journal of Bank Marketing*, *Journal of Financial Services Marketing*, and *the Journal of Educational Technology Systems*. Her research interests include online relationship marketing, fashion and beauty marketing, digital business strategy, electronic learning adoption, entrepreneurship, online branding and advertising, social media marketing, and structural equational modeling in marketing. She can be reached at slboateng@ug.edu.gh.

Chapter 3

Applying Agile Principles in Institutions of Higher Learning: Lessons from the COVID-19 Pandemic

Joshua Ofoeda and James Ami-Narh

Contents

Introduction

COVID-19 continues to cause havoc globally, and many countries feel the impact of the outbreak. With the current global infections hitting 125 million and over 2.7 million deaths, the pandemic has changed our world forever. Up to now, millions of people are still under lockdowns, while many businesses have also collapsed. Therefore, it is expected that the pandemic will have a continued impact on countries, organizations, and individuals for an extensive period (Ågerfalk et al., 2020). Since the virus was declared a global pandemic, governments worldwide have resorted to various ways of minimizing the spread of the virus. Different response methods to deal with the situation have been proposed by experts. Leaders of various countries continue to hold periodic conferences to address their citizens on the measures they have taken to fight the virus (Janssen & van der Voort, 2020). Some of these measures include social distancing, the ban on social gatherings, closure of borders, frequent handwashing with soap under running water, and the use of alcohol-based hand sanitizers. Other measures instituted by governments include restriction of movement of people and the suspension of intra-region public transports. Recent studies have shown that travel restrictions minimize the spread of the virus in nations like China, where the virus originated (Chinazzi et al., 2020).

The pandemic, just like disasters such as earthquakes and war, has put governments, businesses, and universities at risk. Many universities that lacked proper strategies to respond to pandemics, such as COVID-19, were severely exposed. Most university processes were drastically altered. Schools had to close down, resulting in a massive disruption of academic calendars. Conferences at various levels (local and international) were canceled due to travel restrictions, among others (Marinoni & van't Land, 2020; Shamsir et al., 2021). Generally, the effect of the pandemic brought in a sense of urgency for governments and businesses to adapt and recover from the effects of the pandemic. The aftermath shows how some governments have exhibited agility concepts (Janssen & van der Voort, 2020), while others have been criticized for lacking agility traits mainly due to their bureaucratic levels (Dowdy et al., 2017).

On the whole, institutions of higher learning have been criticized for showing less agility than their industrial counterparts, perhaps, because they have become complacent with their achievements and have demonstrated severe rigidity over the years (Menon & Suresh, 2020). Some universities resorted to business continuity plans to recover from disasters. But, there is a lack of research on how institutions of higher learning respond before, during, and after pandemics such as COVID-19 (Dohaney et al., 2020). Academic continuity is crucial for universities after being hit by a disruptive event. There has been some evidence of how some universities have responded to pandemics such as the HINI flu. However, there is still more to learn from this phenomenon, especially from developing country universities (Ekmekci & Bergstrand, 2010). Therefore, there is the need to explain how the universities quickly respond to the COVID-19 pandemic using agile principles to ensure continuity and reduce the spread of the virus. Besides, countries globally have instituted agile measures within a short time to curb the spread of the virus. Understanding the principles from a university perspective will provide us with an excellent opportunity to understand agility (Janssen & van der Voort, 2020).

The agile principle is a term coined from the software engineering domain. Agile is one of the most used process frameworks in the software development process, and its values are based on the agile manifesto. The agile manifesto advocates adaptive preparation, evolutionary development, and early product delivery (Fowler & Highsmith, 2001). Agile methods also focus on a continual process in improving a software product while encouraging flexible responses to change (Collier, 2012). Agile methods prioritize customer satisfaction through initial and continuous software while also altering the development process requirements as used within the software development environment. Again, agile methods also ensure that software developers work closely with the business people throughout the project development process (Beck et al., 2001).

Since the emergence of agile methods, many organizations have been fascinated by its potential to engage organizational stakeholders in adapting to changes and quickly delivering software products (Alec Cram, 2019). Reports suggest that about 95% of companies practice elements of agile development. About 70% of organizations are also believed to use agile approaches to develop their systems (VersionOne, 2016; Alec Cram, 2019). The usefulness of agile methodologies in managing software development teams led to its adaptation into other fields. For instance, educational institutions have adopted agile methods as a means of delivering education, and some of those agile methods have been used to deliver courses such as software engineering courses (Alfonso & Botia, 2005) and mathematics (Duvall et al., 2017). Unlike other software development methodologies like the waterfall approach, agile development embraced the change from the onset. Agile developers accept that software development is shrouded in some form of uncertainty due to the inability of customers to express the features of the software they want from the beginning (Meso & Jain, 2006; Batra, 2020). These principles of change and speed were later expanded to organizational studies (Sambamurthy et al., 2003; Overby et al., 2006; Bi et al., 2012). Since then, agility has been widely accepted in the organizational literature as the practice and approaches facilitating quick responses (Janssen & van der Voort, 2020). Having evolved from dynamic capabilities organizational agility shares similarities with agile principles used in software development (Teece, 2007; Conboy, 2009). Essentially, this study explains how PKU's management constantly worked with the government, health professionals, employees, and customers to respond swiftly to the pandemic, resulting in the closure of schools.

As a response to the COVID-19 pandemic, countries have adopted various measures within short periods. Similarly, since schools were in session during the outbreak, universities also adopted measures to ensure academic work was not disrupted. The response of the universities offers us an excellent opportunity to learn more about agility (Flaxman et al., 2020; Janssen & van der Voort, 2020). In this study, the underpinning issue is the lessons that practitioners and researchers can learn from the pandemic response from universities. The study cannot assess which university did best to respond to the pandemic to keep up with academic work. Considering how context shapes social phenomena like the COVID-19 pandemic, responses might differ from one university to the university. The question in this study is what led to the chosen response from the many alternatives, and most importantly, what can we learn as practitioners and researchers from such responses?

On that basis, the study seeks to explore how a university in a developing country responded to the COVID-19 pandemic to better comprehend agility in crisis response. The outcome of this study is also to provide suggestions to pertinent research issues that involve agility in a context of a developing country and make practical and research suggestions for the future. This study is based on PK University (pseudonym), hereafter referred to as PKU. PKU is a government-owned university in Ghana, West Africa. The choice of Ghana and PKU is because the authors have in-depth knowledge of this context.

Theoretical Guide

Agility

Organizations continue to face intense competition all year round. Besides, the uncertainties in the business environment caused by the COVID-19 pandemic pose a further threat to businesses in their quest to be productive and survive. Such high levels of uncertainties have imbued the notion of agility among many governments, companies, and people around the world (Batra, 2020). Amid these developments, speed and accuracy have become the new currency for governments, educational institutions, and individuals. The need for speed, for instance, has largely been attributed to the rise of digital channels through which goods and services are delivered (Smith, 2020). The likes of Amazon, Uber, Netflix, among others, have demonstrated the need for speed in their operations. On the contrary, companies like Kodak, who have failed to sense and quickly respond to environmental changes, have seen their early demise (Cancialosi, 2020). These intricacies give further credence to operate with speed in an era driven by digital technologies. To ensure speedy response and accuracy, organizations need to ensure working practices and methods that ensure swift response (Beck et al., 2001; Janssen & van der Voort, 2020).

Within organizational studies, agility primarily refers to the ability of organizations to sense changes in the environment and quickly respond to those changes. Agility has been used interchangeably with the word flexibility in recent times (Agarwal et al., 2006; Conboy, 2009). Some early studies suggest that agility could relate to an organization's ability to be proactive (Naylor et al., 1999) and embracing change as it comes (Goldman et al., 1994). The need for agility ensures that organizations survive the turbulent market environment that poses several threats to them. Therefore, organizations invest in IT to help them cope with the pressure and embrace innovative initiatives to respond to market threats and opportunities (Lu & Ramamurthy, 2011). Agility is, therefore, viewed as integral for business success as it allows them to achieve competitive performance in volatile business environments (Fink & Neumann, 2007; Bi et al., 2013). Agility also facilitates timely responses to changes in the business environment (Tallon et al., 2019). Some of these changes include changes in the demands of goods and services and changes in technology development.

Another essential element of organizational agility relates to issues of risks and uncertainties. Because risks relate to known possibilities, organizations can allocate resources to reduce those risks (Batra, 2020). However, uncertainties comprise unknown probabilities. Once organizations do not know something, it becomes challenging to hedge uncertainties with third parties (Batra, 2020). Indeed, COVID-19 is one of those occurrences that have resulted in so much uncertainty.

Situation Faced: General Outlook of PKU's Situation

Despite the negative impact on governments, schools, and other businesses, the pandemic presents limitless learning opportunities. For instance, since the outbreak, we have experienced an exponential increase in the use of the Internet and other web services (Sein, 2020). The use of online meeting platforms like Zoom skyrocketed. Many universities are moving toward online teaching for continuity due to schools' indefinite closure (Mishra et al., 2020). This study relies on the concept of agility to analyze PKU's response to the pandemic. The university had to adapt to respond to the challenges the outbreak came within a short period to ensure continuity of education. Within this context, the study argues that it was necessary to quickly deal with the situation to minimize the spread of the virus. But more importantly, it was prudent to ensure that the delivery of education is not halted because of the closure of schools. As used in this study, a university is a higher learning educational institution where academic research is conducted, and students study for degrees. Amid the outbreak, the onus lied on the university stakeholders to respond and, at the same time, be aware of the uncertainty around the situation. Meanwhile, the uncertainty around the situation provided an opportunity for the university stakeholders to create measures to minimize the transmission of the virus and ensure that academic work continues.

Table 3.1 presents a summary of the major events that took place at PK University. The table also shows an overview of the national front events that affected PKU operations directly or indirectly. Essentially, specific regulations and policies at the national level inform what PKU does. Directives from the government, Ministry of Education, and other bodies affect the operations of PKU. For

Table 3.1 The Unfolding of Major Events at PKU

Dates in 2020	Major Events that Took Place
March 11	• The NCTE issues directives to all public universities regarding COVID-19
March 12	• Ghana's health ministry confirms the first two COVID-19 cases
March 13	• PKU shuts down elevators and bans mass gathering to prevent the spread of the virus • PKU management and health directorate issue preventive measures • PKU directs all lecturers to mount their lecture notes, slides, and reference materials on the school's learning management platform • Public Service Commission issues workplace contingency measures
March 15	• President of Ghana addresses the nation (bans all social gathering and ports) • Management of PKU Shuts down university campus • NCTE instructs all public universities to submit contingency plans on how ICT and learning management platforms can be deployed to complete the academic semester
March 16	• PKU presents facilitators and students with a comprehensive user guide to the school's learning management platform
March 18	• PKU commences online teaching and learning via its LMS and other complementary platforms like Whatsapp, Email, Zoom, and Google meet • University Teachers Association of Ghana (UTAG)—National issues communique to all public universities regarding the lockdown
March 19	• Head of civil service issue a workplace contingency plan
March 21	• MTN Ghana provides free connectivity to several online learning channels to support home learning
March 23	• Data issues—Students and other stakeholders raise concerns
March 24	• Media briefing with the minister of education (update on Covid-19)
March 26	• The University Teachers Association of Ghana (UTAG) issues an update on COVID-19
March 27	• President of Ghana addresses the nation and announces restrictions on selected areas in Ghana
April 3	• PKU collaborates with a network service provider to provide free data to its LMS
April 24	• A new deadline for students to pay their fees before writing the virtual examinations
May 18–June 8	• Commencement of end of semester virtual examination
July 23	• Deadline for marking of exams questions
July 1–31	• Supplementary virtual learning (online) examination
September 2–5	• Graduation for all qualified final year students
January 2021	• Commencement of 2020–2021 academic year

instance, directions from the Education Ministry and the National Council for Tertiary Education (NCTE), to a large extent, shifted much responsibility to the universities regarding how they can complete the academic year and graduate their students. Such commitment was meant to enable the universities to adapt to the COVID-19 conditions and make decisions that best fit individual universities. Since public universities are autonomous and have specific mandates, it was imperative to choose strategies that suit their context. The NCTE directive on March 15, 2020, to all public universities, provided some evidence of this approach. This approach presented universities with opportunities that will keep them running during the closure of schools. Such a directive gave PKU the necessary mandate to continue teaching and learning online, including conducting a virtual examination.

Stakeholders at PKU had different views on the approach adopted by management. For instance, some students complained about the burden of poor Internet connectivity from their homes, whereas those with reliable Internet connectivity also lamented the high cost of Internet bundles. Other groups complained they could not access the learning management platform of the university because of their inability to pay their school fees. The final group of people believed it was not ideal for teaching and conducting exams during the pandemic because of the fear that is associated with the virus. Critically, the students aver that learning from home and writing an end-of-semester examination during the pandemic could negatively affect their performance. Based on these issues, some media houses joined the complaining students to criticize PKU's management. The main criticisms rested on the decision of the university to continue with online exams during the pandemic. This plan was to compel the university to revert its decision to conduct online exams. The online examination as necessitated by the pandemic seems to be the first among most of these universities hence the backlash.

Actions Taken and Results Achieved

Educational institutions across the globe have been hit unawares by the COVID-19 virus. Many schools are still living with the consequences of the virus. The surprise element presented calls for schools to act amid the uncertainties that surround the outbreak. For instance, there were doubts about when a vaccine will be available for all and when schools resume face-to-face education (something that dominated most universities in the developing country). To respond to the changes and challenges that COVID-19 presents to nations and particularly universities, the following issues emerged.

1. The high cost of Internet issues—who pays for the high cost of data during online learning exams?
2. Financial issues—what happens to students who cannot access the Learning Management System (LMS) due to their inability to pay fees?
3. The psychological issues—is this the right time to write the online exams?

The High Cost of Internet Issue

By the end of April 2020, more than 1.2 billion students are believed to be out of the classroom. Globally, more than 91% of students have been affected by the pandemic due to the closure of schools (Li & Lalani, 2020). Most of these students have been directed to continue education from home. Such directions further heighten the need for Internet access across the affected countries. Various Internet technologies have also enabled families and friends to keep up with loved ones. Businesses are also leveraging meeting platforms such as zoom to keep up with partners and employees (Sein, 2020). However, an overarching issue has to do with Internet access. According to UNESCO, about 826 million students kept out of school during the pandemic have no computers. More so, 706 million learners have no Internet access at home. The numbers seem high in Sub-Saharan African (SSA) countries. The study reports that 89% of learners in these countries do not have computers at home, whiles 82% do not have Internet access (UNESCO, 2020). A recent study also found that students faced Internet connectivity issues during the closedown of universities in Ghana (Henaku, 2020).

PKU had to adapt to these challenges that confront its major stakeholders (students). Despite the challenges, all the stakeholders do, however, agree on the abnormal times we leave in. The uncertainty generated by the virus demands adaptability to ensure continuity. To ensure that the fit between PKU and the environment is not diminished (Greenwood et al., 2017; Janssen & van der Voort, 2020), PKU came to the following resolution. First, PKU partnered with a leading telecommunication company to provide Internet access to staff and students. Primarily, the free data allows staff and students to download and upload learning materials to the learning management free of charge. Students who were not registered on the network were encouraged to purchase the provider's SIM card to enjoy the benefits. Students were also encouraged to use their smartphones if they had no personal computer.

Financial Issues

Existing research has shown that organizations such as PKU are not required to respond to every single change in the environment, as presented by COVID-19. However, an organization's failure to respond to the issues in time could significantly damage the organization. While it is essential to respond quickly, sometimes, quick decisions could compromise the quality of the decision-making process (Janssen & van der Voort, 2020). In PKU, an initial assessment of the effect of the pandemic on the university was conducted. Because the school uses its internally generated funds to fund most developmental projects, it was crucial to seriously analyze the financial concerns of students and bear in mind the consequences. A recent study reports that COVID-19 continues to impact the finances of students and families. Students, especially those in developing countries, continue to owe schools. This is because their financial sources have been greatly affected by the pandemic (Upoalkpajor & Upoalkpajor, 2020).

PKU embarked on removing the barriers within its structures. Barriers and bureaucracies are typical of most government institutions. Interestingly, removing such barriers ensures a flatter institution (Waite et al., 2015). Consequently, the following measures were instituted to ensure that students were not pressured unduly. First, the management directed lecturers to suspend deadlines for assignments on the learning management platform. Initially, students complained of their inability to submit exercises, projects, and assignments on the platform because they owed school fees. As a university policy, only students who paid their fees were given access to the platform. Second, the management issued a directive that extended the deadline for the payment of school fees. The directive was to ensure that students had ample time to complete paying their fees before the examination took place. Third, before the exams, the management directed lecturers to conduct supplementary exams on the virtual platform. This directive was in anticipation that students might be unable to submit their exams on the deadline dates.

The Psychological Issues

The psychological conditions of students during this pandemic cannot be overemphasized. Students are believed to suffer from some anxiety disorders as a result of the outbreak. Critically, it is the fact that the increased number of cases across the world has elicited some concern about possible infections. Therefore, this has increased anxiety among students (Bao et al., 2020; Cao et al., 2020). In a recent study in China, Cao et al. (2020) found that about 25% of college students suffered from anxiety because of the pandemic. Such anxiety, which is necessitated by the fear of being infected, is also believed to negatively affect their studies and future employment opportunities (Wang et al., 2020). Per these concerns, PKU was not oblivious to the effects of the pandemic on students' ability to continue school.

Management, therefore, continuously engaged student leadership on the need to complete the academic semester. Students were entreated to bear with management in those hard times as prudent measures were taken that would benefit all stakeholders. Through several engagements, PKU issued a directive that exams will take place online. PKU's decision was the first in its history, as face-to-face exams have been the norm for decades. Ideally, physical examinations at PKU took place between 1 and 3 hours, depending on the course. However, the pandemic presented issues that needed a fitting response. On this basis, the examination was conducted via the school's LMS. With this, students had the liberty to research and answer the questions. Students had up to 48 hours (two days) to submit responses to each examination question of a course. This notwithstanding, PKU was also proactive in creating emails for the various causes. This approach ensured that students who could not send their answers through the LMS do so through the designated emails. Such provisions went down well with the various stakeholders, hence the virtual examination.

On the whole, all courses had about a 93% response rate during the exams. This shows that a greater number of the student population could submit their exams through the LMS or the designated course email. Besides, supplementary exams were conducted for those who were unable to take part in the main exams. The initiative also took into account the work of staff. Lecturers mainly needed some form of motivation to deliver their services to students. Past research suggests that teacher motivation is needed during these trying times, apart from learners (Upoalkpajor & Upoalkpajor, 2020). Considering that lecturers had to work from home, management provided lecturers with data packages to do their work.

Lessons Learned and Implications for Theory and Practice

Theoretical Implications

The COVID-19 pandemic seems to have provided institutions of higher learning opportunities to become flexible and responsive in a short period. It has also provided them with the prospects of learning about agile principles and their importance for survival. The study made some observations as they relate to agility in educational institutions. First, agitations or tensions among various stakeholders nearly constrained PKU's desire to demonstrate agility on time. Mukerjee (2014) contends that, whereas agility is necessary for universities, most universities cannot achieve it because of tensions within and outside the organization. For PKU, management had to overcome the tensions quickly to provide an appropriate response to the changes emanated from the pandemic.

The study also found that bureaucracy, known for its slow nature, was also essential for PKU to respond to the pandemic changes. For instance, as a public university, PKU had to close the school after a directive from the central government. This is evident in the president's 15th March address to close social gatherings (see Table 3.1). The closure also gave the school the leeway to adapt to the changes and ensure that it does not cease operations. Janssen and van der Voort (2020) underscored the critical role bureaucracy plays in governments' adaptation to the COVID-19 pandemic.

Another important observation is the willpower of stakeholders, especially university management, to remain flexible amid rigidity and tensions from critical stakeholders like the students. For most developing economies, online education is now gaining ground. Critically, most universities in developing countries are yet to fully adopt electronic learning platforms (Ansong et al., 2017). Traditional face-to-face teaching and learning had been the predominant mode for decades. A distraction of the status seemed uncomfortable to the students. Therefore, they felt it was best to wait until the pandemic was over to continue school. But, the ideal time for schools to reopen had been surrounded by so much uncertainty. It was, therefore, not surprising that students kicked against the online examination from the onset. Previous studies have shown that such an institutional bottleneck could hinder information systems innovations like online education (Naresh & Reddy, 2015). Another thought worthy of attention is the role of strong institutions in spearheading agility. The PKU management demonstrated this as all other universities were in limbo as to what would happen to them. The existence of institutions might not be enough to become agile, as Janssen and van der Voort (2020) suggested. But the strength and commitment to become agile is also very notably crucial for survival.

PKU's approach could further be attributed to the "double-loop learning" model. According to Argyris (1991), "double-loop learning" contrasted the idea of "single-loop learning," which entails repeating the same problem without any form of change in technique and without ever interrogating the goal. Argyris used the thermostat analogy to explain the difference between the two terms. The study suggests that an excellent example of single-loop learning is "when a thermostat turns on the heat on itself given that the temperature in a room drops below 68 degrees" (Argyris, 1991, p. 4). On the contrary, a thermostat that asks why it is set at 68 degrees and can discover other economic temperatures in achieving the goal of heating the room would be engaging in double-loop learning (Argyris, 1991, p. 4). Principally, the model provides a structure that enables altering decision-making objectives due to experience (Janssen & van der Voort, 2020).

Typically, most professionals, like lecturers and students, are comfortable with their single-loop models. This is because some of them have acquired the needed skills to learn during face-to-face interactions. Management and students decided on the current situation they found themselves in with a clear goal in mind. As the evidence from the previous sections suggests, the students, for instance, became apprehensive by the decision to conduct online teaching and learning. They, therefore, set to blame the management. Equally, management also issued directives to lectures to make their study materials accessible to students in the interim. According to Argyris (1991), such issues are commonplace with single-loop learning. As posited, these issues depict agility characteristics as it involved generating quick responses by making decisions following the pandemic. The double-loop learning model details a reflection on organizations to adapt well in the future. The second learning loop encapsulates the decision of organizations to possess adaptability characteristics. An underlying assumption of this step is to ensure that organizations survive through adaptation.

Implications for Practice

The COVID-19 pandemic presents researchers and practitioners with several lessons that can be useful for higher learning institutions in the future. First, there is no strategy globally touted as the best. Responses largely vary depending on the context. Even so, with the various educational institutions, there is no single best response. From the PKU case, the multiple stakeholders had their demands, some of which resulted in tensions. For instance, students' pressures regarding Internet data charges resulted in PKU's adaptation of giving free data through a major Internet service provider to help students access resources on the school LMS.

An additional lesson from this study is that responses could change over time. The spread of the pandemic globally showed how responses could be adapted over a certain period. Some responses that were seen to be effective initially might not yield results at the later stages. At this period, learning and monitoring the situation are quintessential (Janssen & van der Voort, 2020). Therefore, organizations need to possess these capabilities (thus, learning and monitoring). Such capabilities ensure that organizations have a broader perspective of the issues and not waiting for the government to do everything. While other universities were waiting in the PKU case, PKU and its stakeholders ensured that education continued. The management of PKU outlined strategies that ensured that all stakeholders coped with the situation. For instance, PKU changed its earlier position on insisting on the deadline date for which students were expected to pay their tuition fees. The previous position experienced resistance from the student body. Based on this, and through monitoring events, the PKU management had to alter that position by extending the deadline to ensure that students were not disadvantaged. PKU also introduced two different supplementary examinations (the first-ever in its history) for those who could not write the regular examinations due to financial, psychological, and Internet connectivity issues.

Third, PKU's approach concerns how it is important to be agile but still maintain stability and remain relevant at the same time. Previous studies suggest that adaptive strategies have the propensity to challenge stability (Janssen & van der Voort, 2016). In the wake of the pandemic where schools were closed, higher learning institutions needed to demonstrate some form of stability to respond. Considering the pressure of the pandemic on universities, it is not ideal to panic and change organizational structures. Instead, they need to become innovative in ensuring that the structures are maintained and ensuring that the systems work. Generally, changing structures and decision-making takes a longer time but established mechanisms tend to work well. This is because stakeholders can cope with them since they are familiar with them. Organizations that possess strong systems and structures are better positioned to respond to crises.

Fourth, the pandemic and subsequent lockdown, which has forced educational institutions to move their services online, have resulted in the presence of a variety of strategies. As evident in the case of PKU, various strategies reemphasize the assumptions that underpin the evolutionary game theory. Agents in a game have the liberty to choose from a variety of strategies. The idea of having multiple strategies also reveals which strategy is the most abundant (Gokhale & Traulsen, 2011). With past evidence, PKU selected the ideal alternatives that maintained a fit with its Ghanaian context. Meanwhile, the involvement of many institutions in the selection of the appropriate strategy, however, could lead to confusion and can be counterproductive. The PKU case shows that educational institutions can leverage multiple ways to become agile in a crisis, such as COVID-19. The pandemic has not spared any country across the globe. Every country has been affected uniquely, and it becomes difficult to make comparisons. Each Ghanaian university was allowed to propose contingency plans that can help students complete the semester. Whereas others waited to see a reduction in the cases before continuing school, PKU quickly responded by proposing measures that enabled students to continue school from home. Universities in other contexts could challenge such strategies as adopted by PKU in response to the pandemic. As indicated by Denning (2018), this study cannot conclude that one strategy is the best, and others are wrong.

The fifth lesson from this study points to how the NCTE shifted responsibility to the individual universities. Besides issuing directives to all universities to adhere to COVID-19 protocols, the NCTE called on the various universities to adapt to their contexts and use resources (e.g., e-learning platform) at their disposal to ensure continuity. The mandate of the NCTE is to oversee the administration of tertiary education in Ghana. Therefore, their collaboration with the various universities was fundamental. Considering the pandemic, the universities and the NCTE needed to collaborate while adapting to the situation. The role of collaboration to aid in the decision-making process has also been well established in past research (Wang et al., 2018).

Another lesson from this study points to the need for universities in developing countries to invest in their information systems capabilities. PKU's readiness necessitated the need to adopt online education as it invested in its LMS. Investments were made in areas such as software and hardware infrastructure. Infrastructure issues mainly focused on hardware, compatibility, and connectivity (Zhang et al., 2009). As Batra (2020) suggests, companies that invest in such capabilities perform better in turbulent environments like those we currently witness. Whereas PKU successfully responded to the changing needs and brought the academic semester to an end successfully, others wrote their exams physically. Others had to wait for months to conduct their exams. This is because organizations were unprepared and unable to develop the needed capabilities to respond to the pandemic changes (Worley & Jules, 2020). In certain contexts, such unpreparedness from the other universities could lead to extinction because they were unprepared for the situation (Tilman, 2019).

Finally, sector-level strategic responses in crises such as COVID-19 are influenced by national-level responses. Concerning the fact that all institutions are affected by government policy, schools and other institutions had to wait for the president to issue an official statement based on which they can design or alter theirs.

Implications to Policy

For institutions of higher learning, policy formulation is critical to their operations. Like Ghana, universities globally have different structures and mandates, which distinguishes them from one another. At the height of the pandemic, the government acknowledged the peculiar mandates, focus, and strengths of these universities. Hence, the need to allow them to institute measures that will support their peculiar mandate and structures. The lessons from the study provide a stepping stone for educational policymakers to have contingency plans in place to ensure continuity in the wake of pandemics such as COVID-19. In other contexts, such as the United States, universities have adopted various business continuity plans such as extreme weather conditions and other disasters (Kapucu & Khosa, 2013; Dohaney et al., 2020). Such plans aim to manage disruptions after disasters. Pandemics such as COVID-19 seem to be far from over. As a result, universities should provide distinct policies on how to continue their operations amid such pandemics. One such policy is the strengthening of institutions and providing robust online platforms that can support teaching and learning. It is imperative to understand the dynamics in the contextual environment and offer appropriate policies by relaxing institutional structures to provide greater efficiency and consistency in teaching and learning. Understanding these dynamics feeds into policymakers' activities as they can use the insights to mitigate rigidity which is very common in most government institutions. For instance, many students may not be able to return to school due to the impact of the pandemic on their finances. As a result, enrollment could be affected in the coming years. Policies that can ensure that these people continue school is needed to bridge the inequality gap, especially in developing country universities.

Conclusion

The COVID-19 pandemic continues to have a devastating effect on governments and institutions across the world. With so many students out of school due to the virus, the situation is becoming a "new normal". Despite this, the outbreak has also presented educational institutions, especially universities, an opportunity to adapt and become agile in the wake of the pandemic. The study analyzed the response to the COVID-19 pandemic of a university in a developing country to gain richer insights into agile education in practice. Specifically, the study investigated concepts that relate to timing, collaboration, and stability. The PKU approach showed that agility, indeed, involves tenants of sensing and responding to changes in the environment. The outcomes also indicate that agility and adaptability can go hand in hand (Janssen & van der Voort, 2020).

This theoretical guide of this study explains how agility originated from the software development discipline and later applied in organizational studies. The nature of agility, therefore, takes an adaptive approach that involves some form of contingency methods. In such cases, organizations demonstrate high levels of tolerance to address the inconsistencies of the pandemic, as evidenced in the case of PKU. While acknowledging the ability to sense for changes and be tolerant, the ability of organizations to provide rational responses to the changes is vital. Meanwhile, it is also imperative for organizations to offer sound analysis for decisions during turbulent times. Centralized and decentralized mechanisms, coupled with innovation, science, and politics, are also needed in this regard (Janssen & van der Voort, 2020). For instance, concerning science, PKU had to listen to health experts to minimize the spread of the virus, especially among the few employees who provide essential services such as the school hospital. With this assertion in mind, the study presents critical questions and issues that could be addressed in future research.

Future Research and Practice Directions

With the claims made in this study, this section presents some future research directions. The first is to understand how other higher learning institutions respond to the changes emanating from COVID-19 amid several contradictions. As we have observed in this study, the focus was on a university in a developing country. A greater and deeper contextualization of the issues may provide other insightful findings to shape the agility debate. For instance, in PKU, there have been some agitations from stakeholders, and one of such agitation was due to technical challenges of the LMS. But how would schools with robust systems respond to the pandemic amid the uncertainties?

Another crucial area for future research concerns how higher learning institutions, especially those in developing countries, are institutionalizing the changes brought by COVID-19? In essence, we ask, how are managers of higher institutions institutionalizing the "new normal?" With the pandemic still with us, governments and leadership of universities perhaps have learned several lessons. But how do these lessons enable them to institutionalize the positive new measures? For instance, in the case of PKU, future research could analyze managers' role and power in institutionalizing the responses generated during the pandemic. What will be some of the consequences of institutionalizing some of these policies? Finally, with design science research influencing information systems practice (Rai, 2019), we ask how the outcomes of this study will influence the design of information systems within organizations, in general, and higher learning institutions in particular?

References

Agarwal, A., Shankar, R., & Tiwari, M. (2006). Modeling the Metrics of Lean, Agile and Leagile Supply Chains: An ANP-Based Approach. *European Journal of Operational Research, 173*, 211–225.

Ågerfalk, P., Conboy, K., & Myers, M. (2020). Information Systems in the Age of Pandemics: COVID-19 and Beyond. *European Journal of Information Systems, 29*(3), 203–207.

Alec Cram, W. (2019). Agile Development in Practice: Lessons from the Trenches. *Information Systems Management, 36*(1), 2–14.

Alfonso, M. I., & Botia, A. (2005, April). An Iterative and Agile Process Model for Teaching Software Engineering. In *18th Conference on Software Engineering Education & Training (CSEET'05), April 18–20, 2005* (pp. 9–16). IEEE, Ottawa, ON.

Ansong, E., Boateng, R., & Boateng, S. (2017). The Nature of E-Learning Adoption by Stakeholders of a University in Africa. *E-Learning and Digital Media, 1*(18).

Argyris, C. (1991). Teaching Smart People How to Learn. *Harvard Business Review, 69*(3), 99–109.

Bao, Y., Sun, Y., Meng, S., Shi, J., & Lu, L. (2020). 2019-nCoV Epidemic: Address Mental Health Care to Empower Society. *The Lancet, 395*(10224), e37–e38.

Batra, D. (2020). The Impact of the COVID-19 on Organizational and Information Systems Agility. *Information Systems Management, 37*(4), 361–365.

Beck, K., Grenning, J., & Martin, R. (2001). *Manifesto for Agile Software Development*. https://agilemanifesto.org/

Bi, R., Davison, R., Kam, B., & Smyrnios, K. (2013). Developing Organizational Agility Through It and Supply Chain Capability. *Journal of Global Information Management (JGIM), 21*(4), 38–55.

Cancialosi, C. (2020, March 12). *Organizational Agility and Resilience- Two Critical Sides of The Same Coin.* Retrieved August 8, 2020, from www.forbes.com/sites/chriscancialosi/2020/03/10/organizational-agility-and-resiliencetwo-critical-sides-of-the-same-coin/#6e0af44d614a

Cao, W., Fang, Z., Hou, G., Han, M., Xu, X., Dong, J., & Zheng, J. (2020). The Psychological Impact of the COVID-19 Epidemic on College Students in China. *Psychiatry Research, 287*, 112934.

Chinazzi, M., Davis, J. T., Ajelli, M., Gioannini, C., Litvinova, M., Merler, S., & Viboud, C. (2020). The Effect of Travel Restrictions on the Spread of the 2019 Novel Coronavirus (COVID-19) Outbreak. *Science, 368*(6489), 395–400.

Collier, K. (2012). *Agile Analytics: A Value-Driven Approach to Business Intelligence and Data Warehousing.* Upper Saddle River, NJ: Addison-Wesley Professional.

Conboy, K. (2009). Agility from First Principles: Reconstructing the Concept of Agility in Information Systems Development. *Information Systems Research, 20*(3), 329–354.

Denning, S. (2018, January 28). *What is Strategic Agility?* www.forbes.com/sites/stevedenning/2018/01/28/what-is-strategic-agility/#9e20b55a0b1b

Dohaney, J., Roiste, D., Salmon, R., & Sutherland, S. (2020). Benefits, Barriers, and Incentives for Improved Resilience to Disruption in University Teaching. *International Journal of Disaster Risk Reduction, 50*, 101691.

Dowdy, D., Rieckhoff, K., & Maxwell, J. (2017, May 25). *How the Public Sector Can Remain Agile Beyond Times of Crisis.* Retrieved August 12, 2020, from www.mckinsey.com/industries/public-and-social-sector/our-insights/how-the-public-sector-can-remain-agile-beyond-times-of-crisis

Duvall, S., Hutchings, D., & Kleckner, M. (2017). Changing Perceptions of Discrete Mathematics through Scrum-based Course Management Practices. *Journal of Computing Sciences in Colleges, 33*(2), 182–189.

Ekmekci, O., & Bergstrand, J. (2010). Agility in Higher Education: Planning for Business Continuity in the Face of an H1N1 Pandemic. *SAM Advanced Management Journal, 75*(20).

Fink, L., & Neumann, S. (2007). Gaining Agility through IT Personnel Capabilities: The Mediating Role of IT Infrastructure Capabilities. *Journal of the Association for Information Systems, 8*(8), 440–462.

Flaxman, S., Mishra, S., Gandy, A., Unwin, H. J., Mellan, T. A., Coupland, H., & Bhatt, S. (2020). Estimating the Effects of Non-Pharmaceutical Interventions on COVID-19 in Europe. *Nature.* https://doi.org/10.1038/s41586-020-2405-7

Fowler, M., & Highsmith, J. A. (2001). The Agile Manifesto. *Software Development, 9*(8), 28–35. http://users.jyu.fi/~mieijala/kandimateriaali/Agile-Manifesto.pdf

Gokhale, C., & Traulsen, A. (2011). Strategy Abundance in Evolutionary Many-Player Games with Multiple Strategies. *Journal of Theoretical Biology, 283*(1), 180–191.

Goldman, S., Nagel, R., & Preiss, K. (1994). *Agile Competitors and Virtual Organizations: Strategies for Enriching the Customer*. New York: Von Nostrand Reinhold.

Greenwood, R., Oliver, C., Lawrence, T. B., & Meyer, R. E. (2017). *The Sage Handbook of Organizational Institutionalism*. London: Sage Publications.

Henaku, E. (2020). COVID-19: Online Learning Experience of College Students: The of Ghana. *International Journal of Multidisciplinary Sciences and Advanced Technology*, *1*(2), 54–62.

Janssen, M., & van der Voort, H. (2016). Adaptive Governance: Towards a Stable, Accountable and Responsive Government. *Government Information Quarterly*, *33*(1), 1–5.

Janssen, M., & van der Voort, H. (2020). Agile and Adaptive Governance in Crisis Response: Lessons from the COVID-19. *International Journal of Information Management*, https://doi.org/10.1016/j.ijinfomgt.2020.102180.

Kapucu, N., & Khosa, S. (2013). Disaster Resiliency and Culture of Preparedness for University and College Campuses. *Administration & Society*, *45*, 3–37.

Li, C., & Lalani, F. (2020, April 29). *The COVID-19 Pandemic has Changed Education Forever*. Retrieved February 6, from www.weforum.org/agenda/2020/04/coronavirus-education-global-covid19-online-digital-learning/

Lu, Y., & Ramamurthy, K. (2011). Understanding the Link between Information Technology Capability and Organizational Agility: An Empirical Examination. *MIS Quarterly*, *35*(4), 931–954.

Marinoni, G., & van't Land, H. J. (2020). The Impact of Covid-19 on Higher Education Around the World. *IAU Global Survey Report, International Association of Universities*, *2*(2).

Menon, S., & Suresh, M. (2020). Organizational Agility Assessment for Higher Education Institution. *The Journal of Research on the Lepidoptera*, *51*(1), 561–573.

Meso, P., & Jain, R. (2006). Agile Software Development: Adaptive Systems Principles and Best Practices. *Information Systems Management*, *23*(3), 19–30.

Mishra, L., Gupta, T., & Shree, A. (2020). Online Teaching-Learning in Higher Education during Lockdown Period of COVID-19 Pandemic. *International Journal of Educational Research Open*. https://doi.org/10.1016/j.ijedro.2020.100012

Mukerjee, S. (2014). Organizational Agility in Universities: Tensions and Challenges. In T. Fitzgerald (Ed.), *Advancing Knowledge in Higher Education: Universities in Turbulent Times* (pp. 15–25). Hershey, PA: IGI Global.

Naresh, B., & Reddy, B. (2015). Challenges and Opportunity of E-Learning in Developed and Developing Countries- A Review. *International Journal of Emerging Research in Management & Technology*, *4*(6).

Naylor, J., Nairn, M., Berry, D., & Integrating, 1. L. (1999). Leagility: Integrating the Lean and Agile Manufacturing Paradigm in the Total Supply Chain. *Engineering Costs and Production Economics*, *62*, 107–118.

Overby, E., Bharadwaj, A., & Sambamurthy, V. (2006). Enterprise Agility and the Enabling role of Information Technology. *European Journal of Information Systems*, *15*, 120–131.

Rai, A. (2019). Engaged Scholarship: Research with Practice for Impact, Editor's Comments. *MIS Quarterly*, *43*(2), iii–viii.

Sambamurthy, V., Bharadwaj, A., & Grover, V. (2003). Shaping Agility Through Digital Options: Reconceptualizing the Role of Information Technology in Contemporary Firms. *MIS Quarterly*, (27), 237–263.

Sein, M. K. (2020). The Serendipitous Impact of COVID-19 Pandemic: A Rare Opportunity for Research and Practice. *International Journal of Information Management*, *55*, 102164. https://doi.org/10.1016/j.ijinfomgt.2020.102164

Shamsir, M., Krauss, S., Ismail, I., Jalil, H., Johar, M., & Rahman, I. (2021). Development of a Haddon Matrix Framework for Higher Education Pandemic Preparedness: Scoping Review and Experiences of Malaysian Universities During the COVID-19 Pandemic. *Higher Education Policy*, 19(1), 1–40. https://doi.org/10.1057/s41307-020-00221-x

Smith, G. (2020, July 1). *Seven Steps To Creating Business Agility in Your Organization*. Retrieved August 8, 2020, from www.forbes.com/sites/forbesbusinesscouncil/2020/07/01/seven-steps-to-creating-business-agility-in-your-organization/#5e60d5063f49

Tallon, P., Queiroz, M., Coltman, T., & Sharma, R. (2019). Information Technology and the Search for Organizational Agility: A Systematic Review with Future Research Possibilities. *Journal of Strategic Information Systems*, *28*, 218–237.

Teece, D. (2007). Explicating Dynamic Capabilities: The Nature and Microfoundations of (Sustainable) Enterprise Performance. *Strategic Management Journal, 28*(13), 1319–1350.

Tilman, L. M. (2019). *Agility: How to Navigate the Unknown and Seize Opportunity in a World of Disruption.* Arlington, VA: Missionday.

UNESCO. (2020, April 21). *Startling Digital Divides in Distance Learning Emerge.* Retrieved June 3, 2020, from https://en.unesco.org/news/startling-digital-divides-distance-learning-emerge

Upoalkpajor, J.-L., & Upoalkpajor, C. (2020). The Effects of COVID-19 on Education in Ghana. *Asian Journal of Education and Social Studies, 9*(1), 23–33.

VersionOne. (2016). *10th Annual State of Agile Report.* Alpharetta, GA: CollabNet.

Waite, T., Nisbet, M., & Vanorny, S. (2015, 415). *Achieving Agility in Higher Education: Four Critical Transformations.* Retrieved January 2, 2021, from https://evolllution.com/opinions/achieving-agility-higher-education-critical-transformations/

Wang, C., Horby, P., Hayden, F., & Gao, G. (2020). A Novel Coronavirus Outbreak of Global Health Concern. *The Lancet, 395*(10223), 470–473.

Wang, C., Medaglia, R., & Zheng, L. (2018). Towards a Typology of Adaptive Governance in the Digital Government Context: The Role of Decision-Making and Accountability. *Government Information Quarterly, 35*(2), 306–322.

Worley, C., & Jules, C. (2020). COVID-19's Uncomfortable Revelations About Agile and Sustainable Organizations in a VUCA World. *The Journal of Applied Behavioral Science, 56*(3), 279–283.

Zhang, J., Li, H., & Ziegelmayer, J. L. (2009). Resource or Capability? A Dissection of SMEs' IT Infrastructure Flexibility and Its Relationship with IT Responsiveness. *Journal of Computer Information Systems, 50*(1), 46–53.

Authors' Profile

Joshua Ofoeda is a PhD candidate at the Operations and Management Department of the University of Ghana Business School. Joshua is currently a lecturer at the University of Professional Studies, Accra, where he teaches courses such as Information Systems and Electronic Commerce. His research interests are information systems development, digital platforms, e-government, e-commerce, digital economy, and IT ethics.

James Tetteh Ami-Narh is a senior lecturer and currently the Director of Information Services and Technology Directorate, University of Professional Studies, Accra (UPSA). With a diverse background, he strongly believes in the contribution that technology makes to the lives of people and organizations. As an information system professional with 20 years of experience, James has taught several information systems-related courses on professional programs such as ACCA, CIMA, ICSA, CA Ghana, and MBA MIS. His research interest is in information systems management, information technology professional practice, e-commerce, e-health, and green computing.

DOING BUSINESS IN EMERGING ECONOMIES

Reflections and Future Directions

Chapter 4

Emerging Trends in Digital Transformation in the Public Sector for Service Innovation

Kofi Agyenim Boateng and Akua Peprah-Yeboah

Contents

DOI: 10.4324/9781003152217-6

Overview

The transforming power of contemporary digital technologies continues to open organizations and institutions—including those in the public sector—up for many possibilities of service innovation (Alaimo et al., 2020; Alaimo & Kallinikos, 2017; Wiredu et al., 2019). The service innovation possibilities have inspired governments—especially those from the developing world—to embark on a radical process of electronic-driven transformation of their institutions in what some government officials christen as "Digital Agenda" (Mansell, 2014, p. 203). Ghana is one such developing country that has hooked on to the digital agenda catchphrase and has accordingly, in recent times, accelerated the pace of digital transformation meant to shape the direction of service innovation in many aspects of public sector operations. The application of the digital transformation technologies in the public sector suggests a new paradigm of service innovation.

The direction of service innovation in the administration of the public sector is supposed to be consistent with the rising expectations of the citizenry (Mergel et al., 2019). These growing expectations can be seen in innovative public service delivery functions that occasion transparency, identity, speed, convenience, context-awareness demands, and participation, among others. These outcomes of the digitally transformed public sector via innovative service delivery reinforce the varied means by which digital technologies can be applied to meet the dynamic needs of the citizenry in diverse and meaningful societal arrangements. The new pattern of service innovation identifies with multifaceted intentions such as popularizing government projects across the country, bridging the digital divide (Venkatesh & Sykes, 2013) as well as making life a lot more comfortable and convenient for the general population. In view of this, it is uncommon for ordinary citizens to miss the unmistakable forces underlying the digital transformation agenda in the provision of public sector service innovation.

Digital transformation enthusiasts continue to advance their views on the application of technologies in shaping societies, institutions, and businesses (see, for example, Li et al., 2018; Mergel et al., 2019; Vial, 2019; Margiono, 2020). To this end, digital transformation scholars have focused attention on matters of how enduring lessons can be learned from the implementation of information systems projects (Majchrzak et al., 2016a), the determination of business models resulting from digital transformation (Berman, 2012; Remane et al., 2017), the sustainability of "digital" itself in entrepreneurship and its allied business models (Bican & Brem, 2020), among a host of others. All of these studies have discussed one form of digital transformation project or another at any given point in time to underscore their vital significance.

However, what appears to be prominently missing from these research efforts are works that take on the challenge to present many of these implemented digital transformation projects and view them simultaneously from the standpoint of ongoing results. Doing this provides an opportunity to contribute to the growing body of literature on digital transformation, especially regarding public sector service innovation. Again, analyzing these digital transformation projects in terms of the simultaneity of their outcomes to account for the underlying forces in both the ontological and epistemological understanding in the literature constitutes an inextricable aspect of the aspirations of this study. We are thus sensitized to this research question: Why does the government initiate digital transformation projects in the public sector through innovative services for citizens? Teasing out an appropriate response to the research question provides an avenue for contributing toward knowledge and understanding by way of digital innovations and their relationship with digital transformation.

It is crucial to consider how finding a response to the research question also drives us to a cross-analysis of eight recently implemented digital transformation projects between 2010 and 2019. In the course of this digital transformation scrutiny, we construct a vignette and contextualize themes that emerge from them based on the motivation and the diversity of the scenarios that accompany the rollout of the projects. As a result of constraints of space, we endeavor to provide a brief but rich account of the particular digital transformation project ahead of the thematic lessons—it has to offer—toward the overall contribution of the study. The overarching reason that reinforces the rationale for this study is inspired by the observation that the prevailing explanation of digital transformation in service innovation has an orientation of "one project at a time" (Matt et al., 2015; Schweer & Sahl, 2017; Vogelsang et al., 2018). And the researchers are of the view that such an orientation misses a fundamental point from a "broader perspective" logic.

The chapter is structured along these lines. Following the introduction is the second section that provides a scholarly rendition of the contemporary digital transformation literature and relates it to service innovation practices. The third section outdoors the presentation of the eight vignettes developed to bring out the societal preference for some aspects of digital transformation this study is seeking to unearth. In the fourth section, we present our philosophical lens, interpretive philosophical assumption, for scrutinizing how digital transformation shapes service innovation within the public sector. Following that, we synthesize all the narratives from the digital transformation projects to underscore the fundamental predispositions that occasion their implementation, and finally, we draw lessons and implications from the digital agenda discourse for both research and practice.

Digital Transformation: A Literature Callout

The concept of digital transformation, acknowledged elsewhere as "the fourth Industrial Revolution" (Siebel, 2019, p. 18), has been examined extensively in recent times (Vial, 2019). Various perspectives have, therefore, emerged on what constitutes digital transformation. To Majchrzak et al. (2016b), for instance, digital transformation is the profound societal and industrial changes brought about by digital technologies, while Haffke et al. (2016) focus on the process involved in digital transformation and point out that it entails the digitization of sales and communication channels and the augmentation or replacement of an organization's physical offerings with digital alternatives.

However, digital transformation goes beyond digital innovation. The concept and practice of digital transformation are not upgrading software or undertaking a supply chain improvement project, but intentionally creating a digital shock to what may be a reasonably functioning system (Andriole, 2017). Thus, it can be said to be the strategic overhaul of business activities, processes, competencies, and models to take advantage of the opportunities that digital technologies offer (Demirkan et al., 2016).

The lack of consensus on the definition of digital transformation is clear from literature. Vial (2019) examined twenty-three unique definitions of digital transformation and bemoaned the lack of conceptual precision in the various definitions. However, he noted the idea that digital transformation is primarily explained as it relates to the organization and is defined in terms of the use of "digital technologies". The difference among definitions mostly relates to the specific types of technologies involved and the nature of the transformation taking place (Andriole, 2017; Piccinini et al., 2015). Drawing on these observations, it is noted elsewhere that digital transformation is "a process that aims to improve an entity by triggering significant changes to its properties through combinations of information, computing, communication, and connectivity technologies" (Vial, 2019, p. 118). For the purposes of the current study, we adopt Vial's (2019) definition because it gives a clear and concise description of the concept while incorporating aspects of the various perspectives of digital transformation.

Remane et al. (2017) note that digital transformation occurs as a response to the diffusion of digital technologies such as cloud computing, mobile Internet, social media, and big data that fit with the popular SMACIT (Social, Mobile, Analytics, Cloud, and the Internet of Things) acronym (Sebastian et al., 2017). Typically, digital transformation employs a combination of these technologies. For instance, a firm might employ an algorithm that tailors its marketing strategy to customer preferences (Günther et al., 2017). Such an algorithm may use customer mobile phones and social media data to understand customer behavior (Newell & Marabelli, 2015). These technologies enable real-time monitoring and updating and transformation of production processes and customer relations (Porter & Heppelmann, 2014). Another aspect of digital transformation is the emergence of platform economies that create value by connecting people and entities (Mergel et al., 2019). Here, the core business model aims at facilitating the communication between external producers and consumers as is the case of online markets like Amazon.

The main advantage of digital transformation projects is in their ability to create "hyperconnectedness and collaboration of consumers and organizations across the gamut of value chain activities: co-design, co-creation, co-production, co-marketing, co-distribution and co-funding" (Berman, 2012, p. 6). Ultimately, digital transformation disrupts the status quo in service delivery and creates an entirely new business model, gaining new market shares, entering new markets, attracting new customers, and dropping those who are not contributing to the financial bottom line (Mergel et al., 2019). Further, organizational culture and structures at the organizational and intra-organizational level benefit from digital transformation (Nograsek & Vintar, 2014). Administrative processes, for instance, are improved through enhanced coordination between departments, agencies, institutions, both private and public (Cordella & Tempini, 2015).

Service Innovation in a Digitized Public Sector

Although the concept of innovation in business has been around for decades, its application to the public sector burgeoned after Osborne and Gaebler's (1992) seminal work, *Reinventing Government* (RG), nearly three decades ago. Prior to this, the term innovation was mainly used in relation to entrepreneurship in the private sector. According to Schumpeter (1934, 1942), innovation has three critical aspects: entrepreneurship, "creative destruction" that brings about novelty and value, and individual or collective value generation. Thus, in essence, innovation is the creation of something new to create value. This value creation could be a new application of an existing tool or technology, a new perspective or way of thinking, a new method, among others. Despite having a unique institutional structure, different from the private sector, the public sector can still benefit from a private sector-like entrepreneurial drive. The motivations, risks, rewards, incentives, and constraints faced by the public sector, especially in contemporary times, call for the adoption of innovations to achieve their aim of contributing to economic growth and prosperity (Bertot et al., 2016).

With the ever-evolving needs of the populations they serve, the public sector has had to adopt novel methods that recognize challenges and find fast, cheap, and consensus-based solutions to them (UNECE, 2017). One emerging trend in this regard is embarking on digital transformation in governance with different nomenclatures such as *digital government, e-government, online government*, and *Internet-based government* (Rosenberg, 2018; Wirtz & Daiser, 2018). Digital government can be described as governments' attempt to use innovative digital means to solve social, economic, political, and other problems, while transforming themselves in the process (Janowski, 2015). However, the approach by West (2005) underscores the technological aspect of the meaning of the concept of digital government by focusing on the employment of electronic communication gadgets such as computers and the Internet in public service delivery.

Service innovation in the public sector comes in seven different strands (see Table 4.1) (Bertot et al., 2016) that are mutually exclusive and target a specific aspect of the public service. However,

Table 4.1 Digital Public Service Innovation Framework

	transparent	Participatory	Anticipatory	Personalized	Co-created	Context-aware	Context-Smart
Can agencies disseminate information (one-way) to citizens?	x	x	x	x	x	x	x
Can agencies and citizens engage in (two-way) discrete interactions?	x	x	x	x	x	x	x
Can agencies and citizens engage in linked interactions (transactions)?	x	x	x	x	x	x	x
Can agencies coordinate internally (seamlessly) between themselves?	x	x	x	x	x	x	x
Can citizens know about how service decisions are made by the government?	x	x					
Can citizens participate in service decision-making by the government?		x					
Can government initiate (proactively) service delivery to citizens?			x				
Can citizens choose how they wish to receive services from the government?				x			
Can government and citizens engage in collaborative service delivery?					x		
Is the service provider(s) aware of the service delivery context?						x	x
Is the service provider(s) utilizing context awareness for better service delivery?							x

Source: Adapted from Bertot et al. (2016).

combinations of these innovations can be employed to further enhance their effectiveness. For example, a public sector service can employ digital innovations toward a more personalized and context smart service, thus offering services that consider the preferences of the intended beneficiary as and when change becomes imperative or as the situation demands.

Digital transformation of public sector service innovation is often associated with wider reforms within the sector (Clegg, 2007) aimed at enhancing efficiency and policy effectiveness and reducing bureaucracy (Kamarck & Kamarck, 2007). The relationship between digital innovation and value creation in the public sector is mediated by "public service delivery capability, public engagement capability, co-production capability, resource-building capability, and public-sector innovation capability" (Pang et al., 2014, p. 187). Digital transformation for service innovation draws on these five capabilities to reduce conflicts among competing values (Evans, 2019). ICT-related innovation can promote public sector values "mainly through transforming the relationship between government and citizens, improving democratic outcomes such as transparency and public participation, assisting in meeting collective expectations of the public, and enabling knowledge exchange and collaboration across different organizations" (Karkin et al., 2018, p. 1).

Governments have found varying rational narratives for embarking on digital transformation in the public sector (Beniwal & Sikka, 2013). Such logical narratives can range from population demands, fulfillment of political campaign promises following an electoral victory, meeting the aspirations of public servants (Masiero, 2018), as well as coming to terms with the requirements of local and global businesses for mutual collaboration. In some situations, too, aligning with the expectations of multinational development agencies such as the IMF or the World Bank orchestrate the need to digitally transform the public sector with service innovation operations. These e-government outcomes have become increasingly popular due to the greater role information technologies continue to play in inspiring digital transformation for public sector innovative practices.

Digital transformation in these innovative practices translates into the possibilities of supplanting existing work processes, supporting organizational decision-making and communication as well as improving public service delivery via the design and application of new methods. The target of these innovative practices addresses some fundamental concerns of governments. These primary concerns find expression in heightened efficiency, enhanced effectiveness, increased accountability (Masiero & Bailur, 2021) such as is in the case of democratization and citizen involvement at the local level plus a means of decentralization of centralized operations. Despite reported favorable outcomes of digital transformation in the public sector through innovative service delivery (see, for example, Dunleavy et al., 2006a), there are worrying difficulties that sometimes even make governments hesitant in implementing digital transformation projects. The digital divide (Patankar et al., 2017), reinforces the differences between the information-haves and information-have-nots, archiving and preservation of information challenges, security and privacy concerns are but some of the enduring worries connected with digital transformation projects in all societies.

Digital Transformation Vignettes

Part of the overriding objective of this chapter is to join the current digital transformation conversation and understand how it makes a meaningful contribution to societal life in many of its diverse manifestations, such as the delivery of innovative service in the public sector. Highlighting these varied manifestations involves an analytical juxtaposition of eight vignettes of implemented digital transformation projects. The construction of the eight vignettes is purely informed by the three-purpose criteria advanced by Barter and Renold (2000). According to the pair, the criteria seek "to allow actions in context to be explored, [second] to clarify people's judgments, and [finally] to provide a less personal and therefore less threatening way of exploring sensitive topics" (p. 1). It remains the abiding conviction of this study that the choice of vignettes to illustrate the digital transformation in the delivery of service innovation in the public sector is relevant on, at least, two counts.

Fundamentally, a vignette is applied to scrutinize belief systems and attitudinal shifts about multifaceted topical issues (Aujla, 2020). And vignettes are also suitable and appropriately relevant for qualitative research techniques (Bradbury-Jones et al., 2014) such as the orientation this chapter assumes. Each of the eight digital transformation projects was picked for its inclusion in this study for reasons that justified their implementation by the Government of Ghana. The rationale for the implementation of the projects—at least from the point of view of the government—is deeply rooted in the need to transform the workings of the supervising or implementing agencies, departments or institutions concerned. Transforming the lives of those aspects of public sector institutions has service innovation at the center of the offerings they render to the citizenry. The government's digital agenda for transforming the public sector via the instrumentality of service innovation has such targeted outcomes as flexible and convenient seamless financial services operations in the form of mobile money interoperability (MMI). Systems with context-awareness functionality such as Ghana Post GPS have both latent and direct objective for providing information accuracy at both normal and emergencies.

The implementation of systems of technology, to provide transparency and speed as an attempt to minimize corrupt and fraudulent practices, and instill a certain degree of fairness in those systems also features in some of the rationales for digital transformation interventions. Digital transformation projects such as discussed in some of the vignettes in the following sections, see, for example, vignettes 4, 5, 6, 7, and 8 bear testimony of the underlying motivations presently under consideration. All of the implemented digital transformation projects have a common character by way of scope. The scope finds expression in their area of operations, i.e., sectoral, inter-sectoral, and multisectoral. All of the chosen digital transformation projects have been in implementation for some reasonable amount of time to gauge their use among the intended population. However, what this study shied away from, and which is purposeful, is an attempt to determine their success or otherwise from the stakeholders involved. The authors believe these success or failure issues are beyond the immediate preoccupation of this chapter.

Vignette 1: National Digital Property Addressing System

The National Digital Property Addressing System dubbed Ghana Post GPS (Global Positioning System) with a nickname: Jack Where Are You? is a mechanism that divides Ghana into 5 meter squared grids and assigns a unique identifier to each grid to serve as an address for the location. The system, sponsored by the Government of Ghana, was designed by a Ghanaian information technology firm and deployed by the Ghana Post Company Ltd. with support from the National Information Technology Agency. The system uses a web and smartphone application (Asaase[1] GPS), with additional offline capabilities, to generate a unique GPS address for every 5 meter by 5 meter space within the borders of the country. The digital address generated is a distinctive nine-digit code made up of two letters denoting the Region, a three-digit postal code for the area, and a four-digit code for the specific location. Currently, all institutions that undertake public data collection such as the Social Security and National Insurance Trust, the Driver and Vehicle

Licensing Authority (DVLA), and the Registrar General's Department accept the digital address. In fact, other state agencies such as National Identification Authority, Ghana Revenue Authority, and Electoral Commission require all registrants and clients to provide their digital addresses. The system facilitates the ease of finding locations, which is critical for emergency responders like the police and ambulance services. The Ghana Post GPS app comes with an innovative panic button that can be used to signal the Police, Fire, and Ambulance services and give real-time location information in the event of imminent danger. The system also has benefits for local governance as it can be used to locate a property for taxation and levying purposes. In the financial sector, verification of the addresses of customers for account opening and loan applications is facilitated by the digital address system. Online marketers also use the system to facilitate the location of customers for easy delivery of goods.

Justification for Inclusion: Information Accuracy, Digitized Location Address, Context-awareness Functionality

Vignette 2: Mobile Money Interoperability

Ghana's MMI system, the first of its kind in Africa, was introduced by the country's central bank in May 2018 to facilitate the transfer of value from one person to another person via a mobile device. Interoperability refers to the functionality of software, like mobile money applications, to communicate and make use of information between and among different entities. Thus, MMI enables mobile money users in Ghana to send and receive money to and from one another, regardless of the network provider they subscribe to. Previously, the telecommunication companies that deployed the mobile money wallet service operated as closed systems, allowing transfers between wallets on the same network only. As a result, a third-party payment provider was needed to facilitate the transactions across networks. With the advent of MMI, however, mobile money users can transfer money to mobile wallets on other networks, from mobile money wallets to bank accounts and vice versa, and from an e-zwich[2] card to a mobile money wallet and vice versa. This feature, coupled with the already existing interoperable features of the e-zwich card, means that e-zwich cardholders can perform transactions at any financial institution without having an account with them. Thus, the functionality of the mobile money wallet is made similar to that of a bank account. The MMI is expected to drive financial inclusion, by increasing service reach, lowering transaction cost, and reducing reliance on the transportation of bulk cash for otherwise mundane transactions. The Government of Ghana introduced the MMI as part of its commitment to making the Ghanaian economy less cash-driven.

Justification for Inclusion: Financial Inclusion and Convenient Transactions, Flexible Financial Settlements

Vignette 3: The Ghana Interoperable Quick Response Code System

Another public sector-led innovation introduced in furtherance of the drive toward digital transformation is Ghana's Interoperable Quick Response Code and the proxy payment solution. Designed by a global payments solutions provider established in 1995 and operating in 90 countries worldwide, together with the Ghana Interbank Payment and Settlement Systems (GhIPSS), the solution provides a centralized switching service for QR code payments by all participants. The QR code system permits the transfer of money between customers of Financial Institutions, Fintechs, and Mobile Money Operators by scanning a quick response code with their smartphones. The QR Code and Proxy Pay systems are designed to increase financial inclusion by making secure, convenient, and affordable financial services available to the vast majority of people. Ghana is the first country in Africa to harmonize its QR Code payment systems at a national level. Unlike unique or individual QR codes for electronic payments, the Ghana Interoperable Quick Response Code is universal, making it possible for customers to make payments to merchants from various funding sources on any platform. The proxy payment solution is a layer of the GhIPSS's Instant Pay system that offers a unique alias or proxy identifier in the form of mobile phone numbers as part of individual and corporate account details at financial institutions. The proxy identifier is linked to the account such that a transfer made to that mobile phone number is automatically credited to the linked bank account in the domiciliary financial institution. By this, businesses, for instance, can receive payments from customers irrespective of the financial institution they are associated with. Customers who do not own bank accounts but have mobile money accounts can still make transfers straight into the bank accounts of vendors.

 Justification for Inclusion: Speed, Financial inclusion, Flexible Financial Settlements

Vignette 4: The Paperless Port System

The Customs Division of the Ghana Revenue Authority (GRA), in partnership with a private community network provider, developed and deployed the Ghana Customs Management System which instituted a means paperless (computerized) clearing across all the customs entry points in the country. The paperless port system is a common digital platform for all actor groups in the ports' goods clearing process, i.e., all parties involved in the evaluation, classification, inspection, and permitting of imports and all related activities. The actor groups include the customs, clearing agents, importers, and port authorities as well as all Ministries, Departments, and Agencies that issue permits before goods are imported into the country. In view of this, unauthorized and unqualified middlemen (usually referred to locally as *Goro*[3] *boys*) are concomitantly eliminated as they do not have access to the system. The paperless port-clearing system means that majority of the processes involved in the importation of goods are web-based, thus minimizing paperwork. Currently, documents such as declarations, receipts for duties and taxes, fees, or port charges paid are still required to be presented in hard copy. Ultimately, the system is expected to be completely paperless with all documents presented electronically. Additionally, an i-transit electronic tracking service has been deployed to install tracking devices on cargo ships that transit in the country to help the GRA track shipments and ensure that they leave the shores of Ghana to their intended destinations.

 Justification for Inclusion: Transparency, Speed and Less Corrupt Practices

Vignette 5: Digital Health Care Systems

In 2019, the Ghana government contracted an American drone company to establish a drone medical delivery service in the country. The service makes on-demand delivery of medical supplies and equipment to the Ministry of Health and GHS-approved facilities from different distribution points around the country. Thus, essential medical products and services are made available to health care facilities in a seamless and timely fashion especially during emergencies. Since 2019, the drone project has increased access to medical supplies for close to 15 million people most of whom are in hard-to-reach rural areas. The drone service has been especially instrumental in the delivery of personal protective gear, test kits, and other supplies necessary for fighting the COVID-19 pandemic. Before the outbreak, the service transported about 200 types of medical products such as blood, protective equipment, vaccines, and anti-venoms to several health facilities. This would have been extremely difficult because of the long, dangerous, and occasionally inaccessible road that would have caused loss of lives due to the associated delays and preventable accidents that characterize such journeys. Given this encouraging scenario, the government has expressed the intention to expand the drone service to provide routine medication to the homes of patients to reduce the pressure on medical facilities and risk to patients during the pandemic.

Justification for Inclusion: Enhanced Accessibility to Emergency Health Services and Speed

Vignette 6: Electronic Case Management System

Launched in March 2019 by the President of Ghana, the Paperless Courts or Electronic Case Management System (ECMS) also known as E-Justice, digitalizes the otherwise manual courts' registry filing systems. The entire justice process, from the filing of cases to the execution of court decisions, is automated. The system creates an e-docket for each case filed where all court proceedings and other related issues are recorded and preserved. Court users are registered as "business partners" on the system and are enabled to file cases, make complaints, track the status of ongoing cases, and even make online and mobile money payments for court transactions. Further, the system has a feature that instantly prompts court users via short message service (SMS) and email, whenever there are changes in court schedules and adjournments. Receipts for all court-related transactions are also sent as alerts. The introduction and implementation of the ECMS are expected to be a panacea for the characteristic challenges of the manual court filing system such as duplication of suit numbers, illegible handwritten documents, and the often bureaucratic processes involved in the transfer of documents through the court system that prolongs processing times. The e-docketing system facilitates easy access to information by authorized parties to the cases. It also creates an easily accessible electronic library of cases for referencing by lawyers and judges. Overall, the electronic portals are meant to improve the court experience of users and limit the human-to-human interactions that breed corruption. In the end, the system encourages compliance with policies and improves the security and privacy of cases and other allied services.

Justification for Inclusion: Transparency, Speed, Fairness, and Efficiency

Vignette 7: Digital Vehicle Registration System

The DVLA has launched a Vehicle Registration System that automates the vehicle registration process that hitherto was primarily manual. The Vehicle Registration System is expected to streamline the registration process and eliminate any potential redundancies. The digital registration infrastructure enables clients to complete their vehicle registration processes in an hour to reduce long queues that characterize the registration process, especially, at the start of the New Year. To make registration easy and paperless, the DVLA system has been connected to the paperless port system. The essence of this connection is to make the process less burdensome through the use of the chassis numbers of vehicles to track the custom and import documentations. The authority has also developed an online database that automatically stores all registered vehicles and the issue of new driver's licenses. Additionally, the process for the issuance of new licenses has been enhanced. The mandatory computer-based test can now be written in six Ghanaian languages: Twi, Ga, Dagbani, Hausa, Nzema, and Ewe. Including the local languages increases access for those who would, otherwise, be excluded because they cannot speak the English language. The new system makes use of the latest technologies for the production of more secure driver identification licenses that can potentially be integrated with other national identification systems, including the national identification cards, passports, and social security numbers, with an improved guarantee for securing data and the license. According to the DVLA, under the new system, it should take a maximum of up to three weeks to obtain a license in Ghana. There is also a premium service option for issuing the same-day license upon a successful test result.

Justification for Inclusion: Speed and Efficient Service Delivery

Vignette 8: Ghana Electronic Procurement System

The Ghana Electronic Procurement System (GHANEPS), launched in April 2019, is the first of its kind in the West African sub-region. The system facilitates public procurement processes via a web-based, collaborative platform that offers a secure, interactive, dynamic environment for carrying out all classes of procurement processes irrespective of their complexity or value. With this system, prospective contractors register, prepare, and submit their tenders online. The tenders are then evaluated and contracts are awarded electronically. The system also enables users to create and manage their catalogs and framework agreements, partake in auctions and make payments and track tender applications in real time. The current system is an improvement on the web-based Unit Cost of Infrastructure Budget Estimator Tool, launched by the Public Procurement Authority in 2017. The primary aim of the GHANEPS is to combat corruption by minimizing the direct human interactions involved in government tendering processes. According to the World Bank—which sponsored the project—as much as US$100million will be saved annually, through the transparency offered by the GHANEPS. The Procurement Act, 2016, Act 914 has been introduced to accommodate the use of electronic tools in public procurement processes and practices.

Justification for Inclusion: Transparency, Minimization of Corrupt Practices

Discussion—An Interpretive Perspective of Digital Transformation

Having presented the vignettes to demonstrate the contextual account of the various public sector innovation practices occasioned by a digital transformation drive, we now turn our attention to discuss the themes that characterize and motivate the digital transformation agenda such as identification, privacy, interoperability, transparency, convenience, speed, flexibility, participation, and context-awareness. These themes are discussed with interpretative philosophy in mind. The essence of the interpretive philosophy is to explain and determine the relevance of the research question: Why does the government initiate digital transformation through innovative services for citizens? The interpretive orientation has the potential to offer a richer and contextually sensitive understanding of the motivating rationalities that emerge from a wide spectrum of perspectives informing digital transformation in public sector service innovation.

The interpretive perspective is crucial because it draws inspiration from subjectivism and constructivism to which Goodman (1978) maintains any one classification of social reality can be articulated in one of several ways. One of such ways is the point that the interpretivist school of thought is premised on the idea that reality is not given and that it is a negotiation process conditioned and influenced by an individual's beliefs, suppositions, and practices generated by a sense of social, cultural, historical, and personal biases. These personal biases should then permit a reflexive pattern to be established in the process that reinforces Walsham's (1993, pp. 4–5) claim that interpretive IS research strategies focus on "producing an understanding of the context of the information system, and the process whereby the information system influences and is influenced by the context".

It is now obvious that the matters and motivations concerning digital transformation and public sector service innovation are quite diverse and complicated to determine a single, inflexible, and finely distinct outlook. The diverse and complicated nature of the forces driving digital transformation projects in this study, so far, is evidenced by the varied nature of the vignettes describing implemented innovative public sector services. The novel public sector services reveal the moving factors that account for their implementation, for instance, the implementation of the national ID system has motivating factors quite different from the rollout of the digital health care delivery system.

It is fair to admit, however, that the rationale for the implementation of some digital transformation projects also finds similar meaning or expression in others. Thus, some projects in question are radically different from others by both contents of the application and by design. To be sure, the interpretivist direction accepts the multiplicity of viewpoints concerning any specific social reality. Making sense in the interpretivist tradition is an activity that involves shared cognitive mechanisms for the establishment of personal reality (Searle, 1995). The personal reality postulation is consistent with Weber's who is particularly concerned with the thought of "exploratory understanding" in addition to a "correct causal interpretation of concrete course of behaviour" (Weber, 1949, p. 35, 40). The following discussions are sensitized by the interpretivist viewpoint in conjunction with the themes that are drawn out from the presented vignettes.

Identification and Privacy Issues in Digital Transformation

The public sector has often be characterized by, and accused of, being inefficient, unpleasantly poor, and stubbornly bureaucratic in the delivery of service to the citizenry (Persson & Goldkuhl, 2010; Dunleavy et al., 2006a). With these unfavorable attributes, the public sector comes across as being impervious to change and innovation. However, the national digital transformation projects described in the vignettes signify a radically different public sector. Evidence suggests the current wave of digital transformation makes the public sector accommodative of change and innovation. For instance, the digitized national identification (ID) card provides a database that validates attributes of individuals to confirm their identity. This was not the scenario in the recent past, at least, prior to the implementation of the national identification system. Apart from affording the individuals to prove their identity to state institutions qua agencies and private organizations such as financial establishments, the use of a digital ID system is assumed to provide immense benefits to citizens and businesses. The government sees the issue of the digital ID system as a means of innovating the delivery of public services through its digital transformation. Using the digital ID system in this manner enables a less corrupt means of welfare payments to the elderly in society in a program destined, Livelihood Empowerment Against Poverty. From the standpoint of governance, the application of technology in this innovative fashion reinforces administrative efficiency such as minimizing paperwork, reducing processing times, and lessening the incidence of fraud.

Besides, digital ID provides support for businesses and the citizenry the advantage of streamlining business registration processes as legitimate identification for common transactions such as opening a bank account and clearing cheques at the banks. Previously, such a simple exercise as opening a bank account would involve banks relying heavily on landmarks in establishing the location of a customer. These landmarks range from more perennial artifacts such as electricity poles, electric transformers to objects as fleeting as kiosks of mobile phone top-up vouchers, or electricity rechargeable kiosks or food vendor shelters. Using these as landmarks are so unreliably risky to the extent that if for any reason, these food vendors are unable to operate, one is highly likely to miss their way to a given location.

It is apropos to highlight the point that the use of these digital systems as a means of identification is bedeviled with some protracting challenges. For instance, the use of smartphones to generate one's digital address presupposes the user to have a certain level of formal education. And in a country where illiteracy is, still quite high in people of ages 15 years and above (approximately 21%),[4] the phenomenon of the digital divide has the potential to unfavorably affect some people's ability to generate their digital addresses. The cost of affording a smartphone combined with unstable network connectivity is all part of a monumental challenge to the government's digital transformation efforts. In such a situation, even if there is a strong desire to have one's digital address enrolled on the national database, such a yearning would only become short-lived. Last, but by no means least, all manner of privacy concerns have been raised against the means of populating the database system in the national identification project. Some of these privacy concerns are occasioned by the fact that building a national database should not be entrusted to individuals to populate it, rather such an exercise should be the charge of a national agency to ensure a commendable level of integrity.

Transparency or Fraud in Public Sector Innovation?

On top of the government's agenda of bringing innovative public service delivery through digital transformation is the need to open up state institutions to the general public in the name of transparency and inhibiting fraudulent practice. Given this government's aspiration, in Ghana, for example, there is in operation at the ports in Tema and Takoradi, a technology-labeled Paperless Port System that is meant to ease congestion at the ports and quicken the operation of clearing of goods and other allied functions. What would, in hitherto, take months to clear, now only need some few hours or a day to do so, something that has received praise from the customers who have experienced this speedy, reasonably transparent clearance at the ports. The determination of the right amount in clearing one's goods, too, is now far more transparent than what was the norm some time ago. There is an online platform that the customers interface with to know the amount involved in clearing their stuff. In most instances, middlemen—some of whom used to take advantage of unsuspecting customers in dubious clearing charges—caused delays and inconvenience them in the process. The E-justice system carries the same transparency appeal in its design and application for all the user stakeholders, such as clients and their lawyers. When the public sector provides such innovative services for the citizenry, opportunities for fraud get to be minimized as the prevailing transparent conditions within which services are provided make little room for such unwholesome practices to blossom.

Speed, Convenience, and Flexibility of Digital Innovation

In all of the digital transformation aspirations, matters of speed, convenience, and flexibility constitute an abiding desire, both from the standpoint of the served and the server (service provider). In this connection, citizens find it ever more appealing to partake in innovative public services with a foundation typified by the speed, convenience, and flexibility with which to access and make use of public services. This appeal is crucial for sustaining the long-term acceptance and use of digital transformation projects by the citizenry. On the other hand, it also ensures the continuous interest of the government in initiating steps to expand the frontiers of their application and use by the citizenry in other akin digital transformation endeavors. The implementation of MMI, the first of its kind on the African continent, attests to this point. Mobile money transactions, indeed, started from Kenya as M-Pesa in 2007. However, Ghana's version of MMI is the first of its kind in Africa at the time of implementation in 2018. With Ghana's brand of MMI, one can undertake funds transfer from a bank account onto a mobile money wallet, and the reverse is also possible, even though prior arrangement with the bank for activation of this particular reverse service is a prerequisite.

This interoperable fund transfer facility provides opportunities for financial inclusion. Financial inclusion presupposes the removal of the inhibitions that are used to characterize the movement of funds from a bank account to a mobile money wallet and vice versa. In sum, mobile financial transactions guarantee speed, convenience, and flexibility in financial transactions for a sizeable segment of the population. The convenience and flexibility encourage banking on the move with implications for reinvigorating the socioeconomic activities in society.

Context-Awareness and Participation in Digitized Public Sector Innovation

Digitally-enabled context-aware innovative public services present a favorable appeal to the implementation and use of digital transformation projects. Occasionally identified as "ubiquitous government" due to its characterization of anywhere anytime computing possibilities (Yoo, 2010), context-aware digital services enable pervasive use of diverse personalized purposes. The customized service provides chances for individuals to become an inextricable part of the digitized public sector service innovation process. A typical illustration of this scenario is the use of the Ghana Post GPS for not only generating a unique digital address but also rely on the artifact's digital capabilities to access personalized emergency services in times of need. For instance, the Ghana Post GPS allows a user to activate an emergency service, like the police, ambulance, and fire by pressing the relevant button on their mobile phone to request appropriate emergency service. Thus, at the instantiation of a particular emergency service, the GPS functionality enables the police, ambulance, or fire tenders to identify and locate where the request for emergency service is initiated. With this location identifier, the user does not have to go through the sometimes tortuous and inconvenient process of using unreliable landmarks to direct the requested emergency service to where they can be located. For, the technology is adapted to intelligent codes driven by a sense of the user's context or geographical designation. The crucial nature of this service has made it possible for the GP GPS to have an offline version so that even without an Internet connection, its use for the generation of personalized digital addresses is still active.

Implications for Practice and Research

This chapter has accounted for the link between the knowledge of digital innovations and development by means of an illustration of an implemented digital technology projects in terms of vignettes. Theoretically, the chapter contributes to the broader debate about the distinctive focus of digital transformation projects in terms of the underlying rationale that drive their implementation. Ipso facto, digital transformation projects are sensitive to contextual factors that account for the matters that condition their implementation across situational and contextual circumstances. Future research should also focus on employing either a quantitative or even mixed research technique to determine the extent to which digital transformation projects can register a more widespread appeal among the citizenry.

In terms of practice, the encouraging widespread acceptance of digital transformation projects notwithstanding, it is appropriate to suggest that some of these public sector innovation services should be designed and implemented with the average user in terms of technological sophistication mind. Bearing such a crucial factor in mind is important in broadening the appeal such technologies would hold for the intended average user. Therefore, again, the government needs to intensify their efforts at making education accessible to all. Since education is the common denominator that applies to all digital transformation projects, without education, it will always be difficult for the average person to use a digital transformation project in a meaningful manner.

Conclusion

Thus far, this study has presented a painting of a motley of issues instigating digital transformation in bringing innovation into services rendered to the citizenry in the public sector. In doing this, eight differently implemented digital transformation projects have been analyzed to draw themes based on the motivating rationale. The motivating rationale emphasizes the underlying conditions and factors of the application and use of the various technologies that embody the content and focus of the digital transformation projects. The content and configuration of these projects encourage broad acceptance and ensure ongoing participation and widening patronage in the public sector's digitally transformed innovative services.

Notes

1. Asaase is an Akan (an ethnic group in Ghana) rendition of earth.
2. E-zwich refers to Ghana's National Switch and Smart card payment system that offers interoperability to deposit-taking institutions.
3. Goro is a Hausa word for cola-nut interpreted locally as a token in exchange for a favor or rendered service.
4. http://uis.unesco.org/en/country/gh

References

Alaimo, C., & Kallinikos, J. (2017). Computing the Everyday: Social Media as Data Platforms. *Information Society*, *33*(4), 175–191. https://doi.org/10.1080/01972243.2017.1318327

Alaimo, C., Kallinikos, J., & Valderrama, E. (2020). Platforms as Service Ecosystems: Lessons from Social Media. *Journal of Information Technology*, *35*(1), 25–48. https://doi.org/10.1177/0268396219881462

Andriole, S. J. (2017). Five Myths about Digital Transformation. *MIT Sloan Manage*, *58*(3), 20–22.

Aujla, W. (2020). Using a Vignette in Qualitative Research to Explore Police Perspectives of a Sensitive Topic: "Honor"-Based Crimes and Forced Marriages. *International Journal of Qualitative Methods*, *19*, 1–10. https://doi.org/10.1177/1609406919898352

Barter, C., & Renold, E. (2000). I Wanna Tell You a Story: Exploring the Application of Vignettes in Qualitative Research with Children and Young People. *International Journal of Social Research Methodology*, *3*(4), 307–323. https://doi.org/10.1080/13645570050178594

Beniwal, V., & Sikka, K. (2013). E-governance in India: Prospects and Challenge. *International Journal of Computer and Communication Technology*, *4*(3), 1–5.

Berghaus, S., & Back, A. (2016). *Stages in Digital Business Transformation*. Mediterranean Conference on Information Systems (MCIS). Paphos, Cyrpus: University of Nicosia, Nicosia. http://aisel.aisnet.org/mcis2016%5Cnhttp://aisel.aisnet.org/mcis2016

Berman, S. J. (2012). Digital Transformation: Opportunities to Create New Business Models. *Strategy and Leadership*, *40*(2), 16–24. https://doi.org/10.1108/10878571211209314

Bertot, J., Estevez, E., & Janowski, T. (2016). Universal and Contextualized Public Services: Digital Public Service Innovation Framework. *Government Information Quarterly, 33*(2), 211–222.

Bican, P. M., & Brem, A. (2020). Digital Business Model, Digital Transformation, Digital Entrepreneurship: Is there a Sustainable "Digital"? *Sustainability (Switzerland), 12*(13), 1–15. https://doi.org/10.3390/su12135239

Bradbury-Jones, C., Taylor, J., & Herber, O. R. (2014). Vignette Development and Administration: A Framework for Protecting Research Participants. *International Journal of Social Research Methodology, 17*(4), 427–440. https://doi.org/10.1080/13645579.2012.750833

Clegg, S. (2007). Something is Happening Here, but You Don't Know What It Is, Do You, Mister Jones? In *ICT in the Contemporary World. Information Systems and Innovation Group*, London School of Economics and Political Science.

Cordella, A., & Tempini, N. (2015). E-Government and Organizational Change: Reappraising the Role of ICT and Bureaucracy in Public Service Delivery. *Government Information Quarterly, 32*(3), 279–289.

Demirkan, H., Spohrer, J. C., & Welser, J. J. (2016). Digital Innovation and Strategic Transformation. *IT Professional, 18*(6), 14–18.

Dunleavy, P., Margetts, H., Bastow, S., & Tinkler, J. (2006a). New Public Management is Dead—Long Live Digital-Era Governance. *Journal of Public Administration Research and Theory, 16*(3), 467–494. https://doi.org/10.1093/jopart/mui057

Evans, O. (2019). Digital Government: ICT and Public Sector Management in Africa. In J. Sebestova, Ž. Rylková, P. Krejčí & M. Lejková (Eds.), *New Trends in Management: Regional and Cross-border Perspectives* (pp. 269–286). London: London Scientific.

Goodman, N. (1978). *Ways of Worldmaking*. Indianapolis: Hackett Publishing Company.

Günther, W. A., Rezazade Mehrizi, M. H., Huysman, M., & Feldberg, F. (2017). Debating Big Data: A Literature Review on Realizing Value from Big Data. *Journal of Strategic Information Systems, 26*(3), 191–209. https://doi.org/10.1016/j.jsis.2017.07.003

Haffke, I., Kalgovas, B. J., & Benlian, A. (2016). The Role of the CIO and the CDO in an Organization's Digital Transformation. *International Conference of Information Systems*, Dublin, Ireland from December 11–14, 2016. Atlanta, GA: Association for Information Systems.

Janowski, T. (2015). From Electronic Governance to Policy-driven Electronic Governance—Evolution of Technology Use in Government. In J. A. Danowski & L. Cantoni (Eds.), *Communication and Technology* (pp. 425–439). Berlin: De Gruyter Mouton.

Kamarck, E. C., & Kamarck, E. C. (2007). *The End of Government . . . as We Know It: Making Public Policy Work*. Boulder, CO: Lynne Rienner Publishers.

Karkin, N., Yavuz, N., Cubuk, E. B. S., & Golukcetin, E. (2018, May). The Impact of ICTs-related Innovation on Public Values in Public Sector: A Meta-analysis. In *Proceedings of the 19th Annual International Conference on Digital Government Research: Governance in the Data Age* (pp. 1–9). Article No. 20. May 30–June 1, 2018, Delft, the Netherlands. New York: Association for Computing Machinery.

Li, L., Su, F., Zhang, W., & Mao, J. (2018). Digital Transformation by SME Entrepreneurs: A Capability Perspective. *Information Systems Journal, 28*, 1129–1157.

Majchrzak, A., Markus, L. M., & Wareham, J. (2016a). Designing for Digital Transformation: Lessons for Information Systems Research from the Study of ICT and Societal Challenges. *MIS Quarterly: Management Information Systems, 40*(2), 267–277. https://doi.org/10.25300/MISQ/2016/40

Majchrzak, A., Markus, M. L., & Wareham, J. (2016b). Designing for Digital Transformation: Lessons for Information Systems Research from the study of ICT and Societal Challenges. *MIS Quarterly, 32*(2), 205–225. https://doi.org/Article

Mansell, R. (2014). Here Comes the Revolution—the European Digital Agenda. In K. Donders, C. Pauwels, & J. Loisen (Eds.), *The Palgrave Handbook of European Media Policy* (1st ed., pp. 202–217). London: Palgrave Macmillan.

Margiono, A. (2020). Digital Transformation: Setting the Pace. *Journal of Business Strategy, January*. https://doi.org/10.1108/JBS-11-2019-0215

Masiero, S. (2018). Explaining Trust in Large Biometric Infrastructures: A Critical Realist Case Study of India's Aadhaar Project. *Electronic Journal of Information Systems in Developing Countries, 84*(6), 1–15: e12053. https://doi.org/10.1002/isd2.12053

Masiero, S., & Bailur, S. (2021). Digital Identity for Development: The Quest for Justice and a Research Agenda. *Information Technology for Development*, *27*(1), 1–12.

Matt, C., Hess, T., & Benlian, A. (2015). Digital Transformation Strategies. *Business and Information Systems Engineering*, *57*(5), 339–343. https://doi.org/10.1007/s12599-015-0401-5

Mergel, I., Edelmann, N., & Haug, N. (2019). Defining Digital Transformation: Results from Expert Interviews. *Government Information Quarterly*, *36*(4), 101385. https://doi.org/10.1016/j.giq.2019.06.002

Newell, S., & Marabelli, M. (2015). No TitleStrategic Opportunities (and Challenges) of Algorithmic Decision-Making: A Call for Action on the Long-Term Societal Effects of 'Datification.' *Journal of Strategic Information Systems*, *24*(1), 3–14.

Nograsek, J., & Vintar, M. (2014). E-Government and Organisational Transformation of Government: Black Box Revisited? *Government Information Quarterly*, *31*(1).

Osborne, D., & Gaebler, T. (1992). *Reinventing Government*. New York, NY: Penguin Press.

Pang, M. S., Lee, G., & DeLone, W. H. (2014). IT Resources, Organizational Capabilities, and Value Creation in Public-sector Organizations: A Public-value Management Perspective. *Journal of Information Technology*, *29*(3), 187–205.

Patankar, R., Vyas, S., & Tyagi, D. (2017). Archiving Universal Digital Literacy in Rural India. In *Proceedings of the 10th International Conference on Theory and Practice of Electronic Governance (ICEGOV '17)* (pp. 528–529). New York: Association for Computing Machinery.

Persson, A., & Goldkuhl, G. (2010). Government Value Paradigms-Bureaucracy, New Public Management, and E-Government. *Communications of the Association for Information Systems*, *27*(1), 45–62. https://doi.org/10.17705/1cais.02704

Piccinini, E., Hanelt, A., Gregory, R. W., & Kolbe, L. M. (2015). Transforming Industrial Business: The Impact of Digital Transformation on Automotive Organizations. 2015 *International Conference on Information Systems: Exploring the Information Frontier*, ICIS 2015, September, Fort Worth, TX from December 13–16, 2015. Atlanta, GA: Association for Information Systems.

Porter, M. E., & Heppelmann, J. E. (2014). How Smart, Connected Products are Transforming Competition. *Harvard Business Review*, *92*(11), 64–88.

Remane, G., Hanelt, A., Nickerson, R. C., & Kolbe, L. M. (2017). Discovering Digital Business Models in Traditional Industries. *Journal of Business Strategy*, *38*(2), 41–51. https://doi.org/10.1108/JBS-10-2016-0127

Rosenberg, D. (2018). Use of e-Government Services in a Deeply Divided Society: A Test and an Extension of the Social Inequality Hypotheses. *New Media & Society*, 21(2), 1461444818799632.

Schumpeter, J. A. (1934). *The Theory of Economic Development*. Cambridge, MA: Harvard University Press.

Schumpeter, J. A. (1942). *Capitalism, Socialism e Democracy*. New York, NY: Harper and Row.

Schweer, D., & Sahl, J. (2017). *The Digital Transformation of Industry—The Benefit for Germany* (pp. 23–31). https://doi.org/10.1007/978-3-319-31824-0_3

Searle, J. R. (1995). *The Construction of Social Reality*. London: Penguin Books.

Sebastian, I. M., Moloney, K. G., & Ross, J.. (2017). How Big Old Companies Navigate Digital Transformation. *MIS Quarterly Executive*, *16*(3), 197–213.

Siebel, T. M. (2019). *Digital Transformation: Survive and Thrive in an Era of Mass Extinction*. New York: RosettaBooks.

UNECE. (2017). *Innovation in the Public Sector. United Nations Publication Issued by the Economic Commission for Europe*. New York: United Nations. https://unece.org/DAM/ceci/publications/Innovation_in_the_Public_Sector/Public_Sector_Innovation_for_web.pdf

Venkatesh, V., & Sykes, T. A. (2013). Digital Divide Initiative Success in Developing Countries: A Longitudinal Field Study in a Village in India. *Information Systems Research*, *24*(2), 239–260. https://doi.org/10.1287/isre.1110.0409

Vial, G. (2019). Understanding Digital Transformation: A Review and a Research Agenda. *Journal of Strategic Information Systems*, *28*(2), 118–144. https://doi.org/10.1016/j.jsis.2019.01.003

Vogelsang, K., Liere-Netheler, K., Packmohr, S., & Hoppe, U. (2018). Success Factors for Fostering a Digital Transformation in Manufacturing Companies. *Journal of Enterprise Transformation*, *8*(1–2), 121–142. https://doi.org/10.1080/19488289.2019.1578839

Walsham, G. (1993). *Interpreting Information Systems in Organizations*. Chichester: Wiley.

Weber, M. (1949). *The Methodology of the Social Sciences*. Glencoe, IL: Free Press.

West, D. M. (2005). *Digital Government: Technology and Public-Sector Performance*. Princeton, NJ: Princeton University Press.

Wiredu, G. O., Boateng, K. A., & Effah, J. K. (2019). Technology Media, Service Innovation and the Shaping of Executive Cognition. *Proceedings of the 5th African Conference on Information Systems & Technology, Addis Ababa, Ethiopia. African Conference on Information Systems & Technology, Ghana Institute of Management and Public Management, Accra, Ghana*.

Wirtz, B. W., & Daiser, P. (2018). A Meta-analysis of Empirical e-Government Research and Its Future Research Implications. *International Review of Administrative Sciences*, *84*(1), 144–163. doi:10.1177/0020852315599047

Yoo, Y. (2010). Computing in Everyday Life: A Call for Research on Experiential Computing. *MIS Quarterly*, *34*(2), 213–231.

Authors' Profile

Dr. Kofi Agyenim Boateng is a senior lecturer at the Department of Supply Chain and Information Systems, Kwame Nkrumah University and Science and Technology, Ghana. He is an interpretive researcher who examines the adoption and use of information systems in organizations and public sector institutions. He has over 20 publications spanning journals, book chapters, and conference papers.

Akua Peprah-Yeboah is a lecturer at the Department of Accounting and Finance, Kwame Nkrumah University and Science and Technology, Ghana. Her research explores financial literacy, corporate performance, and financial reporting.

Chapter 5

Old Roots into New Trees: Artisan Entrepreneurship in Cyprus

Burcu Toker and Burak Erkut

Contents

Introduction

Research into artisan entrepreneurship became a trend in the recent seven years (Pret & Cogan, 2019). Artisan entrepreneurs, who are defined as "individuals who produce and sell products or services which possess a distinct artistic value resulting from a high degree of manual input" (p. 3), are known to be revolutionizing traditional craft sectors. Artisan entrepreneurship process is known to involve making handcrafted goods or services and is associated with manual techniques and traditions (Ferreira et al., 2018). In particular, a growing interest in homemade goods and services that have a

DOI: 10.4324/9781003152217-7

cultural component resulted in the emergence of the artisan entrepreneurship worldwide (Ratten et al., 2019). According to Boukas and Chourides (2016), small islands have a number of characteristics that make them unique, these are especially with "their authentic mosaic of resources and altering their ecosystem and social fabric" (p. 27). The authors pose the question of whether development without harming these unique characteristics is possible for small islands, and come to the conclusion that the competitiveness of small islands lies in sustainable development "since their scarce resources are under threat due to their direct exposition at the global forces, as well as the overdevelopment and frequently unruled expansion" (Boukas & Chourides, 2016, p. 39). One of the unique characteristics of small islands is their traditions and traditionally handcrafted goods and services, and Cyprus as a small island is known to have a rich culture that emerged out of different civilizations having ruled the island for centuries. As Cyprus lies at the crossroads between East and West, due to its strategic location, it was ruled by many civilizations throughout history, the Assyrians, Egyptians, Persians, Romans, Arabs, Lusignan Dynasty, Venetians, Ottomans, and the British.

Cyprus was particularly known to have an economy based on traditional sectors such as producing goods and services with manual techniques, having large groups of artisans and craftsmen in the economy, and playing a key role in exporting some of the handcrafted goods to other countries (Kokko & Kaipainen, 2015). Nevertheless, over time, the presence of traditional sectors diminished in Cyprus and the island became a mass tourism island with a significantly big white-collar community (Kokko & Kaipainen, 2015; Boukas & Chourides, 2016). Recent studies identify that there is a growing interest in becoming entrepreneurially active among university students and graduates in Cyprus (Kaya et al., 2019; Polyviou et al., 2019). Based on this background, the present study poses the question of how artisan entrepreneurship scene is changing in Cyprus by focusing on the product development processes of artisan entrepreneurs, their motivations, and the conditions in which they are performing their entrepreneurial activity. To be more specific, their career choices, impact of their families and their choices of studies, and their financing models have been asked. The rest of the chapter is organized as follows: The authors explain the concept, followed by the methodology. Afterward, the findings are presented, followed by a discussion, concluding remarks, and practical and policy implications as well as future research and practice directions.

Concept Explanation

The theoretical underpinning of this chapter is entrepreneurship that is the driving force behind the economic change (Erkut, 2020). The point of departure for entrepreneurial activity is the subjective knowledge of the individual, which is unique to each and every person, and can be turned into a competitive advantage in the marketplace (Erkut, 2016). Among many forms of entrepreneurial activity, the chapter focuses on artisan entrepreneurship. Artisan entrepreneurship is not a new concept to the world. On the contrary, manual production techniques, resulting in products that have an artistic value, are known ones since centuries. Even though artisan entrepreneurship as a concept is pretty new to the entrepreneurship research, there is already a growing interest in understanding artisan entrepreneurs and placing them in a country-specific context. Pret and Cogan (2019) focus on a systematic literature review on artisan entrepreneurship and identify that future research needs to focus on a bigger variety of craft industries to understand our knowledge on artisan entrepreneurs and inform policymaking on this topic. Since this topic is even after a growing interest largely absent from the entrepreneurship literature, there is a need to understand artisan entrepreneurship more in detail (Ferreira et al., 2018). Pret and Cogan (2019) also found out that artisan entrepreneurs engage in cooperation with other businesses and even with some competitors. Flanagan et al. (2017) emphasized that artisan entrepreneurs engage in cooperative behavior, that is to say, they may be cooperating with their competitors to promote the growth of the artisan industry. In their findings, the authors identified that breweries were recommending competing breweries to their own customers.

Even though a lot has been written regarding the early forms of commercial exchange, which was even present in the preindustrial age, our knowledge of the social, historical, and anthropological concepts which led to the emergence of the first forms of entrepreneurs, who did not simply focus on a pure exchange process, is limited (Edward et al., 2020). In this sense, artisan entrepreneurship is different from the traditional entrepreneurial perspective since the former not only has a purely economic motivation but very often relies on valuing the traditions of a community by conceptualizing its business idea as a part of a social mission (Ratten et al., 2019). This way of entrepreneurial thinking differs from the basic approach of an arbitrage-entrepreneur according to Kirzner (Erkut, 2016); rather, it is a more hybrid concept, combining economic goals with social missions, which can be associated with social entrepreneurship. According to Cater et al. (2017), artisan entrepreneurs can be associated with creating a social value through their business conceptions and practicing their business in terms of a prosocial way.

Artisan entrepreneurship involves interpreting or reinterpreting the traditions of a particular community. Recently, Floris et al. (2020) investigated how firms in traditional sectors innovate, by focusing on two small family bakeries. They identified four strategies of innovating in traditional sectors, which are radical innovations, embodiment of tradition, reinterpretations of tradition, and retro-innovations. Investigated by Arias and Cruz (2019), artisan entrepreneurs were found out to be relevant for developing countries. The authors mention that investigating the emergence process of artisan entrepreneurship deserves further attention (Arias & Cruz, 2019). Ramadani et al. (2019) investigated artisan entrepreneurship in a transition economy setup in Macedonia. They found out that financial results are extremely sensitive to the behaviors of the owners of enterprises in this setup. In particular, regarding artisan entrepreneurship in transition economies, the authors found out that networking is not only very valuable for success but also very important for the financial results (Ramadani et al., 2019). The authors advise that future research should be conducted on understanding the motivation of artisan entrepreneurs.

A particular issue in understanding entrepreneurial activity is understanding the role of perceptions (Erkut, 2016; Erkut, 2018). According to Erkut (2016), the process of product innovation and the corresponding market-shaping process can be viewed as a cyclical process of four phases, consisting of perception of information, turning this into knowledge, conceptualizing the knowledge with capabilities, and the emergence of an artifact, with which the cycle goes back to the initial phase of the perception of information. This evolutionary economic model bridges the gap between the streams of research of product innovation and market shaping and is relevant for understanding the motivations, aspirations, and perceptions of artisan entrepreneurs. According to Erkut (2018), innovations and, more specifically, product innovations are very much contingent events that cannot be described by a mere "success story" phenomenon. Therefore, for understanding artisan entrepreneurs' stories, a more contingent approach needs to be implemented.

Of course, entrepreneurship research needs to deliver some guidelines for policymaking, as it is often perceived equally by scholars and policymakers alike. However, little has been written regarding the role of policymaking for the support of artisan entrepreneurship. One exception is the case of Wellalage and Reddy (2020), who mention that introducing more external finance sources for small and medium enterprises should be a target for policymaking in small island countries. Boukas and Chourides (2016) also have policy implications that can be viewed as supporting artisan entrepreneurs. According to the authors, policymakers should understand crises and sustainability as "evolving systemic configurations" (p. 33), for which policymaking and entrepreneurs should be prepared. They conclude that this should involve a communication of all stakeholders for a stronger policymaking effort to respond to the changes. Teixeira and Ferreira (2019) emphasize the importance of artisanal products since, according to the authors, these products contribute to the regional competitiveness within a country as well as to the development of tourism in that country. Similarly, Toker and Rezapouraghdam (2021) highlight the importance of using local food in the tourism strategy of the country. According to the authors, local food can help a local community to emphasize sustainable development by using local ingredients, and it can also create a competitive advantage in tourism by means of educating tourists about the uniqueness of local food. With regard to artisan entrepreneurship in traditional sectors, the suggestion by Toker and Rezapouraghdam (2021) implies that developing and retaining a competitive advantage in tourism can be obtained by enhancing the interaction of artisan entrepreneurs with tourists to educate the latter and increase their knowledge about Cyprus by experiencing the local uniqueness of the island's traditions.

Methodology

A qualitative methodology was adopted to explore the topic of entrepreneurship in traditional sectors of Cyprus. For this purpose, semi-structured interviews were performed with active entrepreneurs in these sectors. These semi-structured interviews enabled authors to understand the entrepreneurial motivation, vision, and perspectives, which provided insightful details about this unique type of entrepreneurial activity. The semi-structured interviews were conducted based on the relevant spheres of interaction of the entrepreneurs with their environment. These are, the product innovation-market shaping nexus as highlighted in Erkut (2016), the impact of family and university as highlighted in Gao et al. (2021) and Kaya et al. (2019) respectively, the role of their target groups (Kahn & Baum, 2020), career choice (Liguori et al., 2019) and a day in their entrepreneurial life (Kramvig & Førde, 2020).

Regarding the data sample, a total of six entrepreneurs participated in the survey, all of them residing and working in Cyprus. The criteria of selection included being an active artisan entrepreneur, residing and working in Cyprus, and focusing on artisan entrepreneurship in traditional sectors of Cyprus. Regarding their experience in traditional entrepreneurship, this group was very useful and information-rich. The sample size indicates that the authors selected a convenience sample to explore the topic (Neuman, 2014).

Participants ranged in age from 20–29 to 60–69.1 of the participants is in the age range of 20–29, two of the participants are in the age range of 30–39, one of them is in the age range of 40–49, one of them is in the age range of 50–59, and one of them in the age range of 60–69.

Three entrepreneurs are male, three entrepreneurs are female. All of them are married, with one of them having one child, three of them having two children, one of them having three children, and one of them having no children. This indicates that all of them have some sort of familiar responsibilities (McGowan et al., 2012).

Table 5.1 provides details of the respondents' current businesses and previous experiences.

The research was conducted primarily with the aim of understanding the motivations, expectations, and drivers of traditional entrepreneurship in Cyprus. Semi-structured interviews were conducted over a five-month period between August 2019 and December 2019. Since qualitative data can be very chaotic and tortuous, the authors followed the advice of Merriam (1988) to collect and analyze qualitative data in a concurrent way. Interviews were conducted and analyzed one by one.

Table 5.1   Details About the Respondent Entrepreneurs

ID	Type of Business	Years of Entrepreneurial Activity	Education	Background
P1	Handmade traditional Cypriot chairs	1–3	High school (natural sciences)	Continuing father's business
P2	Sourdough bread, probiotic tea, superfood spread, good quality coffee	3–5	Master's in Law	Lawyer
P3	À la carte and Cypriot dishes as well as boutique hotel	1–3	Master's in Education Science	Teacher
P4	Ornamentals made out of traditional material felt	5+	Bachelor's in Preschool Teaching	Teacher
P5	Local food and sweets	5+	Bachelor's in Public Management	Public Servant
P6	Lefkara lace Lapta lace	5+	Master's in Tourism Marketing	Continuing family business

Findings

From Idea to Product Development

Regarding what product they are offering, P1 said that he is manufacturing traditional chairs with wicker and wood materials. P2 said that he has a broad range of products including sourdough bread, probiotic tea, healthy spreads, and good quality coffee. P3 said that she is active in both offering à la carte and Cypriot dishes in the restaurant as well as rooms in her boutique hotel. P4 said that she is also having a broad range of products, mainly made of traditional material of felt, using felt to manufacture door ornamentals for newborn babies, memorial books, baskets, and other ornamentals. P5 said that she is offering local food. These are cordial, green walnuts in syrup, bitter orange in syrup, eggplant in syrup, ashure (also known as Noah's pudding), and paluze (sweet jelly made of grapes or carob extract). P6 said that he is making Cyprus handmade lace such as Lefkara lace and Lapta lace. All of the participants are focusing on handmade, traditional manufacturing methods. Of course, for some of the participants, their initial ideas to become entrepreneurially active differ from their current product range. For example, P2 said that he initially only wanted to offer superfood spread series, whereas P4 said that she initially only did some ornaments for her son's birthday; later on, after people recognized these inspirational handmade ornaments, they asked her to manufacture what they had in their mind for their special days. P1 said that initially he wanted to offer couches and sofas in addition to traditional chairs; currently, he is only offering the latter. On the other hand, P3, P5, and P6 seem to have realized what they had in their mind; P3's initial idea was to open a location, where all her beloved ones as well as her family could gather, whereas P5's initial idea was to learn how to make traditional food and continue to spread out the traditions. P6, on the other hand, took over the family business which was already focusing on Cyprus handmade lace; however, he implemented a product diversification strategy to reach out new and different customer groups. He imagined whether Cyprus handmade lace could have a more functional use, for example, at the cover of a diary or as covers for wine bottles.

Participants were asked how they developed their idea further in their minds. P1 already knew how to manufacture wooden chairs from the teaching of his father and other relatives who were already handmade manufacturing these. P2 focused on grinding different sorts of nuts and superfood by using a traditional stone mill, then using local recipes to create superfood spreads. He started selling the products before he opened his first store. Then, he moved the product range to his current store to reach out to more people. P3 mentioned that her family previously owned the building in which her current restaurant and boutique hotel are located. After losing beloved members of her family, she missed them a lot, and seeing the building empty and desolate made her very sad. Her initial idea of gathering her beloved ones and family members in a location and remembering their losses was realized in this building. P4 said that she already followed people from social media who were doing their own creations using felt. Later on, she established her own Instagram page to reach out to people. P5 said that she started to cook these traditional foods first for her family and sold whatever was in excess. From that point onwards, she adjusted the quantity of production corresponding to the increased demand. P6 said that he focused on making a diary with a cover of a handmade Lefkara lace, through which the Lefkara lace had a comeback. He also designed Lefkara lace to fit on covers for wine bottles which became a good gift alternative. Right after the authors conducted an interview with P6, when the pandemics started, the authors observed that P5 adapted the products to the COVID-19 situation. To be more specific, during the COVID-19 pandemics, he manufactured cotton masks with handmade Lefkara lace and Lapta lace on them.

Regarding their sources of inspiration for their current products or product ranges, P1 said that this was his father's job, from whom he took the inspiration. P2 said that his inspiration was focusing on health, which, according to him, is the real wealth. P3 said that her main inspiration was having a space to represent Cypriot culture in the Walled City of Lefkosa, especially emphasizing the ancestors' generation and their efforts in building the Cypriot culture. P4 said that her inspiration was the period of her pregnancy. She took pregnancy leave from the place she was working, and when she was back to work, she faced some difficulties, upon which she resigned and started her current entrepreneurial activity. P5 said that she imagined to make traditional food for herself and her family. Out of this hobby, her current entrepreneurial activity emerged. P6 was already familiar with his family's business, which was established by his mother and his father.

Regarding which Cypriot traditions were forming the base of their inspiration, P1 answered this question by pointing out to the Cypriot tradition of wicker weaving. P2 said the tradition of cooperative baking of sourdough bread is as old as 5,000 years in Cyprus, and this has liberated people and nurtured them in the correct way over centuries. P3 said that her inspiration was to represent both Cypriot dishes and traditional chair manufacturing in an international platform. P4 said that the tradition forming the base of her inspiration was Cypriot handicraft manufacturers that are an important component of the culture. P5 said that especially serving the guests fruits preserved in syrup accompanied by Cypriot coffee is an important element in the local culture. Apart from that, both paluze and ashure are also important elements of the local culture.

P6 said that it was Cyprus handmade lace tradition which kickstarted the business idea.

Whether there are others in the family who are interested in continuing their entrepreneurial activity, only P1 said that his son is interested in continuing it. Whereas all the others rejected it, P2 emphasized that even though nobody in his family currently focuses on continuing his entrepreneurial activity, his grandmother's baking talent was a further inspiration for him to continue this family tradition. P5 gave the examples of her mother, grandmother, and aunts, who were all very active in cooking local food. P6 said that both his mother and father were involved in the business.

On this occasion, participants were asked what kind of talents were required for manufacturing their products. P1 said that in addition to physical power, a focused mind and love are required. P2 said that especially knowing the contents as well as health impacts of products and their interactions with each other are required. In addition, production discipline, choosing the correct combination of purchasing and job requirements, and using senses in a balanced combination are required. P3 said that a good quality of service, hygiene as well as a healthy customer management policy are the required skills for her activity. P4 said that what is required is using her own intuitions and love to manufacture her products. She especially believes in trial-and-error processes to optimize her products. P5 answered this question with naming three talents, which are patience, thoroughness, and being able to cook. P6 mentioned that a broad knowledge of Cyprus handmade lace is required for his business.

Family and University Impact

Whether they learned anything from their family that was useful for their current entrepreneurial activity, P1 said that living a peaceful and happy life was something that he learned from his family and something that is useful for his entrepreneurial activity; whereas P2 said that his family's expertise in export management gave him useful insights. P3 said that she learned to embrace good quality and be honest with her family. According to P3, her family's belief is that the true path of positive energies can enlighten one's life in all aspects. P4 said that the problems she faced within her family made her stronger toward her life's challenges. After facing family problems, she never gives up easily when she starts with something new. In addition, her current entrepreneurial activity needs patience and convincing the buyer side—skills that she excelled in after she faced problems in her own family. P5 said that to preserve cordial and fruits or vegetables in syrup for a long time, she learned some methods from her family. P6 said that the supply chain was already established by his family, so he built upon it to diversify products and give handmade lace a more functional use.

In addition, they were asked to answer at which stage their family supported their entrepreneurial activity. P1 and P2 both said that their families supported their entrepreneurial activities both materially and morally. P3 not only made a similar comment but also mentioned that it is a family enterprise; therefore, she works together with her family members. P4 also mentioned that her family supported her a lot, especially by purchasing her products and sharing these on social media and introducing her products to other customer groups. This initial support was welcomed by close friends of her family members. Once she reached a critical mass, her family's moral support continued. P5 answered this question by stating that her family supported her during the cooking and packaging of the local food she offers. P6 mentioned that during the manufacturing, marketing, and logistics processes, he made use of his family's support.

Participants were also asked, whether their field of studies (either in the case of high school studies, for P1, or their university studies, for P2, P3, P4, P5, and P6) proved anything useful for their current entrepreneurial activity. P1, who is a high-school graduate from the natural sciences department, said that it was the curiosity which proved itself to be useful in his current entrepreneurial activity. Because of the curiosity, he faced during his high-school studies, he was able to understand how current youngsters' interests are shaped. P2, who has a postgraduate degree in law, said that his studies gave him a perspective to see the big picture. P3 who has a postgraduate degree in Educational Sciences said that her studies were helpful for stress management, building up healthy relationships, fulfilling the responsibilities toward customers to the full extent as well as understanding the customer psychology. P4 who has a Bachelor's degree in preschool teaching said that both her studies and her current entrepreneurial activity are shaped by her inclination toward children. According to P4, it makes her happy to create products for children. P5, who has a Bachelor's degree in public management, said that it was entrepreneurship, self-consciousness, and the fact that production is important both for the household and for the family were the important concepts which she learned from her field of studies that is useful for her current entrepreneurial activity. P6, who has a Master's degree in tourism marketing, said that particularly for marketing purposes, his studies contributed to his current business.

Target Group

For their products, participants were asked who were the initial target groups and whether these groups differ from their current customer groups. In addition, they were also asked whether there was a different target group for every product. P1 said that he imagined the owners of coffee shops, restaurants, pubs as well as those persons who were interested in having traditional chairs in their home kitchens. P1's initial target groups are in line with his current customer groups, and depending on needs, there are different groups of customers for different products. P2 initially imagined two target groups; those who seek healthy products and those with diabetes. He admits that there was no special marketing strategy for those with diabetes; a mere word-of-mouth strategy was not sufficient to reach out this target group. P2 added that the initial strategy was for products to be consumed jointly since every product has a different health benefit. Nevertheless, different groups of people buy different products from him. P3 said that she imagined of locals who are mature and respectful, and this target group turned out to be her current customers, even though, there are different customers for different dishes she offers. P4 said her initial target group was mothers of newborns who looked for decoration for celebrating the birth of their babies. Even though currently this target group turned out to be one of her customer groups, it is not the single one. In addition, she makes decorations out of traditional felt material for weddings, engagement parties, henna nights, and birthdays, so the organizers of these events are her additional customer groups. As celebration ornaments can be different according to purposes, for every product, she has a different customer group. P5 said that both tourists and locals were her initial target groups, and these two target groups turned out to be her current customers. She added that for every product, there is a different customer sub-group within these two groups. P5 also mentioned that she was interested in extending her customer groups to new ones. P6 imagined firms and other corporate establishments to be the initial target groups for the diversified products. He successfully reached out to these target groups. He also said that for every product, there is a different target group.

A Day in Their Entrepreneurial Life

Participants were asked to describe what a day in their entrepreneurial life looks like. P1 described that activities differ from chopping wood to building the basic skeleton of the chair and later on weaving the wicker on it. Later on, he polishes the chair and makes some other technical arrangements for it before it is ready. P2 described that he starts at 8 in the morning for putting together his sourdough, and it takes up to 12 hours to produce the sourdough bread. P3 said that even though her entrepreneurial life is very busy and stressful, she enjoys every moment of it because she sees it not as a job but as a hobby, through which she is doing something which makes her happy, she gets to know new people and feels herself at her second home. P4 said that especially during her pregnancy, there was no routine in her entrepreneurial activity. Because she already had her first child, and together with her husband she had responsibilities for her home, it was both tiring and long lasting. Especially during the final months of her pregnancy, she focused on finishing her orders as fast as possible since there could be a surprise at any moment. Nevertheless, she manages to keep up with both her family responsibilities and her entrepreneurial activity. P5 mentioned that she is a public servant, working 8 hours per day, and she does her entrepreneurial activity after work. Admitting that she has a lot of stress in the government office she is working in, she relaxes after work by focusing on her entrepreneurial activity. P6 said that he starts the day by opening his store, going outside to market his products, and return to the store before large groups of customers come to the store by noon.

Career Choices

Participants were asked to answer what they would have done if they were not currently doing this particular entrepreneurial activity. P1 answered this by becoming a shepherd, P2 answered it by stating that only God would know it, P3 answered it with teaching, and P4 answered it by baking, adding that since she already has two children, she would have chosen something that she could have done at home. P5 said that she would have been again in production or manufacturing duties, as manufacturing things gives her a different kind of joy. P6 answered this question by mentioning that he would be marketing products although he wouldn't know what he would market if he were not doing his current job.

In addition, they were asked whether they started their current entrepreneurial activity as out of an opportunity or out of a need. P1, P2, and P5 stated that for them, this was an opportunity-based entrepreneurial activity. In addition, P2 also stated that it was also his passion, but basically, he recognized that there was a need for these products, but nobody was offering them, whereas P5 stated that these traditions were almost forgotten, so she saw an opportunity in transmitting the traditions to new generations. P3 stated that it was a need-based entrepreneurial activity, whereas P4 stated that it was both. She left her job, which she enjoyed a lot, because of her pregnancy—this led her to think of something that she could do at home, whereas she also needed some material support, and it was a hard time for her family. She combined both to proceed with her current entrepreneurial activity. P6 stated that it was already an established business, but when he took over, he noticed that there are opportunities that were yet to be utilized.

Regarding how they financed their current job, P1 said that his father left him everything necessary in his testament. P2 said that it was both his own savings, some credit he got but also some help he received. P3 said that it was both her own savings and some credit she got from a bank. P4 said that because at the start she did not have any material, it was hard to finance it out of her savings. Nevertheless, the more she produced, the more she could earn to buy additional materials. P5 also says that she started this activity with her own savings, and the more she sold, the more she could invest into her entrepreneurial activity. P6 said that it was by equity financing.

They were asked whether they were satisfied with the current status of their entrepreneurial activity or if they wanted to develop it further. P1 said that he wanted to develop it further with his children. P2 said that he wanted to develop it further. P3 said that even though she is happy with the current status, she believes that development is a gradual process that goes on forever. P4 said that for all her products, she got positive feedback and is continuously developing it further. P5 said that she is just at the start of her entrepreneurial activity that she has a lot to learn and develop her product portfolio further. P6 said that he is satisfied with the current status of his entrepreneurial activity, but there is a bigger potential than already discovered.

Participants were also asked when they wanted to continue with their current entrepreneurial activity. P1 said that he wanted to continue with it until he dies, and P2 said that he wanted to continue with it as long as it lasts. P3 and P5 said that they wanted to continue with it as long as they are in good health, and P4 said that even though nowadays she is having a break due to her children's issues, she would soon continue with it. P6 said that he wants to continue with it for 15–20 years.

Whether they wanted to continue their entrepreneurial activity in Cyprus, P1, P2, P4, and P5 gave a positive answer, whereas P3 did not provide an answer. Similarly, participants were asked whether they were missing anything from their previous job. P1 and P2 gave a negative answer to this question. P3 did not respond, whereas P4 said that she wanted children always to be in her life and she loved teaching. P5 said that through her job as a public servant, she gets to know a lot of new people, which is something interesting for her. P6 said that he aims to continue his entrepreneurial activity in Cyprus, covering all parts of it—for which he is in contact with potential business partners.

On a scale of 1–10, participants were asked to give a number of how much they are missing their previous life (1=never, 10=always). P1, P2, and P5 crossed 1; P3 did not respond; P6 crossed 6; and P4 crossed 10. Again, on a scale of 1–10, participants were asked whether they were happy with the decision of becoming entrepreneurially active (1=very unhappy, 10=very happy). P1, P4, and P5 crossed 10; P2 crossed 7; P6 crossed 9; and P3 did not respond.

Discussion and Conclusion

Pret and Cogan (2019) mention that artisan entrepreneurs in a small island setup can be a new source of competitiveness and regional development that can contribute to tourism, gross domestic product growth, and job opportunities by conceptualizing the cultural heritage of their native small islands. This was the motivation of this chapter, which focused on exploring artisan entrepreneurs of Cyprus that focus on Cypriot traditions and interpret these in their entrepreneurial activities. The authors conducted six semi-structured interviews over a five-month period with six artisan entrepreneurs. Research highlights can be summarized as follows.

First, all interviewees provided some level of a formal education that is differing from their current entrepreneurial activity. All of them had previously white-collar jobs. Nevertheless, they identified some entrepreneurial opportunities in utilizing elements of Cypriot culture and traditions and giving them a more functional use. This change in their careers also resulted in a change in their lifestyle. This revolutionizing attempt turned an almost-dead industry of traditional sectors into a dynamic industry with great visibility. This conclusion is in line with the findings of Pret and Cogan (2019), who mention that for artisan entrepreneurs, altruistic goals such as valuing the traditions and culture of a society can be perfectly in line with economic goals of being entrepreneurially active. In addition, Pret and Cogan's (2019) observation of artisan entrepreneurs being lifestyle-oriented is supported by this study. The study also delivers new evidence on how product innovation and market shaping are inseparable from each other, highlighting why many economists consider the product innovation-market shaping nexus as a black box (Erkut, 2020).

Second, all interviewees started their current entrepreneurial activity by perceiving their environment and perceiving a gap that needs to be filled in their environment. In all of the cases, their identification of a market gap goes back to a Cypriot tradition. This conclusion is line with the findings of Teixeira and Ferreira (2019), who mention that artisan entrepreneurs are keeping traditions belonging to specific locations alive and innovating out of these traditions to strengthen the identity, reputation, and competitiveness of their home locations. In addition, this conclusion also supports the observations of Erkut (2016, 2018) regarding the role of perceptions as a starting point of innovative, entrepreneurial activities.

Third, all interviewees mainly relied on own sources of financing and financed their activities out of their own pocket. Only two of them got an additional credit from a bank. This means that even though preserving the culture of a country, and valuing it in business ideas are important societal goals, artisan entrepreneurs have a hard time to find external sources of funding. This is in line with the findings of Flanagan et al. (2017), who found out that artisan entrepreneurs face a hard time to find out external sources of finance due to their both newness and smallness. This is also in line with the findings of Kaya et al. (2019) regarding the difficulties of finding external sources of financing for entrepreneurial activities in Cyprus.

Fourth, all kinds of innovative activities for traditional sectors could be identified among interviewees. As mentioned earlier, according to the taxonomy of Floris et al. (2020), there are four forms of innovating in traditional sectors. These types of innovations, and the identification of interviewees with respect to the types of innovations they are offering, can be seen in Table 5.2.

As a result of the interviews, P1 was identified as a retro-innovator since traditional Cypriot chairs were well known to older generations but brand new to younger generations; P2 was identified both as a retro-innovator for providing the sourdough bread to younger generations who consider it as a new product and as a radical innovator for inventing superfood spreads based on traditional, natural, and local ingredients; P3 was identified both as a provider of an embodiment of traditions, since she is providing Cypriot food, and as a radical innovator since she turned a chair making atelier into a restaurant that has the name "the Chair maker"; P4 was identified as reinterpreting traditions

Table 5.2   Innovations and Their Types

ID	Type of Product	Type of Innovation
P1	Handmade traditional Cypriot chairs	Retro-innovation: Handmade traditional Cypriot chairs are known products for older generations, but brand-new products for new generations
P2	Sourdough bread, probiotic tea, superfood spread, good quality coffee	Retro innovation: Sourdough bread Radical innovation: Superfood spread
P3	À la carte and Cypriot dishes as well as boutique hotel	Embodiment of traditions: Cypriot food Radical innovation: Turning a chair making atelier into a restaurant
P4	Ornamentals made out of traditional material felt	Reinterpretation of traditions: Modern decorations out of traditional material
P5	Local food and sweets	Embodiment of traditions: Local sweets
P6	Lefkara lace and Lapta lace	Retro innovations: Lefkara lace, Lapta lace Radical innovations: Diaries and protective masks with Lefkara motives

since felt is a traditional material, but ornaments are modern-day decorations; P5 was identified as a provider of embodiment of traditions since the tradition of making local sweets is valued in her business; and P6 was identified as both a provider of retro-innovations since Lefkara lace and Lapta Lace are known to older generations, but new to younger ones, and as a radical innovator, since diaries and masks with Lefkara lace and Lapta Lace are elements are new-to-the-world products. Even though the lines between these four categories in the taxonomy of Floris et al. (2020) may be blurred, this colorful view and categorization of artisan entrepreneurs show us how dynamic and multifaceted the artisanal entrepreneurial activities in small islands can be.

Practical and Policy Implications

First implication is the emergence of a dynamic and new artisan entrepreneurship sector in Cyprus. This emergence, so far, was done on its own and without any systematic support of a government program or any other financial incentive. Policymakers should focus on understanding the financial and technical needs of artisan entrepreneurs and design corresponding financial and technical support programs for strengthening artisan entrepreneurs, whereas practitioners should focus on creating new business models involving traditions and culture as new sources of innovation in their entrepreneurial mindset. So far, practical approaches to entrepreneurship had two domains of being either technological or social, but traditions and culture can also nurture the entrepreneurship scene by giving new ideas based on old traditions, hence, providing sources or inspirations of product innovations.

Second implication is the role of traditions and customs in artisan entrepreneurial activities in Cyprus. The authors observed that these customs and traditions were known to artisan entrepreneurs due to elder members of their families, but there is neither a standardization attempt nor any systematic guideline for describing traditions and customs for entrepreneurial activity. Even though entrepreneurs are known for reinterpreting some traditions, some sort of guideline for describing entrepreneurs what are the standards of a particular traditional manufacturing method may be necessary, as future generations may also be interested in these and they may not find the chance to ask the elderly about it.

Third implication is the potential of spillover effects in artisan entrepreneurial activities. In line with Curtis' (2016) observation that artisan entrepreneurship may create spillover effects, there is plenty of room for designing an entrepreneurial ecosystem as well as regional clusters for the emergence and establishment of artisan entrepreneurs. Policymakers should keep in mind that not the attempts of mass tourism, which, in long turn, may damage the country's authenticity, but emphasizing the local and the authentic properties of their country would be the long-run competitive advantage on a global level. However, since this chapter's perspective was based on a convenience sampling strategy with six entrepreneurs, a more systematic research with bigger samples is required to build a knowledge base for action.

Future Research and Practice Directions

Of course, the study has a number of limitations. Since no previous work was done regarding artisan entrepreneurship in Cyprus, the study only focused on a convenient sample of six entrepreneurs to explore this topic. Future research should be done on a quantitative basis with a bigger sample. Second, the study did not ask artisan entrepreneurs their perspectives of entrepreneurial ecosystems in Cyprus. This should be done by focusing on the literature around Global Entrepreneurship Monitor in future studies.

For practitioners, an immediate direction of practice would be to focus on traditions and culture as a source of innovations for entrepreneurial practice. As often represented in the literature, entrepreneurial activities rely on technology, but these are misrepresented to be new technologies only. The results show that old or traditional technologies can also provide a fertile ground for entrepreneurial activities.

References

Arias, R. A. C., & Cruz, A. D. (2019). Rethinking Artisan Entrepreneurship in a Small Island: A Tale of Two Chocolatiers in Roatan, Honduras. *International Journal of Entrepreneurial Behavior & Research*, *25*(4), 633–651.

Boukas, N., & Chourides, P. (2016). Niche Tourism in Cyprus: Conceptualising the Importance of Social Entrepreneurship for the Sustainable Development of Islands. *International Journal of Leisure and Tourism Marketing*, *5*(1), 26–43.

Cater, J., Collins, L., & Beal, B. (2017). Ethics, Faith, and Profit: Exploring the Motives of The US FairTrade Social Entrepreneurs. *Journal of Business Ethics*, *146*(1), 185–201.

Curtis, R. B. (2016). Ethical Markets in the Artisan Economy: Portland DIY. *International Journal of Consumer Studies*, *40*(2), 235–241.

Edward, J., Bendickson, J. S., Brent, J. J., Baker, B. L., & Solomon, S. J. (2020). Entrepreneurship within the History of Marketing. *Journal of Business Research*, *108*, 259–267.

Erkut, B. (2016). Product Innovation and Market Shaping: Bridging the Gap with Cognitive Evolutionary Economics. *Indraprastha Journal of Management*, *4*(2), 3–24.

Erkut, B. (2018). The Emergence of the ERP Software Market between Product Innovation and Market Shaping. *Journal of Open Innovation: Technology, Market, and Complexity*, *4*(3), 23. https://doi.org/10.3390/joitmc4030023

Erkut, B. (2020). Hayek on Product Innovation and Market Shaping: Opening the Black Box. *Liberal Düşünce Dergisi*, *25*(100), 169–189. https://doi.org/10.36484/liberal.757980

Ferreira, J., Sousa, B. M., & Goncalves, F. (2018). Encouraging the Subsistence Artisan Entrepreneurship in Handicraft and Creative Contexts. *Journal of Enterprising Communities: People and Places in the Global Economy*, *13*(1/2), 64–83. https://doi.org/10.1108/JEC-09-2018-0068

Flanagan, D. J., Lepisto, D. A., & Ofstein, L. F. (2017). Coopetition Among Nascent Craft Breweries: A Value Chain Analysis. *Journal of Small Business and Enterprise Development*, *25*(1), 2–16. https://doi.org/10.1108/jsbed-05-2017-0173

Floris, M., Dettori, A., & Dessi, C. (2020). Innovation within Tradition: Interesting Insights from Two Small Family Bakeries. *Piccola Impresa/Small Business*, *1*, 70–92. http://dx.doi.org/10.14596/pisb.344

Gao, J.-L., Dong-Sheng, L., & Conway, M.-L. (2021). Family Support and Entrepreneurial Passion: The Mediating Role of Entrepreneurs' Psychological Capital. *Social Behavior and Personality*, *49*(3), 1–15. https://doi.org/10.2224/sbp.9791

Kahn, M. J., & Baum, N. (2020). Entrepreneurship and Formulating Business Plans. In N. Baum & M. Kahn (Eds.), *The Business Basics of Building and Managing a Healthcare Practice* (pp. 37–43). Springer. https://doi.org/10.1007/978-3-030-27776-5_6

Kaya, T., Erkut, B., & Thierbach, N. (2019). Entrepreneurial Intentions of Business and Economics Students in Germany and Cyprus: A Cross-Cultural Comparison. *Sustainability*, *11*(5), 1437. http://dx.doi.org/10.3390/su11051437

Kokko, S., & Kaipainen, M. (2015). The Changing Role of Cultural Heritage in Traditional Textile Crafts from Cyprus. *Craft Research*, *6*(1), 9–30.

Kramvig, B., & Førde, A. (2020). Stories of Reconciliation Enacted in the Everyday Lives of Sámi Tourism Entrepreneurs. *Acta Borealia*, *37*(1/2), 27–42.

Liguori, E., Winkler, C., Vanevenhoven, J., Winkel, D., & James, M. (2019). Entrepreneurship as a Career Choice: Intentions, Attitudes, and Outcome Expectations. *Journal of Small Business & Entrepreneurship*, *32*(4), 311–331. https://doi.org/10.1080/08276331.2019.1600857

McGowan, P., Lewis Redeker, C., Cooper, S. Y., & Greenan, K. (2012). Female entrepreneurship and the management of business and domestic roles: Motivations, expectations and realities. *Entrepreneurship & Regional Development*, *24*(1/2), 53–72.

Merriam, S. B. (1988). *Case Study Research in Education: A Qualitative Approach* (1st ed.). San Francisco, CA: Jossey-Bass.

Neuman, W. L. (2014). *Social Research Methods*. Essex: Pearson Education.

Polyviou, A., Eteokleous, P., Dikaiakos, D. M., & Kassinis, I. G. (2019). *Entrepreneurship in Cyprus: National Report 2018/2019*. Global Entrepreneurship Monitor. Retrieved May 4, 2021, from https://gnosis.library.ucy.ac.cy/bitstream/handle/7/61641/GEM%20Report%202019-Web.pdf?sequence=1&isAllowed=y ()

Pret, T., & Cogan, A. (2019). Artisan Entrepreneurship: A Systematic Literature Review and Research Agenda. *International Journal of Entrepreneurial Behavior & Research*, *25*(4), 592–614. https://doi.org/10.1108/IJEBR-03-2018-0178

Ramadani, V., Hisrich, R. D., Dana, L.-P., Palalic, R., & Panthi, L. (2019). Beekeeping as a Family Artisan Entrepreneurship Business. *International Journal of Entrepreneurial Behavior & Research*, *25*(4), 717–730.

Ratten, V., Costa, C., & Bogers, B. (2019). Artisan, Cultural and Tourism Entrepreneurship. *International Journal of Entrepreneurial Behavior & Research*, *25*(4), 582–591. https://doi.org/10.1108/IJEBR-05-2018-0319

Teixeira, S., & Ferreira, J. J. M. (2019). Entrepreneurial Artisan Products as Regional Tourism Competitiveness. *International Journal of Entrepreneurial Behavior & Research*, *25*(4), 652–673. https://doi.org/10.1108/IJEBR-01-2018-0023

Toker, B., & Rezapouraghdam, H. (2021). Intangible Cultural Heritage and Management of Educational Tourism. In V. G. Costa, A. A. Moura, & M. D. R. Mira (Eds.), *Handbook of Research on Human Capital and People Management in the Tourism Industry* (pp. 199–216). IGI Global. https://doi.org/10.4018/978-1-7998-4318-4.ch010

Wellalage, N. H., & Reddy, K. (2020). Determinants of Profit Reinvestment Undertaken by SMEs in the Small Island Countries. *Global Finance Journal*, *43*, 100394. https://doi.org/10.1016/j.gfj.2017.11.001

Authors' Profile

Burcu Toker holds BSc and Msc in Industrial Engineering and PhD in Business Management. She is currently an associate professor and Vice Rector at Bahçeşehir Cyprus University. She also serves as Head of Department and researcher at the Business Administration Department of the Faculty of Economics, Administrative and Political Sciences at the same university. Formerly, she was lecturer, researcher and Head of Department at Industrial Engineering Departments of Girne American University and Cyprus International University. Her main research interests include systems analysis and design, systems improvement, quality improvement, statistical analysis, and qualitative and quantitative research methods.

Burak Erkut holds a BSc in Economics and Management Science and an MSc in Economics from Leipzig University as well as a PhD from Dresden University of Technology (TU Dresden). He is currently an Assistant Professor at Bahçeşehir Cyprus University. He also serves as the Director of Vocational School and Deputy Director of the Institute of Social and Applied Sciences at the same university. He is a fellow of the Institute for Research in Economic and Fiscal Issues (IREF) in France. Previously, he worked as a post-doctoral research fellow at the Chair of Economic Policy and Economic Research of TU Dresden. His main research interests include evolutionary economics, economics of innovation, and entrepreneurship.

Chapter 6

The Missing Links for Project Success: Evidence from an Emerging Economy

Saviour Ayertey Nubuor, Kwasi Dartey-Baah, and Yvonne Ayerki Lamptey

Contents

DOI: 10.4324/9781003152217-8

Introduction

There have been several house construction projects over the years to reduce the housing deficit in Ghana. However, most of those construction projects have faced problems like poor workmanship and ruin of the structures within a short period of time, mainly due to ineffective construction project leadership (Amponsah, 2010). In 2016, contribution of the construction industry to gross domestic product in Ghana was 13.7% (Ghana Statistical Service, 2017). Further, it employed 2% of the youth in the country (Darko & Lowe, 2016). Thus, if appropriate attention is given to the leadership challenges bedeviling the construction industry, it could largely contribute to the development of Ghana.

Ofori and Toor (2012) have observed that leadership is the missing component in the strive for construction industry development. Ofori (2015) added that the nature or environment of the construction sector, particularly in developing countries, creates a need and makes it essential for understanding the role of leadership. Studies have shown that outcome of any project is linked to employee's attitude toward the project and the leadership of that project (Dumdum et al., 2002; Dvir et al., 2002). Transformational leadership style (TFL) is linked with the behaviors of employees and their performance. Transformational leadership conveys an affirmative change in their followers (Morgan, 2012; Berson & Avolio, 2004; Lee, 2005).

Extant literature has covered studies on leadership patterns and success of projects to some extent (Aga et al., 2016; Deichmann & Stam, 2015; Liphadzi et al., 2015; Jiang, 2014). Nevertheless, these studies mostly focused on developed economies with little attention on Africa and West Africa in particular. Accordingly, there is a lacuna of knowledge first on whether TFL impact project success (PS) within the house construction sector of Ghana; second, team building (TB) plays a mediating role in the relationship between TFL and successful completion of projects within the house construction sector. Based on these gaps, this chapter aims at investigating how TFL affects the success of house construction sector projects in Ghana by considering TB as the mediating variable between TFL and PS. The chapter contributes to leadership and construction project literature and practice in three main ways; first, the authors developed a consolidated model to unveil the nature of the relationship between TFL on PS. The model graphically depicts the mediating role played by TB in the connection between TFL and success of projects. Second, we replicate the direct impact of TFL on PS by bringing out the reasoning behind the relationship with the support of social exchange theory (SET), hence, supporting the robustness of previous findings. Third, the chapter has uncovered the much-needed contextual reality in the house construction sector of Ghana by examining the role played by TB in the process of leader's influence on PS. This chapter, therefore, enhances knowledge and practice in the domain of leadership and success of projects.

The structure of this chapter is as follows; the background from a theoretical perspective is elucidated, and the hypothesized relationships are defined after the introduction. Next is the methodology and results of the analysis. Afterward, discussion on the main findings and the contributions to theory and practice are elaborated. Finally, study limitations, future research directions, and conclusions are presented.

Review of Literature and Research Hypotheses

Synopsis of Leadership in Africa

In the words of Northouse (2016, p. 6; 2018), leadership is "a process whereby an individual influence a group of individuals to achieve a common goal". Leadership in most African countries, specifically, SSA is similar. Prebendalism, patrimonialism, in-group collectivism, ethnic, religious, and family ties drive the actions of most leaders in Africa (Aryee, 1994, as cited in Dartey-Baah, 2015a, 2015b). This assertion is also supported by the work of Montgomery (1987) and Kuada (2008). Kuada (2010) argued that the culture in which African leaders are nurtured influences their style of leadership and relationship with their followers. The impact of culture in the behavior of African leaders could be seen in both corporate organizations and State-Owned Enterprises. This avowal is highly applicable in the Ghanaian and Sub-Sahara African context.

Leadership in State Owned Enterprises in modern Ghana is largely characterized by the use of governmental powers to reward political loyalists, the distribution of contracts and jobs to party affiliates among others (Sandbrook & Oelbaum, 1997; Hale & Fields, 2007). Muchiri (2011) asserted that there are leadership styles that are more useful within the SSA context and one of them is transformational leadership. This is because TFL pays heed to the needs of the followers. The use of TFL is more relevant in sectors like the house construction environment where there is a high propensity to focus on accomplishment of tasks rather than care for the human resources. Within the Ghanaian context, leaders are seen as organizational representatives and thus must show supportive behaviors toward their followers in all organizations (Dartey-Baah & Addo, 2018; Howieson, 2019; Alblooshi et al., 2020).

It is suggested that African leaders should not directly import the leadership behaviors of the West or East but identify and make use of leadership behaviors that works best within the African context taking into consideration the culture dynamics.

The Construction Industry in Ghana

Historically, colonialism left in its wake elements of foreign construction styles in Ghana. During the colonial times, the designs for various infrastructure works and housing were "exotic"- foreign materials and designs, human resources among others were used in the industry. Currently, one can find traces of some of these facilities in areas like "James Town", "Asylum Down" among others in the Greater Accra Region. After the independence of Ghana, however, there was a gradual shift from the adoption of a whole foreign style and technique to a merger with some traditional values and techniques even though there was a large reliance on foreign expertise and machines (Amponsah, 2010).

According to Amponsah (2010), there are two main sectors within the industry in Ghana. These are (1) the formal sector and (2) the informal sector. The formal sector is made up of large, capital intensive and technically complex projects. Such projects need the expertise of technocrats and mostly imported equipment and machines. These projects are usually carried out by the government, real estate companies, and multinational corporations. On the other hand, the major clients of informal sector are individuals, families, and small-scale enterprises. The activities of the industry have a lot of significance to the achievement of the national socioeconomic development goals of providing infrastructure, accommodation, and employment. This is reflected in the construction of hospitals, schools, townships, offices, houses, and other buildings (Ofori, 2006). Owing to the diversified nature of the construction industry, this chapter focused on residential (housing) construction projects within the industry in Ghana.

Social Exchange Theory and Effect of Transformational Leadership on Project Success

SET commenced in the late 1950s and progressed in the early 1960s with the contributions of renowned scholars like George Homans, John Thibaut, Harold Kelley, and Peter Blau (Cropanzano & Mitchell, 2005; Emerson, 1976). SET is primarily about the social exchanges and interactions that generate obligations within the relationship. It involves inter-dependent interactions where the actions and reactions of one person depend on the other person (Emerson, 1976). The basic ideas are based on (1) rules and norms of exchange, (2) resources exchanged, and (3) relationships that emerge. In practical terms, the theory posits that where an action has been rewarded in the past, followers think that if such an action is repeated, there is a higher possibility for one to receive a reward, and for that matter, they would like to repeat actions that will attract rewards based on the rules of engagement (Homans, 1958). Transformational leadership deals with the relationship exchanges that can take place between any leader and his/her followers; therefore, SET has been used as the theoretical lense in this chapter.

In leadership, one of the most common and comprehensive theories is the full range theory of leadership developed by Avolio and Bass (2004). As per these scholars, full range leadership is made up of three constructs, namely, TFL, transactional, and laissez-faire leadership styles. Avolio and Bass (2004) as well as Burns (1995) contended that as concepts, transformational, and transactional leaderships are distinctive with different dimensions. Laissez-faire is viewed as non-leadership in the sense that it allows the followers to act on their own without a hands-on direction from the leader. Owing to the nature of the laissez-faire style, it is squabbled that this style is embedded in management by exception inactive measurement dimension of transactional leadership (Avolio & Bass, 2004). This study made use of TFL.

According to Northouse (2016), the application of TFL style leads to an improvement in the outcomes for organizations. To Shamir et al. (1998), TFL establishes a higher level of commitment from both leaders and followers in achieving the organizational vision and objectives. It is about inspiring project team members to give their best effort and contribution by promoting mutual understanding and respect. There are three main steps when using TFL: (1) clarifying the value and significance of tasks to the followers, (2) urging the followers to strive beyond self-interest toward organizational interest, and (3) stimulating followers' self-worth and self-actualization needs (Bass, 1985). TFL has four interrelated dimensions, namely, inspirational motivation, idealized influence, intellectual stimulation, and individualized considerations (Bass, 1998).

Project success has been described differently by various researchers. This is because the word success is so broad and difficult to define and obtain common agreement (Jugdev & Moller, 2005). Keeping in line with the research objectives, this study used success of a project as the capability of it to meet the requirements in terms of time, budget, quality, as well as the stakeholders.

Once the tasks are assigned to members of a project by a leader, a social exchange begins between the leader who assigns the tasks and the members who accepted those tasks. Whenever the social exchange experienced between a leader and his/her follower is cordial, the followers will reciprocate with an amicable attitude toward work, and invariably, this will inure to the accomplishment of project goals. If the leader exhibits negative social exchange relationship (e.g., disrespect and the absence of motivation and rewards) with project team members, they will not give their best effort for achieving organizational PS (Yang et al., 2011, 2013; Anantatmula, 2010). Literature provides evidence to support the assertion that transformational leadership behaviors by project managers lead to improved PS (Scott-Young & Samson, 2008; Zwikael & Unger-Aviram, 2010). Transformational leaders create a positive social exchange environment where team members aim at achieving the targets set toward PS (Sohmen, 2013; Burke et al., 2006).

Team building is considered as a construct which can be used in different contexts. In project environment, it constitutes activities that enhance interpersonal relationships, task clarity, and the use of identifying problems and solving them (Klein et al., 2009; Salas et al., 1999). Where the project manager adopts TFL, he/she influences TB by (1) clarifying the limits and exclusions of tasks assigned to team members; (2) giving the free will for team members to explore out of curiosity and make decisions on their own; (3) sharing both information and knowledge within a team and the

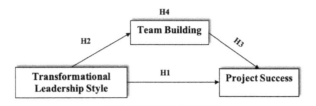

Figure 6.1 Conceptual model.

organization as a whole so that specific, measurable, attainable, realistic, and time-bound decisions can be made; (4) motivating and fostering positive team spirit (Iii, 2000). As opposed, when there is no effective transformational leadership, even the teams with right capabilities will not achieve PS (Sohmen, 2013; Klein *et al.*, 2009; Burke *et al.*, 2006). The practice of transformational style leadership by project leaders empowers and motivates teams to achieve success in projects (Burke *et al.*, 2006; Sohmen, 2013). Therefore, TFL style is required to build team spirit and work toward PS.

Project success is improved when there is team cohesiveness as a result of TB (Jacques *et al.*, 2013; Somech, 2006). A study by Aga *et al.* (2016), using a survey involving 224 development-related project managers in non-governmental organizations (NGOs) of Ethiopia, showed that TB affects the success of projects within the NGO.

Given that transformational leadership has the good of the team members in mind and achieves that through effective communication, goal clarity, problem-solving techniques, and interpersonal skills, team members get a sense of belongingness and commit to the assigned tasks to achieve PS (Zhu *et al.*, 2005). In sum, transformational leadership can improve the probability of PS by fostering TB (Yang *et al.*, 2011; Morgeson *et al.*, 2010). Based on SET and the empirical evidence discussed, we posit that:

H_1—Transformational leadership style has a positive effect on success of a project within the house construction sector of Ghana.

H_2—Transformational leadership style has a positive influence on TB within the house construction sector of Ghana.

H_3—Team building has a positive influence on PS within the house construction sector of Ghana.

H_4—Team building plays a mediating role in the relationship between TFL style and PS within the house construction sector of Ghana.

Building on the literature review and theoretical perspectives, we present the conceptual relationship between the variables in this research. This relationship is shown in Figure 6.1.

Methodology

Participants and Procedure

The survey respondents were simple random sampled from ten well-established construction companies working on housing projects (e.g., Appolonia affordable housing project at Oyibi; Borteyman affordable housing project at Tema among others) in Ghana. The authors focused on team members and project beneficiaries like civil engineers, project managers with rich experience in house construction management. The homogeneity of respondents informed the use of simple random sampling technique. The selected companies have over ten years' work experience in house construction projects in Ghana.

Before conducting the mass scale study, we tested the standardized questionnaire on 50 house construction project team members on-site. We used the pilot study responses to revise the questionnaire items with the guidance of construction project management professionals to enhance the readability and clarity. The questionnaire was self-administered on-site after the leadership of the selected companies permitted us to engage the respondents. All the questions were close-ended with a section requesting for the email addresses and telephone numbers of the respondents. Each participant took a minimum of 20 minutes to respond to all the questions. Three hundred and ten project team members initially responded to the questionnaire. Out of the 310 respondents, only the responses of 287 participants (civil engineers, project beneficiaries, and project professionals) were used in the analysis. This is because the remaining questionnaire was either not complete or not correctly answered.

Majority of the respondents (96.9%) were males. This is because construction projects are seen as male-oriented jobs or careers in Ghana. As far as educational qualifications are concerned, 56.8% were bachelor's degree holders, followed by 16.2% holding master's degree while 27% had higher national diploma (HND). Regarding age, 50.9% were between 21 and 30 years, 35.9% between 31 and 40 years, and the remaining 13.2% were 41 years and above. On project experience, 47.0% of the respondents had 1–5 years and 34.8% 6–10 years, while the balance counted more than ten years' experience in the field. It could be deduced from the considerable experiences of the respondents that they have substantial practical knowledge of construction project management and hence qualified as respondents.

Measures

Transformational leadership style was measured by using the five-point Likert multifactor leadership questionnaire which was developed by Bass and Avolio (1993). The scale ranges from "1 = not at all" to "5 = frequently if not often". The subscales for each of the dimensions of transformational leadership (i.e., inspirational motivation, idealized influence, intellectual stimulation, and individualized considerations) were reduced to four items that highly measured the constructs within Ghana. The authors used the composite of the dimensions in the study. Originally, the items range from 5 and above. The respondents were requested to think about their direct leader and tick (√) the boxes that best described him/her. A sample item of transformational leadership included "My leader instills pride in me for being associated with her/him". It must be emphasized that the full-range scale was not used because not all of the items accurately measure the constructs from the pilot study.

Twelve items on a five-point Likert scale instrument which was developed based on the meta-analysis by Klein *et al.* (2009) and the study by Aga *et al.* (2016) was used to measure TB. The scale ranges from "1 = not at all" to "5 = frequently/often". A sample item included "Conducting training programs on communication skills for the project team".

Project success was measured by employing a 12 items measurement scale encompassing client and stakeholders' satisfaction, time, cost, performance, client use, and effectiveness. These measurements were adapted from the project implementation profile by Pinto and Slevin (Slevin & Pinto, 1986) and a multidimensional construct of PS based on the views of project leaders. These measures fall in line with prior studies (Pinto & Prescott, 2010; Bryde, 2008).

Sample item included "The project was completed according to the budget allocated". The measurements of PS were based on a five-point Likert scale ranging from "1 = strongly disagree" to "5 = strongly agree".

Results

Analysis of Moment Structure (AMOS) version 22 was used to run Structural Equation Modeling (SEM) while Statistical Package for Social Sciences (SPSS) version 22 was used to do the preliminary analysis that assured the suitability of data for SEM. Having conducted the preliminary analysis, we constructed the measurement model to check validity of constructs. This was followed by constructing the structural model which enabled test of hypotheses. Bootstrapping approach was employed to examine the significance of the specific indirect effects (Preacher & Hayes, 2008).

Preliminary Analysis

We used aggregated response in the analysis. First, the responses were coded and entered into Microsoft Excel for screening. Means of non-missing responses within a specific construct were used to replace missing values (Hair *et al.*, 2010). Afterward, the data were exported to SPSS for multivariate assumptions, external validity, multicollinearity, and reliability tests. These checks were done to make the raw data usable for the data analysis and interpretation as recommended by Hair *et al.* (2010). Subsequently, the data were loaded into AMOS for SEM.

Sampling adequacy and measurement validity were done through principal axis factoring. This was performed to identify the common dimensions within the constructs (Hair *et al.*, 2006). To measure the general sampling adequacy of the constructs, the Kaiser–Meyer–Olkin (KMO) and Bartlett's test of Sphericity were done. The KMO value was 0.840, and Bartlett's test of Sphericity was significant ($P < 0.001$) (Kaiser, 1970). This showed that correlations existed among the items, and the data are suitable for factor analysis. Absolute skewness values for all the constructs were within +1 to –1. This was an indication that there was no issue with normality of data. Significant results of linearity test proved that all the constructs are sufficiently linear. There was no multicollinearity issue since the Variation Inflation Factor (VIF) values were below the cutoff of 3 (Hair *et al.*, 2006). The reliability of the scales (TFL: $\alpha = 0.94$; PS: $\alpha = 0.94$; TB: $\alpha = 0.92$) was all above the threshold value of 0.7 (Nunnally, 1978). The mean, standard deviation, and correlation values are given in Table 6.1.

Table 6.1   Means, Standard Deviations, and Correlations

Variable	TFL	PS	TB	Mean	Standard Deviation
TFL	1.000**	-	-	2.09	1.05
PS	.470**	1.000**	-	2.21	1.10
TB	.606**	.405**	1.000**	1.93	0.91

** Correlation is significant at the 0.01 level (1-tailed); TFL—transformational leadership style; PS—project success; TB—team building.

Confirmatory Factor Analysis

The measurement model is made up of transformational leadership, PS, and TB. We used first-order constructs in the model since we did not use the dimensions of the constructs in hypothesizing. The fit indices of the measurement model indicate a good model fit (χ^2/df = 1.43, P = 0.000, NFI = 0.91, TLI = 0.94, CFI = 0.94, RMSEA = 0.03). All the standardized regression weights are above 0.7 and significant (p < 0.001) and Average Variance Extracted (AVE) values of the constructs surpass the threshold value of 0.5 confirming the convergent validity of concerned constructs (Chin, 2003). An adequate internal consistency of the measures was evident since composite reliability values of the constructs exceeded the threshold value of 0.7 (Chin, 2003). Discriminant validity was also evident since the square root of AVE is greater than the inter-factor correlations (Gefen & Straub, 2005). Table 6.2 shows the values of AVE on the diagonal cells, composite reliability values, and the inter-construct correlations.

The Structural Model and Testing of Hypotheses

The hypotheses that propose direct impacts between variables were tested by using SEM results. The mediation test was performed by using 5,000 bootstrap samples with 95% bias-corrected confidence interval (Cheung & Lau, 2008). Further, we followed the recommendations of Hayes (2013) to assess the specific indirect effect of TB in the link between TFL and PS. We developed two models (the hypothesized mediation model and the direct paths only model). It can be seen from Table 6.3 that the hypothesized model showed better model fitness (χ^2/df = 1.32, GFI = 0.98, CFI = 0.97, TLI = 0.95, NFI = 0.92, RMSEA = 0.03) than that of the direct path only model. Thus, we used the hypothesized model to test the hypotheses.

Figure 6.2 shows the final structural model that displays path coefficients between variables. We hypothesized (hypothesis 1) that TFL positively influences PS within the house construction sector of Ghana. It is evident that TFL positively influences house construction PS (β = 0.17, t = 3.07, P < 0.05), thereby supporting the acceptance of hypothesis 1. Hypothesis 2 postulated that TFL style positively influences TB within the house construction sector in Ghana and hypothesis 3 stated that TB positively influences success of projects within the house construction sector of

Table 6.2 AVE Values, Composite Reliability, and Inter-Construct Correlations

Variable	TFL	PS	TB	AVE	CR
TFL	**0.73**	-	-	0.54	0.89
PS	0.36	**0.75**	-	0.56	0.94
TB	0.37	0.47	**0.71**	0.51	0.90

Table 6.3 Fit Indices of Hypothesized Model and Alternative Model

Model	χ^2/df	GFI	CFI	TLI	NFI	RMSEA
Hypothesized model	1.32	0.98	0.97	0.95	0.92	0.03
Alternative model (direct paths only)	2.42	0.86	0.94	0.94	0.91	0.06

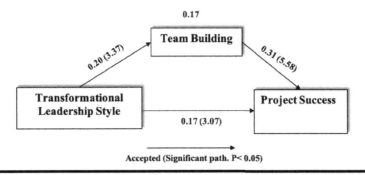

Figure 6.2   Tested model with path coefficients (t-values in parenthesis).

Table 6.4   The Mediation Effect of TB on TFL and PS

Model	Without Mediating Variable			With Mediating Variable		
	Variables	Estimate	p-value	Variables	Estimate	P-value
Default model	TFL → PS	0.231	0.001	TFL → TB → PS	0.17	0.002

Table 6.5   Bootstrapping Results for the Indirect Effects

Parameter			A × B Result at 95% Confidence Level				
			Estimate	Lower	Upper	P-value	Result
TB	←	TFL	.196	.104	.286	.001	Supported
PS	←	TFL	.171	.263	.080	.003	Supported
PS	←	TB	.309	.423	.197	.001	Supported

Note: Bootstrapping based on N = 5,000 subsamples.

Ghana. The results showed that TFL positively influences TB (β = 0.20, t = 3.37, P < 0.01) and also, TB positively affects the PS (β = 0.31, t = 5.58, P < 0.01), thus, providing enough evidence to support hypotheses 2 and 3.

We tested two models, one without the mediator and the other with the mediator, to detect the possibility of an indirect effect of TFL on PS through TB. It could be seen from Table 6.4 that with no mediation variable included, the standardized regression weight of the default model was 0.231 (P < 0.05). The standardized regression weight decreased from 0.23 to 0.17 at 95% confidence level once TB was introduced in the model as the mediator. This shows that TFL's influence is partially mediated by TB. As portrayed in Table 6.5, bootstrapping results in Process Macro supplemented the significant effect of TB in mediating the significant relationship between TFL and success of construction projects since the upper and lower limits of the confidence intervals do not contain zero (Hayes, 2013; Preacher & Hayes, 2004, 2008). Accordingly, hypothesis 4 which states that TB mediates the relationship between TFL style and success of a project within the house construction sector of Ghana was supported.

Discussion

The motive of this chapter is to examine the influence of TFL on the success of house construction projects using TB as the mediating variable between TFL and PS. In support of studies by Yang *et al.* (2011) and Anantatmula (2010) who found that TFL has an influence on PS, this research empirically proved that, indeed, TFL has a positive influence on success of projects within an emerging economy.

The authors believe that people naturally prefer to do their best where they are appreciated and feel that there is a higher incentive for their growth and development. These findings are in line with the study by Keegan and Hartog (2004). In the context of emerging economies particularly in Africa, most leaders prefer to use people to achieve the outcomes of tasks without much attention to the welfare of the people they are using. Most of the time, the leaders in emerging economies particularly in Africa feel they are doing the employees a favor by employing them, and for that matter, they should be used to do any task. Such thinking does not promote a good work relationship among employees and their leaders. Such mental orientation which is born out of greed and obstinate attachment to certain traditions is outmoded, and this chapter makes it clear that, instead of leaders being task oriented, they should be people oriented through the application of TFL and success on projects will be achieved. In practice, organizational leaders should know the state of their employees by checking on them to see whether they are making progress in their professional and social life as a whole or whether there are some weaknesses or issues that need to be addressed. This lesson is applicable in not only the construction industry which is the main context of this chapter but also other industries.

As conceptualized, TB partially mediated the relationship between transformational leadership and success of house construction projects. This indicates that the use of TFL by project leaders and managers within the house construction sector requires that due attention is given to TB to ensure PS; consequently, in assessing the influence of TFL on PS, it is important to include TB as a likely mediator. This finding is in congruence with the results of a study by Burke *et al.* (2006) and McDonough III (2000). Why is it that in emerging economies like Ghana among others, most leaders do not give attention to building the capacity of their teams or in the context of organizations, employees? At the end of the day, it is the enhanced capacity or skill of the team that will create value to the organization. Despite these, some leaders in emerging economies do not seek the betterment of their employees.

This chapter has demonstrated that, for various projects, particularly house building projects to be successful, there is a clarion call to focus on building the team with the requisite skills needed, and they will contribute to the success of the projects undertaking by the organization. Obviously, a sub-skilled employee will produce a sub-standard result. In addition, by TB, the researchers meant conditions such as organizational strategies, authority relationships, resources, and performance management systems should build synergy and promote team knowledge, skills, and capabilities.

Besides, teams have internal structures that shape the behavior of members and influence performance. Most often, the structure defines the roles, norms, team's cohesiveness, and conformity, thus, leadership should incorporate appropriate team structures that will enhance the performance of the members and obviously contribute to the success of various project tasks within the organization. For example, the team structure should promote "groupthink" decision-making process that ensures team cohesiveness, concurrence and prevents opinions that might cause destructive conflict. The transformational leader should create teams whose members can work intensely on specific and common tasks using their positive synergy and complementary skills. There should be clear goals, relevant skills, mutual trust, unified commitment, effective communication, and internal and external support (sound infrastructure such as proper training, reasonable measurement system) within teams by the transformational leader to enhance successful project execution.

Empirically, the influence of TFL has not been adequately studied within the house construction context of developing countries in Africa including Ghana. Most studies are from the developed economies with little research from emerging economies (Aga *et al.*, 2016; Deichmann & Stam, 2015; Liphadzi *et al.*, 2015). The findings of this chapter fill the knowledge lacuna in the existing literature on influence of leadership on PS in the house construction sector of Ghana. Also, this study extends theories in the field of organizational leadership in a developing country context. Significantly, the chapter projected the theory of organizational leadership and its influence on the successful outcome of projects in the construction industry of a developing economy.

Conclusion

In the growing research area of leadership and construction PS, this chapter endeavored to examine; how TFL influences construction PS within an emerging country context. Specifically, based on SET, the research developed a conceptual model. The findings revealed that TFL positively influences the success of projects in the construction sector of Ghana. Further analysis revealed that TB partially mediated the relationship between transformational leadership and success of projects. Our study extended the literature on leadership and its influence on construction PS, particularly within projectized organizations like the house construction sector; however, generalizing these findings for all types and sizes of construction sectors and other industries may require further investigation.

Practical and Policy Implications

1. The practical application of the findings is that project leaders within the house construction sector should concentrate more on developing transformational leadership capabilities, which directly and indirectly impact house construction projects' success. Construction companies should create an environment where transformational leadership training, in particular, would be given to management so that this type of behavior would spread across the entire structure of the project. This practice can be extrapolated in other industries.
2. Team building should be given due consideration in construction projects as it directly impacts the success of projects. However, it was observed that many project leaders in developing economies do not take the development of team members seriously, and there is a clarion call to move away from that backward view of leadership to one that empowers and develops project team members.
3. Leaders can build their teams by offering training, arranging seminars, and other TB activities to enhance team cohesion and productivity.
4. For policy, we suggest that management of construction projects should establish standards within the human resource policy manual that focus on hiring project managers with transformational leadership qualities to ensure a higher probability of success.
5. Academics and practitioners can use this chapter to guide their investigations into leadership styles and their influence on PS within various organizational contexts.

Future Research and Practice Directions

Even though this chapter demonstrated that TFL positively influences PS within the house construction sector of Ghana, there are some future research directions worth noting. First, the study mainly used the quantitative methodology to come out with the results. However, other factors could not be measured quantitatively; as such, an additional study using a case study, the mixed methodology, and action research would be highly commendable. Second, the aggregated data were gathered from respondents within the house construction sub-section of the construction industry; an extension of the study to cover respondents in other sub-areas like mining, road construction, among others, may give alternative results.

For practitioners, it is evident from this chapter that the major problem of construction project failure in emerging economies, in particular, is leadership. Indeed, leadership is the lifeblood of organizational PS. If project leaders and managers, civil engineers, project beneficiaries, and project professionals in developing nations consciously deploy the leadership style that builds and develops team members rather than the style that exploits them, there's hope for successful stories of PS in emerging economies. The model that we have developed in this study can serve as a practical guide when faced with challenges regarding the appropriate style of leadership to be used. Enough of the blame game when projects fail; let's put into action these recommendations so that others can also learn best practices from emerging economies.

Acknowledgment

We thank the editors, copyeditors, and the anonymous reviewers for their constructive criticisms, suggestions, and directions throughout the process. We also appreciate the financial support from the University of Ghana Business School's Research and Conference Committee.

Competing Interests: The authors have no competing interests to declare.

References

Aga, D. A., Noorderhaven, N., & Vallejo, B. (2016). Transformational Leadership and Project Success: The Mediating Role of Team-Building. *International Journal of Project Management, 34*(5), 806–818.

Alblooshi, M., Shamsuzzaman, M., & Haridy, S. (2020). The Relationship between Leadership Styles and Organizational Innovation: A Systematic Literature Review and Narrative Synthesis. *European Journal of Innovation Management*, Vol. ahead-of-print No. ahead-of-print. https://doi.org/10.1108/EJIM-11-2019-0339

Amponsah, R. (2010). *Improving Project Management Practice in Ghana with Focus on Agriculture, Banking and Construction Sectors of the Ghanaian Economy*. RMIT Thesis.

Anantatmula, V. S. (2010). Project Manager Leadership Role in Improving Project Performance. *Engineering Management Journal, 22*(1), 13–22.

Aryee, J. R. A. (1994). *An Anatomy of Public Policy Implementation*. Brookfield: Ashgate Publishing Company.

Avolio, B. J., & Bass, B. M. (2004). *Multifactor Leadership Questionnaire*. London: Mind Garden.

Bass, B. M. (1985). Leadership Performance Beyond Expectations. *Academy of Management Review, 12*(4), 5244–5247.

Bass, B. M. (1998). *Transformational Leadership: Industrial, Military, and Educational Impact*. Mahwah, NJ: Lawrence Erlbaum Associates.

Bass, B. M., & Avolio, B. J. (1993). Transformational Leadership and Organizational Culture. *Public Administration Quarterly, 17*(1), 112–121.

Berson, Y., & Avolio, B. J. (2004). Transformational Leadership and the Dissemination of Organizational Goals: A Case Study of a Telecommunication Firm. *Leadership Quarterly, 15*(5), 625–646.

Bryde, D. (2008). Perceptions of the Impact of Project Sponsorship Practices on Project Success. *International Journal of Project Management, 26*(8), 800–809.

Burke, C. S., Stagl, K. C., Klein, C., Goodwin, G. F., Salas, E., & Halpin, S. M. (2006). What Type of Leadership Behaviors are Functional in Teams? A Meta-Analysis. *Leadership Quarterly, 17*(3), 288–307.

Cheung, G. W., & Lau, R. S. (2008). Testing Mediation and Suppression Effects of Latent Variables. *Organizational Research Methods, 11*(2), 296–325.

Chin, W. W. (2003). Issues and Opinions on Structural Equation Modeling. *Embo Journal, 11*(12), 4261–4272.

Cropanzano, R., Anthony, E., Daniels, S., & Hall, A. (2016). Social Exchange Theory: A Critical Review with Theoretical Remedies. *Academy of Management Annals, 11*, 1–38.

Cropanzano, R., & Mitchell, M. S. (2005). Social Exchange Theory: An Interdisciplinary Review. *Journal of Management, 31*, 874–900.

Darko, E., & Lowe, A. (2016). *Ghana's Construction Sector and Youth Employment*. ODI Working Paper. London: Overseas Development Institute.

Dartey-Baah, K. (2015a). Political Leadership in Ghana: 1957 to 2010. *African Journal of Political Science and International Relations, 9*(2), 49–61.

Dartey-Baah, K. (2015b). Resilient Leadership: A Transformational-Transactional Leadership Mix. *Journal of Global Responsibility, 6*(1), 99–112.

Dartey-Baah, K., & Addo, S. (2018). Leaders as Organisational Representatives: A Structural Model. *African Journal of Economic and Management Studies, 10*(2), 148–168.

Deichmann, D., & Stam, D. (2015). Leveraging Transformational and Transactional Leadership to Cultivate the Generation of Organization-Focused Ideas. *Leadership Quarterly, 26*(2), 204–219.

Dumdum, U. R., Lowe, K. B., & Avolio, B. J. (2002). A Meta-Analysis of Transformational and Transactional Leadership Correlates of Effectiveness and Satisfaction: An Update and Extension. In B. Avolio & F. Yammarino (Eds.), *Transformational and Charismatic Leadership: The Road Ahead* (pp. 35–66). New York: Elsevier Science.

Dvir, T., Eden, D., Avolio, B. J., & Shamir, B. (2002). Impact of Transformational Leadership on Follower Development and Performance: A Field Experiment. *Academy of Management Journal, 45*, 735–744. https://doi.org/10.2307/3069307

Emerson, R. M. (1976). Social Exchange Theory. *Annual Review of Sociology, 2*(7), 335–362.

Gefen, D., & Straub, D. (2005). A Practical Guide to Factorial Validity Using Pls-Graph: Tutorial and Annotated Example. *Communications of the Association for Information Systems, 16*(1), 91–109.

Ghana Statistical Service. (2017). *Provisional 2016 Annual Gross Domestic Product*. Accra, Ghana: GSS. https://www2.statsghana.gov.gh/docfiles/GDP/GDP2017/April/Annual_2016_GDP_April%20 2017_Edition.pdf.

Hair, J. F., Black, W. C., Babin, B. J., & Anderson, R. E. (2010). *Multivariate Data Analysis* (7th ed.). Upper Saddle River, NJ: Prentice Hall.

Hair Jr, J. F., Black, W. C., Babin, B. J., Anderson, R. E., & Tatham, R. L. (2006). *Multivariate Data Analysis* (6th ed.). Upper Saddle River, NJ: Pearson-Prentice Hall.

Hale, J. R., & Fields, D. L. (2007). Exploring Servant Leadership Across Cultures: A Study of Followers in Ghana and the USA. *Leadership, 3*(4), 397–417.

Hayes, A. F. (2013). *Introduction to Meditation, Moderation, and Conditional Process Analysis: A Regression-Based Approach*. New York: Guilford Press.

Homans, G. C. (1958). Social Behavior as Exchange. *American Journal of Sociology, 63*(6), 597–606.

Howieson, W. B. (2019). What is Leadership?—An Academic Perspective. In *Leadership* (pp. 35–149). Bingley: Emerald Group Publishing Limited. https://doi.org/10.1108/978-1-78769-785-020191003

McDonough E. F. III (2000). Investigation of Factors Contributing to the Success of Cross- Functional Teams. *Journal of Product Innovation Management , 17 (3),* 221–235.

Jacques, P. H., Garger, J., & Thomas, M. (2013). Assessing Leader Behaviors in Project Managers. *Management Research News, 31*(31), 4–11.

Jiang, J. (2014). The Study of the Relationship between Leadership Style and Project Success. *Social Science Electronic Publishing, 1*(1), 51.

Jugdev, K., & Moller, R. (2005). A Retrospective Look at Our Evolving Understanding of Project Success. *IEEE Engineering Management Review, 34*(3), 110–110.

Kaiser, H. F. (1970). A Second Generation Little Jiffy. *Psychometrika, 35,* 401–415.

Keegan, A. E., & Hartog, D. N. D. (2004). Transformational Leadership in a Project-Based Environment: A Comparative Study of the Leadership Styles of Project Managers and Line Managers. *International Journal of Project Management, 22*(8), 609–617.

Klein, C., Diazgranados, D., Salas, E., Le, H., Burke, S. C., & Lyons, R., et al. (2009). Does Team Building Work? *Small Group Research, 40*(2), 181–222.

Kuada, J. (2008). Social Resources and Entrepreneurial Activities in Africa. *International Journal of Social Entrepreneurship, 1*(1), 27–55.

Kuada, J. (2010). Culture and Leadership in Africa: A Conceptual Model and Research Agenda. *African Journal of Economic and Management Studies, 1*(1), 9–24.

Lee, J. (2005). Effects of Leadership and Leader-Member Exchange on Commitment. *Leadership & Organization Development Journal, 26*(8), 655–672.

Liphadzi, M., Aigbavboa, C., & Thwala, W. (2015). Relationship between Leadership Styles and Project Success in the South Africa Construction Industry. *Procedia Engineering, 123*(1–2), 284–290.

McDonough, E. F. III (2000). Investigation of Factors Contributing to the Success of Cross-Functional Teams._ *Journal of Product Innovation Management, 17(3),* 221–235.

Montgomery, J. D. (1987). Probing Managerial Behaviour: Image and Reality in Southern Africa. *World Development, 15*(7), 911–29.

Morgan, T. L. (2012). *An Examination of Project Managers' Leadership Contributions to Project Success Using Critical Success Factors.* Dissertations & Theses—Gradworks.

Morgeson, F. P., Derue, D. S., & Karam, E. P. (2010). Leadership in Teams: A Functional Approach to Understanding Leadership Structures and Processes. *Journal of Management, 36*(1), 5–39.

Muchiri, M. K. (2011). Leadership in Context: A Review and Research Agenda for Sub-Saharan Africa. *Journal of Occupational and Organizational Psychology, 84*(3), 440–452.

Northouse, P. G. (2016). *Leadership: Theory and practice* (7th ed.). Thousand Oaks, CA: Sage Publications.

Northouse, P. G. (2018). *Leadership: Theory and Practice.* Los Angeles, CA: Sage Publications.

Nunnally, J. C. (1978). *Psychometric Theory.* New York: McGraw-Hill.

Ofori, D. (2006). *Problems of Project Management: Theory, Evidence and Opinion from Ghana.* Monograph. Accra: Ghana Universities Press.

Ofori, G. (2015). Nature of the Construction Industry, Its Needs and Its Development: A Review of Four Decades of Research. *Journal of Construction in Developing Countries, 20*(2), 115–135.

Ofori, G., & Toor, S. R. (2012). Leadership and Construction Industry Development in Developing Countries. *Journal of Construction in Developing Countries, 17*(48), 1–21.

Pinto, J. K., & Prescott, J. E. (2010). Planning and Tactical Factors in the Project Implementation Process. *Journal of Management Studies, 27*(3), 305–327.

Preacher, K. J., & Hayes, A. F. (2004). SPSS and SAS Procedures for Estimating Indirect Effects in Simple Mediation Models. *Behavior Research Methods, Instruments, & Computers, 36*(4), 717–731.

Preacher, K. J., & Hayes, A. F. (2008). Asymptotic and Resampling Strategies for Assessing and Comparing Indirect Effects in Multiple Mediator Models. *Behavior Research Methods, 40,* 879–891.

Salas, E., Rozell, D., Mullen, B., & Driskell, J. E. (1999). The Effect of Team Building on Performance: An Integration. *Small Group Research, 30*(3), 309–329.

Sandbrook, R., & Oelbaum, J. (1997). Reforming Dysfunctional Institutions Through Democratization? Reflections on Ghana. *The Journal of Modern African Studies, 35*(4), 603–646.

Scott-Young, C., & Samson, D. (2008). Project Success and Project Team Management: Evidence from Capital Projects in the Process Industries. *Journal of Operations Management, 26*(6), 749–766.

Shamir, B., Zakay, E., Breinin, E., & Popper, M. (1998). Correlates of Charismatic Leader Behavior in Military Units: Subordinates' Attitudes, Unit Characteristics, and Superiors' Appraisals of Leader Performance. *Academy of Management Journal, 41*(4), 387–409.

Slevin, D. P., & Pinto, J. K. (1986). The Project Implementation Profile: New Tool for Project Managers. *Project Management Journal, 17.*

Sohmen, V. S. (2013). Leadership and Teamwork: Two Sides of the Same Coin. *Journal of Information Technology & Economic Development, 4*(2), 1–18.

Somech, A. (2006). The Effects of Leadership Style and Team Process on Performance and Innovation in Functionally Heterogeneous Teams. *Journal of Management Official Journal of the Southern Management Association, 32*(1), 132–157.

Yang, L. R., Huang, C. F., & Wu, K. S. (2011). The Association Among Project Manager's Leadership Style, Teamwork and Project Success. *International Journal of Project Management, 29*(3), 258–267.

Yang, L. R., Wu, K. S., & Huang, C. F. (2013). Validation of a Model Measuring the Effect of a Project Manager's Leadership Style on Project Performance". *KSCE Journal of Civil Engineering, 17*(2), 271–280.

Zhu, W., Chew, I. K. H., & Spangler, W. D. (2005). CEO Transformational Leadership and Organizational Outcomes: The Mediating Role of Human—Capital-Enhancing Human Resource Management. *Leadership Quarterly, 16*(1), 39–52.

Zwikael, O., & Unger-Aviram, E. (2010). HRM in Project Groups: The Effect of Project Duration on Team Development Effectiveness. *International Journal of Project Management, 28*(5), 413–421.

Authors' Profile

Saviour Ayertey Nubuor is a lecturer and researcher in the Department of Organization and Human Resource Management at the University of Ghana Business School. He holds a PhD in Management Science and Engineering focusing on Project Management from Wuhan University of Technology, Wuhan, People's Republic of China. He is a Project Management Professional (PMP) and a member of the Project Management Institute (PMI) of the United States. He was a co-founder and director of projects and administration for Africa-China Business Group Ltd. He has published in reputable peer-reviewed journals and serves as a consultant for both private and public institutions. His research focuses on project management, leadership, and human resource management.

Kwasi Dartey-Baah is an associate professor at the Department of Organization and Human Resource Management (OHRM) in the University of Ghana Business School. He holds a PhD in Leadership and Human Resource Development from Trinity College Newburgh, United States, and Canterbury University, United Kingdom, and engineering degrees from Kwame Nkrumah University of Science and Technology, Ghana, and the Imperial College, London. He has considerable research and consultancy experience in project management and leadership development. He has published in high-impact journals including Leadership and Organizational Development Journal, International Journal of Law & Management, and African Journal of Economic and Management Studies in his area of research. Key themes in his research are Leadership, Corporate Social Responsibility, Safe Work Environments, and Organizational Culture.

Yvonne Ayerki Lamptey is a senior lecturer with the Department of Organization and Human Resource Management at the University of Ghana Business School. Her PhD in Business Studies focuses on employment relations. Yvonne is a professional member of the Institute of Human Resource Management Practitioners, Ghana. She has served as a consultant and conducted training for private and public institutions. She has published in international per review journals on union relations, organizational behavior, corporate leadership, and the informal sector. Her research focus is on employment relations, strategic human resource management, and organizational behavior.

Chapter 7

When Internationalization Goes Awry: The Separation of Policy and Practice in Intellectual Property

Symeon Mandrinos and Calvin W. H. Cheong

Contents

Introduction

The bilateral dispute between China and the United States over intellectual property rights (IPRs) has created an environment of conflicting national interests on intellectual property standards, leading to increasingly tense trade relations. Under these circumstances, many firms—American, Chinese, or others—have had to adapt and make quick decisions whether to remain in or exit the market. The United States' primary area of concern is the arbitrary and often discriminatory enforcement of intellectual property laws and standards in China. Specifically, the United States took particular interest in the pervasiveness of institutional influence hidden among a complex decentralized governance framework (Li & Alon, 2020) that lack the necessary institutions and agencies at the local or domestic level to drive and sustain IPR reforms and conformity efforts (Brander et al., 2017). Matters are exacerbated by the inherently opaque nature of IPRs and standards, making it difficult to identify prevailing practices, draw meaningful connections between policies and outcomes, and measuring the effectiveness of policy implementation (Bromley & Powell, 2012; Wijen, 2014).

Despite the concerns raised by US lawmakers, recent years have seen China undergoing a shift toward upholding and protecting IPRs by complying with formal, international regulations (Lu, 2021; Peng et al., 2017), in what can be described as a transition from opaque to translucent policy (Altman et al., 2019). By establishing minimum intellectual property standards, China has been able to protect its local intellectual property through the provision of guidance for improving judicial protection, besides lowering the costs of IPRs protection (Lu, 2021). This has allowed the country to leverage on its institutional influence by providing foreign firms with an acceptable level of IPRs (Peng et al., 2017), thereby creating an environment, that at least on the surface, complies with international standards. The establishment of three specialized IP courts in Beijing, Guangzhou, and Shanghai marked a new trajectory of development for IP protection in China (Lu, 2021) that ensures IPRs remain beneficial to all stakeholders from the ongoing relationships (Peng et al., 2017). However, even though protection of IP rights plays a vital role in encouraging independent innovation and optimizing a favorable environment for innovation and invention, it is, rather surprisingly, unbeneficial toward reducing international IP conflicts (Li, 2016; Phillips, 2011). Recent years, especially during the period of tense, Sino-American trade relations saw a number of US entrepreneurs deciding to deinternationalize and return to the United States after flocking to China to start their tech businesses in the late 2000s and early 2010s (Areddy, 2018).

After two years of conflict, both the United States and China agreed to minimize their policy and institutional "distance" on trade, culminating in a trade deal that was signed in January 2020 with IPRs as a key component of the trade agreement (Bisio et al., 2020; Zhang, 2020). With the trade agreement in place, both countries effectively recognized internationalization as a key factor for economic growth. The challenge to both countries is to put in place policies that stimulate mutual home/host market engagement since their present institutional distance creates institutional and policy implementation challenges (Kostova et al., 2020) and is not sufficiently conducive to foster an equitable trade relationship. Firms caught in this tussle face the challenge of devising an appropriate strategy that is suitably competitive yet, do not place it under increased scrutiny by their respective governments.

Theoretically, these challenges are reflected in the Institutional Theory perspectives of organizational institutionalism and institutional economics. Organizational institutionalism places emphasis on a firm's need for corporate legitimacy that despite the deep institutional distance and opacity of policy between two countries, a firm (un)willingly submits to institutional demands and comply with regulatory pressures (Kostova et al., 2020). Institutional economics, on the other hand, focuses on the difference in institutional environments, and the degree of support provided by local institutions toward economic activities (Kostova et al., 2020). While both perspectives are highly relevant to the context of this chapter, we focus on the organizational institutionalism perspective as it is more closely related to the complexity of issues arising out of the establishment and enforcement of IPRs such as institutional and/or regulatory pressures and inconsistencies, (in)voluntary compliance, and corporate legitimacy. Specifically, we explore how firms elect to decouple and/or deinternationalize due to pressures related to the enforcement of IPRs policies.

In this chapter, we show that in a field rife with opaque policies and procedures (as is the case of IPRs), firms face additional strategic complexities as the interests of the "nation-state", firm, and the need for corporate legitimacy exist in a constant state of tension. When exposed to institutional pressures, firms naturally succumb and align their interest with those of the state. State interests, however, are often detrimental to the firm, evoking some form of strategic response from the firm to remain tenable. We argue that these responses are reflected in the firm's decision to (un)intentionally decouple and/or (in)voluntarily deinternationalize. Because strategic responses (e.g., deinternationalization and decoupling) are typically implemented as a series of maneuvers to achieve the objectives laid down by an institutional policy (Evans, 1991), we argue that when firms are controlled by institutional complexities arising out of opacity, their need to comply drives their export responses.

This chapter represents the first attempt to highlight the importance of decoupling and deinternationalization, which will aid formal institutions and policymakers in understanding the impact of intellectual property standards and regulations on export-oriented firms. To this end, further refinements can be made to existing policies to ensure that firms are not discouraged from expansion and innovation because of stricter regulatory enforcement. This chapter is also an important step toward deescalating trade tensions and fostering more harmonious and mutually beneficial bilateral relations through the introduction and fair implementation of transparent intellectual property standards that will encourage internationalization in an increasingly global community. Theoretically, adopting the IPRs context also helps explain the practical value of decoupling and deinternationalization, making these previously ambiguous terms more approachable thanks to our efforts to examine the institutional logic and institutional complexity that exist to specify the diversity of their elements.

Institutional Theory

The institutional theory explains how the environment impacts upon firms with other market actors, and interact with institutions (He et al., 2013; Scott, 2014). According to the theory, there are three pillars of the institutional environment: the regulative, the normative, and the cognitive dimensions (North, 1990; Scott, 1995), where all forms of institutions can manage interactions and influence decision-making (Kostova & Zaheer, 1999; Scott, 1995). Perhaps, the most well-known of the three pillars of institutional acceptability are those introduced by Scott (1995) who showed that institutional policies (i.e., the regulative) such as the existing rules and regulations in a particular environment may promote conformity and compliance behavior in some parties while restricting behavior in others based on institutional pressures. The cognitive pillar, meanwhile, places emphasis on a generally shared perception of what is typical or taken for granted (e.g., locally acceptable business practices). The normative pillar is the value system that defines what is appropriate for market actors, even in the absence of legal or other obligations (e.g., sociocultural norms and beliefs) where institutions are able to influence organizational as well as individual actions through normative pressures (Scott, 1995, 2014). The discussion in this chapter will primarily be based on the regulative pillar.

Decoupling and Deinternationalization

The theory of decoupling emerged from a series of observations that sought to determine the reasons why firms chose to (not) implement a range of policies (Meyer & Rowan, 1977). Deinternationalization, meanwhile, is often considered as a firm's strategic response to reduce participation in international operations (Benito & Welch, 1997). Central to a firm's decision to decouple or deinternationalize is its willingness and/or ability to conform and comply with a diverse range of institutional policies. Conformity and compliance with institutional policies, however, are the key drivers in a firm's response toward achieving legitimacy. Conformity refers to the firm's voluntary response to the meeting and/or exceeding (informal/social) norms and obligations not (yet) codified in standards and law. Compliance, in contrast, constitutes the firm's mandatory completion of legal or formal obligations, often at the barest minimum levels of institutional acceptability (Durand et al., 2019). Decoupling then can best be described as a firm's "policy-practice" response when they adopt policies in form but not in substance through acts of ceremonial compliance to avoid institutional pressures (Mandrinos et al., 2019).

The motivations behind decoupling come in two forms: ceremonial compliance and substantive compliance. Ceremonial compliance occurs when firms avoid institutional demands emerging from government policies by pursuing outward business practices while portraying an inward business orientation in line with government policies. In other words, decoupling as a firm's response arising from ceremonial compliance is simply a charade of international business. Substantive compliance, in contrast, occurs when firms comply and engage with institutional pressures emerging from government policies by pursuing business practices and portraying a business orientation that is consistent with government policies (i.e., inward practice–inward policy and outward practice–outward policy) (Lim & Mandrinos, 2020; Mandrinos et al., 2019). Figure 7.1 illustrates the matrix of decoupling characteristics based on the relationship between ceremonial/substantive compliance. Decoupling motivated by substantive compliance is, therefore, regarded as a true reflection of business engagement in international markets (Lim & Mandrinos, 2020; Mandrinos et al., 2019). More importantly, decoupling is arguably less harmful when it maintains a pro-international business orientation, thereby contributing to internationalization.

The alternative, however, is dangerous. When institutional pressures mount, as a result of say, increasingly convoluted policies or opaque processes, firms that are motivated through substantive compliance may be forced to deinternationalize. Defined as a firm's strategic response to reduce participation in international operations (Benito & Welch, 1997), deinternationalization represents a serious threat to international business besides undermining the firm's international position (Choquette, 2019; Gnizy & Aviv, 2018; Lim & Mandrinos, 2020; Sapouna et al., 2018; Sousa & Tan, 2015; Yayla et al., 2018). The competitive edge these firms have built over the years may, as a result, be extinguished in the firms' pursuit of legitimacy through either substantive or

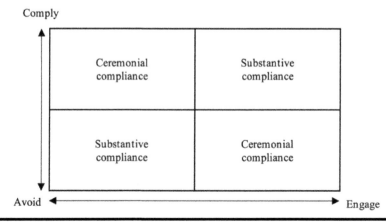

Figure 7.1 Matrix of decoupling characteristics.

ceremonial compliance. Consequently, caution needs to be exercised when devising policies to ensure that firms on the brink of decoupling are incentivized to pursue internationalization. Firms considering deinternationalization meanwhile need to be given assurance that their rights and interests are protected to mitigate threats of deinternationalization and escalating trade tensions besides encouraging further innovation.

Our description of decoupling and deinternationalization is well illustrated by the bilateral dispute between China and the United States over IPRs. Both countries recognize internationalization as a key factor for industrial competitiveness and economic growth and thus need to put in place policies and programs to stimulate export modes and local firm involvement in such activities. However, the inconsistent, convoluted policies and opaque processes within both countries' intellectual property standards and laws create a barrier that disincentivizes many firms from internationalizing. Firms intending to comply with either country's intellectual property laws will have to choose between a ceremonial or substantive level of compliance. An American firm, for example, will be in substantive compliance with American IP laws given the strict enforcement locally. If it intends to expand to China, the firm may choose to ceremonially or substantively comply with Chinese IP laws. A ceremonial compliance with Chinese laws will likely hasten the firm's market entry but due to lax enforcement of IPRs, the firm may soon lose its competitive edge. A substantive compliance, meanwhile, will be costly and may be subject to greater scrutiny by regulatory authorities. Either way, the firm may be deterred from internationalizing, or if already internationalized, may be encouraged to deinternationalize. There are, of course, other possible scenarios to compliance. We summarize these in Table 7.1 to illustrate the range of decoupling characteristics and their respective international business outcomes.

Bilateral policies (or in this case, intellectual property laws) need to be strategic and targeted to the extent that it promotes economic growth and industrial competitiveness between countries, regardless of their level of development. Inconsistent standards, legal constraints, and bureaucratic processes create legitimacy criteria that vary in complexity, leading to confusion as firms desperately try to conform (North, 1990). In the name of national interest, nation-states need to rise to the challenge of stimulating investment in internationalization activities by introducing policies and programs that not only are comprehensive but also consistent in form and application with all aspects of business and trade law, whether local or international. This will align local laws with international certifiable standards. Presently, this is not the case. Loopholes between local and international IP standards abound, undermining their effectiveness (Boiral, 2003; Christmann & Taylor, 2006) and allowing firms to bypass regulations that compromise their competitiveness and economic positions (Papageorgiadis et al., 2013) during times of market tension and other disruptions (Suddaby, 2010). These issues need to be addressed to create a more equitable playing field for trade between nations.

Table 7.1 Decoupling Characteristics and International Business Outcomes

Compliance	Policy		Practice	Reality	Effect
Ceremonial	Inward	Avoid	Engage	Charade	Internationalization
	Outward	Comply	Avoid	Charade	Deinternationalization
Substantive	Inward	Comply	Avoid	Truth	Deinternationalization
	Outward	Comply	Engage	Truth	Internationalization

Institutional Pressure and Complexity

Ever since the Statute of Anne of 1710 began providing legislative protection on modern intangible assets, intellectual property laws and standards have posed significant regulatory challenges on the path of internationalization (Patterson, 1966; Peng et al., 2017). However, it was not until the end of the nineteenth century—when the United States became the largest net producer of intellectual properties—did the markets begin to demand better safeguards against internationalization for the country's IPRs. Under these circumstances, the institutional boundaries target the same well-defined domain, and therefore, both country and firm must be cognizant of and responsive to whom exerts institutional pressures upon whom they are dependent. Neither the "nation state" nor firms can detach themselves from its institutional settings. As these two different interests co-exist in tension, the firm will have to eventually decide on its level of compliance with intellectual property laws. This is a particularly important decision to make since the firm's (non)compliance with IPRs has a significant impact on its costs and benefits of doing business, especially at the international level (Li & Alon, 2020; Peng, 2013; Peng et al., 2009, 2017). Making distinction between export firms and IPRs is, however, difficult since both are joined together through a unique configuration of policy elements that are (or at least supposed to be) mutually supportive to achieve completeness (Peng, 2013; Peng et al., 2017; Rugman & Verbeke, 2000; Verbeke, 2013).

Unfortunately, institutional responses to these circumstances are in a constant state of evolution. Thus, in fields undergoing a transitional phase—such as the enforcement of IPRs at the international level—there is no clear prioritization and dominant logic to guide institutional pressures. Due to the lack of a definitive framework that organizes and prioritizes an optimal balance between state and firm interests, it is common to see the firm's interests (in)voluntarily coalesce with national interests when a strategic decision needs to be made on which institutional pressures to satisfy. Presently, however, there exists a significant institutional overlap among the regulatory bodies overseeing IPRs. Although these bodies are bound by the same IP laws, their actions when enforcing these laws differ significantly, introducing unnecessary complexity and creating confusion among firms. To illustrate, there are four main forms of IPRs namely copyright (to protect creative expression), patent (to protect inventions or innovations), trademark (to protect brands, logos, and by extension, trading reputations of the undertakings), and trade secrets (Farrand, 2017; Parr, 2018). Each of these IPRs offers tailored solutions to meet the diverse needs and demands of the market. However, each also requires the firm to meet unique sets of criteria before the IPR can be granted. The layers of complexity between the criteria for each IPR create an environment that is inconducive for effective compliance and enforcement. To make matters worse, the agencies responsible for enforcing these IPRs in the case of the United States and China actively compete against one another, and to establish a system of domination, it accommodates firm responses (e.g., IPR compliance) that serve the agency's interests, effectively withholding IP protection from firms with a more legitimate need.

Intentional–Unintentional Decoupling

The complexity of and pressures from the various institutions (i.e., IPRs agencies) are bound to elicit a decoupling response from the firm. The firm's decoupling response, however, may be intentional or unintentional, depending on the motivations behind the response. Decoupling is intentional when firms deliberately choose to ceremonially comply, i.e., symbolically adopt or buy in to institutional pressures (de Bree & Stoopendaal, 2020; Fung et al., 2011; Jamali, 2010; Luiz & Callum, 2014)—a common response, particularly among foreign firms and investors. In countries with a high level of institutional pressure and control such as China, this typically takes the form of firms understating or leaving out certain income items by under-reporting import taxes (Fung et al., 2011). Foreign firms intentionally decouple from institutional demands through differential tax treatments by manipulating trade figures and overstating import invoices to reduce tariff costs while repatriating capital to China (Fung et al., 2011).

In countries where regulatory controls are weak or have a wide "grey area" in legal interpretation and enforcement, multinational enterprises instead see themselves as victims of an uncertain business and legal environment (Luiz & Callum, 2014). Their decision to deliberately bypass institutional demands to achieve some semblance of compliance is driven by the belief that it is the weak policies and poor enforcement that led to this response. Ultimately, however, an appropriate level of compliance is never achieved as seen in many firms' attempts to comply with any international compliance standards. On the one hand, compliance signals a firm's commitment to conform to societal expectations which can certainly help generate corporate and institutional legitimacy and enhance firm outcomes. On the other hand, the inconsistencies between each country's legal institutions and policies provide ample opportunities for multinational enterprises to ceremonially comply with, or in some cases, avoid regulations altogether (Jamali, 2010).

Decoupling, however, may not always be intentional. Although the various IPR agencies aim to ensure firms achieve compliance, the lack of consensus or conflicting interests between them may lead to poor implementation and enforcement (Gondo & Amis, 2013; Kavali et al., 2001; Lee et al., 2010; Li et al., 2013), creating inconsistent applications of the law which ultimately discourages compliance (Perezts & Picard, 2014). Despite a firm's best intentions to properly comply with legal requirements, the weak and poorly worded standards and procedures prevent them from realizing any of the purported benefits of the IPRs (Crilly et al., 2012; Gondo & Amis, 2013; Sandholtz, 2012). The result is an unintentional decoupling where firms accept a particular practice or procedure as appropriate but do not accept it as intended (Gondo & Amis, 2013; Kavali et al., 2001; Lee et al., 2010; Li et al., 2013).

Although institutional pressures should be treated by firms as *the floor* (Kavali et al., 2001), when policies are weak or improperly enforced, it creates a smokescreen—an opaque field—that allows firms to influence policies to secure favors (e.g., public contracts). Left unchecked, weak monitoring systems and prejudicial evaluations by the authorities encourage firms to put more effort into influencing institutional pressures in their favor (Kavali et al., 2001). The opaque relationship between institutions and firms eventually causes firm practices to likewise turn opaque, making regulatory oversight difficult. Firms, as a result, fail to recognize how their interactions with institutions are preventing them from realizing the true nature and outcome of their decisions. To illustrate, when firms cannot accurately determine the degree of arbitrariness in local policies due to the high opacity, they underestimate their exposure to the authorities' arbitrary behavior, hampering their ability to devise effective policy responses, and cope with the external environment which creates a disconnect between the adoption of institutional constraints demanded by regulatory officials and the firm's actual level of compliance (Lee et al., 2010). This eventually causes an unintentional decoupling since firms—faced with complex and arbitrarily enforced policies—are reluctant to engage with government officials and, as a result, diminishes their ability to influence institutional pressures. These concerns are amplified in China owing to its diverse institutional environment characterized by regional or provincial variations. Although institutional pressures are stipulated by the central Chinese government, the degree of protection and the effectiveness of enforcement lies with the provincial judges and authorities. Such inconsistencies often result in a vicious circle where firms, in their pursuit of legitimacy, resort to misguided efforts of compliance due to the inconsistencies in the application of law at the international, national, and regional levels. This, however, opens the firm's response to suspicion which reduces their ability to obtain institutional protection and support, thereby jeopardizing their efforts for legitimacy (Li et al., 2013).

Voluntary–Involuntary Deinternationalization

A firm's headway into the international markets does not typically follow an incremental, linear path. Rather, the process of internationalization is often wrought with tribulations caused by institutional pressures and complexities that often require the firm to (in)voluntarily take devolutionary steps to withdraw from international operations (e.g., foreign divestment and export withdrawals) as part of its long-run strategic response. That is, they deinternationalize. Although deinternationalization often carries connations of failure (Choquette, 2019; Gnizy & Aviv, 2018; Lim & Mandrinos, 2020; Sapouna et al., 2018; Sousa & Tan, 2015; Yayla et al., 2018), it is not necessarily a voluntary one. Firms are generally reluctant to restrict or abandon export markets (Gnizy & Aviv, 2018; Turner, 2012; Velázquez-Razo & Vargas-Hernánde, 2011; Vissak & Francioni, 2013) for no firm wants inherently to fail in its process of internationalization. Far from being a signal of the firm's failure, deinternationalization can more accurately be regarded as a response that corrects previous (voluntary or involuntary) failures.

Institutional pressures distract firms away from their core competencies, effectively undermining firm interests which result in these failures that trigger deinternationalization. Over the years, these institutional pressures have taken the form of export readiness and international orientation (Crick, 2004; Sapouna et al., 2018), political risk, tariffs or exchange rates (Akhter & Choundhry, 1993; Vissak & Francioni, 2013), micro- and macro-economic issues (Crick, 2004), strategic fit, and cultural distance (Sousa & Tan, 2015) among others. As the following examples show, the chain of events leading to deinternationalization is often beyond the firm's control.

Among the various pressures firms may face, political risk is perhaps the most insidious as firms often have no avenues for recourse and are forced to withdraw from a particular market due to political changes (Akhter & Choundhry, 1993). Although forced withdrawals from a host country are often the result of political upheaval within the country itself, events outside the host country may also force firms to withdraw. Despite meeting formal obligations, firms, especially smaller ones, are forced to deinternationalize by discontinuing export activities due to their frustrations and disappointments with export mechanics and support systems available as well as other macroeconomic issues such as unfavorable exchange terms (Crick, 2004). Many of these issues stem from political instability (i.e., political risk) and the inconsistent drafting and application of policy. As Vissak and Francioni (2013) show, a variety of political pressures—including problems with tariffs, unfavorable exchange rates, poor price competition, and an inconducive external environment—trail a firm's path to deinternationalization.

Firms are naturally reluctant to exit a market since, in the eyes of the firm, deinternationalization is a sign of failure that is detrimental to the firm's reputation as well as market outcomes. Frustrations mount when the investment made has been sizeable. However, much like political uncertainties, there are many market-level variables that are beyond a firm's control. Evolving financial considerations and requirements; strategic mismatch due to policy changes; or even boundary conditions such as cultural distance are among the most common (Cheong et al., 2020; Cheong, 2018; Sousa & Tan, 2015). However, if properly guided by internationally oriented mindsets aiming to restructure strategic decisions, (Sapouna et al., 2018), a market exit may be beneficial to the firm as it creates the perception that the firm is meeting its institutional obligations. That is, deinternationalization may, in fact, be considered a strategic response to political uncertainties surrounding the firm which in the long run helps build firm resilience (Vissak & Francioni, 2013). Caution is thus advised in the use of the term "deinternationalization". Despite the negative connotations surrounding its use, deinternationalization can more accurately be described as a strategic long-term maneuver leading to the development of new product lines and greater international expansion.

Although the causes of deinternationalization are multifaceted, the overarching concern that looms over the international business—conflict between the interests of the state and the firm, and inconsistent drafting and application of legal standards—still remain. Institutions, in establishing policy, should pay close attention to the substance rather than form of the policy to minimize consequences on a firm's international development. In our current state (i.e., China vs. the United States), the institutional pressures inherent within and between two countries are not only detrimental to the internationalization of Chinese and American firms, it also affects their bilateral trade and diplomatic relations with and between other countries. Owing to the substantial investments made by both the United States and China in other countries, their (indirect) influence on global diplomacy inhibits the country's ability to react to the ongoing trade dispute, forcing them to take sides, whether economically or legally. What we need, however, is an environment that is conciliatory especially with regard to legal standards. As firms and institutions remain interdependent, every party is duty-bound not to have tangential policy treatments for the same pressures will be implemented when endorsing agreements in other foreign destinations (Chen & Maxwell, 2007). This notion provides an incentive for consistency between the various actors (country–country and country–firm) to ensure nondiscriminatory policy treatment.

Theoretically, deinternationalization takes place primarily through the lens of the regulative pillar of institutional theory. Firms are naturally attracted to establishing operations in countries with higher quality IP enforcement mechanisms. The quality of IPRs, therefore, is a reflection of institutional accountability. As IP standards and regulations gradually turn opaque, it self-legitimizes by creating normative expectations that guide behavior and facilitates institutional change. Firms that are unwilling or fail to comply with what has now become the "norm" must be prepared to face the consequences. With China increasingly recognized as a nation that seeks to integrate with the world economy, both the regulative and normative pillars of institutional theory feature prominently in explaining the drivers of deinternationalization in the face of institutional pressures within the context of IPRs. Under these circumstances then, the normative pillar of institutional theory becomes closely associated with the regulative pillar. As regulations establish and impose specific standards and behaviors expected of firms, unwillingness or failure to abide by these standards may result in deinternationalization. To a lesser yet still important extent, the decision to deinternationalize also suggests a cognitive influence. The cognitive pillar of institutional theory emphasizes the generally shared perception of what is typical or taken for granted. That is to say, the decision to deinternationalize could also be driven by the firm's general perception of the quality of say, IPRs in a country. As the quality of legal and regulatory standards are a representation of the country to the world, actions taken by various market actors within the country in response to these standards may influence firms—locally and abroad—to remain, enter, or exit the market.

Discussion

This chapter is an attempt to integrate and develop an understanding of the tensions experienced by international firms in the face of pressure from national institutions as well as institutional

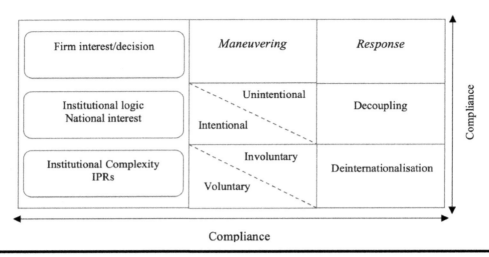

Figure 7.2 Theoretical framework.

complexities that stem from conflicting IPRs agencies. Theoretically, this chapter has shown how organizations interpret their behavior and provided guidelines on how organizations may react to situations where interests and decisions may ideally but not necessarily coincide. We illustrate our theoretical framework in Figure 7.2.

Thus far, we have shown how firms experience institutional complexity when they are exposed to regulatory pressures that—to achieve institutional legitimacy—drive the firm's interest toward those of the nation-state. We posit that the dual tension of national interests and institutional complexities (as evidenced by IPR agencies) evoke an export maneuvering response by the firm in the form of an (un)intentional decoupling or an (in)voluntary deinternationalization. That is, when the firm's interests and decisions are restricted or even controlled by institutional complexity, it is the firm's compliance or desire to comply that drives these responses.

Figure 7.2 provides a useful integrating framework to explain decoupling and deinternationalization by relating the institutional logic (i.e., national interest) and institutional complexity (i.e., IPRs standards and policies) concepts applied in two different categories (Maneuvering—Response). To illustrate, a firm's strategic maneuvering responses are primarily motivated by the amalgamation of firm interests and managerial decisions. These maneuvers and responses can range from the day-to-day operating decisions and activities to firm-wide strategic decisions such as product development or even international expansion. When facing pressure to align the firm's interests and comply with those of the nation-state, the firm's available set of maneuvers are reduced to either intentional or unintentional forms of decoupling. Pressure to comply or align with national interests is relatively common, even in countries that are more economically liberalized. However, when we throw institutional complexities into the mix, the firm's ability and willingness to comply take on a different form. In an environment where various institutions (i.e., IPRs agencies, local judiciary, and law enforcement) adopt an arbitrary stance on the application of IP standards and laws, compliance becomes difficult if not impossible. Add to this the various other factors beyond the firm's control (e.g., local and international political risk, financial requirements, evolving sociocultural expectations), firms are then faced with the harsh reality that will have to deinternationalize, whether voluntary or otherwise, to remain a going concern.

Conclusion

In this chapter, we extended our understanding of decoupling and deinternationalization in the context of intellectual property conflicts between the United States and China. There are many overlaps between the two, and although both terms are commonplace in the literature, we have yet to find a clear demarcation between them until now. Their distinctions are, indeed, subtle and evolving, hence the need for practical rather than theoretical context. Suffice to say, the preceding discussion has achieved this. Despite our intentions to focus on the practical, we also provide theoretical implications to inspire further academic discussion. Our effort should empower policymakers with insights that can be used to reinvigorate policies, so they not only encourage internationalization but also mitigate decoupling and deinternationalization. In the same vein, as IPRs are a fragile intangible asset with which to work, this relation cannot be relegated to second place in the field of international business. If we understand the interaction between IPRs, decoupling, and deinternationalization, we might be able to translate into building circuits that offer the knowledge of a better international business policy-practice perspective.

References

Akhter, S. H., & Choundhry, Y. A. (1993). Forced Withdrawal from a Country Market: Managing Political Risk. *Business Horizons, 36*(3), 47–54.

Altman, E. J., Nagle, F., & Tushman, M. L. (2019). *Managed Ecosystems and Translucent Institutional Logics: Engaging Communities.* Working Paper 19–096. Boston, MA: Harvard Business School.

Areddy, J. T. (2018). American Entrepreneurs Who Flocked to China are Heading Home, Disillusioned. *Wall Street Journal, 8.*

Benito, G. R., & Welch, L. (1997). De-Internationalization. *Management International Review, 37*(2), 7–25.

Bisio, V., Horne, C., Listerud, A., Malden, K., Nelson, L., Salidjanova, N., & Stephens, S. (2020). *The U.S.-China "Phase One" Deal: A Backgrounder.* Washington, DC: U.S.-China Economic and Security Review Commission. https://www.uscc.gov/sites/default/files/2020-02/U.S.-China%20Trade%20 Deal%20Issue%20Brief.pdf

Boiral, O. (2003). ISO 9000: Outside the Iron Cage. *Organization Science, 14*(6), 720–737.

Brander, J., Cui, V., & Vertinsky, I. (2017). China and Intellectual Property Rights: A Challenge to the Rule of Law. *Journal of International Business Studies, 48*(7), 908–921.

Bromley, P., & Powell, W. W. (2012). From Smoke and Mirrors to Walking the Talk: Decoupling in the Contemporary World. *The Academy of Management Annals, 6*(1), 483–530.

Chen, C.-S., & Maxwell, T. A. (2007). The Dynamics of Bilateral Intellectual Property Negotiations: Taiwan and the United States. *Government Information Quarterly, 24*(3), 666–687.

Cheong, C. W. H. (2018). Religiosity and Corporate Risk-Taking. *Asian Journal of Finance and Accounting, 10*(2), 81–113.

Cheong, C. W. H., Lee, M., & Weissmann, M. A. (2020). Credit Access, Tax Structure and the Performance of Malaysian Manufacturing SMEs. *International Journal of Managerial Finance, 16*(4), 433–454.

Choquette, E. (2019). Import-Based Market Experience and Firms' Exit From Export Markets. *Journal of International Business Studies, 50*(3), 423–449.

Christmann, P., & Taylor, G. (2006). Firm Self-Regulation Through International Certifiable Standards: Determinants of Symbolic Versus Substantive Implementation. *Journal of International Business Studies, 37*(6), 863–878.

Crick, D. (2004). U.K. SMEs Decision to Discontinue Exporting: An Explanatory Investigation into Practices within the Clothing Industry. *Journal of Business Venturing, 19*(4), 561–587.

Crilly, D., Zollo, M., & Hansen, M. T. (2012). Faking it or Muddling through? Understanding Decoupling in response to Stakeholder pressures. *Academy of Management Journal, 55*(6), 1429–1448.

de Bree, M., & Stoopendaal, A. (2020). De- and Recoupling and Public Regulation. *Organisation Studies*, *45*(5), 599–620.

Durand, R., Hawn, O., & Ioannou, I. (2019). Willing and Able: A General Model of Oganizational Responses to Normative Pressures. *Academy of Management Review*, *44*(2), 299–320.

Evans, J. S. (1991). Strategic Flexibilty for High Technology Manoeuvres: A Conceptual Framework. *Journal of Management Studies*, *28*(1), 69–89.

Farrand, B. (2017). Bold and Newly Independent, or Isolated and Cast Adrift? The Implications of Brexit for Intellectual Property Law and Policy. *Journal of Common Market Studies*, *55*(6), 1306–1321.

Fung, H.-G., Yau, J., & Zhang, G. (2011). Reported Trade Figure Discrepancy, Regulatory Arbitrage, and Round-Tripping: Evidence from the China—Hong Kong Trade Data. *Journal of International Business Studies*, *42*(2), 152–176.

Gnizy, I., & Aviv, S. (2018). Reverse Internationalization: A Review and Suggestions for Future Research. In L. C. Leonidou, C. S. Katsikeas, S. Samiee, & A. Bilge (Eds.), *Advances in Global Marketing. A Research Anthology*. Cham, Switzerland: Springer.

Gondo, M. B., & Amis, J. M. (2013). Variation in Practice Adoption: The Roles of Conscious Reflection and Discourse. *Academy of Management Review*, *30*(2), 225–247.

He, X., Brouthers, K. D., & Filatotchev, I. (2013). Resource-Based and Institutional Perspectives on Export Channel Selection and Export Performance. *Journal of Management*, *39*(1), 27–47.

Jamali, D. (2010). MNCs and International Accountability Standards Through an Institutional Lens: Evidence of Symbolic Conformity or Decoupling. *Journal of Business Ethics*, *95*(4), 617–640.

Kavali, S., Tzokas, N., & Saren, M. (2001). Corporate Ethics: An Exploration of Contemporary Greece. *Journal of Business Ethics*, *30*(1), 87–104.

Kostova, T., Beugelsdijk, S., Scott, W. R., Kunst, V. E., & Chua, C. H. (2020). The Construct of Institutional Distance through the Lens of Different Institutional Perspectives: Review, Analysis, and Recommendations. *Journal of International Business Studies*, *51*(4), 467–497.

Kostova, T., & Zaheer, S. (1999). Organizational Legitimacy Under Conditions of Complexity: The Case of the Multinational Enterprise. *The Academy of Management Review*, *24*(1), 64–81.

Lee, S.-H., Oh, K., & Eden, L. (2010). Why Do Firms Bribe? Insights from Residual Control Theory into Firms' Exposure and Vulnerability to Corruption. *Management International Review*, *50*(6), 775–796.

Li, J. (2016). The Transplanting of IP Laws. *Journal of Intellectual Property Law and Practice*, *11*(9), 717–718.

Li, J., Vertinsky, L., & Zhang, H. (2013). The Quality of Domestic Legal Institutions and Export Performance Theory and Evidence from China. *Management International Review*, *53*(3), 361–390.

Li, S., & Alon, I. (2020). China's Intellectual Property Rights Provocation: A Political Economy View. *Journal of International Business Policy*, *3*, 62–72.

Lim, W. M., & Mandrinos, S. (2020). Decoupling in International Business: A Rejoinder on Internationalization and De-inernationalization. *Journal of International Business Education*, *15*.

Lu, T. (2021). The Case Guidance System in China: A Practical Guide to Intellectual Property Cases. *Journal of Intellectual Property Law and Practice*, 1–6.

Luiz, J. M., & Callum, S. (2014). Corruption, South African Multinational Enterprises and Institutions in Africa. *Journal of Business Ethics*, *124*(3), 383–398.

Mandrinos, S., Mahdi, N. M. N., & Liew, C. S. L. (2019). Decoupling in International Business. *Journal of General Management*, *44*(4), 220–231.

Meyer, J., W., & Rowan, B. (1977). Institutionalized Organizations: Formal Structure as Myth and Ceremony. *American Journal of Sociology*, *83*(2), 340–363.

North, D. C. (1990). *Institutions, Institutional Change and Economic Performance*. Oxford: Oxford University Press.

Papageorgiadis, N., Cross, A. R., & Alexiou, C. (2013). The Impact of the Institution of Patent Protection and Enforcement on Entry Mode Strategy: A Panel Data Investigation of U.S. firms. *International Business Review*, *22*(1), 278–292.

Parr, R. L. (2018). *Intellectual Property: Valuation, Exploitation and Infringement Damages* (5th ed.). Hoboken, NJ: John Wiley & Sons Inc.

Patterson, L. (1966). The Statute of Anne: Copyright Misconstrued. *Harvard Journal on Legislation*, *3*(2), 223–256.

Peng, M. W. (2013). An Institution-Based View of IPR Protection. *Business Horizons, 56*, 135–139.

Peng, M. W., Ahlstrom, D., Carraher, S. M., & Shi, W. (2017). An Institution-Based View of Global IPR History. *Journal of International Business Studies, 48*(7), 893–907.

Peng, M. W., San, S. L., Pinkham, B., & Chen, H. (2009). The Institution-Based View as a Third Leg for a Strategy Tripod. *Academy of Management Perspectives, 23*(3), 63–81.

Perezts, M., & Picard, S. (2014). Compliance or Comfort Zone? The Work of Embedded Ethics in Performing Regulation. *Journal of Business Ethics, 131*(4), 833–852.

Phillips, J. (2011). The Panda Plan: China's Path to Progress. *Journal of Intellectual Property Law and Practice, 6*(3), 133.

Rugman, A. M., & Verbeke, A. (2000). Multinational Enterprises and Public Policy. In C. C. Millar, R. M. Grant, & C. J. Choi (Eds.), *International Business: Emerging Issues and Emerging Markets* (pp. 21–43). London: Palgrave Macmillan.

Sandholtz, K. W. (2012). Making Standards Stick: A Theory of Coupled vs. Decoupled Compliance. *Organization Studies, 33*(5–6), 655–679.

Sapouna, P., Dimitratos, P., Larimo, J., & Zucchella, A. (2018). Market Withdrawal, International Orientation and International Marketing: Effects on SME Performance in Foreign Markets. In L. C. Leonidou, C. S. Katsikeas, S. Samiee, & B. Aykol (Eds.), *Advances in Global Marketing: A Research Anthology* (pp. 281–303). Cham, Switzerland: Springer.

Scott, W. R. (1995). *Institutions and Organizations.* Thousand Oaks, CA: Sage Publications.

Scott, W. R. (2014). *Institutions and Organizations: Ideas, Interests and Identities* (4th ed.). Thousand Oaks, CA: Sage Publications.

Sousa, C. M. P., & Tan, Q. (2015). Exit from a Foreign Market: Do Poor Performance, Strategic Fit, Cultural Distance, and International Experience Matter? *Journal of International Marketing, 23*(4), 84–104.

Suddaby, R. (2010). Challenges for Institutional Theory. *Journal of Management Inquiry, 19*(1), 14–20.

Turner, C. (2012). Deinternationalization: Towards a Coevolutionary Framework. *European Business Review, 24*(2), 92–105.

Velázquez-Razo, P. N., & Vargas-Hernánde, J. G. (2011). The Strategy of De-Internationalization of the SMEs of the Footwear in the Area Metropolitana De Guadalajara. *Business Management Dynamics, 1*(1), 12–23.

Verbeke, A. (2013). *International Business Strategy* (2nd ed.). Cambridge, UK: Cambridge University Press.

Vissak, T., & Francioni, B. (2013). Serial Nonlinear Internationalization in Practice: A Case Study. *International Business Review, 22*(6), 951–962.

Wijen, F. (2014). Means versus Ends in Opaque Institutional Fields: Trading off Compliance and Achievement in Sustainability Standard Adoption. *Academy of Management Review, 39*(3), 302–323.

Yayla, S., Yeniyrta, S., Uslaya, C., & Cavusgil, E. (2018). The Role of Market Orientation, Relational Capital, and Internationalization Speed in Foreign Market Exit and Re-Entry Decisions Under Turbulent Conditions. *International Business Review, 27*(6), 1105–1115.

Zhang, J. J. (2020). The U.S. and China Finally Signed a Trade Agreement. Who Won? *The Washington Post.*

Authors' Profile

Symeon Mandrinos is a lecturer at Swinburne University of Technology Sarawak. He holds a PhD in Business Administration from the University of Essex. His main research interests are Theory of the Firm and International Business. He is currently an Associate Researcher with Universiti Malaysia Sabah and has contributed to different research projects on both national and regional levels. Previously, he was an associate researcher for the Global Entrepreneurship Research and Innovation Centre and a Regional Liaison (Eastern Europe) for Universiti Malaysia Kelantan. Prior to academia, Symeon was an Export Manager in the Fast-Moving Consumer Goods industry.

Calvin W. H. Cheong holds a PhD in Finance from Monash University. His research focuses on practical and practicable international and corporate finance issues, and social and economic development. Prior to academia, Calvin was also the senior partner of a multinational consulting firm. He is currently a senior lecturer at Sunway University, Malaysia, and Adjunct Research Fellow at Swinburne University of Technology, Sarawak. He is also the associate editor and a member of the Editorial Board for a few journals of high repute.

MANAGING THE CONSUMER EXPECTATIONS AND BEHAVIOR

Chapter 8

Leveraging Cultural Artifacts in Corporate Branding in a Developing Economy

Sheena Lovia Boateng

Contents

DOI: 10.4324/9781003152217-11

Introduction

Over the years, scholars have sought to test concepts and theories in branding research and marketing strategies to examine the myriad effects of brand elements on branding outcomes. Some of these efforts have contributed to enhancing our comparative understanding of brand elements, including brand name, brand logo, and brand slogan. For instance, Rybaczewska et al. (2020) confirmed the role and influence of slogans, the effectiveness of which emerged to be dependent on the stage of the customer decision-making process. At the same time, Kohli and LaBahn (1997) identified the impact of brand name on sales, inducing trial and fostering long-term brand success. Similarly, comparing the prevalence of brand logos and slogans in firm advertising, Wilson (2020) found that, regardless of the advertising medium, logo use is greater than slogan use. However, studies of this nature present a limited perspective, often failing to make theoretical advances and offering few implications for utilizing these elements to achieve the firm's objectives. Attempts of this nature blur our understanding of the true nature of brand element design and the significant ways in which the nature and structure of the individual elements differ from one another.

Furthermore, even though the prominence of brand name, logo, and slogan for firms is widely acknowledged, a close inspection of branding literature revealed relatively limited empirical research on what goes into the design of these elements and their individual effects on customer perceptions (Kaur & Kaur, 2019). More so, the impact of these elements on brand image and their effectiveness in influencing firm outcomes (such as customer loyalty and purchase intention) have received little attention, especially in the context of emerging and developing economies. For example, as an intangible cue, the significance of corporate or brand image in Asian cultures (Amin et al., 2013) and its effect on loyalty have been echoed in research (Kaur & Kaur, 2019). However, studies on building brand image often tend to be silent on cultural cues as reflected in the brand name, logo, and slogan (Kaur & Kaur, 2019).

Further, though some brand elements, such as brand name and brand logo, are relatively overt and easy to observe, they can also sometimes be difficult to understand. A deeper insight into the underpinning cues facilitates comprehension of the message or culture being communicated (Burkus, 2014). This chapter argues that the utilization of specific cultural artifacts in the formulation of brand elements creates specific cues which influence consumer perceptions and decisions (Erdem & Swait, 2004; Utz et al., 2011). For example, Wilson (2020) found that brand logos, unlike slogans, integrated more territorial and cultural symbols in their design, thereby facilitating consumer perceptions of brand credibility.

Thus, the contribution this article makes is, first, in empirically examining the design of a firm's brand name, brand logo, and brand slogan, as well as their effects on brand image and customer loyalty through the application of the cue utilization theory. Second, it examines the relationship of these under-researched brand elements with brand image and customer loyalty. The study also investigates the mediating role of brand image in enhancing the relationship between these brand elements and customer loyalty. Third, these relationships are explored in the context of a developing economy, where such research is yet to gain visibility. The need for more research in emerging and developing markets has been viewed as an opportunity for new theoretical as well as practical and managerial implications (Burgess & Steenkamp, 2006).

Although the conceptual framework captures some relations that have been previously tested, the integration of multifaceted relationships between the constructs identified in the present study provides an important extension of prior research (Nyadzayo & Khajehzadeh, 2016; Quoquab et al., 2019). The rest of the chapter is structured as follows. The next two sections deal with the application of the cue utilization theory and the use of cultural artifacts as cues in firm branding.

The subsequent section covers the literature review, conceptual model, and hypotheses development. It is then followed by the methodology and the results of the data analysis performed using Structural Equation Modeling (SEM). The last section concentrates on discussing the findings and offers both theoretical and pragmatic implications as well as conclusions.

Application of the Cue Utilization Theory

The cue utilization theory is applied in this study to explain the use of cultural artifacts in designing corporate brand elements, namely, brand names, symbols, and slogans, to influence consumer behavior. These cultural artifacts play the role of cues that are utilized by the firm to create unique brand associations in the minds of customers. The theory, which is often used to explain consumer preferences and behavior in marketing (Bruwer et al., 2017; Mishra et al., 2020), posits that the pairing of a "cue" and a consumption good or service creates cue-based complementarities. These cues elicit changes in consumer preference. Thus, their inclusion in the firms' branding strategy raises the marginal utility derived by consumers from the consumption of the firm's product or service (Laibson, 2001).

Cue utilization theory has been used in several studies (Choi et al., 2018; Wang et al., 2016) to explain how specific brand cues are used to send signals to consumers to influence how they judge the quality of a firms' product or service. Two main types of cues are espoused that can be used to influence consumer preferences and choice, namely, high-scope cues and low-scope cues (Wang et al., 2016). High-scope cues such as brand name, slogan, and logos (Miyazaki et al., 2005; Wilson, 2020) have been found to be relatively more reliable and effective, especially when paired with other low-scope cues like product price and warranties which can be easily manipulated (Purohit & Srivastava, 2001). Researchers aver that, when consumers are presented with several cues of both kinds, they rely more on high-scope cues to make decisions (Hu et al., 2010; Utz et al., 2011).

In this study, cultural artifacts used in designing brand elements such as a firm's brand name, logo, and slogan have been conceptualized as high-scope cues. According to Hatch and Rubin (2006), brands possess a symbolic power to engage all stakeholders, including customers. Hence, the skillful management of cultural artifacts as part of the brand story can add value and foster organizational cultures that characterize what the firm's brand stands for (Hatch & Rubin, 2006). Existing research indicates that artifacts representing the unique culture of the target audience are often harnessed in the design of the firm's brand elements, particularly, logos (Hankinson, 2015; Wilson, 2020). The association of these cultural artifacts, conceptualized as high-scope cues, with the firm's brand, as well as products and services they offer, creates cue-based complementarities. Thus, the utilization of these cultural artifacts enables brands to signal and reinforce certain desirable attributes among customers, including perceptions of reliability, credibility, and expertise that influence their behavior (Erdem & Swait, 2004).

Cultural Artifacts as Branding Cues

Literature provides evidence of the utilization of cultural artifacts as part of corporate branding efforts (Ashworth & Kavaratzis, 2015; Fierro & Aranburu, 2019; Wilson & Liu, 2010). For instance, in their study on shaping Halal into a brand, Wilson and Liu (2010) determined that Halal is recognized as an effective element in branding, marketing, and product development.

Halal is an Arabic word linked to Islamic culture, the basic acceptance and understanding of which is central to every Muslim's belief. According to Camarero et al. (2012), individuals often find their identity in cultural artifacts. Thus, by utilizing cultural artifacts like Halal as cues to communicate brand values, firms can get customers to connect with their brand on an individual level and create positive associations with it (Ashworth & Kavaratzis, 2015). In line with this, the Consolidated Bank Ghana (CBG) was branded using "Adinkra symbols", which were developed by the Asante tribe of Ghana and can be found on various items including clothing, art, and jewelry everywhere in the country (Coppens et al., 2011). Based on Ghanaian folklore, these symbols encapsulate worldviews, incisive observations of human behavior, and interactions between humans and nature (Owusu, 2019). Each Adinkra symbol has a basic meaning with expansive interpretations that are applicable to different contexts—hence their unique applicability in the bank's branding efforts.

The CBG was established when the Bank of Ghana dissolved and rebranded five insolvent universal banks in the Ghanaian banking sector. Some of them were undercapitalized and beyond rehabilitation, including Beige Bank Limited, Construction Bank Limited, the Royal Bank Limited, Sovereign Bank Limited, and UniBank Ghana Limited (Frimpong, 2018). The bank's branding strategy was anchored on one specific Adinkra symbol, called **Nkonsonkonson** (see Figure 8.1), which means "chain link" in Asante Twi, a language spoken by about 15 million people in Ghana. The symbol represents unity, community, and human relations and was incorporated into the branding of CBG to communicate these values in an attempt to restore customer confidence in the new bank created out of the five collapsed banks and solidify its position in the Ghanaian banking system.

Specifically, the **Nkonsonkonson** symbol was incorporated into the name of the bank, using the word "Consolidated" to communicate the values of togetherness and oneness. It was also directly incorporated into the bank's logo (see Figure 8.2) to depict the value of strength perfected in unity, given that five individual banks were brought together to become one. The logo is portrayed as four hands holding in unison, with the **Nkonsonkonson** symbol in the center, and the letters CBG next to it. The brand slogan also follows suit, employing the phrase "We stand with you" to highlight the bank's commitment to stand with its customers in unity as a collective in

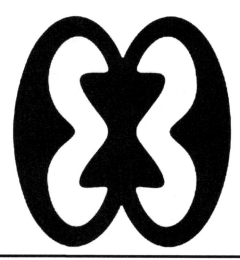

Figure 8.1 Nkonsonkonson (Adinkra symbol).

Figure 8.2   Consolidated Bank Ghana Logo.

forging ahead toward a brighter future. The bank's use of the Adinkra symbol, a core element of the Ghanaian culture, as part of their branding strategy is consistent with the findings of researchers like Malai and Speece (2005), who found that culture influences customer perceptions of brand name, as well as the strength of the relationship between a firm's brand name and the loyalty of their customers.

Literature Review and Hypotheses Development

Customer Loyalty

Customer loyalty refers to a customers' attachment and commitment to a firm, product, service, or brand (Uncles et al., 2003). Specifically, in terms of service delivery, customer loyalty is described as customers' observed behaviors that are characteristic of their attachment and commitment to a brand (Gefen, 2002). Customer loyalty encompasses all customer behavior that depicts their desire to enhance an existing relationship with a brand. This includes their willingness to consistently repatronize that brand over time, regardless of other competing brands (Oliver, 1999; Palmatier et al., 2006). Firm branding strategies have been observed in literature to have significant effects on customer loyalty (Grewal et al., 2004; Le et al., 2014). For instance, Rubio et al. (2017) assert that brand name is one of the key determining factors of a customer's loyalty to a retailer. Similarly, Quoquab et al. (2019) found that customers consider the Halal logo as a reputation builder that directly and indirectly affects their loyalty to fast-food brands in Malaysia. Thereby, establishing corporate branding elements, such as brand name, brand logo and slogan, and brand image, as noteworthy predictors of customer loyalty. However, Keller (2008) asserts that firms need to have a good balance of both verbal and visual brand elements to enhance each brand element's individual contribution.

Brand Image

Brand image is a strategic tool firms utilize to influence consumers' brand choices and build brand equity (Bian & Moutinho, 2011). It is often conceptualized in literature to comprise both cognitive and affective components, including the perceptions that consumers have about a brand in their memory and the emotions they associate with it (Low & Lamb, 2000; Salinas & Pérez, 2009). Furthermore, according to Aranda et al. (2015), a brand image may consist of tangible and intangible components that can be applied to both products and services. Faircloth et al. (2001) assert that firms can contribute significantly to building enhanced brand equity by creating the desired brand image. For example, Jin et al. (2012) found that developing a positive brand image among full-service restaurants influences customer loyalty. Similarly, Nyadzayo and Khajehzadeh (2016) attest to the efficacy of brand image and its crucial role in driving customer loyalty. At the same time, Han et al. (2019) determined that brand image is unavoidable in enhancing customer loyalty. Thus, the hypothesis is the following:

H_1—Brand image positively affects customer loyalty.

Brand Name

Brand name is the principal and most prominent brand element possessed by a firm. It is the part of a brand that can be verbalized and often contains elements such as words, numbers, or letters (Hu et al., 2012). Brand name plays a differentiator role that enables customers to distinguish between various brands based on their unique attributes. This is exhibited by the careful and intricate brand name screening and selection processes that are utilized by firms (Lerman & Garbarino, 2002). According to Ranchhod et al. (2011), brand name influences the brand and how it is viewed globally. It provides product recognition and facilitates product and service decision-making among customers.

According to Aaker (1991), a consumer's appreciation of a firm's brand image is initially derived from the brand name in tandem with the associations that it brings forth. Thus, brand name has a strong impact on customer loyalty and has been found to have a positive effect on consumers' perceptions of a brand's image, particularly in the fashion industry (Park & Lennon, 2009; Selnes, 1993). More so, Malai and Speece (2005) aver that service providers can encourage customer loyalty by building a strong brand name. Therefore, the study hypothesizes that:

H_2—Brand name positively affects brand image.
H_5—Brand name positively affects customer loyalty.

Brand Logo

Brand logo refers to the various graphic and typeface elements that a firm uses, sometimes in conjunction with its name, as a form of identification (Henderson & Cote, 1998). Together, they form an intricately designed brand element that often incorporates territorial and cultural symbols as well as elements of expertise. Besides brand name, brand logos are the next most used brand signals that enable consumers to recognize and recall brands and cognitively process relevant brand-related information (Wilson, 2020). As stated by Valek (2020), they are a marker of a firm's intended brand message that plays a pivotal role in the success of its marketing efforts. It is intended to create brand likability and memorability among customers, along with a strong sense of familiarity upon exposure (Pham et al., 2012).

Brand logos have been found in literature to have a significant impact on consumer perceptions and behavior. For instance, Japutra et al. (2015) determined that a firm's brand logo could predict customers' satisfaction and trust. Kaur and Kaur (2019) also found that a firm's brand logo plays a key role in enhancing its brand image. Furthermore, in a study conducted among Muslim fast-food consumers, Quoquab et al. (2019) found that the Halal logo influences customer loyalty both directly and indirectly. Hence, the following hypotheses:

H_3—Brand logo positively affects brand image.
H_6—Brand logo positively affects customer loyalty.

Brand Slogan

Brand slogans are often an abridged form of a brand's competitive positioning statement and play a crucial role in communicating a brand's essence. These messages bring brands closer to their consumers, improving firms' identities and making them more attractive (Kohli et al., 2007, 2013). Nonetheless, brand slogans are most effective when paired with the brand name of the firm (Wilson, 2020). In a study comparing the slogans used by firms in global and domestic markets on their websites from 2007 to 2013, Anwar (2015) established that slogans go through evolutionary changes on account of diverse market conditions and firms' corporate communications and identities.

According to Rybaczewska et al. (2020), simple and memorable slogans can affect consumer brand perceptions and enhance brand equity, thereby increasing product sales. To achieve this, firms often incorporate short catchy words that are easy to internalize and recall to create a deeper psychological connection between customers and the brand. For instance, Strutton and Roswinanto (2014) found that, by managing brand slogans, firms can achieve desirable branding outcomes. For a firm's brand slogan to influence its brand image, Park et al. (1986) opine that the slogan must emphasize strong and unique brand associations. Thus, it is hypothesized that:

H_4—Brand slogan positively affects brand image.
H_7—Brand slogan positively affects customer loyalty.

Mediating Role of Brand Image

Researchers have confirmed the positive effect of brand image on performance-related variables such as purchase intention and customer loyalty (Lee & Lee, 2018; Raji et al., 2019). More so, several other researchers, including Hussein et al. (2018) and Akroush et al. (2016), have demonstrated the mediating effects of brand image on customer loyalty as an outcome in the presence of various predictor variables. For instance, He and Lai (2014) found that consumers' perceptions of brands' legal and ethical responsibilities may enhance brand loyalty through the creation of positive functional and symbolic brand images.

Similarly, Kaur and Soch (2018), in a study of Indian mobile phone users, found the corporate image to be a complete mediator in the relationship between their trust and attitudinal loyalty toward mobile phone service providers. Additionally, in the context of service delivery, Hussein et al. (2018) found that brand image mediates the effects of the physical and social environment on customer loyalty. For this reason, the study hypothesizes that:

H_8—Brand image mediates the relationship between brand name and customer loyalty.
H_9—Brand image mediates the relationship between brand logo and customer loyalty.
H_{10}—Brand image mediates the relationship between brand slogan and customer loyalty.

Figure 8.3 depicts the conceptual framework for the study, presenting the hypothesized relationships discussed earlier.

Method

Sample and Data Collection

The respondents in this study were the customers of the five insolvent universal banks, including Beige Bank Limited, Construction Bank Limited, the Royal Bank Limited, Sovereign Bank

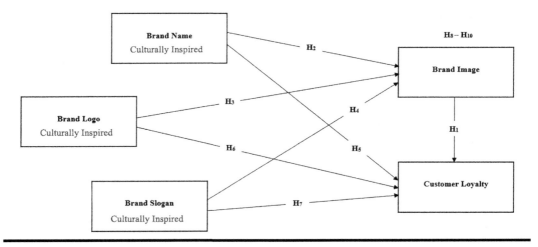

Figure 8.3 Conceptual model.

Limited, and UniBank Ghana Limited that were dissolved and rebranded to create the CBG. All the assets of the dissolved banks were transferred to CBG, along with all their branches, Automated Teller Machines (ATMs), staff, and customers. Overall, responses obtained from a total of 392 CBG customers were utilized for the purposes of this study.

An assessment of demographic information gathered, including respondents' gender, age, education level, and the number of years they had saved with their erstwhile bank, indicated that the majority of the respondents were male (51%), with females accounting for 49%. The dominant age group was 18–30 years (82.1%), with 83.7% of them having tertiary education. Overall, 66.3% of the entire sample indicated they have been saving with their erstwhile bank for less than 5 years, followed by those who had been saving with their banks between 5 and 10 years (31.4%) and then 11 years and above (2.3%). The study adopts a quantitative approach, using the survey technique to test the research hypotheses presented earlier (Creswell, 2014).

Measures

A pool of measurement items was drawn from previous literature on corporate branding to adequately reflect the context of the study. The Cronbach's alpha values of the resulting scales for each construct were found to be above 0.8, thereby satisfying statistical requirements (Hair et al., 2006). Brand name impact was measured using five items adapted from Le et al. (2014) and measured on a Likert scale ranging from 1—"Strongly disagree" to 5—"Strongly agree". Brand logo impact was measured by asking customers to rate their perceptions regarding the CBG logo on a scale ranging from 1 to 5 based on seven parameters adapted from Peterson et al. (2015). These include Negative change/Positive change; More unfavorable/More favorable; Irrelevant/Relevant; Unimportant/Important; Bad/Good; Means nothing to me/Means a lot to me; and Dislike/Like.

Brand slogan, adapted from Briggs and Janakiraman (2017), was coded as a dichotomous variable (0 = No; 1 = Yes), measuring whether or not the customers believed that the CBG slogan was easy to recall. For brand image, seven items were adapted from Salinas and Pérez's (2009) study and employed for measurement using a Likert scale ranging from 1—"Strongly disagree" to

5—"Strongly agree". Similarly, customer loyalty was measured with six items adapted from Hsieh and Li (2008) using the same Likert scale.

Analysis and Results

Data gathered were analyzed using the two-step approach to SEM recommended by Anderson and Gerbing (1988) to establish a measurement model and structural model.

Measurement Model

Confirmatory Factor Analysis (CFA) was performed on the data gathered via AMOS 24 to assess the reliability and validity of the constructs and scales used. A measurement model was estimated, consisting of four latent factors to achieve this purpose, as presented in Figure 8.3. The reliability and validity of the brand slogan construct were not reported as it was measured as a categorical variable. The Composite Reliability (CR) for each construct exceeded the acceptable level of 0.70 (Bagozzi & Yi, 2012). In addition, the Average Variance Extracted (AVE) for each construct accounted for more than 0.50 of the total variance (Fornell & Larcker, 1981), suggesting that convergent validity is established for each construct (Bagozzi et al., 1991). These are presented in Table 8.1.

Additionally, a discriminant validity test was conducted by means of a Heterotrait–Monotrait (HTMT) ratio of correlations analysis. Furthermore, the individual inter-construct correlations were compared with the square root of the AVEs for each construct, according to Fornell and Larcker's (1981) criterion. The results revealed that the square root of the AVEs for each construct was higher than the individual inter-construct correlations as recommended by Fornell and Larcker (1981) (see Table 8.2). Furthermore, all the HTMT values for each construct fell below the recommended threshold of 0.90 (Henseler et al., 2015) (see Table 8.3).

Thereby, confirming discriminant validity, model fit was evaluated using χ^2 (392) = 200.03, $p \leq 0.001$, χ^2/df = 1.77, CFI = 0.97, TLI = 0.97, RMSEA = 0.044.

Structural Model and Direct Path Analysis

A path analysis was subsequently performed through the estimation of a structural model in AMOS 24 after the measurement model was confirmed to test the hypothesized direct relationships between the variables. The model fit statistics revealed a good fit with χ^2 (392) = 217.77; $p \leq 0.001$; χ^2/df = 1.73; CFI = 0.97; TLI = 0.96; RMSEA = 0.043. Each hypothesized relationship was examined based on path significance, as presented in Table 8.4 and graphically depicted in Figure 8.4.

The estimates for the test of direct relationships (see Table 8.4) capture the findings of the tests for H_1 through to H_7. As can be observed from the table, all the hypotheses (H_1, H_2, H_3, H_4, H_6), except for H_5 and H_7, were supported. Thus, brand image was found to have a significant positive effect on customer loyalty (β = 0.55, $p \leq 0.001$) (H_1), while brand name was found to have a significant positive effect on brand image (β = 0.34, $p \leq 0.001$) (H_2) and an insignificant effect on customer loyalty (β = 0.10, p = 0.103) (H_5). At the same time, the results revealed that brand logo has a significant positive effect on both brand image (β = 0.25, $p \leq 0.001$) (H_3) and customer loyalty (β = 0.14, $p \leq 0.01$) (H_6). In turn, brand image was significantly influenced by brand slogan

Table 8.1 Psychometric Properties

Construct and Measurement Items		β	t Value (Significance)	CR	AVE	α
Brand Name				0.84	0.58	0.84
The new bank name is a meaningful one	BN2	0.92	Fixed			
I think the new brand name is a favorable one	BN3	0.71	15.22***			
The new name chosen is a good brand name	BN4	0.87	15.20***			
The brand name is distinctive	BN5	0.82	11.32***			
Brand Logo				0.85	0.59	0.85
Irrelevant/relevant	BL2	0.89	Fixed			
Means nothing to me/means a lot to me	BL3	0.93	12.61***			
Dislike/like	BL4	0.90	14.05***			
Bad/good	BL5	0.85	13.76***			
Brand Image				0.84	0.57	0.84
This bank is nice	BI4	0.67	Fixed			
This bank has a personality that distinguishes it from its competitors	BI5	0.71	12.15***			
This bank does not disappoint its customers	BI6	0.81	13.41***			
This bank is one of the best banks in the sector	BI7	0.81	13.40***			
Customer Loyalty				0.84	0.52	0.84
I will patronize any new service introduced by the bank in the future	CL1	0.70	Fixed			
I will say positive things about the bank when I talk to my friends or relatives about banking	CL2	0.69	12.09***			
I will recommend this bank to my friends or relatives when they need relevant information	CL3	0.73	12.72***			
I will encourage my good friends or relatives to patronize this bank's services	CL4	0.74	12.80***			
This bank will be my first choice when I need to use any financial service	CL5	0.74	12.80***			

Note: n = 392; ***p ≤ 0.001.

Table 8.2   Convergent and Discriminant Validity Measures

Construct	1	2	3	4
1. Brand Name	**0.76**			
2. Brand Logo	0.47***	**0.77**		
3. Brand Image	0.48***	0.44***	**0.75**	
4. Customer Loyalty	0.43***	0.44***	0.67***	**0.72**
Mean	3.48	3.42	3.40	3.57
Standard Deviation	0.84	1.01	0.76	0.64

Note: Square roots of Average Variances Extracted (AVE) are on the diagonal (in bold); correlations are off the diagonal. The AVEs for each construct are far greater than the corresponding inter-construct square correlations, thereby supporting discriminant validity.

Table 8.3   Assessment of Discriminant Validity Using HTMT Analysis

Constructs	1	2	3	4
1. Brand Name				
2. Brand Logo	0.480			
3. Brand Image	0.527	0.460		
4. Customer Loyalty	0.435	0.441	0.677	

Notes: All the HTMT ratio of correlations values are under 0.90 (Henseler et al., 2015).

Table 8.4   Results of Direct Path Analysis

Hypothesis	Path Description	β	t Value	Results
H_1	Brand Image → Customer Loyalty	0.55	7.33***	Supported
H_2	Brand Name → Brand Image	0.34	5.21***	Supported
H_3	Brand Logo → Brand Image	0.25	3.82***	Supported
H_4	Brand Slogan → Brand Image	-0.17	-3.38***	Supported
H_5	Brand Name → Customer Loyalty	0.10	1.63	Not Supported
H_6	Brand Logo → Customer Loyalty	0.14	2.39**	Supported
H_7	Brand Slogan → Customer Loyalty	-0.03	-1.70	Not Supported

***$p \leq 0.001$, **$p \leq 0.01$, *$p \leq 0.05$.

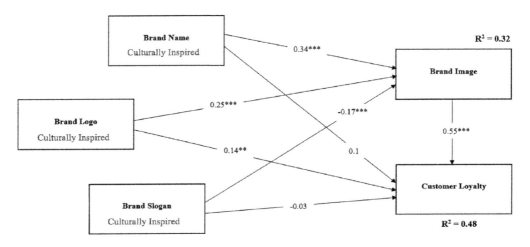

Notes: Model fit statistics: $\chi^2(392) = 217.77$; p < 0.001; $\chi^2/df = 1.73$; CFI = 0.97; TLI = 0.96; RMSEA = 0.043.
**p < 0.01; ***p < 0.001

Figure 8.4   Conceptual model.

(β = -0.17, p ≤ 0.001) (**H₄**) which, in contrast, had an insignificant effect on customer loyalty (β = -0.03, p = 0.482) (**H₇**).

These findings demonstrate that brand name, brand logo, and brand slogan are among the minimum requirements for the banking firms that seek to create a positive brand image for themselves, particularly among their customers. However, to directly influence customer loyalty, concerted efforts need to be made by the bank to create a compelling brand logo and build a positive brand image among the customer base. Nonetheless, the insignificant relationship between brand name, brand slogan, and customer loyalty may be the result of a less literal application of the cultural cue utilized (the **Nkonsonkonson** symbol) in their design. This is evident in the significant direct effect of brand logo on customer loyalty, given that the **Nkonsonkonson** symbol was directly incorporated into its design. As such, brand logo seems to benefit from the customers' familiarity with the Adinkra symbol and what it stands for, thereby directly influencing their loyalty to the bank (Erdem & Swait, 2004; Wilson, 2020).

Mediation Analysis

Subsequently, a mediation analysis was conducted using a bootstrap sample of 2,000, the outcome of which is presented in Table 8.5, highlighting the presence of full mediating relationships between the hypothesized constructs. It can be observed from the table that H₈, H₉, and H₁₀ are all supported (see Table 8.5), indicating that brand image fully mediates the relationship between brand name, logo, slogan, and customer loyalty. The direct path from brand name to customer loyalty and the indirect path through brand image were each found to be significant, thus, providing support for **H₈**. The direct path from brand logo to customer loyalty and the indirect path through brand image were also significant. Likewise, the direct path from brand slogan to customer loyalty and the indirect path through brand image have been found significant, thereby providing support for **H₉** and **H₁₀**.

Table 8.5   Results of Mediation Analysis

Relationship	Hypothesis	Direct without Mediator (p value)	Direct with Mediator (p value)	Indirect Effect	Mediation Type
Brand Name → Brand Image → Customer loyalty	H_8	0.29 (***)	0.10 (0.17)	***	**Full Mediation**
Brand Logo → Brand Image → Customer loyalty	H_9	0.28 (**)	0.14 (0.09)	**	**Full Mediation**
Brand Slogan → Brand Image → Customer loyalty	H_{10}	-0.13 (**)	-0.03 (0.49)	***	**Full Mediation**

***$p \leq 0.001$, **$p \leq 0.01$, *$p \leq 0.05$.

These findings are consistent with previous research, such as by Hussein et al. (2018) and Akroush et al. (2016) who emphasized the mediating role of brand image in the effect of various predictor variables on customer loyalty in firm–customer interactions. They also corroborate the outcome of studies conducted by scholars such as Rybaczewska et al. (2020) and Ranchhod et al. (2011), demonstrating the indirect effect of brand elements, including brand name, brand logo, and brand slogan, on customer decision-making as a result of their brand perceptions.

Discussion and Conclusions

This study sought to assess the role of cultural artifacts utilized as cues in designing brand name, brand logo, and brand slogan in facilitating loyalty among customers and the mediating effect of brand image in this relationship. A review of extant literature indicated that previous studies have largely neglected the nature and formulation of specific brand elements and the ways in which the nature and structure of these individual elements impact customer perceptions and branding outcomes. Further, the review revealed a limited application of relevant theories in examining the individual effects of these brand elements as well as the implications for utilizing specific cues to design and formulate these elements. Hence, the study sought to apply the cue utilization theory in examining the design and formulation of brand name, logo, and slogan using cultural artifacts, and their individual effects on brand image and customer loyalty. The findings provide support for eight out of ten hypotheses specified in this study, thereby presenting significant implications for theory and practice.

The initial hypotheses posited that brand name, brand logo, and brand slogan would positively influence brand image and customer loyalty. In this regard, the study's findings affirm the existence of a positive and direct effect of these elements on brand image, confirming the findings of the previous research. These include the assertion made by Ranchhod et al. (2011) that brand name influences how a brand is perceived globally, which, according to Malai and Speece (2005), significantly affects customer loyalty among service providers, including banks. The findings also reinforce the assertions of Kaur and Kaur (2019) and Japutra et al. (2015) regarding the positive effects of brand logo on customer perceptions, including enhancing brand image and customer trust. Likewise, the findings support the significant influence of brand slogan on brand image, which, per Park et al. (1986), is emphasized through strong and unique brand associations. In the case of this research, strong and unique brand associations are introduced by incorporating the **Nkonsonkonson** Adinkra symbol, a Ghanaian cultural artifact, into the formulation of the brand elements including the name, logo, and slogan of the CBG bank. Through the application of the cue utilization theory, the study provides evidence for the effectiveness of cultural artifacts like the Adinkra symbols including **Nkonsonkonson** as branding cues to communicate the values of the firm that facilitates the creation of positive associations and individual level connections with customers (Ashworth & Kavaratzis, 2015).

However, in terms of the effect on customer loyalty, only brand logo was found to have a significant effect. The confirmation of the effect reinforces the assertions of Wilson (2020) claiming that besides brand name, brand logos are the most impactful brand elements that enable customers to recognize and recall brands as well as cognitively process brand-related information. It shows that, of the three brand elements, brand logos that incorporate cultural artifacts as cues have the capacity to communicate the necessary signals to elicit customer loyalty. This can be attributed to the fact that brand logos are intricately designed brand elements that often integrate territorial and cultural symbols. Hence, by design, the brand logo serves as a marker of a firm's intended brand message, establishing likability and memorability among customers (Pham et al., 2012; Valek, 2020).

Furthermore, the mediating role of brand image in the relationships between brand name, brand logo, brand slogan, and customer loyalty was all confirmed. This outcome presents the importance of brand image in examining the impact of the three brand elements on customer loyalty. Thus, the study concludes that the effects of these three brand elements on bank customer loyalty are primarily achieved through brand image perceptions. These significant mediating effects demonstrate that brand image is a noteworthy enabler when it comes to the effect of brand name, logo, and slogan on bank customer loyalty. Consequently, firms in the banking industry can enhance their brand image by actively incorporating cultural artifacts that are relevant to their target customers in the design of their brand elements, which are geared toward achieving customer loyalty.

More so, the bank's brand name, logo, and slogan, all of which are incorporated in the **Nkonsonkonson** symbol, are confirmed as high-scope cues. This is consistent with the tenets of the cue utilization theory as applied in this study, which emphasizes the reliance of customers on high-scope cues for decision-making in consumption situations as corroborated by Utz et al. (2011) and Hu et al. (2010). Thereby, these findings reiterate the important role of cultural artifacts as cues in firm branding. As such, through the skillful management of cultural artifacts as part of brand element design, banks can create high-scope cues that reinforce a positive brand image among their customer base (Erdem & Swait, 2004; Hatch & Rubin, 2006). The use of the **Nkonsonkonson** Adinkra symbol in the design of CBG's brand elements communicates the integrity, credibility, and continuity of the brand, which will enable the bank to gain and maintain customers' attention and interest.

Theoretical and Practical Implications

This study provides contributions to the literature on key brand elements (name, logo, and slogan) and their impact on brand image and customer loyalty. Through the application of the cue utilization theory, the study validates the impact of incorporating cultural artifacts as cues in the creation and formulation of corporate brand elements. This implies that, by incorporating cultural artifacts that represent the unique culture of their target audience, service firms can communicate positive brand attributes and ensure customer loyalty (Hankinson, 2015; Wilson, 2020). Despite the depth of the existing research on brand elements, the empirical literature has placed limited emphasis on the individual contributions of these brand elements to achieving firm outcomes. This study has empirically confirmed the assertions of several scholars, including Malai and Speece (2005) and Valek (2020), arguing that well-designed brand elements create positive brand perceptions among customers. Based on the findings outlined in this study, the following recommendations are proposed:

1. High-scope cues that cannot be easily manipulated—brand name, brand logo, and brand slogan—are critical in any rebranding or repositioning strategy of banks or other firms. These branding elements underpin brand image perceptions which also have a significant impact on customer loyalty. Firms must focus their investment efforts and resources on the design of their brand elements to create positive perceptions and influence customer behavior in connection to the brand.
2. Cultural artifacts depict accepted worldviews and incisive observations of human behavior that consumers can easily relate to. In collectivist societies such as Ghana, Nigeria, India, and Indonesia, common goals, group loyalty, and interconnectedness between people are encouraged. Firms, like banks, in such societies, are more likely to gain from cue-based complementarities when the brand elements are inspired by cultural artifacts. Moreover, firms need to make a comprehensive effort to research key cultural artifacts in a given cultural context to avoid misunderstanding among target customer groups.
3. Then again, among the three brand elements, brand logos that incorporate cultural artifacts as cues have a better capacity to communicate the necessary signals to directly elicit customer loyalty. Thus, in leveraging cultural artifacts, managers should consider starting with the brand logo.
4. Still, the importance of the other two elements, brand name and brand slogan, should not be ignored by firms working in developing economies. The comprehensive effort put into all three brand elements enhances the likelihood of customer loyalty and positive brand perception as a result of the creation of a coherent brand image.

Limitations and Future Research Directions

In terms of the limitations, the study focused on examining the design of brand elements (name, logo, and slogan) of a firm in the banking sector, and their impact on brand image and customer loyalty. It would be interesting for future studies to look at the nuances of brand element design and formulation for other firms in both banking and other sectors. Moreover, this study focused on the utilization of cultural artifacts, particularly Adinkra symbols from Ghana, as cues in the design of the brand elements for a Ghanaian bank. Future research can examine other cues utilized by firms in banking or other sectors as part of their brand element design to communicate specific brand attributes to their target audiences.

References

Aaker, J. (1991). The Negative Attraction Effect? A Study of the Attraction Effect Under Judgment and Choice. In R. H. Holman & M. R. Solomon (Eds.), *Advances in Consumer Research* (Vol. 18, pp. 462–469). Provo, UT: Association for Consumer Research.

Akroush, M. N., Jraisat, L. E., Kurdieh, D. J., AL-Faouri, R. N., & Qatu, L. T. (2016). Tourism Service Quality and Destination Loyalty—The Mediating Role of Destination Image from International Tourists' Perspectives. *Tourism Review, 71*(1), 18–44.

Amin, M., Isa, Z., & Fontaine, R. (2013). Islamic Banks: Contrasting the Drivers of Customer Satisfaction on Image, Trust, and Loyalty of Muslim and Non-Muslim Customers in Malaysian. *International Journal of Bank Marketing, 31*(2), 79–97.

Anderson, J. C., & Gerbing, D. W. (1988). Structural Equation Modeling in Practice: A Review and Recommended Two-Step Approach. *Psychological Bulletin, 103*(3), 411–423. https://doi.org/10.1037/0033-2909.103.3.411

Anwar, S. T. (2015). Company Slogans, Morphological Issues, and Corporate Communications. *Corporate Communications: An International Journal, 20*(3), 360–374.

Aranda, E., Gómez, M., & Molina, A. (2015). Consumers' Brand Images of Wines: Differences between Two Leading Spanish Denominations of Origin. *British Food Journal, 117*(8), 2057–2077. https://doi.org/10.1108/BFJ-08-2014-0299

Ashworth, G. J., & Kavaratzis, M. (2015). Rethinking the Roles of Culture in Place Branding. In M. Kavaratzis, G. Warnaby, & G. J. Ashworth (Eds.), *Rethinking Place Branding* (pp. 119–134). Springer. https://doi.org/10.1007/978-3-319-12424-7_9

Bagozzi, R. P., & Yi, Y. (2012). Specification, Evaluation, and Interpretation of Structural Equation Models. *Journal of the Academy of Marketing Science, 40*(1), 8–34.

Bagozzi, R. P., Yi, Y., & Phillips, L. (1991). Assessing Construct Validity in Organizational Research. *Administrative Science Quarterly, 36*(3), 421–458.

Bian, X., & Moutinho, L. (2011). The Role of Brand Image, Product Involvement, and Knowledge in Explaining Consumer Purchase Behaviour of Counterfeits. *European Journal of Marketing, 45*(2), 309–566.

Briggs, E., & Janakiraman, N. (2017). Slogan Recall Effects on Marketplace Behaviors: The Roles of External Search and Brand Assessment. *Journal of Business Research, 80*, 98–105.

Bruwer, J., Chrysochou, P., & Lesschaeve, I. (2017). Consumer Involvement and Knowledge Influence on Wine Choice Cue Utilisation. *British Food Journal, 119*(4), 830–844.

Burgess, S. M., & Steenkamp, J. -B. E. M. (2006). Marketing Renaissance: How Research in Emerging Markets Advances Marketing Science and Practice. *International Journal of Research in Marketing, 23*(4), 337–356. http://dx.doi.org/10.1016/j.ijresmar.2006.08.001

Burkus, D. (2014, December 2). *How to Tell if Your Company Has a Creative Culture* [online], [In:] "Harvard Business Review". https://hbr.org/2014/12/how-to-tell-if-your-company-has-a-creative-culture

Camarero, C., Garrido-Samaniego, M. J., & Vicente, E. (2012). Determinants of Brand Equity in Cultural Organizations: The Case of an Art Exhibition. *The Service Industries Journal, 32*(9), 1527–1549.

Choi, H. S., Ko, M. S., Medlin, D., & Chen, C. (2018). The Effect of Intrinsic and Extrinsic Quality Cues of Digital Video Games on Sales: An Empirical Investigation. *Decision Support Systems, 106*, 86–96.

Coppens, L. C., Verkoeijen, P. P. J. L., & Rikers, R. M. J. P. (2011). Learning Adinkra Symbols: The Effect of Testing, *Journal of Cognitive Psychology, 23*(3), 351–357.

Creswell, J. W. (2014). *Research Design Qualitative, Quantitative, and Mixed Methods Approaches.* Thousand Oaks, CA: Sage Publications.

Erdem, T., & Swait, J. (2004). Brand Credibility, Brand Consideration, and Choice. *Journal of Consumer Research, 31*(1), 191–198.

Faircloth, J. B., Capella, L. M., & Alford, B. L. (2001). The Effect of Brand Attitude and Brand Image on Brand Equity. *Journal of Marketing Theory and Practice, 9*(3), 61–75.

Fierro, A., & Aranburu, I. (2019). Airbnb Branding: Heritage as a Branding Element in the Sharing Economy. *Sustainability, 11*(1), 74. https://doi.org/10.3390/su11010074

Fornell, C., & Larcker, D. F. (1981). Evaluating Structural Equations Models with Unobservable Variables and Measurement Error. *Journal of Marketing Research, 18*(1), 39–50.

Frimpong, E. D. (2018, August 1). BoG Collapses 5 Banks into Consolidated Bank Ghana Ltd. *Graphic.* www.graphic.com.gh/business/business-news/bog-collapses-5-banks-into-consolidated-bank-ghana-ltd.html

Gefen, D. (2002). Customer Loyalty in E-Commerce. *Journal of the Association for Information Systems, 3*(1), 27–51.

Grewal, D., Levy, M., & Lehmann, D. (2004). Retail Branding and Loyalty: An Overview. *Journal of Retailing, 80*(4), ix–xii.

Hair, J. F., Black, W. C., Babin, B. J., Anderson, R. E., & Tatham, R. L. (2006). *Multivariate Data Analysis.* Upper Saddle River, NJ: Pearson University Press.

Han, H., Yu, J., & Kim, W. (2019). Environmental Corporate Social Responsibility and the Strategy to Boost the Airline's Image and Customer Loyalty Intentions. *Journal of Travel & Tourism Marketing, 36*(3), 371–383.

Hankinson, G. (2015). Rethinking the Place Branding Construct. In M. Kavaratzis, G. Warnaby, & G. J. Ashworth (Eds.), *Rethinking Place Branding* (pp. 13–31). Springer. https://doi.org/10.1007/978-3-319-12424-7_9

Hatch, M. J., & Rubin, J. (2006). The Hermeneutics of Branding. *Journal of Brand Management, 14*(1/2), 40–59.

He, Y., & Lai, K. K. (2014). The Effect of Corporate Social Responsibility on Brand Loyalty: The Mediating Role of Brand Image. *Total Quality Management & Business Excellence, 25*(3/4), 249–263. https://doi.org/10.1080/14783363.2012.661138

Henderson, P. W., & Cote, J. A. (1998). Guidelines for Selecting or Modifying Logos. *Journal of Marketing, 62*(2), 14–30.

Henseler, J., Ringle, C. M., & Sarstedt, M. (2015). A New Criterion for Assessing Discriminant Validity in Variance-Based Structural Equation Modeling. *Journal of the Academy of Marketing Science, 43*, 115–135. https://doi.org/10.1007/s11747-014-0403-8

Hsieh, A., & Li, C. (2008). The Moderating Effect of Brand Image on Public Relations Perception and Customer Loyalty. *Marketing Intelligence & Planning, 26*(1), 26–42. https://doi.org/10.1108/02634500810847138

Hu, J., Liu, X., Wang, S., & Yang, Z. (2012). The Role of Brand Image Congruity in Chinese Consumers' Brand Preference. *Journal of Product & Brand Management, 21*(1), 26–34.

Hu, X., Wu, G., Wu, Y., & Zhang, H. (2010). The Effects of Web Assurance Seals on Consumers' Initial Trust in an Online Vendor: A Functional Perspective. *Decision Support Systems, 48*, 407–418.

Hussein, A. S., Hapsari, R. D. V., & Yulianti, I. (2018). Experience Quality and Hotel Boutique Customer Loyalty: Mediating Role of Hotel Image and Perceived Value. *Journal of Quality Assurance in Hospitality & Tourism, 19*(4), 442–459.

Japutra, A., Keni, K., & Nguyen, B. (2015). The Impact of Brand Logo Identification and Brand Logo Benefit on Indonesian Consumers' Relationship Quality. *Asia-Pacific Journal of Business Administration, 7*(3), 237–252. https://doi.org/10.1108/APJBA-10-2014-0124

Jin, N. P., Lee, S., & Huffman, L. (2012). Impact of Restaurant Experience on Brand Image and Customer Loyalty: Moderating Role of Dining Motivation. *Journal of Travel & Tourism Marketing, 29*(6), 532–551.

Kaur, H., & Kaur, K. (2019). Connecting the Dots between Brand Logo and Brand Image. *Asia-Pacific Journal of Business Administration, 11*(1), 68–87.

Kaur, H., & Soch, H. (2018). Satisfaction, Trust and Loyalty: Investigating the Mediating Effects of Commitment, Switching Costs and Corporate Image. *Journal of Asia Business Studies, 12*(4), 361–380. https://doi.org/10.1108/JABS-08-2015-0119

Keller, K. L. (2008). *Strategic Brand Management: Building, Measuring, and Managing Brand Equity* (3rd ed.). Upper Saddle River, NJ: Pearson/Prentice Hall.

Kohli, C., & LaBahn, D. W. (1997). Creating effective brand names: A study of the naming process. *Journal of Advertising Research, 37*, 67–75.

Kohli, C., Leuthesser, L., & Suri, R. (2007). Got Slogan? Guidelines for Creating Effective Slogans. *Business Horizons, 50*(5), 415–422.

Kohli, C., Thomas, S., & Suri, R. (2013). Are You in Good Hands? Slogan Recall: What Really Matters. *Journal of Advertising Research, 53*(1), 31–42.

Laibson, D. I. (2001). A Cue-Theory of Consumption. *Quarterly Journal of Economics, 116*(1), 81–119.

Le, A. N. H., Cheng, J. M. S., Kuntjara, H., & Lin, C. T. J. (2014). Corporate Rebranding and Brand Preference. *Asia Pacific Journal of Marketing and Logistics, 26*(4), 602–620.

Lee, J., & Lee, Y. (2018). Effects of Multi-Brand Company's CSR Activities on Purchase Intention Through a Mediating Role of Corporate Image and Brand Image. *Journal of Fashion Marketing and Management, 22*(3), 387–403. https://doi.org/10.1108/JFMM-08-2017-0087

Lerman, D., & Garbarino, E. (2002). Recall and Recognition of Brand Names: A Comparison of Word and Nonword Name Types. *Psychology and Marketing, 19*(7–8), 621–639.

Low, G. S., & Lamb, C. W. (2000). The Measurement and Dimensionality of Brand Associations. *Journal of Product & Brand Management, 9*(6), 350–370.

Malai, V., & Speece, M. (2005). Cultural Impact on the Relationship Among Perceived Service Quality, Brand Name Value, and Customer Loyalty. *Journal of International Consumer Marketing, 17*(4), 7–39. https://doi.org/10.1300/J046v17n04_02

Mishra, S., Malhotra, G., & Saxena, G. (2020). In-Store Marketing of Private Labels: Applying Cue Utilisation Theory. *International Journal of Retail & Distribution Management, 49*(1), 145–163. https://doi.org/10.1108/IJRDM-04-2020-0152

Miyazaki, A. D., Grewal, D., & Goodstein, R. C. (2005). The Effect of Multiple Extrinsic Cues on Quality Perceptions: A Matter of Consistency. *Journal of Consumer Research, 32*, 146–153.

Nyadzayo, M. W., & Khajehzadeh, S. (2016). The Antecedents of Customer Loyalty: A Moderated Mediation Model of Customer Relationship Management Quality and Brand Image. *Journal of Retailing and Consumer Services, 30*, 262–270.

Oliver, R. L. (1999). Whence consumer loyalty? *Journal of Marketing, 63*(4), 33–44.

Owusu, P. (2019). Adinkra Symbols as "Multivocal" Pedagogical/Socialization Tool. *Contemporary Journal of African Studies, 6*(1), 46–58.

Palmatier, R. W., Dant, R. P., Grewal, D., & Evans, K. R. (2006). Factors Influencing the Effectiveness of Relationship Marketing: A Meta-Analysis. *Journal of Marketing, 70*(4), 136–153.

Park, C. W., Jaworski, B. J., & McInnis, D. J. (1986). Strategic Brand Concept-Image Management. *Journal of Marketing, 50*(4), 135–145.

Park, M., & Lennon, S. J. (2009). Brand Name and Promotion in Online Shopping Contexts. *Journal of Fashion Marketing and Management, 13*(2), 149–160. https://doi.org/10.1108/13612020910957680

Peterson, M., AlShebil, S., & Bishop, M. (2015). Cognitive and Emotional Processing of Brand Logo Changes. *Journal of Product & Brand Management, 24*(7), 745–757. https://doi.org/10.1108/JPBM-03-2015-0823

Pham, L., Pallares-Venegas, E., & Teich, J. E. (2012). Relationships between Logo Stories, Storytelling Complexity, and Customer Loyalty. *Academy of Banking Studies Journal, 11*(1), 73–92.

Purohit, D., & Srivastava, J. (2001). Effect of Manufacturer Reputation, Retailer Reputation, and Product Warranty on Consumer Judgments of Product Quality: A Cue Diagnosticity Framework. *Journal of Consumer Psychology, 10*(3), 123–134.

Quoquab, F., Sadom, N. Z. M., & Mohammad, J. (2019). Driving Customer Loyalty in the Malaysian Fast-Food Industry: The Role of Halal Logo, Trust and Perceived Reputation. *Journal of Islamic Marketing, 11*(6), 1367–1387. https://doi.org/10.1108/JIMA-01-2019-0010

Raji, R. A., Rashid, S., & Ishak, S. (2019). The Mediating Effect of Brand Image on the Relationships between Social Media Advertising Content, Sales Promotion Content and Behaviuoral Intention. *Journal of Research in Interactive Marketing, 13*(3), 302–330.

Ranchhod, A., Gurău, C., & Marandi, E. (2011). Brand Names and Global Positioning. *Marketing Intelligence & Planning, 29*(4), 353–365.

Rubio, N., Villaseñor, N., & Yagüe, M. J. (2017). Creation of Consumer Loyalty and Trust in the Retailer Through Store Brands: The Moderating Effect of Choice of Store Brand Name. *Journal of Retailing and Consumer Services, 34*, 358–368.

Rybaczewska, M., Jirapathomsakul, S., Liu, Y., Chow, W. T., Nguyen, M. T., & Sparks, L. (2020). Slogans, Brands and Purchase Behaviour of Students. *Young Consumers, 21*(3), 305–317. https://doi.org/10.1108/YC-07-2019-1020

Salinas, E. M., & Pérez, J. M. P. (2009). Modeling the Brand Extensions' Influence on Brand Image. *Journal of Business Research, 62*(1), 50–60.

Selnes, F. (1993). An Examination of the Effect of Product Performance on Brand Reputation, Satisfaction and Loyalty. *European Journal of Marketing, 27*(9), 19–35.

Strutton, D., & Roswinanto, W. (2014). Can Vague Brand Slogans Promote Desirable Consumer Responses? *Journal of Product & Brand Management, 23*(4/5), 282–294. https://doi.org/10.1108/JPBM-02-2014-0507

Uncles, M. D., Dowling, G. R., & Hammond, K. (2003). Customer Loyalty and Customer Loyalty Programs. *Journal of Consumer Marketing, 71*(1), 67–83.

Utz, S., Kerkhof, P., & Van Den Bos, J. (2011). Consumers Rule: How Consumer Reviews Influence Perceived Trustworthiness of Online Stores. *Electronic Commerce Research and Applications, 11*, 49–58.

Valek, N. S. (2020). Drawing a Destination Logo from Memory and Its Influence on the Destination Perception. *Journal of Destination Marketing & Management, 16*, 100436. https://doi.org/10.1016/j.jdmm.2020.100436

Wang, Q., Cui, X., Huang, L., & Dai, Y. (2016). Seller Reputation or Product Presentation? An Empirical Investigation from Cue Utilization Perspective. *International Journal of Information Management, 36*(3), 271–283.

Wilson, J. A. J., & Liu, J. (2010). Shaping the Halal into a Brand? *Journal of Islamic Marketing, 1*(2), 107–123. https://doi.org/10.1108/17590831011055851

Wilson, R. T. (2020). Slogans and Logos as Brand Signals within Investment Promotion. *Journal of Place Management and Development.* Advance online publication. https://doi.org/10.1108/JPMD-02-2020-0017

Author's Profile

Dr. Sheena Lovia Boateng is a lecturer at the Department of Marketing and Entrepreneurship at the University of Ghana Business School. She is a fellow of the Academy of Marketing Science. She also served as a member of the Editorial Advisory Board for the Emerald Emerging Markets Case Study Journal, Emerald Publishing Limited, UK, from 2018 to 2020. She has published seven journal publications, five books, six book chapters, four published conference papers, and one industry report. Her academic work has been published in the *International Journal of Bank Marketing, Journal of Financial Services Marketing*, and *the Journal of Educational Technology Systems*. Her research interests include online relationship marketing, fashion and beauty marketing, digital business strategy, electronic learning adoption, entrepreneurship, online branding and advertising, social media marketing, and structural equational modeling in marketing. She can be reached at slboateng@ug.edu.gh.

Chapter 9

Assessing the Mobile Money Value Creation in the Agriculture Value Chain: Evidence from a Developing Economy

Qudiratu Ngmenensoa Ishak and Acheampong Owusu

Contents

DOI: 10.4324/9781003152217-12

Introduction

There is a growing indication that the agricultural value chain is confronted by challenges including network limitations, delays in money transfers and payments, unreliable communication, and misdirected parcels containing money sent via public transport (Au & Kauffman, 2008). It is difficult to transfer money in rural areas where many agricultural activities take place as banks are mostly located in urban centers (Kikulwe et al., 2014). Also, informal methods of transferring money which could include people keeping money on themselves while on a journey or sending it through bus drivers are prone to theft and highway robberies (Hughes & Lonie, 2007; Kim et al., 2010). On the other hand, money sent via family and friends sometimes never reach its intended receivers (Sander, 2003).

Recognizing these difficulties underscored the need for mobile-enabled money transfers over the past few years to improve the way financial activities are conducted along the agricultural value chain (Babcock, 2015). In developing countries, the use of mobile-enabled money transfers has been particularly facilitated through the speedy spread of mobile phones. Also, the reduction in the cost of mobile phones and the availability of low-cost credit cards have provided avenues for mobile phone usage beyond voice communication (Orozco, 2003; Sekabira & Qaim, 2016). It is increasingly becoming easier for actors along the agricultural value chain to reduce the amount of time and money spent on traveling to urban areas to gain access to the capital they require to invest in agriculture. This situation is because of the arguably large number of mobile money agents in many rural areas. This study, therefore, aims at assessing the value created in using mobile money services along the agricultural value chain in Ghana.

The agricultural value chain encompasses a set of actors: input dealers, farmers, aggregators, processors, and retailers, who add value to agricultural products at each stage (FAO et al., 2010). However, the literature on agricultural value chains and the use of mobile money seem to focus mostly on one of these stakeholders. For instance, with a focus on smallholder farmers, Kikulwe et al. (2014) analyzed the benefits associated with using mobile money services on activities of households of smallholder farms in Kenya. Similarly, Kirui et al. (2013) in their examination of the effect of mobile money transfer on the activities of agricultural households focused on the household of the farmer. It has arguably become necessary for research to be conducted to fill this identified gap in knowledge and offer a representation of perspectives of the different actors involved in the agricultural value chain.

Also, studies on mobile money seem to focus on factors affecting its adoption and acceptance, mostly. They seldom explored the outcomes and value creation opportunities from the use of this new payment pathway. For instance, Ngumbu and Mulu-mutuku (2018) analyzed the adoption of mobile money services by women entrepreneurs in Kenya. The same can be said for Mallat and Tuunainen (2008), who explored the adoption of mobile payment systems by merchants and discuss factors that drive and inhibit their adoption. Afshan and Sharif (2016) also analyzed mobile banking and intention for adoption using the untapped (behavioral, environmental, and technological) dimensions of mobile banking acceptance by following a more comprehensive approach. These studies demonstrate the seeming concentration on studying the factors affecting the adoption and acceptance of mobile money services with less emphasis on value creation, outcomes, or benefits.

This study assessed the value created in using mobile money services along the agricultural value chain in Ghana, which is in response to the gaps identified in the literature. This study focused on the value created in using mobile money transfer services along the agricultural value chain and the factors affecting value creation in using mobile money transfer services along the agricultural value chain in Ghana. The study, therefore, addressed the following research questions:

1. What is the value created in using mobile money transfer services along the agricultural value chain in Ghana?
2. What factors influence mobile money transfer services along the agricultural value chain in Ghana?

This study extended the literature of mobile money and agricultural research from a multi-stakeholder perspective with emphasis on the literature on the outcomes or value created in using mobile money in agriculture. It demonstrated the use of the transaction cost theory, particularly the actor motivation cost component in determining commitments in transactions.

Literature Review

Mobile money may be described as a financial tool based on the use of a mobile phone than be used to transfer money in a quick and safe manner to different geographical locations (Gosavi, 2018). The Ghanaian mobile money business comprises MTN Mobile Money operated by Scancom Ghana, Airtel Money, and Tigo Cash operated by AirtelTigo Ghana, and Vodafone Cash operated by Vodafone Ghana (Cobla & Osei-Assibey, 2018; Yaokumah et al., 2017). The mobile money ecosystem includes Mobile Network Operators, agents, banks, customers, competitors, merchants, and regulators (Tobbin, 2011; Jenkins, 2008).

Mobile Money Use and Benefits

There is a myriad of reasons for using mobile money. Some of these uses are savings (Sekabira & Qaim, 2016), borrowing (Gosavi, 2018), sending and receiving money, paying bills, and purchasing airtime among many others. These uses are described as functional transactions (Davidson & Pénicaud, 2011). Costs and delays associated with the trading of goods and services are greatly lessened, thereby supporting the growth of business transactions. Cobla and Osei-Assibey (2018) and Batista and Vicente (2017) indicated that mobile money transfer services enhance the transfer of money by making it relatively faster and less expensive.

Furthermore, mobile money is facilitating the growth of cashless economies as customers are beginning to carry more cash on mobile money accounts than on themselves for transactions (Kikulwe et al., 2014). Transaction costs, risks of robbery attacks, leakages, and overheads are also reduced by mobile money since customers are no longer required to pay transport fares to urban areas, to access financial services. This situation has a positive effect on agriculture (Kirui et al., 2013). The swiftness of mobile money, coupled with its liquidity, offers significant benefits in determining how quickly funds are accessed for transactions along the agricultural value chain (Stuart & Cohen, 2011).

Several factors influence the use of mobile money. These factors could, however, increase or decrease the benefits of using mobile money. Some of these factors are:

1. Financial literacy—Research has shown that the utilization of financial services is proportional to an increase in the levels of education, particularly financial education (Nunoo & Andoh, 2011; Cole et al., 2011).

2. The quality of substitute financial services—Research shows mobile money is capable of yielding benefits or creating value if there is low quality in the services provided by banks and also alternate remittance channels like debit and credit cards (Mas & Ng'weno, 2010).
3. Regulations—The regulations set to oversee mobile money activities can either constrain or facilitate the deployment and eventual creation of value by mobile money service (WEF, 2011; Heyer & Mas, 2011).

The Agricultural Value Chain

An agricultural value chain refers to all the series of organizations, activities, people, and processes that an agricultural product goes through on its journey from the point of origin to the final consumer. The chain may be broken down into various actors, as shown in Figure 9.1.

The input supply stage involves distributing genetic materials used to produce crops or livestock. For example, seeds or breeding stock is used to produce the main agricultural products (MoFA, 2011). The production stage is where the land is prepared, crops are planted, fertilizers are applied, and weeding and harvesting of the crops among other practices take place (Tchale & Keyser, 2010). Aggregation involves the buying of agricultural produce from smallholder farmers to accumulate a large quantity for sale or processing. The processing stage is where agricultural produce is converted into finished goods and finally sold in its raw or polished state at the retail stage (Akramov & Malek, 2012). A synthesis of the literature on the agricultural value chain is presented in Table 9.1.

Table 9.1 indicates that the literature on agricultural value chains and the use of mobile money seem to primarily focus on one of the multiple stakeholders. For instance, Kikulwe et al. (2014) focused mainly on one stakeholder—the smallholder farmer—during their analysis of the benefits of mobile money transfer usage on the activities of smallholder farm households in Kenya. Also, studies focusing on mobile money services mostly focus on factors that affect the adoption and acceptance of the mobile money system to the neglect of the outcome and benefits of mobile money technology. For instance, Ngumbu and Mulu-mutuku (2018) analyzed the adoption of mobile money services by women entrepreneurs in Kenya. The current study is thus justified by examining the phenomenon from multiple stakeholder perspectives.

Underpinning Theory and Conceptualization of Factors Investigated

The core aim of this study is to assess the value created in using mobile money services in the agricultural value chain in Ghana. The value assessed by this study is mainly in the area of reduced operational cost, enhanced commitments in transactions, and enforcement of compliance of agreements. Hence, there is a need to make use of a theory that can help the study achieve its

Figure 9.1 The stages in the agricultural value chain.

Source: Tchale and Keyser (2010).

Table 9.1   Related Literature

Research Paper	Context	Research Participants	Theory	Methodology	Gaps Identified
Babcock (2015)	Uganda, Zambia, Ghana	Farmers	No theory/ Model	Qualitative	Need to extend the study to the other actors who work with farmers and their use of digital finance with farmers
Kikulwe et al. (2014)	Kenya	Farmers and households	Conceptual framework	Quantitative	Research using a multistakeholder approach rather than focusing on only farmers and their households
Kirui et al. (2013)	Kenya	Farm households	Conceptual framework	Quantitative	Need to examine the effect of using well-known mobile money innovations announced after Mobile Money services such as Pesa-Pap and Pesa-Connect on the welfare of smallholder farmers
Sekabira and Qaim (2016)	Uganda	Farm households	Conceptual Framework	Quantitative	The need to analyze the usage of mobile money among the various actors of the agricultural value chain.
Grossman and Tarazi (2014)	Ghana	Farmers	No theory/ Model	Qualitative	Need to extend the study to the other actors who work with farmers and their use of digital finance with farmers
Batista and Vicente (2017)	Mozambique	Farmers	No theory/ Model	Quantitative	Their test structure, which was constrained by statistical power, can be refined further as far as creating an increasingly explicit variety that can be interpreted vigorously as social network pressure

purpose. The transaction cost theory presents a way to assess this value in one of its components known as actor motivation costs.

Actor motivation costs involve the costs of having asymmetrical or incomplete information and a commitment that is imperfect in a transaction. It emanates from opportunism: one of the two major assumptions of human behavior in the transaction cost theory: bounded rationality and opportunism (Williamson, 1981). Opportunism describes the inadequate or contorted information disclosure among parties undertaking a transaction. Opportunism assumes that people are not just rationally bounded; they, in some cases, show opportunistic conduct (Douma & Schreuder, 2008). It demonstrates that contemplation of personal circumstances with cleverness will guide human actors in the trade relationship. This incorporates practices that could include swindling, lying, and unpretentious types of agreement violations (Williamson, 1985).

In Transaction Cost Theory, the presence of opportunistic tendencies increases transaction costs through monitoring conduct, securing assets, and ensuring that the other party does not take part in astute conduct (Grover & Malhotra, 2003). These costs influence the enforcement of mechanism compliance and decision-making and add to the loss of agreements and disputes associated with legally binding contracts (Pare, 2003).

Boateng (2011) focused on the other component of the transaction cost theory—coordination costs—in his study on assessing the impact of mobile phones on micro-trading activities. Coordination costs are the costs involved in searching for goods or services, suppliers, customers, and ensuring compliance of contracts and other agreements after contracts (Wigand et al., 1997). Coordination costs were used as a basis for assessing how mobile phones were used in micro-trading transactions to generate benefits and effects.

The current study, in contrast to Boateng (2011), focused on actor motivation costs. It used actor motivation cost as a basis for exploring how mobile money is helping actors along the agricultural value chain to enhance commitments in transactions. This was achieved by examining how the use of mobile money along the agricultural value chain helps reduce or eliminate opportunism among actors, which is one of the causes of actor motivation costs in the transaction cost theory. The reduction or elimination of opportunism in transactions would contribute to enhancing commitments in transactions which would, in turn, facilitate decision-making and enforce compliance of agreements

Research Methodology

A qualitative approach guided by the critical realism paradigm involving a case study was adopted for this study. This helped appreciate particular issues through the investigation of the behavior and perspectives of the people in certain situations as well as the context within which they perform specific actions (Kaplan & Maxwell, 2005). An agricultural firm that performs activities at different stages on the agricultural value chain and has used mobile money services for at least a year in their business was chosen for the study. Further, the agricultural company (hereinafter referred to as Agro Company Limited) was selected because of their mobile money service usage for agriculture-related transactions for at least a year. The operations of the company also fall under at least one stage of the agricultural value chain for maize production.

The maize value chain was selected because it has all of the stages in the agricultural value chain as described by Tchale and Keyser (2010). Additionally, maize is the largest produce and most widely consumed cereal in Ghana, and its production has seen an increasing trend since 1965 (Morris et al., 1999). The aforementioned explanation offers a description for the selection of the case study so that researchers who may wish to transfer the findings of this study to other contexts can be guided (Lincoln & Guba, 1985). This was also in line with Benbasat et al. (1987) who advised that studies on firm-level phenomena require site selection that is based on the features of the organization while ensuring that there is enough information to assist in achieving the objectives of the study.

Based on the critical realism research philosophy and a case study approach, data from multiple sources were combined to generate the findings of the research (Benbasat et al., 1987). Using these multiple sources of data allowed for the triangulation of data which could enhance the credibility of data, one of the criteria for demonstrating the trustworthiness of qualitative research (Lincoln & Guba, 1985). Evidence gathered from the case was mainly through interviews. However, direct observation, working documents, and archival records from the case study firm were used to complement the data collected through the interviews. The authors used interviews because they provided the opportunity to access first-hand information from respondents along the agricultural value chain who were involved directly in using mobile money for transactions. The questions comprised both open- and close-ended types of questions. The data were collected over a period of one month. A total of 11 respondents were used for this study. Table 9.2 outlines the distribution of personnel who were interviewed for the study.

The interviews were conducted to solicit their first-hand views on the research objectives. The interviews were recorded with a Samsung Galaxy J7 Duo smartphone as the voice recording device after obtaining permission from the respondents together and also through note-taking in a book. The notes taken were used as guidelines for the follow-up questions. Each interview lasted not less than 45 minutes and not more than 1 hour.

Using the Transaction Cost Theory and the research purpose as guides, Miles et al.'s (2014) data analysis approach was adopted; the approach highlights four key components for analysis: data collection, data condensation, data display, and drawing and verification of conclusions. This description of the study methods and steps taken throughout demonstrates the dependability and confirmability of the study which also forms part of the criteria for demonstrating the trustworthiness of qualitative research (Lincoln & Guba, 1985).

Table 9.2 Distribution of Respondents for the Study

Division	Role of Personnel	Number of Respondents
Division one (Mechanization Services) Total = 6 respondents	Head of Division One	1
	Deputy head of Division One	1
	IT officer	1
	Farmers who regularly requested tractor services	2
	Tractor Owner	1
Division Two (Input supply, Production, Aggregation, and Retail) Total = 5 respondents	Head of Division 2	1
	Deputy head of Division 2	1
	Accounts	1
	Outgrower farmers	2

Profile of Agro Company Limited

Agro Company Limited was established and incorporated in 2004 under the laws of the Ghana Private Company Act of 1962. The company operates in both the northern and southern sectors of Ghana. The company has two divisions. One division is involved in the provision of mechanization services at the production stage of the agricultural value chain while the other division is involved in input supply, production, aggregation, and retail. These activities are all in the aim of increasing productivity, incomes, and the standard of living of farmers within the country.

Findings

Uses of Mobile Money Service within the Agriculture Value Chain

The participants were initially asked to indicate the significant agricultural activities for which mobile money services were required.

The analysis of the responses, therefore, revealed that mobile money was used for two activities: provision of tractor services to smallholder farmers and the transactions with tractor owners as indicated by the Head of Division One:

> mobile money is the main focus of this division, which is providing tractor services to smallholder farmers. The farmers who request our services pay us via mobile money.

A tractor owner operating within Division One also indicated that:

> As tractor owners, we are paid our incomes from the tractor services provided via mobile money.

The respondents corroborated this finding within the Division Two of the case institution. Thus, mobile money was used in the transactions of four agricultural activities, namely, the supply of inputs, provision of tractor services, aggregation of products from out-growers, and the sale of agricultural produce. The Deputy Head of Division Two asserted that:

> Largely, we use mobile money to pay our out-growers, pay our suppliers from whom we receive input supplies, and receive payment from some customers who buy inputs from us. We also use mobile money to receive payment for the tractor services we render to customers and in sending money to our drivers to buy fuel while transporting our supplies to us.

Also, a farmer who is an out-grower within Division Two indicated that:

> as for me, I use mobile money a lot in my activities as a farmer. Most of the people who buy my farm produce, including Agro Company—Division Two, pay me through mobile money. So, I save the money in my wallet and use it later to pay for agricultural inputs such as seeds and fertilizer as well as my transactions.

The Role of Mobile Money in Value Creation within the Case Firm

The extensive use of mobile money service has helped the firm to provide transparency, which goes a long way in building trust and strengthening the relationship between them and the tractor owners were examined.

Respondents indicated that:

> Mobile money has helped to keep and provide financial records to tractor owners whom we work with, thereby providing transparency.
>
> [Deputy Head: Division One]

This is also an indication of a source of financial inclusion for smallholder farmers in rural areas who were previously unbanked as a Smallholder farmer indicated that:

> *It has helped me to build a financial history for myself. I am able to keep a record of the agricultural services that I pay for with mobile money transactions and serves as financial trail or records for me when I am asked for credit facilities from financial institutions.*

Another smallholder farmer also indicated that mobile money had helped them see the need to save while using their mobile money wallets as the medium.

> because I know I will use mobile money to pay for tractor services and other services when the farming season starts, I leave the majority of the money I receive as payment for my agricultural produce on my mobile money wallet as savings. So, when the farming season starts, I use it to pay for the services and inputs I need.

Agro Company Limited, on the other hand, has been able to create value in terms of reduction in operation costs and expansion, which are attributed to the use of mobile money services. The Head of Division One asserted that:

> we used to have a staff in each region of Ghana to receive payments for the tractor services rendered. However, through the use of mobile money services, payments are directly sent to us in the head office. Our operational cost has reduced since we no longer have to keep staff in each of the locations to receive payments.

In terms of operational efficiency, the deputy head of Division One indicated that:

> We also now have reduced occurrences of theft. We experienced a few cases of theft in the beginning when operators were the ones collecting the money on site. Some of them would collect the money and would not record it. Mobile money has helped to curb this by providing payment trails for all transactions.

Furthermore, trust has been built through the use of mobile money with other actors along the agricultural value chain. As a result of this trust, the relationships between these actors have been strengthened.

our suppliers now trust that they will receive payments via mobile money as we always do when they supply us with inputs. Hence, they are not scared to supply us with inputs on credit. It is also the same with the wholesalers and retailers who buy agricultural produce from us to go and sell. We have also come to trust that they will pay us via mobile money as they always do as such, we are not scared to give them the produce on credit.

[Deputy Head—Division Two]

Factors that Affect Value Creation in Using Mobile Money at Agro Company Limited

The study explored the factors enabling the company to use mobile money with the other actors along the value chain to create value as stated by respondents from the company. Among the factors highlighted were:

availability and reliability of network coverage, rules, and regulations governing mobile money and mobile money Interoperability. Others include the availability of third-party service providers in the system such as Hubtel, and the availability of mobile money vendors are the factors that greatly affect our use of mobile money to create value.

[IT Officer—Division One]

for me, it is mainly the reliability of the network which is available in so many places, including my farms. Also, there are mobile money vendors all around so I can easily deposit and withdraw money. Mobile is also easy to use and very convenient. My only problem is the commission charged, but it is not too bad.

[Out-grower farmer—Division Two]

In the communities, is it is easier for our farmers and other people we work with to use mobile money. This is because they do not have to pay for transportation or walk long distances to come to the town to use a bank since there are mobile money vendors in almost all the communities so they just go there and they take their money. Hence, it's very convenient for the people that they work with.

[Head—Division Two]

A summary of the findings from the analysis is shown in Table 9.3.

Discussions

The following subsections are organized in response to the two research objectives of this study.

Mobile Money in Value Creation

From the findings, the value created from the use of mobile money focuses primarily on reduction in actor motivation costs as described from the transaction cost theory. The findings show that mobile money is helping actors along the agricultural value chain to enhance commitments

Table 9.3 Summary of Case Findings

Agricultural Activities	Value Created	Factors Affecting Value Creation
1. Provision of tractor services • Receiving payment for tractor services provided to farmers **2. Transactions with tractor owners** • Paying tractor owners their revenue from tractor services provided **3. Supply of inputs** • Paying Suppliers • Sending money to drivers conveying supplies for fuel while on the journey • Receiving payment from farmers and retailers who buy their agricultural inputs • Paying for machinery part replacement from sellers • Receiving payment for tractor services provided to farmers **4. Aggregation of produce from out-growers** • Paying smallholder farmers (out-growers) for agricultural produce aggregate **5. Sale of farm produce** • Receiving payment from customers (Poultry farmers, Wholesalers, Retailers)	**1. Reduction in operational cost** • No need for staff to be stationed in locations to collect money for tractor services • Reduced risk of theft • No more need to send another vehicle with fuel to help a truck carrying inputs stranded on the road as a result of insufficient funds to buy fuel • No need for staff to go around to collect money from customers who buy on credit **2. Strengthening of relationships** • Creating transparency and establishing trust by providing financial records • Building of trust • No more fear in selling on credit **3. Expansion of business** • Farmers' ability to save money on their mobile money wallets for the next season's agricultural activities • Ability to continuously onboard more customers as mobile money technology is scalable • The willingness of more suppliers and customers to do business with them because of their convenient payment system **4. Increased revenue** • Sale of agricultural inputs and produce to more customers in the hinterlands	1. Network Coverage and Reliability 2. The convenience of the service 3. Mobile Money Interoperability 4. Commission Charged 5. Availability of third-party service providers in the system such as Hubtel 6. Rules and regulations governing mobile money 7. The availability of mobile money vendors

in transactions by making and receiving payments through mobile money to facilitate decision-making and enforce compliance of agreements hence, reducing actor motivation costs. This value can be categorized into Operational, Relational, and Strategic. These forms of value are associated with the suggested benefits of ICT use in trade or commerce (Boateng et al., 2008).

Concerning operational value, the findings indicated that the costs of operations had reduced since there was no longer the need for staff to be stationed or go around regions to collect money for tractor services as well as no need for customers to pay through the banks. Mobile money is less expensive than many alternatives to cash (McKay & Pickens, 2010; Okello et al., 2012). Again, using mobile money services has reduced the risk of carrying huge cash on trips to hinterlands to pay farmers or to other regions to buy agricultural inputs. This situation has led to a reduced risk of theft and armed robbery. The need to send another vehicle with fuel to help a truck carrying inputs stranded on the road as a result of insufficient funds to buy fuel has also been reduced since mobile money was now used. This, therefore, affirms that connecting actors along the agricultural value chain to a cash transfer system which is an electronic payment system could bring about significant impact via reduced transaction costs, overheads, and leakages (Lochan et al., 2010).

The operational value created led to relational value. This was a result of creating transparency and building trust among all the parties involved in agricultural transactions using mobile money. The mobile money system also provided a financial report for all the parties. This situation affirms that mobile money use among actors of the agricultural value chain helps strengthen relationships and build trust (Babcock, 2015).

Also, mobile money is a convenient and accessible method to keep financial records (Stuart & Cohen, 2011). This form of value is crucial as it helps actors along the agricultural value chain to enhance commitments in transactions to facilitate decision-making and enforce compliance with agreements. The result is a reduction in actor motivation costs.

Furthermore, from the findings, the relational value has progressively led to strategic value creation along the agricultural value chain. A critical value that mobile money use has helped create as asserted by Batista and Vicente (2017) is creating and promoting a saving culture among farmers, especially smallholder farmers. This is because, farmers, especially smallholders, are beginning to save money on their mobile money wallets after they receive payments for their agricultural produce for their next farming season. Consequently, these farmers are expanding their business as they are more prepared for the upcoming farming seasons and plan out their spending behavior. This, therefore, confirms that mobile money services enable users to keep money through a bank account or a mobile money account with the mobile network provider (Solin & Zerzan, 2010). Hence, mobile money transfer has become a convenient method of saving money, in addition to sending and receiving payments (Contini et al., 2011). Input suppliers are also able to sell agricultural inputs and produce to more customers in the hinterlands as a result of mobile money use. More suppliers and customers are more willing to do business with companies using mobile money because of their convenient payment system and thereby expanding their reach. This confirms that agricultural enterprises can expand when relationships among the various actors are strengthened (Grossman & Tarazi, 2014). Also, for companies like Agro Company Limited who use the mobile money platform to deal with many customers, mobile money offers them the ability to continuously enroll more customers as the mobile money technology is scalable.

Factors Affecting Value-Creation in Mobile Money Use

The study revealed that certain factors had enabled mobile money to be used in creating value along the agricultural value chain and some other factors which have reduced or inhibited value creation.

The enabling factors are network coverage and reliability, the convenience of the service, the availability of the mobile money vendors, mobile money interoperability, availability of third-party service providers in the system such as Hubtel, and rules and regulations governing mobile money. This is crucial as it affirms that network coverage and reliability are essential factors that promote the use of mobile money services in the agriculture sector. Other factors such as the convenience of the service, the availability of the mobile money vendors, and rules and regulations guarding mobile money operation as specified by the appropriate regulators are important factors to the successful use of mobile money to create value in agriculture (Kirui et al., 2013; Babcock, 2015). Factors such as the quality of other financial services among others that were identified as factors that could influence the use of mobile money along the agricultural value chain (Mas & Ng'weno, 2010) were not found to be essential factors to respondents.

The inhibiting factors, on the other hand, included network failures, commission charges, and fear of fraud. This confirms the assertion that network failures are a significant factor that hinders mobile money use (Senso & Venkatakrishnan, 2013). This finding also confirms that network challenges, particularly in rural areas, are a crucial challenge to users of mobile money (Ndunge, 2011). Also, factors from literature such as level of financial literacy and commission charged (Cole et al., 2011; Nunoo & Andoh, 2011), which were viewed to hinder mobile money use was not established in this study to inhibit or reduce the value created in using mobile money services. People in rural areas with little or no formal education found mobile money very convenient to use as they memorize mobile money options and procedures. The issue of the commission charged by the network operators did not seem to hinder mobile money as farmers maintained that they would have had to spend more than the commission charged for traveling to a nearby town to access their cash. The agricultural company also mentioned that they used mobile money merchant sim cards registered in the company's name, which allows for transactions with large sums of money at no cost.

A summary of the findings found in Figure 9.2 shows mobile money usage within the agricultural value chain, including the value created and the factors that affect value creation.

Conclusions

This study sought to assess the value created in using mobile money services along the agricultural value chain in Ghana. A qualitative case study of an agro-enterprise was, therefore, conducted. This agro-enterprise has been operating in Ghana since 2004. Analysis of the data collected indicated that mobile money was used to perform activities such as the supply of agricultural inputs, production, and aggregation along the agricultural value chain. Other actors along the agricultural chain who do not use mobile money but interact with the actors who perform the aforementioned activities could consider using mobile money in their financial transactions as an alternative method of reducing risks in financial transactions.

The study explored the value created in using mobile money services along the agricultural value chain. From the findings, the value generated from the use of mobile money focuses primarily on reduction in actor motivation costs in the transaction cost theory. This value can be categorized into Operational, Relational, and Strategic. The cost of operations was considerably reduced since there was no longer the need for staff to be stationed or go around the regions to collect money for tractor services as well as no need for customers to pay through the banks. Also, the use of mobile money services has reduced the risk of carrying huge cash on trips to hinterlands to pay farmers or to other regions to buy agricultural inputs, and this has led to a reduced risk of

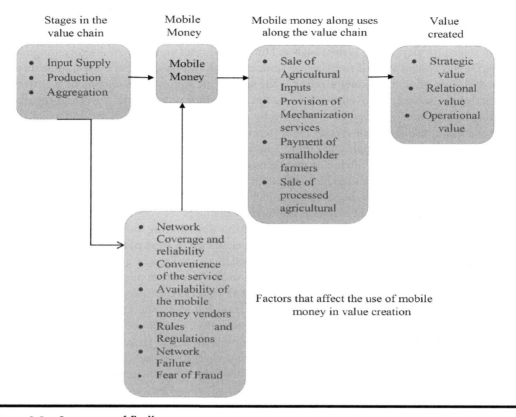

Figure 9.2   Summary of findings.

theft and armed robbery. Therefore, actors along the agricultural value chain who wish to create the same or similar value could consider using mobile money.

The final objective was to explore the factors that influence mobile money transfer services along the agricultural value chain in Ghana. The enabling factors for mobile money use in value creation were network coverage and reliability, the convenience of the service, the availability of the mobile money vendors, mobile money interoperability, availability of third-party service providers, and rules and regulations governing mobile money. Additionally, the inhibiting factors included network failures, commission charges, and fear of fraud. The finding also emphasizes that network challenges, particularly in rural areas, are a crucial challenge to users of mobile money. Also, factors from literature such as the level of financial literacy and commission charged that was viewed to hinder mobile money use did not hinder or reduce the value created in using mobile money services as claimed by respondents. They maintained that they would have had to spend more than the commission charged for traveling to a nearby town to access their monies. Hence, agribusinesses who have plans of using mobile money for their transactions can use this as a guide to assess themselves to see if they have the enabling factors and if they can withstand the inhibiting factors before they use the service. It could also help allay their fears of not being able to use the service because of the low level of financial literacy of other actors and commission charged.

Implications of the Study

Concerning implications for theory, this study has extended the literature of mobile money and agricultural research from a multistakeholder value chain perspective. The literature reviewed primarily focused on one actor being the farmers. This study has contributed toward the understanding of mobile money usage among multiple stakeholders along the agricultural value chain. The literature on the use of mobile money services in agricultural activities, especially among actors along the agricultural value chain, is arguably limited in developing countries like Ghana; hence, the contribution from this study is timely. This research has demonstrated the use of the transaction cost theory, particularly the actor motivation cost component in determining commitments in transactions. There is limited literature on the outcome or benefits of mobile money use as compared to its adoption and acceptance. As a result of this, there is limited literature on the use of the transaction cost theory to assess the outcome of mobile money use; hence, this study helped in addressing this gap.

With regard to practical implications, since the study demonstrates the dominant activities that mobile money is used for and the value that is created in using mobile money along the agricultural value chain, this could encourage actors along the agricultural chain who do not use mobile money but interact with the actors who perform the aforementioned activities to use mobile money in their financial transactions. This would help them create the value discussed earlier. Additionally, the enabling factors for value creation from mobile money use include network coverage and reliability, regulations, service convenience, and availability of mobile money vendors whilst the inhibiting factors included network failures and fear of fraud. Again, from the study, the level of financial literacy and commission charged did not necessarily hinder or reduce the value created in using mobile money services. This could serve as a guide to agribusinesses who have plans of using mobile money for their transactions to know if they have the enabling factors and if they can withstand the inhibiting factors before they use the service. It could also help allay their fears of not being able to use the service because of low level of financial literacy of other actors and commission charged.

In terms of policy, this study has demonstrated the importance of mobile money use along the agricultural value chain in a developing economy. It has also provided useful insights into the dominant agricultural activities performed using mobile money, the value created, and the inhibiting factors. This study can, therefore, guide agricultural businesses and telecommunication companies to discuss and adopt policies that create additional value for actors along the agricultural value chain while reducing the effect of the inhibiting factors. These policies could be geared toward reducing the commission charged or cost involved in using mobile money to provide additional operational value, additional security features to reduce the incidence of fraud and provision of stable network in areas of unstable network.

Future Research and Practice Directions

First, this study focused on one agricultural company, its employees and customers; hence, the use of a smaller sample size. Additionally, the study could not cover all the stages of the agricultural value chain especially, the processing of the agricultural produce. There is a need for research into agricultural processing companies who use mobile money to assess the value created in using mobile money in their transactions with other actors along the agricultural value chain. There is also the need for research into the agricultural value chains of other crops aside from maize. This will deepen the understanding of whether the value created from mobile money usage is dependent on the type of product being moved along the supply chain. Again, the outcomes of the qualitative study may be limited in scope and generality. Therefore, upcoming studies could examine the phenomenon in a quantitative context to improve scope and generality.

References

Afshan, S., & Sharif, A. (2016). Acceptance of Mobile Banking Framework in Pakistan, *Telematics and Informatics*, (33), 370–387.

Akramov, K., & Malek, M. (2012). *Analyzing Profitability of Maize, Rice, and Soybean Production in Ghana: Results of PAM and DEA Analysis*. Ghana Strategy Support Programme Working Paper No. 0028. Washington, DC: International Food Policy Research Institute.

Au, Y., & Kauffman, J. (2008). The Economics of Mobile Payments: Understanding Stakeholder Issues for an Emerging Financial Technology Application. *Electronic Commerce Research and Applications 1*(7), 141–164.

Babcock, L. (2015). *Mobile Payments: How Digital Finance is Transforming Agriculture*. Wageningen: Technical Centre for Agricultural and Rural Cooperation.

Batista, C., & Vicente, P. C. (2017). *Improving Access to Savings through Mobile Money: Experimental Evidence from Smallholder Farmers in Mozambique* (No. novaf: wp1705). Carcavelos, Portugal: Universidade Nova de Lisboa, Faculdade de Economia, NOVAFRICA.

Benbasat, I., Goldstein, D. K., & Mead, M. (1987). The Case Research Strategy in Studies of Information Systems. *MIS Quarterly, 11*(3), 369–386.

Boateng, R. (2011). Mobile Phones and Micro-trading Activities—Conceptualising the Link. *Info, 13*(5), 48–62.

Boateng, R., Heeks, R., Molla, A., & Hinson, R. (2008). E-Commerce and Socio-Economic Development: Conceptualizing the Link. *Internet Research, 18*(5), 562–92.

Cobla, G. M., & Osei-Assibey, E. (2018). Mobile Money Adoption and Spending Behaviour: The Case of Students in Ghana. *International Journal of Social Economics, 45*(1), 29–42. https://doi.org/10.1108/IJSE-11-2016-0302.

Cole, S., Sampson, T., & Zia, B. (2011). Prices or Knowledge? What Drives Demand for Financial Services in Emerging Markets? *The Journal of Finance, 66*(6), 1933–1967.

Contini, D., Crowe, M., Merritt, C., Oliver, R., & Mott, S. (2011). *Mobile Payments in the United States, Mapping Out the Road Ahead*. Proceedings of the Mobile Payments Industry Workshop, Federal Reserve Banks.

Davidson, N., & Pénicaud, C. (2011). *State of the Industry: Results from the 2011 Global Money Adoption Survey*. London: Mobile Money for the Unbanked, GSMA.

Douma, S., & Schreuder, H. (2008). *Economic Approaches to Organizations* (4th ed.). Harlow, England: Financial Times/Prentice Hall.

FAO, IFAD, & ILO. (2010). *Agricultural Value Chain Development: Threat or Opportunity for Women's Employment?* Gender and Rural Employment Policy Brief #4. www.fao.org/docrep/013/i2008e/i2008e04.pdf

Gosavi, A. (2018). Can Mobile Money Help Firms Mitigate the Problem of Access to Finance in Eastern Sub-Saharan Africa? *Journal of African Business, 19*(3), 343–360. https://doi.org/10.1080/15228916.2017.1396791

Grossman, J., & Tarazi, M. (2014, June). *Serving Smallholder Farmers: Recent Developments in Digital Finance*. Focus Note 94. Washington, DC: CGAP.

Grover, V., & Malhotra, M. K. (2003). Transaction Cost Framework in Operations and Supply Chain Management Research: Theory and Measurement. *Journal of Operations Management, 21*, 457–473.

Heyer, A., & Mas, I. (2011). Fertile Grounds for Mobile Money: Towards a Framework for Analyzing Enabling Environments. *Enterprise Development and Microfinance, 22*(1). SSRN: https://ssrn.com/abstract=1593389.

Hughes, N., & Lonie, S. (2007, April). *M-PESA: Mobile Money for the "Unbanked" Turning Cell Phones into 24-Hour Tellers in Kenya*. Innovations: Technology, Governance, Globalization. Industry Workshop. Federal Reserve Banks, Como, Italy. Information and Communication Technologies, MIT Press 2 (1–2), 63–81.

Jenkins, B. (2008). *Developing Mobile Money Ecosystems*. Washington, DC: IFC and the Harvard Kennedy School.

Kaplan, B., & Maxwell, J. A. (2005). *Qualitative Research Methods for Evaluating Computer Information Systems Evaluating the Organizational Impact of Healthcare Information Systems* (pp. 30–55). New York: Springer.

Kikulwe, E. M., Fischer, E., & Qaim, M. (2014). Mobile Money, Smallholder Farmer and Household Welfare in Kenya. *PLoS One, 9*(10).

Kim, C., Mirsobit, M., & Lee, I. (2010). An Empirical Examination of Factors Influencing the Intention to Use Mobile Payment. *Computers in Human Behavior, 26*(3), 310–322.

Kirui, O. K., Okello, J. J., Nyikal, R. A., & Njiraini, G. W. (2013, May). Impact of Mobile Phone-Based Money Transfer Services in Agriculture: Evidence from Kenya. *Quarterly Journal of International Agriculture, Humboldt-Universitaat zu Berlin, 52*(2), 1–22.

Lincoln, Y., & Guba, E. G. (1985). *Naturalistic Inquiry*. Newbury Park, CA: Sage.

Lochan, R., Ignacio, M., Radcliffe, D., Supriyo, S., & Tahilyani, N. (2010, December). The Benefits to Government of Connecting Low-Income Households to an E-Payment System: An Analysis in India. *Lydian Payments Journal, 2*. London, United Kingdom. http://ssrn.com/abstract=1725103

Mallat, N., & Tuunainen, V. K. (2008). Exploring Merchant Adoption of Mobile Payment Systems: An Empirical Study 1. *E-Service Journal, 6*(2), 24–57.

Mas, I., & Ng'weno, A. (2010). Three Keys to M-PESA's Success: Branding Channel Management and Pricing. *Journal of Payments Strategy & Systems, 4*(4), 352–370.

McKay, P., Claudia, P., & Pickens, M. (2010). *Branchless Banking 2010: Who's Served? At What Price? What's Next?* Focus Note 66. Washington, DC: Consultative Group to Assist the Poor.

McKay, C., & Pickens, M. (2010). *Branchless Banking 2010: Who's Served? At What Price? What's Next?* [Focus Note 66]. Washington, DC: CGAP.

Miles, M. B., Huberman, A. M., & Saldana, J. (2014). *Qualitative Data Analysis: A Methods Sourcebook* (3rd ed.). Los Angeles, CA: Sage.

Ministry of Food and Agriculture (MoFA). (2011). *Agriculture in Ghana. Facts and Figures (2010)*. Ghana: Statistical, Research and Information Division, Ministry of Food and Agriculture.

Morris, M. L., Tripp, R., & Dankyi, A. A. (1999). *Adoption and Impacts of Improved Maize Production Technology: A Case Study of the Ghana Grains Development Project*. Economics Program Paper 99-01. Mexico, DF: CIMMYT.

Ndunge, K. (2011). *Benefits and Challenges of Using Mobile Money to Reduce Poverty*. New York, USA: Houghton College.

Ngumbu, C., & Mulu-Mutuku, M. (2018). *Determinants of Awareness and Adoption of Mobile Money Technologies: Evidence from Women Micro Entrepreneurs in Kenya*. Women's Studies International Forum 67 (July 2017) (pp. 18–22). Amsterdam, the Netherlands: Elsevier.

Nunoo, J., & Andoh, F. K. (2011). *Sustaining Small and Medium Enterprises through Financial Service Utilization: Does Financial Literacy Matter?* Paper presented at the 2012 Annual Meeting, August 12–14, 2012, Seattle, Washington, 123418.

Okello, J., Kirui, O. K., Njirani, G. W., & Gitonga, Z. M. (2012). Drivers of Use of Services: Observations on Customer Usage and Impact from M-PESA. CGAP Brief Smallholder Farmers in Kenya, *Journal of Agricultural Science*, 111–124.

Orozco, M. (2003). *Worker Remittances: An International Comparison*. Working Paper Commissioned by the Multilateral Investment Fund, Inter-American Washington, DC: Development Bank.

Pare, D. J. (2003). Does this Site Deliver? B2B E-Commerce Services for Developing Countries. *Information Society, 19*(2), 123–134.

Sander, C. (2003). *Migrant Remittances to Developing Countries—A Scoping Study: Overview and Introduction to Issues for Pro-Poor Financial Services*. Prepared for DFID, London, UK

Sekabira, H., & Qaim, M. (2016). *Mobile Money, Agricultural Marketing, and Off-Farm Income in Uganda*. Global Food Discussion Paper 82, University of Göttingen. www.uni-goettingen.de/de/213486.html

Senso, N. C., & Venkatakrishnan, V. (2013, December). Challenges of Mobile Phone Money Transfer Services' Market Penetration and Expansion in Singida District, Tanzania. *International Journal of Research in Management & Technology (IJRMT), 3*(6). ISSN: 2249–9563.

Solin, M., & Zerzan, A. (2010). *Mobile Money Methodology for Assessing Money Laundering and Terrorist Financing Risk.* GSMA Discussion Paper. www.gsma.com/mobilefordevelopment/wpcontent/uploads/2012/03/amlfinal35.pdf

Stuart, G., & Cohen, M. (2011). Cash-In, Cash-Out: The Role of M-PESA in the Lives of Low-Income People. *Financial Services Assessment.* the United States, Mapping out the Road Ahead.

Tchale, H., & Keyser, J. (2010). *Quantitative Value Chain Analysis: An Application to Malawi.* Policy Research Working Paper (WPS) 5242. Washington, DC: The World Bank. http://documents.worldbank.org/curated/en/909391468272372680/pdf/WPS5242.pdf

Tobbin, P. (2011). *Understanding Mobile Money Ecosystem: Roles, Structure and Strategies.* Proceedings—2011 10th International Conference on Mobile Business, ICMB 2011, pp. 185–194. https://doi.org/10.1109/ICMB.2011.19

WEF (World Economic Forum). (2011). *Mobile Financial Services Development Report.* www.weforum.org/issues/mobile-financial-services development.

Wigand, R., Picot, A., & Reichwald, R. (1997). *Information, Organization and Management: Expanding Markets and Corporate Boundaries.* Chichester: John Wiley & Sons.

Williamson, O. E. (1981). The Economics of Organization: The Transaction Cost Approach. *The American Journal of Sociology, 87*(3), 548–577.

Williamson, O. E. (1985). *The Economic Institutions of Capitalism.* New York: Free Press.

Yaokumah, W., Kumah, P., & Okai, E. S. A. (2017). Demographic Influences on E-Payment Services. *International Journal of E-Business Research (IJEBR), 13*(1), 44–65.

Authors' Profile

Qudiratu Ngmenensoa Ishak holds an MPhil in Management Information Systems at the Department of Operations and Management Information Systems of the University of Ghana Business School (UGBS). She has a background in Computer science and Geography. Her research interests include e-agriculture, financial technologies, electronic business, social media, and the digital economy. Qudiratu can be reached at qudirat18ishak@gmail.com.

Acheampong Owusu holds a PhD in Information Systems from the Limkokwing University of Creative Technology, Cyberjaya, Malaysia. He is a lecturer at the Department of Operations and Management Information Systems at the University of Ghana Business School. His research interests include Business Intelligence (BI) Systems and Analytics, Technology Diffusion, Cloud Computing, and E-commerce. Acheampong has published several research articles in peer-reviewed journals. He can be reached at aowusu@ug.edu.gh.

Chapter 10

Examining Fintech Adoption in the Banking Sector of a Developing Country

Fred Pobee and Eric Ansong

Contents

Introduction

Economies worldwide and financial landscapes have seen rapid advances with digital technology. Financial technology, also known as FinTech, has become a buzzword and has gained significant attention in the finance industry. Fintech, according to Gai et al. (2018), refers to the use of technological devices, such as tablets and smartphones, to provide financial services. Fintech can be credited for the reduced financial service cost, increased reach of more people by financial firms, and reduced face-to-face interactions, especially for fostering economic development during the COVID-19 pandemic (World Bank, 2020). The global investment in FinTech totaled $57.4 billion for the second half of 2018, a remarkable increase from $28 billion for the second half of 2017 (KPMG, 2019). These statistics show increasing FinTech innovation investments by technology firms and large financial institutions (Chen et al., 2019).

FinTech is driving financial inclusion among developed countries' financial markets; however, its adoption lags among consumers in developing countries (Walton, 2014). Simultaneously, many African economies seem to be at the tail end of the financial innovation spectrum (Johnson & Walton, 2018). According to Miraz and Ali (2018), the global drive toward the Internet of Things secures the future of FinTech. There is evidence to show that the prolific use of FinTech can remodel financial inclusion, particularly in developing economies (Coeckelbergh & Reijers, 2015; Kshetri, 2017). Public choices on financial inclusion have increased with FinTech. It is reported that development in FinTech will advance e-commerce market growth (Polasik et al., 2015). Transaction cost and transaction time are significantly reduced through disintermediation (Dwyer, 2015). Nonetheless, De Filippi (2014) posits that the adoption of FinTech by end users will make it realize its top prospect, without which the impact of FinTech will remain minimal.

Nevertheless, despite the extensive interest in FinTech, very little is currently known about factors influencing its adoption in developing countries. This chapter provides an understanding of technology and behavioral factors that influence FinTech innovation adoption in Ghana. The literature on FinTech innovation in Ghana is predominantly focused on mobile money (Chauhan, 2015; Narteh et al., 2017; Senyo & Osabutey, 2020; Upadhyay & Jahanyan, 2016) to the detriment of other FinTech innovations. This chapter focuses on e-zwich—a FinTech innovation that allows savvy cardholders and merchants to load, spend funds, and settle various financial transactions. These financial transactions include withdrawal of cash, payment of goods and services, transfer of money, receipt of salaries, payment of wages, and payment of bills from any e-zwich point of sales or ATM nationwide.

Due to the limited research and unexposed technological and behavioral antecedents of e-zwich adoption, proper theoretical and practical claims cannot be made about its adoption. This research adopts a multiple theory approach to uncover the factors influencing Ghana's e-zwich adoption by integrating the Technology Acceptance Model (TAM) and Prospect Model. Even though many models and frameworks have been utilized in studying factors that influence technology acceptance, TAM has been observed to be arguably the most reliable of them (Dillon & Morris, 1996). While TAM evaluates the technology factors (Davis, 1989), the prospect theory evaluates the behavioral factors that influence its use (Tversky & Kahneman, 1986). Similar to Liu and Forsythe's (2010) research, this chapter arguably represents the first attempt to integrate two dominant theories—the TAM and the Prospect Theory—to gain a more in-depth understanding of why consumers, including those who perceive considerable risk in Fintech innovations, would choose to continue to use the e-zwich services in Ghana. Thus, the underlying research question is: what are the factors influencing e-zwich adoption in Ghana? This chapter uncovers the factors influencing the use of FinTech innovation from the Ghanaian context. This research's findings on e-zwich adoption would be vital to research and practice. Second, it points out the effect of both enablers and inhibitors in the use of FinTech innovation.

Background and Theoretical Foundation

FinTech was introduced first in Ghana in 1997, allowing holders to engage in cashless transactions introduced by the then Social Security Bank (Kelly, 2020; Mawuli, 2020). Eleven years later, Ghana's government launched the e-zwich, a national and interoperable smart payment system that allowed cashless transactions (Breckenridge, 2010). The FinTech industry of Ghana has witnessed a tremendous revolution to embrace smartphones and applications in transactions. Currently, 11 million active users of electronic and digital channels for mobile payment have been reported in Ghana (Kelly, 2020). The regulator of payment systems, the Bank of Ghana (BoG), reports that about 71 FinTech companies operate in the country. Some examples of Ghanaian FinTech companies include ExpressPay, Slydepay, Hubtel'spayment, Zeepay, InvestMobile, Bloom Impact, Paysail, and G-Monet (Kelly, 2020; Mawuli, 2020).

The chief executive officer's characteristics, business characteristics, and FinTech payment characteristics are predictors of FinTech payment services diffusion in a small and medium enterprise setting (Coffie et al., 2020). The literature on FinTech in Africa has predominantly focused on FinTech payment services diffusion's antecedents because of its contribution to economic development (Fanta et al., 2016; Makina, 2019; Yermack, 2018). Despite these studies, current SSA studies have focused chiefly on mobile money (Batista & Vicente, 2020; Munyegera & Matsumoto, 2016; Senyo & Osabutey, 2020), a type of FinTech innovation that allows financial transactions via mobile devices (Donovan, 2012). In Ghana, there has been minimal focus on the diffusion of other FinTech innovations such as e-zwich; thus, strong theoretical and practical claims cannot be made about e-zwich adoption drivers. Given the importance of the e-zwich payment system, this chapter measures the factors that account for its adoption. The focus on e-zwich is the seemingly relatively low infrastructure for use (supports both online and offline transactions) compared to other FinTech innovations that require sophisticated ICT infrastructure that only supports online transactions.

However, it must be emphasized that the e-zwich payment system scheme is a groundbreaking interbank settlement system launched by the BoG to enhance connectivity to banking and retail financial services in Ghana. At the outlets of other e-zwich financial institutions, e-zwich cardholders may conduct banking and retail transactions. One notable feature of e-zwich is its ability to facilitate online and offline transactions, enabling cardholders to connect with e-zwich services in all parts of the country, whether or not the region has a strong communication network.

Research Framework and Hypothesis Development

According to Wu and Wang (2005), an enriched understanding of individuals' behavioral intention to adopt technology is attained when two or more technology acceptance frameworks are integrated. Besides Wu and Wang (2005), other researchers have echoed the importance of incorporating models to provide a holistic understanding of a phenomenon (Fichman, 2004; Lyytinen & Rose, 2003). As a result, this chapter incorporates perceived ease of use (PEOU) and perceived usefulness (PU) from the TAM and perceived risk, agent trust, and service trust from the prospect theory to enrich understanding of the factors that influence e-zwich acceptance and use in Ghana. TAM and prospect theory's unique antecedents provide a robust standpoint to uncover the factors that influence e-zwich adoption. More so, these models set off each other to answer the research question. While TAM uncovers technology adoption drivers (Davis, 1989; Dillon & Morris, 1996), the prospect theory uncovers technology adoption inhibitors (Tversky & Kahneman, 1986). The research model developed for this research is presented in Figure 10.1.

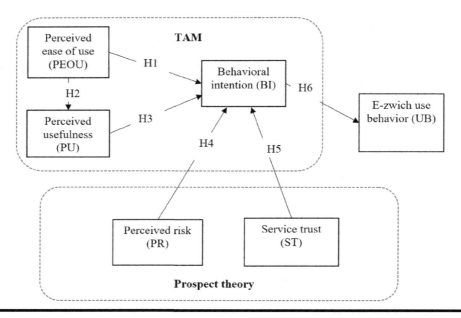

Figure 10.1   Research model.

Technology Acceptance Model

Proposed by Davis (1989), TAM predicts users' acceptance and use of technology. Due to its significant predictive power, TAM has been argued by Mathieson (1991) to have an empirical advantage over some models like the theory of planned behavior. TAM has been employed to investigate online shopping (Gefen et al., 2003), e-commerce (Pavlou, 2003), cloud computing (Gangwar et al., 2015; Sharma et al., 2016), and acceptance of commercial mobile services (Jiang & Deng, 2011; Narteh et al., 2017; Wei et al., 2011). As echoed by Davis (1989), an individual's behavioral intention to accept and use technology and system is influenced by two factors: PEOU and PU.

PEOU measures the degree of ease associated with using technology (Davis, 1989; Rogers, 1995). This factor describes the extent to which an individual believes that using technology would be free from mental and physical stress. The literature has suggested a significant effect of PEOU on behavioral intention (Kamal et al., 2020; Narteh et al., 2017; Rafique et al., 2020; Rahman et al., 2017). Davis (1989) modeled a significant effect of PEOU on PU. Yoon (2016) clarified the significant effect of PEOU on PU. In the e-zwich service, PEOU is conceptualized as the easiness to register, make a payment, and access customer services. This chapter, therefore, hypothesizes that

H₁—*PEOU of the e-zwich system will significantly influence users' behavioral intention in Ghana.*
H₂—*PEOU of the e-zwich system will have a significant influence on perceived usefulness.*

PU measures the degree to which an individual believes that using technology or a system will bring some gains in his job by making it easier, quicker, and better (Davis, 1989). The literature has suggested a significant relationship between PU and behavioral intention (Narteh et al., 2017;

Padashetty & Krishna, 2013; Rafique et al., 2020; Rahman et al., 2017; Zhou, 2011). This chapter hypothesized that

H3: PU of the e-zwich system will significantly influence users' behavioral intention in Ghana.

The Prospect Theory

The prospect theory has been used to predict human behavior in many domains; however, it has not been explicitly employed to predict behavior related to e-zwich adoption. In a recently published study, Senyo and Osabutey (2020) applied the prospect theory to explain mobile money adoption. Developed by Kahneman and Tversky (1979), the prospect theory explains how consumers choose from alternatives with some elements of uncertain outcomes or risks. As a behavior theory, the prospect theory holds that consumers' decisions are dependent on gains and losses associated with the particular behavior rather than the outcome (Kahneman & Tversky, 1979).

The prospect theory has been employed extensively in psychology and behavioral economics. The theory has also been used as a theoretical lens in information systems research to know and understand the risks associated with technology use (Li & Shimizu, 2018; Xiao, 2020). E-zwich services, just like other online payment systems, have the inherent risk that deters people from using the innovation. Consequently, it is essential to understand the effect of such risks; thus, this chapter determines whether perceived risk and service trust affect behavioral intention to use e-zwich innovation. Constructs of the prospect theory utilized for this chapter include Perceived risk and Service trust.

According to Pavlou (2003), perceived risk refers to users' cognizance of uncertainty associated with technology use. Due to most technology activities' online nature, online transactions present some risks (Abubakar et al., 2019). Some recently published studies have investigated the effect of perceived risk on mobile payment (Chopdar et al., 2018; Liébana-Cabanillas et al., 2019; Senyo & Osabutey, 2020). Senyo and Osabutey (2020) suggested that perceived risk negatively impacts behavioral intention to adopt a FinTech innovation in Ghana. Contrariwise, extant studies (e.g., Baganzi & Lau, 2017; Tobbin & Kuwornu, 2011) reported a significant influence of perceived risk on behavioral intention to adopt FinTech innovations. These results present findings that suggest that the effect of perceived risk on behavioral intention is inconsistent and inconclusive. This chapter, therefore, hypothesized that

H4: Perceived risk influences users' behavioral intention to use e-zwich services.

As opined by Manuel (2015), service trust refers to the belief in the service provided by a vendor. In online transactions, trust becomes a complex issue. People who use online payment systems are mostly those who have some level of trustworthiness in the service. On the other hand, some people do not ascribe to online payment systems due to service trust issues (Grohmann et al., 2018). Some studies have investigated the impact of trust on Fintech adoption (Baganzi & Lau, 2017; Chauhan, 2015; Osei-Assibey, 2015). However, the focus of these studies has been on service provider trust rather than service trust. A good and reputable service provider is not enough to guarantee good service. It is essential to assess service trust in tandem to service provider trust. Senyo and Osabutey (2020) explored the effect of service trust on behavioral intention to adopt FinTech; however, they focused on mobile money innovation to the detriment of other FinTech innovation kinds such as e-zwich. This chapter, therefore, hypothesized that

H5: Service trust influences users' behavioral intention to use e-zwich services.

Methodology of the Study

According to Nardi (2018), quantitative research helps obtain objective results through statistical, mathematics, or numeric analysis of data collected through polls, questionnaires, and surveys. This chapter, therefore, adopted the quantitative research approach with the survey strategy to respond to the hypotheses.

The convenience data sampling technique was employed to collect data for the chapter. An online survey containing 20 items was used to collect data from a randomly sampled adult population in the Greater Accra region of Ghana between October and December 2020. The questionnaire was in two parts. The first part gathered data on the respondents' demographics (age, gender, educational level, and marital status). The second part was on the questions related to the hypothesized variables on the factors that may influence the adoption of e-zwich innovation. The questionnaire was pilot-tested with ten respondents. The pilot test was to ensure that the items reflect the chapter's objective, and it was proven so by the pilot survey. In estimating the sample size, this research followed the Hair et al. (2011) rule, which suggests that the sample size should be ten times the largest number of the hypothesized path in a research model. In the research model developed for this chapter, the largest number of the hypothesized path is six. Therefore, by employing the ten times rule, a sample size of 60 (i.e., 6 × 10) is considered sufficient. There was, however, the need to collect adequate data that represents the population to achieve generalization. The questionnaire was distributed to 300 through an online survey system to adults in Ghana on a convenience sampling basis. From this, 264 responses were fully completed and returned and were deemed suitable for this chapter.

Given that the required sample size was 60, the number of responses collected was sufficient for this chapter. Homogeneity variance test for the pilot and main data collection was performed with a one-way ANOVA. The results revealed that the two data groups were homogenous, i.e., they did not differ statistically. The assumption of homogeneity of the variance was, therefore, met. The Common Method Variance (CMV) bias was tested with Harman's Single Factor Test. The test indicated the absence of CMV bias because the total variance for a single factor was less than the 50% threshold, as suggested by Podsakoff et al. (2003).

The survey items were measured on a five-point Likert scale ranging from 1 "strongly disagree" to 5 "strongly agree". For the measurement of the TAM variables, items were adopted from Davis (1989); however, the items were revised to understand the factors influencing Ghanaians e-zwich adoption. The following number of items were used to measure the variables; PEOU—4 items; PU—4 items; BI—3 items. For the measurement of the Prospect model variables, items were adopted from Senyo and Osabutey (2020). The following number of items were used to measure the variables; Perceived risk—5 items, service trust—4 items. The data were analyzed using partial least square Structural Equation Modeling (PLS-SEM).

Data Analysis and Results

The respondents' demographic profile (Table 10.1) reveals that 55%, representing 145 of the respondents, were males while 45%, representing 119, were females. The majority of the respondents (92), representing 35% of the sample size, were within the age bracket of 25–30. Respondents within the age range of 18–24 and 31–40 accounted for 23% of the sample size, respectively. The demographic characteristics of the respondents for the chapter are outlined in Table 10.1.

Table 10.1 Demographic Characteristics of Respondents

Variable	Frequency (n=264)	Percentage (%)
Gender		
Male	145	55
Female	119	45
Age		
18–24	61	23
25–30	92	35
31–40	61	23
41–50	50	19
Marital status		
Single	106	40
Married	132	50
Divorced	26	10
Educational level		
Senior high	3	1
Bachelor's degree	118	45
Master's degree	115	44
Doctorate	10	4

Measurement Model Estimation

The validity and reliability of the multiple item scale were tested using the maximum likelihood estimation technique of CFA. The result indicated high and acceptable factor loadings above the threshold of 0.70 suggested by Hair et al. (2010). Each construct showed an acceptable internal consistency level with Cronbach's alpha estimates ranging from 0.789 to 0.867 (Hair et al., 2010). An adequate internal consistency of each construct's multiple items was achieved with composite reliability above 0.70 (Hair et al., 2010). Bagozzi and Yi (2012) and Hair et al. (2010) indicated that the Average Variance Extracted (AVE) of all constructs must be greater than or equal to 0.50. The AVE of the constructs in Table 10.2 is above 0.50, explaining a large portion of the variance.

The AVE indices (Table 10.3) were above the constructs' squared correlation and other constructs in the model, which indicates a good discriminant validity (Chin et al., 2003).

Model Goodness of Fit

The root mean squared error of approximation (RMSEA), comparative fit index (CFI), chi-square/ degree of freedom, goodness of fit (GFI), and normed fit index (NFI) indices were used to assess

Table 10.2   Factor Loadings and Reliability Analysis

Constructs	Codes	Loadings	Cronbach's alpha	CR	AVE
Perceived ease of use	PEOU1	0.832	0.814	0.825	0.637
	PEOU2	0.801			
	PEOU3	0.709			
	PEOU4	0.822			
Perceived usefulness	PU1	0.818	0.867	0.868	0.676
	PU2	0.826			
	PU3	0.811			
	PU4	0.880			
Perceived risk	PR1	0.711	0.789	0.781	0.577
	PR2	0.783			
	PR3	0.876			
	PR4	0.859			
	PR5	0.742			
System trust	ST1	0.836	0.849	0.842	0.729
	ST2	0.82644			
	ST3	0.855			
	ST4	0.781			
Behavioral intention	BI1	0.875	0.856	0.852	0.701
	BI2	0.839			
	BI3	0.872			

Table 10.3   Discriminant Analysis

	PEOU	PU	PR	ST	BI
PEOU	*0.799*				
PU	0.163	*0.822*			
PR	0.463	0.526	*0.759*		
ST	0.252	0.102	0.301	*0.853*	
BI	0.574	0.312	0.437	0.295	*0.837*

Note: Diagonal elements (italics) in the matrix represent the square root of AVE.

Table 10.4   The Model of Fit

Goodness of Fit	Recommended Threshold	SEM Value	Remark
Root mean squared error of approximation	≤ .10	0.054	Good fit
Comparative fit index	≥ .90	0.975	Good fit
Chi-square/degree of freedom	≤ 3.0	2.67	Good fit
Goodness of fit	≥ .90	0.925	Good fit
Normed fit index	≥.90	0.943	Good fit

the model fit. As revealed in Table 10.4 and suggested by Hoyle and Panter (1995), overall model fit indexes' conditions were met.

Structural Model Estimation

The structural model estimation results confirmed H1, H2, H3, H4, H5, and H6. More so, 59.2% of the predicted variance in behavioral intention was explained by the model. Similarly, 47.8% of actual use was explained by the model. Perceived ease of use explained 40.4% of the variance in PU. As shown in Figure 10.2, PEOU has a significant positive effect on behavioral intention ($\beta = 0.251$, $p < 0.01$). The results show a significant positive effect of PEOU on PU ($\beta = 0.359$, $p < 0.05$). PU has a significant positive effect on behavioral intention ($\beta = 0.472$, $p < 0.05$). Perceived risk and service trust both have a significant positive effect on behavioral intention ($\beta = 0.243$, $p < 0.05$) and ($\beta = 0.279$, $p < 0.05$), respectively. The behavioral intention has a significant positive effect on use behavior ($\beta = 0.223$, $p < 0.01$).

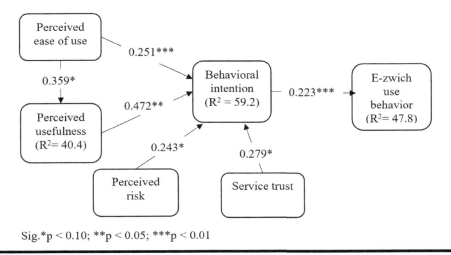

Sig.*p < 0.10; **p < 0.05; ***p < 0.01

Figure 10.2   Results of the structural model.

Table 10.5 Summary of Results

Structural Linkage	Beta Estimate	t Values	Supported
H1: PEOU ⟶ BI	0.251	5.21	Yes
H2: PEOU ⟶ PU	0.359	3.32	Yes
H3: PU ⟶ BI	0.472	4.51	Yes
H4: PR ⟶ BI	0.243	2.72	Yes
H5: ST ⟶ BI	0.279	2.93	Yes
H6: BI ⟶ UB	0.223	4.98	Yes

Discussion

This chapter's findings revealed that PEOU has a significant positive influence on behavioral intention. This finding implies that Ghanaians' perceived ease with using e-zwich increases their intention to adopt the innovation. This finding is consistent with extant studies on innovation adoption (e.g., Kamal et al., 2020; Narteh et al., 2017; Rafique et al., 2020; Rahman et al., 2017). Consistent with previous studies (Rahman et al., 2017; Yoon, 2016; Zhou, 2011), this chapter confirmed a significant positive influence of PEOU on PU. This finding indicates that Ghanaians' PEOU associated with using e-zwich significantly influences the innovation's PU.

The chapter's findings also confirmed a significant positive relationship between PU and behavioral intention, a position that corroborates prior studies (Narteh et al., 2017; Padashetty & Krishna, 2013; Rafique et al., 2020). This finding implies that the gains that e-zwich innovation brings to Ghanaians (e.g., easy and quick money transfer) increase the behavioral intention to use the innovation.

Similarly, perceived risk has a significant positive influence on behavioral intention. This finding supports Tobbin and Kuwornu (2011) claim and Baganzi and Lau (2017), suggesting that the cognizance of uncertainty associated with using e-zwich innovation by Ghanaians significantly impacts behavioral intention to use the innovation. Consistent with previous studies (Baganzi & Lau, 2017; Chauhan, 2015; Osei-Assibey, 2015), the finding of this research revealed a significant positive effect of service trust on behavioral intention. This finding implies that the belief in the e-zwich innovation service to Ghanaians significantly influences e-zwich adoption. Finally, behavioral intention to use e-zwich showed a significant positive effect on the actual use. This finding implies that Ghanaians' subjective probability of adopting e-zwich innovation positively and significantly leads to the actual use of the e-zwich innovation. The summary of the structural model results is presented in Table 10.5.

Conclusion and Research Implications

Although several models have been used to explore technology acceptance, TAM is the most widely used and generally accepted theory to explain technology acceptance. Nevertheless, new questions have emerged concerning its specific configuration in the case of actual behavior, including perceived risks and trust. There is a call by some researchers, including Alambaigi and Ahangari (2016), to advance understanding of how the TAM may be improved or modified to reflect the full complexity of acceptance processes better. In this regard, this chapter sought to explore the factors that influence the adoption of e-zwich in Ghana using the TAM and the prospects theory.

This chapter showed that users' PEOU, PU, perceived risks, and trust in the services influence their intention to adopt the e-zwich services. Again, the intention to use e-zwich influences the actual usage of the system.

Implications to Research

This chapter presents some theoretical contributions. First, there is a dearth of studies that employ the TAM to investigate e-zwich adoption. As a result, this chapter extends the use of the TAM to explore e-zwich adoption. Despite TAM being employed to study mobile payment in general (e.g., Chauhan, 2015), few studies have applied TAM constructs in the context of e-zwich innovation adoption. Second, the research provides a multitheory approach to comprehend the factors influencing e-zwich adoption by integrating the TAM and the prospect model. TAM's constructs focus chiefly on technology adoption enablers and do not account sufficiently for deterrents or inhibitors of technology adoption. By combining the TAM and the prospect model, the new model brings a risk or deterrent perspective to e-zwich adoption.

This chapter may serve as a useful reference source for both undergraduate and postgraduate students pursuing degree programs in Information Systems. This chapter highlights the factors that influence the adoption of a Fintech innovation in Ghana. Findings from this chapter may form the bedrock on discussions on Fintech adoption in developing economies.

Practical Implications

The findings of this research also present some practical implications. The findings point to the significance of PEOU and PU to behavioral intention. Based on the research findings, the following suggestions can be adduced for practitioners in the Fintech sector:

- It is suggested that practitioners consider issues related to ensuring the easiness of using the e-zwich services. Thus, usage of the system should be free of effort (Davis, 1989). According to the Interaction Design Foundation (2021), users must be able to tap to find within three seconds of accessing the system's interface to ensure ease of use. Also, users should find the system so familiar that they are intuitive. It is thus best to start with user research to understand users and the contexts in which they will encounter and use the system.
- Another issue worth considering is the significant role of users' perception of the system being useful to their intention to use it. This refers to the perception that the system will enhance the performance of a task. Zalla (2014) asserts that perception is a key to interpreting and understanding products and services. The author also posits that the most critical issue to consider in system design is user perception that the system will be useful to them. In this regard, practitioners in the Fintech sector must ensure that the various features of the innovations, including uses, are well marketed to users. As discovered in this chapter, users' PU influences behavioral intention to adopt e-zwich services. E-zwich service providers must highlight the usefulness and gains that accompany e-zwich innovation and ensure consistent service redesign to drive adoption and use.
- The chapter points to the significant importance of perceived risk and service trust to behavioral intention. With this in light, e-zwich service providers must continuously ensure that the service provided is trustworthy devoid of negative service trust issues to drive the adoption and use of e-zwich services in Ghana.

Policy Implications

The chapter's implication to policy governing Fintech adoption and implementation within the developing economy context is worth noting. Fintech thrives on effective regulations and laws. Policymakers in Ghana, for instance, have enacted various Acts to protect and regulate the Fintech industry. The Payment Systems and Services Act of 2019 (Act 987) of Ghana provides the basic legal regulatory framework for Fintech firms. Others include the Anti-Money Laundering Act of 2008 (Act 749), the Data Protection Act of 2012 (Act 843), and the Electronic Transactions Act of 2008 (Act 772) (The International Comparative Legal Guides, 2020). These acts and legal frameworks are expected to govern Fintech adoption and implementation. It is, therefore, recommended that policymakers in other developing economies replicate this in their jurisdictions.

Future Research and Practice Directions

First, this research adopted a convenience sampling method of data collection (nonprobabilistic approach). This approach may not necessarily capture the populations' view. Future research could investigate e-zwich adoption with a probabilistic data sampling approach. Second, the chapter was conducted with data collected in Ghana. It is unknown how well the model and its results may apply to other developing and developed country contexts due to social peculiarities. As a result, future research can apply the model to other developed and developing countries to improve the findings' generalizability.

The chapter's practical implications have already been discussed, but the following suggestions for practitioners within the Fintech sector are worth noting.

- The first crucial issue in the Fintech sector is effective planning, where all the ideas about the given system are to be collected to provide detailed information for developers. Effective planning helps provide an early insight into the current trends, the target market, and competitors. Again, planning will allow practitioners to become familiar with regulatory and legal requirements for operating within the sector. In this vein, it is recommended that practitioners effectively plan for projects within the Fintech sector to achieve the needed results and outcomes.
- The second most important issue worth noting is paying attention to users' PU, PEOU, perceived risks, and service trust in Fintech implementation. These issues are very critical for the success of Fintech, especially from the developing economy perspective.

References

Abubakar, Y. A., Hand, C., Smallbone, D., & Saridakis, G. (2019). What Specific Modes of Internationalization Influence SME Innovation in Sub-Saharan Least Developed Countries (LDCs)? *Technovation, 79*, 56–70.

Alambaigi, A., & Ahangari, I. (2016). Technology Acceptance Model (TAM) as a Predictor Model for Explaining Agricultural Experts' Behavior in Acceptance of ICT. *International Journal of Agricultural Management and Development, 6*(2), 235–247.

Baganzi, R., & Lau, A. (2017). Examining Trust and Risk in Mobile Money Acceptance in Uganda. *Sustainability, 9*(12), 22–33. https://doi.org/10.3390/su9122233

Bagozzi, R. P., & Yi, Y. (2012). Specification, Evaluation, and Interpretation of Structural Equation Models. *Journal of the Academy of Marketing Science, 40*(1), 8–34.

Batista, C., & Vicente, P. C. (2020). Improving Access to Savings through Mobile Money: Experimental Evidence from African Smallholder Farmers. *World Development, 129*. Article 104905. https://doi.org/10.1016/j.worlddev.2020.104905

Breckenridge, K. (2010). The World's First Biometric Money: Ghana's E-Zwich and the Contemporary Influence of South African Biometrics. *Africa, 80*(4), 642–662.

Chauhan, S. (2015). Acceptance of Mobile Money by Poor Citizens of India: Integrating Trust into the Technology Acceptance Model. *Info, 17*(3), 58–68.

Chen, M. A., Wu, Q., & Yang, B. (2019). How Valuable is FinTech Innovation? *The Review of Financial Studies, 32*(5), 2062–2106.

Chin, W. W., Marcolin, B., & Newsted, P. (2003). A Partial Least Squares Latent Variable Modeling Approach for Measuring Interaction Effects: Results from a Monte Carlo Simulation Study and an Electronic-Mail Emotion/Adoption Study. *Information Systems Research, 14*(2), 189–217.

Chopdar, P. K., Korfiatis, N., Sivakumar, V. J., & Lytras, M. D. (2018). Mobile Shopping Apps Adoption and Perceived Risks: A Cross-Country Perspective Utilizing the Unified Theory of Acceptance and Use of Technology. *Computers in Human Behavior, 86*, 109–128.

Coeckelbergh, M., & Reijers, W. (2015). Cryptocurrencies as Narrative Technologies. *ACM SIGCAS Computers and Society, 45*(3), 172–178.

Coffie, C. P. K., Hongjiang, Z., Mensah, I. A., Kiconco, R., & Simon, A. E. O. (2020). Determinants of FinTech Payment Services Diffusion by SMEs in Sub-Saharan Africa: Evidence from Ghana. *Information Technology for Development*, 1–22.

Davis, F. D. (1989). Perceived Usefulness, Perceived Ease of Use, and User Acceptance of Information Technology. *MIS Quarterly, 13*(3), 319–340.

De Filippi, P. (2014). Bitcoin: A Regulatory Nightmare to a Libertarian Dream. *Internet Policy Review, 3*(2), 1–11.

Dillon, A., & Morris, M. G. (1996). User Acceptance of Information Technology: Theories and Models. *Annual Review of Information Science and Technology (ARIST), 31*, 3–32.

Donovan, K. (2012). Mobile Money for Financial Inclusion. In *Information and Communications for Development* (pp. 61–73). https://doi.org/10.1596/978-0-8213-8991-1

Dwyer, G. P. (2015, April). The Economics of Bitcoin and Similar Private Digital Currencies. *Journal of Financial Stability, 17*, 81–91.

Fanta, A. B., Mutsonziwa, K., Goosen, R., Emanuel, M., & Kettles, N. (2016). *The Role of Mobile Money in Financial Inclusion in the SADC Region*. FinMark Trust Policy Research Papers (03|3). https://wp-content/uploads/2017/03/mobilemoney-and-financial-inclusion-in-sadc.pdf

Fichman, R. (2004). Going Beyond the Dominant Paradigm for Information Technology Innovation Research: Emerging Concepts and Methods. *Journal of Association of Information Systems, 5*(8), 314–355. https://doi.org/10.17705/1jais.00054

Gai, K., Qiu, M., & Sun, X. (2018, February). A Survey on FinTech. *Journal of Network and Computer Applications, 103*, 262–273.

Gangwar, H., Date, H., & Ramaswamy, R. (2015). Understanding Determinants of Cloud Computing Adoption Using an Integrated TAM-TOE Model. *Journal of Enterprise Information Management, 28*(1), 107–130.

Gefen, D., Karahanna, E., & Straub, D. (2003). Trust and TAM in Online Shopping: An Integrated Model. *MIS Quarterly, 27*(1), 51–90.

Grohmann, A., Klühs, T., & Menkhoff, L. (2018, November). Does financial Literacy Improve Financial Inclusion? Cross-Country Evidence. *World Development, 111*, 84–96.

Hair, J. F., Black, W. C., Babin, B. J., & Anderson, R. E. (2010). *Multivariate Data Analysis* (7th ed.). Singapore: Pearson Education Ltd.

Hair, J. F., Ringle, C. M., & Sarstedt, M. (2011). PLS-SEM: Indeed, a Silver Bullet. *Journal of Marketing Theory and Practice, 19*(2), 139–152. https://doi.org/10.2753/mtp1069-6679190202

Hoyle, R. H., & Panter, A. T. (1995). Writing about Structural Equation Models. In *Structural Equation Modeling: Concepts, Issues, and Applications*. Thousand Oaks, CA: Sage Publications.

Interaction Design Foundation. (2021). *Ease of Use*. Retrieved April 6, 2021, from www.interaction-design.org/literature/topics/ease-of-use

Jiang, G., & Deng, W. (2011). An Empirical Analysis of Factors Influencing the Adoption of Mobile Instant Messaging in China. *International Journal of Mobile Communications*, 9(6), 563–583.

Johnson, K. A., & Walton, A. J. (2018). Exploring Perceptions of Bitcoin Adoption: The South African Virtual Community Perspective. *Interdisciplinary Journal of Information*, 13, 165–182.

Kahneman, D., & Tversky, A. (1979). Prospect Theory: An Analysis of Decision Under Risk. *Econometrica*, 47, 263–291.

Kamal, S. A., Shafiq, M., & Kakria, P. (2020, February). Investigating Acceptance of Telemedicine Services through an Extended Technology Acceptance Model (TAM). *Technology in Society*, 60, 101212. https://doi.org/10.1016/j.techsoc.2019.101212

Kelly, J. (2020). *Fintech*. Retrieved April 6, 2021, from www.addisonbrightsloane.com/articles/fintech-2020/

KPMG. (2019). *Pulse of Fintech H1'19- Global Trends*. Retrieved March 10, 2021, from https://home.kpmg/xx/en/home/campaigns/2019/07/pulse-of-fintech-h1-19-global-trends.html

Kshetri, N. (2017). Will Blockchain Emerge as a Tool to Break the Poverty Chain in the Global South. *Third World Quarterly*, 38(8), 1710–1732.

Li, Z., & Shimizu, A. (2018). Impact of Online Customer Reviews on Sales Outcomes: An Empirical Study Based on Prospect Theory. *The Review of Socionetwork Strategies*, 12(2), 135–151.

Liébana-Cabanillas, F., Molinillo, S., & Ruiz-Montañez, M. (2019, February). To Use or not to Use, that is the Question: Analysis of the Determining Factors for Using NFC Mobile Payment Systems in Public Transportation. *Technological Forecasting and Social Change*, 139, 266–276.

Liu, C., & Forsythe, S. (2010). Sustaining Online Shopping: Moderating Role of Online Shopping Motives. *Journal of Internet Commerce*, 9(2), 83–103.

Lyytinen, K., & Rose, G. (2003). The Disruptive Nature of Information Technology Innovations: The Case of Internet Computing in Systems Development Organizations. *MIS Quarterly*, 27(4), 557–595.

Makina, D. (2019). The Potential of FinTech in Enabling Financial Inclusion. In *Extending Financial Inclusion in Africa* (pp. 299–318). Academic Press. https://doi.org/10.1016/B978-0-12-814164-9.00014-1

Manuel, P. (2015). A Trust Model of Cloud Computing Based on Quality of Service. *Annals of Operations Research*, 233(1), 281–292.

Mathieson, K. (1991). Predicting User Intentions: Comparing the Technology Acceptance Model with the Theory of Planned Behavior. *Information Systems Research*, 2(3), 173–191.

Mawuli, A. J. (2020). *Fintech in Ghana: Financial Inclusion and the Drive towards a Cashless Economy*. Retrieved April 6, 2021, from www.jbklutse.com/fintech-in-ghana/

Miraz, M. H., & Ali, M. (2018). Applications of Blockchain Technology Beyond Cryptocurrency. *Annals of Emerging Technologies in Computing*, 2(1), 1–6.

Munyegera, G. K., & Matsumoto, T. (2016, March). Mobile Money, Remittances, and Household Welfare: Panel Evidence from Rural Uganda. *World Development*, 79, 127–137. https://doi.org/10.1016/j.worlddev.2015.11.006

Nardi, P. M. (2018). *Doing Survey Research: A Guide to Quantitative Methods*. Oxfordshire, England: Routledge.

Narteh, B., Mahmoud, M. A., & Amoh, S. (2017). Customer Behavioral Intentions Towards Mobile Money Services Adoption in Ghana. *The Service Industries Journal*, 37(7–8), 426–447.

Osei-Assibey, E. (2015). What Drives Behavioral Intention of Mobile Money Adoption? The Case of Ancient Susu Saving Operations in Ghana. *Economics*, 42(11), 962–979.

Padashetty, S., & Krishna, S. V. (2013). An Empirical Study on Consumer Adoption of Mobile Payments in Bangalore City: A Case Study. *International Journal of Arts, Science & Commerce*, 4(1), 54–57.

Pavlou, P. A. (2003). Consumer Acceptance of Electronic Commerce: Integrating Trust and Risk with the Technology Acceptance Model. *International Journal of Electronic Commerce*, 7(3), 69–103.

Podsakoff, P. M., MacKenzie, S. B., Lee, J. Y., & Podsakoff, N. P. (2003). Common Method Biases in Behavioral Research: A Critical Review of the Literature and Recommended Remedies. *Journal of Applied Psychology*, 88(5), 879–903. http://doi:10.1037/0021-9010.88.5.879

Polasik, M., Piotrowska, A. I., Wisniewski, T. P., Kotkowski, R., & Lightfoot, G. (2015). Price Fluctuations and the Use of Bitcoin: An Empirical Inquiry. *International Journal of Electronic Commerce*, 20(1), 9–49.

Rafique, H., Almagrabi, A. O., Shamim, A., Anwar, F., & Bashir, A. K. (2020). Investigating the Acceptance of Mobile Library Applications with an Extended Technology Acceptance Model (TAM). *Computers & Education*, 145, 103732.

Rahman, M. M., Lesch, M. F., Horrey, W. J., & Strawderman, L. (2017 November). Assessing the Utility of TAM, TPB, and UTAUT for Advanced Driver Assistance Systems. *Accident Analysis & Prevention*, 108, 361–373.

Rogers, E. M. (1995). *Diffusion of Innovations* (4th ed.). New York: Free Press.

Senyo, P. K., & Osabutey, E. L. (2020, December). Unearthing Antecedents to Financial Inclusion through FinTech Innovations. *Technovation*, 98, 102155.

Sharma, S. K., Al-Badi, A., Govindaluri, S., & Al-Kharusi, M. (2016). Predicting Motivators of Cloud Computing Adoption: A Developing Country Perspective. *Computers in Human Behavior*, 62, 61–69. https://doi.org/10.1016/j.chb.2016.03.073

The International Comparative Legal Guides. (2020). *Ghana: Fintech Laws and Regulations*. London: Global Legal Group. https://iclg.com/practice-areas/fintech-laws-and-regulations/ghana

Tobbin, P., & Kuwornu, J. K. (2011). Adoption of Mobile Money Transfer Technology: Structural Equation Modeling Approach. *European Journal of Business and Management*, 3(7), 59–77.

Tversky, A., & Kahneman, D. (1986). Rational Choice and the Framing of Decisions. *Journal of Business*, 59(4), 251–275.

Upadhyay, P., & Jahanyan, S. (2016). Analyzing User Perspective on the Factors Affecting Use Intention of Mobile-Based Transfer Payment. *Internet Research*, 26(1), 38–56.

Walton, J. (2014). Cryptocurrency Public Policy Analysis. *SSRN Electronic Journal*. https://papers.ssrn.com/sol3/papers.cfm?abstract_id=2708302

Wei, G., Xinyan, Z., & Yue, M. (2011, May). Notice of Retraction: A Literature Review on Consumer Adoption Behavior of Mobile Commerce Services. *2011 International Conference on E-Business and E-Government (ICEE)*, IEEE, Shanghai, China, 6–8 May 2011. New York: IEEE Computer Society, 1–5.

World Bank. (2020). Fintech Market Reports Rapid Growth During COVID-19 Pandemic. *Press Release*. www.worldbank.org/en/news/pressrelease/2020/12/03/fintech-market-reports-rapid-growth-during-covid-19-pandemic

Wu, J. H., & Wang, S. C. (2005). What Drives Mobile Commerce? *Information & Management*, 42(5), 719–729.

Xiao, F. (2020, November). Evidence Combination Based on Prospect Theory for Multi-Sensor Data Fusion. *ISA Transactions*, 106, 253–261.

Yermack, D. (2018). FinTech in Sub-Saharan Africa: What has Worked Well, and What has not (No. w25007). *National Bureau of Economic Research*. https://doi: 10.3386/w25007

Yoon, H. (2016). User Acceptance of Mobile Library Applications in Academic Libraries: An Application of the Technology Acceptance Model. *The Journal of Academic Librarianship*, 42(6), 687–693. https://doi.org/10.1016/j.acalib.2016.08.003

Zalla, M. (2014). *Five Fundamentals of Great Design: Perception*. Retrieved April 6, 2021, from https://landor.com/five-fundamentals-of-great-design-perception

Zhou, T. (2011). An Empirical Examination of Users' Post-Adoption Behavior of Mobile Services. *Behaviour & Information Technology*, 30(2), 241–225.

Authors' Profile

Frederick Pobee is currently a PhD candidate in Business Administration in the Faculty of Business and Economics, University of Pécs, Hungary. He obtained his Master of Philosophy (MPhil) in Management Information Systems from the University of Ghana, Legon. His research interests include digital innovation, e-commerce adoption, e-learning, innovation-based entrepreneurship, and financial inclusion. Frederick Pobee can be contacted at pobee.fred@gmail.com.

Eric Ansong is a senior lecturer in Information Systems at Wisconsin International University College, Ghana. He holds a PhD in information systems. His research interests cover the Digital

Economy, Digital business strategy, technology-mediated teaching and learning, and Design science. He has published many research articles in peer-reviewed academic journals and books and has presented papers in international conferences that include the Hawaii International Conference on System Sciences (HICSS). He can be reached via eric.ansong@wiuc-ghana.edu.gh. His ORCID ID is http://orcid.org/0000-0002-0262-3485.

DEVELOPING RESILIENT ECONOMIES AND INSTITUTIONS

IV

Chapter 11

A Scientific Decision-Making Framework to Aid the Selection of Leadership Styles for Project Success

Saviour Ayertey Nubuor and Kwasi Dartey-Baah

Contents

DOI: 10.4324/9781003152217-15

Introduction

There have been several instances of construction project failures in Ghana as a result of poor or ineffective leadership style deployment. Ofori and Toor (2012) observed that leadership is "the missing ingredient in the recipe for industry development". They added that the nature or environment of the construction industry particularly in developing countries makes the need for appropriate leadership more essential.

Similarly, projects can only be viewed as successful if the project goals are achieved and the needs of stakeholders are adequately satisfied. Past research on leadership have demonstrated that it is questionable whether the skill of the project team is fully utilized by the project manager/ leader. So, the question is, which style of leadership is appropriate and likely to ensure construction project success in Ghana? How do we select the leadership styles among the numerous styles available? Owing to the fact that there are conflicting opinions and judgments on the appropriate leadership style for project success, it is expedient to adopt a more robust and acceptable decision-making model to select the leadership style. This reinforces the use of MCDM-AHP.

The analytic hierarchy process is applicable in decision-making processes across disciplines according to Liu and Hai (2005). AHP is capable of structuring complex decision-making hierarchically particularly in situations where there are conflicting opinions and judgments on an issue. In essence, the AHP is used in this chapter to select the leadership style because of the following reasons: (1) Once the AHP is introduced and used as the method for decision-making, the results are in a general sense accepted. This is because the method is based on mathematics and seen as objective and reliable even though it has some limitations. (2) AHP is ideal to get a consolidated result for inputs from several diverse respondents using the geometric mean. (3) It helps in hierarchical structuring of decision problems which aids in easy understanding of the decision process. (4) There is a possibility of combining multiple inputs from several respondents to a consolidated outcome (Liu and Hai, 2005). However, despite the aforementioned advantages in the usage of AHP, people are used to ranking or stating their agreement and disagreement on decision problems rather than pair-wise comparison in arriving at decisions in Ghana.

The structure of this chapter is arranged as follows: the background from a theoretical perspective is elucidated after the introduction. Next is the AHP process for leadership which includes the results and analysis. Afterward, the main findings, contributions, and implications for practitioners and limitations of the study are elaborated.

Literature Review and Theoretical Perspectives

MCDM-AHP Decision Theory

Decision-making (DM) is an action that explores a solution fulfilling the constraints of a problem among several alternatives. It has been the subject of active research in many different fields and studied from several points of view. DM might be seen as a problem-solving activity which is terminated when a satisfactory solution is found. Thus, DM can be viewed as a reasoning or emotional process which can be objective or subjective, based on explicit or tacit assumptions (Uehara et al., 2011).

A classical DM focuses on some key elements like (1) a set of alternatives or available decisions, a set of states of nature that defines the framework of the problem; (2) a set of utility values, each one associated with a pair which is composed of an alternative and a state of nature; and (3) a function that establishes the expert's preferences regarding the plausible results (Uehara et al., 2011).

The classical decision-solving process entails; the identification of the decision and objective, identification of alternatives, development of the model structure, uncertainties and preferences, gathering of information, rating of the alternatives, choosing the best alternatives, sensitivity analysis if needed, and the making of a decision (Uehara et al., 2011). Where a single individual decides on a complex problem, there might be quite a number of errors that will be associated with that decision. A number of people deciding on a complex problem will produce a better result than a single person. There is a need to decide to maximize value based on the number of criteria or attributes that are available.

Most well-known and fastest growing branches of DM since the 1980s is Multi-criteria Decision-Making (MCDM). This is because DM has changed over the years from one decision-maker and one goal to several decision-makers with several goals. In the early part of the 1980s, MCDM models are used on computers with the help of decision support systems. Current studies, however, focus more on finding good instead of completely optimal solutions to problems (Dyer et al., 1992).

MCDM opined that the decision-maker is required to make a choice within a number of options called alternatives or criteria. These alternatives or criteria are believed to have objective functions which are known (Dyer et al., 1992). There are two main streams of MCDM. These are Multi-Objective Decision-Making (MODM) and Multiattribute/Multicriteria Decision-Making (MADM/MCDM). MODM is used where solution spaces are continuous and problems must satisfy one or more conflicting objectives usually through mathematical programming. On the other hand, MADM/MCDM is applicable where there are discrete solution spaces and the finite number of alternatives requiring the use of ranking procedures. MCDM is used in this chapter because it is much more relevant and is frequently used in practice than MODM. Also, it has become an important part of DM theories and within the scope of management science.

There are a number of methods used within MCDM analysis. Some include Analytical Hierarchical Process (AHP), Analytical Network Process (ANP), Multi-Attribute Utility Theory (MAUT), Technique of Order Preference Similarity to Ideal Solution (TOPSIS), Preference Ranking Organization Method for Enriched Evaluation, Elimination and Choice Expressing Reality, Data Envelopment Analysis, Measuring Attractiveness by a Categorical Based Evaluation Technique (Kumar et al., 2017), among others. The method to be used depends largely on the problem, that is, whether it is a choice, ranking, sorting, or description problems.

The general procedure for the use of MCDM analysis entails, defining a system with objectives to be met, finding all the criteria affecting the system based on the objectives, seeking alternative systems to meet the need of objectives, setting priorities or weights to the alternatives, selecting the MCDM method for the purpose, and then finally finding and presenting an optimal alternative for evaluation (Kumar et al., 2017). This procedure is depicted in Figure 11.1

Among all the methods, AHP has been used in this study to select the leadership styles. AHP is "a theory of measurement through pairwise comparisons and relies on the judgments of experts to derive priority scales" (Saaty, 2008). AHP is used because the respondents understand its use and applicability. Second, the selection of leadership style is a ranking problem, and third, the use of other methods which the respondents are not familiar will be problematic. These and many other reasons underpin the use of AHP in this research. Also, AHP incorporates mathematics and psychology in coming out with a good decision. In AHP, the concept of Eigenvalue is applied.

AHP is developed by Saaty (2008) and used when the decision-maker is unable to build a utility function. There are four main phases for ranking the alternatives in AHP. These are structuring

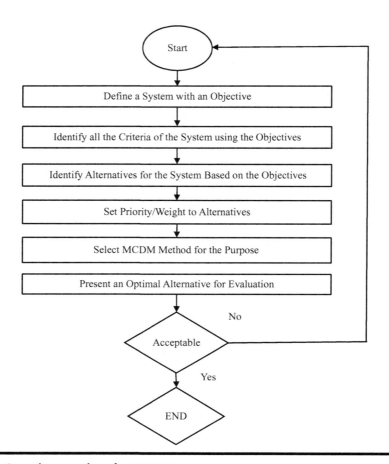

Figure 11.1 Generic procedure for MCDM.

Source: Kumar et al. (2017).

of the MCDM problem, computation of the scores/priorities based on pairwise comparisons, checking of consistency, and finally doing a sensitivity analysis. The main processes used in AHP are shown in Figure 11.2.

MCDM methods, particularly AHP, have been used in different areas such as management science, operations management, resource management, and others. For example, AHP was used to help the selection of houses for buyers, examine the attributes of the location of houses, housing investments, land suitability for residential housing construction, and the selection of various policies to aid DM (Kumar et al., 2017). Zendeh et al. (2011) used AHP to select appropriate leadership styles in their research. Therefore, MCDM-AHP is suitable and has been used to select the leadership styles in this study.

The Concept of Leadership

Some philosophers argue that leaders are born (Great Man Theory: 1840s), to some, leaders have unique traits (Traits Theory: 1930s-1940s), to the point that others think anyone can be

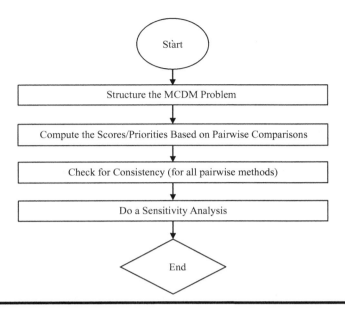

Figure 11.2   Basic procedure for AHP.

Source: Kumar et al. (2017).

made a leader (Behavioral Theories: 1940s–1950s), or based on a situation, a leader can emerge (Contingency Theories: 1960s). Leadership is an enigma, one may not be able to clearly define it, but there is no doubt that when it exists one will see it. One of the greatest challenges is the exhibition of appropriate leadership in the industry, academia, economic, and political settings.

Owing to the fact that leadership is an enigma, many scholars and writers have used different classification systems to explain the dimensions of it (Fleishman et al., 1991). From Western history, we have authors like Plato, Machiavelli, Hobbes, Locke, among others (Collinson, 1998), and in the history of the East, we have Confucius as well as Xunxi (Collinson et al., 2000).

Essentially, leadership is the ability to influence people toward the attainment of organizational goals. Leadership is reciprocal, occurring among people. Leadership is dynamic and involves the use of power to achieve or get things done (Yukl, 1989). Leadership is essential because the success or failure of an organization depends on it. There is probably no topic more important to business success today than leadership (Burns, 1978; Senge, 1990).

Other scholars conceptualize leadership as the focus of group processes where the leader is the fulcrum of change, and the will of the group is taken into consideration. Some conceptualize leadership from the view of personality perspectives where the leader is seen to have certain traits that help them to influence others. Also, some authors describe leadership in terms of power relationship, transformational processes, and from skills perspective (Bass, 1990a, 1990b). This study made use of the leadership conceptualization from the transformational, group processes, personality, and power relationship perspectives.

Some leadership behaviors that have been identified as important for effective leadership in a variety of situations are task-oriented behavior (transactional leadership), people-oriented behavior (transformational leadership), and ethically oriented behavior (ethical leadership) among others. Every organization has human resources as one of the most important resources for achieving the organizational objectives; however, the realization of these objectives hinge on the exhibition of appropriate behaviors by the leader. In other words, within this pool of human resources, leadership is crucial to make the best out of every situation. These leaders have unique features such as intelligence, physical stamina, self-confidence, integrity, sociability, tenacity, diplomacy, and tact, desire to achieve among others which are worth studying (Bass, 1990b).

Leadership Styles

Leadership style depends largely on the context or the situation in which the leader finds him/herself. Some of the most popular and comprehensive leadership styles are obtained from the full-range leadership theory developed by Avolio and Bass (2004). To them, full-range leadership is made up of three second-order constructs, namely, transformational, transactional, and laissez-faire. The authors argued that transformational and transactional leadership are separate concepts which have different dimensions even though Burns (1995) sees transformational and transactional leadership to be opposite constructs. Laissez-faire is viewed as nonleadership in the sense that it allows the followers to act on their own without a proactive direction from the leader. Owing to the nature of the laissez-faire style, it is argued that it is embedded in management by exception passive dimension of transactional leadership (Avolio & Bass, 2004).

Other researchers have posited that transformational and transactional leadership styles are the most widely known constructs of the full-range leadership theory which have effects on organizational outcomes (McColl-Kennedy & Anderson, 2002).

The Concept of Project Success

Project success has been described differently by various researchers. This is because the word success is a word that is so general and wide in nature that it is difficult to define and obtain mutual agreement. Jugdev and Müller (2005) in their article mentioned that defining what success means in a project context is like gaining consensus from a group of people on the definition of a "good art". Generally, the views on project success have evolved over the years from simple definitions that were limited to the implementation phase of the project life cycle to definitions that reflect an appreciation of success over the entire project and product life cycle to include value creation to the stakeholders (Jugdev & Müller, 2005).

According to Lim and Mohammed (1999), two distinctions must be considered before answering what constitutes project success. The first distinction is the difference that exists between project success and project management success. Project success is measured against the overall project's objective, whereas project management success is measured by the traditional measures of time, cost, and performance. The second distinction is the difference between project success criteria and project success factors. While project success criteria are the measures by which the project is evaluated to determine its failure or success (Lim & Mohammed, 1999; Terry, 2002), project success factors are the inputs to the management system that lead to the success of the project either directly or indirectly (Terry, 2002).

Construction Projects, Leadership, and Project Success

In 2016, the contribution of the construction industry to gross domestic product in Ghana was 13.7% (Ghana Statistical Service, 2017). Further, it employed 2% of the youth in the country (Darko and Lowe, 2016). Ofori and Toor (2012) have observed that leadership is the missing component in the strive for construction industry development. Ofori (2015) added that the nature or environment of the construction sector, particularly in developing countries, creates a need and makes it essential for understanding the role of leadership. Studies have shown that outcome of any project is linked to the leadership style of the project leader (Dumdum et al., 2002; Dvir et al., 2002).

Thus, if appropriate attention is given to the leadership challenges bedeviling the construction industry among others in emerging economies, it could largely contribute to sustainable development. Although project success has been described differently by various researchers, completion of project on time, cost, quality, and meeting stakeholder expectations are used as a measure of project success in this study.

Data Collection Methods

The study was undertaken using some companies in the construction industry of Ghana (for example, X-cell construction, KLOGG Ghana Limited, and Pakons Construction) to ascertain what leadership styles are prevalent and what constitute project success. The study made use of a Multi-Criteria Decision Making Analytic Hierarchical Process (MCDM-AHP) using the Saaty scale, an in-depth interview, and focus group discussions with purposively sampled experts in the field to select the leadership style that is appropriate for project success. The interview was conducted using three construction project management experts, the AHP used 21 project management professionals, and the focus group discussion was done among the construction project team members together with relevant project stakeholders. The discussion focused on what constitutes project success, whether project management methodologies are employed in their company and the type of leadership styles that they think their leaders exhibit and which of the leadership styles they prefer.

AHP Model Development for Leadership Style Selection Process

The objective of the study is to develop an AHP model to select two main leadership styles among the numerous styles used in project management within the construction industry of Ghana. In compliance with the qualitative and quantitative data collection for AHP after the pattern of Saaty (2008), the following steps have been followed.

Step 1: Define the Objective or Goal

The goal of this study is to choose two main leadership styles that influence project success.

Step 2: Define the Elements in Criteria, Sub-Criteria, and Alternatives

A semi-structured in-depth interview was conducted with three project management professionals from X-cell construction, KLOGG Ghana Limited, and Pakons Construction. These respondents are represented on Table 11.1 as respondent 1 (R1), respondents 2 (R2), and respondent 3 (R3) to evaluate the criteria for choosing leadership styles for project management and project success. The respondents were asked to add any other criterion that they felt was useful in addition to the "Iron

Table 11.1 Criteria and Alternative Selection

	R1	R2	R3	Average									
Criteria				1	2	3	4	5	6	7	8	9	
Budget	9	7	8										8.0
Time	8	7	7										7.3
Scope	9	9	7										8.3
Team	7	7	5										6.3
Project type	8	6	4										6.0
Alternatives													
TFL	9	8	9										8.7
TSL	9	7	8										8.0
EL	7	8	6										7.0

Triangle" criteria. The selection of the five (5) criteria was based on their importance and ability to meet the objective of the study. To avoid too many complex criteria that would make the pairwise comparison difficult and to avoid unnecessary delays in this cross-sectional research, five (5) of the criteria were selected (see Table 11.1). The respondents were asked to rate the criteria using the famous ratio scale developed by Saaty (2008).

Also, the small size criteria selection was in conformity with what Tam and Tummala (2001) recommended for the selection of criteria in AHP. After the results from the respondents were evaluated, the criteria were identified and averaged. Based on the popular iron triangle measure of project success in literature and a ranking above 7 using the Saaty (2008) AHP scale, three main criteria were selected. These were budget, time, and scope. These criteria were clear and self-explanatory; thus, no sub-criteria were used. Following the same procedure used in the selection of the criteria, three leadership styles were selected. These were transformational (TFL), transactional (TSL) and ethical leadership (EL) styles. The explanation of the criteria and alternatives are given in Table 11.2.

Step 3: Develop the AHP Model

Based on step 2, the Analytic Hierarchy Model is shown in Figure 11.3. The model contained three criteria and three alternatives in a three-level hierarchy, starting with the goal, criteria, and alternatives.

The criteria had been identified and a pairwise comparison was made. The comparison was made two at a time using the three criteria in the second level of the hierarchy. This was followed by the pairwise comparison at the third level to show how important they were with reference to the goal (see Table 11.3).

Table 11.2   Explanation of Criteria and Alternatives

Criteria	ID	Explanation
Budget	B	The sum of money required to complete the project. It is used to measure the leadership style's ability to complete a project on budget
Time	T	The total duration of the project. It is used as a criterion to measure the leadership style's ability to complete the project on schedule
Scope	S	The overall requirements of a project. In this study, meeting of stakeholders' requirement is part of the scope. The leadership style adopted can influence the meeting of project scope
Alternatives		An element is strongly favored, and its dominance is demonstrated in practice
Transformational Leadership	TFL	People oriented style of leadership
Transactional Leadership	TSL	Task oriented style of leadership
Ethical Leadership	ETL	Leadership influenced by respect for ethical beliefs and values

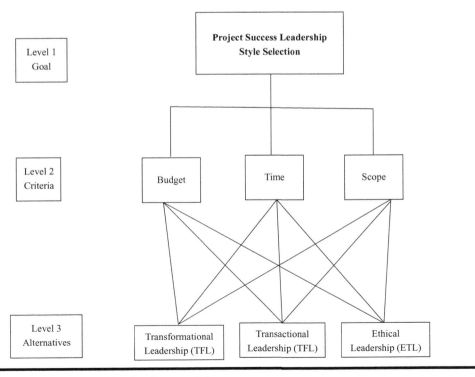

Figure 11.3   AHP leadership selection model.

Table 11.3   Decision Hierarchy with Consolidated Priorities

Goal	Level 1 Criteria	Glb Prio.	Transformational Leadership	Transactional Leadership	Ethical Leadership
Leadership Style Selection	Budget 0.498	49.8%	0.570	0.267	0.163
	Time 0.355	35.5%	0.609	0.262	0.129
	Scope 0.147	14.7%	0.589	0.277	0.134
		1.0	59.0%	26.8%	14.2%

From Table 11.3, the respondents gave 0.498 (49.8%) preference to budget, 35.5% to time, and 14.7% to scope. The local weights under level 1 were based on normalized pairwise comparison, and the global weights were obtained from the local weights. All normalization calculations had been done by the Business Performance Management Singapore (BPMSG) software. It could be deduced that the experts saw completing a project on budget as the first criteria in selecting the leadership style; this was followed by time and scope. It was worth noting that many of the projects in Ghana were not completed on budget, and this informed why the experts selected budget as the top priority. It must be emphasized here that these results were consistent since the software used calculated the consistency index (CI) and then suggested necessary modifications that were made during the CI checks.

Step 4: Make a Pairwise Comparison of Each Group

As required, the priority weight of each criterion was determined by using an AHP survey approach. The survey consisted of all the elements in each of the levels of the formulated AHP model. The survey was administered via the Internet with the aid of bpmsg.com (a web-based AHP solution developed by Klaus D. Goepel). The web links for the criteria and alternatives generated by BPMSG were emailed to all the respondents to gather the pairwise comparison judgments. The pairwise comparison was to determine the relative weight of each criterion and alternative using the nine-point scale developed by Saaty (1980).

According to Dalalah (2011), the geometric mean of all matrices is relevant to form the geometric mean matrix. In as much as the arithmetic mean could be used, this study made use of the geometric mean since a ratio scale was used in the study by Aragon et al. (2012). AHP has been used in diverse DM problems, and the calculations are as follows:

$$A = \left(a_{ij}\right) = \begin{bmatrix} a_{11} & a_{12} & \cdots & a_{1n} \\ a_{21} & a_{22} & \cdots & a_{2n} \\ \vdots & \vdots & \vdots & \vdots \\ a_{n1} & a_{n2} & \cdots & a_{nn} \end{bmatrix} = \begin{bmatrix} 1 & a_{12} & \cdots & a_{1n} \\ \dfrac{1}{a_{12}} & 1 & \cdots & a_{2n} \\ \vdots & \vdots & 1 & \vdots \\ \dfrac{1}{a_{1n}} & \dfrac{1}{a_{2n}} & \cdots & 1 \end{bmatrix} \tag{1}$$

$$G_{ij} = \left[\prod_{x-1}^{10} a x_{ij} \right]^{1/n} \quad \forall i, j \tag{2}$$

From this equation (1 and 2), a_{12} represents a_{12} element of first respondent matrix A in that order. This is followed by a synthesized matrix, which is shown in (3).

$$a_{ij} = \left(\frac{a_{ij}}{\text{sum of jth column}} \right) \tag{3}$$

Subsequently, $W = (w_1, w_2, w_3 \ldots w_n)$ is a weight of priority which are computed using Saaty's eigenvector procedure.

$$w_n = \left(\text{Sum of ith row} / n \right) \tag{4}$$

Saaty (2000) demonstrated the relationship between evaluation matrix A and weight vector. The relative weights are given by the right eigenvector (ω) corresponding to the largest eigenvalue (λ_{max}), as:

$$A\omega = \lambda_{max}\omega \tag{5}$$

From Saaty's postulations, if the pairwise comparisons are completely consistent, the matrix A will have rank 1 and $\lambda_{max} = n$. In this scenario, the weights are obtained by normalizing any of the rows or columns of A (Kumar & Dash, 2014). Undoubtedly, the quality, validation, and acceptance of the AHP result are in sync with the consistency of the pairwise comparison judgments (Saaty, 2008). There are many ways to validate the AHP procedure, but this study used the eigenvalue method to check the consistency of results. The consistency is defined by the relation between the entries of A: $a_{ij} \times a_{jk} = a_{ik}$ (Saaty, 2008; Kumar & Dash, 2014). To avoid inaccurate subjective judgments, the authors check the consistency to verify the rationality and logic of the matrix as cited by Dalalah et al. (2011). The CI is calculated, using equation (6):

$$CI = \left[\frac{\lambda_{max} - n}{n - 1} \right] \tag{6}$$

where λ_{max} represents the maximum variance of the matrix. The study made use of the average of all λ and assumes it as the maximum variance feasible and then calculates CI and CR and check the consistency. Using the consistency ratio (CR), the authors made judgments on whether the evaluations are sufficiently consistent. The CR is calculated as the ratio of the CI and the random index (RI) as indicated in Table 11.4 and equation (7).

According to Saaty (2008), the number 0.1 is the accepted upper limit for CR, and if the final CR exceeds this value, the evaluation procedure has to be repeated to improve the consistency.

$$CR = \left[\frac{CI}{RI} \right] \tag{7}$$

Table 11.4   Random Index

N	1	2	3	4	5	6	7	8	9	10
RI	0.00	0.00	0.58	0.90	1.12	1.24	1.32	1.41	1.45	1.45

Source: Saaty (2008).

Table 11.5   Consolidated Decision Matrix of Nodes

Consolidated Decision Matrix			
Budget	CR	0.009168	
	1	2.34719	3.1788
	0.426041	1	1.793742
	0.314584	0.557494	1
Time	CR	0.007941	
	1	2.538543	4.337547
	0.393927	1	2.219405
	0.230545	0.450571	1
Scope	CR	0.015821	
	1	2.409154	3.883972
	0.415083	1	2.331427
	0.257468	0.428922	1

Accordingly, Table 11.5 entails the consolidated decision matrix of the pairwise comparisons following the discussions in steps 1–4. The CR value for budget is 0.009168 and time is 0.0007941 while scope is 0.015821. This is an indication that all the CR scores are less than 0.1 and as such consistent and acceptable (see Table 11.6).

Step 5: Evaluate Alternatives According to the Weighting

After assigning values to all the elements of the criteria, a pairwise comparison was made by the respondents using the alternatives and the criteria. Table 11.5 shows the final scores of each alternative with regards to the criteria and the goal by the respondents. For the purposes of anonymity and confidentiality, the actual names of the respondents have been represented with R, where R stands for respondent. The CR for all the participants was within the acceptable range. Thus, it could be argued that generally the pairwise comparison was consistent, reliable, and acceptable (see Table 11.6).

Step 6: Get Rankings

From Table 11.7, the total score on the bottom of the table is the summation of all the respondents' global weights under the three criteria. So, by inference, transformational leadership ranked as the first alternative followed by transactional leadership and ethical leadership.

Table 11.6   Evaluation of Alternatives by Participants

Name	Transformational Leadership	Transactional Leadership	Ethical Leadership	CR max
Group	0.589535	0.268398	0.142067	0.015821
R1	0.503947	0.414944	0.081109	0.074430
R2	0.410416	0.273943	0.315641	0.055960
R3	0.671382	0.215694	0.112925	0.089538
R4	0.622673	0.291274	0.086054	0.005781
R5	0.705953	0.207837	0.08621	0.074430
R6	0.486943	0.238355	0.274702	0.019086
R7	0.665876	0.217394	0.116729	0.009615
R8	0.354078	0.316345	0.329577	0.055981
R9	0.70032	0.205807	0.093873	0.055971
R10	0.6315	0.265228	0.103272	0.089538
R11	0.617615	0.215352	0.167033	0.019126
R12	0.47149	0.189963	0.338546	0.019107
R13	0.640225	0.252276	0.107499	0.076728
R14	0.410416	0.273943	0.315641	0.055960
R15	0.39784	0.203872	0.398289	0.019088
R16	0.6315	0.265228	0.103272	0.089538
R17	0.677473	0.242974	0.079553	0.009619
R18	0.443238	0.427553	0.129208	0.019088
R19	0.493444	0.404785	0.10177	0.089455
R20	0.549939	0.209848	0.240213	0.019107
R21	0.698717	0.210895	0.090388	0.089538

Table 11.7   Criteria and Alternative Weights and Rankings

Crit/Alt	pGlb	Transformational Leadership	Transactional Leadership	Ethical Leadership
Budget	49.8%	0.570016	0.2667	0.163285
Time	35.5%	0.609344	0.261902	0.128755
Scope	14.7%	0.589244	0.276593	0.134162
Group Result		0.589535	0.268398	0.142067
Ranking		59.0%	26.8%	14.2%

Step 7: Identify the Leadership Style from the Ranking

In view of the global ranking, the summary of the relative weights was presented in Table 11.5. It could be deduced that among the alternatives, transformational leadership had the highest weight and ranking (59%). This was followed by transactional leadership (26.8%) and ethical leadership (14.2%). Transformational leadership style was the best alternative in terms of the budget, time, and scope criteria, thus, based on the goal, these two leadership styles (transformational and transactional leadership styles) were selected.

Sensitivity Analysis of Result

Sensitivity analysis was carried out to identify the effect of changes in the priority of criteria on the alternatives, that is, the leadership styles. It could be seen that the sensitivity analysis was robust with transformational leadership ranking high, followed by transactional leadership and ethical leadership (see Figure 11.4). A change from 60.9% by absolute −59.6% will change the ranking between transformational leadership and transactional leadership.

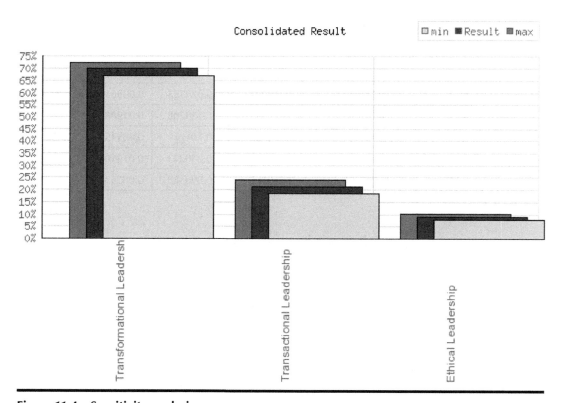

Figure 11.4 Sensitivity analysis.

Conclusion

The purpose of this chapter was to come out with a scientific DM model for project leaders, practitioners, and academics. The interviews and focus group discussions revealed the following: First, the leadership styles exhibited by leaders depend on the situation in which the leaders find themselves and the relationship that exists among the leadership and the project team members. Also, it is observed that the team members prefer a leader who gives clear objectives and care about them as team members.

On the other hand, some of the project managers interviewed focused on achieving project success by ensuring that the teamwork and achieving the targets set for the project led to transactional leadership. Second, it is discovered that there is inadequate knowledge on project management methodologies, particularly the application of best practices from project management institutes. Third, project success depended on meeting the budget, completing the project on time, the satisfaction of the clients, among others. Finally, others talked about the fact that weak leadership, political interference, corruption, and misappropriation of funds within the industry are the causes of project failure in Ghana, especially the failure of public-funded projects.

Further, it is empirically evident that the goal of the study and, for that matter, the AHP model have been achieved. The results obtained through AHP were valid and reliable. This is because the evaluation criteria align with the objective; the pairwise comparisons were obtained through informed judgments and consistency. This research presented the step-by-step procedure in identifying the significant criteria for the construction project management leadership style selection process. Hence, transformational and transactional leadership styles are seen as the ideal leadership styles for construction project success in an emerging economy, specifically Ghana.

Future Research and Practice Directions

It could be deduced from this chapter that project managers that exhibit the elements of transformational and transactional leadership styles based on the situation could influence the success of construction projects in an emerging economy. The AHP model used in this study simplifies the complex decision of selecting leadership styles among a number of options.

The proposed model can be applied to assist and enhance DM regarding leadership style selection and adoption for project success within the construction industry. The application can be done by following the objective criteria used in the study. The process can be replicated by practitioners to make informed decisions when faced with complex issues. Academics and practitioners can use this chapter to understand the different DM models available to them when making complex decisions. In addition, this chapter can be used by academics and practitioners to guide their investigations into multicriteria DM models.

It must be emphasized that although AHP is one of the well-known methods for multicriteria DM, it has its limitations. For example, pairwise comparison is difficult and time-consuming when there are too many criteria and alternatives. Also, the use requires the respondents to have substantial knowledge of pairwise comparisons; as such, research should make it a point to educate respondents on the concept of pairwise comparisons when using the AHP Model. Hartwich (1999) noted that AHP does not provide sufficient guidelines on how to structure the problem, the formation of the levels for the criteria and alternatives, and the aggregation of group opinion when globally dispersed and under the constraints of time. Future studies can undertake longitudinal research to enrich the field of decision science since this is scarce within the field. Nevertheless, researchers can replicate this study in other industries.

Acknowledgments

We thank the editors, copyeditors, and anonymous reviewers for their constructive criticisms, suggestions, and directions throughout the process. We also appreciate the financial support from the University of Ghana Business School's Research and Conference Committee.

Competing Interests: The authors have no competing interests to declare.

References

Aragon, T. J., Dalnoki-Veress, F., & Shiu, K. (2012). *Deriving Criteria Weights for Health Decision Making: A Brief Tutorial*. Berkeley, CA: Center for Infectious Disease Control.

Avolio, B. J., & Bass, B. M. (2004). *MLQ: Multifactor Leadership Questionnaire. Manual and Sampler Set* (3rd ed.). Redwood City, CA: Mind Garden.

Bass, B. M. (1990a). *Bass & Stodgill Handbook of Leadership: Theory, Research, and Managerial Applications* (3rd ed.) New York: Free Press.

Bass, B. M. (1990b). From Transactional to Transformational Leadership. *Organizational Dynamics*, (3), 19–31.

Burns, J. M. (1978). *Leadership*. New York: Harper & Row.

Burns, J. M. (1995). Transactional and Transforming Leadership. In J. T. Wren (Ed.), *The Leader's Companion: Insights on Leadership through the Ages* (pp. 100–101). New York: The Free Press.

Collinson, D. (1998). *Fifty Major Philosophers*. London: Routledge.

Collinson, D., Plant, K., & Wilkinson, R. (2000). *Fifty Eastern Thinkers*. London: Routledge.

Dalalah, D., Hayajneh, M., & Batieha, F. (2011) A Fuzzy Multi-Criteria Decision-Making Model for Supplier Selection. *Expert Systems with Applications*, 38(7), 8384–8391.

Darko, E., & Lowe, A. (2016). *Ghana's Construction Sector and Youth Employment*. ODI Working Paper. London: Overseas Development Institute.

Dumdum, U. R., Lowe, K. B., & Avolio, B. J. (2002). A Meta-Analysis of Transformational and Transactional Leadership Correlates of Effectiveness and Satisfaction: An Update and Extension. In B. Avolio & F. Yammarino (Eds.), *Transformational and Charismatic Leadership: The Road Ahead* (pp. 35–66). New York: Elsevier Science.

Dvir, T., Eden, D., Avolio, B. J., & Shamir, B. (2002). Impact of Transformational Leadership on Follower Development and Performance: A Field Experiment. *Academy of Management Journal*, 45, 735–744. https://doi.org/10.2307/3069307

Dyer, J. S., Fishburn, P. C., Steuer, R. E., et al. (1992). Multiple Criteria Decision-Making, Multiattribute Utility-Theory—the Next 10 Years. *Management Science*, 38(5), 645–654.

Fleishman, E. A., Mumford, M. D., Zaccaro, S. J., et al. (1991). Taxonomic Efforts in the Description of Leader Behavior: A Synthesis and Functional Interpretation. *Leadership Quarterly*, 2(4), 245–287.

Hartwich, F. (1999). *Weighing of Agricultural Research Results: Strength and Limitations of the Analytic Hierarchy Process (AHP)*. A Discussion Paper. Stuttgart, German: Universitat Hohenheim. https://entwicklungspolitik.uni-hohenheim.de/uploads/media/DP_09_1999_Hartwich_02.pdf

Jugdev, K., & Müller, R. (2005). A Retrospective Look at Our Evolving for Project Success. *Project Management Journal*, 36, 19–32.

Kumar, A., & Dash, M. K. (2014). Criteria Exploration and Multi—Criteria Assessment Method (AHP) of Multi—Generational Consumer in Electronic Commerce. *International Journal of Business Excellence*, 7(2), 213–236.

Kumar, A., Sah, B., Singh, A. R., et al. (2017). A Review of Multi Criteria Decision Making (MCDM) Towards Sustainable Renewable Energy Development. *Renewable and Sustainable Energy Reviews*, 69, 596–609.

Lim, C. S., & Mohammed, M. Z. (1999). Criteria for Project Success: An Exploratory Re-Examination. *International Journal of Project Management, 17*(4), 243–248.

Liu, F. H. F., & Hai, H. (2005). The Voting Analytic Hierarchy Process Method for Selecting Supplier. *International Journal of Production Economics, 97*(3), 308–317.

McColl-Kennedy, J. R., & Anderson, R. D. (2002). Impact of Leadership Style and Emotions on Subordinate Performance. *Leadership Quarterly, 13*, 545–559.

Ofori, G. (2015). Nature of the Construction Industry, Its Needs and Its Development: A Review of Four Decades of Research. *Journal of Construction in Developing Countries, 20*(2), 115–135.

Ofori, G., & Toor, S. R. (2012). Leadership and Construction Industry Development in Developing Countries. *Journal of Construction in Developing Countries, 17*(1), 1–21.

Saaty, T. L. (1980). *The Analytic Hierarchy Process.* New York: McGraw-Hill.

Saaty, T. L. (2000). *Fundamentals of Decision Making and Priority Theory with the Analytic Hierarchy Process* (Analytic Hierarchy Process Series, Vol. 6). Pittsburgh: RWS Publications.

Saaty, T. L. (2008). Decision Making with the Analytic Hierarchy process. *International Journal of Services Sciences, 1*(1), 83–98.

Senge, P. M. (1990). *The Fifth Discipline: The Art & Practice of the Learning Organization.* New York: Doubleday.

Tam, M. C. Y., & Tummala, V. M. R. (2001). An Application of the AHP in Vendor Selection of a Telecommunications System. *Omega, 29*(2), 171–182.

Terry, C. D. (2002). The "Real" Success Factors on Projects. *International Journal of Project Management, 20*(3), 185–190.

Uehara, C. S., Kahneman, D., & Tversky, A. (2000). *Choices, Values and Frames* (p. 860). Londres: Cambridge University Press. Revista Economía, 2011, *34*(68), 205–207.

Yukl, G. (1989). Managerial Leadership: A Review of Theory and Research. *Journal of Management, 15*, 251–289.

Zendeh, A. B., & Aali, S. (2011). An AHP Approach for Selecting the Suitable Leadership Style. *International Proceedings of Economics Development and Research, 25*, 20–24.

Authors' Profile

Saviour Ayertey Nubuor is a lecturer and researcher in the Department of Organization and Human Resource Management at the University of Ghana Business School. He holds a PhD in Management Science and Engineering focusing on Project Management from Wuhan University of Technology, Wuhan, People's Republic of China. He is a Project Management Professional (PMP) and a member of the Project Management Institute (PMI) of the United States. He was a co-founder and director of projects and administration for Africa-China Business Group Ltd. He has published in reputable peer-reviewed journals and serves as a consultant for both private and public institutions. His research focuses on project management, leadership, and human resource management.

Kwasi Dartey-Baah is an associate professor at the Department of Organization and Human Resource Management (OHRM) in the University of Ghana Business School. He holds a PhD in Leadership and Human Resource Development from Trinity College Newburgh, United States, and Canterbury University, United Kingdom, and engineering degrees from Kwame Nkrumah University of Science and Technology, Ghana, and the Imperial College, London. He has considerable research and consultancy experience in project management and leadership development. He has published in high-impact journals, including *Leadership and Organizational Development Journal, International Journal of Law & Management*, and *African Journal of Economic and Management Studies* in his area of research. Key themes in his research are Leadership, Corporate Social Responsibility, Safe Work Environments, and Organizational Culture.

Chapter 12

What Factors Drive Ethical Decision-Making of Prospective Accountants?

Gabriel Korankye and Francis Aboagye-Otchere

Contents

DOI: 10.4324/9781003152217-16

Introduction

Ethics has become a very topical issue and consistently prominent in academic discussions for decades. In accounting, however, discussions have been heightened in recent times partly due to the stern criticisms faced by the accounting profession following several reported unethical practices by some accountants (Craft, 2013; Patterson & Rowley, 2019). A few of such high-profiled cases with the direct involvement of accountants include the Enron, Arthur Anderson case of 2001, the WorldCom scandal of 2002, the Freddie Mac scandal of 2003, the Lehman Brothers scandal of 2008, and the Satyam scandal of 2009. In Ghana, both public and private sector institutions have had their fair share of unethical conducts mostly with the involvement of accountants. Apart from the fact that these unethical practices negatively affect the accounting profession's image, the occurrence of such acts has huge implications on the institutions, sometimes leading to their eventual collapse. For a profession that prides itself with integrity as its core value, maintaining high ethical standards for its professional members has become more than necessary in minimizing the involvement of accountants in unethical practices at the workplace.

Scores of academic literature have looked into determinants of unethical behavior, and the outcomes indicate that social consensus, the magnitude of consequences, and demographic factors influence the ethical decision-making process of accountants (Guffey & McCartney, 2008; Pierce & Sweeney, 2010; Robin et al., 1996; Stanga & Turpen, 1991). Further, studies in the area of ethics have focused on developing frameworks and models to explain ethical behavior. Two main works have been prominent. First is the moral intensity model which captures how the characteristics of a moral issue itself may influence an individual's ethical decision-making (Douglas & Kevin, 2002; Sweeney & Costello, 2009). Studies employing this model have yielded contradictory results. While Leitsch (2006) suggests that there is no significant relationship between moral intensity and moral sensitivity. On the other hand, Sweeney and Costello (2009) find a significant relationship between moral intensity and the three stages of ethical decision-making process. The second model is Robin et al.'s (1996) perceived importance of an ethical issue (PIE) model. This model proposes that the level of relevance that an individual attaches to an ethical issue or dilemma will affect one's decision-making. While some argue that this is an improvement on the moral intensity construct, works employing this model are limited (Guffey & McCartney, 2008; Haines et al., 2008; Robin et al., 1996).

Patterson et al. (2019) and Ferrell and Fraedrich (2015) posit that our world today is full of complex ethical scenarios that require individuals to make complex ethical decisions daily. The scores of calls for business and more specifically, accounting students to be introduced to the rapidly changing political, legal, and ethical environment around them has been consistent and predates the twenty-first century. In the 1950s, the Carnegie and Ford Foundation commissioned academic work on business education which was further modified by the American Assembly of Collegiate Schools of Business in 1974. This led to a subsequent modification of their curricula and the introduction of "ethical considerations" for the very first time (Harris, 1991). Since then, the need for ethics has been heightened in business and accounting practice and education. Similarly, there has been an increase in research in these areas (Apostolou et al., 2016; Guffey & McCartney, 2008; Haron et al., 2014; Ismail & Yussof, 2016; Obalola & Adelopo, 2012; Pierce & Sweeney, 2010; Simpson et al., 2016; Stonciuviene & Naujokaitiene, 2013; Sweeney & Costello, 2009; Ziegenfuss & Singhapakdi, 1994).

Generally, studies surrounding ethics and, more specifically, determinants of ethical decision-making have widely focused on using either the demographic or individual characteristics, moral intensity attached to a particular ethical issue, or perceived importance attributed to an ethical issue (Baird et al., 2006; Boateng & Agyapong, 2017; Costa et al., 2016; McCuddy & Peery, 1996). A few scholars may have also investigated the effect of personal values but measured its impact on ethical behavior only. This study focuses on a conceptual analysis of the complexity of ethical decision-making in light of the PIE model.

The Concept of Ethical Decision-Making

Accountants encounter morally charged situations and hence make ethical judgment and decisions in their daily activities and operations (Lincoln & Holmes, 2011). An ethical decision is defined as "a decision that is legally and/or morally acceptable, and an unethical decision is illegal and/or morally unacceptable to the society at large" (Guffey & McCartney, 2008; Johnston, 2010). Ethical decision-making is deemed as a process (Jones, 1991). The ethical decision-making process is theoretically explained by Rest's (1986) model. This model was couched out of a number of studies and theories which sought to explain ethical development and behavior from different standpoints. The model sought to harmonize the efforts and outcomes of all the prior attempts (Lincoln & Holmes, 2011).

Rest's model shows that the ethical decision-making process of an individual is made of four stages. That is moral sensitivity, moral judgment, moral motivation or intention, and moral character or action or behavior. The stages are a decision schema and occur sequentially (Haines et al., 2008). That is an individual makes a judgment after recognizing a moral issue; then after, the individual will make up his or her mind to carry out an ethical behavior (Haines et al., 2008).

Ethical Decision-Making and Individual Characteristics

Individual characteristics such as age, gender, level of education, course major, exposure to ethics knowledge, and experience among others have been outlined to be important determinants of ethical decisions and ethical status of persons (Guffey & McCartney, 2008; Modarres & Rafiee, 2011; Pan & Sparks, 2012; Sweeney & Costello, 2009). Evidence from literature on gender and ethical decision-making (Brunton & Eweje, 2010; Guffey & McCartney, 2008; Pierce & Sweeney, 2010) suggests that females are more ethical, in judgment and action, compared to their male counterparts. This has been attributed to the edge of men for competitive success and as a result may resort to unethical means to achieve this success (Guffey & McCartney, 2008). Also, women are perceived to be more caring and concerned about hurting others compared to men and hence are more likely to be more ethical (Pierce & Sweeney, 2010). There are, however, a few studies that posit that there is no evidence to support the relationship between gender and ethical decision-making (Harris, 1989; McCuddy & Peery, 1996).

Aside from gender, other studies have identified age (Modarres & Rafiee, 2011; Pierce & Sweeney, 2010), level of education, level of experience (Modarres & Rafiee, 2011), and familiarity with ethical codes (Costa et al., 2016) to have a significant influence on ethical judgment and intentions of individuals. Pierce and Sweeney (2010) argue that the younger generation is less ethical, compared to the older ones. Similarly, those with a lower level of education as well as a few years of experience tend to be more unethical in judgment and intention (Modarres & Rafiee, 2011). It is, therefore, imperative for organizations and professional bodies to target the young, less experienced, and those with little ethical education when designing ethical training programs.

Moral Intensity and Ethical Decision-Making

Jones (1991) in his seminal study identified six (6) dimensions of moral intensity and these are "Magnitude of Consequences, Temporal Immediacy, Social Consensus, Proximity, Probability of Effect, and Concentration of Effect" (Dorantes et al., 2006; Douglas et al., 2001; Haines et al., 2008; Lincoln & Holmes, 2011; Sweeney & Costello, 2009). Haines et al. (2008) argue that moral intensity is monotonic and thus any change in any of the components will result in an overall change in the moral intensity of an ethical situation.

Magnitude of consequence refers to the quantum of benefit or harm of the action on people. The higher the benefit or harm the action will have on people, the higher the magnitude of consequence or vice versa. The effect on the ethical judgment and/or behavior will be dependent on whether the consequence is harmful or beneficial. The proponents defined social consensus as the extent to which society approves or disapproves of an action. If the action is socially acceptable, then it has a higher social consensus. This implies that an individual will engage in an action with a high social consensus. The third dimension, probability of effect, focuses on the likelihood that the consequence of the action will happen or not. Probability of effect has a negative effect on ethical actions. That is, if an action has a high probability of effect, then there is a high possibility that the outcome will occur and hence deter people from engaging in such an unethical act.

The time lag between action and consequence is what is termed as temporal immediacy by Jones (1991). The shorter the time between the event and the effect, the higher the immediacy and the less likelihood one may engage in that action. Proximity refers to the relationship that exists between the perpetrator and the victim of the unethical action. This relationship may be social, psychological, physical, or cultural. The closer the victim is to the agent of the action, the less likely the agent will engage in it. The last dimension is concentration of effect which is defined as the number of people that will be affected by the given outcome of the action. The higher the number of people to be affected, the higher the concentration of effect, and the more likely it is to make an ethical decision. It is believed that all the dimensions influence the various components of moral decision-making process of individuals (Haines et al., 2008; Lincoln & Holmes, 2011; Sweeney & Costello, 2009).

Some studies surrounding ethical decision-making have sought to find out the impact of the moral intensity construct on ethical decision-making process (Dorantes et al., 2006; Douglas et al., 2001; Douglas & Kevin, 2002; Haines et al., 2008; Leitsch, 2006; Lincoln & Holmes, 2011; Sweeney & Costello, 2009). For instance, in studying the ethical decision-making of service academy students, Lincoln and Holmes (2011) found that there is a significant relationship between social consensus and moral intensity, moral judgment, and intention to act ethically. Also, they found that Proximity has a significant effect on only moral awareness, also moral judgment and intention to act are affected by magnitude of consequence and probability of effect (Lincoln & Holmes, 2011).

Notwithstanding the enormous subscription to "moral intensity" as one of the dominant determinants of Rest's four-stage decision-making process, there has been some resistance against it. The critics of the construct argue that moral intensity only focuses on the facts of the matter. As such, if the facts change, an individual's judgment of an ethical issue might change, ignoring the decision-maker's moral cognition (Haines et al., 2008; Robin et al., 1996). Therefore, to consider the personal judgment of the individual decision maker, opponents proposed another theory or construct, the PIE. The PIE construct considers the perception of the individual about the issue ahead of the facts of the matter, and as a result, the moral situation may change but the ethical position of the actor may not (Haines et al., 2008; Robin et al., 1996).

Perceived Importance of an Ethical Issue

In recent times, PIE, otherwise known as Perceived Personal Values or Perceived Personal Relevance, has become prevalent in ethical decision-making literature (Guffey & McCartney, 2008). This construct was derived by Robin et al. (1996) as an extension of the moral intensity construct established by Jones (1991). Prior literature has featured PIE in diverse ways (Guffey & McCartney, 2008; Haines et al., 2008; Johnston, 2010; Robin et al., 1996; Singhapakdi, 1999). These researchers argue that PIE influences ethical decision-making in almost the same way as Jones' moral intensity construct. Beyond this overlap, PIE, more importantly, considers the individual's perception of an ethical issue (Haines et al., 2008). Thus, PIE considers "an individual's values, beliefs, needs, perceptions, special characteristics of the situation, and the personal pressures existing" in an ethical decision-making situation. Whiles Jones' model focuses on characteristics of the moral issue, the PIE model considers the individual factors and perceptions (Guffey & McCartney, 2008; Robin et al., 1996).

In examining the impact of PIE on ethical decision-making, Robin et al. (1996) examined the responses of some advertising managers in the United States. The results showed that an individual's level of PIE has a significant influence on the ethical judgment and behavioral intention of the person. Similarly, a study investigating the impact of PIE on ethical decision-making among marketing professionals revealed that all PIE dimensions have a significant positive relationship with ethical decision-making (Singhapakdi, 1999). This implies that individuals with high PIE are less likely to engage in unethical behavior, whereas individuals with low PIE were more likely to engage in immoral behavior.

In the accounting context, a study by Guffey and McCartney (2008) revealed that PIE is significantly related to ethical judgment and behavioral intention of accounting students to act ethically or unethically. Similarly, Haines et al. (2008) examined the influence of PIE on the four stages of the ethical decision-making process and found that PIE is a predictor of moral judgment. In effect, the level of perceived relevance or importance that one attaches to an ethical issue is very key in determining how one will act in the face of such a situation.

In as much as PIE is seen as a key determinant of ethical decision-making, there are a few contradicting views. For instance, Haines et al.'s (2008) study, on the one hand, confirmed the findings of Guffey and McCartney (2008) and Robin et al. (1996). On the other hand, the study finds no relationship between PIE and moral obligation, and PIE and moral intent. Further investigations revealed that moral obligation happens after a judgment has been made, and also moral obligation is a significant determinant in the variation in moral intent (Haines et al., 2008).

Ethical Behavior

Ethics is a person's morals, values, or principles. Ethical behavior is, however, defined as the conscious effort by an individual to do the right or moral thing even in the absence of rules and supervision (Alleyne et al., 2013). That is, a person standing by his/her values and convinced to apply them even when no one is watching. The collective ethical behaviors of the people in an organization become its ethical culture, and it is somewhat driven by the ethical behavior of the leadership.

Most studies have considered the effect of organizational factors and cultures as determinants of ethical behavior (Akaah & Lund, 1994; Bebi & Xhindi, 2017; Douglas et al., 2001). However, researchers have explored moral development and ethical behavior not only from a cognitive-development perspective, which is the most dominant approach in moral development, but also from behavioral, social, and psychoanalytic perspectives (Lincoln & Holmes, 2011). That not-withstanding, individual or personal values are not overridden by these factors.

Personal Values

Individual characteristics and personal values are very key factors that influence the ethical behavior of a person (Longenecker et al., 2004). Social adaptation theorists define values as "a type of social cognition that facilitates an individual's adaptation to the environment" (Fritzsche & Oz, 2007). Flowing from that, personal values are seen to be the "deep-seated, pervasive, core-beliefs or guiding principles that transcend specific situations to direct or propel human behavior in decision-making" (Alleyne et al., 2013). Considering the definitions, it is right to argue that it is inadequate for researchers to look at moral development only from a cognitive-development point of view, which is arguably the most predominant approach in moral development. However, it is important to consider other relevant perspectives, especially social and behavioral points of view (Holmes et al., 2012). It is opined that values are the most abstract social cognition. However, it is believed that values serve as the basis for attitude development and, subsequently, specific decision-making (Fritzsche & Oz, 2007).

Studies on personal values have concentrated on a broad spectrum of values. For instance, a study designed to determine the effect of ethical values (altruism, self-enhancement, traditional, and openness) on organizational commitment showed that there exists a positive significant relationship between the values and organizational commitment (Hunt et al., 1989). The authors further argue that corporate ethical values are a composite of both policies (whether formal or informal) and individual values of the managers (Hunt et al., 1989). Further, another study in the United States investigated the effect of altruistic values, self-enhancement values, traditional values, and openness on the dimensions of ethical decision-making (Fritzsche & Oz, 2007). The results revealed that there is a positive relationship between altruistic values and ethical decision-making, whereas self-enhancement is negatively related to ethical decision-making (Fritzsche & Oz, 2007). The authors suggest that other values should be investigated to find out how they may also influence the ethical behavior of individuals (Fritzsche & Oz, 2007; Hunt et al., 1989).

This implies that the profession and an organization seeking to maintain high ethical standards are better off admitting an individual exhibiting altruistic and traditional values rather than one who shows self-enhancement and openness to change. This is because the altruistic person is more leaned toward justice and equality, while the individual exhibiting self-enhancement values is egoistic. Aside from these values, there are other fundamental values which might be relevant in building ethical individuals and, more importantly, accounting professionals, and some of these are discussed in later sub-sections.

Ethical Judgment of Accounting Students

Tomorrow's accountants are the accounting students of today. These students, as accounting professionals in the future, will be responsible for making certain top-level financial and accounting decisions in various industries and sectors of the economy. Literature suggests that ethical students will grow into ethical professionals (Guffey & McCartney, 2008). It is, therefore, pertinent to consider them when making any efforts to improve ethical decision-making among accountants.

Several studies have investigated the ethical decision-making of accounting students, most of which does a comparison between accounting and other student groups (Alleyne et al., 2013;

Apostolou et al., 2016; Boateng & Agyapong, 2017; Guffey & McCartney, 2008; Harris, 1989, 1991; Leitsch, 2006; Sweeney & Costello, 2009). Generally, it has been found that comparatively accounting students exhibit higher levels of ethical decision-making than other groups of students. For instance, a study by Harris (1991) revealed that business students exhibit higher ethical values than their nonbusiness counterparts. Alleyne et al. (2013) also found that accounting students tend to be more ethical in their decision-making than their nonaccounting colleagues. This can be attributed to the continuous exposure of accounting students to ethics. Hence, ethics in business, and specifically, accounting education might be the way to improve the ethical position of the profession.

Ethics in Accounting Education

In response to calls by the International Accounting Education Standards Board's, most professional accounting bodies and accounting educators across the world have tried to imbibe in their curricula, ethics education. These calls have been reiterated and reinforced after the numerous scandals in the late 1990s and early 2000s. In the same vein, accounting institutions and professional bodies in Ghana have also endeavored to abide by this directive and not be left out. Following that, about 74% of the universities in Ghana, as of 2016, had ethics as part of their curricula for business students. Even though ethics may not be a stand-alone course but rather, a part of another course (embedded), it is mostly core (Simpson et al., 2016). This indicates the level of importance attached to the course.

The question has now shifted from including ethics in education to whether it should be a stand-alone course or an embedded one. The second is whether or not to make ethics a core subject for students (Gandz & Hayes, 1988; Whitla, 2011). According to Gandz and Hayes (1988) and Whitla (2011), making ethics an elective course will result in selection bias and also send a signal that the course is only voluntary. Also, there have been arguments that embedding ethics in another course reduces the importance and focus being placed on it. However, Guffey and McCartney (2008) argue that ethics in institutions is not just about introducing the course but, most importantly, the delivery and/or how it is taught. To be able to deliver the course to achieve improved ethical standards, it is also important to understand the basis of making unethical judgment and decisions.

Theoretical Review

Theories have been rarely applied in ethical decision-making literature and ethics studies as a whole. Nonetheless, there have been a few theories that have been employed to explain the determinants of ethical behavior and ethical decision-making by individuals. The most predominantly used theory in this area of research is Rest's (1986) four-stage ethical decision-making model.

Rest's Four-Stage Ethical Decision-Making Model

Rest's four-stage ethical decision-making model is the most common, widely used, and validated model in ethics literature (Haines et al., 2008; Robin et al., 1996). The model is made of four stages of the individual decision-making process. The first is "recognizing a moral issue" and the last is "engaging in moral behavior". The model is shown in Figure 12.1.

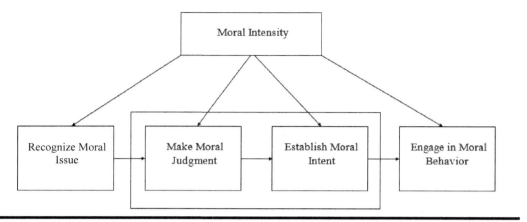

Figure 12.1 Rest's four-stage ethical decision-making model.

Recognition of a moral issue which is the first stage of the ethical decision model is also known as Moral Sensitivity or Moral Awareness. According to Rest (1986), moral sensitivity is one's capability to identify that an issue has in it an ethical dilemma. In other words, it is a process of recognizing the moral content in a situation and subsequently validating the moral perspective of the decision maker. Recognizing a moral issue involves the individual realizing that his/her actions have the potential to positively or negatively affect other people. That is their actions may harm or benefit others (Lincoln & Holmes, 2011; Robin et al., 1996).

The second stage of Rest's (1986) model is moral judgment, which involves the formulation and evaluation of the alternative solutions available to a moral issue. This step in the process calls for the individual to reason through the possible choices and their potential consequences to find out which is more or most ethically sound (Guffey & McCartney, 2008; Lincoln & Holmes, 2011; Robin et al., 1996).

Stage three of the model involves the establishment of a moral intention. The intention of the individual to choose a moral decision over other possible solutions representing different values is termed as moral intention (or moral motivation). This component of the ethical decision-making process involves committing to choosing a moral value. For example, an individual may recognize two solutions to a dilemma: one that will result in personal power and one that is right morally. The choice of morality over personal power by the individual, in this instance, represents moral motivation (Lincoln & Holmes, 2011; Robin et al., 1996).

Moral behavior (or moral action) is the last stage of Rest's model. Moral action points to the final behavior of the individual in an ethical situation. This stage focuses on the final action of an individual in an ethical situation. The moral action stage of the decision-making process involves the ability, courage, and determination to follow through with the moral decision (Lincoln & Holmes, 2011; Robin et al., 1996).

Moral Intensity

According to Jones (1991), moral intensity refers to "a construct that captures the extent of issue-related moral imperative in a situation". This construct is made up of six components, which helps in describing a moral issue. Moral intensity varies with variations in the underlisted components.

These components are magnitude of consequence, social consensus, probability of effect, temporal immediacy, proximity, and concentration of effect.

Modifications to Rest's Four-Stage Ethical Decision-Making Model

In an effort to adequately answer the question "what factors influence ethical decision-making", a number of models have emerged from Rest's four-stage ethical decision-making model which has been the basis for most, if not all, ethical decision-making models (Lau et al., 2013; Loyens & Maesschalck, 2010). Among the many models that have been developed, we mention a few prominent ones. First is the person–situation interactionist model by Trevino in 1986 (Loyens & Maesschalck, 2010). This model considers personal factors as moral development, ego, strength, and locus of control among others, and situation factors (or moderators) such as organizational culture, moral content of organizational culture, job context, and characteristics of the job. Trevino's work added to existing works by introducing and emphasizing on the interacting effects of the situational factors (Trevino, 1986).

Subsequently, works by Hunt and Vitell (1986) and Stead et al. (1990) have provided another modification to Rest's (1986) model by introducing ethical ideologies, that is, deontological and teleological evaluations, to the model. They define deontological ideology as how inherently right or wrong an option is, while consequential ethics is referred to as teleological evaluation. That is, one's choice is dependent on what is best for the whole (Hunt & Vitell, 2006; Stead et al., 2016). Furthermore, Tan (2002) introduced another dimension to Rest's (1986) and Jones' (1991) models, calling it the issue–risk–judgment (IRJ) model. The IRJ suggests that aside from moral judgment and moral intensity, an individual's ethical decision-making is influenced by perceived risk of the situation (Tan, 2002).

The aforementioned models, among others, that have been developed as a modification to Rest's (1986) and Jones' (1991) models are skewed toward the relationship between personal characteristics, firm characteristics, and situational characteristics, neglecting the individuals' values, convictions, and perceptions (Guffey & McCartney, 2008; Haines et al., 2008; Lau et al., 2013; Loyens & Maesschalck, 2010). This may be due to the external nature of the personal, organizational, and situational characteristics, making it easy to observe and/or measure. However, this creates a gap in literature.

Theoretical Framework

This present study proposes a framework (Figure 12.2) that captures the individual's values and perceptions of an ethical issue as determinants of ethical judgment and ethical behavior. In modifying Rest's model, moral intensity is replaced with Robin et al.'s (1996) empirically validated construct, PIE. Also, the personal values included in the framework are the set of values proposed by Scott as integral to ethical development (Akaah & Lund, 1994).

Perceived Importance of an Ethical Issue

The PIE construct was propounded by and subsequently empirically tested by Robin et al. (1996). It differs from other theories by considering among other things, the beliefs, needs, perceptions, values, special characteristics of the situation, and existing personal pressures in the ethical decision-making process. Unlike Jones (1991) model (moral intensity) which only focuses on the characteristics of the issue or situation at hand, PIE goes further to include the individual traits of the decision maker.

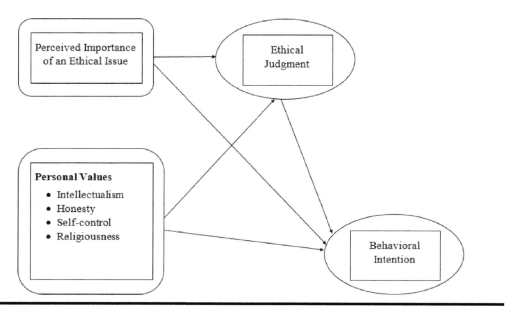

Figure 12.2   Model for ethical decision-making.

After proposing the theory, Robin et al. (1996) tested the construct empirically. Employing a scenario-based questionnaire, they found that there is a significant relationship between PIE and ethical judgment. The study showed that people who are high in terms of PIE are less likely to engage in unethical behavior, whereas people who are low in terms of PIE are more likely to engage in unethical actions. Further studies have also tested this model empirically and have come out with similar results. For instance, Haines et al. (2008) surveyed 235 business students, and their results and findings supported that of Robin et al. (1996). Also, Guffey and McCartney (2008) surveyed 397 accounting students and came up with similar findings. Hence, it can be deduced that PIE is a useful and more comprehensive measure of perceived relevance of an ethical issue.

Thus, the level of significance that one attaches to a particular situation will influence the person's ethical judgment and behavior. The more relevant one deems a situation to be the less likely the individual will be unethical about it. As such, organizations should place a premium on situations and any issue that reflects some element of ethics to ensure that the decision-maker values the issue.

Personal Values

As has been established in earlier discussions, personal values can be a key determinant of decision-making and by extension behavior. Hence, the study adopts Scott's (1965) personal values scale and incorporates it in the ethical decision-making model. This study, in answer to Shafer et al.'s (2001) recommendations, employs Scott's (1965) personal values scale of subscales measuring intellectualism, honesty, self-control, and religiousness.

Intellectualism

Intellectualism is an important component of the makeup of an individual, especially students. It is defined as the ability of an individual to understand, discern and reason is termed as intellectualism (Alleyne et al., 2013). Using correlation analysis, Alleyne et al. (2013) revealed that there is a significant relation between intellectualism and ethical behavior. That is, if an individual is perceived to have a high sense of understanding, discernment, and reasoning, then the person will be more ethical in his or her decision-making and behavior.

Honesty

To be honest means to shy away from deceit, being truthful and sincere, and/or morally correct and vitreous (Wells & Molina, 2017). Wells and Molina (2017) posit that honesty is a very important value that is upheld by most people, including professionals. Furthermore, a study by Finegan (1994) revealed that honest students were more ethical in judgment and subsequent behavior. An honest person is genuine and trustworthy and hence will be ethical in decision-making. Organizations should, therefore, seek to recruit honest people into their institutions. Also, it is in the right direction for the accounting profession to have as one of its fundamental principles, integrity which is underpinned by honesty. It has, however, been argued that deceit and dishonesty are resorted to at times due to the complex nature of some situations and the world at large (Wells & Molina, 2017).

Self-Control

Self-control can be defined as one's ability to manage emotions, impulse, and behavior (Baumeister & Line, 2000; Martijn et al., 2002). Self-control is deemed to be a very important element of human characteristics. It is also believed that one key to pursuing distant goals is the ability to override and change dominant reactions (Baumeister & Line, 2000; Martijn et al., 2002). As the saying goes, "self-control is a virtue", and it is an important feature that guides the action of individuals.

Some prior literature suggests that people who exercise self-control are depleted of their strength or energy and hence unable to continue exercising this value. This, in turn, reduces their moral awareness (Gino et al., 2011). That notwithstanding, Alleyne et al. (2013) believe that self-control has a significant relationship with ethical behavior. The virtue of self-control aids individuals to pause and think through their actions before performing them, hence making them more ethical in judgment and behavior.

Religiousness

In studying ethics, the focus has been on the philosophical and social aspects while little attention is paid to the religious aspect of it (Longenecker et al., 2004). Religious nature of an individual is perceived to help determine the difference between right and wrong (Modarres & Rafiee, 2011). Christians, Muslims, and other religions are guided by their Bible, Qur'an, and other Holy books, respectively, which shapes their decision-making and actions (Modarres & Rafiee, 2011). Extant literature suggests that religious virtue plays a significant role in developing accountants' ethical perspectives. Modarres and Rafiee (2011) and Longenecker et al. (2004) posit that accountants, business managers, and professionals as a whole, who believe in the Supreme Being, God, strive to do what is right and holy in His eyes and hence create a moral imperative which supersedes just human institutions.

There are two dimensions of religiosity, extrinsic and intrinsic (Singhapakdi et al., 2013). Extrinsic religiosity is the act of worshiping a Supreme Being for selfish needs. Contrarily, intrinsic religiosity encompasses the act of worshiping a Supreme Being based on spiritual and inherent motivations (Singhapakdi et al., 2013). An empirical study by Singhapakdi et al. (2013) revealed that managers who are of high intrinsic religiosity are very ethical in intentions, while managers who exhibited higher extrinsic religiosity were unethical in their intentions (Singhapakdi et al., 2013). Thus, people who are genuinely religious (intrinsic) will be more ethical in their judgment and exhibit ethical behavior due to their true commitment to the values of their religion.

Practical and Policy Implications

First, the different dimensions of personal values (that is, intellectualism, honesty, self-control, and religiousness) have implications on the ethical judgment of accounting students. Given the importance of these values, firms should put in place recruitment process that can select for them, candidates of who exhibit highly acceptable values. Also, for firms and the accounting profession to ensure and promote good ethical behavior, continuous professional development and training programs should project these values. Educators may develop a curriculum that focuses on ethics and the development of values among the accounting students based on the model of ethical decision-making developed in this study. This will help cultivate the values earlier in these future professionals. Recruitment processes of firms should include integrity checks which will help the organization to choose people who uphold such values in high esteem since such values are critical to one's ethical decision-making process.

PIE is also deemed to influence the ethical judgment and behavior of accounting students. This implies that the level of relevance placed on an issue matter. As such, if an individual attaches a high level of relevance to an ethical issue, the person will be more critical of an unethical action and will subsequently desist from such behaviors. Accounting students and professionals should be trained and encouraged to see ethical issues as high premium and important matters. This will help create a culture of giving high relevance to such issues of ethical dilemma and subsequently ensuring good ethical judgment and behavior. Further, training institutions for accountants and organizations should have a culture of ethics that places ethics at the helm of affairs or hold ethics in high esteem. Members and, most importantly, leadership of such organizations and institutions should be fully committed to this organizational culture to encourage prospective accountants to learn from their examples. In addition, institutions that train accountants and firms that employ these young accountants should be meticulous in their planning process, identify the possible ethical issues in the process, and coach these prospective accountants on how to deal with such ethical dilemmas.

Finally, judging an issue ethically will result in behaving ethically in that situation. In effect, leadership and management of professions and organizations should pay attention to the judgments and comments individuals pass on issues of ethical substance. This is because these judgments are likely to influence the individuals' final action. Following this, prospective accountants should also be trained to appropriately evaluate and judge ethical situations. Also, recruitment process of firms should also consider an assessment of the ethical judgment of prospective accountants. This will aid the organization in determining the ethical position of these young accountants and hence inform the choice of candidates for certain positions in the firm.

Future Research and Practice Directions

This study sought to discuss the complexity of ethical decision-making among accountants while drawing more attention to the PIE model. The study also develops a more complex and inclusive model that explains ethical decision-making from a more value standpoint. Also, through an in-depth analytical literature review, we discuss quite some trends in empirical research, make practical inferences, and point out some areas that are lacking in prior literature. Some clear issues include the overemphasis on the impact of demographic factors on ethical decision-making and behavior, the overdependence on primarily two theories in discussions on ethics and ethical decision-making, and the limited empirical work on the role values and philosophical orientations play in the ethical decision-making process.

The following recommendations are, therefore, outlined for consideration in future research. First, research in ethics and ethical decision-making should move away from demographic characteristics and focus more attention on other factors that are relevant to decision-making. Second, future research may concentrate attention on investigating more into values and ethical decision-making and ethical behavior. Further, we encourage more efforts to be channeled into developing new models, frameworks, and theories that explain ethical decision-making. This will bring more nuance into the discussions on ethics and reduce the overdependence on Rest's (1986) four-stage decision-making model and Jones' (1991) moral intensity construct. Finally, more experimental rather than a survey, research is encouraged in future studies. Since ethics is a very sensitive and more practical area, more depth can be achieved, and knowledge is developed if studies in this area employed the experimental approach to research. We believe that will assist researchers the opportunity to have subjects or participants experience ethical dilemmas firsthand and monitor their actions and reactions.

References

Akaah, I. P., & Lund, D. (1994). The Influence of Personal and Organizational Values on Marketing Professionals' Ethical Behavior. *Journal of Business Ethics*, 13(6), 417–430.

Alleyne, P., Cadogan-McClean, C., & Harper, A. (2013). Examining Personal Values and Ethical Behaviour Perceptions between Accounting and Non-accounting Students in the Caribbean. *The Accounting Educators' Journal*, XXIII, 47–70.

Apostolou, B., Dorminey, J. W., Hassell, J. M., & Rebele, J. E. (2016). Accounting Education Literature Review (2015). *Journal of Accounting Education*, 35(1), 20–55.

Baird, J. E., Zelin, I., & Brennan, P. J. (2006). Academic Major, Gender, Personal Values, and Reactions to an Ethical Dilemma. *Journal of Business Case Studies (JBCS)*, 2(2), 73–82.

Baumeister, R. F., & Line, J. J. E. (2000). Self-Control, Morality and Human Strength. *Journal of Social and Clinical Psychology*, 19(1), 29–42.

Bebi, L., & Xhindi, T. (2017). The Impact of Organizational Factors on Ethical Decision Making Process of Albanian Accountants. *European Journal of Multidisciplinary Studies*, 6(2), 95–101.

Boateng, E. A., & Agyapong, D. (2017). Gender and Ethical Behaviour of Accounting Students : An Empirical Evidence of University of Cape Coast. *Research Journal of Finance and Accounting*, 8(4), 49–56.

Brunton, M., & Eweje, G. (2010). The Influence of Culture on Ethical Perception Held by Business Students in a New Zealand University. *Busines Ethics: A European Review*, 19(4), 349–362.

Costa, A. J., Pinheiro, M. M., Ribeiro, M. S., Costa, A. J., Pinheiro, M. M., & Ethical, M. S. R. (2016). Ethical Perceptions of Accounting Students in a Portuguese University: The Influence of Individual Factors and Personal Traits. *Accounting Education*, 25(4), 327–348.

Craft, J. L. (2013). A Review of the Empirical Ethical Decision-Making Literature: 2004–2011. *Journal of Business Ethics*, 117(2), 221–259.

Dorantes, C. A., Hewitt, B., & Goles, T. (2006). Ethical Decision-Making in an IT Context: The Roles of Personal Moral Philosophies and Moral Intensity. *39th Hawaii International Conference on System Sciences*, 00(C), 1–10.

Douglas, P. C., Davidson, R. A., & Schwartz, B. N. (2001). The Effect of Organizational Culture and Ethical Orientation on Accountants' Ethical Judgments. *Journal of Business Ethics*, 34(1), 101–121.

Douglas, R., & Kevin, P. (2002). The Role of Moral Intensity in Ethical Decision Making. *Business & Society*, *41*(1), 84–117.

Ferrell, O. C., & Fraedrich, J. (2015). *Business Ethics: Ethical Decision Making & Cases*. Toronto: Nelson Education.

Finegan, J. (1994). The Impact of Personal Values on Judgments of Etliical Behaviour in the Workplace. *Journal of Business Ethics*, *13*(9), 747–755.

Fritzsche, D. J., & Oz, E. (2007). Personal Values' Influence on the Ethical Dimension of Decision Making. *Journal of Business Ethics*, *75*(4), 335–343.

Gandz, J., & Hayes, N. (1988). Teaching Business Ethics. *Journal of Business Ethics*, *8*(3), 657–665.

Gino, F., Schweitzer, M. E., Mead, N. L., & Ariely, D. (2011). Unable to Resist Temptation: How Self-Control Depletion Promotes Unethical Behavior. *Organizational Behavior and Human Decision Processes*, *115*(2), 191–203.

Guffey, D. M., & McCartney, M. W. (2008). The Perceived Importance of an Ethical Issue as a Determinant of Ethical Decision-Making for Accounting Students in an Academic Setting. *Accounting Education*, *17*(3), 327–348.

Haines, R., Street, M. D., & Haines, D. (2008). The Influence of Perceived Importance of an Ethical Issue on Moral Judgment, Moral Obligation and Moral Intent. *Journal of Business Ethics*, *81*(2), 387–399.

Haron, H., Ismail, I., Ibrahim, D. N., & Na, A. L. (2014). Factors Influencing Ethical Judgement of Auditors in Malaysia. *Malaysian Accounting Review*, *13*(2), 47–86.

Harris, J. R. (1989). Ethical Values and Decision Processes of Male and Female Business Students. *Journal of Education for Business*, *64*(5), 234–238.

Harris, J. R. (1991). Ethical Values and Decision Processes of Business and Non-Business Students: A Four-Group Study. *The Journal of Legal Studies Education*, *9*(1), 215–232.

Holmes, K., Marriott, L., & Randal, J. (2012). Ethics and Experiments in Accounting: A Contribution to the Debate on Measuring Ethical Behaviour. *Pacific Accounting Review*, *24*(1), 80–100.

Hunt, S. D., & Vitell S. (1986). A General Theory of Marketing Ethics. *Journal of Macromarketing* (Spring), *26*(2), 5–16.

Hunt, S. D., & Vitell, S. J. (2006). The General Theory of Marketing Ethics: A Revision and Three Questions. *Journal of Macromarketing*, *26*(2), 143–153.

Hunt, S. D., Wood, V. R., & Chonko, L. B. (1989). Corporate Ethical and Commitment Organizational in Marketing. *Journal of Marketing*, *53*(3), 79–90.

Ismail, S., & Yussof, S. H. (2016). Cheating Behaviour among Accounting Students: Some Malaysian Evidence. *Accounting Research Journal*, *29*(1), 20–33.

Jones, T. M. (1991). Ethical Decision-Making by Individuals in Organizations: An Issue-Contingent Model. *Academy of Management Review*, *16*(2), 366–395. http://dx.doi.org/10.2307/258867

Johnston, M. M. (2010). *Perceived Importance of an Ethical Situation (PIE) on Ethical Judgment and Intention*. Honors Program Theses. 29. University of Northern Iowa, Cedar Falls, IA. https://scholarworks.uni.edu/hpt/29

Lau, G. K. K., Yuen, A. H. K., & Park, J. (2013). Toward an Analytical Model of Ethical Decision Making in Plagiarism. *Ethics and Behavior*, *23*(5), 360–377.

Leitsch, D. L. (2006). Using Dimensions of Moral Intensity to Predict Ethical Decision-making in Accounting. *Accounting Education: An International Journal*, *15*(2), 135–149.

Lincoln, S. H., & Holmes, E. K. (2011). Articles Ethical Decision Making: A Process Influenced by Moral Intensity. *Journal of Healthcare, Science and the Humanities*, *I*(1), 55–69.

Longenecker, J. G., Mckinney, J. A., & Moore, C. W. (2004). Religious Intensity, Evangelical Christianity and Business Ethics: An Empirical Study. *Journal of Business Ethics*, *55*(1), 373–386.

Loyens, K., & Maesschalck, J. (2010). Toward a Theoretical Framework for Ethical Decision Making of Street-Level Bureaucracy: Existing Models Reconsidered. *Administration and Society*, *42*(1), 66–100.

Martijn, C., Tenbült, P., Merckelbach, H., Dreezens, E., & de Vries, N. K. (2002). Getting a Grip on Ourselves: Challenging Expectancies about Loss of Energy after Self-Control. *Social Cognition*, *20*(6), 441–460.

McCuddy, M. K., & Peery, B. L. (1996). Selected Individual Differences and Collegians' Ethical Beliefs. *Journal of Business Ethics*, *15*(1), 261–272.

Modarres, A., & Rafiee, A. (2011). Influencing Factors on the Ethical Decision Making of Iranian Accountants. *Social Responsibility Journal*, *7*(1), 136–144.

Obalola, M., & Adelopo, I. (2012). Measuring the Perceived Importance of Ethics and Social Responsibility in Financial Services: A Narrative-Inductive Approach. *Social Responsibility Journal*, *8*(3), 418–432.

Pan, Y., & Sparks, J. R. (2012). Predictors, Consequence and Measurement of Ethical Judgments: Review and Meta-analysis. *Journal of Business Research*, *65*(1), 84–91.

Patterson, L., & Rowley, C. (2019). Ethical Management and Leadership: A Conceptual Paper and Korean Example. *Asian Journal of Business Ethics*, *8*(1), 1–24.

Pierce, B., & Sweeney, B. (2010). The Relationship between Demographic Variables and Ethical Decision Making of. *International Journal of Auditing*, *14*(1), 79–99.

Rest, J. R. (1986). *Moral Development: Advances in Research and Theory*. New York: Praeger.

Robin, D. P., Reidenbach, E. R., & Forest, P. J. (1996). The Perceived Importance of an Ethical Issue as an Influence on the Ethical Decision-making of Ad Managers. *Journal of Business Research*, *35*(1), 17–28.

Scott, W. A. (1965). *Personal Values Scale. Values and Organisations*. Chicago: Rand McNally College Publishing Company.

Shafer, W. E., Morris, R. E., & Ketchand, A. A. (2001). Effects of Personal Values on Auditors' Ethical Decisions. *Accounting, Auditing & Accountability Journal*, *14*(3), 254–277. https://doi.org/10.1108/EUM0000000005517

Simpson, S. N. Y., Onumah, J. M., & Oppong-Nkrumah, A. (2016). Ethics Education and Accounting Programmes in Ghana: Does University Ownership and Affiliation Status Matter? *International Journal of Ethics Education*, *1*(1), 43–56.

Singhapakdi, A. (1999). Perceived Importance of Ethics and Ethical Decisions in Marketing. *Journal of Business Research*, *45*(1), 89–99.

Singhapakdi, A., Vitell, S. J., Lee, D.-J., Nisius, A. M., & Yu, G. B. (2013). The Influence of Love of Money and Religiosity on Ethical Decision-Making in Marketing. *Journal of Business Ethics*, *114*(1), 183–191.

Stanga, K. G., & Turpen, R. A. (1991). Ethical Judgments on Selected Accounting Issues: An Empirical Study. *Journal of Business Ethics*, *10*(1), 739–747.

Stead, W. E., Worrell, D. L., & Stead, J. G. (1990). An Integrative Model for Understanding and Managing Ethical Behavior in Business Organizations. *Journal of Business Ethics*, *9*(3), 233–242.

Stead, W. E., Worrell, D. L., & Stead, J. G. (2016). Managing Ethical Behavior in Business jeanGamJsL. *Journal of Business Ethics*, *9*(3), 233–242.

Stonciuviene, N., & Naujokaitiene, J. (2013). Formation of the Ethics of Professional Accountants from a Moral Standpoint: Analysis of Decisive Factors and their Influence. *European Scientific Journal*, *1*(1), 106–115.

Sweeney, B., & Costello, F. (2009). Moral Intensity and Ethical Decision-Making: An Empirical Examination of Undergraduate Accounting and Business Students. *Accounting Education: An International Journal*, *18*(1), 75–97.

Tan, B. (2002). Understanding Consumer Ethical Decision Making with Respect to Purchase of Pirated Software. *Journal of Consumer Marketing*, *19*(2), 96–111.

Trevino, L. K. (1986). Ethical Decision Making in Organizations: A Person-Situation Interactionist Model. *The Academy of Management Review*, *11*(3), 601.

Wells, D. D., & Molina, A. D. (2017). The Truth about Honesty. *Journal of Public and Nonprofit Affairs*, *3*(3), 292–308.

Whitla, P. (2011). Integrating Ethics into International Business Teaching: Challenges and Methodologies in the Greater China Context. *Journal of Teaching in International Business*, *22*(3), 168–184.

Ziegenfuss, D. E., & Singhapakdi, A. (1994). Professional Values and the Ethical Perceptions of Internal Auditors. *Managerial Auditing Journal*, *9*(1), 34–44.

Authors' Profile

Mr. Gabriel Korankye is a lecturer with the Department of Accounting, University of Professional Studies, Accra. He has a Master of Philosophy (MPhil) in Accounting and a Bachelor of Science

(BSc) in Administration (Accounting) from the University of Ghana Business School (UGBS). He had his Senior High Education at Prempeh College, one of the best Senior High Schools in Ghana. Gabriel previously worked as a teaching assistant at the UGBS and also as Tutor at the distance education unit of the University of Ghana. He has teaching experience in Financial Accounting and Reporting as well as Audit and Assurance. Gabriel's areas of research interest are behavioral accounting and finance, accounting information systems, and accounting and business education. He has a working knowledge in Structural Equation Modelling (specifically, the partial least squares technique).

Dr. Francis Aboagye-Otchere is a senior lecturer at the Department of Accounting of the University of Ghana Business School (UGBS). He has extensive experience in university level teaching, executive and adult training, organizational and financial restructuring, design, redesign, and improvement of business processes. He previously served as the Head of Department and Coordinator for Accounting. Prior to joining UGBS, he worked as a consultant with Kwame Asante & Associates-Representative of Arthur Andersen. His research focuses on Corporate Governance and Disclosure Practices, Internet Financial Reporting, Earnings Management, and Corporate Social Responsibility Reporting. His teaching experience span across Financial Accounting and Reporting, International Accounting, Accounting Theory, Healthcare Accounting, and Control and Business Finance at both graduate and undergraduate levels.

Chapter 13

The Motivation to Engage in Fraud by Individuals at the Workplace

Theodora Aba Abekah Koomson and
Godfred Matthew Yaw Owusu

Contents

DOI: 10.4324/9781003152217-17

Introduction

The world has been hit by several corporate scandals that has resulted in massive losses to affected firms. Research into the collapse of these otherwise vibrant firms suggests different kinds of fraudulent activities by key persons in the corporation to be one main underlining factor (Low et al., 2008; Tang & Sutarso, 2013). The occurrence of fraud in businesses continues to heighten and the 2016 report on Crime Surveys by PricewaterhouseCoopers indicates that one of every three organizations has suffered from fraud in some shape or form (PwC, 2016). Like the rest of the world, Africa has had its fair share of these corporate collapses resulting from fraudulent activities with the case of Steinhoff in South Africa being, arguably, the most notable one. Indeed, the 2018 Report to the Nations by the ACFE classifies the African continent as the second largest in the world in terms of the number of reported fraud cases by business organizations (ACFE, 2018). Most of the firms sampled from Africa for this report were from emerging economies.

Within the Ghanaian context, for instance, the financial sector experienced what has been described by many as its most turbulent moment in the country's history largely due to fraudulent activities. Between 2017 and 2019 alone, a total of 16 universal banks had collapsed as a result of the banking cleanup exercise carried out by the Bank of Ghana (BoG) with several savings and loans and microfinance companies also going down. Per the BoG records, the monetary values of fraud cases for the year 2016 aggregate to the equivalent of $44,789,725 (BoG, 2019). As an emerging economy, the effects of these fraud cases in Ghana have been felt not only by the affected firms but also by individuals connected to the firm and the country at large. Due to the huge financial and nonfinancial effects usually associated with corporate failures, the need to devote maximum attention to issues of fraud within organizations and develop ways of mitigating the occurrence of fraud has been highlighted by major stakeholders in the business community (Owusu et al., 2020). Consequently, discussions on fraudulent activities by key personnel in business organizations have heightened in recent times.

While the term fraud appears to have an obvious meaning to the average person, the conceptualization of fraud in the literature has been described to be complex. It has been suggested that fraud can mean different things to different people under different circumstances (Vaisu et al., 2003). Depending on the professional and social orientation of an individual and the prevailing circumstance at the time of the occurrence of an act, that act may be considered fraudulent or not (reference). By implication, the same act that may be classified as fraudulent in one instance may not be deemed as fraudulent in other instances based on the unique prevailing circumstance and reference to other considerations. Due to the different ways by which fraud can be conceptualized, it is important to take into consideration when discussing the phenomenon, the uniqueness of the person or group defining it, and exactly what is being referred to.

Conceptualization of Fraud in the Literature

The literature is rich with several meanings of fraud from different perspectives, by different researchers, and some identifiable bodies. Silverstone and Sheetz (2007) define fraud simply to mean harm, wrongdoing, and deceit while Zervos (1992, p. 199) considers fraud simply as "the art of deception for gain". Gilbert (1997) considers acts of deceits including intentional distortion of the truth, misrepresentation, or concealment of a material fact that can help a person to gain an unfair advantage over another to secure something of value or deprive another of a right as fraud. Smith (2001) defines fraud, from the business perspective, to involve acts that can be as trivial as an employee having an extended lunch break without permission, to large-scale misappropriation of funds by a company accountant involving many millions of dollars. From a criminal perspective, fraud is conceptualized to mean "a generic category of criminal conduct that involves the use of dishonest or deceitful means in order to obtain some unjust advantage or gain over another" (Smith, 2001, p. 1).

Organized bodies such as The International Auditing and Assurance Standards Board (IAASB) and The Association of Certified Fraud Examiners (ACFE) have also defined fraud in diverse ways. The IAASB, for instance, defines fraud as "an intentional act by one or more individuals among management, those charged with governance, employees, or third parties, involving the use of deception to obtain an unjust or illegal advantage" (ISA 240, 2009, p. 5). The ACFE, on the other hand, defines fraud as "a knowing misrepresentation of the truth or concealment of material fact to cause detriment to another" (ACFE, 2018, p. 6).

Although there appears to be different definitions for the phenomenon fraud, central to these definitions is the fact that fraud remains an act of deceit usually perpetrated against an entity or a person, by an individual or a group of individuals for personal gains or to benefit their organizations. Again, common to the definitions of fraud is the fact that the act of deception is purposeful and not by accident, and it is meant to cause harm to another (a person or an entity) or deprive another of something (Koomson et al., 2020).

Fraud in Corporations

The issue of fraud continues to attract the attention of researchers globally due to the increasing growth in reported cases of fraud within organizations and its negative impact on the sustainability of businesses. The effect of fraud is huge and includes both financial and nonfinancial effects. Globally, organizations lose about 5% of their revenues to fraud every year (ACFE, 2018). Due to the huge financial losses usually associated with corporate failures, the need to devote attention to issues of fraud within organizations and develop ways of mitigating the occurrence of fraud has been highlighted by major stakeholders in the business community (Owusu et al., 2020). Consequently, discussions on fraudulent activities by key personnel in business organizations have heightened in recent times.

Perpetrators of Fraud

Fraud against corporations can be committed both internally and externally. Fraud by external parties comes in a variety of schemes. External parties to a firm can exploit weak internal controls in that firm to take away the resources of the firm. For instance, external perpetrators can steal money from a firm when there are poor access controls to the cash safe (Mui & Mailley, 2015). Organizations also face dangers of security breaks and burglaries of property by outsiders, hacking, and information theft, among others. In some instances, external perpetrators of fraud against organizations are former employees of the firm who try to take advantage of their prior knowledge of the organization (Mui & Mailley, 2015).

While the prevalence of external fraud and its impact on business success cannot be underestimated, fraud perpetrated internally has been acknowledged to be the most pervasive against businesses in recent times (Gullkvist & Jokipii, 2013; Mustafa & Youssef, 2010; Zahari et al., 2020). Internal fraud occurs when those trusted to protect the assets and resources of an organization purposely misuse or misapply the organization's resources and assets for their own enhancement (ACFE, 2016). Perpetrators of internal fraud may, therefore, be the executives, employees, and managers of organizations. In literature, internal fraud is commonly referred to as "Occupational Fraud". Occupational fraud, i.e., internally perpetuated fraud, is believed to be the largest and most prevalent threat organizations and the global economy are confronted with (ACFE, 2018).

Common Forms of Fraud at the Workplace

Literature acknowledges different forms of fraud that can occur at the workplace. The most widely used classification of fraud is the Occupational Fraud and Abuse Classification System, developed by the ACFE. This classification distinguishes between three common forms of fraud that occur within an organization as corruption, financial statement fraud, and asset misappropriation (ACFE, 2016).

Corruption

Corruption as a form of fraud is explained by ACFE (2012, p. 2) to include "schemes that result in abuse of power or influence by an individual in a business transaction in a way that violates the individual's duty to the employer in order to gain a direct or indirect benefit". Such schemes include, but not limited to, bribery, embezzlement, and forgery (Gorsira et al., 2018). The Association of Certified Fraud Examiners reports that corruption represents about 38% of fraud perpetrated internally against organizations, making it the second most common form of occupational fraud (ACFE, 2018).

Financial Statement Fraud

Financial statement fraud, which accounts for about 10% of occupational fraud, is the least common of the three occupational fraud schemes in terms of frequency of occurrence but often results in the highest of losses. Financial statement fraud includes deliberate adjustments to a firm's financial statements to mislead users of financial information by portraying a false image of the firm (ACFE, 2018; Robinson & Aria, 2018). Unlike some unintentional errors that may lead to misstatements in the financial statements of firms, the perpetrators of financial statement fraud carefully plan these modifications to the financial statement to their benefit (Robinson, 2018). Financial statement fraud can be broadly classified into three: change in accounting methods, fiddling with managerial estimates of cost and accelerated or delayed revenue, and expenditure recognition (Beasley et al., 2000). Although the least in terms of occurrence, financial statement fraud often results in the most losses to organizations (ACFE, 2018).

Asset Misappropriation

Asset misappropriation is the third and most prevalent fraud that occurs in organizations and basically refers to all activities that result in the misuse or theft of an organization's resources that are classified as misappropriation of assets (ACFE, 2012). Compared to the other forms of fraud, asset misappropriation is generally easier to commit and hence can be committed by all individuals within a firm. This to a large extent explains why asset misappropriation has been found to be the most prevalent form of fraud by existing studies (ACFE, 2018; ACFE, 2016; Padgett, 2015). Asset misappropriation schemes are mainly grouped into two: cash misappropriation and misappropriation involving inventory and all other assets. The latter has five sub misappropriation schemes: theft of cash on hand; theft of cash receipts in the form of skimming or cash larceny; fraudulent disbursements in the form of billing, payroll, or expense reimbursement schemes, check, and payment tampering and register disbursement; and misuse of assets; and larceny of assets (ACFE, 2018). Although asset misappropriation may not result in huge direct losses as with financial statement fraud, misappropriating assets rids firms of resources that could have been used for the enhancement of performance and subsequent increase in profitability levels (ACFE, 2016).

ACFE (2018) reports that asset misappropriation cases increased by about 6% since their 2016 report to 89%. In addition to its dominance, asset misappropriation is a phenomenon that is of great importance to the Accounting discipline, especially in the field of Auditing. The current professional audit standards ISA 240 extends auditors' responsibility for fraud detection to include asset misappropriation.

Theoretical Perspective on Fraud

Several theories have been employed by researchers in examining fraud including the Fraud Scale, Fraud Cube, Fraud Square, and ABC of white-collar crime among others. However, the two most dominant theories that have frequently been employed by several studies on fraud are the Fraud Triangle Theory (FTT) and the Fraud Diamond Theory (FDT).

Fraud Triangle Theory

Considered the most popular theory in fraud research, the FTT is a refined version of a concept originally propounded by a renowned criminologist, Donald R. Cressey. Cressey (1953) explores the reasons for which people commit fraud, focusing on the motivation for individuals to violate trust. Findings of the study suggest that trusted individuals may violate trust when confronted with some pressures which can't be shared with others; when they are able to justify the reason for violating trust; and when they find situations that create an opportunity to violate trust (Cressey, 1953). Three interrelated factors: Pressure, Rationalization, and Opportunity are identified by Cressey (1953) to be the main determinants of fraudulent acts by individuals. These three factors together constitute the component of the FTT.

Although Cressey's FTT has been widely used and supported by several empirical studies, some researchers have criticized the FTT for being limited in some regards. The FTT has been argued to be inadequate in deterring, preventing, and detecting fraud as two tenets of the theory, pressure and rationalization, cannot be observed (Albrecht, 1991; Mui & Mailley, 2015). Albrecht (1991) also argues that the FTT only focuses on a micro view of the perpetrator's disposition. Due to the difficulty in determining an individual's pressure and rationalization, some researchers suggest that factors such as the perpetrator's capabilities and other nonfinancial factors which are not included in the FTT be introduced to the fraud literature (Wolfe & Hermanson, 2004; Kassem & Higson, 2012; Melorose et al., 2015; Ruankaew, 2016; Sujeewa et al., 2018; Vousinas, 2019).

It is on the basis of the aforementioned limitations that the FDT was introduced.

Fraud Diamond Theory

In response to the criticisms raised against the FTT, Wolfe and Hermanson (2004) introduced a fourth factor which is observable, Capability, to the FTT to assess the abilities an individual possesses or a position of advantage that can enable the person to engage in a fraudulent act. The inclusion of Capability introduces a nonfinancial factor to the fraud theory which captures the fraud perpetrator's personal abilities (Kassem & Higson, 2012; Wolfe & Hermanson, 2004). A new fraud theory, the FDT, emerged with four elements: Pressure, Rationalization, Opportunity, and Capability to be a better tool for preventing and detecting fraud (Wolfe & Hermanson, 2004). With the influx of new trends in the occurrence of fraud and some limitations leveled against the FDT, a new fraud theory emerged: the S.C.O.R.E. model.

Stimulus, Capability, Opportunity, Rationalization, and Ego Model (the S.C.O.R.E. Model)

Although the FTT and FDT are the most widely used models for explaining why people commit fraud, recent studies suggest that the FTT and the FDT should not be seen as the sufficiently reliable models (Lokanan, 2015; Vousinas, 2019). Some criticisms raised against the FTT and FDT include they not being able to meet all considerable social changes as they are more than a decade old (Lokanan, 2015; Vousinas, 2019), hence the need for a new model for examining fraud. A more recent theory, the S.C.O.R.E. model, was developed by Vousinas (2019) to address some of the inherent limitations of the FTT and FDT. Vousinas (2019) argues that apart from the four known predictors of fraud based on the FTT and FDT, the ego of an individual should also be considered when investigating the determinants of fraud. The S.C.O.R.E. model consequently postulates that five factors may account for why individuals engage in fraud: stimulus/pressure, capability, opportunity, rationalization, and ego. The S.C.O.R.E. model is shown pictorially in Figure 13.1.

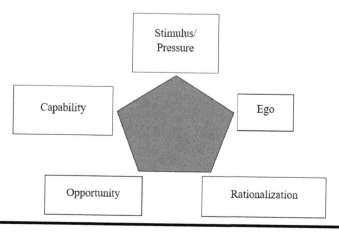

Figure 13.1 The S.C.O.R.E.

Source: Vousinas (2019).

Pressure (Stimulus)

Pressure is explained as a nonshareable problem that motivates a person to commit fraud (Cressey, 1953). The pressure to commit fraud arises when an individual is faced with financial and nonfinancial burdens that may drive him/her to engage in fraudulent activities (Cressey, 1953). Albrecht et al. (2006) conclude that all individuals in the organization, be it the executive, management, or employees, experience some form of pressure. Individuals faced with such pressures tend to seek interim options to solve their problems, and engaging in fraudulent activities becomes a possible alternative (Albrecht et al., 2010; Skousen Omar & Mohamad Din, 2010). According to Hasnan et al. (2008), pressure is exerted from either the external environment to meet certain financial goals or a personally generated desire to attain some financial targets. This pressure need not be real; once the individual believes he or she is being pressured, it is likely to influence that individual to engage in fraudulent activities to come out of such pressures (Albrecht et al., 2006).

Pressure may seem different depending on the position of an individual in an organization. For example, a manager may be under pressure to meet some targets and hence manage earnings to escalate profits reported in the financial statement, whereas a treasurer, due to personal pressure, may take home some money from the cash safe of the firm (Said et al., 2017).

Opportunity

Another important factor that influences individuals to commit fraud is the existence of "opportunity" to engage in the fraudulent act. When organizations trust certain individuals to be in charge of some important roles within the organization with little or no supervision, it may create an opportunity for the occurrence of fraud (Omar & Din, 2010). Also, an organization with a weak internal control system lacks measures to detect and prevent fraud, has no sanctions for fraud perpetrators to deter others, or lacks an audit trial presents an opportunity for its employees to commit fraud (Kassem & Higson, 2012). Similar to pressure, opportunity can be real or not. Once an individual believes that such opportunities exist, he or she may take advantage to engage in fraudulent activities (Albrecht et al., 2006).

Kumar et al. (2018) report that if over time, organizations fail to seal opportunities for the occurrence of fraud, some workers in the organization may see it as a signal of "slack organizational culture" and eventually take advantage of these opportunities. To the extent that organizations cannot control individual factors such as financial and personal pressures, an important avenue for minimizing the occurrence of fraud is to avoid creating an opportunity for fraud (McClurg & Butler, 2006; Ruankaew, 2016).

Rationalization

Perpetrators of fraud often have a mindset that makes them give excuses to justify their actions (Hooper & Pornelli, 2010). Rationalization is explained as an attitude of an individual that makes him or her justify immoral acts they engage in as needful (Abdullah & Mansor, 2015). As argued by Jackson et al. (2010), if a person is not able to provide justifications for his or her wrongdoings, it is unlikely that individual will engage in acts considered to be unethical such as fraud. According to Rae and Subramanian (2008), people often rationalize to justify unethical behaviors because they lack personal integrity and moral reasoning.

Individuals give several rationalizations for their fraudulent behaviors. Some people have a belief that once their actions do not hurt others directly, or their actions will help achieve an ultimate good, it is not fraudulent. In a typical work environment, when people perceive to be underpaid, they consider fraudulent acts against their organization as a form of compensation to them. As a result, people develop rationalizations such as "I deserve a bonus or a raise but did not get one" and "I am underpaid, the organization owes me" which makes engaging in fraudulent acts easier (Cressey, 1953; Ramamoorti, 2008; Said et al., 2017; Zikmund, 2008). Rationalization, therefore, enables perpetrators of fraud to justify their actions to make them acceptable to themselves and protect their belief and self-image as honest, innocent persons who were unfortunate to be caught up in a critical situation and not criminals (Cressey, 1953; Said, Asry, et al., 2018).

Capability

Capability encompasses the "personal traits and abilities that play a major role in whether fraud may occur even with the presence of the other three elements of the fraud triangle theory" (Wolfe & Hermanson, 2004, p. 1). The key argument espoused by this study is that most of the fraudulent acts that led to massive loss of resources occurred because people with the right capabilities were involved. As explained by the authors, the relevance of the construct capability in explaining fraudulent activities of individuals stems from the fact that while the existence of an opportunity opens the doorway to fraud, and notwithstanding the fact that pressure and rationalization can draw the person toward it, a person must have the capability to recognize the open doorway as an opportunity to take advantage of it. Thus, the ability to recognize the existence of the opportunity alone is not enough to commit fraud unless an individual is well positioned to take advantage of that opportunity. A fraud perpetrator should, therefore, have the skills and ability to actually commit the fraud.

Wolfe and Hermanson (2004) explained capability to encompass six elements: position, smartness, confidence, coercion, effective lying, and dealing with stress. First, the person should be in a position or perform a function within the organization that grants him access to the assets of the organization and allows him or her to commit fraud. Often, this position is not enjoyed by others in the organization and hence provides an advantage that can be exploited by the individual to commit fraud. For example, a store's manager is in a better position to abuse the assets of an organization since he keeps and reports on the assets in stock. Again, performing a function repetitively increases one's knowledge and control of the process over time and hence the capability of the individual to commit fraud heightens.

Second, the fraud perpetrator should be smart enough to notice there exist and then take advantage of the weaknesses in the internal system (Wolfe & Hermanson, 2004). Most of the reported fraud cases have intelligent and creative minds behind them. The ACFE affirms this in their report to the nations when they found that about 51% of fraud perpetrators had at least a bachelor's degree (ACFE, 2016).

The person to perpetrate the fraud must also have the confidence that he will not be caught, and the cost that would accrue to him would be minimal. The fraud action would be considered less costly when the confidence of the perpetrator is high. Also, the perpetrator should be someone who can convince others to go along or look away to enhance a fraud. The perpetrator also needs to be a consistent liar to be able to keep the stories he or she makes to cover up for the fraud meaningful. Finally, committing fraud comes with the constant fear of being detected and its related consequences of shame and punishment. Dealing with this feeling daily can be very stressful. The perpetrator must, therefore, be good in dealing with stress (Wolfe & Hermanson, 2004).

Ego

Vousinas (2019) argues that the social pressures individuals face force them to engage in fraudulent activities primarily to keep their ego. Because people cherish and do not want to lose their reputation, especially one of power, they may or may not involve themselves in certain activities just to keep their ego (Vousinas, 2019). On the positive side, people who want to maintain their reputation may not want to tarnish their integrity and hence would be conscious not to engage in actions that suggest otherwise. Such individuals are less likely to engage in activities considered unethical or immoral. On the other hand, people can also go to the extreme to do anything just to keep their status in life. Such extremes may include engaging in fraudulent acts.

Individuals delight in the belief that they are outsmarting the world when their first crimes were successful and undetected. This makes them feel superior to others and boost their ego. They, therefore, engage again and again in such fraudulent activities as far as they are not being caught having the excitement of tricking the world (Vousinas, 2019). Duffield and Grabosky (2001) also suggest that aside from financial pressure, ego could be another motivation for fraud. The two streams of ego: power over people and power over situations could cause individuals to commit fraud.

Vousinas (2019) argues that ego appears to be a common trend in some of the most recent shocking frauds and provides instances of fraud cases where ego is seen to play a role. First is the case of Russell Wasendorf, founder of Peregrine Financial Group, who admitted in a suicide note that "I guess my ego was too big to admit failure. So, I cheated". Second, the oversized ego of Robert Allen Stanford, owner of Stanford Financial Group, was responsible for the $7bn global Ponzi scheme. The third is the Ponzi scheme considered the largest financial fraud in the history of United States: the Bernie Madoff's $65bn scam. Madoff's ego was too huge for him to accept failure and stated that "I refused to accept the fact, could not accept the fact, that for once in my life I failed".

Discussion

This section discusses the application of the S.C.O.R.E. model to both the fraud literature and practice. How the model explains the determinants of fraud is highlighted, and a conceptual framework is developed as a guide for future research. On the basis of the proposed conceptual framework, this section also suggests practical guidelines on how the model can be used in determining the occurrence of fraud at the workplace.

Drawing from the tenets of the S.C.O.R.E. model, this chapter proposes that five factors can influence an individual to commit fraud at the workplace: pressure, rationalization, opportunity, capability, and ego. The predicted relationship between these factors and fraud is developed into a conceptual model as presented in Figure 13.2.

Pressure and Fraud

From theoretical perspective and existing empirical evidence on fraud, it has been established that when individuals are faced with intense pressure be it financial or nonfinancial, they tend to find ways to alleviate such pressures. Engaging in fraudulent activities becomes an option once it presents an intervening solution to their problem. Based on this premise, and consistent with the evidence provided by some other related studies, this chapter argues that pressure may be associated with the motivation to engage in fraud at the workplace. Empirical evidence from several studies supports the claim that pressure positively influences fraud at the workplace (Albrecht et al., 2010; Cressey, 1953; Omar & Mohamad Din, 2010; Ruankaew, 2016; Said et al., 2017).

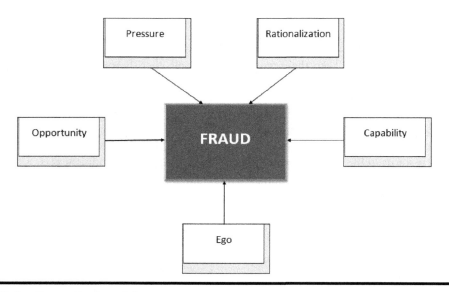

Figure 13.2   Conceptual model.

Rationalization and Fraud

The chapter argues that when individuals hold beliefs that fraudulent activities are needful and harm no one directly and are able to justify their actions, there is a higher propensity for that person to engage in fraud. For instance, a frequently cited justification for fraud at the workplace is the belief that it is a means of compensating oneself for poor remuneration by the employer. People with such mindsets easily rationalize their actions through their inner conviction hold the view that engaging in acts deemed fraudulent may be worthwhile in their unique circumstances while maintaining the belief that they have done nothing wrong. Ghafoor et al. (2019), Kassem and Higson (2012), Said, Asry, et al. (2018), Kazemian et al. (2019), Vousinas (2019), and Wolfe and Hermanson (2004) all provide empirical support that rationalization has a positive relationship with fraud.

Opportunity and Fraud

When opportunities for fraud exist in organizations (the existence of loopholes for exploitation), especially in the form of weak internal control measures, the motivation to engage in fraudulent activities in the workplace is usually high. Some individuals may take advantage of the slacks in the internal control mechanisms to commit fraud because they believe there is a lower likelihood of being exposed. When the internal controls are strong, however, it serves as a deterrent to the occurrence of fraud. The rate of fraud is higher when individuals perceive that certain opportunities for the occurrence of fraud are not sealed in the organization (Holtfreter, 2004; Jokipii, 2010; Le & Tran, 2018).

Capability and Fraud

Fraud is often easier to commit when the perpetrator occupies a position of influence that gives the person access to the assets of the firm. Such individuals often have the capacity to exploit weaknesses within the organization, are often confident of not being exposed and even when caught, may be able to escape the consequences. As pointed out by Wolfe and Hermanson (2004), along with pressure, opportunity, and rationalization, the fraud perpetrator must have the capability to recognize an open door as an opportunity and take advantage of it. There have been several studies that conclude that the capability of an individual to commit fraud is a determinant of the occurrence of fraud (Mackevičius & Giriūnas, 2013; Albrecht et al., 1995; Kassem & Higson, 2012; Abdullahi & Mansor, 2015).

Ego and Fraud

People sometimes attach a strong sense of importance to building a status which they wish to maintain mainly because of how the perceptions of others affect their ego. Vousinas (2019) reports that to maintain their status in life, especially one of power, and keep their egos, some individuals are prepared to go any length, including engaging in fraudulent acts. Being egoistic is, therefore, associated with the likelihood of the occurrence of fraudulent activities. Findings from some existing studies demonstrate that ego has a positive relationship with the occurrence of fraud (Koomson et al., 2020; Pedneault et al., 2012).

Implications to Practice and Policy

The argument in this chapter has important implications for practice and policymakers. The chapter highlights certain factors that may be responsible for the occurrence of fraud in firms. The proposed conceptual framework, as shown in Figure 13.1, can be adopted by managers as a guide to look out for the influencers of fraud in their firms.

With reference to the impact of pressure, managers of firms can examine the reasonableness of the workload of their employees, the key performance indicators assigned to them, and the timelines to deliver. This will guard against having employees posed with too much pressure from the workplace in addition to some pressures they may be facing outside of work. The firm can also have a strong human resource support system that investigates personal financial and nonfinancial problems of its employees and develop ways to help its employees. This will reduce the likelihood of employees resorting to fraud as the only way out of such pressures.

A frequent basis of rationalizing fraud as discussed in this chapter is the fact that employees feel underpaid. To reduce the rate at which employees will rationalize certain fraudulent acts as needful, as proposed by the conceptual model, managers of firms should ensure that employees are treated fairly, especially in terms of remuneration and other compensation schemes. Therefore, when employees are paid well, it minimizes the risk of having some employees commit fraud in the workplace using inadequate pay as a justification.

The opportunity to commit fraud is, perhaps, one area firms can control the most to minimize the level of fraud committed within the firm. Organizations can put in place strong internal control mechanisms that seals all loopholes within the firm that makes committing fraud easy. Again, firms can have stringent measures of dealing with fraud perpetrators who are caught to serve as a deterrent to others to reduce the occurrence of fraud. Given that there is a limit to which firms can control other factors that are more personal to the perpetrators of fraud, firms should leverage on sealing the opportunities that may exist within the workplace to reduce the ease to commit fraud.

The capabilities of individuals within an organization are often derived from the level of trust the firm has in them and how much access the firm allows such individuals to have to the resources and books of the firm. With the knowledge that individuals can abuse the trust placed in them to engage in fraud because they are in the capacity to, firms should be mindful of the level of autonomy given to management and employees and how much access they have to assets of the firm.

During recruitment, firms should endeavor to look out for traits that foster fraud in the workplace. For instance, the proposition that individuals who are egoist in nature often tend to engage in fraudulent activities just to keep their status could be a relevant guide to managers in identifying such traits during recruitment. Such traits, when identified prior to employment, will help managers avoid hiring such individuals to minimize the risk of the occurrence of fraud.

Again, an understanding of these push factors (pressure, rationalization, opportunity, capability, and ego) could be a useful tool to policymakers in mapping up strategies aimed at reducing the occurrence of fraud at the workplace by individuals.

Future Research and Practice Directions

An important way to extend the knowledge on fraud is for future studies to examine other determinants of fraud aside from those identified in this chapter. For instance, research on how organizational commitment, culture, personality traits, and other behavioral traits influence individuals to commit fraud would enrich the fraud discourse.

Again, the factors found to influence employees to commit could be a guide to organizations in developing strategies to reduce the occurrence of fraudulent acts within their firms.

Conclusion

The involvement of employees, managers, and sometimes owners of organizations in perpetrating fraud against their own organizations has been on the rise, and this has generated intense research interest in internally perpetrated fraud. Most existing research has studied the phenomenon of fraud mainly through the lens of the FTT and the FDT. The chapter shares some new insights into fraud discourse by proposing a new framework based on a new fraud theory, the S.C.O.R.E. model. Accordingly, it is predicted that from the perspective of the S.C.O.R.E. model, five broad factors: pressure, rationalization, opportunity, capability, and ego, may be associated with the motivation to engage in fraudulent behavior at the workplace.

Thus, this chapter opines that individuals engage in fraudulent acts at the workplace, first, because of certain financial or nonfinancial pressures they face either at work or from family and friends; second, when they can justify their actions as not wrong or consider such wrongful acts as compensation for work done; third, when the internal control systems of their firms fails to prevent, detect, and deter fraud; fourth, when they occupy positions in the organization that give them access to the resources of the firm or have certain traits that gives them the capability to commit fraud; and fifth, when they have an egoistic nature to maintain their status in society.

References

Abdullahi, R., & Mansor, N. (2015). Fraud Triangle Theory and Fraud Diamond Theory. Understanding the Convergent and Divergent for Future Research. *International Journal of Academic Research in Accounting, Finance and Management Science, 1*, 38–45.

Albrecht, C., Turnbull, C., Zhang, Y., & Skousen, C. J. (2010). The Relationship Between South Korean Chaebols and Fraud. *Management Research Review, 33*(3), 257–268.

Albrecht, W. S. (1991). Fraud in Government Entities: The Perpetrators and the Types of Fraud. *Government Finance Review, 7*(6), 27–30.

Albrecht, W. S., Hill, N. C., & Albrecht, C. C. (2006). The Ethics Development Model Applied to Declining Ethics in Accounting. *Australian Accounting Review, 16*(1), 30–40.

Albrecht, W. S., Williams, T. L., Wernz, G. W. (1995). *Fraud: Bringing Light to the Dark Side of Business*. Burr Ridge, IL: Irwin.

Association of Certified Fraud Examiners. (2012). *Report to the Nations on Occupational Fraud and Abuse: 2012 Global Fraud Study*.

Association of Certified Fraud Examiners. (2016). *Report to the Nations on Occupational Fraud and Abuse: 2016 Global Fraud Study*. Austin, TX: Association of Certified Fraud Examiners.

Association of Certified Fraud Examiners (ACFE). (2018). *2018 Global Fraud Study: Report to the Nation on Occupational Fraud and Abuse Asia-Pacific Edition* (pp. 1–28). Austin, TX: Association of Certified Fraud Examiners.

Beasley, M. S., Carcello, J. V., Hermanson, D. R., & Lapides, P. D. (2000). Fraudulent Financial Reporting: Consideration of Industry Traits and Corporate Governance Mechanisms. *Accounting Horizons, 14*(4), 441–454.

BoG. (2019). *Bank Fraud Swallows GHS44.4m; GHS19.1m Staff-Aided—BoG Report*. Accra, Ghana: Bank of Ghana.

Cressey, D. R. (1953). The Criminal Violation of Financial Trust. *American Sociological Review, 15*(6), 738–743.

Duffield, G., & Grabosky, P. (2001). *The Psychology of Fraud. Trends and Issues in Crime and Criminal Justice*. Canberra: Australian Institute of Criminology.

Ghafoor, A., Zainudin, R., & Mahdzan, N. S. (2019). Factors Eliciting Corporate Fraud in Emerging Markets: Case of Firms Subject to Enforcement Actions in Malaysia. *Journal of Business Ethics, 160*(2), 587–608.

Gilbert. (1997). *Pocket Size Law Dictionary—Black. Gilbert Law Summaries Staff*. San Diego, CA: Harcourt Brace Legal and Professional Publications.

Gorsira, M., Steg, L., Denkers, A., & Huisman, W. (2018). Corruption in Organizations: Ethical Climate and Individual Motives. *Administrative Sciences, 8*(1), 4.

Gullkvist, B., & Jokipii, A. (2013). Perceived Importance of Red Flags Across Fraud Types. *Critical Perspectives on Accounting, 24*(1), 44–61.

Hasnan, S., Abdul Rahman, R., & Mahenthrian, S. (2008). Management Predisposition, Motive, Opportunity, and Earnings Management for Fraudulent Financial Reporting in Malaysia (December 15, 2008).

Holtfreter, K. (2004). Fraud in US Organizations: An Examination of Control Mechanisms. *Journal of Financial Crime, 12*(1), 88–96.

Hooper, M. J., & Pornelli, C. M. (2010). *Deterring and Detecting Financial Fraud: A Platform for Action*. Washington, DC: Center for Audit Quality. https://www.thecaq.org/wp-content/uploads/2019/03/deterring-and-detecting-financial-reporting-fraud-a-platform-for-action.pdf

ISA. (2009). *International Standard on Auditing 240: The Auditor's Responsibilities Relating to Fraud in an Audit of Financial Statements*. New York, NY: International Auditing and Assurance Standards Board (IAASB).

Jackson, K., Holland, D., Albrecht, C., & Woolstenhulme, D. (2010). Fraud Isn't Just for Big Business: Understanding the Drivers, Consequences, and Prevention of Fraud in Small Business. *Journal of International Management Studies, 5*(1), 160–164.

Jokipii, A. (2010). Determinants and Consequences of Internal Control in Firms: A Contingency Theory-Based Analysis. *Journal of Management & Governance, 14*(2), 115–144.

Kassem, R., & Higson, A. (2012). The New Fraud Triangle Model. *Journal of Emerging Trends in Economics and Management Sciences, 3*(3), 191–195.

Kazemian, S., Said, J., Nia, E. H., Vakilifard, H., & Futter, A. (2019). Examining Fraud Risk Factors on Asset Misappropriation: Evidence from the Iranian Banking Industry. *Journal of Financial Crime, 26*(2), 447–463.

Koomson, T. A. A., Owusu, G. M. Y., Bekoe, R. A., & Oquaye, M. (2020). Determinants of Asset Misappropriation at the Workplace: The Moderating Role of Perceived Strength of Internal Controls. *Journal of Financial Crime, 27*(4), 1191–1211.

Kumar, K., Bhattacharya, S., & Hicks, R. (2018). Employee Perceptions of Organization Culture with Respect to Fraud—Where to Look and What to Look for. *Pacific Accounting Review, 30*(2), 187–198.

Le, T. T. H., & Tran, M. D. (2018). The Effect of Internal Control on Asset Misappropriation: The Case of Vietnam. *Business and Economic Horizons, 14*(4), 941–953.

Lokanan, M. E. (2015). Challenges to the Fraud Triangle: Questions on its Usefulness. *Accounting Forum, 39*(3), 201–224.

Low, M., Davey, H., & Hooper, K. (2008). Accounting Scandals, Ethical Dilemmas and Educational Challenges. *Critical Perspectives on Accounting, 19*(2), 222–254.

Mackevičius, J., & Giriūnas, L. (2013). Transformational Research of the Fraud Triangle. *Ekonomika, 92*(4), 150–163.

McClurg, L. A., & Butler, D. S. (2006). Workplace Theft: A Proposed Model and Research Agenda. *Southern Business Review, 31*(2), 25–34.

Melorose, J., Perroy, R., & Careas, S. (2015). the New Fraud Diamond Model- How Can It Help Forensic Accountants in Fraud Investigation in Nigeria? *Statewide Agricultural Land Use Baseline 2015, 1*(4), 129–138.

Mui, G., & Mailley, J. (2015). A Tale of Two Triangles: Comparing the Fraud Triangle with Crime Triangle. *Accounting Research Journal, 28*(1), 45–58.

Mustafa, S. T., & Youssef, N. B. (2010). Audit Committee Financial Expertise and Misappropriation of Assets. *Managerial Auditing Journal, 25*(3), 208–225.

Omar, N. B., & Mohamad Din, H. F. (2010). *Fraud Diamond Risk Indicator: An Assessment of its Importance and Usage.* CSSR 2010–2010 International Conference on Science and Social Research, (July 2005), 607–612.

Owusu, G. M. Y., Bekoe, R. A., Anokye, F. K., & Okoe, F. O. (2020). Whistleblowing Intentions of Accounting Students. *Journal of Financial Crime, 27*(2), 477–492.

Padgett, S. (2015). About the Association of Certified Fraud Examiners and the Report to the Nations on Occupational Fraud and Abuse. *Profiling the Fraudster*, 239–242.

Pedneault, S., Silverstone, H., & Rudewicz, F., & Sheetz, M. (2012). *Forensic Accounting and Fraud Investigation for Non-Experts.* Hoboken, NJ: John Wiley and Sons.

PricewaterhouseCoopers. (2016). *Adjusting the Lens on Economic Crime. Global Economic Crime Survey* (pp. 9–18). London: PricewaterhouseCoopers.

Rae, K., &. Subramanian, N. (2008). Quality of Internal Control Procedures: Antecedents and Moderating Effect on Organizational Justice and Employee Fraud. *Managerial Auditing Journal, 23*(2), 1–43.

Ramamoorti, S. (2008). The Psychology and Sociology of Fraud: Integrating the Behavioral Sciences Component into Fraud and Forensic Accounting Curricula. *Issues in Accounting Education, 23*(4), 521–533.

Robinson, H. (2018). *An Analysis of the SEC's Prosecution of Financial and Accounting Related Fraud.* USF St. Petersburg campus Honors Program Theses (Undergraduate). St. Petersburg, FL: University of South Florida St. Petersburg. https://digitalcommons.usf.edu/honorstheses/241

Robinson, W. N., & Aria, A. (2018). Sequential Fraud Detection for Prepaid Cards Using Hidden Markov Model Divergence. *Expert Systems with Applications, 91*, 235–251.

Ruankaew, T. (2016). Beyond the Fraud Diamond. *International Journal of Business Management and Economic Research, 7*(1), 474–476.

Said, J., Alam, M. M., Ramli, M., & Rafidi, M. (2017). Integrating Ethical Values into Fraud Triangle Theory in Assessing Employee fraud: Evidence from the Malaysian Banking Industry. *Journal of International Studies, 10*(2), 170–184.

Said, J., Asry, S., Rafidi, M., Obaid, R. R., & Alam, M. M. (2018). Integrating Religiosity into Fraud Triangle Theory: Empirical Findings from Enforcement Officers. *Global Journal Al Thaqafah, 8*(1), 131–143.

Silverstone, H., & Sheetz, M. (2007). *Forensic Accounting and Fraud Investigation for NonExperts* (2nd ed.). Hoboken, NJ: John Wiley & Sons.

Smith, R. G. (2001). *Defining, Measuring, and Reporting Fraud Risk within Your Organization.* IIR Conferences, Applying Risk Management to Implement a Proactive Fraud Prevention Strategy in Financial Services. Parkroyal Darling Harbour, 19–20.

Sujeewa, G. M. M., Yajid, M. S. A., Azam, S. M. F., & Dharmaratne, I. (2018). The New Fraud Triangle Theory— Integrating Ethical Values of Employees. *International Journal of Business, Economics and Law, 16*(5).

Tang, T. L. P., & Sutarso, T. (2013). Falling or Not Falling into Temptation? Multiple Faces of Temptation, Monetary Intelligence, and Unethical Intentions Across Gender. *Journal of Business Ethics, 116*(3), 529–552.

Vaisu, L., Warren, M., & Mackay, D. (2003). Defining Fraud: Issues for Organizations from an Information Systems Perspective. *7th Pacific Asia Conference on Information Systems*, 10–13.

Vousinas, G. L. (2019). Advancing Theory of Fraud: The S.C.O.R.E. Model. *Journal of Financial Crime, 26*(1), 372–381.

Wolfe, D. T., & Hermanson, D. R. (2004). The Fraud Diamond: Considering the Four Elements of Fraud: Certified Public Accountant. *The CPA Journal, 74*(12), 38–42.

Zahari, A. I., Said, J., & Arshad, R. (2020). Organizational Fraud: A Discussion on the Theoretical Perspectives and Dimensions. *Journal of Financial Crime, 27*(1), 283–293.

Zervos, K. (1992). Responding to Fraud in the 1990s. *Complex Commercial Fraud*, 199–209.

Zikmund, P. E. (2008). Reducing the Expectation Gap. *The CPA Journal, 78*(6), 20–25.

Authors' Profile

Theodora Aba Abekah Koomson is a young academic with the Department of Accounting, University of Ghana Business School. Her research interest mainly focuses on issues in Behavioral Accounting and Finance. She has journal articles that cut across diverse issues with a keen interest in Ethics and Fraud. One of the papers she coauthored, "Temptation and the Propensity to Engage in Unethical Behavior", was awarded the outstanding paper of the year 2020 by the *International Journal of Ethics and Systems* and Emerald Publishing in their 2020 Literati Awards.

Godfred Matthew Yaw Owusu is an associate professor and researcher with the Department of Accounting, University of Ghana Business School. He is an active researcher who specializes in the use of structural equation modeling techniques in understanding topical behavioral Accounting and Finance issues. He has published several papers in reputable journals focusing predominantly on tax compliance, whistleblowing, fraud, ethics, financial behavior, and financial well-being of individuals.

Chapter 14

Developing Nexus Managerial Resilience Using Spiritual Intelligence: An Investigation of Malaysia's Transformation to Industry Revolution 4.0

Jegatheesan Rajadurai, Vathana Bathmanathan, Amar Hisham Jaaffar, and Revin Rajan

Contents

Introduction

Since the beginning of IR 4.0 in 2011, especially in the manufacturing sector, IR 4.0 has quickly spread and been adapted to become the most common agenda among industrialists, employers, and policymakers. Some scenarios are already taking place, while others are predicted to happen in the near future. While the old economy is seen as a vertical, authoritative relationship, the new economy is more of a horizontal, trusting collaboration. Mass production is an element of the past; the new approach sees more mass collaboration. The proximity of an organization's resources was

DOI: 10.4324/9781003152217-18

previously important, but in the new economy, it is less significant. In the old, the structure was rigid, but it is now more flexible. Instead of a capitalist model, businesses in the new economic model will be based on profit-sharing.

Malaysia is relatively new to IR 4.0 and is endeavoring to implement measures to deal with the challenges that come with it. Researchers have expressed their views and interpretations of how the world should respond and why the global business culture should be concerned about the implementation of IR 4.0. This is an extremely challenging domain, encompassing interconnection between the Internet of Things and Cyber-Physical Systems which blend sensors, software, processors, and communication technology to create "things" that have the potential to provide information and, ultimately, add value to manufacturing practices (Mohamad et al., 2018).

Inextricably linked with IR 4.0 is the Nexus generation. The Nexus generation is a cohort born in years between 1980 and 2000 (Bathmanathan et al., 2018). This cohort is also known as the Millennials, Gen Y, or Echo Boomers (Jorgensen & Bradley, 2003; Nizam et al., 2014; San et al., 2015). This generation is considered to be the Internet or dot.com generation (Chaney et al., 2017; Gardiner et al., 2013; Jorgensen & Bradley, 2003) and is known for their inclination to use technology (Bathmanathan et al., 2018). Nexus generation is also known to have an individualistic behavior (Grant, 2017; Jerome et al., 2014) that they prefer to set their own timeline and excel in a flexible environment where there is a balance between their social and work life (Jerome et al., 2014). Consequently, the Nexus generation tends to be employed by IR 4.0 companies. The Nexus generation is also the generation that is moving up the corporate ladder and finding itself in positions such as supervisors, managers, or middle-level management. The Nexus generation is facing several managerial challenges thrown up by IR 4.0. In the competitive environment that we are witnessing today, they are now, unfortunately, trapped in the unenviable position of having to cope with managing operational staff relations in a sensitive and empathic manner on a daily basis, yet at the same time, having to meet the demands of their employers to generate profits and meet targets (Hossain et al., 2018; Puteh et al., 2015). Most of the literature on IR 4.0 in Malaysia has focused on technological advancement, the digital revolution, and human capital hard skills, but very few researchers have investigated the problems related to human capital soft skills and the support services that are crucial to maintaining and growing IR 4.0, thereby benefiting the nation economically (Sani, 2019; Queiri & Dwaikat, 2016; Chin & Liu, 2014).

Issues of IR 4.0 in Malaysia

There are several issues that are inherent in IR 4.0 in Malaysia. First, the transformations observed in the IR 4.0 environment have posed serious challenges to the Nexus generation's managerial confidence, capabilities, and resilience. Managerial resilience is the ability to persist and effectively adapt to adversity or bounce back from difficult events or situations (Grotberg, 1996); Tusaie and Dyer (2004). An employee's resilience is also seen as both a psychological construct focusing on individual adaptive resources and a socially constructed multidimensional concept influenced by an environmental context such as a workplace (Wanberg & Banas, 2000). Although the Nexus generation is found to be technologically savvy, the IR 4.0 environment is seen to pose a challenge to this generation's managerial resilience. This is because the members of this generation have been reported to lack critical-thinking, problem-solving skills, leadership skills, and lifelong learning skills, and they are unable to cope with the rapid changes in the IR 4.0 business environment (Sani, 2019; Queiri & Dwaikat, 2016; Chin & Liu, 2014). They also have been reported as not being socially adaptive and/or competent adaptive and displaying a low level of personal competence (Queiri & Dwaikat, 2016; Chin & Liu, 2014). In addition to these personal negatives and challenges, they have to deal with organizational challenges relating to the slowness of several organizations to adopt new processes brought about by the IR 4.0 revolution and to deal with legacy issues of companies. Nexus middle managers are further stressed due to the mismatch of their expectations with those of Gen X and the late Baby Boomer cohort of employers (Sani, 2019; Queiri & Dwaikat, 2016). In addition, IR 4.0 companies focus on profits and place tremendous pressure on middle managers who are struggling with the effects of globalization. The Nexus generation, trapped at the middle management level, is the most seriously affected having to manage staff relations while responding to employers' demands for profits and efficiency. Consequently, members of the Nexus generation are extremely stressed, resulting in early retirements and premature resignations.

Second, IR 4.0 entails the introduction of the Internet of Things, Cyber-Physical Systems, Big Data, the Data Warehouse Server, and other programs. Companies faced intense pressure to use IR 4.0 digital technologies which subsequently change their current business model and new business mindset (Lekan et al., 2020). Besides the digital transformation strategies of IR 4.0, the transformation of human capital in the organization is also every important to ensure that it is ready to face these changes. Among the fears faced by employees are the fear of being replaced by technology and an incapability to perform the new assigned duty (Bordeleau & Felden, 2019). This condition leads to a self-preservation behavior among employees which is often viewed as anger, irrationality, or refusal to make changes (Hernandez, 2021).

Middle managers in these companies, who are mostly from the Nexus generational cohort, are prone to this kind of behavior including working faster, responding to situations in real time, and competing aggressively with other companies to snare contracts (Sani, 2019; Asree et al., 2010; King et al., 2001; Nyberg et al., 2014; Puspanathan et al., 2017; Ulrich & Dulebohn, 2015; Bonekamp & Sure, 2015; Kergroach, 2017). This has impacted middle managers significantly by placing enormous workplace pressure on them.

Third, the advancement of IR 4.0 is also a threat to young managers as the machinery and software algorithms which were used to perform sophisticated analysis and decision-making processes in the past can now function without the human factor (Ford, 2009). This development has altered the way organizations work and behave toward their existing employees. The rapid growth of IR 4.0 has meant that conventional and familiar job requirements have now become fragmented and demand additional and different skillsets for middle managers (Puspanathan et al., 2017; Kergroach, 2017). This shift from a labor-intensive production system to a technologically intensive production system has not only made businesses more efficient but also caused millions to lose their positions as the advancement in cybernetics brought about by IR 4.0 made many jobs obsolete (Puspanathan et al., 2017). Many researchers believe that managers are immensely fearful of the impact of job obsolescence that automation will soon replace these managers, thereby creating a climate of fear, uncertainty, anguish, and insecurity among many middle managers (Puspanathan et al., 2017; Asree et al., 2010; King et al., 2001; Nyberg et al., 2014; Ulrich & Dulebohn, 2015).

Fourth, to meet the expectations of IR 4.0 and remain relevant to their employers and positions, many middle managers are extremely stressed due to the pressure to acquire the necessary skills to stay employed (Puspanathan et al., 2017). Businesses have reported that many of their managers are experiencing high levels of mental anguish, stress, depression, and demotivation, resulting in a decline in both performance and productivity.

Malaysian Employers' Federation executive director Datuk Shamsuddin Bardan agreed that there is already a visible increase in the number of workplace-related depression cases in the country

(Ganesan et al., 2017). Depression will be the number one disability by 2030 and is expected to deplete workplace productivity (Ganesan et al., 2017). Depression is a leading cause of economic loss at the individual, family, employer, health system, and national level due to direct and indirect health costs, absenteeism, lost productivity while at work, and decreased income—all of which can result in a reduced national economic output (Thye, 2019). The government and employers must be aware that neglecting psychosocial factors in the workplace is not only bad for the individual worker but also directly affects the productivity and output of any organization (Thye, 2019).

It then comes as no surprise that the issues stated earlier such as the IR 4.0 transformation, workplace pressure, job obsolescence, and workplace-related depression have affected the resilience of middle managers enormously. This has led to premature resignations, early retirement, and managers departing to set up their own enterprises (Puteh et al., 2015). This situation is grave and all too prevalent among young managers and has been of great concern to Human Resource Managers in Malaysia as reported frequently in the Malaysian dailies such as The New Straits Times, The Star, and The Edge, among others (Queiri et al., 2014). Ultimately, companies will lose their experienced managers and be faced with managerial shortages, as well as the possibility of being forced to relocate their businesses elsewhere. If this happens, a direct and negative consequence will be felt by the Malaysian economy (Queiri et al., 2014). Datuk Shamsuddin Bardan stated that there must be a holistic way of handling the issue to benefit both employers and employees. Fortunately, multinational companies are strategizing many new initiatives to implement "work-life balance" in their organizations (Ganesan et al., 2017); however, such initiatives are less common among local companies. This problem is seen to arise due to a lack of employer understanding of young managers' growth mindsets and behavior in the workplace (Sani, 2019; Puteh et al., 2015; Eisner, 2005).

An inordinate focus on productivity and performance by employers has created "mental torture for these middle-level managers", stated Malaysian Trade Union Council Secretary-General J. Solomon (Ganesan et al., 2017). He added that many employers set unrealistic goals, and the stressed middle managers are forced to clock in for long working hours to meet these targets (Ganesan et al., 2017). This obviously represents another challenge and a heightened sense of insecurity on the part of the Nexus generation. As the Baby Boomer generation approaches retirement and Generation X opts for early retirement or promotion to top management levels, the positions in middle management have now fallen directly on the shoulders of the Nexus generation. Companies and employers capitalize on this generation's characteristics to achieve material success at the expense of middle manager well-being. IR 4.0 has meant that many Nexus generation middle level managers have had pressure brought to bear on them to make their companies more profitable, often by making the companies more "mean and lean". This situation makes work difficult to cope with in the present environment, thus affecting their managerial abilities and behaviors. As a result, some Nexus managers resort to taking frequent medical leave as they are too depressed and demotivated to work (Ganesan et al., 2017). Employers should manage the people side of change as conscientiously as the solution design, assisting impacted groups of employees due to IR 4.0 to be ready and willing to give full commitment toward the changes (Nielsen et al., 2021). As IR 4.0 may have a negative impact on employee well-being, particularly on employees from the Nexus generation, the involvement of employees in the change process is very important to overcome this negative impact (De Jong et al., 2016).

The Nexus generation cannot be put under pressure caused by extreme working conditions, unlike Gen X and the Baby Boomer generations. Queiri and Dwaikat (2016) found that work overload, role ambiguity, job stress, job attitude, and work life conflict have contributed to Nexus generation members leaving employment soon after they have been employed. They will not hesitate to quit their jobs if they are unhappy with their work environment (Queiri et al., 2014; Chin & Liu, 2014). Job loyalty is not their priority (Sani, 2019; Queiri et al., 2014; Chin & Liu, 2014). Managers in this cohort are seen to quit their jobs more often than other generations (Yusoff et al., 2013; Raman et al., 2011; Sujansky & Ferri-Reed, 2009). On average, Nexus members are found to only remain in their positions for approximately 18 months compared to other generational cohort members who remain for an average of 4 years (Queiri et al., 2015). This is believed to be due to Nexus members' sensitivity to their employers' feedback regarding performance (Twenge et al., 2012). The author suggests that this could be the catalyst for their intention to leave employment.

Despite the literature on IR 4.0 tending to focus on human capital hard skills, infrastructural readiness, technological advancement, and digital transformation, it is evident from the discussion earlier that IR 4.0 in Malaysia is not without problems in its operational, functional, managerial divisions, and support services. Premature resignations by the Nexus cohort, early retirements, and departures to set up their own enterprises are challenges IR 4.0 companies encounter due to workplace pressure, job obsolescence, and workplace-related depression experienced by the Nexus generation middle managers (Sani, 2019; Queiri & Dwaikat, 2016; Queiri et al., 2014; Chin & Liu, 2014). Nexus employee turnover has been problematic in Malaysia since 2012 (Downe et al., 2012). Researchers investigated some factors that caused this situation (Queiri et al., 2014; Downe et al., 2012); however, they failed to investigate the root cause—the lack of managerial resilience. As such, inculcating managerial resilience among the Nexus generation middle managers is the first step toward developing a personal relationship between employers and the Nexus generation middle managers to ensure Nexus retention in these companies.

Equally worrying for IR 4.0 was the subject of recent comments by Dato Shamsuddin bin Badan and reported in the Free Malaysia Today. He said that a study by an industry research firm, International Data Corporation (IDC), found that Malaysia's undergraduates were unprepared for IR 4.0. IDC reported that 63% of the undergraduates failed to articulate what IR 4.0 was and 30% of the undergraduates felt completely unprepared for an IR 4.0 work environment. Even more concerning is that more than 50% of them felt that IR 4.0 organizations were not ready for a new generation joining the workforce, citing these companies' unwillingness to adopt new frameworks as reasons for their opinions (Aris, 2019). Therefore, these are not only problems for those already in the IR 4.0 workforce, there are those who are feeling alienated and excluded outside the workforce, thereby depriving IR 4.0 of a potentially valuable source of recruitment.

Discussion

The traditional organizational management mindset, which focused on financial rewards as a means of retaining their managers, has proven to be inadequate for the retention of Nexus managers given their distinctive characteristics discussed earlier (Queiri et al., 2014). The Nexus generation is a critical, highly valued resource for the successful management of global businesses (Tiwari et al., 2018). Young managers need to have their minds, hearts, and souls in the right place and know how to use them to be resilient in the present competitive environment (Tiwari et al., 2018). Contemporary management thought is that spiritually intelligent managers are an asset to an organization as they have the ability to get the best out of people which leads to a workplace that is fulfilling for employees (Puspanathan et al., 2017).

Spiritual intelligence, based on the work of previous researchers, has four dimensions: critical existential thinking, personal meaning production, transcendental awareness, and conscious state of expansion (Amram & Dryer, 2008; Anwar & Osman-Gani, 2015; King, 2008). Critical Existential Thinking is the ability to create meaning based on a deep understanding of existential questions (Anwar & Osman-Gani, 2015; Amram, 2007). It is the ability to interpret the meaning and reason of life and worldly issues such as one's presence, reality, death, and one's relationship to the universe (King, 2008). Personal Meaning Production is a person's ability to stimulate both the physical and psychological experience of the person along with personal meaning that comes from a sense of satisfaction (King, 2008). It is the capacity to infer individual importance and reason from all physical and mental encounters, including the ability to produce and expect a reason for one's existence (Anwar & Osman-Gani, 2015). Transcendental Awareness is the ability to understand one's relationship with a higher power, all the creatures, man, and the environment (King, 2008; Vaughan, 2002). This includes the ability to recognize positive measurements of the self, others, and the physical world amid typical conditions of awareness, joined by the ability to recognize their connection to one's self and to the physical world (Anwar & Osman-Gani, 2015; King, 2008). Conscious State of Expansion is the ability to enter a state of spiritual awareness or even higher (King, 2008). It is the capacity to move around at a higher level of spiritual awareness at one's own discretion (Anwar & Osman-Gani, 2015; King, 2008). Since people are born with the capacity for spirituality, and when they combine spirituality with their professional career, they tend to see Conscious State of Expansion, not as a job, but as a mission (Baldacchino, 2008). In the workplace, Spiritual intelligence helps managers in the context of relationships and enables them to align personal values with a clearer sense of purpose that demonstrates a higher level of integrity in work (Chin et al., 2011).

A spiritually intelligent manager creates an environment of cooperation and trust. This type of manager will ensure performance is achieved through empathy, awareness, understanding, and support, targeting the innate strengths of the manager instead of driving their Nexus managers with cold calculations for profits and impressive bottom lines. It is from this crucial perspective that the researchers of this study believe a new perspective in management is required in shifting from a performance management approach based on materialism to a performance management approach based on spiritualism.

Spiritual intelligence provides a unifying framework for one's whole life, especially one's inner life. In particular, the aim is to bring about a state of functioning characterized by harmony, as opposed to conflict, presumably a place where all a Nexus manager's strivings and impulses are coordinated in service of an overarching purpose that is perceived as having deep personal meaning.

Therefore, it is the contention of the researchers of this study that spiritual intelligence is the way forward to strengthen the managerial resilience of the Nexus generation. It is imperative that this new concept of managerial resilience be investigated thoroughly to determine the effect its presence has on employees, the possible benefits inherent in this new concept, and the best way to develop it. If companies fail to do this, there will be serious implications for the future well-being of individuals, businesses, and the sustainability of IR 4.0 and the Malaysian economy. The Nexus Managerial Resilience Index (NeMRI) for Malaysian Nexus generation middle managers will act as a guide for Malaysian IR 4.0 companies to gauge the likelihood of early retirements, premature resignations within the middle manager cohort, and compare them on an annual, bian-nual, or quarterly cycle as deemed necessary by the companies. Companies must invest in building Nexus Managerial Resilience by employing spiritual intelligence to ensure their managers are retained. The schematic diagram mentioning the relationship between the spiritual intelligence and Managerial resilience is shown in Figure 14.1.

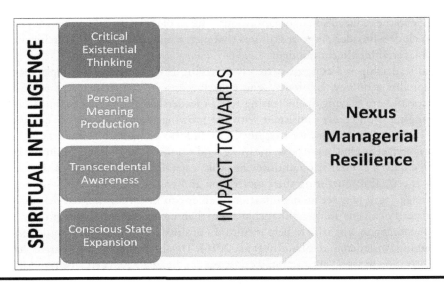

Figure 14.1   Nexus managerial resilience and spiritual intelligence.

Implications to Practitioners

There are several implications resulting from investigating the influence of spiritual intelligence on managerial resilience. First, there will be a change in the business culture that changes the way management views its organization, especially how it should be structured and managed to suit the radically changing industrial platform where machines and people communicate with one another. In the traditional management system, the vision of the company becomes the starting point for any setting of organizational goals. With the approach of incorporating spiritual intelligence into the management, the purpose of the organization is now viewed from the strategic direction of the organization whereby managerial spiritual behavior becomes an entity of strategic management. With the ever-growing pressure on companies to introduce Environmental Social Governance (ESG) elements into their operations, spiritual behavior guides managers at the operational level to be more aware of their connectedness with fellow humans and the natural environment they are all a part of. All business decisions will be based on a harmonious mix of materialism, spirituality, and environmentalism. This way of thinking will build managerial resilience by finding sustainable ways to run businesses and embrace collective action in decision-making. This contention has been raised in previous studies (Anwar & Osman-Gani, 2015; King, 2008). However, it has not been investigated in depth because this form of thinking is abstract and did not sit well with a business culture that focused entirely on materialism.

Second, investigating the influence of spiritual intelligence on managerial resilience will require a new leadership framework in which senior management will recognize the positive attributes of their middle managers in relation to their own self, their relationship with others, and their existence in the physical world (Anwar & Osman-Gani, 2015; King, 2008). The physical world in this context would be the IR. 4.0 environment. This way of thinking will change the landscape of the corporate leadership development framework which will now focus on the "leading self", "leading others", and "leading business" competencies in the dynamic IR 4.0 industry, especially due to the reduced size of organizations. The whole managerial competency concept will change to include a broader range of skill sets that merge intangible spiritual intelligence with the existing managerial intelligent quotient.

Spiritual leadership is a concept currently emerging globally and slowly replacing the profit-oriented capitalist economy. Existential and consciousness behaviors are fast becoming a norm in companies and are playing an increasing role in leadership and management decisions when pursuing long-term outcomes consistent with the growing interest in the ESG framework and reporting. The managerial behavior that involves this form of leadership framework will encourage middle managers to find a purpose, meaning, and readiness for the changes in the IR 4.0 work place which entails a combination of different skills, capabilities, and strategies (Piccarozzi et al., 2018). This is crucial to nurturing their motivation and engagement in their work environment. Middle managers will now see an organization as an environment for them to develop their competencies instead of an environment that challenges their competencies. Consequently, a "Work as Worship" phenomenon will arise to help inculcate a positive learning and innovative environment for the emerging work demand (Shamim et al., 2016). This is an altered mental state that increases intrinsic motivation at work. As a result, work stress can be easily reduced when middle managers discover a mission and passion for what they do.

Third, the influence of spiritual intelligence on managerial resilience will mean that future trainers and business education providers will need to include knowledge and attainment levels of spiritual intelligence in their respective curriculum development, program delivery, and program learning outcomes. The business education providers and learners will undergo a complete paradigm shift in terms of their value systems resulting in a mindset that views business as a multidirectional entity comprising ESG factors designed to achieve a sustainable business as opposed to the present unbalanced single directional flow aimed solely at producing a profitable business.

From the perspective of the practitioner, the influence of spiritual intelligence on Nexus managerial resilience will develop a personal spiritual leadership at the individual level, organizational spiritual leadership at the team level, and sustainability in spiritual leadership at the organizational level (Samul, 2020). To overcome the challenges regarding IR 4.0 such as new business models and change management, the element of spiritual intelligence can be embedded in the organization's HRM practices and policies by raising a leader's awareness of spirituality and sustainability, creating a positive workplace environment based on spirituality and inculcate the awareness and attitudes of employees toward sustainability. The outcomes of the HRM practices and policies embedded with spirituality including a sustainable workplace, spiritual workplace, and spiritual values can be a tool to adapt the challenges brought by the IR 4.0 and encourage a corporative rather than individualistic behavior.

Furthermore, the Nexus managerial resilience armed with spiritual intelligence can become the change agent for their company in facing the pressure of IR 4.0 by ensuring a smooth transitioning toward digital transformation strategies in their businesses. Besides the necessary skills regarding IR 4.0, spiritual intelligence capital is vital as a complimentary skill that should not be neglected by companies. Finally, face IR 4.0, companies are recommended to train their employees in spiritual intelligence and can use a train-the-trainer approach, as they will become a change agent to train their colleagues.

Conclusion

As we know, companies cannot change environmental dynamics; therefore, they will continue to move at an ever-increasing pace. However, companies can help ease the situation by investing in and supporting the managerial resilience of their Nexus generation managers who are struggling to cope with the current business environment (Jahn et al., 2012; Puspanathan et al., 2017). In Malaysia, Nexus employees made up over 68.2% of the total workforce in 2018 (Hossain et al., 2018). However, many of their work values are either unknown to, or not taken seriously by, their employers, thus there are very few retaining strategies in place in many organizations (Hossain et al., 2018). It is clear that Nexus managers who experience a better fit with their organizations are less likely to resign (Queiri et al., 2014). It might appear that being socially responsible is in conflict with the intention to attain growth and profits; however, a resilient manager can guarantee some distinct competitive advantages (Asree et al., 2010; Zakaria et al., 2015; King et al., 2001; Nyberg et al., 2014; Ulrich & Dulebohn, 2015). As more companies recognize the advantages of having resilient middle managers, it will then be a corporate expectation and standard of performance for IR 4.0 companies.

Establishing a NeMRI will help Malaysian IR 4.0 companies understand the factors that affect Malaysian Nexus Managerial Resilience and enable them to be more aware of the managerial challenges of the Malaysian Nexus generation. Spiritual Intelligence advocates good performance by way of thinking outside the box, acting with empathy and concern for others, and not to be confined by a myopic, objective performance metric. Although an "index" is viewed by some professionals as reducing the employee's personality and strength of character into a singular metric, the authors of this chapter believe otherwise. There are four dimensions of spiritual intelligence, and they are critical existential thinking, personal meaning production, transcendental awareness, and the conscious state of expansion. Each of these dimensions is measured by several metrics or indicators. Given that the recommendations of the authors are to use spiritual intelligence as a means to achieve managerial intelligence, creating an index simply averages out the influence of all these dimensions and their respective metrics into a single digit that makes it easy for senior management to understand and use the index as a means to assess the managerial resilience of their middle managers. The index can also be used to periodically gauge the likelihood of middle managers leaving the organization, that is, on a monthly, quarterly, biannually, or yearly basis and alerts senior management of such a likelihood taking place before it becomes too late.

This index will then allow IR 4.0 companies to adapt their company expectations to accommodate the Nexus generation's managerial dynamics and complexities. Thus, further quantitative research can contribute to the creation of a NeMRI, which will assist employers of IR 4.0 companies to be responsive to the needs of Nexus managers. This index and the knowledge of the Spiritual Intelligence variables influencing Nexus generation and Managerial Resilience will enable IR 4.0 companies to restrategize their company's goals and objectives to accommodate Nexus expectations and dynamics. This index will also enable IR 4.0 companies to support Nexus Managerial Resilience efforts and provide invaluable indicators for employers or government when it comes to meeting Malaysia's National Policy for IR 4.0 (Skills and Talent: Up-skilling Existing & Producing Future Talents), Sustainable Development Goals 2030 (Good Health and Wellbeing; Decent Work and Economic Growth; Societal Harmony and Happiness), and Shared Prosperity Vision 2030 (Human Capital; Social Capital) in the next decade.

Acknowledgment

The authors wish to acknowledge the Ministry of Higher Education, Malaysia, who funded the project under the Fundamental Research Grant Scheme (FRGS), grant code Ref: FRGS/1/2020/SS02/UNITEN/02/1 which contributed to ideas that were presented in this chapter.

References

Amram, Y. (2007, August 17–20). *The Seven Dimensions of Spiritual Intelligence: An Ecumenical Grounded Theory*. Proceeding of the 115th Annual Conference of the American Psychological Association, pp. 1–9.

Amram, Y., & Dryer, C. (2008). *The Integrated Spiritual Intelligence Scale (ISIS): Development and Preliminary Validation*. Paper presented at the 116th annual conference of the American Psychological Association, Boston, MA.

Anwar, M. A., & Osman-Gani, A. M. (2015). The Effects of Spiritual Intelligence and its Dimensions on Organizational Citizenship Behaviour. *Journal of Industrial Engineering and Management, 8*(4), 1162–1178.

Aris, N. A. (2019, August 17). *Malaysia Ill-Prepared for IR 4.0, Employers Group Agrees*. Free Malaysia Today (FMT). www.freemalaysiatoday.com/category/nation/2019/08/17/malaysia-ill-prepared-for-ir-4-0-employers-group-agrees/

Asree, S., Zain, M., & Razalli, M. R. (2010). Influence of Leadership Competency and Organizational Culture on Responsiveness and Performance of Firms. *International Journal of Contemporary Hospitality Management, 22*(4), 500–516.

Baldacchino, D. R. (2008). Spiritual Care: Is it the Nurse's Role? *Spirituality and Health International, 9*(4), 270–284.

Bathmanathan, V., Rajadurai, J., & Sohail, M. S. (2018). Generational Consumer Patterns: A Document Analysis Method. *Global Business and Management Research, 10*(3), 958–970.

Bonekamp, L., & Sure, M. (2015). Consequences of Industry 4.0 on Human Labour and Work Organisation. *Journal of Business and Media Psychology, 6*(1), 33–40.

Bordeleau, F. È., & Felden, C. (2019). *Digitally Transforming Organisations: A Review of Change Models of Industry 4.0*. Proceedings of the 27th European Conference on Information Systems.

Chaney, D., Touzani, M., & Ben Slimane, K. (2017). Marketing to the (new) Generations: Summary and Perspectives. *Journal of Strategic Marketing, 25*(3), 179–189. http://doi.org/10.1080/0965254X.2017.1291173

Chin, A., & Tong, D. Y. K. (2011). The Roles of Emotional Intelligence and Spiritual Intelligence at the Workplace. *Journal of Human Resources Management Research, 2011*, 1–9.

Chin, T., & Liu, R.-H. (2014). An Exploratory Study on Workforce Development Strategies by Taiwan-invested OEMs in China. *Asian Social Science, 10*(4), 233.

De Jong, T., Wiezer, N., de Weerd, M., Nielsen, K., Mattila-Holappa, P., & Mockałło, Z. (2016). The Impact of Restructuring on Employee Well-Being: A Systematic Review of Longitudinal Studies. *Work & Stress, 30*(1), 91–114.

Downe, A. G., Loke, S.-P., Ho, J. S.-Y., & Taiwo, A. A. (2012). Corporate Talent Needs and Availability in Malaysian Service Industry. *International Journal of Business and Management, 7*(2), 224.

Eisner, S. P. (2005). Managing Generation Y. *SAM Advanced Management Journal, 70*(4), 4.

Ford, M. (2009). *The Lights in the Tunnel: Automation, Accelerating Technology and the Economy of the Future*. Sunnyvale, CA: Acculant Publishing.

Ganesan, J., Mun, L. K., & Raman, K. (2017). Determinants of Organisational Commitment Among Generation-Y in the Malaysian SMEs. *Modern Applied Science, 11*(12).

Gardiner, S., Grace, D., & King, C. (2013). Challenging the Use of Generational Segmentation through Understanding Self-Identity. *Marketing Intelligence & Planning, 31*(6), 639–653. http://doi.org/10.1108/MIP-06-2012-0062

Grant, G. B. (2017). Exploring the Possibility of Peak Individualism, Humanity's Existential Crisis, and an Emerging Age of Purpose. *Frontiers in Psychology, 8*, 1478. https://doi.org/10.3389/fpsyg.2017.01478

Grotberg, E. (1996). The International Resilience Project: Research and application. In E. Miao (Ed.), *Proceedings of the 53rd Annual Convention, International Council of Psychologists: Cross-Cultural Encounters*. Taipei, Taiwan: General Innovation Service.

Hernandez, A. M. (2021). Global Transformation Towards Sustainability—Clusters of Current Scholarly Discourse. In *Taming the Big Green Elephant* (pp. 21–41). Wiesbaden: Springer VS.

Hossain, M. I., Limon, N., Amin, M. T., & Asheq, A. S. (2018). Work Life Balance Trends: A Study on Malaysian GenerationY Bankers. *IOSR Journal of Business and Management, 20*(9), 1–9.

Jahn, E. J., Riphahn, R. T., & Schnabel, C. (2012). Feature: Flexible Forms of Employment: Boon and Bane. *The Economic Journal, 122*(562), F115–F124.

Jerome, A., Scales, M., Whithem, C., & Quain, B. (2014). Millennials in the Workforce: Gen Y Workplace Strategies for the Next Century. *E-Journal of Social & Behavioural Research in Business, 5*(1), 1.

Jorgensen, B. (2003). Baby Boomers, Generation X and Generation Y? *Foresight, 5*(4), 41–49. http://doi.org/10.1108/14636680310494753

Kergroach, S. (2017). Industry 4.0: New Challenges and Opportunities for the Labour Market. *Форсайт, 11*(4 (eng).

King, A., Fowler, S., & Zeithaml, C. (2001). Managing Organizational Competencies for Competitive Advantage: The Middle-Management Edge. *Academy of Management Perspectives, 15*(2), 95–106.

King, D. B. (2008). *Rethinking Claims of Spiritual Intelligence: A Definition, Model, and Measure.* A Dissertation Presented in Partial Fulfillment of the Requirements for the Degree of Master of Science, Trent University, Peterborough, ON.

Lekan, A., Aigbavboa, C., Babatunde, O., Olabosipo, F., & Christiana, A. (2020). Disruptive Technological Innovations in Construction Field and Fourth Industrial Revolution Intervention in the Achievement of the Sustainable Development Goal 9. *International Journal of Construction Management*, 1–12.

Mohamad, E., Sukarma, L., Mohamad, N. A., Salleh, M. R., Rahman, M. A. A., Rahman, A. A. A., & Sulaiman, M. A. (2018). *Review on Implementation of Industry 4.0 Globally and Preparing Malaysia for Fourth Industrial Revolution.* Paper presented at the Proceedings of Design & Systems Conference 2018, p. 28.

Nielsen, K., Dawson, J., Hasson, H., & Schwarz, U. V. T. (2021). What about Me? The Impact of Employee Change Agents' Person-Role Fit on Their Job Satisfaction During Organisational Change. *Work & Stress, 35*(1), 57–73.

Nizam, N. Z., Rajiani, I., Mansor, N., & Yahaya, S. N. (2014). Understanding Green Purchasing Behavior among Gen Y in Malaysia by Examining the Factors Influenced. *Interdisciplinary Journal of Contemporary Research in Business, 6*(2), 1–14. http://journalarchieves37.webs.com/181-194jun14.pdf

Nyberg, A. J., Moliterno, T. P., Hale Jr, D., & Lepak, D. P. (2014). Resource-Based Perspectives on Unit-Level Human Capital: A Review and Integration. *Journal of management, 40*(1), 316–346.

Piccarozzi, M., Aquilani, B., & Gatti, C. (2018). Industry 4.0 in Management Studies: A Systematic Literature Review. *Sustainability, 10*(10), 3821.

Puspanathan, C. A., Ramendran SPR, C., Muthurajan, P., & Singh, N. S. B. (2017). Perceptions of Generation Y Undergraduate Students on Career Choices and Employment Leadership: A Study on Private Higher Education Institutions in Selangor. *Malaysian Online Journal of Educational Sciences, 5*(3), 46–59.

Puteh, F., Kaliannan, M., & Alam, N. (2015). Assessing Gen Y Impact on Organizational Performance: An Analysis from top Management Perspective. *Journal of Administrative Science, 12*(1), 47–59.

Queiri, A., & Dwaikat, N. (2016). Factors Affecting Generation Y Employees' Intention to Quit in Malaysian's Business Process Outsourcing Sector. *Journal of Sustainable Development, 9*(2), 78–92.

Queiri, A., Fadzilah, W., Yusoff, W., & Dwaikatt, N. (2014). Generation-Y Employees' Turnover : Work-Values Fit Perspective Generation-Y Employees. *Turnover: Work-Values Fit Perspective, 9*(11), 199.

Queiri, A., Yusoff, W. F. W., & Dwaikat, N. (2015). Explaining Generation-Y Employees' Turnover in Malaysian Context. *Asian Social Science, 11*(10), 126.

Raman, G., Ramendran, C., Beleya, P., Nodeson, S., & Arokiasamy, L. (2011). Generation Y in Institution of Higher Learning. *International Journal of Economics and Business Modelling, 2*(2), 142–154.

Samul, J. (2020). Spiritual Leadership: Meaning in the Sustainable Workplace. *Sustainability, 12*(1), 267.

San, L. Y., Omar, A., & Thurasamy, R. (2015). Online Purchase : A Study of Generation Y in Malaysia. *International Journal of Business and Management, 10*(6), 1–7. http://doi.org/10.5539/ijbm.v10n6p298

Sani, R. M. (2019). Adopting Internet of Things for Higher Education. In A. Raman & M. Rathakrishnan (Eds.), *Redesigning Higher Education Initiatives for Industry 4.0* (pp. 23–40). Hershey, PA: IGI Global.

Shamim, S., Cang, S., Yu, H., & Li, Y. (2016,). Management Approaches for Industry 4.0: A Human Resource Management Perspective. In *2016 IEEE Congress on Evolutionary Computation (CEC)* (pp. 5309–5316). IEEE.

Sujansky, J., & Ferri-Reed, J. (2009). *Keeping The Millennials: Why Companies Are Losing Billions in Turnover to This Generation- and What to Do About It.* Hoboken, NJ: Wiley.

Thye, L. L. (2019, July). Mental Health in the Workplace. *The Star.* Retrieved January 2, 2020, from www.thestar.com.my/opinion/letters/2019/07/15/mental-health-in-the-workplace

Tiwari, S., Wee, H.-M., & Daryanto, Y. (2018). Big Data Analytics in Supply Chain Management between 2010 and 2016: Insights to Industries. *Computers & Industrial Engineering, 115,* 319–330.

Tusaie, K., & Dyer, J. (2004). Resilience: A Historical Review of the Construct. *Holistic Nursing Practice, 18*(1), 3–10.

Twenge, J. M., Campbell, W. K., & Freeman, E. C. (2012). Generational Differences in Young Adults' Life Goals, Concern for Others, and Civic Orientation, 1966–2009. *Journal of Personality and Social Psychology, 102*(5), 1045.

Ulrich, D., & Dulebohn, J. H. (2015). Are We There Yet? What's Next for HR? *Human Resource Management Review, 25*(2), 188–204.

Vaughan, F. (2002). What is Spiritual Intelligence? *Journal of Humanistic Psychology, 42*(2), 16–33.

Wangberg, C. R., & Banas, J. T. (2000). Predictors and Outcomes of Openness to Changes in a Reorganizing Workplace. *Journal of Applied Psychology, 85*(1), 132–142. doi:10.1037/0021-9010.85.1.132

Wan Yusoff, W. F., Queiri, A., Zakaria, S., & Raja Hisham, R. R. I. (2013). *Generation-Y Turnover Intention in Business Process Outsourcing Sector.* Kota Kinabalu: ICMEF.

Zakaria, I. B., Mohamed, M. R. B., Ahzahar, N., & Hashim, S. Z. (2015). A Study on Leadership Skills of Project Manager for a Successful Construction Project. *International Academic Research Journal of Social Science, 1*(2), 89–94.

Authors' Profile

Jegatheesan Rajadurai is an associate professor in the Department of Business and Management, College of Business Management and Accounting, Universiti Tenaga Nasional (UNITEN). He has had 30-year experience teaching courses in business, marketing, and management. He has supervised several doctoral candidates to the successful completion of their programs and has been invited to be an external examiner for doctoral candidates at other universities. His research interests are in tertiary education, green marketing, sustainability management, energy management, Gen Y behaviors, social sciences, and stakeholder analysis. He is, and has been, a Project Leader of many national and university grants schemes.

Vathana Bathmanathan (PhD) is a senior lecturer at Universiti Tenaga Nasional (UNITEN). She began her career at UNITEN in May 2000 as an executive. After 14 years of administrative experience, she moved to the academic and research field in 2014. Prior to her venture into academic and research, she had trained many graduates who are currently holding high-level positions in various organizations. Vathana specializes in Green Marketing, Gen Y behavior, green purchasing behavior, and studies on Sustainability and Food Waste. Besides teaching and conducting research, she also holds managerial positions which includes Quality Manager and Open Distance Learning MBA Coordinator.

Amar Hisham Bin Jaaffar (PhD) has 5-year experience working as a researcher of studies related to organizational behavior. His research has focused on the proactive environmental behavior of employees and firms in Malaysia. Among the important topics that have been studied by him over the past years is the positive environmental deviance behavior of environmentally sensitive industries in Malaysia. Currently, he is teaching Business and Management subjects for bachelor's in business students and Research Methodology subjects for Master and PhD students. He is also supervising a Master and PhD student in the area of organizational behavioral related studies.

Revin Rajen has been a Corporate Trainer and Management Consultant, is the Founder CEO of Asia Centre for Leadership and Civilization, and is currently setting up a global Virtual Blended Learning (VBL) platform. Revin has been engaged in projects focusing on High-Performance Culture, Organizational Transformation, and Complex Adaptive Leadership. Companies he has worked with include UBS, Maybank, Ambank, UOB, Exxon Mobil, and Alstom Asia Pacific. His publications include Foundation of Success, Dreams of Destiny, and Change Starts With Me. Revin is a much sought after platform speaker and has hosted a TV program called "Power To Succeed" sponsored by Tenaga Nasional.

Chapter 15

From Cradle to Maturity: How Digital Enterprises in Developing Economies Strategize to Survive

Eric Ansong

Contents

DOI: 10.4324/9781003152217-19

Introduction

The digital economy has redefined business strategy into a term referred to as "Digital Business Strategy". This new phenomenon started with the Information Technology (IT) Strategy which was viewed as a functional-level strategy—a subset of the entire business strategy (Bharadwaj et al., 2013). Now, the survival of the entire digital business rests on the digital business strategy being implemented. On the other hand, there has been a silence on the dimensions of digital business strategy, especially in the digital economy where digital enterprises are not restricted to the traditional business models and practices. These digital enterprises are not restricted to developing a business strategy using the established legacy systems but to go further and adopt new concepts and techniques to exploit their markets. A major issue for strategists includes developing a digital business strategy framework that holistically meets the various dimensions of the business needs, especially as the firm goes through the different stages of growth.

It has also been observed that most new enterprises are unable to survive beyond 42 months after they are established (Allen et al., 2007). This phenomenon is prevalent in most developing economies. In Africa as a whole, only 13% of enterprises survive beyond 42 months after their establishment. The cause of this phenomenon has been attributed to the type of digital business strategy being implemented. Politicians, academics, and other agencies have made calls for African governments to make efforts to avert the high business discontinuation rates. This situation brings to the fore the need to review the digital business strategy of digital enterprises that have survived beyond the 42-month threshold to identify the various dimensions which matter along the different stages of growth. This will lead to the development of a digital business strategy framework that shows the trajectory of strategic actions to be taken by start-up enterprises in the quest to survive and mature.

The Dimensions of Digital Business Strategy

Digital business strategy has been seen to be a multidimensional concept which deals with the various directions a business may pursue to survive and remain profitable. This assertion is corroborated by Drnevich and Croson (2013) in the special edition of MIS Quarterly on digital business strategy where four major dimensions were highlighted: Coordination, Flexibility, Governance, and Competence.

Coordination

The coordination dimension of digital business strategy deals with the digital enterprise's ability to cooperate, collude, or coordinate with rival firms. This prevents or limits new competitors from entering into the industry and exerts authority over both customers and suppliers.

Governance

In terms of the Governance dimension of digital business strategy, the focus is on using Information Technology in managing and monitoring supplier networks and the performance of contracts between the human resources of the firm. For instance, Dawson et al. (2016) examined factors that influenced IT-based innovations in organizations and discovered that it was very critical for the whole team to approach innovation as a unit to achieve success.

Competence

The competence dimension of digital business strategy, on the other hand, emphasizes the capabilities and the resources which the firm uses to capture and create value. The firm may acquire these capabilities and resources by consciously building them—through inheritance or chance (Drnevich & Croson, 2013). In the competence-based perspective, the focus is mostly on the balance existing between the creation of value and its capture. This serves as the mechanism for determining the economic benefits of investments for the firm.

Flexibility

Finally, the flexibility dimension highlights the ability of digital enterprises to quickly respond to changes that occur both internally (inside) and externally (outside) which leads to an improvement in efficiency and effectiveness. Highlighting the dynamic nature of digital technologies which requires that products are quickly produced, Henfridsson et al. (2014) assert that firms need to adopt a digital business strategy that will enable them to be flexible and stay competitive. A major advantage of flexibility is the ability to adapt to new situations at minimal costs and also being able to seize opportunities quickly (Drnevich & Croson, 2013).

The Stages of Growth of the Firm

The review of literature on growth models highlighted numerous multistage models which attempt to explain the growth of firms using a diverse array of features. Dodge et al. (1994) assert that the overriding consensus in the various models is the predictable pattern of changes that occur in the different stages of the development of the organization. Growth models may categorize the stages based on:

1. The sequence of activities that outline how changes occur over time.
2. A progression that is hierarchical and irreversible.
3. A wide range of activities and structures in the firm.

Dodge et al. (1994) postulate that the life cycle of firms is seen to consist of between three and ten stages. In their study, a four-stage growth model was utilized—(1) entrepreneurial, (2) collectivity, (3) formalization and control, and (4) structure elaboration and adaption. It has been asserted that the growth pattern of small businesses is known to be S-shaped, and the most critical stages are the first three stages. In this regard, the first three stages, as provided by Dodge et al. (1994), are adapted for reviewing the case start-up digital enterprise for this piece.

The first stage involves the entrepreneur directly performing all the business activities. The second stage occurs where there are supervised operations—the entrepreneur employs and directly supervises the employee(s) as the business expands. Phase 3 is the indirect supervision stage—employees are not directly supervised. Team heads are utilized at this stage.

Case Study: Digix Enterprise

Digix (a pseudonym) is a Ghanaian digital enterprise that began its operations in 2011 as an e-book publisher. Initially, the start-up published e-Journals for higher educational institutions

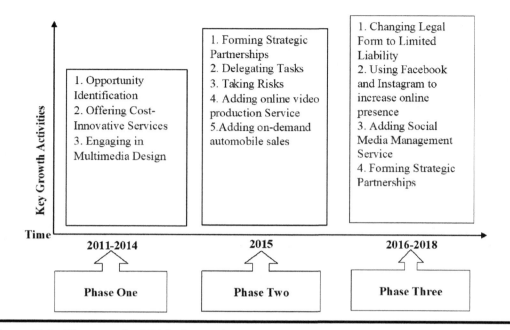

Figure 15.1 The growth of Digix Enterprise.

through an online e-book platform. The digital enterprise registered as a sole proprietorship firm in 2011 and, later in 2017, became a limited liability company. With an initial two employees (owner and assistant), the enterprise currently has seven employees which include the owner who is also the manager; a content validator who doubles as a marketer; an administrator who also serves as an assistant to the manager; and four part-time employees.

The Growth of Digix Enterprise

The digital enterprise has grown through the three major phases from its year of establishment (2011) to its present status in 2017. Figure 15.1 shows the growth process of the digital enterprise.

Digital Business Strategy in Phase One

The creativity and commitment of the founder characterized the first stage in the growth of the digital enterprise. The most dominant dimension in the founding phase of the digital business is Governance. The focus of the governance dimension is the ability of the digital enterprise to allocate resources to create and capture value efficiently. The analysis of data revealed that, in the first phase of growth of the digital enterprise, the entrepreneur was actively involved in its operations. Again, the entrepreneur's high level of innovation contributed to the survival of the firm. This finding is corroborated by Liu et al. (2015), who postulated that the level of innovation of the founder influences the way resources are managed for the firm to remain competitive. Similarly, Glassman et al. (2015) identified the business owner's strategic decisions such as Internet filtering and monitoring systems to be effective ways of promoting better compliance which leads to employee empowerment and resource replenishment.

Another crucial digital business strategy dimension in the first phase of growth is Competence. The significant capital of digital businesses in the first stage of growth is the intellectual skill of the owner(s) and some technological resources. Alden (2011) asserts that most digital enterprises rely heavily on the innovative skills and expertise of the owner(s) in the first stage of growth. Besides, Biberhofer et al. (2019), in their study, argued that the sustainability of firms is dependent upon the competencies and the more in-depth knowledge levels of the entrepreneur.

In terms of flexibility, the output of the strategic action is the ability of the digital enterprise to be agile; adapt to the changing conditions in the industry. In the first phase of growth, the digital enterprise adopted a simple business model which was agile enough to survive in the economy. Besides, the commitment of the business owner also contributed to the survival of the business. This finding is not different from the globally influential digital enterprises such as Amazon, Facebook, Uber, and Airbnb—which started with highly committed entrepreneur(s) with a simple business model which involved a single product or service.

Digital Business Strategy in Phase Two

The digital enterprise developed in the second phase of its growth. The delegation of tasks characterized this phase as the business expanded and engaged more workers and customers. The most dominant digital business strategy dimension in the second phase of growth was Flexibility. In the second phase of growth, the digital enterprise acquired some experience, which helped it become agile and survive. This experience is mostly gained with the knowledge capital of the firm through knowledge codification and articulation. Through this experience, the enterprise identified opportunities within the market. For instance, Sia et al. (2013) discovered that managers acquire some experience, which helps them cultivate leadership for digital transformation, after operating in the industry for some years. Again, in Hay-Smith's (2008) study on two young Scottish entrepreneurs, he discovered that through their ingenuity and creativity, these entrepreneurs were able to set up a hugely successful brewery in 2007 even in the face of the global recession.

Another dominant dimension of digital business strategy in the developing phase of growth is Competence. In the second phase of growth, the firm relied on its reputation, financial, and human resources to stay competitive and survive. Enough financial and human resources became available to the digital enterprise in the second phase of growth. In explaining this phenomenon, Chuang and Lin (2017) argue that the ability of the digital enterprise to combine human, business, and technological resources effectively helps it achieve profitability and continue its growth. This assertion is also corroborated by Trkman (2010), who identified the success factors for businesses to be the effective management of all resources.

Digital Business Strategy in Phase Three

The third phase of growth is the maturity stage. This stage is characterized by expansion, delegation, and coordination. The most significant dimension of digital business strategy in this phase is Coordination. In the third phase of growth, the digital enterprise vertically integrated its products and services. The digital enterprise offered a package of services and products which were complementary to each other. In the case of the digital enterprise in this study, it offered lecture video production and the management of the e-learning platform as a package. In addition, the digital enterprise was able to manage its relationship with external entities such as the regulatory bodies and suppliers. Zhao and Xia (2014) argue that the ability of the organization to work with trading partners determines its market readiness.

Another significant digital business strategy dimension in the third phase is Flexibility. The third phase of growth is characterized by decentralization and delegation. Initially, all decisions and activities were performed by the owner of the digital enterprise. At the maturity stage of the business, employees are assigned roles and responsibilities. This assertion is not different from the finding of Zaheer et al. (2018) who discovered that one of the strategies for the survival of digital enterprises was a "lean start-up" (one or two initial employees). Functions are centralized initially, but as the firm grows, other personnel are employed, and tasks are decentralized. Also, the firm continues to discover new opportunities as it grows in the third phase.

Competence is another significant digital business strategy dimension in the third phase. The third phase of growth is also characterized by the ability of the firm to manage the available resources, which include financial, human, physical, and IT resources. In terms of human resources, the digital enterprise grows and employs personnel to take up roles in the business. Again, the firm reinvests its profits, which allows an increased financial resource to be available. Nevo and Wade (2010), for instance, conducted a study on identifying a firm IT assests which played strategic roles for competitive advantage. It was discovered that these IT assets could only be used to achieve strategic advantages when other organizational resources are available and combined with them, leading to the creation of IT-enabled resources. Dawson et al. (2016) assert that the whole team must approach innovation as a unit to succeed in the digital economy.

The Digital Business Strategy Model for the Growth of the Firm

Three major growth events were identified in the case. The first event—the founding stage—was characterized by the initial digital business strategic actions. The second event—the development stage—was also marked by digital business strategic actions aimed at delegating some business activities as it develops. The third event—the maturity stage—was also characterized by the digital business strategic actions geared toward coordinating the business activities as it matured.

Four major dimensions were highlighted in the review of digital business strategy literature— governance, flexibility, coordination, and competence. These four dimensions form the pillars for a digital business strategy framework. The governance dimension of digital business strategy deals with the ability of the digital enterprise to allocate resources to create and capture value efficiently. The flexibility dimension, however, highlights the ability of the digital enterprise to respond quickly to changes that occur in both the internal and external environments leading to an improvement in efficiency and effectiveness. The competence dimension emphasizes the capabilities and the resources which the firm uses to capture and create value. The coordination dimension focuses on the ability of the digital enterprise to cooperate, collude, or coordinate with other external agencies such as rival firms and regulators to prevent or limit new competitors from entry and exert authority over both its customers and suppliers. These four dimensions arguably focus on the various facets of digital business strategy.

In another breadth, it was realized that the levels of significance of the dimensions of the digital business strategy differ at the various stages of growth of the digital enterprise. Consequently, digital enterprises tend to give different focus or attention to the dimensions as the firm navigates from one growth stage to another.

Table 15.1 shows that, comparatively, the most important digital business strategy dimensions in the first phase of growth of a digital enterprise are Governance and competence. This can be attributed to the focus of the digital enterprise in the first phase of growth, which is the founding stage, where the entrepreneur's vision comes to life. The entrepreneur directly supervises all

Table 15.1 Significant Dimensions of Digital Business Strategy

Phases of Growth	Significant Dimensions of Digital Business Strategy
Phase One: Founding stage	**Governance dimension** *Entrepreneurs' ownership:* The direct involvement of the owner/entrepreneur in the operations of the business enhanced the survival of the business. *Level of innovation:* This refers to the new service/product being introduced onto the market. A higher level of innovation creates opportunities in the market for the business.
	Competence dimension *Intellectual resources:* The start-up capital for the business in the first phase is the intellect/skills of the owner/founder. This influences the ability to combine the other resources to maximize output. *Technological resources:* As a digital enterprise, technological devices such as Laptops, internet among others are the primary resources.
Phase two: Developing stage	**Flexibility dimension** *Experience accumulation:* The digital enterprise accumulates a vast amount of experience from the first phase, which is applied to adjusting the business model. *Opportunity discovery:* based on the accumulation of experience, the digital enterprise can identify business opportunities in the industry.
	Competence dimension *Reputation:* A major resource available in the second phase of growth is the reputation or brand the digital enterprise builds for itself in the first phase of growth. High quality and trustworthy brand attract customers. *Financial and human resources*: Start-up capital is expected to have accrued some profits which are expected to be reinvested into the digital enterprise in the second phase. In addition, more human resources become available to the enterprise as it grows in the second phase.
Phase three: Maturity stage	**Coordination dimension** *Integrated services:* The digital enterprise in the maturity stage integrates its services with customers by providing related products or services in packages. These integrated services are aimed at helping to reduce the bargaining power of the customers and increasing the switching cost. *Government and regulatory support:* The digital enterprise, in the maturity stage of growth, benefits from favorable policies and interventions from industry supervisors and government agencies.

activities in the start-up firm. The most significant activity in the first phase is the ingenuity of the founder(s). This finding is corroborated by Liu et al. (2015), who postulated that the level of innovation influences the way resources are managed for the firm to remain competitive. On the other hand, Flexibility was the most crucial dimension in the second phase of growth. Coordination was, however, the most dominant digital business strategy dimension in the third phase of growth.

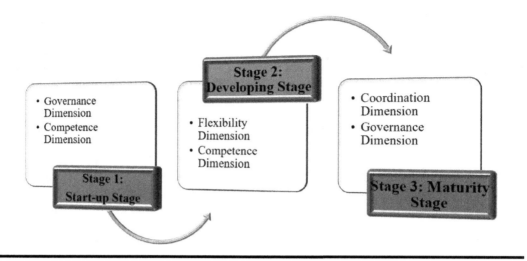

Figure 15.2   Digital business strategy framework.

The Digital business strategy framework for the growth of the digital enterprise showing the relevant digital business strategy dimensions at the various stages of growth is presented in Figure 15.2.

Conclusion and Implications

The main aim of this position chapter was to develop a framework that outlined the various strategic actions a start-up firm should take as it moves along the various stages of growth. These digital strategic actions were necessary to aid the firm to navigate and survive in the digital economy.

It is envisaged that start-up firms who wish to operate within a similar context of the case enterprise may consider the various significant dimensions to survive and grow. The framework is thus useful to entrepreneurs who wish to develop a digital business strategy to survive and grow beyond the 42-month survival threshold.

Implications of the Study

This chapter is arguably one of the initial studies to view digital business strategy from a multi-dimensional perspective, such as governance, flexibility, coordination, and competence. In this regard, the strategic actions of the case firm were reviewed to identify the most significant digital business strategy dimensions at each stage of the growth of the digital enterprise. Therefore, a digital business strategy model was developed, which is a novelty in the field of Information Systems. This model may, therefore, be used in future studies on reviewing the strategic actions of digital enterprises.

In addition, this chapter highlights the success story of how a digital enterprise is thriving in a very competitive and unstructured digital economy of a developing country. This is meant to bring fierce competition as well as opportunities to the attention of current and hopeful digital entrepreneurs. These enterprises are thus creating jobs and providing business solutions locally that would hitherto be sought from more developed economies. There is, therefore, a need for some legal frameworks to be established to cushion these enterprises from the fierce competition that stagnates their growth. Furthermore, infrastructure and financial support should be given to these enterprises to develop and employ more people. Finally, more accelerator and incubator programs should be set up to provide exposure for the innovative ideas of these enterprises and enable them to attract funding from alternative sources.

References

Alden, E. (2011). Primum Non Nocere: The Impact of Dodd-Frank on Silicon Valley. *Berkeley Business Law Journal*, *8*(2), 107–127.

Allen, E., Langowitz, N., Elam, A. E., & Dean, M. (2007). *The Global Entrepreneurship Monitor (GEM) 2007 Report on Women and Entrepreneurship Executive Summary.* www.gemconsortium.org.

Bharadwaj, A., El Sawy, O. A., Pavlou, P. A., & Venkatraman, N. (2013). Digital Business Strategy: Toward a Next Generation of Insights. *MIS Quarterly*, *37*(2), 471–482. https://doi.org/10.25300/MISQ/2013/37:2.3

Biberhofer, P., Lintner, C., Bernhardt, J., & Rieckmann, M. (2019). Facilitating Work Performance of Sustainability-Driven Entrepreneurs through Higher Education: The Relevance of Competencies, Values, Worldviews and Opportunities. *The International Journal of Entrepreneurship and Innovation*, *20*(1), 21–38.

Chuang, S. H., & Lin, H. N. (2017). Performance Implications of Information-Value Offering in E-Service Systems: Examining the Resource-Based Perspective and Innovation Strategy. *Journal of Strategic Information Systems*, *26*(1), 22–38. https://doi.org/10.1016/j.jsis.2016.09.001

Dawson, G. S., Denford, J. S., & Desouza, K. C. (2016). Governing Innovation in US State Government: An Ecosystem Perspective. *The Journal of Strategic Information Systems*, *25*(4), 299–318.

Dodge, H. R., Fullerton, S., & Robbins, J. E. (1994). Stage of the Organizational Life Cycle and Competition as Mediators of Problem Perception for Small Businesses. *Strategic Management Journal*, *15*(2), 121–134.

Drnevich, P. L., & Croson, D. C. (2013). Information Technology and Business-Level Strategy: Toward an Integrated Theoretical Perspective. *Management Information Systems Quarterly*, *37*(2), 483–509.

Glassman, J., Prosch, M., & Shao, B. B. M. (2015). To Monitor or Not to Monitor: Effectiveness of a Cyberloafing Countermeasure. *Information & Management*, *52*(2), 170–182.

Hay-Smith, J., Mørkved, S., Fairbrother, K. A., & Herbison, G. P. (2008). Pelvic Floor Muscle Training for Prevention and Treatment of Urinary and Faecal Incontinence in Antenatal and Postnatal Women. *Cochrane Database of Systematic Reviews*, *8*(4). https://doi.org/10.1002/14651858.CD007471

Henfridsson, O., Mathiassen, L., & Svahn, F. (2014). Managing Technological Change in the Digital Age: The Role of Architectural Frames. *Journal of Information Technology*, *29*(1), 27–43. https://doi.org/10.1057/jit.2013.30

Liu, J., Kauffman, R. J., & Ma, D. (2015). Competition, Cooperation, and Regulation: Understanding the Evolution of the Mobile Payments Technology Ecosystem. *Electronic Commerce Research and Applications*, *14*(5), 372–391.

Nevo, S., & Wade, M. R. (2010). The Formation and Value of IT-Enabled Resources: Antecedents and Consequences of Synergistic Relationships. *MIS Quarterly*, *34*(1), 163–183.

Sia, S. K., Soh, C., & Weill, P. (2013). How DBS Bank Pursued a Digital Business Strategy. *MIS Quarterly*, *27*(2), 471–662.

Trkman, P. (2010). The Critical Success Factors of Business Process Management. *International Journal of Information Management*, *30*(2), 125–134.

Zaheer, H., Breyer, Y., Dumay, J., & Enjeti, M. (2018). Straight from the Horse's Mouth: Founder's Perspective on Achieving 'Traction' in Digital Start-Ups. *Computers in Human Behavior*, *2018*, 1–13.

Zhao, K., & Xia, M. (2014). Forming Interoperability through Interorganizational Systems Standards. *Journal of Management Information Systems*, *30*(4), 269–298.

Author's Profile

Eric Ansong is a senior lecturer in Information Systems at Wisconsin International University College, Ghana. He holds a PhD in information systems. His research interests cover the Digital economy, Digital business strategy, technology-mediated teaching and learning, and Design science. He has published a number of research articles in peer-reviewed academic journals and books and has presented papers in international conferences which include the Hawaii International Conference on System Sciences (HICSS). He can be reached via eansong003@st.ug.edu.gh, eric.ansong@wiuc-ghana.edu.gh. His ORCID ID is http://orcid.org/0000-0002-0262-3485.

INNOVATION AND HEALTHCARE

Chapter 16

"Get Checked. Go Collect"— Improving Patients' Access to Chronic Medication

Ricardo Kettledas and Thomas Anning-Dorson

Contents

Introduction

The effect of inequality in healthcare is very apparent—limited chance of longer, healthier lives. Inequality in the healthcare system does not happen by chance. It is usually socially and institutionally engineered and is usually beyond the control of the disadvantaged. It is possible to cure this social anomaly if there is a will of the people and institutions—both social and government—to deal with it. The fundamental causes of inequalities in health care include political prioritization and decision-making, and societal proclivity toward equity and fairness. These two affect equality in income, power, and wealth distribution which perpetuate poverty, marginalization, and discrimination. These things have dire consequences on healthcare delivery and access.

DOI: 10.4324/9781003152217-21

According to the World Health Organization (WHO) (2018),

> Health inequities are differences in health status or the distribution of health resources between different population groups, arising from the social conditions in which people are born, grow, live, work and age. Health inequities are unfair and could be reduced by the right mix of government policies.

South Africa, one of the most unequal countries on earth, has attempted to improve equity in healthcare through varied interventions (Stats SA, 2020). The South African National Development Plan has set 2030 as the year it achieves Universal Health Coverage (UHC). The achievement of this will bring a significant shift in the equity of health services provision in the country. The health system within South Africa has perpetuated the inequality which is widespread in different facets of the economy (Winchester & King, 2018; Mhlanga & Garidzirai, 2020). There have been calls for urgent action to improve the plight of the masses, who are usually at the end of social and health injustice (Valiani, 2020; Kollamparambil, 2021). This is a common feature in emerging and developing economy contexts (Tosam et al., 2018). Management scholars and practitioners in private for-profit and public, nonprofit entities must seek to advance simple but effective methods in dealing with the challenges in such contexts.

We analyze how distinctive value is delivered in an emerging economy—South Africa, through a simple value assessment model (Need–Value–Reaction Model). The framework assumes that creating meaningful value requires a basic understanding of the needs/problems before creating a solution to meet those needs. The last bit of the model assesses the reaction toward delivering value from the intended recipients of the value and the competition. We briefly explain the elements of the model here.

Needs—Needs are necessities of life such that it is critical for an organism's survival and to live a healthy life. Needs are fundamental problems that threaten livelihood. Needs create a state of deprivation that threatens existence and quality thereof. Consumer/citizens needs are, therefore, a requirement for existence. Deficiency needs arise due to deprivation and motivate people when they are unmet (McLeod, 2007). Needs cause persons to act to have a chance of survival and good living. There may be different ways of satisfying needs, but what service providers should pursue is the best way that deals with the root cause. What is derived out of need fulfillment can be termed as value to the person that seeks it.

Value—Value is a critical consequence of need. It is what drives actions and all we do. Graeber (2005) defines value as to how an individual actor's actions take on meaning, for the actor herself/himself (p. 37). The outcome of the process of satisfying needs is the value that the value recipient largely determines. The level of importance one places on the need and how that influences the eventual quality of life will affect the significance of value sought.

Reaction—Need–Value relationship will always cause a reaction. Since needs create a state of deprivation, any attempt to meet what is sought will receive a reaction, be it positive or negative. When the value created to satisfy that need meets the satisfaction threshold of that need, there will be a positive reaction, while a negative reaction is observed if the threshold is not met. Needs inherently shape expectations. The value sought to meet the specific requirements of a need will receive a reaction base on the expectations beforehand. For instance, customers will boycott an outlet/product/service if the expected value from such a brand does not meet the expectations. When needs are not appropriately met, the tension created as a result of seeking a better life is reignited.

This chapter shares lessons from how South Africa has successfully implemented a Centralized Chronic Medication Dispensing and Distribution (CCMDD) system that has created a seamless process for patients to collect their chronic medications. The rest of the chapter is structured as follows. The following section explains the need or problem at hand and why the intervention needs to be implemented. After that, the next section explains what was done and the constituents of the intervention or value that was offered. This is done by explaining the value composition and value delivery mechanism. The chapter concludes with some important policy and managerial lessons.

The Problem within the South African Healthcare System

The stubborn inequality problem in South Africa has created a two-tier healthcare system. There is a massive divide between private and public health services regarding access, equity, and quality of care for the population. South Africa's estimated mid-year population for 2020 was at 59.62m. Only a tiny percentage of the South African population, about 16%, can afford to buy private healthcare services and access to quality healthcare. This select few are the so-called South African middle class and the rich. They are the ones with good-paying jobs, business owners, and the political elite who can afford to have a medical aid fund.

According to Genesis Medical Scheme (2021), the cost of a comprehensive medical aid plan ranges from R 2175 to R 4061 per month. Meanwhile, Business Insider SA (2021) indicates that the total number of persons employed in South Africa increased from 9.56 million in Q3 to 9.64 in Q4 2020. This represents just about 16% of the 59.62 million as per the mid-year estimates by the government. The average salary of the employed in 2020 was about R 23,000. These persons may, therefore, be able to afford private medical aid. Comparatively, the rest of the population, which is about 50 million, struggle to take care of their health needs. In fact, according to Statista (2021), the average household income in the country is R 2,831 per month. This further shows the wide gap between the haves and the have-nots and the extent to which they can adequately cater to their health needs.

In a WHO report, the chairman of the South African Medical Association, Dr. Mphata Norman Mabasa, describes the state of healthcare inequalities in the following words:

> I've seen many instances of patients in the public health system dying when hospitals can't keep them longer. If you've got money, you can buy and save lives. In the public sector, for example, kidney dialysis is rationed . . . even within the private sector, members on low-cost schemes come off worse, with a narrower range of services covered and patients needing to spend a higher proportion of their incomes.

Keeton (2010) also indicates another critical issue is the marked disparity between urban and rural care, with many rural patients having to travel into cities to access services. However, both the poor in the urban and rural areas suffer the same healthcare challenge. The key issue here is that a significant section of the population cannot afford and does not have access to good healthcare. They rely on the already overcrowded public healthcare clinics with limited resources. Such patients often have to get up at the crack of dawn and take multiple taxis just to get to the front of the queue in the hope of getting quick and easy medical services. Often, this is done purely on hope as there are no guarantees on whether they will even make it through the doors, and if they do, they are often told that the medicines they so desperately need are out of stock.

The primary need or problem faced by many in South Africa is inequitable access to health services. In an attempt to improve the plight of many, there have been investments in healthcare over the past years. The challenge has been that there is only a slight improvement observed in the quality of healthcare delivery in the country. New approaches have to be adopted to achieve the all-important UHC. One of the biggest challenges facing the healthcare system is the constant and daily overcrowding of facilities. In this piece, we ask a simple question: Do all of the patients crowding the healthcare facilities need to see a doctor or queueing for other reasons? It was found that some of the patients' queueing for long hours only need to get access to their prescribed medicines. They do not require clinical care or advice from a doctor or nurse on each visit but merely need to collect their prescriptions.

This is the nature of the beast the country faces in terms of healthcare. There must be something done to isolate the specific needs within groups if there are to be a meaningful solution to the health problems within the larger population. No country has an unlimited amount of resources to deal with all of its challenges. In the same vein, South Africa's healthcare problems cannot be solved instantaneously. There is the need to apply some innovative measures to the limited resources to achieve significant gains judiciously. There is the need to isolate and define the specific needs within different groups to provide meaningful solutions to the populace.

The Intervention—Value on Offer

The Value Composition

Acknowledging the challenge faced by the country, an innovative program was conceptualized a few years ago to deal with a specific need that borders on access to critical medicines for a segment of the population. This was done through a well-thought-out plan to isolate needs and bring in the private sector to enhance the efficient distribution of medication to chronic patients. This was implemented by the Department of Health.

One of the core mandates of the National Department of Health is to establish a health system based on decentralized management, principles of equity, efficiency, sound governance, internationally recognized standards of research, and a spirit of enquiry and advocacy which encourage participation. Based on that the Department created and implemented a program that sought to address the challenges regarding access to critical medicines. The success of this program is based on the proper management of the relationship among need–value–reaction.

Within the public sector, it is important always to acknowledge that there is heterogeneity within the population (market). The difference in needs within the population requires a careful segmentation approach to isolate what is critical and the actions needed to be successful at policy or program implementation. With the present case, the Department identified a small segment of the healthcare market and created a solution that generated new value to the customer. The new value on offer is the introduction of a new innovative model for patients to go and collect their medicines at their convenience when needed.

The segmentation–targeting–positioning framework presents a vital tool for public sector marketing management. Segmentation means identifying possible homogenous groups into a broader market. Such homogenous groups should have similar needs and should share some characteristics, which are usually descriptors. These characteristics may be based on geography, demography, economic, psychography, behavior, among others. It must be noted that the descriptors should only follow the similarity of needs. Thus, after similar needs have been grouped, the practitioner can then further group persons based on the descriptors.

Targeting describes the act of selecting which segments (based on needs and descriptors) to focus your attention on. Within the public sector, there are numerous challenges faced by practitioners. The targeting stage becomes an important point that should be tackled carefully. One needs to consider the resource availability, the critical nature of the needs, and the possible success before selecting a target, especially in the public sector context. Positioning focuses on how the customer views and assesses the service relative to the competition. One's ability to position a service in the public sector space determines the possible uptake of the service or behavior. It needs careful planning on explaining the rationale and the benefits through a well-thought-out communication program.

Through segmentation, we could quickly identify a subset of the population who are patients who do not need to see the doctor on each visit to the clinic. All they require is to gain access to their medicines to continue with their daily lives. One essential step in the segmentation process is to perform needs analysis, which comprises collecting patient data. The clinical data obtained from various clinical programs confirmed the high burden of "stable" chronic patients in the healthcare system. By way of example, South Africa has about 7.7m patients who required antiretroviral medicines for HIV monthly. The aim is to stabilize, treat, and ensure that they remain in care to improve their quality of life. Stable chronic patients can manage their condition, such as high blood pressure, themselves through a combination of lifestyle changes and their prescribed medication.

For this targeted segment, the marketing intent was to bridge the gap between the public and private sectors and promote synergy between the two sectors to achieve a common goal. Public sector facilities are overcrowded, understaffed, and operated limited hours. To improve patient access to needed medicines, especially for patients on chronic medication and assist with decongesting public clinics, the Department implemented the Centralised Chronic Medication Dispensing and Distribution (CCMDD) program. The program allowed enrolled patients to pick up their medication from private sector partners' outlets. By bringing in the private sector, there is a creation of additional footprint and extended operating hours, which promotes access and convenience as the key value on offer.

The Value Delivery Mechanism

The CCMDD Program, also called "Get Checked. Go Collect", allows for the effective distribution of government-issued medication for free at collection points dotted across the country through a public–private partnership. It started in the Umzinyathi District within the KwaZulu-Natal Province, with its 55 public health facilities as a pilot. The program targeted the millions of South Africans with chronic conditions such as diabetes, HIV, or high blood pressure.

The program adopts a seamless process to cut down on the challenges faced at the public clinics. The basic criteria to enroll on this program are to have a chronic condition and test results within the normal range. A healthcare worker will register the patient, and an SMS sent with information on the medication and collection details. Collection requires an ID card and CCMDD Collection Card. A patient can collect three months' worth of medication at a go and visit the clinic twice a year. On these visits, the patient is checked by the healthcare personnel to have the script renewed.

The convenience comes from the country's over 200 pickup points through retail and pharmaceutical chains. This is the significant private sector partnership that has contributed significantly to the success of the program. Patients can also collect their parcels from the adherence club or churches, mosques, community halls, and private doctors' rooms. A patient has to choose which outlet is best suited based on the location of work or home.

The "Get Checked. Go Collect" program eliminates the long-distance travel and waiting time in long queues at public facilities. For the frail and old, one can nominate two persons to do the pickup. This was particularly helpful for those with weaker immune systems who may be in isolation due to their increased risk of COVID-19 infection. The system is such that there are seldom medicine shortages at these pickup points. This eliminates the possibility of treatment interruptions which helps in keeping patients' condition stable.

As at the end of June 2020, a total of 3.6m patients had been registered on the program with a weekly average of 20,000 patients per week. The various radio and social media campaigns and print media (banners and flyers in clinics in local languages for different regions) had resulted in steady and positive growth over the past year.

A patient was quoted in a media report saying:

> before the CCMDD implementation, with my hours at work, I use to pay people to collect my medication at the clinic. Sometimes, the nurses would refuse to allow this, and if that would happen, I would sometimes go days without medication. This has caused me to default twice, but now, with the CCMDD program, the defaulting days are over. I don't stress myself anymore because my time is flexible, and it takes less than 20 minutes for me to get to a Clicks pharmacy to collect my ART and go back to work.

The achievement of the program is predicated on the fact that the system isolated the needs and focused on a small segment of the total patient pool. The Department is in the process of targeting its campaigns to more deep rural areas and taxi ranks. The success of this approach has led to a new drive of moving away from curative models to preventative care UHC.

Policy and Managerial for Practitioners

The success of profit-centered and nonprofit-centered ventures is based on understanding the real problem at hand. In management and for ventures involving humans, the most important element is the need—the pivot around which problems can be defined. The need–value–reaction model used in this chapter has helped assess how to evaluate the value in different situations. The case of CCMDD offers some valuable lessons going forward. We highlight some of them in the following paragraphs

One of the key challenges of management in the current dispensation is the lack of rigor in problem identification and definition. Solutioning requires a thorough understanding of what is inhibiting progress—meeting societal needs, increasing profitability, changing behavior, or increasing adoption of a desired technology. Root-cause analysis has been an important management practice that must be applied at all times. The rationale behind this is to put out the fire from the base. It is meant to help avoid designing solutions from symptoms but the cause. A lot of countries, especially developing and emerging ones and their agencies, throw monies at developmental problems without a proper understanding of the root of these problems. Policymakers must learn to understand the basis of public needs. Needs analysis is the most critical element of the value creation process. Getting to know what the needs help in providing valuable products and services to intended customers. As indicated in the introduction, needs are the motivators for all actions. Dissatisfaction with public service is a result of needs not being met. The challenge is that resources are finite, and all needs cannot be solved at a go. Needs analysis in the public sector allows policymakers to prioritize the most important needs.

Another important lesson that is linked to the above is the heterogeneity within our customer base. While needs analysis is an important function in the value creation process, recognizing the fact that customer needs may differ helps in isolating which needs are to be met first. In the afore-mentioned case, while South Africa faces several healthcare challenges, the needs of the citizens are not homogenous. Usually, developmental challenges are looked at and assessed at a higher level without paying attention to the details, which usually informs policy actions. The proverbial "forest and the singleness of each tree within the forest" becomes important in designing solutions in the public space. Segmentation is critical in the effective application of the highly constrained resource of states, governments, and businesses. An important lesson for managers in private and public enterprises or agencies is to divide customers (market) based on needs before applying the descriptors. Since needs are the basis for value creation, starting with it helps isolate the different elements at play. Usually, needs cut across different demographic groupings. Managers and policymakers must base the segmentation on needs before further grouping via demographic, geographic, and psychographic variables.

Another important lesson that the "Get Checked. Go Collect" program offers is that solutions should target eliminating fundamental bottlenecks after appropriately isolating needs. One of the biggest crises for the South African healthcare system was overcrowding and long queues. The program isolated the needs of chronic medication patients and removed the bottleneck as regard access to medication. All these categories of patients want were access to their periodic medication. They did not have to join the ones who needed to see a physician.

Additionally, the bottleneck for such patients was the absence of convenience. The pro-gram created a seamless process that allowed patients to spend less than five minutes to get their medications. One of the best ways to offer value in the public space is through the elimination of bottlenecks. While the bureaucratic system is put in place to check corruption (arguably the biggest problem of developing countries), this same system instead fosters what it is meant to fight and deny citizens from accessing real value even when they can afford it. The critical question that policymakers should ask, which is also critical to profit conscious enterprises, is how we can offer the value sought in the most convenient manner? What increases the pain points of our clients? How can we improve on our processes to delight our clients? In developing economies, the concept of "phygital" becomes even more critical. As we transition into the digital world, our lack of infrastructure and the preparedness of the popu-lace should lead us to find solutions that blend the "physical and the digital". Convenience should be sought at the intersection of the digital and the physical realities to deal with public and business challenges.

Do the simple things first. Targeting the low-hanging fruits by doing the simple things first creates space to deal with the monster challenges in public policy. While the challenges of the South African healthcare system are of monstrous proportions, dealing with some basic issues of overcrowding and providing chronic medications go a long way to dealing with the monster. The simple things were reducing or eliminating queues, providing access to medication, and increas-ing public healthcare workers with morale. Additionally, they used the existing channels of value delivery within the healthcare value chain. If citizens can use retail outlets such as "Pick n Pay" and "Shoprite" for money transfers and other collections, why couldn't they do so with the medi-cation collection? If religious canters of worship are trusted places for the people, why couldn't they access their medications from there? Doing simple things first and finding value delivery partners became the important success factors for the program. Emerging economy contexts have their systems and structures that support value delivery. Leveraging on these existing structures, which are trusted by the citizens and supported by their social institutions, allows for effective value delivery. Policymakers should design solutions based on the existing value chain—thereby cutting down on cost—and social institutions such that citizens would participate in the value creation and delivery process.

The success of the "Get Checked. Go Collect" program is also based on the effective communication of the policy. The intended audience was trained on the process of registration and collection, the benefits of subscribing, dealing with frequently asked questions, media campaign, and constant monitoring of communication effectiveness. While value creation is key, the communication of the value created is equally important. Most often than not, policy failures result from a lack of an effective communication plan. Value is definitely created for a market—an audience—this market must be aware of the benefits the solution provided deliver. Failure of many innovations in both commercial and not-for-profit ventures can be attributed to a lack of understanding of the value on offer to the market. According to Maes et al. (2012), the relational aspect of value management is highly critical as it determines the extent of uptake of every value. The relational mechanism establishes social interaction, active participation, and collaboration among internal and external stakeholders through norms, values, and shared beliefs. The program's ability to bring in the private sector and customer testimonials enhanced the reach of the program. It is important in the public sector to go beyond persuasion and build dialogue to engender trust. Managers in both the public and private sectors should seek to inform, listen, and respond to any issue which is considered critical and valuable to the audience.

Conclusion

This chapter has highlighted the importance of segmentation in the effective value creation and delivery process. Drawing from a healthcare program implemented in an emerging market economy to solve one of the difficult changes in the economy's healthcare system, the chapter shares useful lessons for both practitioners and researchers. South Africa is one of the most unequal countries in the world. Unfortunately, the countries healthcare sector is one of the sectors which suffers greatly as a result of this inequality. While the well-to-do are well taken care of through exorbitant health insurance premiums, the poor suffers through lack of access.

This chapter has shared lessons from a healthcare program that has afforded millions of patients' access to chronic medication in an emerging economy. The National Health Department of South Africa implemented a centralized medication dispensing and distribution program which allowed chronic patients to have access to their periodic medications seamlessly. The success of this program was based on a needs analysis which allowed the Health Department to segment based on health needs at the various healthcare centers. A simple process of registration and collection was then developed to move the collection from healthcare centers, thereby reducing overcrowding and long queues. The program leveraged on existing value delivery chains of the healthcare system and other sectors to deliver a valuable service to over three million patients.

This chapter has offered important lessons for both practitioners in profit-oriented sectors and not-for-profit sector practitioners as well. The chapter has provided a useful tool that helps determine the effectiveness of a value creation and delivery process. The tool also helps evaluate how to effectively use an entity-limited resource to meet the most pressing or profitable needs. The chapter offers that existing value delivery chains can afford public sector practitioners to adequately meet the needs of the public in a more convenient manner.

References

Business Insider SA. (2021, March 30). *This Is the Average Salary in SA—and it's Not Keeping Up with Inflation.* Retrieved May 6, 2021, from www.businessinsider.co.za/average-salary-in-south-africa-2021-3-2#:~:text=The%20average%20monthly%20salary%20earned%20in%20South%20Africa%20was%20R23,was%20higher%20during%20that%20time

Genesis Medical Scheme. (2021). *Best and Worst Medical Aid Schemes in SA—with Prices.* www.genesismedical.co.za/best-worst-medical-aid-schemes-south-africa-prices/

Graeber, D. (2005). Value: Anthropological Theories of Value. In J. G. Carrier (Ed.), *A Handbook of Economic Anthropology* (pp. 439–454). Cheltenham: Edward Elgar Publishing.

Keeton, C. (2010). Bridging the Gap in South Africa: The South African Government's Proposed National Insurance Scheme Aims to Tackle the Stark Divide in Health Care between Rich and Poor. *Bulletin of the World Health Organization, 88*(11), 803–805.

Kollamparambil, U. (2021). Socio-economic Inequality of Wellbeing: A Comparison of Switzerland and South Africa. *Journal of Happiness Studies, 22*(2), 555–574.

Maes, K., De Haes, S., & Van Grembergen, W. (2012). The identification and Definition of Value Management Practices used to Deploy is Investments. In *MCIS (Short Papers)* (p. 34).

McLeod, S. (2007). Maslow's Hierarchy of Needs. *Simply Psychology, 1*, 1–8.

Mhlanga, D., & Garidzirai, R. (2020). The Influence of Racial Differences in the Demand for Healthcare in South Africa: A Case of Public Healthcare. *International Journal of Environmental Research and Public Health, 17*(14), 5043.

Statista. (2021). *Household Disposable Income in South Africa from 1990 to 2019.* Retrieved May 6, 2021, from www.statista.com/statistics/874035/household-disposable-income-in-south-africa/#:~:text=In%202019%2C%20South%20African%20households,about%2034%2C037%20South%20African%20Rand.

Stats SA. (2020). *How Unequal is South Africa?* www.statssa.gov.za/?p=12930&gclid=CjwKCAjwhMmEBhBwEiwAXwFoEbGH1qiSJOxlBSUIcSkS8wUZTapsn-UADMrJify0wwFi775y0Y9LahoCOeoQAvD_BwE; accessed on April 29, 2021

Tosam, M. J., Chi, P. C., Munung, N. S., Oukem-Boyer, O. O. M., & Tangwa, G. B. (2018). Global Health Inequalities and the Need for Solidarity: A View from the Global South. *Developing World Bioethics, 18*(3), 241–249.

Valiani, S. (2020). Structuring Sustainable Universal Health Care in South Africa. *International Journal of Health Services, 50*(2), 234–245.

WHO. (2018). *Health Inequities and their Causes.* Retrieved April 2, 2021, from www.who.int/news-room/facts-in-pictures/detail/health-inequities-and-their-causes

Winchester, M. S., & King, B. (2018). Decentralization, Healthcare Access, and Inequality in Mpumalanga, South Africa. *Health & Place, 51*, 200–207.

Authors' Profile

Ricardo Kettledas is a qualified Pharmacist who also holds certificates in Project Management and Financial Management and is studying for his MBA at Wits Business School. He has over 20 years of professional working experience across the wider healthcare spectrum including healthcare information systems. Ricardo has experience working with cross-functional teams and multiple stakeholders both locally and internationally. Ricardo is currently the CCMDD National Program Coordinator where he provides leadership and coordinates processes related to the provision of an alternative chronic medication access program for public sector patients. This entails policy development and implementation; monitoring and evaluation (M&E) involving implementation of a web-based monitoring system for the program; and stakeholder liaison at all levels including the National Department of Health (NDoH) and key funders.

Thomas Anning-Dorson (PhD) is an associate professor at the Wits Business School, University of the Witwatersrand, Johannesburg, South Africa. He also serves a Researcher with The Fairwork Foundation, Oxford Internet Institute, University of Oxford, and a fellow at McGill University, Canada, on the QES Program. His research interest spans the digital economy, innovation, marketing, strategy, value, and emerging markets.

Chapter 17

Predictive Model for Early Detection of Mother's Mode of Delivery with Feature Selection

Emmanuel Awuni Kolog, Oluwafemi Samson Balogun,
Richard Osei Adjei, Samuel Nii Odoi Devine,
Donald Douglas Atsa'am, Oluwaseun Alexander
Dada, and Temidayo Oluwatosin Omotehinwa

Contents

DOI: 10.4324/9781003152217-22

Introduction

Childbirth is a significant aspect and experience in life, especially for women (Namujju et al., 2018; Loke et al., 2015), and means for procreation. This, for generations, has been the exclusive perquisite of women. From the day of conception, essential care is expected to be given that would lead to the delivery of healthy newborns (Shah et al., 2009). Accordingly, this is critical for reducing occurrences of mortality for mother and newborn survival which sadly is not the case in most low- and middle-income countries (WHO, 2010), as seen in developing countries. A negative experience during childbirth may result in unwanted ramifications (Namujju et al., 2018). To this end, it can be said that the climax of childbirth is the period of delivery, which often is a critical decision to make for many mothers (Namujju et al., 2018; Loke et al., 2015) and thus the mode of delivery which affects the success rate of having to safeguard the lives of both mother and child (Shah et al., 2009).

Over the years, although advances in medicine have provided alternatives, the mode of delivery can be classified into two main categories: *Vaginal* and *Caesarean Section* (*C-section*). It is reported that the mode of delivery may present major concerns from health to finance to both mother and child (Lavender et al., 2012). Globally, even though the natural method for delivery via vaginal delivery is higher, C-section deliveries are seen to be on the increase (Zamani-Alavijeh, 2017; Lavender et al., 2012). However, it is well documented in literature that there are instances where a caesarian section has been requested by expectant mothers or suggested without medical indication (Zamani-Alavijeh, 2017; Shi et al., 2016; Lavender et al., 2012), in both middle- and high-income countries (Mazzoni et al., 2016). Varying reasons have been associated with opting for either vaginal or C-section modes of delivery including health risk factors for mother or child, mothers' preference and beliefs, prevention of injuries, and fear (Zamani-Alavijeh, 2017; Shi et al., 2016; Lavender et al., 2012).

This is the milieu that World Health Organization (WHO) advocates for, where countries are to ensure caesarean section deliveries are between 10% and 15% of all births as findings indicate no significant improvement in mortality rates for both mother and child, in cases higher than 10% (WHO, 2015). While some reports indicate several adverse health risks and conditions in children born through cesarean delivery (Keag et al., 2018; Polidano et al., 2017), others present contrary findings (Gondwe et al., 2018). WHO (2019) reports that, globally, about 94% of all maternal deaths occur in countries of low and lower middle-income status. The worst affected in this regard are countries within the Sub-Saharan Africa and South Asia region accounting for about 86% of maternal mortality in 2017. Sub-Saharan Africa recorded approximately two-thirds of those maternal-related deaths (WHO, 2019).

Several factors are suggested in extant literature that may influence the decision to opt for a particular mode of delivery (Loke et al., 2015). Predominantly, the mode of delivery is in the purview of the expectant mother (Loke et al., 2019; Shi et al., 2016; Moffat et al., 2007). Although some mothers, based on previous expectations and experiences, have fears or are uncomfortable to make the decision, do so with guidance or expert advice from medical personnel (Shi et al., 2016; Moffat et al., 2007), especially in countries with well-developed healthcare (Loke et al., 2019), and among others (Zamani-Alavijeh, 2017; Shi et al., 2016; Loke et al., 2015). Nonetheless, the choice of mode of delivery is still an issue of argument (Zandvakili et al., 2017) and dependent on number of factors, both personal and impersonal characteristics or features of the mother which have been addressed in our study. To this end, the features when carefully observed could influence the decision and, thus, provide medically relevant and accurate suggestions that would help expectant mothers prepare adequately for the birth of their child. Accordingly, such practices would help provide quality care and decrease chances of maternal and child mortality, especially in Africa (Shah et al., 2009), providing sound recommendations for neonatal care, expectant mothers, and childbirth (Namujju et al., 2018).

This chapter seeks to explore the likely factors that can be used in predicting the possible and most optimal option in the choice or preference on the mode of delivery using a machine learning approach. By implication, our study provides a pragmatic step toward identification of optimal features to consider in predicting the most suitable mode of delivery, which, in turn, would yield near optimal results in terms of safety during childbirth. This would lead to a reduction in the morbidity, mortality, and adverse outcomes at delivery for both mother and child.

Background

Childbirth

Approximately, 303,000 maternal mortalities occurred globally in 2015, with just 1% occurring outside the regions of low- and middle-income countries (WHO, 2015; Alkema et al., 2016). According to WHO, 66.3% of such mortalities happened in Sub-Saharan Africa (WHO, 2015). Nigeria, a Sub-Saharan African country accounted for 19% of the global maternal mortalities, with approximately 58,000 mortalities occurring in 2015. Nigerian women experience a high maternal mortality ratio of approximately 814 maternal deaths per 100,000 live births (WHO, 2015) and a 1 in 22 lifetime risk of maternal death (Alkema et al., 2016). The ratio in maternal mortality between the southern regions and the northern regions is 1:10 because of poor health indicators and conditions in the Northern part of Nigeria (NPC and ICF International, 2014).

In Nigeria, several factors account for the high maternal mortalities and ratio. These include a low number of skilled birth attendants—with just 45% of births handled by skilled healthcare workers in 2015 (Alkema et al., 2016)—poor attitudes of healthcare personnel on pregnant woman, and the choice of healthcare facility (Esimai et al., 2002; Uzochukwu et al., 2004; Osubor et al., 2006). The high levels of maternal morbidity and mortality are due to poor and inadequate patronage of maternal healthcare services in Nigeria. A study on the number of antenatal visits of pregnant women in Nigeria in 2013 suggests that only 51.1% of participants completed a minimum of four antenatal care visits with 36% of births occurring in a healthcare center (NPC and ICF International, 2014).

Moreover, another critical impediment is that the quality of healthcare facilities and providers is perceived to be poor in Nigeria (Idris et al., 2013; Bawa et al., 2004; Osubor et al., 2006; Esimai et al., 2002; Uzochukwu et al., 2004). A study conducted in the Southern part of Nigeria by Osubor et al. (2006) posits that healthcare facilities owned by the federal government often provide poor-quality maternity services coupled with poorly trained staff and unavailability of qualified healthcare professionals during childbirth (Osubor et al., 2006).

Pregnant women are often encouraged to stick to their antenatal schedules even if there is no present or imminent risk associated with childbirth. Globally, there is a paradigm shift in the maternal and childbirth program from a narrow focus on survival to the incorporation of drivers for thriving and transformation (Renfrew et al., 2014; Tuncalp et al., 2015). Such change is consistent with the third Sustainable Development Goal—including but not limited to women and child health agenda 2016–2030 (United Nations, 2015). Similar agendas are being championed by WHO regarding high-quality healthcare for pregnant women and childbirth period (Tuncalp et al., 2015). With the positive impact of antenatal care on childbirth in mind, the WHO released a comprehensive guidance on antenatal care for a safe, positive, and incident-free pregnancy experience in 2016 (WHO, 2016).

Tikmani et al. (2019) argue that antenatal care is a relevant opportunity to determine and treat pregnancy-related complications and provide programs and solutions targeted at enhancing the health and survival of mothers and new borns (Tikmani et al., 2019). Within the context of antenatal care for pregnant women through childbirth, structured preparation, and programs (Gagnon & Sandall, 2007) aimed to aid in dealing with the physical and emotional changes (Simkin, 2000) experienced by pregnant women during childbirth have been considered. Numerous antenatal programs and interventions have been proven to positively impact childbirth; exercises to prevention of lumbopelvic pain (Kashanian et al., 2009; Garshasbi et al., 2005; Kluge et al., 2011), methods of improving self-control and autonomy during labor (Bergström et al., 2010; Kimber et al., 2008), and research associated with pelvic floor muscle exercises for urinary incontinence (Hay-Smith et al., 2008).

A study conducted by Karabulut et al. (2016) suggests that antenatal care significantly increases the degree of acceptance of pregnancy in women and decreases the fear and anxiety associated with childbirth (Karabulut et al., 2016). Antenatal education is a potential treatment for fear (Serçekuş & Başkale, 2016; Badaoui et al., 2019) and helps to alleviate post-traumatic stress disorder symptoms (Gökçe İsbir et al., 2016). Nonmedical antenatal care refers to a range of nonmedical services available to women during pregnancy which are aimed at supporting women and prepare them for the birth and the postpartum period (Ludwig et al., 2020). In some developed countries, pregnancy-specific yoga, antenatal classes, gymnastics courses, and other related exercises and courses for pregnant women and breastfeeding classes are considered as nonmedical antenatal care targeted at pregnant women to prepare them for childbirth (Ludwig et al., 2020).

Related Works

At childbirth, a quick decision may have to be taken regarding the most suitable mode of delivery for the patient. In general, there are two modes: vaginal (Normal) delivery and Cesarean delivery (Hrycyk et al., 2016). While the vaginal or "natural" delivery is preferable, the Cesarean delivery—which involves the use of surgical operations with considerably higher risks—is increasingly being used even when it is medically not required (Kamat et al., 2015; Rydahl et al., 2019).

Studies have found that there is a strong association between the age of a woman and cesarean section delivery (Abbas et al., 2018). Some authors claim that women who had previously delivered via cesarean section are more likely to deliver subsequently via similar mode (Fitzpatrick et al., 2019), and those (women with cesarean history) who chose planned-vaginal delivery are prone to severe medical complications (Rydahl et al., 2019). All of these, coupled with the fact that Cesarean deliveries are on the increase, have made it a public health problem worldwide (Lipschuetz et al., 2020). A review of existing literature highlights how machine learning algorithms have been successfully used to tackle issues related to cesarean deliveries—one approach is in forecasting mother's mode of child delivery. Over the years, several academic papers have been published and numerous machine learning applications developed (Abbas et al., 2018).

In a quest to reduce the cesarean delivery rate, a group of researchers applied machine learning techniques to predict successful vaginal births after previous cesarean deliveries using a cohort of about 10,000 parturients (women-in-labor) with 1 (one) previous cesarean delivery. These women were preallocated into low-, medium-, and high-risk groups. The results showed a vaginal delivery success rate of 97.3%, 90.9%, and 73.3% in the low-, medium-, and high-risk groups, respectively (Lipschuetz et al., 2020).

In another example, Kamat et al. (2015) successfully applied two data classification algorithms (Naive Bayes and ID3) to determine the mother's mode of delivery based on the following features: age, BMI, Systolic blood pressure, diastolic blood pressure, glucose-fasting, parity, BPD (around 29 weeks), fundal height (around 29 weeks), cervical length (around 29 weeks), and neonatal weight (from the previous pregnancy). Naive Bayes was reported to have higher accuracy. On a similar note, Kavitha and Balasubramanian (2018) implemented the Decision Tree (a machine learning model) to forecast the mode of delivery by using the following features: age, height, BMI, child weight, HBP, sugar, thyroid, toxemia, multiple pregnancies, breech presentation, and sleep disturbance. Accuracies of about 100% and 99.50% were achieved—on training and testing datasets, respectively.

The aforementioned research works demonstrate the fact that machine-learning algorithms can be used in the prediction of mother's mode of delivery in advance, thereby making it possible to avoid unnecessary cesarean operations. They also show that if the insights gleaned from the analyses of certain risk factors (or features) are carefully communicated to medical staff—e.g., via modern reporting interfaces—the chances of patients having successful vaginal deliveries will be significantly increased.

Methodology

Dataset

The dataset used for this work is secondary. Information on pregnant women who came for delivery in some public and private hospitals in Northern Nigeria were considered. The dataset variables are length of stay of pregnant women after delivery, age of mother, educational qualification, occupation, number of procedures, number of diagnoses, mode of delivery (normal or vaginal delivery and cesarean), parity, mother's weight, and child's weight. As a matter of the Government open data initiative, the data are freely available upon request. The data have been coded in such a way that mothers cannot be personally identified to ensure data confidentiality and anonymity. Table 17.1 represents the various attributes and their respective descriptions.

Methods and Machine Learning Classifiers

The method used in this chapter is quantitative. Thus, machine learning was employed to select feature attributes and as well build the predictive models. The predictive model was built based on ML classification. The target variable (mode of delivery) had only two tags: *Normal* and Cesarean. Hence, the technique was a binary text classification. Before building the predictive models, we preprocessed the data to ensure error-free data. We cleaned the data, explored the correlation among the various attributes that were selected, and eventually built the predictive model. Machine learning capabilities such as Pandas, numpy, matplotlib, and Scikit with Python programming were leveraged for this study. The four ML algorithms used in this study are described as follows.

Table 17.1 Description of the Feature Attributes

	Attribute	Description
NoV	Number of Visits	This is the number of visits to the hospital during antenatal
MoW	Mother's Weight	This is the pregnant woman's weight
NoP	Number of Procedures	These are some assisted delivery procedures that take place during labor and after delivery
NoD	Number of Diagnoses	This is the number of times the pregnant woman was diagnosed before and after delivery
HT	Hospital Type	This is the type of hospital the pregnant woman attended for delivery
LoS	Length of Stay	This is the length of stay in the hospital by the pregnant woman after delivery
Age	Mother's Age	This is the age of the pregnant woman
Loc	Location (residential)	This the location of the residence of the pregnant woman
Ocu	Occupation	This is the job category of the pregnant woman
EoQ	Educational Level	This is the highest academic qualification obtained by the pregnant woman
Parity	Parity	This is number of times the mother had given birth
MoD	Mode of Delivery	This is the form of delivery for the pregnant women, e.g., Normal and Cesarean birth

Naïve-Bayes: According to Li and Li (2020), naïve-Bayes is a supervised machine-learning classification algorithm based on Bayesian rule. The assumption entails that the prior probability and conditional probability of each attribute in the class are known. In this chapter, the required task is to predict the natural or cesarean mode of delivery, C_i (where C_1 = natural and C_0 = cesarean mode of delivery) given that its predictor variables are $d_1, d_2, ..., d_p$ as $P(C_i | d_1, d_2, ..., d_p)$. The Bayesian formula for estimating this probability is given in equation (1). From the equation, $P(C_i)$ is known as the prior probability of the outcome, $P(d)$ is defined as the predictor variable probability, and $P(d|C_i)$ is the conditional probability or likelihood, while $P(C_i|d)$ is called the posterior probability.

$$P\left(C_i | d\right) = \frac{P\left(C_i\right) P\left(d | C_i\right)}{P\left(d\right)} \tag{1}$$

$$Posterior = \frac{Prior \times likelihood}{Evidence} \tag{2}$$

Support Vector Machine (SVM): The SVM algorithm finds a linear classifier that separates the training data with the largest margin. The major goal of the SVM is to find a hyperplane in the instance space, and it can classify different types of test instances. Cortes and Vapnik (1995) described SVM also known as Support vector machine as a two-category model. Assuming that x_i is the training input, y_i is the training output, w is the weight vector, b is the intercept, m is the size of the dataset, the hyperplane can be written as:

$$y = w^T x + b, (x_i, y_i) \in D$$
$$\text{If } y = w^T x_i + b \geq 1, y_i = +1$$
$$\text{Else if } y = w^T x_i + b \leq -1, y_i = -1$$

The optimization problem is written as:

$$\min_{w,b} \frac{1}{2} \|w^2\| \tag{3}$$
$$\text{Subject to } y_i \left(w^T x_i + b \right) \geq 1, i = 1, 2, ..., m$$

Random Forest: Breiman (2001) and Liaw and Wiener (2002) describe random forest algorithm as a type of ensemble machine learning method which can be applied in classification, regression, and outlier detection. Random forest is a classifier consisting of a collection of independently generated decision trees. The model is trained, and the out-of-the-bag error is estimated given a set of input and outputs. We can estimate the importance $I(x_i)$ for each variable. First, compute the difference $R(x_i)$ between errors obtained for the initial order and the random order (Ricordeau & Lacaille, 2010).

$$R(x_i) = \text{Error with random order of } x_i - \text{Error with initial order of } x_i \tag{4}$$

$$\text{The results is normalized to obtain } I(x_i) = 100 \times \frac{R(x_i)}{\Sigma_k R(x_k)} \tag{5}$$

K-Nearest Neighbor: According to Song et al. (2017) and Chen (2018), k-Nearest Neighbor (KNN) is a simple machine learning algorithm that stores all available cases and classifies new cases based on a similarity measure. The algorithm is used to solve problems related to classification, regression, and pattern recognition. It classifies data based on the distance between classes in the training data and testing data (Giri et al., 2016). Depending on the nature of the data, the KNN uses distance measures such as Minkowski, Manhattan, and Euclidean. Considering the structure of the data in this chapter, the Euclidean distance shown in equation (6) is the most appropriate:

$$Dist(X, Y) = \sqrt{\Sigma_{i=1}^{D} (X_i - Y_i)^2} \tag{6}$$

where X (predictor variable) and Y (response variable) are the two attributes. Given the selected nearest neighbors, the KNN uses the following voting approaches to classify the test sample:

1. Majority voting: $y = arg \max_v \sum_{(x_i, y_i) \in D_z} \delta(v, y_i)$

2. Distance-weighted voting: $y = arg \max_v \sum_{(x_i, y_i) \in D_z} w_i \delta(v, y_i)$

where $\delta(v, y_i)$ is an indicator function, D_z is the set of nearest neighbors of the test sample, and the weight $w_i = 1 / d(X, x_i)^2$.

Experiment

Data Preprocessing

The data were preprocessed to identify possible missing data, errors, and abnormal outliers in the data. There were few missing data of which *Expectation–Maximization* (EM) algorithm was applied to replace the missing data. The EM algorithm incorporates statistical considerations to compute the "most likely," or "maximum-likelihood" source distribution that would have created the observed projected data, including the effects of counting statistics (Dempster et al., 1997). After cleaning and preparing the data, we applied a normalization technique to normalize the data to a range of (0,1). Data normalization refers to rescaling the various instances of the data to a standard range such as (0,1). The technique is often applied to attributes of varying scales. The technique ensures uniformity of the data which prevents bias and skewness.

Feature Selection

To produce an optimized performance of the various ML algorithms, we proposed a feature selection technique that considers the expert knowledge of medical professionals. The outcome from selecting the features is compared with other results obtained from performing principal component analysis (PCA). Irrelevant feature attributes are likely to decrease the accuracy of the ML models and increase the chances of overfitting (Brownlee, 2019; Kolog et al., 2018). In our approach, five medical professionals were tasked to rank the various attributes from the dataset vis a vis the mode of child delivery. All the selected medical practitioners have been in the medical profession for at least ten years with competencies in obstetrics. The experts were tasked to rank the various predictive attributes from the scale of 1–5, where 1 is least important and 5 is the most important. This approach encompasses knowledge and experiences of the medical practitioners for the feature selection. To the best of our knowledge, this technique has not adequately been explored in the context of feature selection for machine learning classification. The equations (8) and (9) are formulas for computing the aggregated mean rank (*Mean$_r$*) of each of the attributes (LoS, Age, Loc, Edu, Parity, NoV, MoW, NoP) ranked by the medical experts, E_i ($i = 1, 2, \ldots n$). From the equations, the total number of experts is denoted by n. The criterion for selecting the various attributes is based on equation (10).

$$Mean_r = \frac{\sum_{i=1}^{n} E_i}{n} \tag{9}$$

The criterion for the feature selection:

$$\begin{cases} True, & if\ Mean_r \geq 3 \\ \\ \\ False, & if\ Mean_r < 3 \end{cases} \tag{10}$$

Table 17.2 Feature Selection

Attributes	Health Experts Ranking							PCA Rank
	E1	E2	E3	E4	E5	Mean	Selection	
Hospital type (HT)	1	1	2	2	2	**2.0**	**False**	**2**
Length of stay (LoS)	5	4	5	4	4	**4.4**	True	1
Mother's age (Age)	5	5	5	4	4	**4.6**	True	1
Location (residential) (Loc)	3	3	3	3	4	**3.2**	True	2
Occupation (Ocu)	1	2	1	1	1	**1.0**	**False**	**3**
Educational level (EoQ)	3	4	3	4	5	**3.4**	True	1
Parity (Parity)	4	4	3	4	5	**4.0**	True	1
Number of visits (NoV)	3	3	2	3	3	**3.1**	True	1
Mother's weight (MoW)	4	4	4	4	3	**3.8**	True	1
Number of procedure (NoP)	3	4	5	4	4	**4.0**	True	1
Number of diagnosis (NoD)	4	3	3	4	3	**3.4**	True	1

Additionally, Python script was developed by leveraging the capabilities of the PCA in Scikit-learn to select the features. The result was compared with our approach in Table 17.2. As shown in Table 17.2, except for the attributes: *hospital type*, *location (residence)*, and *occupation*, all the other attributes were found to have strong predictive strength. However, only *Hospital type* and *occupation* were dropped from the subset used for classification modeling. It is to be noted that our feature selection approach and that of the PCA resulted to similar feature subset.

Classification Model

The experimental data containing the selected feature attributes were divided into two, for model construction and testing. One part of the data, which is 80%, was used as training set, while the remaining 20% used to test the models. The instances of the training data were used to train the various ML algorithms. The data were slightly imbalanced as the number of Cesarean modes of delivery was greater than the Normal modes of delivery (refer to Table 17.3). The imbalanced nature of the data prompted the need to use the train/test technique. An imbalanced classification problem is an example of a classification problem where the distribution of observations across the known classes is biased or skewed. Imbalanced classifications pose a challenge for developing the predictive model as most of the ML algorithms used for classification were designed around the assumption of an equal number of examples for each class. Data imbalance has a higher tendency to influence the performance of the algorithms and reduce the accuracy levels. We treated the data imbalance by reducing the difference between the normal and caesarian modes of delivery in the training data set. Figure 17.1 shows a block diagram that summarizes the steps and the processes employed in the experiments. By using Scikit-learn capabilities in Python, the training data were pipelined into the algorithms for learning which resulted in the creation of a model. Thus, the remaining 20% instances of the test data were used to test the model.

Precision, Recall, F1-score, and the Area under Receiver Operating Characteristics curve (AROC) were computed to ascertain the performance of the algorithms. These measures were originated through the evaluation of the binary classification. In binary classification, Precision asks the question of what proportion of positive (thus cesarean) identifications, during classification, was actually correct? On the other hand, the Recall attempts to ask the question, what proportion of actual positives was identified correctly? Therefore, given that real positive (p) and negative (n) cases in the data (normal and caesarian), the Precision, Recall, and F1-score can be computed as in equations (11)–(13), where *tp* is *true positive*, *fp* is *false positive*, and *fn* is *false negative*.

$$Precision = \frac{tp}{tp + fp} \tag{11}$$

$$Recall = \frac{tp}{tp + fn} \tag{12}$$

$$F1 - score = 2 \times \frac{Precision \times Recall}{Precision + Recall} \tag{13}$$

The ROC is an important measure for ascertaining the predictive strength of a model developed from training ML algorithms. The ROC is a probability curve and area under the curve (AUC) represents the degree or measure of separability of discriminatory. It tells how much the model is capable of distinguishing between classes (thus Normal and Cesarean). The AUC is often computed in a range either (0, 100%) or (0, 1) where the higher the value or score the better the discriminatory strength. By analogy, in this study, the higher the AUC, the better the model in distinguishing between Normal and Cesarean modes of delivery. In ROC curve, the true positive rate (TPR) is plotted on the y-axis, while the false positive rate (FPR) is on the x-axis.

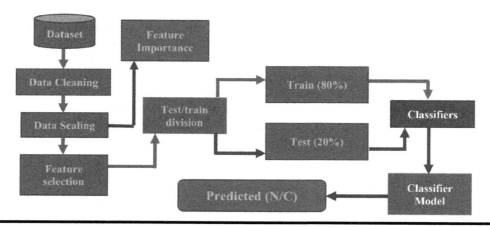

Figure 17.1 Classification model.

Results and Analysis

Descriptive and Correlation

Table 17.3 contains the demographic profiles of the participants. The demographic breakdown of the participants shows that majority of pregnant women are within the ages of 15–25 years, reside

Table 17.3   Demographic Profiles of the Participants

Attributes	Scale	Frequency	Percentage (%)
Age	15–25	370	52.8
	26–35	252	35.9
	36–45	76	10.8
	Above 45	3	0.4
Location (residential)	Rural	487	69.5
	Urban	214	30.5
Educational qualification	No education	220	31.4
	Primary	122	17.4
	Secondary	162	23.1
	NCE/OND	152	21.7
	Degree/HND	45	6.4
Parity	0–4	630	89.9
	5–10	71	10.1
Mode of delivery	Normal delivery	300	42.7
	Cesarean delivery	401	57.3
Hospital type	Public hospital	400	57.1
	Private hospital	301	42.9
Mother weight	Below 40	7	1.0
	40–60	493	70.3
	61–80	168	24.0
	81–100	33	4.7
	Above 100	0	0
Length of stay	1–4	644	91.9
	5–10	43	6.1

(Continued)

Table 17.3   (Continued)

Attributes	Scale	Frequency	Percentage (%)
	Above 11	14	2.0
Number of visits	0–4	538	76.7
	5–10	153	21.8
	Above 11	10	1.4
Number of procedures	0–4	647	92.3
	5–10	53	7.6
	Above 11	1	0.1
Number of diagnosis	0–4	645	92.0
	5–10	54	7.7
	Above 11	2	0.3

in the rural areas, with no education, with 0–4 number of children, use public hospitals, within the weights of 40–60 kg, stay within 1–4 days in the hospital before and after delivery, and visit for antenatal 0–4 times.

Table 17.4 shows the correlation among the various selected feature attributes. Generally, there is a significant linear relationship between the feature attributes. However, the correlation among the individual attributes varied. For instance, while there exists weak correlation between the age and length of stay ($r = -0.107$), there exists a strong correlation between the number of procedures and number of diagnoses ($r = 0.799$).

Classification and Model Evaluation

Table 17.5 shows the computed parameters for the performance of the algorithms. From the table, the Precision, Recall, Weighted average, and Accuracy of the algorithms are shown. The accuracies of all the algorithms are impressive on the dataset as all the scores are beyond 90%, which goes beyond the acceptable threshold of the 70% (Landis & Kouch, 1977). However, the performances of these algorithms are not equal, with slight variations. With respect to the performance, SVM and NB yielded the best performance (A = 97%) followed by the KNN (A = 96%)) and RF (A= 95%). These scores show that SVM and NB are the best performing algorithms for predicting mother's mode of delivery in the dataset used in the study.

We investigated the performance of each of the algorithms. The Recall, Precision, and F1-scores of both the SVM and NB were found to exhibit the same predictive strength for the *Normal* and *Cesarean* mode of delivery. As indicated in the table, 82% proportion of the instances of the data (for *Cesarean*) were identified by the algorithms (SVM and NB), while only 82% of the identified data were correctly predicted. Similarly, 98% proportion of the instances of the *Normal* modes of delivery were also identified by the algorithms (SVM and NB), while only 98% of the identified instances of the data were correctly predicted. The F1-scores for SVM were 82% for *Normal* mode of delivery and 98% for Cesarean mode of delivery. These values are the same for the NB.

Table 17.4 Correlation among the Various Feature Attributes

	LoS	Age	Loc	EdL	Parity	NoV	MoW	NoP	NoD
LoS Sig.	1	0.024 0.528	-0.107 0.005*	0.105 0.005*	-0.108 0.004*	0.032 0.397	-0.013 0.728	0.022 0.563	-0.020 0.624
Age Sig.		1	-0.140 0.000*	0.172 0.000*	0.655 0.000*	-0.030 0.422	0.490 0.000*	-0.058 0.126	-0.120 0.001*
Loc Sig.			1	-0.317 0.000*	0.010 0.782	-0.115 0.002*	-0.140 0.000*	-0.005 0.888	-0.017 0.646
Edu Sig.				1	-0.069 0.067	0.231 0.000*	0.198 0.000*	-0.053 0.165	-0.042 0.263
Parity Sig.					1	-0.143 0.000*	0.349 0.000*	-0.066 0.083	-0.075 0.048*
NoV Sig.						1	0.020 0.590	0.384 0.000*	0.396 0.000*
MoW Sig.							1	-0.045 0.238	-0.112 0.003*
NoP Sig.								1	0.799 0.000*

Table 17.5 Classifier Performance

Classifiers	Measures	With Selected Features			Accuracy
		Normal	Cesarean	Weighted Average	
KNN	Precision	0.97	0.88	0.96	**96%**
	Recall	0.99	0.84	0.96	
	F1-score	0.98	0.84	0.96	
RF	Precision	0.78	0.97	0.95	**95%**
	Recall	0.64	0.98	0.96	
	F1-score	0.70	0.98	0.96	
NB	Precision	0.82	0.98	0.97	**97%**
	Recall	0.82	0.98	0.97	
	F1-score	0.82	0.98	0.97	
SVM	Precision	0.82	0.98	0.97	**97%**
	Recall	0.82	0.98	0.97	
	F1-score	0.82	0.98	0.97	

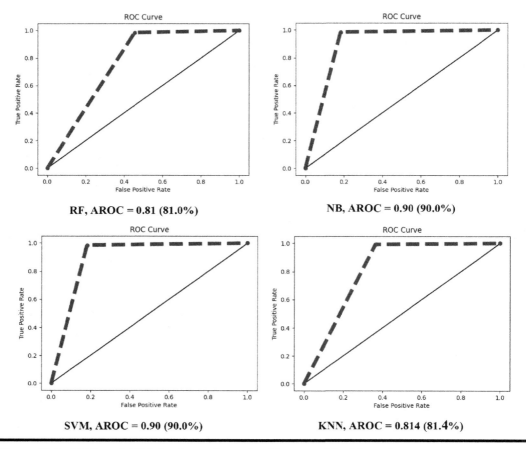

Figure 17.2   ROC and AUC for the various algorithms used in this study.

At the individual classification level, the performance of the KNN was found to be better than the RF algorithm. The Recall scores for KNN and RF are, respectively, 99% and 64% for predicting *Normal* mode of delivery. These scores show that 99% of the instances of the test data were recognized by the KNN algorithm, while only 64% of the instances of the test data were recognized by the RF algorithm. Out of these recognized instances of the data, the accurate predictions of KNN and RF for the normal mode of delivery are 97% and 78%, respectively. It is obvious that the Precision score for RF was below the acceptable threshold of 70%. In the same vein, 84% and 98% of the instances of the *Cesarean* data were recognized by the KNN and RF, respectively, while only 88% and 97% of the recognized instances of the data were correctly predicted. These scores go to show that both algorithms generally performed well with KNN being superior.

Figure 17.2 contains the Receiver operating Characteristics (ROC) curves for the various ML algorithms (SVM, NB, KNN, RF). The ROC curve provides the overall assessment of the predictive models. The area under the curve is termed Area under ROC (AROC). The AROC measures discriminatory power of the predictive model which indicates the ability of the models to classify normal and cesarean modes of delivery. Therefore, the larger the area bounded to the reference line, the better in terms of the predictive models. As indicated in the curves, the top left corner of each of the plots is the "ideal" point—a *FPR* of zero (0), and a *TPR* of one (1). However, it is highly unrealistic to obtain the extreme AROC score of exactly 0 or 1. The acceptable thresholds for the AROC are 0.90–1.0 = *excellent*, 0.80–0.90 = *good*, 0.70–0.80 = *fair*, 0.60–0.70 = *poor*, and 0.50–0.60 = *fail* (Kleinbaum & Klein, 2010). The AROC of all the ML algorithms, in this study, are beyond 80% which are all within the acceptable range. However, SVM (AROC = 90%) and NB (AROC = 90%) yielded *excellent* performances while KNN (AROC = 81.4%) and RF (AROC= 81%) yielded *good* performances (Kleinbaum & Klein, 2010). These performances indicate how well the algorithms discriminate on the dataset.

Feature Importance

The selected features, through recursive feature elimination (RFE) technique, were ranked according to their RFE coefficients. Ranking the features was to determine the order of importance of the various attributes. Table 17.6 shows the various attributes with the RFE coefficients. The RFE coefficients are normalized to the range of (0,1) where 1 is the strongest. As indicated in the table, all the predictor attributes are ranked according to the RFE coefficients. The ranking shows *Length of Stay of mothers at the hospital*, the *Number of Visits*, and the *Number of Procedures* they have undergone through as the three most important feature attributes. These three best feature attributes are followed by the *mother's weight, age,* and *number of diagnoses*. The least important feature attributes for predicting the mother's mode of delivery are mother's *Parity, Educational level, and Location (residence)*. Figure 17.3 shows the visualization output of the order of importance according to the RFE coefficients.

Table 17.6 Order of Importance of the Feature Attributes

Rank	Attributes	Abbreviation	Rfe Coefficient
1	**Length of stay**	**LoS**	**0.68270224**
2	**Number of visits**	**NoV**	**0.06460375**
3	**Number of procedure**	**NoP**	**0.04979128**
4	Mother's weight	MoW	0.04843938
5	Mother's age	Age	0.04448104
6	Number of diagnoses	NoD	0.03856442
7	Parity	Parity	0.03301875
8	Educational level	EoQ	0.03099210
9	Location (resident)	LoC	0.00740703

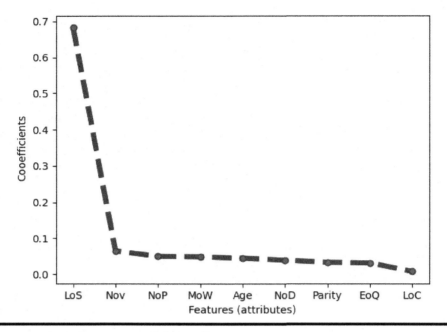

Figure 17.3 Feature importance of the attributes.

Discussions and Implications

Discussion

At childbirth, a decision needs to be taken regarding the most suitable mode of delivery for mothers. Often, certain historical factors account for this decision, some of which are based on individuals' personal choice. Early detection, based on historical data, regarding mother's mode of delivery can help avert possible complications. Early prediction of the right mode of delivery prevents/reduces mortality rate. In this study, secondary data containing attributes and the mode of child delivery was analyzed to predict mother's mode of delivery using a machine learning technique namely, classification. Classification algorithms have been categorized as linear methods, nonlinear methods, rules and trees, or ensembles of trees (Brownlee, 2016). A classification algorithm should not be applied to a problem domain without first spot-checking to evaluate its appropriateness for the task. The four classifiers selected for the experiments in this study fall within the nonlinear methods and ensembles of trees. The predictive accuracy evaluation shows that the nonlinear methods are more appropriate for the task of predicting delivery mode in pregnant women.

As noted in Table 17.5, the SVM and NB, which are nonlinear methods, exhibited the highest predictive accuracy of 97% each. These were closely followed by another nonlinear method, the KNN, with predictive accuracy, 96%. The ensemble of tree method, namely, the RF, exhibited the least predictive accuracy of 95% among the tested classifiers. Though the linear methods were not deployed for experiment in the present study, a previous study deployed logistic regression which is a linear method for a similar investigation. Alavifard et al. (2019) used logistic regression to develop a model for predicting the likelihood of vaginal birth following labor induction among women. The model yielded a predictive accuracy of 81%. Putting this study side by side with our study, it is instructive to note that classifiers within the nonlinear methods are the most appropriate to deploy for tasks of this nature.

Feature selection is the process of ranking predictor variables using numeric values to indicate the importance of each attribute in predicting the outcome variable (Bodur & Atsa'am, 2019). Dataset variables that rank low should be eliminated before model construction to improve on model performance. Basically, feature ranking algorithms utilize any of these three statistical measures to compute the importance of a feature namely, correlation, information gain, and probability distribution (Atsa'am, 2020; Javed et al., 2014). In the correlation-based approach, the linear relationship between an independent variable and the outcome variable is evaluated. An independent variable that exhibits a stronger correlation with the outcome variable is selected as an important feature. In the information-theoretic approach, the mutual information contained in two different attributes is measured, and the attribute with the highest information gain is selected as the most important feature. The probabilistic approach evaluates the dependence between the outcome variable and a predictor variable using probability distribution, and a feature that yields a higher probability value is considered as being important. Several past studies have separately established that relationships exist between length of stay and mode of delivery, number of hospital visits and mode of delivery, and number of procedures and mode of delivery (Campbell et al., 2016; Edozien et al., 2014). These studies confirm the result of the present research where LoS, NoV, and NoP have been selected as the most important attributes in mode of delivery prediction as could be seen in Table 17.6.

Campbell et al. (2016) examined the factors associated with length of stay in the hospital after childbirth among women using maternity data from 92 countries. The study, which deployed the multivariate logistic regression for analysis, discovered that cesarean-section delivery is an important factor associated with LoS. The association between LoS and cesarean section, which is one of the modes of delivery, established by Campbell et al. (2016) corroborates the findings of our study which ranked LoS as one of the important variables in predicting delivery mode in women. In another study, Onwuhafua et al. (2016) investigated the effect of the number of antenatal visits on pregnancy outcomes among a group of 228 pregnant women in Northern Nigeria. The study established various levels of association between LoS and some pregnancy outcomes such as mode of delivery and gestational age at delivery. The association between NoV and mode of delivery established in the study by Onwuhafua et al. (2016) corroborates the results of our study in which NoV has been ranked as one of the important attributes in determining mode of delivery. A study by Edozien et al. (2014) investigated the effect of perineal tear on delivery mode in subsequent pregnancies among women who experienced a third- or fourth-degree perineal tear during previous pregnancies. The study showed that women who experienced a third- or fourth-degree perineal tear during their first birth are more likely to go for elective caesarean section during their second birth compared to women who did not experience this. The findings by Edozien et al. (2014) where perineal tear has been associated with mode of delivery agrees with our study which ranks NoP as one of the important attributes for determining mode of delivery.

Our study has established that parity, educational level of the pregnant woman (EoQ), and location of residence of the pregnant woman (Loc) are not important features in predicting mode of delivery—see Table 17.6. It is instructive to note from Table 17.4 that parity exhibits a negative correlation with LoS, NoV, and NoP. Since LoS, NoV, and NoP have been established to be important attributes in determining mode of delivery, it is logical to conclude that parity is not an important feature going by the negative correlation with the three attributes. A mother's educational level has been established to be associated with some pregnancy outcomes such as the birth weight of a newborn (Mahumud et al., 2017). However, there is no literature evidence to show that this attribute (mother's education) has a particular role to play in predicting mode of delivery. This agrees with the results of our study which ranks EoQ as an unimportant attribute in predicting mode of delivery. Relatedly, the authors have not encountered literature evidence that established an association between location of the residence of a pregnant woman and her likely mode of delivery. This gives credence to our research results in Table 17.6 where Loc is ranked unimportant in predicting mode of delivery.

Implications to Practice

The current study presents interesting implications to practitioners in the medical fraternity, especially in the aspect of childbirth. Early detection, based on historical data, regarding a mother's mode of delivery can help avert possible complications during childbirth. Therefore, the early prediction of the mode of delivery prevents/reduces mortality rate.

In making a choice for the mode of delivery, based on this current study, we recommend to medical practitioners to first consider the history of the mother's length of stay at a health facility, the number of visits to the hospital, and the number of previous cesarean procedures. These were the most critical determinants found toward making decision for mother's mode of delivery. The other important determinants to consider are the mother's weight, mother's age, and the number of diagnoses. However, determinants such as mother's parity, educational level, and location (residence) were less critical in determining the mode of delivery.

The application of this predictive model with such a high degree of accuracy can help physicians and pregnant women to make informed decisions, thereby reducing the risks of complications, morbidity, and mortality rate that could result especially through the misuse of cesarean delivery. Furthermore, the outcome of this study will guide the choice of delivery mode for expectant mothers, thereby reducing the rate of morbidity and mortality associated with childbirth. In effect, the rate of cesarean sections will be reduced, and pregnant women are better prepared mentally, emotionally, and financially for delivery.

Conclusion

This chapter targets medical and healthcare professionals and practitioners, especially those associated with maternal and newborn health and pregnant women. It seeks to guide the choice of delivery mode for expectant mothers to help reduce the rate of morbidity and mortality associated with childbirth. In making a choice for the mode of delivery, length of stay, number of visits to the hospital, and the number of previous cesarean procedures on the expectant mother were found to be critical determinants. We envision that practitioners should consider the most important features found in this study while making decisions on the mode of delivery of pregnant women.

The study proposed a machine-learning technique for predicting the delivery mode of pregnant women. The essence is to reduce the rate of morbidity and mortality associated with childbirth, especially when the delivery mode is cesarean. In a bid to determine an optimal classification algorithm, four models were developed based on SVM, NB, RF, and KNN learning algorithms. We have proposed a feature selection technique that considers the expert knowledge of medical professionals. The most important feature attributes were selected; the models were trained and tested; and their performances were evaluated. The result shows that the most important attributes for predicting a pregnant woman's mode of delivery are the length of stay, number of visits, and number of procedures. The result also shows that SVM and NB performed better than RF and KNN with an accuracy of 97%, 97%, 95%, and 96%, respectively.

Conflict of interest

We declare no conflict of interest.

References

Abbas, S. A., Riaz, R., Kazmi, S. Z., Rizvi, S. S., & Kwon, S. (2018). Cause Analysis of Caesarian Sections and Application of Machine Learning Methods for Classification of Birth Data. *IEEE Access*, *6*(1), 67555–67563. https://doi.org/10.1109/ACCESS.20118.2879115

Alavifard, S., Meier, K., Shulman, Y., Tomlinson, G., & D'Souza, R. (2019). Derivation and Validation of a Model Predicting the Likelihood of Vaginal Birth Following Labour Induction. *BMC Pregnancy Childbirth*, *19*, 130. https://doi.org/10.1186/s12884-019-2232-8

Alkema, L., Chou, D., Hogan, D., Zhang, S., Moller, A. B., Gemmill, A., Fat, D. M., Boerma, T., Temmerman, M., Mathers, C., & Say, L. (2016). Global, Regional, and National Levels and Trends in Maternal Mortality between 1990 and 2015, with Scenario-based Projections to 2030: A Systematic Analysis by the UN Maternal Mortality Estimation Inter-Agency Group. *The Lancet*. *387*(10017), 462–474. https://doi.org/10.1016/s0140-6736(15)00838-7

Atsa'am, D. D. (2020). Feature Selection Algorithm using Relative Odds for Data Mining Classification. In A. Haldorai, & A. Ramu (Eds.), *Big Data Analytics for Sustainable Computing* (pp. 81–106). Hersey, PA: IGI Global. https://doi.org/10.4018/978-1-5225-9750-6.ch005

Badaoui, A., Kassm, S. A., & Naja, W. (2019). Fear and Anxiety Disorders Related to Childbirth: Epidemiological and Therapeutic Issues. *Current Psychiatry Reports*, *21*(4), 27. https://doi.org/10.1007/s11920-019-1010-7

Bawa, S. B., Umar, U. S., & Onadeko, M. (2004). Utilization of Obstetric Care Services in a Rural Community in Southwestern Nigeria. *African Journal of Medicine and Medical Sciences*, *33*(3), 239–244.

Bergström, M., Kieler, H., & Waldenström, U. (2010). Psychoprophylaxis during Labor: Associations with Labor-related Outcomes and Experience of Childbirth. *Acta Obstetricia Gynecologica Scandinavia*, *89*(6), 794–800. https://doi.org/10.3109/00016341003694978

Bodur, E. K., & Atsa'am, D. D. (2019). Filter Variable Selection Algorithm Using Risk Ratios for Dimensionality Reduction of Healthcare Data for Classification. *Processes*, *7*(4), 222. https://doi.org/10.3390/pr7040222

Breiman, L. (2001). Random Forests. *Machine Learning*, *45*(1), 5–32. https://doi.org/10.1023/A:1010933404324

Brownlee, J. (2016). *Supervised and Unsupervised Machine Learning Algorithms*. Machine Learning Mastery, 16(03). San Juan, PR: Machine Learning Mastery. https://machinelearningmastery.com/supervised-and-unsupervised-machine-learning-algorithms/

Brownlee, J. (2019, December 13). *How to Evaluate Machine Learning Algorithms with R*. https://machinelearningmastery.com/evaluate-machine-learning-algorithms-with-r/

Campbell, O. M. R., Cegolon, L., Macleod, D., & Benova, L. (2016). Length of Stay after Childbirth in 92 Countries and Associated Factors in 30 Low-and Middle-income Countries: Compilation of Reported Data and a Cross-sectional Analysis from Nationally Representative Surveys. *PLoS Medicine*, *13*(3), e1001972. https://doi.org/10.1371/journal.pmed.1001972

Chen, S. (2018). K-nearest Neighbor Algorithm Optimization in Text Categorization. *In IOP Conference Series: Earth and Environmental Science*, *108*, 1–5. https://doi.org/10.1088/1755-1315/108/5/052074

Cortes, C., & Vapnik, V. (1995). Support-Vector Networks. *Machine Learning*, *20*, 273–297. https://doi.org/10.1023/A:1022627411411

Dempster, A. P., Laird, N. M., & Rubin, D. B. (1977). Maximum Likelihood from Incomplete Data via the EM Algorithm. *Journal of the Royal Statistical Society: Series B (Methodological)*, *39*(1), 1–38. https://doi.org/10.1111/j.2517-6161.1977.tb01600.x

Edozien, L. C., Gurol-Urganci, I., Cromwell, D. A., Adams, E. J., Richmond, D. H., Mahmood, T. A., & van der Meulen, J. H. (2014). Impact of Third- and Fourth-degree Perineal Tears at First Birth on Subsequent Pregnancy Outcomes: A Cohort Study. *BJOG: An International Journal of Obstetrics & Gynaecology*, *121*(13), 1695–1703. https://doi.org/10.1111/1471-0528.12886

Esimai, O., Ojo, O., & Fasubaa, O. (2002). Utilization of Approved Health Facilities for Delivery in Ile-Ife, Osun State, Nigeria. *Nigerian Journal of Medicine*, *11*(4), 177–179.

Fitzpatrick, K. E., Kurinczuk, J. J., Bhattacharya, S., & Quigley, M. A. (2019). Planned Mode of Delivery after Previous Cesarean Section and Short-term Maternal and Perinatal Outcomes: A Population-based Record Linkage Cohort Study in Scotland. *PLoS Medicine*, *16*(9), 1–26. https://doi.org/10.1371/journal.pmed.1002913

Gagnon, A. J., & Sandall, J. (2007). Individual or Group Antenatal Education for Childbirth or Parenthood, or Both. *Cochrane Database of Systematic Reviews*, *4*(3), 1–52. https://doi.org/10.1002/14651858.CD002869.pub2

Garshasbi, A., & Zadeh, S. F. (2005). The Effect of Exercise on the Intensity of Low Back Pain in Pregnant Women. *International Journal of Gynaecology and Obstetrics*, *88*(3), 271–275. https://doi.org/10.1016/j.ijgo.2004.12.001

Giri, A., Bhagavath, M. V. V., Pruthvi, B., & Dubey, N. (2016). A Placement Prediction System Using k-nearest Neighbor's Classifier. In *2016 Second International Conference on Cognitive Computing and Information Processing (CCIP)* (pp. 1–4). Mysore: IEEE. https://doi.org/10.1109/CCIP.2016.7802883

Gökçe isbir, G., İnci, F., Önal, H., & Yıldız, P. D. (2016). The Effects of Antenatal Education on Fear of Childbirth, Maternal Self-efficacy, and Post-traumatic Stress Disorder (PTSD) Symptoms Following Childbirth: An Experimental Study. *Applied Nursing Research: ANR*, *32*, 227–232. https://doi.org/10.1186/s12887-018-1324-3 10.1016/j.apnr.2016.07.013

Gondwe, T., Betha, K., Kusneniwar, G. N., Bunker, C. H., Tang, G., Simhan, H., Reddy, P. S., & Haggerty, C. L. (2018). Mode of Delivery and Short-term Infant Health Outcomes: A Prospective Cohort Study in a Peri-urban Indian Population. *BMC Pediatrics*, *18*(1), 1–6. https://doi.org/10.1186/s12887-018-1324-3

Hay-Smith, J., Mørkved, S., Fairbrother, K. A., & Herbison, G. P. (2008). Pelvic Floor Muscle Training for Prevention and Treatment of Urinary and Faecal Incontinence in Antenatal and Postnatal Women. *Cochrane Database of Systematic Reviews*, *8*(4). https://doi.org/10.1002/14651858.CD007471

Hrycyk, J., Kaemmerer, H., Nagdyman, N., Hamann, M., Schneider, K., & Kuschel, B. (2016). Mode of Delivery and Pregnancy Outcome in Women with Congenital Heart Disease. *PLoS ONE*, *11*(12), 1–12. https://doi.org/10.1371/journal.pone.0167820

Idris, S., Sambo, M., & Ibrahim, M. (2013). Barriers to Utilisation of Maternal Health Services in a Semi-urban Community in Northern Nigeria: The Clients' Perspective. *Nigeria Medical Journal*, *54*(1), 27–32. https://doi.org/10.4103/0300-1652.108890

Javed, K., Babri, H. A., & Saeed, M. (2014). Impact of a Metric of Association between Two Variables on Performance of Filters for Binary Data. *Neurocomputing*, *143*, 248–260. https://doi.org/10.1016/j.neucom.2014.05.066

Kamat, A., Oswal, V., & Datar, M. (2015). Implementation of Classification Algorithms to Predict Mode of Delivery. *International Journal of Computer Science and Information Technologies*, *6*(5), 4531–4534.

Karabulut, Ö., Coşkuner, P. D., Dogan, M. Y., Cebeci, M. S., & Demirci, N. (2016). Does Antenatal Education Reduce Fear of Childbirth? *International Nursing Review*, *63*(1), 60–67. https://doi.org/10.1111/inr.12223

Kashanian, M., Akbari, Z., & Alizadeh, M. H. (2009). The Effect of Exercise on Back Pain and Lordosis in Pregnant Women. *International Journal of Gynaecology and Obstetrics*, *107*(2), 160–161. https://doi.org/10.1016/j.ijgo.2009.06.018

Kavitha, D., & Balasubramanian, T. (2018). Predicting the Mode of Delivery and the Risk Factors Associated with Cesarean Delivery Using Decision Tree Model. *International of Engineering Sciences and Research Technology*, *7*(8), 116–124.

Keag, O. E., Norman, J. E., & Stock, S. J. (2018). Long-term Risks and Benefits Associated with Cesarean Delivery for Mother, Baby, and Subsequent Pregnancies: Systematic Review and Meta-Analysis. *PLoS Medicine, 15*(1), 1–22. e1002494. https://doi.org/10.1371/journal.pmed.1002494

Kimber, L., McNabb, M., McCourt, C., Haines, A., & Brocklehurst, P. (2008). Massage or Music for Pain Relief in Labour: A Pilot Randomised Placebo-controlled Trial. *European Journal of Pain, 12*(8), 961–969. https://doi.org/10.1016/j.ejpain.2008.01.004

Kleinbaum, D. G., & Klein, M. (2010). Maximum Likelihood Techniques: An Overview. In *Logistic Regression. Statistics for Biology and Health.* New York: Springer.

Kluge, J., Hall, D., Louw, Q., Theron, G., & Grové, D. (2011). Specific Exercises to Treat Pregnancy-related Low Back Pain in a South African Population. *International Journal of Gynaecology and Obstetrics, 113*(3), 187–191. https://doi.org/10.1016/j.ijgo.2010.10.030

Kolog, E. A., Montero, C. S., & Toivonen, T. (2018). Using Machine Learning for Sentiment and Social Influence Analysis in Text. In Á. Rocha, & T. Guarda (Eds.), *Proceedings of the International Conference on Information Technology & Systems (ICITS 2018). ICITS 2018. Advances in Intelligent Systems and Computing. 721* (pp. 453–463). Libertad: Springer.

Landis, J. R., & Koch, G. G. (1977). The Measurement of Observer Agreement for Categorical Data. *Biometrics, 33*(1), 159–174.

Lavender, T., Hofmeyr, G. J., Neilson, J. P., Kingdon, C., & Gyte, G. M. (2012). Caesarean Section for Non-medical Reasons at Term. *Cochrane Database of Systematic Reviews 3*(3), CD004660. https://doi.org/10.1002/14651858.CD004660.pub3

Li, Q. N., & Li, T. H. (2020). Research on the Application of Naive Bayes and Support Vector Machine Algorithm on Exercises Classification. *Journal of Physics: Conference Series, 1437*(1), 1–6. https://doi.org/10.1088/1742-6596/1437/1/012071

Liaw, A., & Wiener, M. (2002). Classification and Regression by Random Forest. *R News, 2*(3), 18–22.

Lipschuetz, M. R., Guedalia, J., Rottenstreich, A., Persky, M. N., Cohen, S. M., Kabiri, D., Levin, G., Yagel, S., Unger, R., & Sompolinsky, Y. (2020). Prediction of Vaginal Birth after Cesarean Deliveries Using Machine Learning. *American Journal of Obstetrics and Gynecology, 222*(6), 613.e1–613.e12. https://doi.org/10.1016/j.ajog.2019.12.267

Loke, A. Y., Davies, L., & Li, S. F. (2015). Factors Influencing the Decision that Women Make on their Mode of Delivery: The Health Belief Model. *BMC Health Services Research, 15*(1), 1–12. https://doi.org/10.1186/s12913-015-0931-z

Loke, A. Y., Davies, L., & Mak, Y. W. (2019). Is it the Decision of Women to Choose a Cesarean Section as the Mode of Birth? A Review of Literature on the Views of Stakeholders. *BMC Pregnancy and Childbirth, 19*(1), 286. https://doi.org/10.1186/s12884-019-2440-2

Ludwig, A., Miani, C., Breckenkamp, J., Sauzet, O., Borde, T., Doyle, I-M., Brenne, S., Höller-Holtrichter, C., David, M., Spallek, J., & Razum, O. (2020). Are Social Status and Migration Background Associated with Utilization of Non-Medical Antenatal Care? Analyses from Two German Studies. *Maternal and Child Health Journal, 24*(7), 943–952. https://doi.org/10.1007/s10995-020-02937-z

Mahumud, R. A., Sultana, M., & Sarker, A. R. (2017). Distribution and Determinants of Low Birth Weight in Developing Countries. *Journal of Preventive Medicine and Public Health, 50*(1), 18.

Mazzoni, A., Althabe, F., Gutierrez, L., Gibbons, L., Liu, N. H., Bonotti, A. M., Izbizky, G. H., Ferray, M., Viergue, N., Vigil, S. I., Denett, G. Z., & Belizan, J. M. (2016). Women's Preferences and Mode of Delivery in Public and Private Hospitals: A Prospective Cohort Study. *BMC Pregnancy and Childbirth, 16*(1), 1–8. https://doi.org/10.1186/s12884-016-0824-0

Moffat, M. A., Bell, J. S., Porter, M. A., Lawton, S., Hundley, V., Danielian, P., & Bhattacharya, S. (2007). Decision Making about Mode of Delivery among Pregnant Women Who Have Previously Had a Caesarean Section: A Qualitative Study. *BJOG: An International Journal of Obstetrics & Gynaecology, 114*(1), 86–93. https://doi.org/10.1111/j.1471-0528.2006.01154.x

Namujju, J., Muhindo, R., Mselle, L. T., Waiswa, P., Nankumbi, J., & Muwanguzi, P. (2018). Childbirth Experiences and their Derived Meaning: A Qualitative Study among Postnatal Mothers in Mbale Regional Referral Hospital, Uganda. *Reproductive Health, 15*(1), 183. https://doi.org/10.1186/s12978-018-0628-y

National Population Commission (NPC) [Nigeria] and ICF International. (2014). *Nigeria Demographic and Health Survey 2013.* https://tinyurl.com/y39a73e2

Onwuhafua, P. I., Ozed-Williams, I. C., Kolawole, A. O., & Adze, J. A. (2016). The Effect of Frequency of Antenatal Visits on Pregnancy Outcome in Kaduna, Northern Nigeria. *Tropical Journal of Obstetrics and Gynaecology*, *33*(3), 317–321. https://doi.org/10.4103/0189-5117.199813

Osubor, K., Fatusi, A., & Chiwuzie, K. (2006). Maternal Health-seeking Behavior and Associated Factors in a Rural Nigerian Community. *Matern Child Health Journal*, *10*(2), 159–169. https://doi.org/10.1007/s10995-005-0037-z

Polidano, C., Zhu, A., & Bornstein, J. C. (2017). The Relation between Cesarean Birth and Child Cognitive Development. *Scientific Reports*, *7*(1), 1–10.

Renfrew, M. J., McFadden, A., Bastos, M. H., Campbell, J., Channon, A. A., Cheung, N. F., Silva, D. R. A. D., Downe, S., Kennedy, H. P., Malata, A., McCormick, F., Wick, L., & Declercq, E. (2014). Midwifery and Quality Care: Findings from a New Evidence-informed Framework for Maternal and Newborn Care. *The Lancet*, *384*(9948), 1129–1145. https://doi.org/10.1016/S0140-6736(14)60789-3

Ricordeau, J., & Lacaille, J. (2010). Application of Random Forests to Engine Health Monitoring. In I. Grant (Ed.), *Proceeding of the 27th Congress of International Council of the Aeronautical Sciences (ICAS)* (pp. 1–10). Nice: ICAS.

Rydahl, E., Declercq, E., Juhl, M., & Maimburg, R. (2019). Cesarean Section on a Rise—Does Advanced Maternal Age Explain the Increase? A Population Register-based Study. *PLOS ONE*, *14*(1), 1–16. https://doi.org/10.1371/journal.pone.0210655

Serçekuş, P., & Başkale, H. (2016). Effects of Antenatal Education on Fear of Childbirth, Maternal Self-efficacy, and Parental Attachment. *Midwifery*, *34*, 166–172. https://doi.org/10.1016/j.midw.2015.11.016

Shah, A., Fawole, B., M'Imunya, J. M., Amokrane, F., Nafiou, I., Wolomby, J. J., Mugerwa, K., Neves, I., Nguti, R., Kublickas, M., & Mathai, M. (2009). Cesarean Delivery Outcomes from the WHO Global Survey on Maternal and Perinatal Health in Africa. *International Journal of Gynecology & Obstetrics*, *107*(3), 191–197. https://doi.org/10.1016/j.ijgo.2009.08.013

Shi, Y., Jiang, Y., Zeng, Q., Yuan, Y., Yin, H., Chang, C., & Pang, R. (2016). Influencing Factors Associated with the Mode of Birth among Childbearing Women in Hunan Province: A Cross-Sectional Study in China. *BMC Pregnancy and Childbirth*, *16*(1), 1–9.

Simkin, P. (2000). The Meaning of Labor Pain. *Birth (Berkeley, Calif.)*, *27*(4), 254–255. https://doi.org/10.1046/j.1523-536x.2000.00254.x

Song, Y., Liang, J., Lu, J., & Zhao, X. (2017). An Efficient Instance Selection Algorithm for k Nearest Neighbor Regression. *Neurocomputing*, *251*, 26–34. https://doi.org/10.1016/j.neucom.2017.04.018

Tikmani, S. S., Ali, S. A., Saleem, S., Bann, C. M., Mwenechanya, M., Carlo, W. A., Figueroa, L., Garces, A. L., Krebs, N. F., Patel, A., Hibberd, P. L., Goudar, S. S., Derman, R. J., Aziz, A., Marete, I., Tenge, C., Esamai, F., Liechty, E., Bucher, S., . . . Goldenberg, R. L. (2019). Trends of Antenatal Care during Pregnancy in Low- and Middle-income Countries: Findings from the Global Network Maternal and Newborn Health Registry. *Seminars in Perinatology*, *43*(5), 297–307. https://doi.org/10.1053/j.semperi.2019.03.020

Tunçalp, Ö., Were, W. M., MacLennan, C., Oladapo, O. T., Gülmezoglu, A. M., Bahl, R., Daelmans, B., Mathai, M., Say, L., Kristensen, F., Temmerman, M., & Bustreo, F. (2015). Quality of Care for Pregnant Women and Newborns-the WHO Vision. *BJOG*, *122*(8), 1045–1049. https://doi.org/10.1111/1471-0528.13451

United Nations. (2015). *UN General Assembly, Transforming our World: The 2030 Agenda for Sustainable Development*. www.unfpa.org/resources/transforming-our-world-2030-agenda-sustainable-development

Uzochukwu, B. S., Onwujekwe, O. E., & Akpala, C. O. (2004). Community Satisfaction with the Quality of Maternal and Child Health Services in Southeast Nigeria. *East African Medical Journal*, *81*(6), 293–299. https://doi.org/10.4314/eamj.v81i6.9178

World Health Organization. (2010). *Maternal, Newborn, Child, and Adolescent Health: Newborn Care at Birth*. www.who.int/maternal_child_adolescent/topics/newborn/care_at_birth/en/

World Health Organisation. (2015). *Trends in Maternal Mortality: 1990 to 2015—Estimates by WHO, UNICEF, UNFPA, the World Bank Group, and the United Nations Population Division*. Geneva: World Health Organization. https://tinyurl.com/y5o7fqr8

World Health Organization. (2016). *WHO Recommendations on Antenatal Care for a Positive Pregnancy Experience*. www.who.int/publications/i/item/9789241549912

World Health Organization. (2019). *Maternal Mortality*. www.who.int/news-room/fact-sheets/detail/maternal-mortality

Zamani-Alavijeh, F., Shahry, P., Kalhori, M., & Araban, M. (2017). Pregnant Women's Preferences for Mode of Delivery Questionnaire: Psychometric Properties. *Journal of Education and Health Promotion*, *6*(1), 1–7. https://doi.org/10.4103/2277-9531.204738

Zandvakili, F., Rezaie, M., Shahoei, R., & Roshani, D. (2017). Maternal Outcomes Associated with Caesarean versus Vaginal Delivery. *Journal of Clinical and Diagnostic Research: JCDR*, *11*(7), QC01–QC04. https://doi.org/10.7860/JCDR/2017/24891.10239

Authors' Profile

Emmanuel Awuni Kolog holds a PhD in computer science with the orientation in human language technologies and MSc in software engineering from the University of Eastern Finland. He is currently a senior lecturer at the University of Ghana. Emmanuel's research interest is multidisciplinary which spans the fields of Text Mining, Affect Detection, Learning Analytics, Machine Learning Applications, and Digital Platforms. He is the recipient of Queen Elizabeth II scholarship to McGill University in Canada. Emmanuel is also an adjunct fellow to the University of Turku plugin campus in the University of Namibia.

Oluwafemi Samson Balogun is a lecturer at the Department of Statistics and Operations Research, Modibbo Adama University of Technology, Yola, Adamawa State, Nigeria, and he is currently a post-doctoral researcher at the School of Computing, University of Eastern Finland. He holds a PhD in Statistics from the Department of Statistics, University of Ilorin, Kwara State, Nigeria. He is a senior research fellow at Centre for Multidisciplinary Research and Innovation (CEMRI), and he is a member of International Biometric Society (IBS), International Statistical Institute (ISI), Nigerian Statistical Association (NSA), and Nigerian Mathematical Society (NMS). He has several conference and journal papers in reputable international bodies, and he is also served as guest reviewers for several journals. His research interest is data science, machine learning, data mining, biostatistics, categorical data analysis, modeling, and probability distribution models.

Richard Osei Adjei is a current student at the Department of Medicine, School of Public Health of Imperial College London. He holds a PhD in Public Health and MSc in Research Chemist from the University of Eastern Finland. He additionally holds PGCE from the Haaga-Helia University of Applied Sciences in Finland. His research interest is multidisciplinary which spans the fields of Exposure Assessment, Affect Detection, Suicidal Behaviors, Health Policy and Analysis, Machine Learning, and Data Science Applications in Public Health. He is a reviewer in Cogent Medicine and has published several articles in scientific journals.

Samuel Nii Odoi Devine is a PhD Candidate at the University of Johannesburg and member of faculty at the Information and Communication Technology of the Presbyterian University College, Ghana. He holds an MSc in Information Technology and BSc in Information and Communication Technology, both with honors. Devine has published articles in reputable journals and presented at conferences. In the year 2019, his paper was nominated with two others for the best paper award at the knowledge management and information systems conference held in Vienna, Austria. He has several years of teaching experience and has been involved in a number of IS projects. His research interest is multidisciplinary, spanning the areas of machine learning applications, NLP, knowledge management, big data, and information security awareness.

Donald Atsa'am is currently a postdoctoral research fellow at the Department of Computer Science and Informatics, University of the Free State, South Africa. He has been a lecturer of Computer Science with the University of Agriculture, Makurdi, Nigeria, since 2012. He holds a PhD in applied mathematics and computer science from the Eastern Mediterranean University, North Cyprus. Donald's research interests are in Data Maning, Machine Learning, and Knowledge Discovery. He has published over 20 articles and book chapters within these areas.

Oluwaseun Alexander Dada is an Information Systems Specialist (Cloud computing) at the Finland Institute for Molecular Medicine (FIMM) in the University of Helsinki. His academic background and work experience span the fields of computer science, educational technology, and business strategy. He is most interested in research related to education, educational technology, data science, business strategy, blockchain, and any aspect of computing (software dev, architecture, cloud).

Temidayo Oluwatosin Omotehinwa is a senior lecturer in the Department of Mathematical Sciences, College of Natural and Applied Sciences, Achievers University, Owo, Nigeria. He holds a PhD in computer science from the University of Ilorin, Ilorin, Nigeria. His research interest includes Machine Learning, Natural Language Processing, Web Programming, Embedded Systems, Internet of Things, Algorithm Design and Cloud Computing. He is a Rank Sheet Certified Programmer. He has authored and/or coauthored articles in refereed journals and conferences. Dr. Omotehinwa is a member of Nigeria Computer Society (NCS) and an associate member of the Institute of Strategic Management (ISMN).

Chapter 18

Decomposing Performance Assessment of Health Systems toward Greater Resilience and Sustainability in Africa

Divine Quase Agozie

Contents

Introduction

Performance assessment of large and complex systems has largely posed challenges to practitioners and researchers (Ungar, 2015; Hosseini et al., 2016). This is observed in the multiplicity of

DOI: 10.4324/9781003152217-23

techniques and frameworks of performance assessment (Thomas et al., 2013). Beyond performance evaluations, current events have also ignited the need to coexamine performance dimensions to meet global and local objectives (Sarre et al., 2014). For example, performance indicators such as system resilience and sustainability have emerged as sensitive global and local goals for all and sundry (Turenne et al., 2019). Particularly in the public health domain, the need for the health system's resilience and sustainability for future generations is an overarching issue across borders. This requires a revised perspective into understanding and assessing resilience and sustainability of systems (WHO, 2020; Olu, 2017).

Early investigations of system resilience from the ecological system's view perceive it to be the measure of disruption absorbed effectively by the system (Holling, 1973). This is because ecological systems face an ever-changing environment, and their ability to survive amidst the disturbances and disruptive pressures establishes their ability to exist for the long term. However, before a system possesses the ability to withstand disruptive pressures, it requires the basis for sustainable existence. Thus, the need for a system to manage and use scarce resources amidst the disturbances to remain viable. These concepts have grown and gained relevance across fields including politics, education, economics, and health (Alblas & Jayaram, 2014). In the global health systems domain, for instance, resilience and sustainability are integrated into the performance requirement measures known as the Sustainable Development Goals (WHO, 2016). Similarly, the global symposium on health systems research and the WHO jointly institutionalized the reporting indicators of resilience and sustainability metrics as areas of competence for health and other related systems (see *Resilient and Responsive Health System for a Changing World*. Vol. 32, Issue suppl_3).

Beyond these, other global institutions like the UN, World bank, the African Development Bank, and some non-governmental stakeholders have jointly impressed the need to increase the resilience and sustainability of productive systems (Turenne et al., 2019; Koffi et al., 2018; UN, 2016). Thus, calls to sustain and build resilient systems have only grown in persistence.

Kieny et al. (2014) observe that continuous improvements begin with understanding system assessment. Thus the understanding of productive system's assessment cannot be underrated. Subsequently, systems improvement requires objective assessment procedure (Afful-Dadzie et al., 2016). Largely, many resilience-related attempt have largely employed unit level indicators (Kruk et al., 2017; Béné et al., 2013). OECD (2017) notes that about two-thirds of performance assessment studies of member states in the EU have been conducted at the hospital level, similar patterns are observed in other non-EU state assessments (Ahluwalia et al., 2017). This beckons the need to contribute to build the capacity of decision-makers to understand and objectively assess key indicators of sustainable and resilient systems (Alameddine et al., 2019; Biddle et al., 2020).

To this end, it is as if examinations that have assessed the performance of health systems, have paid little attention to establishing an objective assessment procedure like determining an acceptable threshold against which actual performance must be compared (Afful-Dadzie et al., 2016) as a start off point. To effectively assess performance, it is imperative to determine whether the systems meet an acceptable performance level to be considered high-performing system. This chapter employs an extension of the Technique for Order Preference by Similarity to Ideal Solution (TOPSIS) framework that allows for the establishment of a local performance level for health systems' resilience and sustainability assessment. It considers resilience and sustainability performance data of African health systems at the macro/political level to uncover the performance of these systems based on a local threshold that will contribute to the continuous evaluation of resilience and sustainability objective.

Background

Determinants of Resilience and Sustainable Health Systems

Resilient systems possess the capacity to maintain core operations and effectively respond to disruptive pressures (Carinci et al., 2015). In essence, health systems show resilience if they are capable of producing positive health outcomes for all actors during and after disturbing events as crises (Braithwaite et al., 2017; Turenne et al., 2019). Resilience amid crisis to sustain positive health outcomes during any kind of disruption be it a breakout, lack of resources, increased demand, or mass casualty occurrences requires proactivity and strategy to for a system to function. Kruk et al. (2015) assert that for the sake of effectiveness, resilience and sustainability objectives must be pursued parallel to each other even before the occurrence of a disruption. For instance, the recent COVID-19 global pandemic clearly exposes why these two objectives ought to be copursued. In that, a common phenomenon to these systems was the fact that sustainable health systems lacked quick response (low resilience) and resilient systems faced acute resource inadequacy (low sustainability) (WHO, 2020). The widespread devastating effects and enormous resilience and sustainability deficit reveals by global health system suggest that resilience and sustainability objects still remain vastly unexplored by many states (WHO, 2020).

Biddle et al. (2020) observe two reasons why resilience and sustainability remain vastly inadequate. First, the recognition that crises demand clarity about actor roles and second, understanding the contributions of factors at different levels of a health system is lacking. For instance, although governments fundamentally support health systems, there is no urgent need to understand how their contributions toward these developments or improvements impact resilience and sustainability of the systems (Braithwaite et al., 2017). Therefore, there is the need for a strategic and network view of health system development efforts across states (Mills, 2017). This is because conditions such as epidemics may not remain bound to a specific location but can go beyond borders. Shocks to a health system in one country can reverberate to others, and the world at large. Therefore, sufficient funding like adequate capital expenditure allocation or acquisition of technology among others may increase health system readiness for service performance, increased efficiency, and productivity, yet is not a sure response to building adequate resilience and sustainability (Olu, 2017; Kruk et al., 2015), yet beyond its borders, it will be inadequate (WHO, 2017; Béné et al., 2013). However, a focused assessment of the additions and increments to the state of resilience and sustainability tells the system's state of readiness (European Commission, 2020).

Departing from the network view of tackling the challenge of attaining resilience and sustainability, Kruk et al. (2015) denotes the need for sufficiently trained workforce, characterized by an increased training and tuning of personnel committed to work in times of crisis. Thus, nations are required to expand public health capacities (like nursing and medical graduates) as an effective response to building resilience (Peters, 2018). The need for a growing and strong health workforce characterized by commitment to emergencies might be difficult and abstract (Cassier-Woidasky, 2013). This establishment begins with training and deployment of sufficient number of medical and clinical personnel to build significant social capital in health systems before a crisis period (Martineau et al., 2017). Moreover, legislation on public health spending and long-term expenditure on public health capabilities is required as these are means of collaborating efforts of public and private stakeholders to determine the roles and responsibilities of these actors toward emergencies (Peters, 2018). Legislation in this regard clarifies the authority of health systems based on the financial allocation determined by statutory specifications. The aforementioned interventions for building resilience and sustainable systems are summarized in Table 18.1.

Table 18.1 Breakdown of Indicator Dimensions

Dimension	Indicator	Sub-Indicators
Resilience (Kruk et al., 2015; Turenne et al., 2019; OECD, 2019)	eHealth Adoption Capital expenditure in the healthcare sector	1. Composite index of eHealth adoption among general practitioners 2. Composite index of eHealth adoption in hospitals 3. Gross fixed capital formation in the health sector as share of GDP
Sustainability (Kruk, 2015; Esty & Cort, 2017)	Medical and Nursing graduates Projection of public expenditure on long-term care	4. Medical graduates per 100,000 population 5. Nursing graduates per 100,000 population 6. Public spending on healthcare as a percentage of GDP 7. Public spending on long-term care as a percentage of GDP

Health Systems Assessment with TOPSIS

Performance assessment indices on the grounds of meaningfulness and objectivity show that many of examinations fail to satisfy fundamental scientific bases for their use in policy decisions (Afful-Dadzie et al., 2016; Singh et al., 2009; Böhringer & Jochem, 2007). For instance, overlooking key scientific processes as normalization, weighting, unit of measurement, and aggregation of indicators to determine composite indices on which performance decisions are made has largely been prevalent (Afful-Dadzie et al., 2016). In this regard, the TOPSIS emerges as an ideal approach for objectively evaluating alternatives with different criteria, while satisfying the scientific processes. For example, based on a benefit (more is preferred) and for a cost (less is better) criteria (Singh & Benyoucef, 2011). TOPSIS, as proposed by Hwang and Yoon (1981), synthesizes both the Multi Attribute Utility Theory (MAUT) and the Analytic Hierarchy Process (AHP) (Alecos & Dimitrios, 2010). Compared to other Multi-Criteria Decision-Making (MCDM) techniques, TOPSIS is one of the most widely used techniques (Dwivedi et al., 2018). It applies processes as normalization, weights to assess the relative closeness of an alternative to hypothetical ideal solutions (the positive ideal and the negative ideal solutions). Using TOPSIS, the best alternative has the longest distance from the negative ideal solution (NIS) and is also the shortest from the positive ideal solution (PIS) (Dwivedi et al., 2018). It is also found to have the least rank reversal among other MCDMs and particularly can accommodate interactions between multiple criteria as costs and benefits (Abirami & Askarunisa, 2017; Govindan et al., 2013). The PIS maximizes the benefit criteria and minimizes the cost criteria, while the NIS maximizes the cost criteria and minimizes the benefit criteria (Wang & Elhag, 2006).

Radenovic and Veselinović (2017) used an AHP-TOPSIS to evaluate the efficiency of health information systems for care services. Shafii et al. (2016) also used a blend of the Fuzzy-Analytic Hierarchy Process (F-AHP) and Fuzzy-TOPSIS to assess the performance of hospital managers on some dimensions of performance. Joumard and Gudmundsson (2010), Patil and Kant (2014), and Avazpour et al. (2013) have used Fuzzy-TOPSIS, AHP, and ANP-TOPSIS, respectively, to assess variants of performance of health systems. Similar TOPSIS applications are also found on sustainability performance assessments. For example, Kucukvar et al. (2014), Demirtas (2013), and Kannan et al. (2014) all used some variants of MCDMs including TOPSIS to assess best renewable energy technology for sustainable energy planning. Very few examinations share similarity with this current one in terms of the application of the TOPSIS extension. Few examinations have considered the determination of a threshold value for comparison. Thus, assessing the performance of health systems on resilience and sustainability practically solves the general problem of health system performance assessment as indicated by Arrow et al. (2012), by determining a minimum acceptable value against which their performance is determined. Further, the framework applied in this chapter allows for the decomposition of the health systems' closeness score to show the contribution of each priority goal determined by the OECD.

Method

The Empirical Model

The TOPSIS methodology developed by Hwang and Yoon (1981) is replicated in the following steps.

Step 1: Transformation of the criteria dimensions into a nondimensional criterion by generating a normalized decision matrix.

For a set $A = \{A^n \mid n = 1, 2, 3 \ldots, k\}$ of n alternatives, under a set $C = \{c_j \mid j = 1, 2, \ldots, m\}$ of m criteria with associated relative weights $W = \{w_j \mid j = 1, 2, 3 \ldots, m\}$. A decision matrix with element x_j^n for $n = 1, 2, 3 \ldots, k$ and $j = 1, 2, 3 \ldots, m$ is formed.

The matrix R of elements r_j^n is the rating for alternative n under criterion j, and w_j be the importance weight assigned to criterion j.

$$r_j^n = \frac{x_j^n}{\sqrt{\sum_{n=1}^{n}\left(x_j^n\right)^2}} \text{ for } n = 1, 2, 3 \ldots, k \text{ and } j = 1, 2, 3 \ldots, m \tag{1}$$

$$R = \begin{bmatrix} r_1^1 & r_2^1 & \cdots & r_m^1 \\ r_1^2 & r_2^2 & \cdots & r_m^2 \\ \vdots & \vdots & \ddots & \vdots \\ r_1^n & r_2^n & \cdots & r_m^n \end{bmatrix}$$

Step 2: This step accounts for the importance weights generated for each criterion in the decision matrix developed in equation (1). The weights w_j is multiplied with the normalized element r_j^n resulting in the weighted normalized matrix elements.

$$v_j^n = w_j * r_j^n, \text{ for } n = 1, 2, 3 \ldots, k \text{ and } j = 1, 2, \ldots, m \tag{2}$$

Step 3: After the weighted normalized elements, it computes the ideal positive A^+ and negative A^- solutions. These solutions serve as hypothetical solutions for comparison purposes. Let J^+ and J^- be a set of more is better and less is better criterion.

$$A^+ = \left\{v_1^+, \ldots, v_m^+\right\} \text{ where } v_j^+ = \left\{\left(max_n v_j^n \mid j \in J^+\right), \left(min_n v_j^n \mid j \in J^-\right)\right\} \tag{3}$$

$$A^- = \left\{ v_1^-, \ldots, v_m^- \right\} \ \textit{where} \ v_j^- = \left\{ \left(min_n \, v_j^n \,\big|\, j \in J^+ \right), \left(max_n \, v_j^n \,\big|\, j \in J^- \right) \right\} \tag{4}$$

Step 4: Here, the separation measures based on the Euclidean distance are computed. The distance from the ideal positive solution S^{n^+} and the ideal negative solution S^{n^-} for each alternative is estimated. The m-dimensional Euclidean distance is used for this computation.

$$S^{n^+} = \sqrt{\sum_{j=1}^{m} \left(v_j^+ - v_j^n \right)^2} \ \text{for} \ n = 1,2,3\ldots, k \tag{5}$$

$$S^{n^-} = \sqrt{\sum_{j=1}^{m} \left(v_j^- - v_j^n \right)^2} \ \text{for} \ n = 1,2,3\ldots, k \tag{6}$$

Step 5: This final step computes the closeness coefficient C^n to be the ideal solution. From the previous step (5), S^{n^+} shows how close an alternative is to the ideal positive solution, whereas in step (6), S^{n^-} shows how far away an alternative is from the ideal negative solution. The two solutions are combined to compute closeness coefficient score for each alternative. This allows for ranking the alternatives based on the S^{n^-} and considering the preference of S^{n^+}. The alternative with the highest coefficient (C^n) is ranked first and continues in descending order.

$$C^n = \frac{s^{n^-}}{s^{n^+} + s^{n^-}} \quad 0 \leq C^n \leq 1 \tag{7}$$

Similarly, alternatives could be ranked in ascending order when S^{n^+} is the focus, thus considering the distance to the positive ideal solution.

$$C^n = \frac{s^{n^+}}{s^{n^-} + s^{n^+}} = 1 - C^n \tag{8}$$

Decomposition Process

Next, the chapter shows the contributions of each dimension. Thus, to know which dimension has been most fulfilled or otherwise. It, therefore, attempts a decomposition of the closeness coefficient.

Assume the weight for criterion j under factor i be w_{ij} and the normalized element in matrix R for criterion j under dimension i for alternative n be r_{ij}^n. Equation (2) then becomes $v_{ij}^n = w_{ij} r_{ij}^n$, for $i = 1,2,3\ldots, p$, $j = 1,2,3\ldots, m_i$, and $n = 1,2,3\ldots, k$. The expression v_{ij}^n now becomes the weighted normalized value of criterion j under factor i for alternative n.

For any alternative n, the criteria could be decomposed into i dimensions by squaring equation (6)

$$\left(S^{n-} \right)^2 = \sum_{i=1}^{p} \sum_{i_j=1}^{m_i} \left(v_{i_j}^- - v_{i_j}^n \right)^2$$

$$v_{i_j}^- = \left\{ \left(min_n \, v_{i_j}^n \,\big|\, j \in J_i^+ \right), \left(max_n \, v_{i_j}^n \,\big|\, j \in J_i^- \right) \right\}$$

$$n = 1,2,\ldots k \ \text{and} \ i = 1,2,\ldots p$$

The squared relative closeness coefficient can be expressed as:

$$
\left(C^n\right)^2 = \frac{\sum_{1_j=1}^{m_1}\left(v_{1_j}^- - v_{1_j}^n\right)^2 + \sum_{2_j=1}^{m_2}\left(v_{2_j}^- - v_{2_j}^n\right)^2 + \sum_{p_j=1}^{m_p}\left(v_{p_j}^- - v_{p_j}^n\right)^2}{\left(s^{n-} + s^{n+}\right)^2}
\tag{9}
$$

Let S_i^{n-} and S_i^{n+} be the total distance from the negative ideal and positive ideal solutions for the set under factor i for alternative n, respectively. Then,

$$
\left(S_i^{n-}\right)^2 = \sum_{i_j=1}^{m_i}\left(v_{1_j}^- - v_{1_j}^n\right)^2
$$

For $n = 1, 2, \ldots, k$, equation (9) can be expressed again as

$$
\left(C^n\right)^2 = \frac{\left(s_1^{n-}\right)^2}{\left(s^{n-} + s^{n+}\right)^2} + \frac{\left(s_2^{n-}\right)^2}{\left(s^{n-} + s^{n+}\right)^2} + \cdots + \frac{\left(s_p^{n-}\right)^2}{\left(s^{n-} + s^{n+}\right)^2}
\tag{10}
$$

Let $(C_i^n)^2$ be the contribution to the overall composite value $(C^n)^2$ by the sub-criteria under dimension i. Then, following equation (7a), equation (10) can be expressed in the following form:

$$
\left(C^n\right)^2 = \left(C_1^n\right)^2 + \left(C_2^n\right)^2 + \cdots + \left(C_p^n\right)^2 \quad n = 1, 2, \ldots, k
\tag{11}
$$

For the two dimensions as in this case, the final composite score based on equation (11) is:

$$
\left(C^n\right)^2 = \left(C_1^n\right)^2 + \left(C_2^n\right)^2 \quad n = 1, 2.
$$

The final composite value for an alternative n can be decomposed into p components, one for each dimension i. By this decomposition, we highlight the contribution of each dimension (resilience and sustainability).

Threshold Determination for a Minimum Acceptable Performance

The threshold is a requirement to determine the minimum acceptable performance expectation of a system (Lancker & Nijkamp, 2000). Only when a system falls above a threshold that it can be judged to have improved. Identifying the threshold helps to keep track with of performance of the health systems to realize their objectives. According to Afful-Dadzie et al. (2016), "achieving the threshold begins with setting the minimum industry standard values for the criteria under consideration and assigning these values as a hypothetical alternative". Which this analysis labels as AU-standard (AUS). It is treated as another alternative added to the list of original alternatives (African states) under assessment. This makes the number of alternatives now $n+1$, and the ($n+1$th) alternative is the AUS.

Thus, assuming $(C^s)^2$ is the square of the closeness coefficient for the systems' standard, an alternative n satisfying the given condition would be judged to have performed well:

$$\left(C^n\right)^2 \geq \left(C^s\right)^2 \tag{12}$$

Thus, $(C^s)^2$ is considered the threshold against which an alternative is compared to determine its actual performance. Afful-Dadzie et al. (2016), notes that, by "assigning the standard values to a new alternative, all attributes of the TOPSIS method are maintained". Hence, the positive and negative ideal alternatives are determined just as before. From the expression, $(C_i^n)^2$ is compared with $(C_i^s)^2$ to determine the performance of an alternative n under a dimension i, relative to the systems standard. Afful-Dadzie et al. (2016) again noted that the result from such comparison under dimension i may not be the same as that obtained when the TOPSIS approach is applied to alternatives being assessed under one-dimensional criterion. This is because in that case there is no interaction effect among dimensions.

Description of Indicators of the Empirical Data

Table 18.2 shows the breakdown of the indicators of resilience and sustainability used in this study's assessment. Data used in this empirical analysis were considered under four broad indicators. The Resilience dimension consisted of eHealth adoption and Capital expenditure for health systems and the Sustainability dimension centered on medical and nursing graduates, and the projection of public expenditure on long-term care. Out of these four indicators, seven sub-indicators were identified as proxies to represent each main dimension (refer to Table 18.2). Three criteria (C1, C2, and C3) assessed eHealth adoption and Capital expenditure under the resilience dimension.

Table 18.2 Criteria and Importance Weights for the Three Dimensions of Performance

Criteria	Symbol	Criteria Weight	Dimension Weight
—Composite index of eHealth adoption among general practitioners	C1	0.2166	**Resilience (0.64)**
—Composite index of eHealth adoption by health systems	C2	0.2044	
—Gross fixed capital formation in the health sector as share of GDP	C3	0.2191	
—Medical graduates per 100,000 population	C4	0.0855	**Sustainability (0.36)**
—Nursing graduates per 100,000 population	C5	0.1827	
—Public spending on healthcare as a percentage of GDP	C6	0.0431	
—Public spending on long-term care as a percentage of GDP	C7	0.0487	

They were also considered as benefits, or "more is better" criteria. Similarly, C4, C5, C6, and C7 criteria were considered benefits making up the sustainability dimension.

Columns 4 and 3, in Table 18.2, show the overall importance weights of each dimension (resilience and sustainability) and the individual weights for the sub-indicators, respectively. The weights were obtained from regression analysis where the regression weights were derived for the indicators in rapid miner analysis software. These weights show sufficient similarity with the OECD/WHO's priority to improve the performance of health systems. Table 18.3 presents the sample data in terms of average values for each criterion used in this study. The compiled data for the analysis compassed an 11-year period from 2008 to 2018. This was largely informed by the availability of data and the quest to minimize missing data challenges. Despite this effort, there were still cases of missing data with some indicators; hence, the average value of the period was used in place of such cases (Noyes et al., 2019). The instances of missing values were found between 2008, 2009, and 2013. These composed approximately 8% of the actual dataset used. The "AU-standard" data for developing the threshold were also extracted from West African Health Organization's *Resilient and Responsive Health System for a Changing World* report. The report contained the average indices for resilient health systems. An extract of the actual dataset employed for the analysis is summarized in Table 18.3.

Table 18.3 Averaged Data Based on the Seven Criteria for 26 Health Systems

Systems	C1	C2	C3	C4	C5	C6	C7
AU-S	1.8	4.5	52	39.1	9892	7.5	5
Botswana	7.65	71.54	36.618	56.21	408.86	9.969	0.685
Burkina Faso	4.897	81.71	70.009	40.055	650.92	9.843	0.313
Cameroon	11.18	61.26	30.982	23.095	1685.7	6.941	0.24
Cabo Verde	13.52	84.49	20.964	88.238	7229.7	9.982	0.181
Chad	19.31	42.96	75.636	34.829	24.259	5.884	0.553
Congo	8.436	80.78	13.464	58.341	464.21	8.805	0.335
DR of the Congo	11.72	75.68	20.964	35.906	328.64	10.62	0.365
Côte d'Ivoire	9.938	80.98	35.918	48.421	362.65	10.73	0.635
Egypt	13	61.67	15.336	23.581	7.0867	8.856	0.613
Equatorial Guinea	15.44	46.21	17.809	34.747	6868.5	7.456	0.4
Ghana	10.92	58.99	43.1	75.973	88313	8.789	0.467
Kenya	6.919	64.89	12.982	33.525	731.08	9.085	0.635
Lesotho	2.377	72.3	32.118	14.905	461.18	7.133	0.398
Madagascar	17.96	46.51	23.745	18.637	188.59	8.764	0.24

(Continued)

Table 18.3 (Continued)

Systems	C1	C2	C3	C4	C5	C6	C7
Malawi	17.01	57.88	52.17	36.306	22.954	5.721	0.208
Mali	23.49	70.89	32.309	17.949	942.89	6.577	0.504
Mauritania	5.738	76.15	33.1	37.859	895.22	10.18	0.124
Mauritius	20.24	54.57	40.745	72.496	11974	8.877	0.635
Morocco	15.05	58.38	15.336	26.558	136.13	6.226	0.459
Namibia	15.33	84.78	32.245	30.721	19.796	9.3	0.116
Niger	10.67	53.01	19.136	56.184	3.1471	7.22	0.435
Nigeria	9.856	72.51	35.136	80.751	139.32	8.325	0.369
Rwanda	19.64	71.37	12.927	20.938	143.07	8.665	0.423
Senegal	4.153	81.16	22.436	32.461	6059.8	9.678	0.381
Seychelles	0.878	73.84	41.745	73.142	968.86	10.83	0.464
South Africa	30.57	50.75	33.218	29.557	7229.7	8.596	0.39

Note: Also included in the data (first row) is the WHO/AU standard. Data available at http://stats. oecd.org/.

Results and Discussions

Table 18.4 presents the performance assessment results for the health systems given the AUS alternative. The overall AUS alternative has a closeness score of 0.032. In essence, this value becomes the threshold value against which all the other alternatives are compared with. Therefore, countries that have closeness scores lesser than 0.032 are considered to have underperformed. Results of the analysis reveal eight systems scored above the threshold value. These include Kenya, Egypt, Côte d'Ivoire, South Africa, Nigeria, DR Congo, Mauritania, and Cabo Verde (in descending order).

The closeness score and percentage distance to or from the threshold hold value as well as the overall rank of all the health systems are shown in Table 18.4. The closeness score is the squared closeness coefficient of all the countries including the AUS as an additional alternative. The percentage difference describes by how much (in percentage distance) an alternative performed relative to the threshold value. Health systems with percentage distance in negative suggest performance below the threshold value. Largely, the analysis reveals that majority of the health systems assessed performed below the threshold value/alternative. In effect, health systems, based on this assessment, are lacking on both objectives. The least performing system fell –2.5% short of the threshold point, and the best performing system exceeded the threshold point by 29.5%. Further observations of the performance levels reveal that, despite the general nonperformance, the systems were not too distant from the threshold value. The average percentage distance for systems beneath the threshold point is –1.63% which suggests marginal underperformance. Figure 18.1 visually displays the earlier scenario of the percentage distances between the countries and the threshold point detailed in Table 18.4.

The threshold value is at point 0 which is the difference between threshold alternative score and itself. The other scores are similarly compared with the threshold value. All but eight systems

Table 18.4 Overall Performance Index Report for All Health Systems

Alternative	Closeness Score	Percentage Difference	Ranking
AU-S	0.032	–	9
Botswana	0.031	–0.001	10
Burkina Faso	0.018	–0.014	15
Cameroon	0.013	–0.019	22
Cabo Verde	0.033	0.001	8
Chad	0.018	–0.014	16
Congo	0.020	–0.012	13
DR of the Congo	0.093	0.061	3
Côte d'Ivoire	0.050	0.018	6
Egypt	0.117	0.085	2
Equatorial Guinea	0.017	–0.015	17
Kenya	0.327	0.295	1
Ghana	0.014	–0.018	20
Lesotho	0.009	–0.023	26
Madagascar	0.025	–0.007	12
Malawi	0.025	–0.007	11
Mali	0.015	–0.017	19
Mauritania	0.039	0.007	7
Mauritius	0.007	–0.025	27
Morocco	0.016	–0.016	18
Namibia	0.012	–0.020	24
Niger	0.014	–0.018	21
Nigeria	0.052	0.020	5
Rwanda	0.010	–0.022	25
Senegal	0.018	–0.014	14
Seychelles	0.013	–0.019	23
South Africa	0.077	0.045	4

outperformed the threshold value. This comparison shows the health systems do not possess sufficient resilience and sustainability. Kruk et al. (2015) opine that health systems in most developing economies lack sufficient physical, human, and information assets that expose them to reduced resilience and sustainability. Thus, the systems may be aware of the sources of threats and emergency risks but do not possess the ability to resist them. Further others lack the awareness and strategic approach required to obtain information technologies and system surveillance to detect and improve their resilience in real time (Khan et al., 2018). Hedberg and Hines (2016) similarly found low levels of resilience among European health systems using the improvement efforts found in the Health System Performance Assessment framework among EU states. They found that the coherent efforts toward facilitating health systems' efficiency is a means of attaining increased resilience. Thus, low levels of resilience will be common among systems where the concept is approached without a strategic plan or pursued as a unit level objective.

Decomposing the Closeness Coefficient Score

To achieve actual resilience and sustainability of a system, it is imperative to decompose both objectives individually to examine performance on each (Hedberg & Hines, 2016). To this end,

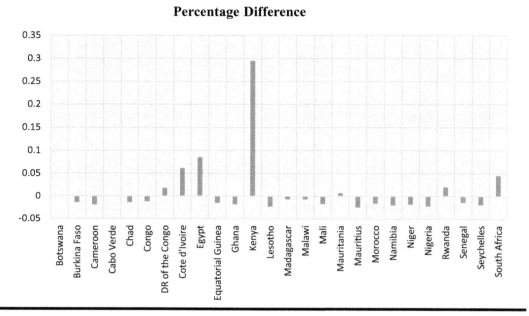

Figure 18.1   Percentage distance relative to threshold.

this analysis assesses the individual contribution of each dimension to the health system's performance by decomposing the closeness score into dimensional closeness scores. This is also to support the fact that these performance dimensions are priority areas of the WHO and other relevant stakeholders in Africa, thus the need ascertain the system's performance under each. This result will inform policy and decision-makers' on how to approach each performance dimension because it offers specific insights into the outcome of the system's efforts toward these objectives. In Table 18.5, the contribution of resilience compared with sustainability of the systems is low for almost all the health systems. 23% of the health systems performed better in resilience compared with sustainability. These alternatives include DR Congo, Egypt, Lesotho, Malawi, Mauritius, and Morocco. The findings somewhat suggest decision-makers have focused quite little on resilience. Further, the findings also provide proof that the objective of health system resilience is neglected among many African health systems. The high-performing systems derived the high-performance scores from their performance on the sustainability objective. It is worthy to note that the threshold value (AU-S) is also decomposed under the two dimensions to show how each health system performed relative to each dimension's threshold.

Overall, the health systems performed better on the sustainability objective or dimension compared with that of resilience. Decomposing the overall performance result, offered a deeper comparison between the threshold alternative with the dimension-specific performance outcomes. This analysis showed the resilience dimension to have the least average closeness score of 0.003 and a dimension relative threshold value of 0.017. Thus, under the resilience dimension, no health system outperformed this dimension-specific threshold. This finding types in with Kittelsen and Keating (2019) who also found health system security and resilience to be lacking across countries globally. Similarly, Kutzin and Sparkes (2016) earlier revealed the limited nature of policy implementations and reforms directed at driving resilience in health systems. Thus, most systems are not resilient due to the limited clarity on the conceptualization of resilience strategies.

Table 18.5   Decomposed Performance Index Report for the Health Systems

Alternative	Resilience	Sustainability	Overall
AU-S	0.017	0.011	0.028
Botswana	0.002	0.007	0.009
Burkina Faso	0.002	0.008	0.01
Cameroon	0.002	0.002	0.004
Cabo Verde	0.004	0.017	0.021
Chad	0.004	0.008	0.012
Congo	0.003	0.004	0.007
DR of the Congo	0.002	0.001	0.003
Côte d'Ivoire	0.003	0.003	0.006
Egypt	0.002	0.001	0.003
Equatorial Guinea	0.003	0.005	0.008
Kenya	0.001	0.324	0.325
Ghana	0.002	0.004	0.006
Lesotho	0.004	0.001	0.005
Madagascar	0.004	0.004	0.008
Malawi	0.007	0.001	0.008
Mali	0.002	0.003	0.005
Mauritania	0.006	0.018	0.024
Mauritius	0.004	0.000	0.004
Morocco	0.005	0.002	0.007
Namibia	0.002	0.003	0.005
Niger	0.002	0.008	0.01
Nigeria	0.005	0.001	0.006
Rwanda	0.002	0.004	0.006
Senegal	0.002	0.008	0.01
Seychelles	0.002	0.002	0.004
South Africa	0.010	0.005	0.015

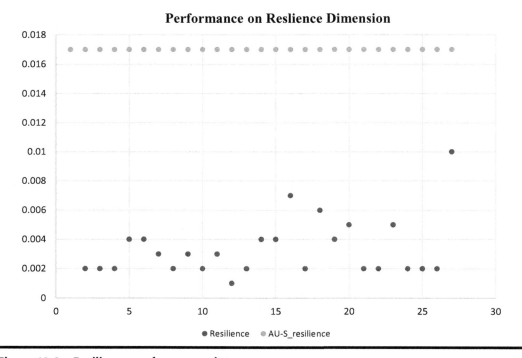

Figure 18.2   Resilience performance plot.

Figure 18.2 shows a graphical performance of the health systems on the dimension of resilience against its threshold value. All points were below the determined threshold value.

Relative to the sustainability dimension, a few health systems showed sufficient performance outcomes (Figure 18.3). It is perceived that sustainability can be achieved using broader strategies such as, strong governance, leadership, increased technology adoption, and direct investments (Taylor, 2017). By this assertion, sustainability can be improved even if it is a broad strategic agenda and not directly focused on health systems only. This notwithstanding the vast differences shown in the performance of the health systems, on both dimensions presents fresh evidence for new investigations by professionals and the researchers into effective strategies for improving resilience of health systems. It is worth noting that Kenyan health system showed the highest performance score of 0.324 that outperformed the threshold value by 31.3%.

A point to note is the difference in the threshold values for each dimension shown in the figures. The threshold values were different for all two dimensions. This is not an indication that the threshold is lowered for or raised for a particular dimension. This occurrence is usual in TOPSIS because of the endogenous nature of the model. Due to the variable nature of the ideal positive and negative solutions, the values are derived from the same alternatives being evaluated when computing the threshold value. Hence, a lower threshold for a dimension does not necessarily translate into an opportunity for passing the performance evaluation for the said dimension. By suggesting the TOPSIS model being endogenous, it means that the model is flexible with resetting the threshold to reflect the developments under a particular dimension.

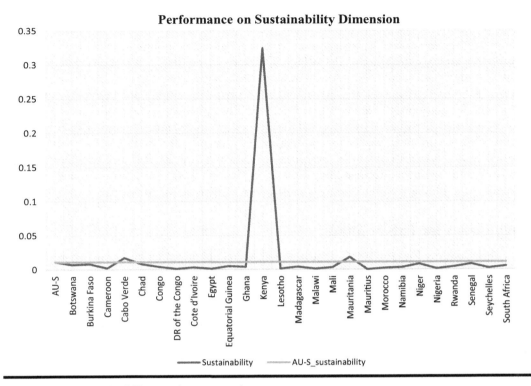

Figure 18.3   Sustainability performance plot.

Implications for Practice

To effectively assess the performance of complex systems, specifically health systems, evaluators, an objective measurement system that determines an inherent minimum level of performance against which actual performance must be compared. This guarantees the feasibility of performance objectives as well as the determination of strategic implementations for the achievement of set objective. This chapter provides a practical procedure for determining micro, meso, and macro performance targets. It also sheds valuable insights on how performance objectives can be decomposed into subunit objectives for unit-specific strategies and implementations for successful accomplishments. Building on the TOPSIS framework, this chapter primarily provides a guide for practitioners and performance evaluation experts who wish to assess performance of organizational objectives at any level of implementation.

Further, health decision-makers and other experts, to reduce the vast variations in the performance of strategic objectives, must employ a networked approach to building resilience and sustainability of health systems within and across Africa. Public health administrators and performance assessment experts must collaborate to reach a consensus on joint strategic objectives and performance assessment metrics for building resilient and sustainable systems.

Conclusion

Most health systems across the African continent have significant ground to cover on the objective of resilience and sustainability of the WHO. This notwithstanding, a few show promising indications of high performance on both dimensions. Notably, Kenya, Egypt, Côte d'Ivoire, South Africa, Mauritania, Nigeria, Cabo Verde, and DR Congo are among these high-performing systems. A decomposition of the overall performance scores, largely revealed similar poor performance outcomes in resilience and sustainability. This is not an encouraging sign for health systems on the African continent, especially considering the current global situation. By inference, the assessed health systems possess low readiness and adaptability to crisis and significant performance deficits for future sustainability. The findings present fresh evidence for the need to revise strategies for building resilient and sustainable health systems across Africa.

Suggestions for Future Study

The conclusions put forward in this chapter unfold several opportunities for future investigations on this subject. First, an extension of this investigation to compass all African states as well as a broader scope of indicators determined for resilience and sustainability will offer a more holistic view of the situation of resilience and sustainability of health systems across the continent. In addition, considering the vast differences obtained in the performance of the health systems on the two objectives considered (resilience and sustainability), it will be even more insightful to understand why the significant differences in performance on the two objectives require a similar strategy. Thus, a qualitative assessment of how the health systems have approached the pursuance of the resilience and sustainability objectives. What similarities and differences exist, and the extent of implementation to discern the potential causes of variations in performance on these objectives among the health systems in Africa.

References

Abirami, A. M., & Askarunisa, A. (2017). Sentiment Analysis Model to Emphasize the Impact of Online Reviews in Healthcare Industry. *Online Information Review, 41*(4), 471–486. https://doi.org/10.1108/OIR-08-2015-0289

Afful-Dadzie, A., Afful-Dadzie, E., & Turkson, C. (2016). A TOPSIS Extension Framework for Re-conceptualizing Sustainability Measurement. *Kybernetes, 45*(1), 70–86.

Ahluwalia, S. C., Damberg, C. L., Silverman, M., Motala, A., & Shekelle, P. G (2017). What Defines a High-Performing Health Care Delivery System: A Systematic Review. *The Joint Commission Journal on Quality and Patient Safety, 43*, 450–459

Alameddine, M. Fouad, F. M., & Diaconu, K. (2019). Resilience Capacities of Health Systems: Accommodating the Needs of Palestinian Refugees from Syria. *Social Science & Medicine, 220*, 22–30.

Alblas, A. A., & Jayaram, J. S. R. (2014). Design Resilience in the Fuzzy Frontend (FFE) Context: An Empirical Examination. *International Journal of Production Research,* 1–19. http://dx.doi.org/10.1080/00207543.2014.899718.

Alecos, K., & Dimitrios, A. (2010). A New TOPSIS-based Multi-criteria Approach to Personnel Selection. *Expert Systems with Application, 37*, 4999–5008.

Arrow, K. J., Dasgupta, P., Goulder, L. H., Mumford, K. J., & Oleson, K. (2012). Sustainability and the Measurement of Wealth. *Environment and Development Economics, 17*(3), 317–353.

Avazpour, R., Ebrahimi, E., & Fathi, M. R. A. (2013). 360 Degree Feedback Model for Performance Appraisal Based on Fuzzy AHP and TOPSIS. *International Journal of Economy, Management and Social Sciences, 2*(11), 969–976.

Béné, C., Newsham, A., Davis, M., 2013. Making the Most of Resilience. IDS, pp. 32. www.ids.ac.uk/publication/making-the-most-of-resilience.

Biddle, L. Wahedi, K., & Bozorgmehr, K. (2020). Health System Resilience: A Literature Review of Empirical Research. *Health Policy and Planning, 35*(8), 1084–1109. https://doi.org/10.1093/heapol/czaa032

Blanchet, K. (2013). Governance of Health Systems. *International Journal of Health Policy and Management, 1*, 177–179

Böhringer, C., & Jochem, P. E. (2007). Measuring the Immeasurable—a Survey of Sustainability İndices. *Ecological Economics, 63*(1), 1–8.

Braithwaite, J., Hibbert, P., Blakely, B., Plumb, J., Hannaford, N., Cameron, J. L., & Marks, D. (2017). Health System Frameworks and Performance İndicators in Eight Countries: A Comparative İnternational Analysis. *SAGE Open Medicine, 5*, 1–10.

Carinci, F., Van gool, K., Mainz, J., Veillard, J., Pichora, E. C., Januel, J., Arispe, M., Kim, S., M., & Klazinga, N. S. (2015). Towards Actionable İnternational Comparisons of Health System Performance: Expert Revision of the OECD Framework and Quality İndicators. *International Journal for Quality in Health Care, 27*(2), 137–146

Cassier-Woidasky, A. K. (2013). *Nursing Education in Germany—Challenges and Obstacles in Professionalization.* Stuttgart: DHBW.

Demirtas, O. (2013). Evaluating the Best Renewable Energy Technology for Sustainable Energy Planning. *International Journal of Energy Economics and Policy, 3*, 23–33.

Dwivedi, G., Srivastava, R. K., & Srivastava, S. K. (2018). A Generalized Fuzzy TOPSIS with İmproved Closeness Coefficient. *Expert Systems with Applications, 96*, 185–195. https://doi.org/10.1016/j.eswa.2017.11.051.

Esty, D. C., & Cort, T. (2017). *Corporate Sustainability Metrics: What Investors Need and Don't Get.* Yale University. Retrieved July 13, 2017, from https://corporatesustainability.org/wp-content/uploads/Corporate-Sustainability-Metrics.pd

European Commission. (2020). *Annual Sustainable Growth Strategy 2021.* European Economic Forecast (Summer 2020), European Economy—Institutional Paper, 132 (July). Regulation (EU) 2021/241 of the European Parliament and of the Council of 12 February 2021 establishing the Recovery and Resilience Facility. http://data.europa.eu/eli/reg/2021/241/oj

Govindan, K., Khodaverdi, R., & Jafarian, A. (2013). A Fuzzy Multi Criteria Approach for Measuring Sustainability Performance of a Supplier Based on Triple Bottom Line Approach. *Journal of Cleaner Production, 47*, 345–354.

Hedberg, A., & Hines, P. (2016). *Addressing the Crisis of Tomorrow: The Sustainability of European Health Systems.* Policy Brief. European Policy Center.

Holling, C. S. (1973). Resilience and Stability of Ecological Systems. *Annual Review of Ecology, Evolution, and Systematics, 4*, 1–23. https://doi.org/10.1146/annurev.es.04.110173.000245.

Hosseini, K., Seyed, M. B., & Ramirez-Marquez, J. (2016). A Review of Definitions and Measures of System Resilience. *Reliability Engineering & System Safety, 4*(2), 47–61

Hwang, C. L., & Yoon, K. (1981). *Multiple Attribute Decision Making: Methods and Applications.* Berlin: Springer.

Joumard, R., & Gudmundsson, H. (2010). *Indicators of Environmental Sustainability in Transport: An Interdisciplinary Approach to Methods.* INRETS report, Recherche R282. INRETS, Bron, France.

Kannan, D., Jabbour, A. B. L. D. S., & Jabbour, C. J. C. (2014). Selecting Green Suppliers Based on GSCM Practices: Using Fuzzy TOPSIS Applied to a Brazilian Electronics Company. *European Journal of Operational Research, 233*(2), 432–447.

Khan, Y., O'Sullivan, T., & Brown, A. (2018). Public Health Emergency Preparedness: A Framework to Promote Resilience. *BMC Public Health, 18*, 1344.

Kieny, M.-P., Evans, D. B., Schmets, G., & Kadandale, S. (2014). Health-system Resilience: Reflections on the Ebola Crisis in Western Africa. *Bull WHO, 92*, 850. https://doi.org/10.2471/BLT.14.149278.

Kittelsen, S. K., & Keating, V. C. (2019). Rational Trust in Resilient Health Systems. *Health Policy and Planning, 34*, 553–557.

Koffi, J. M., & Dubois, J. L. (2018). Formes de résilience et stratégies de politique publique. In E. Grégoire, J.-F. Kobiané, & M.-F. Lange (Eds.), *L'Etat réhabilité en Afrique: réinventer les politiques publiques à l'ère néolibérale* (pp. 319–336). Paris: Karthala.

Kruk, M. E., Ling, E. J., Bitton, A., Cammett, M., Cavanaugh, K., Chopra, M., et al. (2017). Building Resilient Health Systems: A Proposal for a Resilience Index. *BMJ, 357*, j2323. https://doi.org/10.1136/bmj.j2323.

Kruk, M. E., Myers, M., Varpilah, S. T., & Dahn, B. T. (2015). What is a Resilient Health System? Lessons from Ebola. *Lancet, 385*, 1910–1912.

Kucukvar, M., Gumus, S., Egilmez, G., & Tatari, O. (2014). Ranking the Sustainability Performance of Pavements: An İntuitionistic Fuzzy Decision-making Method. *Automation in Construction, 40*, 33–43.

Kutzin, J., & Sparkes, S. P. (2016). Health Systems Strengthening, Universal Health Coverage, Health Security and Resilience. *Bulletin of the World Health Organisation, 94*, 2. https://doi.org/10.2471/BLT.15.165050.

Lancker, E., & Nijkamp, P. (2000). A Policy Scenario Analysis Of Sustainable Agricultural Development Options: A Case Study for Nepal. *Impact Assess. Project Appraisal, 18*(2), 111–124.

Martineau, T., McPake, B., Theobald, S., Raven, J., Ensor, T., & Fustukian, S. (2017). Leaving No One Behind: Lessons on Rebuilding Health Systems in Conflict- and Crisis Affected States. *BMJ Global Health, 2*, e000327. https://doi.org/10.1136/bmjgh-2017-000327.

Mills, A. (2017). Resilient and Responsive Health Systems in a Changing World. *Health Policy Plan, 32*, iii1–iii2. https://doi.org/10.1093/heapol/czx117.

Noyes, J., Booth, A., & Moore, G. (2019). Synthesizing Quantitative and Qualitative Evidence to Inform Guidelines on Complex Interventions: Clarifying the Purposes, Designs and Outlining Some Methods. *BMJ Global Health, 4*, e000893.

OECD. (2017). *Recommendations to OECD Ministers of Health from the High Level Reflection Group on the Future of Health*. Paris, France: OECD/EU. https://www.oecd.org/els/health-systems/Recommendations-from-high-level-reflection-group-on-the-future-of-health-statistics.pdf

OECD. (2019). Long-term Care Spending and Unit Costs. In *Health at a Glance: Indicators*. Paris: OECD. Retrieved May 15, 2020, from www.oecd-ilibrary.org/sites/4dd50c09-en/1/2/11/11/index.html?itemId=/content/publication/4dd50c09-en&mimeType=text/html&_csp_=82587932df7c06a6a3f9dab95304095d&itemIGO=oecd&itemContentType=book.

Olu, O. (2017). Resilient Health System as Conceptual Framework for Strengthening Public Health Disaster Risk Management: An African Viewpoint. *Frontiers in Public Health, 5*, 263. https://doi.org/10.3389/fpubh.2017.00263.

Patil, S. K., & Kant, R. (2014). A Fuzzy AHP-TOPSIS Framework for Ranking the Solutions of Knowledge Management Adoption in Supply Chain to Overcome its Barriers. *Expert Systems with Applications, 41*, 679–693.

Peters, D. H. (2018). Health Policy and Systems Research: The Future of the Field. *Health Research Policy and Systems, 16*. https://doi.org/10.1186/s12961-018-0359-0.

Rađenović, Z., & Veselinović, I. (2017). Integrated AHP-TOPSIS Method for the Assessment of Health Management Information Systems Efficiency. *55*(1), 121–142. https://doi.org/10.1515/ethemes-2017-0008.

Sarre, S., Redlich, C., Tinker, A., Salder, E., Bhalla, A., & McKevitt, C. (2014). A Systematic Review of Qualitative Studies on Adjusting after Stroke: Lessons for the Study of Resilience. *Disability and Rehabilitation, 36*(9), 716–726.

Shafii, M., Hosseini, S. M., Arab, M., Asgharizadeh, M., & Farzianpour, M. (2016). Performance Analysis of Hospital Managers Using Fuzzy AHP and Fuzzy TOPSIS: Iranian Experience. *Global Journal of Health Sciences, 8*(2), 137–155. https://doi.or/10.5539/gjhsv8n2p137

Singh, R. K., & Benyoucef, L. (2011). A Fuzzy TOPSIS Based Approach for e-Sourcing. *Engineering Applications of Artificial Intelligence, 24*(3), 437–448.

Singh, R. K., Murty, H. R., Gupta, S. K., & Dikshit, A. K. (2009). An Overview of Sustainability Assessment Methodologies. *Ecological Indicators, 9*(2), 189–212.

Taylor, C. (2017). *Advancing Resilient Systems for a Sustainable HIV Response*. USAID, Leadership, Management, & Governance Project.

Thomas, E. (2013). A Framework for Assessing Health System Resilience in an Economic Crisis: Ireland as a Test Case. *BMC Health Services Research, 13*, 450

Turenne, C. P., Gautier, L., & Degroote, S. (2019). Conceptual Analysis of Health Systems Resilience: A Scoping Review. *Social Science & Medicine, 232*, 168–180.

Ungar, M. (2015). Qualitative Contributions to Resilience Research. *Quality Social Work, 2*(1), 85–102.

United Nations. (2016). *High-level Panel on the Global Response to Health Crises.* Protecting Humanity from Future Health Crises [internet]. www.un.org/News/dh/ nfocus/HLP/2016-02-05 95

Wang, Y. M., & Elhag, T. M. S. (2006). Fuzzy TOPSIS Method Based on Alpha Level Sets with an Application to Bridge Risk Assessment. *Expert Systems with Applications, 31*(2), 309–319.

World Health Organization. (2016). *Universal Health Coverage: Moving towards Better Health—Action Framework for the Western Pacific Region* [Internet]. Genève: World Health Organization. http://iris. wpro.who.int/bitstream/handle/10665.1/13371/9789290617563_eng.pdf?ua=1.

World Health Organization. (2017, June). *Building Resilience: A Key Pillar of Health 2020 and the Sustainable Development Goals—Examples from the WHO Small Countries Initiative.* [Internet]. p. 101. www.euro. who.int/en/publications/abstracts/building-resilience-a-key-pillar-of-health-2020-and-the-sustainable development-goals-examples-from-the-who-small-countries-initiative-2017

World Health Organization. (2020). *Coronavirus Disease (COVID-19) Technical Guidance: Maintaining Essential Health Services and Systems.* Geneva: World Health Organization. Retrieved May 15, from www.who.int/emergencies/diseases/novelcoronavirus-2019/technical-guidance/maintaining-essential-health-services-and-systems

Author's Profile

Divine Quase Agozie is an assistant lecturer in operations and management information systems department at the University of Ghana Business School and a final year PhD student in information systems at the Cyprus International University. Agozie's research interest concentrates on natural language processing (text mining), online privacy, and sustainable development. He has authored some scholarly articles on privacy fatigue and online engagement on social media. He also has some publications coming up on applications of text mining approaches to data from the advocacy domain for organizational communication.

Chapter 19

Rethinking Patient Empowerment through Online Patient Portals for Managing Diabetes and Hypertension in Ghana

Roger A. Atinga and Anita Asiwome Adzo Baku

Contents

DOI: 10.4324/9781003152217-24

Introduction

Healthcare delivery in the twenty-first century has reached a turning point unparalleled in the past. There is no doubt that patients now have good access to information in the health-seeking process than in the past. Particularly, the emergence of the World Wide Web (www) has caused a fundable change in the way health services are supplied, used, and paid for.

The www has also increased information sources making it easier for patients to use available information to aid treatment and make informed decisions and choices about their condition and how to manage it (Gozali et al., 2014). Recent debate, therefore, emphasizes the need for healthcare providers to consider the adoption of electronic healthcare delivery systems as a vehicle of facilitating access to health services, enabling information sharing between patients and providers and improving health service quality and efficiency (Irani et al., 2009; Kazley et al., 2012). In the era of the pandemic where healthcare facilities are resource strapped and facing challenges of ensuring adequate physical distancing, adherence to the mitigation protocols and optimizing patient flow (Søreide et al., 2020), the need to adopt more innovative patient-oriented technology to care delivery is important. In particular, innovations that seek to decongest clinical settings provide more convenient access to care, enhance patient trust in providers, and ease pressure on health providers at practice settings should be given attention (Lee & Trimi, 2021). Online patient portal system is one such communication and information technology innovation with the potential to improve upon the quality of nonemergency care among patients requiring follow-up checkup. Patient portals are online application systems that enable patients to communicate and interact with health providers (Ancker et al., 2011). Patient portals are typically available online at all times for convenient use by patients. Patients and health providers can use online patient portals to engage each other on treatment decisions, treatment plans and other medical issues (Wootton, 2001).

Patient portals have been shown to lead to improved quality delivery of nonemergency care, reduced readmission and facilitates better therapeutic relations between physicians and patients on needing follow-up care (Griffin et al., 2016; Hjelm, 2005). Patient portals foster better therapeutic relations between the patient and provider, increases medication adherence, and leads to optimal work and patient flow (Goldzweig et al., 2013). Patient portals can empower patients to exhibit responsible behaviors in managing their condition and its progress (Sarkar & Bates, 2014). Wilkinson (1998) defined empowerment as a process of recognizing, promoting, and enhancing a person's abilities to meet their own needs and solve their own problems. In healthcare, patient empowerment is the process of giving the patient control over actions and decisions affecting their lives (Anderson & Funnell, 2010). Patient empowerment has also been conceptualized as the process by which optimal outcomes of healthcare interventions are achieved when patients become active participants in the care giving process (Brennan & Safran, 2003). Empowerment requires the patient to be responsible for themselves and make choices regarding care options determined by the physician (Funnell et al., 1991).

There are several ways of empowering the patient. Notable ones include reciprocal information sharing and communication, patient participation in treatment decisions and care options, and patient control over information regarding their condition and history (Small et al., 2013). When patients are empowered, they become more receptive to therapeutic advice, care options, and adhere to treatment plans. Aujoulat et al. (2007) noted that patients who feel remotely empowered are more likely to integrate better lifestyle and healthy treatment behaviors in their everyday life. Despite the growing importance of patient empowerment, evidence remains limited on how healthcare technology and especially patient portals can empower patients to become therapeutic partners for desired outcomes. Moreover, there is limited empirical evidence drawing linkage between the characteristics of patient portals and patient empowerment among patients with chronic conditions who require frequent contact with health providers. The dearth of research on this subject matter necessitated this study which explored the perceptions of diabetic and hypertension patients about whether the adoption of patient portal can empower them to have self-control over their condition and its management as well as make informed decisions in therapeutic processes.

Methods

Study Setting

Cross-sectional quantitative data were collected in eight referral hospitals across the Greater Accra region of Ghana. The hospital provides inpatient and outpatient care with a combined bed capacity of 356. At the time of the study, diabetes and hypertension cases constituted about 20% of outpatient attendance and 10% of admissions. They were also among the top ten causes of admissions and institutional mortalities. About 90% of the diabetic cases presenting to the facilities were type 2 diabetes which is common among adult populations in Ghana. All diabetic and hypertension patients were physically presenting to the health facilities for care.

Study Participants and Sampling

The study targeted patients 18 years and older who were admitted into diabetes and hypertensive therapy and were subsequently presenting to the hospitals for follow-up care. Opportunistic sampling was used to select respondents. The research team comprising the first author and two research assistants visited each hospital twice a week, each assisted by nurses to recruit participants into the study. Exit interviews were used to collect data. The research team first introduced themselves and the study's aim to the patients while they were on queue for consultation and asked whether they would be interested in participation after completing clinical procedures and consultation with the doctor. An inclusion criterion was if a patient consistently used the Internet and had an email for personal and workplace communication. This criterion was important since patient portal usage requires adequate familiarity with, and use of the Internet. If a patient met this criterion, she/he was contacted at convenient venues within the facility for faced to face interview.

Research Questionnaire

Data were collected using a structured questionnaire developed based on a synthesis of existing literature. The questionnaire was structured into six constructs. The first construct (online communication of medication information) was measured with six items by asking respondents whether they would wish that online portals are used to engage them on medication issues in relation to required doses, frequency of administration and side effects. The second construct (online appointment and visit) was assessed with four questions about online booking, scheduling for consultation and visit reminders. The third construct (online discussion of treatment and care plans) was measured with four items about the need to use online portals to discuss therapeutic issues with the doctor, features care needs, decisions regarding lifestyle, and healthy behaviors.

Table 19.1 Description of Constructs

Variable	No. of Items	Summary Description
Online communication of medication information	6	Sharing online information on medication that includes doses, administration, frequency, timing, and side effects (Hulter et al., 2020; Irizarry et al., 2015)
Online appointment and visit	4	Booking online for visits, scheduling for consultation, and reminder systems for the next visit (Antonio et al., 2020)
Online discussion of treatment and care plans	4	Patient using online portal to discuss therapeutic issues with doctors, future care needs, decisions regarding lifestyle, and healthy behaviors (Alpert et al., 2017; Kelly et al., 2018)
Online previsit planning	2	Online access to patient forms, completion of previsit forms, and progress reports (Antonio et al., 2020)
Online access to information	4	Sharing of vital information relating to risk, education, allergies, medical results, and salient health tips (Goldzweig et al., 2013)
Patient empowerment	2	Patient having self-control over their condition and its management and capacity to make informed decision about treatment (Pekonen et al., 2020)

The fourth construct (online previsit planning) was measured with four items around access to online patient forms, completion of previsit forms, and progress reports. The fifth construct (online access to information) used four items to assess whether the doctor should share information online about risk, education, allergies, medical results, and health tips. The final construct (patient empowerment) was examined with two questions as follows: "the use of online portals would enable me to have self-control over my condition and its management?" and "using online portals will give me the capacity to make informed decision about treatment". Descriptive summary of the construct is shown in Table 19.1. All the questions were placed on a five-point Likert agreement/disagreement scale.

Analysis

Data were analyzed using SPSS 24. Principal component analysis (PCA) with varimax rotation was performed to reduce the number of items into few linearly uncorrelated items. All the 20 items of the six constructs were loaded. However, 15 items were strongly loaded above the recommended 0.5. All but patient empowerment construct produced three items each. The computed Cronbach alpha coefficients of the items produced exceeded the threshold value of 0.7 (Field, 2013) which is an indication that all the items were closely related in measuring each construct. Descriptive statistics of the items produced and the Cronbach alpha values of the constructs are shown in

Table 19.2 Characteristics of Respondents

Characteristic	Description	Quantitative study (n = 280) n (%)
Sex	Male	155 (55.5)
	Female	125 (44.6)
Age (years)	Mean (std. dev.)	45 (14.67)
	Range	38–71
Number of years with the condition	Mean (std. dev.)	5 (8.3)
	Range	
Education	Senior High	132 (47.1%)
	Higher	148 (52.9%)
Know online patient portal	Yes	160 (57.1)
	No	120 (42.9)
Hours of Internet usage in a day	Mean (std. dev.)	7 (3.3)
	Range	5–18

Table 19.2. To determine the association between characteristics of the online portal and the dependent variable (patient empowerment), multivariate regression models were computed. We controlled for knowledge and Internet since they potentially confound the results.

Results

Demographic Characteristics

The majority of the respondents were males (55.5%) had higher education (52.9%) and indicated knowing online portal (67.1%). The mean age and number of years of living with the condition were 45 years and 5 years, respectively. The average daily hours of Internet usage was 7.

Principal Component Analysis

Table 19.3 shows summary results of the Cronbach alpha coefficients as well as the eigenvalues and total variance of the principal component analysis (PCA) model. All the four constructs produced eigenvalues above 1 and with a cumulative total variance of 52%. The significance of the PCA was supported by the Kaiser–Meyer–Olkin (KMO) measure of sampling adequacy (0.841) which exceeded the recommended 0.6 and the significance of the Bartlett's Test of Sphericity ($\chi^2 = 819.918$; df = 171; $P < 0.000$). Results of the factor loadings reporting the distinct items produced and their descriptive statistics are shown in Table 19.4. The mean scores of the items were above 3.0, indicating that respondents somewhat agreed that online portals should be used to

Table 19.3 Cronbach Alphas, Eigenvalues, and Total Variance Extracted

Construct	Cronbach alpha	Eigenvalue	Total Variance Explained
Online communication of medication information	0.80	8.1	9.3.6%
Online appointment and visit	0.82	1.7	8.9%
Online discussion of treatment and care plans	0.74	1.7	8.2%
Online previsit planning	0.76	1.4	6.3%
Online access to information	0.79	1.3	5.8%
Patient empowerment	0.84	1.2	5.4%

communicate medication information, schedule appointment and visit, discuss treatment plans, previsit planning, and share information with the patient. Respondents also held the perception that online portals can empower them to gain control over their conditions and make informed decision on management.

Regression Results

Table 19.4 shows the regression result of the relationship between the online portal attributes (independent variables) and patient empowerment (dependent variables). The overall regression model was statistically significant (F = 109.924; p < 0.001) and produced about 50% of the variance in patient empowerment. Additionally, the VIF values are below cut-off of 10 suggesting the absence of multicollinearity (Field, 2013). This is further supported by the zero-order and partial correlation coefficients. The regression model (summarized in Table 19.5) shows statistically significant association of patient empowerment with online portals for medication information ($\beta = 0.314$; p < 0.01), appointment and visit ($\beta = 0.371$; p < 0.01), discussing treatment plans $\beta = 0.214$; p < 0.05, previsit planning ($\beta = 0.257$; p < 0.05) and information sharing ($\beta = 0.365$; p < 0.01), between the patient and the doctor.

Discussion

Diabetes and hypertensive cases are among the top ten causes of outpatient visits in health facilities in Ghana. In most cases, these conditions do not require hospitalization unless under emergency requiring critical medical attention for resuscitation. In the era of the new normal where hospitals are struggling to maintain adherence to the COVID-19 protocols including physical distancing, it is time to rethink using Information and Communication Technology (ICT) to offer health services to patients with chronic noncommunicable diseases such as diabetes and hypertension who may not necessarily need physical contact with the physician. eHealth tools such as patient portals are instrumental in facilitating remote consultation, monitoring, and visit among patients with chronic conditions in the pandemic era (Lau et al., 2020). This study examined how virtual health service systems such as patient portals can empower patients to gain control over their own health as well as make informed decisions on treatment plans.

Table 19.4 Factor Loadings and Descriptive Statistics

Dimension	Mean	Std Dev.	Factor Loading
Online communication of medication information			
Online patient portals should be used to communicate . . .			
medication doses to patients	2.96	1.277	0.837
medication administration to patients	3.16	1.206	0.709
medication side effects to patients	3.72	1.204	0.803
Online appointment and visit			
I will prefer the use of an online portals for . . .			
booking visits	4.13	1.236	0.652
scheduling for consultation	3.95	0.940	0.679
giving reminder on next visit	3.80	1.107	0.872
Online discussion of treatment and care plans			
I prefer the use of online portals for . . .			
discussing therapeutic issues with the doctor	3.46	1.190	0.628
discussing future care needs with the doctor	2.94	1.205	0.788
discussing healthy behaviors with the doctor	2.89	1.191	0.750
Online previsit planning			
I prefer that opportunity exist to use an online portals for . . .			
accessing my forms	3.39	1.085	0.604
completing my visit forms	3.29	1.052	0.880
knowing progress report before visit	4.02	1.078	0.745
Online access to information			
I prefer to use an online portal for sharing information with the doctor about . . .			
my condition	3.11	1.095	0.611
medical results	3.02	0.085	0.615
health tips	3.92	0.012	0.800
Patient empowerment			
An online portal system will empower me to have self-control over my condition	3.98	0.087	0.752
Online portal system will enable me make informed decision about treatment	4.20	0.008	0.823

Note: Kaiser–Meyer–Olkin Measure of Sampling = 0.841.

Bartlett's Test of Sphericity [χ^2(df) = 819.918(171); $p < 0.000$].

Table 19.5   Multivariate Regression of Association between Patient Empowerment Attributes of Patient Portals

Variables	Standardized Beta	Std. error	t	Correlations		VIF
				Zero order	Partial	
Constant		0.346	2.782**			
Online communication of medication information	0.314	0.085	2.978**	0.505	0.331	1.738
Online appointment and visit	0.371	0.065	4.052**	0.463	0.431	1.311
Online discussion of treatment and care plans	0.214	0.071	2.484*	0.278	0.281	1.165
Online previsit planning	0.257	0.082	2.573*	0.492	0.290	1.568
Online access to information	0.365	0.082	3.361**	0.254	0.368	1.852

Note: **$p < 0.01$; *$p < 0.05$.

Adj. $R^2 = 0.502$.

Dependent variable: Patient empowerment.

The findings of the principal analysis showed that patients would appreciate using a patient portal to communicate medication information about doses, administration, and the side effects of drugs. This finding confirms existing literature that patients prefer online self-service portals that provide instructions about how to go about medication schedule and administration (Lau et al., 2020). It is common for patients with chronic conditions to face challenges about medication regime such as forgetfulness of taking medication as directed, skipping doses or experience limited opportunity to report side effects (Atinga et al., 2018). Instituting patient portals will provide greater opportunity for patients to adequately engage with health providers on problems arising from medication taking and how to manage them (Kruse et al., 2015).

One of the reasons for which patients with chronic conditions often delay at care delivery points is the time taken to navigate previsit procedures like retrieving records and filling out forms. This perhaps explained why the patients preferred using online portals for accessing forms, completing forms before visit, and knowing progress report before actual visit (Ammenwerth et al., 2012). Review studies by Lester et al. (2016) and Roehrs et al. (2017) showed that patients are often concerned by personal information controlled solely by health providers. Access to personal health records online will give the patient greater control over their own information and its management.

Moreover, patients are able to study their personal records for accuracy, completeness, and provide feedback to them before physical visit. Remote completing of records will also minimize waiting hours and enhance service quality experience (Ammenwerth et al., 2012). Closely related to the previsit planning was the finding about appointment before visit that produced strong factor loading. The patients preferred using online patient portals for booking visits, scheduling consultation, and giving reminders on next visit. This finding is not surprising because appointment scheduling systems have been shown to minimize queues, thereby enhancing service quality experience (Prentice et al., 2014). Al-Haqwi and Al-Shehri (2007) also found that patients' positive service experiences were largely influenced by the appointment system which makes care access more convenient and time-saving. Nonetheless, using patient portals for appointment can be problematic when not well managed. Graham et al. (2020), for example, found patient portal services to be associated with patient satisfaction but contributed to missed appointments due to scheduling bugs.

In line with earlier studies (Archer et al., 2011; Lau et al., 2020), the patient had wished for the use of patient online portal services to access information about their condition, medical results, and health tips. This is vital because holding patient medical results because of lack of opportunity to do so often leads to anxiety disorders with a consequential effect on increasing blood pressure level of hypertensive patients (AlKhathami et al., 2017). The patients also indicated that patient portals should be used to discuss treatment decisions, future care needs, and healthy behaviors. Generally, chronic diabetic and hypertensive patients have unique medical needs. They need to adopt and promote consistent healthy lifestyle behaviors including diet, exercise, weight loss, no smoking, and good working habits (Akbarpour et al., 2018). Doing so would require communicating lifestyle decisions and their pros and cons with the provider for counseling (Piette et al., 2003). Adopting an online patient portal system can facilitate such two-way communication more conveniently for effective therapeutic outcomes.

The regression model showed that all the attributes of online patient portal produced statistically association with patient empowerment. Thus, the patient feel empowerment when there is an opportunity to engage and communicate with health providers online about medication issues, appointment and visit, treatment and care plans, previsit planning, and access to information. These findings further strengthen existing evidence highlighting the importance of information communication technology in enabling patients to take coresponsibility in the management of their conditions (Ammenwerth, 2018; Ammenwerth et al., 2019; Risling et al., 2018). The findings further highlight the evolving nature of healthcare delivery. Rather than allowing the patient to present to the health facility for only the physician to decide on the next steps of care, online patient portals can empower the patient to be involved in managing symptoms, medication therapy, and cocreation of medical solutions to health problems.

Conclusion

Whether acknowledged or overlooked, the COVID-19 pandemic and its associated challenges provide lessons to shift from the traditional practices of health service delivery. Just as most functional areas of organizational engagement are going virtual, so it is that healthcare providers can tap on online patient portal to virtually engage patients with chronic conditions without compromising quality and therapeutic effect. In addition, patient portal systems have been shown to contribute significantly to patient empowerment in that they give patients greater control over their condition and decision around management. This was brought to light in this study as positive statistically significant associations were found between the attributes of patient portals and patient empowerment.

Practical Implications

The findings of the study suggest the need for healthcare organization in low- and middle-income countries to adopt patient portals as a stop-gap to the inherent challenges of providing health services under the COVID-19. Furthermore, given that many of the respondents were regular

Internet users, adopting online patient portals such as email or web-based systems to communicate and respond to patient concerns can empower patients to adopt responsible, healthy behaviors. In particular, web-based systems designed with dashboards displaying diabetes and hypertension specific information about medication, history, challenges, allergies, and management is recommended. This will empower patients to make an informed decision and promote adherence to therapeutic pathways.

References

Akbarpour, S., Khalili, D., Zeraati, H., Mansournia, M. A., Ramezankhani, A., & Fotouhi, A. (2018). Healthy Lifestyle Behaviors and Control of Hypertension among Adult Hypertensive Patients. *Scientific Reports*, *8*(1), 1–9.

Al-Haqwi, A. I., & Al-Shehri, A. M. (2007). Appointment System in Primary Care: Opinion of Consumers and Providers. *Journal of Family & Community Medicine*, *14*(3), 99.

AlKhathami, A. D., Alamin, M. A., Alqahtani, A. M., Alsaeed, W. Y., AlKhathami, M. A., & Al-Dhafeeri, A. H. (2017). Depression and Anxiety among Hypertensive and Diabetic Primary Health Care Patients: Could Patients' Perception of their Diseases Control be Used as a Screening Tool? *Saudi Medical Journal*, *38*(6), 621–628.

Alpert, J. M., Dyer, K. E., & Lafata, J. E. (2017). Patient-centered Communication in Digital Medical Encounters. *Patient Education and Counseling*, *100*(10), 1852–1858. https://doi.org/10.1016/j.pec.2017.04.019

Ammenwerth, E. (2018). From eHealth to ePatient: The Role of Patient Portals in Fostering Patient Empowerment. *European Journal of Biomedical Informatics*, *14*(2), 1–4.

Ammenwerth, E., Hörbst, A., Lannig, S., Mueller, G., Siebert, U., & Schnell-Inderst, P. (2019). Effects of Adult Patient Portals on Patient Empowerment and Health-Related Outcomes: A Systematic Review. *MedInfo*, *1*(1), 1106–1110.

Ammenwerth, E., Schnell-Inderst, P., & Hoerbst, A. (2012). The Impact of Electronic Patient Portals on Patient Care: A Systematic Review of Controlled trials. *Journal of Medical Internet Research*, *14*(6), 1–13.

Ancker, J. S., Barrón, Y., Rockoff, M. L., Hauser, D., Pichardo, M., Szerencsy, A., & Calman, N. (2011). Use of an Electronic Patient Portal among Disadvantaged Populations. *Journal of General Internal Medicine*, *26*(10), 1117–1123.

Anderson, R. M., & Funnell, M. M. (2010). Patient Empowerment: Myths and Misconceptions. *Patient Education and Counseling*, *79*(3), 277–282.

Antonio, M. G., Petrovskaya, O., & Lau, F. (2020). The State of Evidence in Patient Portals: Umbrella Review. *Journal of Medical Internet Research*, *22*(11), e23851.

Archer, N., Fevrier-Thomas, U., Lokker, C., McKibbon, K. A., & Straus, S. E. (2011). Personal Health Records: A Scoping Review. *Journal of the American Medical Informatics Association*, *18*(4), 515–522.

Atinga, R. A., Yarney, L., & Gavu, N. M. (2018). Factors Influencing Long-term Medication Non-adherence among Diabetes and Hypertensive Patients in Ghana: A Qualitative Investigation. *PloS one*, *13*(3), e0193995.

Aujoulat, I., d'Hoore, W., & Deccache, A. (2007). Patient Empowerment in Theory and Practice: Polysemy or Cacophony? *Patient Education and Counseling*, *66*(1), 13–20.

Brennan, P., & Safran, C. (2003). Report of Conference Track 3: Patient Empowerment. *International Journal of Medical Informatics*, *69*(2–3), 301–304. https://doi.org/10.1016/s1386-5056(03)00002-9

Field, A. (2013). *Discovering Statistics using IBM SPSS Statistics*. London: Sage Publications.

Funnell, M. M., Anderson, R. M., Arnold, M. S., Barr, P. A., Donnelly, M., Johnson, P. D., Taylor-Moon, D., & White, N. H. (1991). Empowerment: an Idea whose Time has Come in Diabetes Education. *The Diabetes Educator*, *17*(1), 37–41. https://doi.org/10.1177/014572179101700108

Goldzweig, C. L., Orshansky, G., Paige, N. M., Towfigh, A. A., Haggstrom, D. A., Miake-Lye, I., . . . Shekelle, P. G. (2013). Electronic Patient Portals: Evidence on Health Outcomes, Satisfaction, Efficiency, and Attitudes: A Systematic Review. *Annals of Internal Medicine*, *159*(10), 677–687.

Gozali, E., Langarizadeh, M., Sadooghi, F., & Sadeghi, M. (2014). Letter to Editor: Electronic Medical Record, Step toward Improving the Quality of Healthcare Services and Treatment Provided to Patients. *Journal of Ardabil University of Medical Sciences*, *14*(1), 93–96.

Graham, T. A. D., Ali, S., Avdagovska, M., & Ballermann, M. (2020). Effects of a Web-based Patient Portal on Patient Satisfaction and Missed Appointment Rates: Survey Study. *Journal of Medical Internet Research*, *22*(5), 1–8.

Griffin, A., Skinner, A., Thornhill, J., & Weinberger, M. (2016). Patient Portals: Who Uses Them? What Features Do they Use? And Do they Reduce Hospital Readmissions? *Applied Clinical Informatics*, *7*(2), 489.

Hjelm, N. (2005). Benefits and Drawbacks of Telemedicine. *Journal of Telemedicine and Telecare*, *11*(2), 60–70.

Hulter, P., Pluut, B., Leenen-Brinkhuis, C., de Mul, M., Ahaus, K., & Weggelaar-Jansen, A. M. (2020). Adopting Patient Portals in Hospitals: Qualitative Study. *Journal of Medical Internet Research*, *22*(5), 1–12. e16921.

Irani, J. S., Middleton, J. L., Marfatia, R., Omana, E. T., & D'Amico, F. (2009). The Use of Electronic Health Records in the Exam Room and Patient Satisfaction: A Systematic Review. *The Journal of the American Board of Family Medicine*, *22*(5), 553–562.

Irizarry, T., Dabbs, A. D., & Curran, C. R. (2015). Patient Portals and Patient Engagement: A State of the Science Review. *Journal of Medical Internet Research*, *17*(6), 1–15. e148.

Kazley, A. S., Diana, M. L., Ford, E. W., & Menachemi, N. (2012). Is Electronic Health Record Use Associated with Patient Satisfaction in Hospitals? *Health Care Management Review*, *37*(1), 23–30.

Kelly, M. M., Coller, R. J., & Hoonakker, P. L. (2018). Inpatient Portals for Hospitalized Patients and Caregivers: A Systematic Review. *Journal of Hospital Medicine*, *13*(6), 405.

Kruse, C. S., Bolton, K., & Freriks, G. (2015). The Effect of Patient Portals on Quality Outcomes and its Implications to Meaningful Use: A Systematic Review. *Journal of Medical Internet Research*, *17*(2), e44.

Lau, J., Knudsen, J., Jackson, H., Wallach, A. B., Bouton, M., Natsui, S., . . . Avalone, L. (2020). Staying Connected in the COVID-19 Pandemic: Telehealth at the Largest Safety-Net System in the United States: A Description of NYC Health+ Hospitals Telehealth Response to the COVID-19 Pandemic. *Health Affairs*, *39*(8), 1437–1442.

Lee, S. M., & Trimi, S. (2021). Convergence Innovation in the Digital Age And in the COVID-19 Pandemic Crisis. *Journal of Business Research*, *123*, 14–22.

Lester, M., Boateng, S., Studeny, J., & Coustasse, A. (2016). Personal Health Records: Beneficial or Burdensome for Patients and Healthcare Providers? *Perspectives in Health Information Management*, *13*(4), 1–12.

Pekonen, A., Eloranta, S., Stolt, M., Virolainen, P., & Leino-Kilpi, H. (2020). Measuring Patient Empowerment – A Systematic Review. *Patient Education and Counseling*, *103*(4), 777–787. https://doi.org/10.1016/j.pec.2019.10.019

Piette, J. D., Schillinger, D., Potter, M. B., & Heisler, M. (2003). Dimensions of Patient-provider Communication and Diabetes Self-care in an Ethnically Diverse Population. *Journal of General Internal Medicine*, *18*(8), 624–633.

Prentice, J. C., Davies, M. L., & Pizer, S. D. (2014). Which Outpatient Wait-time Measures are Related to Patient Satisfaction? *American Journal of Medical Quality*, *29*(3), 227–235.

Risling, T., Martinez, J., Young, J., & Thorp-Froslie, N. (2018). Defining Empowerment and Supporting Engagement Using Patient Views from the Citizen Health Information Portal: Qualitative Study. *JMIR Medical Informatics*, *6*(3), 1–10.

Roehrs, A., Da Costa, C. A., da Rosa Righi, R., & De Oliveira, K. S. F. (2017). Personal Health Records: A Systematic Literature Review. *Journal of Medical Internet Research*, *19*(1), e13.

Sarkar, U., & Bates, D. W. (2014). Care Partners and Online Patient Portals. *JAMA*, *311*(4), 357–358.

Small, N., Bower, P., Chew-Graham, C. A., Whalley, D., & Protheroe, J. (2013). Patient Empowerment in Long-term Conditions: Development and Preliminary Testing of a New Measure. *BMC Health Services Research*, *13*(1), 1–15.

Søreide, K., Hallet, J., Matthews, J. B., Schnitzbauer, A. A., Line, P. D., Lai, P., . . . Baxter, N. N. (2020). Immediate and Long-term Impact of the COVID-19 Pandemic on Delivery of Surgical Services. *The British Journal of Surgery*, *107*(10), 1250–1261.

Wilkinson, A. (1998). Empowerment: Theory and Practice. *Development in Practice*, *5*(2), 1–8.

Wootton, R. (2001). Telemedicine. *BMJ*, *323*(7312), 557–560.

Authors' Profile

Dr. Roger A. Atinga is a senior lecturer in the Department of Public Administration and Health Services Management, University of Ghana Business School. He holds a PhD in health policy and management. His research is mainly evidence driven toward improving quality, responsiveness, and management practices in health systems and institutions. He has a wealth of teaching and research experience spanning nearly a decade. His research is at the intersection of health policy, health systems management, implementation and healthcare quality, drawing secondary and primary data from health providers, users, and communities. He has attended several peer-reviewed international conferences and presented papers as well as Chaired sessions. He is an author and coauthor of several book chapters and Journal Articles published in peer-reviewed international journals. He is currently an Editorial Board Member of another of international journals.

Anita Asiwome Baku holds a PhD in management from the Putra Business School in Malaysia and is currently a senior lecturer in the Department of Public Administration and Health Services Management at the University of Ghana Business School, Legon. She teaches courses in health services management and her research covers health management, health insurance, social insurance, occupational safety, and health marketing health services. Her writings cover book chapters and journal articles. She is also a reviewer for some international journals is health, social policy, and occupational safety and health.

Chapter 20

Innovation and Healthcare in the Next Decade

Philip Afeti Korto, Anita Asiwome Adzo Baku, Nurudeen Issaka Idrisu, and Nana Akua Boateng-Amartey

Contents

Introduction

The different perceptions held by people inform how they define various concepts and the meanings that are deduced from these concepts. For instance, a horse is viewed as the genus mammalian quadruped to the zoologist, a means of transportation to the traveler, the king of sports to the average person and others, a means of food (Morris, 1965; cited in Rai, 2010). Similarly, various authors have defined innovation differently; hence, no universally accepted definition exists in the literature for the concept of innovation and there is no one best definition for the concept. The definition of innovation is usually context-specific and dependent on the subject area in contention. For instance, Baregheh et al. (2009) define innovation as a process by which an organization transforms ideas into a product or service to compete in its market space. Rogers (2003) defines innovation as an idea, a practice, or a project considered as new by interested persons. The element of change can be observed in the definitions cited. It is, thus, an intentional change to an existing product or service. One may thus define innovation as a conscious effort directed at transforming

DOI: 10.4324/9781003152217-25

an existing product, service, idea, procedure, and something else into a form that serves the desired purpose more appropriately and yields more quality and expeditious results.

Just like innovation in the generic sense of the concept, a plethora of definitions for healthcare innovation in the literature also exist. Globally, however, healthcare innovation can be conceptualized as an intervention aimed at achieving optimal health for people. The WHO defines healthcare innovation as an intentional, value-adding healthcare intervention meant to develop and deliver new or improved healthcare policies, systems, products, and technologies as well as services and healthcare delivery methods that improve the health status of a people (WHO, 2016). According to the organization, a healthcare innovation must respond appropriately to the unmet healthcare needs of a given community, and it must improve efficiency, effectiveness, quality, safety, and affordability of healthcare (WHO, 2016). In keeping with this, Kimble and Massoud (2017) opined that in healthcare, there is often the anticipation that change will result in solving an existing problem. Regardless of the form in which the healthcare innovation is introduced, it is ideally required to solve the healthcare problem for which it was designed. Mindful of the fact that the healthcare innovations may be implemented in the form of new public policies, Korto (2019, p. 238) cautioned poignantly, "regardless of how comprehensive, well-articulated, sound or good an adopted public policy may appear on paper, it is of no use unless the policy is effectively implemented by street-level bureaucrats to solve the societal problem(s) identified". Suffice to say that the usefulness of healthcare innovations lies in their effective and timely application to unmet healthcare needs affecting an entire society or only a segment of it. One may pose a question for example that to what extent has Ghana's Free Maternal Healthcare Policy impacted positively on maternal healthcare affordability and for that matter, maternal mortality ratios in Ghana?

Omachonu and Einspruch (2010) suggest two dimensions of healthcare innovation: the environmental and operational dimensions. These two dimensions are believed to affect or motivate the introduction of healthcare innovations. The environmental dimension encapsulates physician acceptance, organizational culture, regulatory acceptance, partnerships, and collaborations. On the other hand, the operational dimension of healthcare, innovation includes the improvement of clinical outcomes, efficiency, effectiveness, aging population, nursing shortage, patient satisfaction, profitability, patient safety, improved quality, and cost containment (Omachonu & Einspruch, 2010). Globally, the proliferation of healthcare innovation has been aimed at increasing life expectancy, improving diagnostics and treatment options, improving quality of life, efficiency, and effectiveness in healthcare systems (Omachonu & Einspruch, 2010). In the public sector, healthcare innovations take different forms, and they may be small or giant strides made to save lives. For example, Aziato et al., 2019) have noted telemedicine and mobile health (m-health) are two major innovations used in Africa to improve geographical accessibility to healthcare.

It is, however, sad to note that most African countries are not committing monies to finance their healthcare, by extension innovations in the sector, and this may be the reason why most African countries could not achieve the erstwhile Millennium Development Goals (MDGs) by the 2015 deadline. In 2001, for example, African countries signed the African Union's Abuja Declaration, with each member state pledging to allocate not less than 15% of its annual budget to healthcare financing, aside from donor supports in that regard (African Union, 2001; WHO, 2011). Ten years after the Abuja Declaration, the WHO (2011) found that only Rwanda and South Africa had complied with the declaration. Three other countries (Eritrea, Mauritius, and Seychelles) were on track while 27 countries made no progress at all or the progress made was insufficient. The rest of the countries had either reduced their budgetary allocations to healthcare or there was no obvious trend (downward or upward). Al-Bader et al. (2010) posit that even though there is a surge in healthcare innovations and their use globally, it is unclear what African countries are doing to solve their high disease burden status. The authors argue that emerging economies such as Brazil, China, and India have developed business models and low-cost innovations to resolve their healthcare problems (Al-Bader et al., 2010, p. 1). It is, therefore, the responsibility of African countries to finance the introduction of technological healthcare innovations in their healthcare training institutions and healthcare facilities to enable healthcare professionals to be conversant with technological healthcare innovation use.

Touching on the forms of healthcare innovations, Omachonu and Einspruch (2010) reasoned that some innovations may be in the form of an improvement in the service delivery process or the production process while another innovation may be in the form of structural transformations, thereby affecting the internal and external infrastructures to create new models. Largely, the health sector of Ghana has been involved in incremental innovations. Incremental innovation involves the utilization of existing technology to improve service quality. Incremental innovations occur continuously and at varying rates in various service delivery sectors over different periods (Garcia & Calantone, 2002). This may take the form of incremental or small changes to service delivery. One of such incremental innovation examples is the Ghana Health Service's (GHS's) introduction of an electronic health information management software called District Health Information Management System (DHIMS2) to improve its service delivery. DHIMS2 serves as the data warehouse of the GHS and is used for healthcare information management nationwide. DHIMS2 provides for various data entry windows, thereby making it possible for health facility managers to replicate their paper-based data collection tools in electronic forms. The software equally serves as a dashboard that enables cursory monitoring and evaluation of healthcare programs through analysis of key healthcare performance indicators including but not limited to epidemiological patterns, in general, and maternal mortality ratios.

One important aspect of the DHIMS2 software innovation is that it can equally help donors in the health sector of Ghana to monitor performances from afar. For example, using the DHIMS2 software, the Global Fund can monitor and evaluate the effectiveness of its support for treatments for HIV/AIDS, Malaria, and Tuberculosis in Ghana. The future implication of this innovation is that the hospitals under the GHS should be able to issue automated hospital identification (ID) cards to patients. This way, a patient can use ID cards obtained at one public hospital to access healthcare seamlessly at another public hospital. The automated ID card system should be able to reflect the clinical history of the patient irrespective of the hospital that issued the cards. This will cut down on the time doctors use to clerk patients and obtain their clinical history anytime a patient is visiting a particular public hospital for care. The patient's hospital ID should, therefore, be automated like the ATM cards banks issue to their clients. Ghana's health sector's ICT policy, therefore, needs a review to take care of recommendations of this type in the next decade.

Empirical evidence (see Scott & Scott, 2019) also reveals that some African countries such as Rwanda, Ghana, and Malawi have resorted to the use of drones as a means of transporting certain healthcare supplies, especially to remote areas. This is intended to overcome the challenges of transporting blood products, medications, HIV Test Kits, and vaccines to the peripheral part of the country on time. Sustaining these healthcare innovations and further improving on them in the next decade will significantly improve the quality of healthcare delivery. Said differently, sustaining laudable healthcare innovations for the next decade in Africa will not only improve geographical accessibility to healthcare but also reduce mortality ratios, as preventable deaths will no longer occur as is currently happening. In the next decade, various countries including Ghana need to explore other technological advancements that will facilitate the air transport of other healthcare commodities heavier than blood and medications.

The dynamic nature of healthcare and modern technology has necessitated many healthcare innovations and advanced techniques worldwide (Aziato et al., 2019). The caution, however, is that healthcare innovations must not just be introduced but must be effectively implemented to improve the health statuses of the people being served. It is one thing introducing a healthcare innovation and quite another the innovation being appropriate for improving patient outcomes in terms of reducing morbidity and mortality burdens. Globally, healthcare innovations have been associated with new developments in different forms in the healthcare delivery spectrum, and such new developments are aimed at solving health problems that affect an entire community or only a segment of the community (Kimble & Massoud, 2017). Accordingly, Ghana's healthcare innovation applications in the next decade must be patient-centered and user-friendly to produce results that ease the disease burden of the people. It is also imperative that healthcare innovations comply with the legal and regulatory demands in the country. The financial resources that are prerequisites for effective implementation of the innovations to achieve the desired health outcomes must also be made available.

The sustainability of the various healthcare innovations cited in the public sector of Ghana and how impactful they may be in healthcare delivery in the country in the next decade must be a concern for health policymakers, healthcare workers, policy analysts, patient groups, and other stakeholders. Arguably, if these innovations are not sustained, and further strengthened with additional innovations to tackle healthcare problems of the next decade, mortality and morbidity burdens may worsen. In the following paragraphs, issues relating to innovations in the health sector of Low- and Middle-Income Countries (LMICs) developing countries have been discussed and suggestions were made on how to surmount the barriers that embarking to some of these innovations.

Proposed Healthcare Innovations in the Next Decade

The Digitalization of Health for the Next Decade

The digitalization of the health system is one of the many ways of bringing about innovation and improvement in the health sector of LMICs. Several studies have identified the prospects of digitalization and mobile technology in improving the population's access to healthcare in LMICs. Prior to introducing digital healthcare services, some patients such as pregnant women were unable to access maternal and child health services (e.g., antenatal and postpartum services) easily, those suffering from chronic and noncommunicable diseases as well as adolescents also found the services inaccessible (Chib et al., 2015; Shuvo et al., 2015; Sondaal et al., 2016). The digitalization effort should permeate all aspects of the health sector from networking patient records, appointment systems, using digitalized means of contacting patients, providing access, and improving general health outcomes. Many issues plague LMICs and of all these geographical and financial access remain high on the list (Kruk et al., 2018).

Some innovations that the health systems of low- and middle-income countries could adopt include mobile health services known as mHealth. mHealth is the use of mobile telephone technology to provide health services such as educational information, emergency responses, support services, monitoring, and reminders. The benefits of the use of mobile technology in solving health problems have been well documented. Some include increasing geographical and financial access to healthcare and reducing waiting times and cost of transportation. Adopting such innovation and rolling it out to cover the entire population should be the focus of policymakers for the next decade. The rolling out of mHealth services in LMICs especially in Africa is possible because according to Myovella et al. (2020) mobile subscription in Sub-Saharan Africa stood at about 77 persons in every 100 persons in 2018. In Ghana, for instance, the mobile subscription rate stands at about 41 million (National Communications Authority, 2020) with a population of about 30 million. An addition to the current mHealth services that policymakers in LMICs could consider is mConsultation suggested by Griffiths et al. (2020). mConsultation is the use of mobile telephones to consult doctors on a platform created for such purpose Griffiths et al. (2020).

Digitalizing the national health system of LMICs by creating a National Health Information System that compiles patient information for administrative and improvement of patient care for all citizens is one of the ways of using innovation for the next decade. Most emerging economies operate a healthcare system that is publicly funded and fragmented in terms of patient information systems. Some currently still use paper systems for storing patient information. Such a system implies that the patient would have to be telling clinicians their health history (as far as they could remember). A digitalized system is beneficial to the patient, the healthcare facilities, and the health system as a whole, and the policymaker. The information can be used for patient management, hospital planning, development of treatment protocols, and national development planning purposes.

Another health innovation that LMICs could focus on in the next decade is the use of Artificial Intelligence (AI) to reach out to the many people who do not have access to healthcare. AI is defined as the mimicking of human cognition by a computer (Jha & Topol, 2016). AI activities include adoption, learning, reasoning self-correction, and interaction. The use of AI in health holds the potential of increasing accessibility to health, reducing the need for investment in some hardware, increasing compliance to medical regimes, reducing stigmatization among populations easily susceptible to stigmatization because of health conditions such as HIV or mental health issues. Disease spread and conditions could be easily picked up among population groups through AI (Alami et al., 2020). LMICs could invest in AI applications for the next decade to improve health and health outcomes of their populations.

The Use of Crowdsourcing in Solving Health Issues

Crowdsourcing is a process of seeking sustainable solutions to problems that plague a group of people. It is a mechanism that has often been used by developed countries to develop innovative solutions to problems (van Niekerk et al., 2020). These solutions are arrived at through competition where problems are identified and solutions to these problems are solicited and the best solution in terms of how best the problem is solved, in relation to cost is chosen (van Niekerk et al., 2020). The beauty of crowdsourcing is that solutions to problems are provided by people who experience the problem and are thus in a good position to suggest sustainable solutions. In the area of health, crowdsourcing has been identified as having assisted in health promotion, oncology and surgery, and psychiatry (Créquit et al., 2018) and in high-income countries such as the United States, Canada, and Australia (van Niekerk et al., 2020). The use of crowdsourcing as a solution finder is believed to lead to collecting large volumes of data within a short time, saves cost on data collection and researchers have access to data in real time as technology is used to collect the data (Srinivas et al., 2020).

In finding solution to health problems over the next decade, LMICs could adopt this as an innovation in solving the numerous problems that afflict it. This process of involving community members, non-governmental organizations, and social entrepreneurs in solving a health problem will go a long way to reveal innovative approaches that have the buy-in of citizens because the solution emanates from them. Thus, decision-makers would not have to invest so much into research, prior to financing solutions identified. The disease burdens of LMICs could, thus, be greatly reduced through the provision of local initiatives. In addition, crowdsourcing in solving health problems is not a new phenomenon.

Use of Social Innovation to Solve Health Problems

Closely related to the use of crowdsourcing in solving health problems is a concept known as social innovation. Social innovation is a concept that is used to explain new ideas or products that result in a change in the status quo of doing things (Westley & Antadze, 2010). Social innovations are believed to have survived when systems and structures have failed in solving problems (Mulgan et al., 2007). In LMICs where the disease burden is double and attaining the sustainable development goals appear to be impossible for several reasons including limited resources, and more recently the issue of COVID-19, it is important that things are done differently to enable the attainment of the health goals of these countries. Attributes of social innovations include combination of existing ideas or elements, cutting across disciplines, and organizations and leading to the formation of new social relationships (Mulgan et al., 2007).

In the area of health, social innovations in the development of a diagnostic Malaria test kit for schoolchildren in Malawi (Srinivas et al., 2020). This social innovation was aimed at identifying the onset of Malaria among schoolchildren before they even get sick so that early treatment can be administered. Teachers were trained to do the test and administer treatment. In Peru where there exists a high incidence rate of cervical cancer, self-test kits were developed with pictorial description of how-to self-test and given to rural women, who performed the test and mailed the results to a lab in the capital for diagnosis and results communicated back to the women. In the next decade, LMICs could invest in seeking some of these social innovations that are peculiar to their populace to solve issues relating to communicable and noncommunicable diseases.

Summoning Potential Barriers to Innovation in the Next Decade

Innovation for the next decade is susceptible to some barriers that would prevent the efficiency and effectiveness of a health system to achieve its goals. Leonard et al. (2020) have identified seven factors that should be considered by policymakers in their quest to ensure that innovation started is sustainable and beneficial to healthcare seekers. These seven factors include the innovation itself, the institutions, the actors, the network and relationships, the context, the resources, and the knowledge required to ensure successful implementation.

The innovation to be adopted to improve the health system for the next decade in LMICs should be such that it is needs-based, user friendly, and the perceived benefits can be easily observable by the users and the beneficiaries (Aamir et al., 2018; Starmann et al., 2018; Mars & Scott, 2017). In addition, the cost of the innovation should be considered. The cost of acquiring, implementing, and using the innovation could prevent the adoption or use of the innovation and must be part of the considerations in instituting an innovation (Diaconu et al., 2017; Oppong, 2015). Issues of perceived threats (disadvantages of the innovation), benefits of the innovation (improved health status or economic benefits), the ability of the innovation to operate smoothly in the existing healthcare system, thus interoperability of the innovation could serve as a barrier (Starmann et al., 2018). Evidence of the ability of the innovation to do what it is supposed to do affects its credibility, legitimacy, and integrity. Also, the security and privacy offered by the innovation could affect its acceptability (Kiberu et al., 2017). Finally, the durability of the innovation (Diaconu et al., 2017), the need for frequent updates must be carefully considered by policymakers to ensure successful implementation by institutions.

The institutions are the organizational procedures, laws, policies, and practices that regulate innovation in a country (Leonard et al., 2020). For a successful implementation and sustainability of innovation, innovation policies must be aligned with the health goals of the system, supportive, and should not be inconsistent with other policies (Fowkes et al., 2016; Aamir et al., 2018). The regulatory environment must be supportive of the innovation and professionals must be regulated (Diaconu et al., 2017; Tran Ngoc et al., 2018; Bloom et al., 2017). In addition, standards of innovation must be clearly set and enforced to ensure compliance (Kiberu et al., 2017; Puchalski Ritchie et al., 2016). Ensuring the protection of intellectual property such as patent protection, patent monopolies, and the licensing of propriety would lead to more innovations in the health sector (Spicer et al., 2018).

Successful implementation of healthcare innovation in the next decade should be linked to continuous in-service training programs for the implementers. In ensuring knowledge as a facilitator of innovation in healthcare, continuous education in healthcare innovation, in the classroom, as well as on the job is necessary. The dissemination, as well as the quality of that dissemination of innovation to important stakeholders, adds to enhancing knowledge on innovation, thereby reducing the probability of failure of healthcare innovation. Also, improving access to local and international research on innovation increases the chances of success of any healthcare innovation. Building local capacity by advancing local research in innovation and encouraging the implementation of their finding in policymaking enhances innovation (Mbau & Gilson, 2018; Shayan et al., 2019).

Another factor that must be considered in the successful implementation of healthcare innovation is network and relationships. This involves collaborations between all the stakeholders in healthcare innovations. These include healthcare institutions, communities, and healthcare service providers. Clarity of the roles of the various stakeholders must be defined, leadership for the process of innovation must be well established, supportive relationships must be encouraged among stakeholders, collaborations, particularly among researchers and healthcare professionals must be encouraged and partnerships for healthcare innovation forged on effective communication is also important (Tomlinson et al., 2018; Aamir et al., 2018; Tomlinson et al., 2018).

Closely related to network and relationships is the actors involved in the innovation process. The innovation implementation organization may have some organizational cultural practices that may impede or enhance innovation implementation. Positive cultures, such as culture of learning, and compliance are desirable, while culture of resistance to change and discrimination are to be avoided if healthcare innovation is to succeed. Recognizing innovation ownership, monetary appreciation, empowerment, and career advancement facilitates innovation implementation. Attitudes such as confidence, enthusiasm, and trust must be encouraged (McRobie et al., 2017; Tran Ngoc et al., 2018; Mbau & Gilson, 2018).

An understanding of the context of healthcare innovation is also essential. The context connotes the environment within which the innovation is taking place. For the successful implementation and sustainability of healthcare innovation in LMICs, issues of commitment of the political leadership, nonpartisan politicization of the innovation process, reduction of corruption must be considered. Also, if the innovation involves extensive use of healthcare facilities, then care must be taken to ensure equitable distribution of these facilities. Policymakers must take into consideration the sociocultural context of the people to whom the innovation is being suggested. Some of these sociocultural factors include religious and cultural beliefs, issues of gender, and traditional and cultural practices must be examined in the context of the innovation to ensure successful implementation. The literacy level of the population, employment levels, occupations, affordability, and the epidemiological pattern of the population group are all contextual considerations for policymakers and implementers of health innovations for the next decade (Bertone et al., 2018; Bertone et al., 2018; Mbau & Gilson, 2018).

Finally, the resources component of the seven factors that influence innovation implementation success is what is available for the successful implementation of an innovation. These resources relate to financial, human, time, and physical (Leonard et al., 2020). In relation to human resource, the existence of a promoter of the innovation, particularly in the health sector, is important. In addition, health workers involved in the implementation should not be overburdened. Physical infrastructure necessary for the implementation of the innovation must also be available. Sustainable source of funding the innovation must be ensured, and the ability of citizens to pay for the services must be equally considered. Queues, travel time to access the innovation, availability of time for training health professionals must all be considered so that the health innovation is successfully implemented (Cunningham et al., 2016; Spicer et al., 2018; Nielsen et al., 2018; Glasziou et al., 2017; Tran Ngoc et al., 2018).

Conclusion

The attainment of the Sustainable Development Goals by LMICs is hinged on how innovative the managers of the healthcare system are. Continuously doing the same thing appears not to be yielding the desired results. Innovation is critically needed, and healthcare innovation must is acceptable to the citizens and sustainable for the long term. Policymakers in LMICs need not reinvent the wheel on innovation. Benchmarking innovative practices in other countries and learning from the best is the way to go. This is what Rogers (2003) refers to as diffusion of innovation. This chapter has discussed some healthcare invocations for the next decade that would assist policymakers in attaining their health goals through home-grown solutions. A caution on how to overcome possible challenges in the implementation of those innovations has also been suggested.

References

Aamir, J., Ali, S. M., Boulos, M. N. K., Anjum, N., & Ishaq, M. (2018). Enablers and Inhibitors: A Review of the Situation Regarding mHealth Adoption in Low-and middle-income Countries. *Health Policy and Technology*, *7*(1), 88–97.

African Union. (2001). Abuja Declaration on HIV/AIDS, Tuberculosis and other Related Infectious Diseases. OAU/SPS/Abuja/3;27. [Google Scholar]

Alami, H., Lehoux, P., Gagnon, M. P., Fortin, J. P., Fleet, R., & Ahmed, M. A. A. (2020). Rethinking the Electronic Health Record through the Quadruple Aim: Time to Align its Value with the Health System. *BMC Medical Informatics and Decision Making*, *20*(1), 1–5.

Al-Bader, S., Msum, H., Simivu, K., Daar, A. S., & Singer, P. A. (2010). Science-based Health Innovation in Sub-Saharan Africa. *BMC International Health and Human Rights*, *10*(Suppl 1:51), 1–9.

Aziato, L., Ohene, L. A., & Adjei, C. A. (2019). The Societal and Healthcare Context. In E. R. Hinson, K. Osei-Frimpong, O. Adeola, & L. Aziato (Eds.), *Health Service Marketing Management in Africa* (pp. 227–242). New York: Taylor & Francis Group.

Baregheh, A., Rowley, J., & Sambrook, S. (2009). Towards a Multi-disciplinary Definition of Innovation. *Management Decisions*, *47*(8), 1323–1339.

Bertone, M. P., Jacobs, E., Toonen, J., Akwataghibe, N., & Witter, S. (2018). Performance-based Financing in Three Humanitarian Settings: Principles and Pragmatism. *Conflict and Health*, *12*(1), 1–14.

Bloom, N., Van Reenen, J., & Williams, H. (2019). A Toolkit of Policies to Promote Innovation. *Journal of Economic Perspectives*, *33*(3), 163–184.

Chib, A., van Velthoven, M. H., & Car, J. (2015). mHealth Adoption in Low-resource Environments: A Review of the Use of Mobile Healthcare in Developing Countries. *Journal of Health Communication*, *20*(1), 4–34.

Créquit, P., Mansouri, G., Benchoufi, M., Vivot, A., & Ravaud, P. (2018). Mapping of Crowdsourcing in Health: Systematic Review. *Journal of Medical Internet Research*, *20*(5), e187.

Cunningham, P., Gök, A., & Larédo, P. (2016). The Impact of Direct Support to R & D and Innovation in Firms. In *Handbook of Innovation Policy Impact*. Cheltenham: Edward Elgar Publishing.

Diaconu, K., Chen, Y. F., Cummins, C., Moyao, G. J., Manaseki-Holland, S., & Lilford, R. (2017). Methods for Medical Device and Equipment Procurement and Prioritization within Low-and Middle-income Countries: Findings of a Systematic Literature Review. *Globalization and Health*, *13*(1), 1–16.

Fowkes, F. J., Draper, B. L., Hellard, M., & Stoové, M. (2016). Achieving Development Goals for HIV, Tuberculosis and Malaria in sub-Saharan Africa through Integrated Antenatal Care: Barriers and Challenges. *BMC Medicine*, *14*(1), 1–10.

Garcia, R., & Calantone, R. (2002). A Critical Look at Technological Innovation Typology and Innovativeness Terminology: A Literature Review. *Journal of Product Innovation Management*, *19*(2), 110–132.

Glasziou, P., Straus, S., Brownlee, S., Trevena, L., Dans, L., Guyatt, G., . . . & Saini, V. (2017). Evidence for Underuse of Effective Medical Services around the World. *The Lancet*, *390*(10090), 169–177.

Griffiths, F., Watkins, J. A., Huxley, C., Harris, B., Cave, J., Pemba, S., . . . & Sturt, J. (2020). Mobile Consulting (mConsulting) and Its Potential for Providing Access to Quality Healthcare for Populations Living in Low-Resource Settings of Low-and Middle-Income Countries. *Digital Health*, *6*, 1–7. 2055207620919594.

Jha, S., & Topol, E. J. (2016). Adapting to Artificial Intelligence: Radiologists and Pathologists as Information Specialists. *JAMA*, *316*(22), 2353–2354.

Kiberu, V. M., Mars, M., & Scott, R. E. (2017). Barriers and Opportunities to Implementation of Sustainable e-Health Programmes in Uganda: A Literature Review. *African Journal of Primary Health Care & Family Medicine*, *9*(1), 1–10.

Kimble, L., & Massoud, M. R. (2017). What Do We Mean by Innovation in Healthcare? *EMJ Innov*, *1*(1), 89–91.

Korto, P. A. (2019). Managing Policies and Procedures in Healthcare Management. In E. R. Hinson, K. Osei-Frimpong, O. Adeola, & L. Aziato (Eds.), *Health Service Marketing Management in Africa* (pp. 227–242). New York: Taylor & Francis Group.

Kruk, M. E., Gage, A. D., Arsenault, C., Jordan, K., Leslie, H. H., Roder-DeWan, S.,. . Pate, M. (2018). High-quality Health Systems in the Sustainable Development Goals Era: Time for a Revolution. *The Lancet Global Health*, *6*(11), e1196–e1252.

Leonard, E., de Kock, I., & Bam, W. (2020). Barriers and Facilitators to Implementing Evidence-based Health Innovations in Low-and Middle-income Countries: A Systematic Literature Review. *Evaluation and Program Planning*, *82*, 101832.

Mars, M., & Scott, R. E. (2017). Being Spontaneous: The Future of Telehealth Implementation? *Telemedicine and e-Health*, *23*(9), 766–772.

Mbau, R., & Gilson, L. (2018). Influence of Organisational Culture on the Implementation of Health Sector Reforms in Low-and Middle-income Countries: A Qualitative Interpretive Review. *Global Health Action*, *11*(1), 1462579.

McRobie, E., Wringe, A., Nakiyingi-Miiro, J., Kiweewa, F., Lutalo, T., Nakigozi, G., . . . Church, K. (2017). HIV Policy Implementation in Two Health and Demographic Surveillance Sites in Uganda: Findings from a National Policy Review, Health Facility Surveys and Key Informant Interviews. *Implementation Science*, *12*(1), 1–12.

Mulgan, G., Tucker, S., Ali, R., & Sanders, B. (2007). *Social Innovation: What it is, Why it Matters and How it can be Accelerated, Skoll Centre for Social Entrepreneurship*. London: Young Foundation.

Myovella, G., Karacuka, M., & Haucap, J. (2020). Digitalization and Economic Growth: A Comparative Analysis of Sub-Saharan Africa and OECD Economies. *Telecommunications Policy, 44*(2), 101856.

National Communications Authority (NCA). (2020). *Quarterly Statistical Bulletin on Communications in Ghana. April - June 2020*. Accra, Ghana: National Communications Authority. https://www.nca.org. gh/assets/Q2-2020-Statistical-Bulletin-v3.pdf

Nielsen, M. W., Bloch, C. W., & Schiebinger, L. (2018). Making Gender Diversity Work for Scientific Discovery and Innovation. *Nature Human Behaviour, 2*(10), 726–734.

Omachonu, V. K., & Einspruch, N. G. (2010, October). Innovation in Healthcare Delivery Systems: A Conceptual Framework. *The Innovation Journal: The Public Sector Innovation Journal, 15*(1), 1–20.

Oppong, F. C. (2015). Innovation in Income-Poor Environments. *Journal of British Surgery, 102*(2), e102–e107.

Rai, N. (2010, April 28). Law as a Means of Social Change with Reference to Case of Daughter's Right in Parental Property. Available at SSRN: http://ssrn.com/abstract=1597227 or http://dx.doi.org/10.2139/ssrn.1597227

Ritchie, L. M. P., Khan, S., Moore, J. E., Timmings, C., van Lettow, M., Vogel, J. P., . . . Straus, S. E. (2016). Low-and Middle-income Countries Face Many Common Barriers to Implementation of Maternal Health Evidence Products. *Journal of Clinical Epidemiology, 76*, 229–237.

Rogers, E. M. (2003). *Diffusion of Innovations* (5th ed.). New York: Free Press.

Scott, J. E., & Scott, C. H. (2019). Models for Drone Delivery of Medications and other Healthcare Items. In *Unmanned Aerial Vehicles: Breakthroughs in Research and Practice* (pp. 376–392). Hershey, PA: IGI Global.

Shayan, S. J., Kiwanuka, F., & Nakaye, Z. (2019). Barriers Associated with Evidence-based Practice among Nurses in Low-and Middle-income Countries: A Systematic Review. *Worldviews on Evidence-Based Nursing, 16*(1), 12–20.

Shuvo, T. A., Islam, R., Hossain, S., Evans, J. L., Khatun, F., Ahmed, T., . . . Adams, A. M. (2015). eHealth Innovations in LMICs of Africa and Asia: A Literature Review Exploring Factors Affecting Implementation, Scale-up, and Sustainability. *Innovation and Entrepreneurship in Health, 2*, 95–106.

Sondaal, S. F. V., Browne, J. L., Amoakoh-Coleman, M., Borgstein, A., Miltenburg, A. S., Verwijs, M., & Klipstein-Grobusch, K. (2016). Assessing the Effect of mHealth Interventions in Improving Maternal and Neonatal Care in Low-and Middle-income Countries: A Systematic Review. *PloS one, 11*(5), e0154664.

Spicer, N., Hamza, Y. A., Berhanu, D., Gautham, M., Schellenberg, J., Tadesse, F., . . . & Wickremasinghe, D. (2018). 'The Development Sector is a Graveyard of Pilot Projects!' Six Critical Actions for Externally Funded Implementers to Foster Scale-Up of Maternal and Newborn Health Innovations in Low and Middle-Income Countries. *Globalization and Health, 14*(1), 1–13.

Srinivas, M. L., Yang, E. J., Shrestha, P., Wu, D., Peeling, R. W., & Tucker, J. D. (2020). Social Innovation in Diagnostics: Three Case Studies. *Infectious Diseases of Poverty, 9*(1), 1–7.

Starmann, E., Heise, L., Kyegombe, N., Devries, K., Abramsky, T., Michau, L.,. . Collumbien, M. (2018). Examining Diffusion to Understand the How of SASA!, a Violence against Women and HIV Prevention Intervention in Uganda. *BMC Public Health, 18*(1), 1–20.

Tomlinson, M., Hunt, X., & Rotheram-Borus, M. J. (2018). Diffusing and Scaling Evidence-based Interventions: Eight Lessons for Early Child Development from the Implementation of Perinatal Home Visiting in South Africa. *Annals of the New York Academy of Sciences, 1419*(1), 218–229.

Tran Ngoc, C., Bigirimana, N., Muneene, D., Bataringaya, J. E., Barango, P., Eskandar, H., . . . & Olu, O. (2018, August). Conclusions of the Digital Health Hub of the Transform Africa Summit (2018): Strong Government Leadership and Public-Private-Partnerships are Key Prerequisites for Sustainable Scale Up of Digital Health in Africa. In *BMC Proceedings* (Vol. 12, No. 11, pp. 1–7). BioMed Central.

van Niekerk, L., Ongkeko, A., Hounsell, R. A., Msiska, B. K., Mathanga, D. P., Mothe, J., . . . Balabanova, D. (2020). Crowdsourcing to Identify Social Innovation Initiatives in Health in Low-and Middle-income Countries. *Infectious Diseases of Poverty, 9*(1), 1–12.

Westley, F., & Antadze, N. (2010). Making a Difference: Strategies for Scaling Social Innovation for Greater Impact. *Innovation Journal, 15*(2).

World Health Organization (WHO). (2011). *The Abuja Declaration: Ten Years On*. Geneva. www.who.int/ healthsystems/publications/abuja_report_aug_2011.pdf

World Health Organization. (2016). *Innovation*. Retrieved February 2, 2021, from www.who.int/topics topics/innovation/en/

Authors' Profile

Philip Afeti Korto is a seasoned Public Administrator. He is a professional and astute Health Service Administrator who has been practicing for over a decade. He has worked as a Health Service Administrator in the Ghana Health Service for 15 years, where he managed Administration and Support Services at three different hospitals such as Dangme East District, La General, and Achimota Hospitals. His strengths are in management, public policy implementation and writing media articles. Currently, Mr. Korto is an Assistant Registrar at the University of Health and Allied Sciences (UHAS), Ho, Ghana. He is a prolific writer and a Columnist. Philip Afeti Korto holds BSc. Administration (Health Service Administration option) from University of Ghana Business School (UGBS). He also holds a Master of Public Administration from the Ghana Institute of Management and Public Administration (GIMPA). He occasionally gives practical lectures at the University of Ghana Business School (UGBS) upon invitation.

Anita Asiwome Baku holds a PhD in management from the Putra Business School in Malaysia and is currently a senior lecturer in the Department of Public Administration and Health Services Management at the University of Ghana Business School, Legon. She teaches courses in health services management and her research covers health management, health insurance, social insurance, occupational safety, and health marketing health services. Her writings cover book chapters and journal articles. She is also a reviewer for some international journals is health, social policy, and occupational safety and health.

Mr. Nurudeen Issaka Idrisu is an astute Assistant Registrar in the University of Health and Allied Sciences, Ho, Ghana. Previously, he was a Senior Health Service Administrator in the Ghana Health Service and was an educationist as well in the Ghana Education Service. He taught as a teacher for a period of 10 years and also practiced as Health Services Administrator at Achimota Hospital, Ga South Municipal Hospital and Ashaiman Polyclinic of Ghana Health Service with cumulative experience of six years and provided direction and leadership in all matters of Administration. Nurudeen Issaka Idrisu being a seasoned Administrator and a professional has been practicing Administration for over 10 years. He had his professional education as a teacher in Jasikan Training College (now Jasikan College of Education) in Ghana. He holds Bachelor of Arts (Honors) and Master's in Business Administration from University of Ghana Business School (UGBS). He did a short course in Project Management.

Nana Akua Boateng-Amartey is an assistant registrar at the Directorate of Academic Affairs, University of Health and Allied Sciences. Nana Akua completed a Bachelor's Degree in Information Technology at the Royal Melbourne Institute of Technology, Australia, MSc. Business Informatics at the University of Mannheim, Germany, and later pursued a Master's in Business Administration at the Accra Business School, Accra-Ghana. She is a licentiate member of the Chartered Institute of Administrators and Management Consultants, Ghana. Nana Akua worked with SAP Headquarters, Walldorf-Germany in an industrial internship as an Executive Demo Developer from 2008 to 2009. She joined Otto Bauder Haus as an IT Administrator and in Glory Life e.V. Mannheim, Germany, as a Supervisor and Teaching Aide where she facilitated trainings in English, Culture-related activities and projects for individuals on a part-time basis. She also worked with Nyansa Africa Consultancy and ACES Business Concepts as a Learning and Development Consultant from 2014 to 2018.

MAKING HIGHER EDUCATION MORE RESPONSIVE

Chapter 21

Deploying a Computer-Based Registration System in Developing Economy— Lessons Learned

Winfred Ofoe Larkotey

Conents

DOI: 10.4324/9781003152217-27

Introduction

This chapter documents the history of computer-based registration management system adoption of Valley View University, a Seventh-day Adventist institution of higher learning in Accra, Ghana. This institution began as an Adventist Missionary College in 1979 and later named Valley View University College in 1989 became the first private University in Ghana. In 2006, Valley View University became the first chartered private University in Ghana. The admission process was cumbersome and, therefore, moved from various levels to the current online application. The challenge with this system is to persuasively get prospective students to use this system since they continue to use the old system for admission, which had numerous challenges such as missing applications and late delivery of applications.

Registration was done by using the Green Card system. Students had to fill three Green Cards for registration and required seven different officers' signature to complete their registration. The process was cumbersome, and some students took weeks to register. The system was faced with challenges such as long queues during registration, frequently extended registration deadlines, incorrect details, difficulty generating reports, and difficulty keeping records and tracks of records. This led to introducing a new ID system and the "iSchool", which led to registering on the intranet. Students came to campus to report. Challenges such as students finding it difficult to register as well as long queues among others. Finally, the improved "iSchool" that allowed students to register over the Internet and made life easier was introduced. The case study details how this higher learning institution moved from a manual to a computer-based registration system amidst all the challenges.

Situation Faced

Valley View University's registration was manual. Students had to come to campus, pick up three Green Cards, and fill in the courses to register. The following sections describe the challenges and actions that led to the digitalization of the registration system.

Manual Registration Process

In the early years of the University, once the date for the beginning of the semester arrives, both old and new students proceeded to the University to register. By this time, the new students would have spent a week earlier on campus going through another orientation and other formalities.

The registration process involved so many activities, and each student, either old or new, was required to go through. To start with, a student had to pick up three Green Cards from the Admissions and Records office to be filled and submitted back at the end of the registration. Figures 21.1 and 21.2 are the front and back views of the Green Card, respectively.

The student enters his or her account number, semester and academic year of registration, date of registration, student identification number, and grade point average, department, student name, program, the course being majored and minored, sex, place of birth, nationality, marital

VALLEY VIEW UNIVERSITY
CERTIFICATE OF REGISTRATION

A/C No.:

( ) 1st Sem. 20 _____
( ) 2nd Sem. 20 _____
( ) Summer 20 _____

Date _____
ID No. _____
GPA _____
DEPT _____

Name:..Program:........................Major:........................Minor:..................
    Surname   *Other Name(s)*
Sex: ( ) Male   ( ) Female   Birth Place:................................Nationality:..
Marital Status:............................. Residential Status: Residence Hall ☐ Staff Quarters ☐ Community ☐
Baptised SDA? YES ☐ NO ☐ If YES, indicate Conference/Union ....
Non Baptised SDA? .... Other denomination, please specify..
Name & Address of parent:..

Course I.D.	Course No.	Course Title	Sem. Credit	Days	Time	Room	Grade	Quality Points

Are you a
( ) new student?
( ) continuing student?
( ) returnee?, If so indicate the
semester you last attended VVU

Citizenship ☐   Work Attitude ☐

1st Year _____
2nd Year _____
3rd Year _____
4th Year _____

_____ Semester _____

_____
Student's Signature

_____
Registrar

Figure 21.1   Front view of the Green Card.

REGISTRATION CARD

Name: _____   Date: _____

Please secure first the approval of the following (Steps I-VII in sequence) before any line-up of subjects be done:

Step I   **DEPARTMENT HEADS**
        (Subject Line-up)

        _____
          Signature

        Office Stamp

Step II   **VICE PRESIDENT STUDENT ADMIN.**

        Interview _____

        Identification Card _____

Step III **HALL DEAN** _____

        Dormitory Permit _____

Step IV   **LIBRARY**

        Library Card _____

Step V   **WORK COORDINATOR**

        _____

        _____

Step VI   **BUSINESS OFFICE**

        Meal Ticket _____

Step VII **CHAPLAIN**

        _____

Figure 21.2   Back view of the Green Card.

status, and residential status (*residence hall, staff quarters, community*). Other information such as whether baptized SDA or not, the conference one belongs to in case he or she is an Adventist, name and address of parents, the courses being registered for the semester (*Course ID, Course NO, Course Title, Semester Credits, Days, Time, Room*) with the admissions and records department filling the part of the *grade, quality points, citizenship grade (a grade showing how your attitude toward work and activities on campus is which is placed on your transcript)* and *work attitude* on the Green Card at the end of the semester are requested. Other parts that have to be filled on the Green Card are whether you are a new student, continuing student, or a returnee with an indication of the year and semester last attended the level (*1st, 2nd, 3rd, or 4th*), students' signature, and the registrar's signature. All these are found in the front view of the card.

The back view of the Green Card requires the student to write his or her name, the date of registration, and secure the approval (*Signature and Stamp*) of the following people:

■ Department Head
■ Dean, Student Life, and Services
■ Hall Dean (*in case the residence is on campus*)
■ Library (*using the library Card*)
■ Work Coordinator (*if applicable*)
■ Business Office (*to verify if the appropriate school, as well as cafeteria fees where applicable, have been paid*)
■ Chaplain

All these offices' signature and authority stamp would have to be gained for one to have been deemed registered for the semester. This is done by the student moving from one office to the other for approval. Once all three cards have been filled, the student sends all the cards back to the Admissions and Records office. The officer in charge verifies the content of the card and accepts the registration. He or she then takes two of the cards and gives one to the student for their stay. One of the cards from the Admissions and Records department is sent to the students' department to file the grades at the end of the semester.

Challenges of the Green Card System

This system, just like most manual systems, was faced with several challenges, which made the whole registration process strenuous on both students and staff who had to verify and sign all these cards. The following are the challenges:

Long Queues during Registration

Initially, the registration process was not too cumbersome as there were not many students. As the student population increased, the whole process was characterized by long queues, which was not comfortable for both students and staff who were supposed to be signing these cards. "This led to lots of frustration on the part of the student. Later, the trend was that either a student came at the earliest stages of the registration process or the latter part", Mr Samuel Amankwah (*Assistant Registrar- Admissions*).

Frequent Extended Registration Deadlines

Due to the tedious nature of the process, some students could not register within the required period. This led to the University extending its registration for almost every semester to accommodate such scenarios. According to Mr. Tetteh Assion (*an Alumnus*), "there were instances where registration could go far into the semester". This created some amount of difficulty for the records office in processing Green Cards.

Wrong Details

For some students, there were times where the incorrect details, such as the semester and others, were filled. Once this was done and became an oversight for the officer in charge of registration, it became challenging to compute the students' grade for graduation. "There were instances where grades from the department were different from that of the Admission and Records office" (Anonymous).

Difficulty in Generating Reports

The generation of reports during this period was challenging. Be it the transcript of other student scholastic reports, difficulty in the generation of these reports existed. For instance, in the transcript, all the Green Cards about one student will have to be sought out for compilation. This was a daunting task for the few staff at the Admission and Records Office. It became worse when the student who was requesting the report graduated a long time ago. All the same old documents had to be searched for. This resulted in unnecessary delays in the generation of such reports.

Difficulty in Keeping Records and Tracks of Records

The Admissions and Records office has a small office space to be keeping all these Green Cards. This led to them just being left anywhere. There were times where mice and other rodents could destroy cards. This made it difficult for the records to be kept. An Alumna reports,

> I thought I had fulfilled all graduation requirements and had invited my parents, who stayed abroad for my graduation. Upon arriving at the Admission and Records office on the Friday before graduation, I was told I had a course to repeat and could not graduate. I almost collapsed. I was disappointed. To me, I knew I had fulfilled all the requirements. My world came crashing down, especially when my parents had paid so much money to be in Ghana for my graduation.

This was the case of many students during the Green Card era. Students and Admissions and Records officers found it challenging to keep track of students' records.

Actions Taken

To prevent these events from recurring, two faculty members from the computer science department wrote a proposal to the University management on how the University could get brilliant students from the computer science department to develop and introduce an online registration system to streamline all the activities registration. The management, which was then called the Presidents' committee (*PRESCOM*), was made up of five people. At the defense, three of its members bought into the idea of in-house development. The other two suggested either outsourcing or purchase because students could not be allowed to handle their data. Upon Voting, the management decided to let the computer science department build the system. One strong argument that made this idea come to fruition was the concept of "cheap labour" and "if we do not have that confidence in our students to develop this, which organizations will have that confidence to employ them", said Dr. Isaac Wiafe.

Five students made up one first year, three second year, and one third-year student were assembled from the computer science department, with the two faculty members being their liaison with the management to handle the development and implementation of the University Registration Management System dubbed "iSchool". One challenge these students faced was that not all the staff and administrators agreed to develop the system; therefore, requirements gathering was hectic. The students stayed on campus from the year 2004 till July of 2005. Development was done by the end of July 2005. Series of tests began from unit testing to complete testing. The administration decided to now use the registration system at the beginning of the academic year 2005/2006 after several presentations were made to the PRESCOM.

Parallel testing and fading of the old system were the way to go. Some essential staff for the registration process were trained on how to use the system. On the said date where registration began, students picked up one Green Card and filled all the details, brought it to the iSchool desk where the system developers were handling the registration. New student IDs were generated for the new students with the old ones using their old IDs. From there, a student proceeded to one section if continuing or to another area if new for the person's biographic and biometric data to be captured. Both new and continuing students were led through the registration process, and within minutes, most of them were done. This did not come easily as there were some queues at various places. However, it seemed far better than the Green Card Registration System. The administrators were proud to use this system and credited the developers' accounts with five million cedis (*now 500.00 Ghana Cedis*). "For me, this was a happy moment. To see lots of people use the system I have built for the first time, I felt humbled and wanted to do more. It was the beginning of my carrier", Mr Tetteh Assion Kuyona (*One of the Student Developers*). Mr. Kwaku Nyadu (*One of the Student Developers* said, "If the administrators had a little more faith in us, we could have developed the system at a faster rate. This is because we wouldn't have had any impediments".

Results Achieved and Subsequent Challenges

"The initial implementation of this system could not reduce the queues we were having", Mr Timothy Owusu (*the lead Student Developer*). This is because the system only runs on the University's intranet; therefore, students had to come to campus to register. Even though they had been trained, most of these students still found it challenging to register independently. The development team were always at standby to help such students and staff.

The Improved "iSchool"

After five years of implementing the system over the intranet, it was decided by the administration to move it onto the Internet. Students had to pay for their fees at the nearest Prudential Bank, where their account will be synchronized with the University's accounts to allow them for registration. It takes 24 hours for a students' account to be activated for registration. Here, all that a student needs to know is the courses to register for the semester. Figure 21.3 shows the homepage of iSchool.

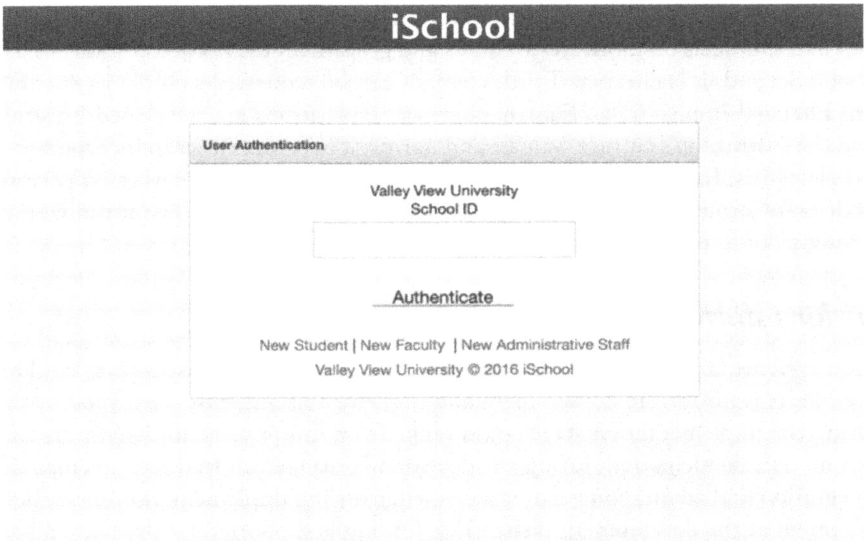

Figure 21.3   Homepage of iSchool.

The student then goes online to https://ischool.vvu.edu.gh/, enters their Student ID, and selects the "iSchool" application. The student then enters his or her password, which, when valid, leads him or her to the student portal. The student clicks on the register icon. A new page is generated, which requires the student to select which semester to register, and the level and clicks on the Submit icon. The list of courses and their credit hours available for that semester and status are displayed. The student selects which classes to register based on the maximum number of credit hours for the semester and level. Once satisfied, the student clicks on the "Register" button to complete the registration process. The student then goes to the report section to print out his or her registration details for the semester.

With the improved iSchool, the student can check his or her courses registered, scholastic report (*unofficial transcript*), a payment plan (*School fees paid and what is owed*), the Time Table for the semester, Grades for the past semester, can make complaints as to what is seen to be wrong, can find notices and announcements, and the students' profile.

The improved iSchool does not necessarily require students to come to campus to register, making it a perfect system. This has taken away the queues that used to characterize the registration system in time past. It has also provided the students with the opportunity to monitor the courses and how well they perform to know how to manage their studies to graduate on time. It is now easier for students to even generate unofficial transcripts and other reports for themselves. This has provided a definite timeline for which registration occurs, thereby taking away frequent extensions of registration. All in all, "the improved iSchool has made life better for us", said Mr Ebenezer Laryea (*Information Technology Services (ITS) Director*). Currently, the ITS department has a team of fully employed developers who constantly improve the iSchool and develop other university needs.

Lessons Learned—Practical and Policy Implications

This case presents several lessons that practitioners can apply in higher education digitalization processes. The case also offers lessons for students. The primary lesson learned from this case is the need to have students handle higher educational institutions' digitalization needs in developing countries. First, this decision motivates students and gives them the needed confidence as they step out of school. Second, it is cheaper. Third, changes can be requested as often as possible without substantial financial implications. Fourth, since these platforms are developed by students who understand the institution's culture, values, and norms, it becomes easier to incorporate them into the digital platforms. In terms of policy, this case suggests the need for laws that govern students whose services are termed cheap labor for such massive projects by higher educational institutions. The following sections provide other lessons from this case.

Reasons for Information Systems Failure

Information systems failure in developing country higher education institutions could be due to minor or major reasons for the development and implementation phases. For most systems, challenges during the implementation stage could range from minor to major issues. This case shows that less or no user participation during the development stage can lead to implementation challenges. Integration and adaptation become a challenge during implementation since there was less user involvement at the development phase. This finding is supported by Bygstad and Munkvold (2011). They suggest that one of the most important challenges between the information system and the related business organization is the concept of integration and adaptation. Businesses find it difficult to fully adapt to the system due to less user participation in the development and the improper handling of the change process.

Businesses have values, culture, and interests cherished and cannot be done away with just by introducing information systems. Digital platforms may have to incorporate these practices to succeed. This is the case of both systems initially implemented by Valley View University. In other words, higher education information systems that are sociotechnical are likely to succeed than those that are skewed toward either technology or social alone. In the case of Valley View University, the initial platform concentrated more on technical rather than social, leading to failure. Therefore, successful information systems development and implementation are dependent on the sociotechnical approach (Coakes et al., 2000; Leonard-Barton & Deschamps, 1988) and maximum user and business participation (Kappelman & McLean, 1994).

Benefits of Digitalizing Higher Educational Institution Registration

Upon implementing the computer-based information system, Valley View University and the student body are benefiting from the following:

- Complete and consistent student records
- Reaching a sizeable prospective student base, therefore, leading to competitive advantage and higher profits
- Students can have access to their information anytime and anywhere
- With a single sign-in, students can have access to all the applications the University subscribes to

The Internet and its applications have seen a sharp growth in its usage over the years, which has changed the way individuals and businesses operate. This technology has provided a different computing platform and opportunities from the traditional standalone information systems. For example, with the use of the Internet, businesses can reach their customers 24/7 (Xiao &

Dasgupta, 2006), different consumers or users of the Internet can exchange information rapidly, and there is general information (Simmers & Anandarajan, 2001), there is an increase in the volume and size of multimedia messages being transmitted over the Internet (D'Ambra & Rice, 2001) and many more. Having gained this ground, several businesses such as Valley View University have relied on the enormous benefits the Internet provides and have used this to their advantage by "running" several applications. The iSchool is one of such technically known web portals (WP). Tatnall (2005) defines a WP as a technology that offers a spectrum of resources and services targeted to a specific user population category through a website, all at one stop. WP's ensure personalization. At Valley View University, students, faculty, and management have access to all resources needed once they log onto the iSchool.

New Technology and Learning Models

According to Osterwalder et al. (2011), a business comprises a conceptual tool containing activities and their relationships expressing a firm's logic. Therefore, an institution must consider which concepts and relationships allow a simplified description and representation of what value is provided to its customers. The strategy and resources required are solely dependent on the institution and its intention to achieve its goals. Developing countries and their institutions are in a very strategic position to gain a competitive advantage.

With the new technologies on the market, several business models are at the disposal of higher learning institutions in developing countries. Some of which are:

- Mobile libraries
- eLearning platforms
- Online library systems
- Admission systems
- Grade implementation systems
- Registration systems
- Transcript management systems

All these systems and many more could be created as individual portlets put together into Web Portals. Higher learning institutions in developing countries should be looking at how Web Portals with a single-sign-in into all the applications could be used to make information dissemination easier.

Effects of Developing the Digital Platforms In-House

In-house digital platform development saves money, and it is easier to incorporate the institution's values, culture, and norms. Also, call for several changes during the use of digital platform becomes easier. Literature on information systems development has looked at the development approaches over several decades. Outsourcing has been one of the significant changes in the information systems field in the last two decades (Rouse & Corbitt, 2007). Several businesses have moved from outsourcing just their peripheral activities (*low-skilled jobs*) to the highly skilled ones. For most companies, outsourcing with the proper organization is seen as one of the main ways the organization gains a competitive advantage. Schwarz et al. (2009) define outsourcing as using an external business to perform some or all of the programming in a country where the client is located. Another definition by Harland et al. (2005) suggests that outsourcing is the process of sourcing activities externally that an organization has the internal capability to perform. The aforementioned definitions suggest that outsourcing occurs when an organization transfers ownership of a product or service that used to be done within the business to another organization to handle.

In-house development, such as in Valley View University, is when the whole activity occurs within the organization. The team is provided with all the logistics that are needed for development. Businesses do this because they have the required IT staff with the requisite skills, time, and resources. The use of students to develop digital platforms has the following effects:

- Generates confidence in the fact that the University is bridging the gap between industry and academia. This is seen when students applied all the practical knowledge received into developing and implementing workable systems.
- It saves money and provides the University with the opportunity to invest in other institution's pressing areas.
- Promotes the Information Systems, Computer Science, and Information Technology programs of the University since students gain that skill. This becomes an important marketing tool for the University, as it has been in Valley View University.

Using the Teaching Case in the Classroom or Training Session

The case explores the challenges of manual processes and digitalization achievements for higher learning institutions in developing countries. It explores how the right management decisions and unwavering support could lead to higher service levels in developing country institutions.

In using this case for teaching and learning purposes, stakeholders would be able to understand clearly:

- The factors that contribute to the failure of information systems in developing country higher educational institutions.
- The values/benefits of digitalizing higher educational institution registration.
- Implications of new technology enabled models for institutions of higher learning in developing countries.
- Effects of developing the digital platforms in-house using students and its implications for developing country higher learning institutions.

Suggested Timeline

Following is the suggested timeline for this case study. The discretion of the lecturer can also be applied to determine other timelines. Alternatively, this case can be analyzed using the sociotechnical theory (Bostrom, & Heinen, 1977).

- Introduction (*The overview and background of the case*): 5–8 minutes
- Actual Reading: 40–50 minutes
- Case Questions: 40–45 minutes
- Question 1: 10 minutes
- Question 2: 10 minutes
- Question 3: 10 minutes

- Question 4: 10 minutes
- Further discussion of essential learning outcomes: 15–20 minutes or as needed

The Following Are Questions That Can Be Discussed Using This Case

1. What are the reasons for information systems failure in most institutions such as Valley View University?
2. What values/benefits would students of higher learning institutions benefit from using computer-based registration systems?
3. What are the implications of new technology-enabled models for institutions of higher learning in developing countries?
4. What are the effects of developing the digital platforms in-house using students, and what are its implications for developing country institutions?

Conclusion

This chapter sought to chronicle the experience of deploying a computer-based registration system in the developing country of Ghana. This chapter offers implications for practitioners such as developers, IT managers, and administrators, especially Higher Education Digitalization. First, this chapter suggests that less or no user participation during the development stage can lead to implementation challenges. Therefore, developers should ensure that users from the various departments where digitalization will be effected are thoroughly engaged with their opinions captured. In this regard, this chapter suggests iterative digitalization approaches for higher educational institutions since this approach requires extensive user involvement. Second, digitalization should not wipe away established cultures, values, principles, and procedures of an institution. If that should happen, users are likely not to use digitalized platforms. In that regard, developers are advised to capture these cultures, values, principles, and procedures of the institution to encourage the use of digital platforms.

From the perspective of university administrators, using students to digitalize Higher Education business processes serves as a cheaper means by which to save money. Aside from saving money, students and other stakeholders feel proud to use digital products that have been developed in-house. In addition, maintenance of such in-house digital platforms becomes easier since the students may be around to help. Finally, for such institutions where programs such as Information Systems, Computer Science, and Information Technology are run, using students to handle in-house digitalization promotes the credibility of the program and serves to advertise the same.

References

Bostrom, R. P., & Heinen, J. S. (1977). MIS Problems and Failures: A Socio-technical Perspective. *MIS Quarterly, 1*(3), 17–32.

Bygstad, B., & Munkvold, B. E. (2011). Exploring the Role of Informants in Interpretive Case Study Research in IS. *Journal of Information Technology, 26*(1), 32–45.

Coakes, E., Lloyd-Jones, R., & Willis, D. (2000). *The New Sociotech: Graffiti on the Long Wall.* London: Springer Verlag.

D'Ambra, J., & Rice, R. E. (2001). Emerging Factors in User Evaluation of the World Wide Web. *Information & Management, 38*(6), 373–384.

Harland, C., Knight, L., Lamming, R., & Walker, H. (2005). Outsourcing: Assessing the Risks and Benefits for Organizations, Organizations, Sectors and Nations. *International Journal of Operations & Production Management*, *25*(9): 831–850.

Kappelman, L. A., & McLean, E. R. (1994, January). User Engagement in the Development, Implementation, and Use of Information Technologies. In *1994 Proceedings of the Twenty-Seventh Hawaii International Conference on System Sciences (4)* (pp. 512–521). Wailea, HI: Piscataway.

Leonard-Barton, D., & Deschamps, I. (1988). Managerial Influence in the Implementation of New Technology. *Management Science*, *34*(10), 1252–1265.

Osterwalder, A., Pigneur, Y., Oliveira, M. A. Y., & Ferreira, J. J. P. (2011). Business Model Generation: A Handbook for Visionaries, Game Changers and Challengers. *African Journal of Business Management*, *5*(7), 22–30.

Rouse, A., & Corbitt, B. (2007). Understanding Information Systems are Outsourcing Success and Risks through the Lens of Cognitive Biases. *Proceedings of the Fifteenth European Conference on Information Systems (ECIS)*, St Gallen, Switzerland, June 7–9. Atlanta, GA: Association of Information Systems.

Schwarz, A., Jayatilaka, B., Hirschheim, R., & Goles, T. (2009). A Conjoint Approach to Understanding IT Application Services Outsourcing. *Journal of the Association for Information Systems*, *10*(10), 1.

Simmers, C. A., & Anandarajan, M. (2001). User Satisfaction in the Internet-anchored Workplace: An Exploratory Study. *JITTA: Journal of Information Technology Theory and Application*, *3*(5), 39.

Tatnall, A. (Ed.). (2005). *Web Portals: The New Gateways To Internet Information and Services*. Hershey, PA: IGI Global.

Xiao, L., & Dasgupta, S. (2006). Organizational Culture and its Business Value: A Resource-based View. *AMCIS 2006 Proceedings*, 92.

Author's Profile

Winfred Ofoe Larkotey, PhD, is a senior lecturer with nine years of experience in consulting and training the youth in the development and use of technology. He holds a Bachelor of Science in computer science from Valley View University, Masters, and a PhD in Information Systems from the University of Ghana. Winfred's research areas are in digital government, mobile platforms, and human–computer interaction, emphasizing government services digitalization. Winfred lectures on Information Systems and other Computer-related courses both at the undergraduate and graduate levels. Dr. Larkotey is a member of the Association of Information Systems and the United Kingdom Association of Information Systems.

Chapter 22

Toward Improving Students' Academic Engagement: The Role of Educational Technology

Abeeku Sam Edu

Contents

DOI: 10.4324/9781003152217-28

Introduction

Information Technology (IT) has increasingly enabled the ease of sharing information among various platforms (Asongu et al., 2019). Significantly, access to information has become available to users to interact and respond through various IT devices. These developments have provided many businesses, the manufacturing, and services sectors, to leverage IT to improve efficiency and enhance business processes. For example, the application of IT has been acknowledged to improve operational excellence and improve the decision-making process and customer relationship management (Laudon & Laudon, 2012; Kassem et al., 2019). This has led to a continuous increase in IT infrastructure to improve and create new business models. Given the advantages and new opportunities IT offers, the Education sector has considerably improved the various aspect of teaching and learning engagements among faculty, students, and administrators using the ubiquitous changes in IT capabilities. In lieu of the pressures from the COVID-19 pandemic, academic engagement was hugely disrupted, which eventually deprived students' opportunities for development. This has further pushed educational institutions to identify initiatives to deploy emerging educational technologies applications and platforms to facilitate academic engagements, mostly for off-campus activities.

More importantly, at the Higher Education Institutions (HEIs), numerous IT applications have been developed to enable teaching and learning (Adarkwah, 2021; Tokareva et al., 2019; Rana & Rana, 2020; Conde et al., 2014; Despotovic-Zrakic et al., 2012; Petrovic et al., 2011; Engelbrecht, 2005; Liaw et al., 2007). Indeed, the use of IT applications and the Internet have become a critical factor for improving the quality of education. Accordingly, many HEIs have developed or adopted dedicated LMS for teaching, learning, and transmitting information through IT application alongside the use of the Internet to enhance instructor–student engagements without limitations to location and time (Woyo et al., 2020; Melo et al., 2020). The Learning Management System platforms have further created an environment for easy access and sharing of information on learning materials for the core and noncore academic activities via the web (Coates et al., 2005). Different Learning Application System platforms are explicitly designed for HEI to address their specific need. Although each platform may appear different, the goal is to engage student–instructors teaching and learning experiences.

A decade ago, these advantages were not available to both instructors and students who relied strictly on hard copies with learning materials. Accessing and sharing information within the educational settings were either difficult or lead to delay and expensive for all stakeholders (Lonn & Teasley, 2009; Domingo & Garganté, 2016). The adoption of LMS platforms by HEIs is, thus, influenced by several factors (Conde et al., 2014). These factors have been categorized as core variables that influence many Information System (IS) adoptions within the information system and technology literature (Hung et al., 2016). It is espoused as the intention to use, perceived usefulness toward the system, users' attitudes toward the implementation of new IS and IT systems and other issues that come with it. These factors are mainly considered as the preimplementation issues that arise toward a system adoption. For example, models and framework such as Technology Acceptance Model (Davis, 1989; (Davis et al., 1989), Technology, Organization, and Environment (Tornatzky & Fleischer, 1990), Institutional Theory (Dacin et al., 2002), and Diffusion of Innovation Theory (Rogers, 2003).

Consequently, these frameworks and models have been used to implement IS and technology innovations, and yet few studies have only considered measuring the success or failures of the systems implemented. Petter et al. (2008) posited that "Acceptance is not equivalent to Success" (p. 2). Thus, how IS and technology systems are properly aligning to organizations objectives and the effect of the system during its actual use of the business process. Therefore, the need to measure the LMS application adopted by HEIs cannot be ignored. In addition, more attention to LMS adoption is primarily toward the institution and learning content rather than its effect on student engagement. As a result, the final users are not well satisfied with the learning chain. A need to access and measure the users' adaptability to a new system goes beyond how implementers perceived some advantages at the adoption stage. Essentially, users' satisfaction is paramount to innovative technology, and as such, students' level of satisfaction and engagement to LMS platforms is imperative. This study, therefore, focuses on exploring the influence of LMS deployment in HEI on students' academic work at the University of Ghana. The study mainly used a Student Management System platform called SAKAI LMS as a case study, currently being adopted at the University of Ghana, Legon, for student academic engagements.

Measuring the usefulness of SAKAI is critical to gain student experiences in using the system. More so, evaluating students' academic engagements with SAKAI LMS will facilitate an avenue for improvement and possible modification of the system based on user feedback. In assessing the effect of SAKAI LMS on students' engagements, the DeLone and MacLean (D&M) model of information system measurement was proposed to assess the extent of SAKAI LMS on student engagement (DeLone & McLean, 2003).

To explore the post-implementation issues of SAKAI LMS as an interactive platform for academic engagement, the study adopted D&M model. The D&M model is an IS theory that significantly evaluates the success of users' acceptance and usage of a system after deployment. More so, the model demonstrates several factors showing how users accept and measure the extent of success of new technology. Few studies have acknowledged the extension of D&M into other areas where technology influences essential activities. Hence, the study proposed the D&M model to evaluate students' engagement due to implementing SAKAI LMS in a higher-learning environment. Specifically, the model used System Quality (SQ), Information Quality (IQ), Service Quality (SERVQ), Digital Literacy (DL), System Usage (SU), and User Satisfaction (US) to examine Student Engagement (SE) represented as net benefits in this study.

The structure of the remaining chapters is organized into six sections. The context of the study is addressed in the second section. The third section focuses on the literature review on IS issues for measuring the successful usage of implemented IS and Technology Innovations. The fourth section deals with the methodology of the study, while the fifth section analyzes the data collected from the field of study, and the sixth section provides discussion of results. Finally, the seventh section presents the conclusions and limitations of the study.

Context of SAKAI LMS Deployment

The use of Technology and IS through the Internet have resulted in significant improvements for most HEI toward teaching and learning. For many HEI, the application of LMS drives how instructors and students manage, share, and access learning materials. Therefore, location and time for accessing these learning materials and communication are not hindrances to student progress. Learning Management Systems currently is being used for both main streams, academic activities, and distant education academic activities. For example, the University of Ghana, for the past five to six years, has adopted the LMS platform known as SAKAI that facilitates teaching and learning environment for its instructors and students. This has seen a perpetual move away to improve the physical learning environment, such as paper-based sharing of educational materials, manual registration of courses, submission of hard copy assignment and project, and communication between students and instructors.

As part of attaining a world-class status as an HEI by 2024, the University of Ghana in 2014 adopted the SAKAI LMS to facilitate learning and official engagement for its various campuses. The campuses include the mainstream undergraduate studies with two categories of students, thus, students on the main campus and students at the city campus. Also, the SAKAI platform has provided opportunities for distant education students across the country and graduate students on the main campus. Therefore, applying SAKAI LMS is a strategic move to provide a teaching and learning platform to meet the increasing demand of students at various locations. SAKAI LMS was started on a pilot basis at the Department of Adult Education and the Department of Distant Education for a year. In 2015, the SAKAI LMS application was fully rolled out at all departments, facilitating the integration of all online applications. Therefore, lecturers can post the syllabi, organize learning materials, announcements, interact with students, and perform test and quizzes online.

SAKAI is an open-source LMS platform uniquely designed to support teaching and learning in HEI. The SAKAI environment includes features that support sharing learning materials and announcement notification. The features include a platform for course overview content, Syllabus, Lessons, Calendar, Announcement, Resources, Test and Quizzes, Markbook, Gradebook, Messages, Polls, Dropbox, Chat Room, Email, Email Archive, Site Info, and Help. Each of these features is available to the need of the user but with authorization content for usage. Instructors have the authorization to add contents relevant to the need of students. Students also have access to all contents created by the instructors but have no authorization to add and delete any content from the site created. However, a student can share contents through platforms such as Dropbox, Chat Room, and Emailing. In SAKAI LMS, each user has his/her worksite called Home and My Workspace provided for storage of personal documents, creating new sites, maintaining schedules, storing resources, and account settings information. It is instructive to emphasize that the deployment of LMS systems in the educational institution is still new in the developing country perspective due to Internet availability, cost, infrastructure, and adaptability.

Related Work

Learning Management Systems are categorized as "enterprise-wide and Internet-based" systems that support a wide range of pedagogical and managing student course engagements. Accordingly, Eom (2014) viewed LMS as "an informal student-centred learning environment, which supports students social and personal needs, facilitate feedback and, most importantly, is interactive". The LMS platforms are categories into two types, open-source platforms and commercial platforms. Open-source LMS platforms include Moodle, Sakai, MyLMS, Claroline, MyGuru2, and ATutor. Connect Edu, Litmos, Blackboard, SumTotal, SuccessFactors, Geo Learning, and Angle learning are categories under the commercial LMS platform. A cursory review of comparing LMS platforms indicates flexibility, accessibility, and user-friendly for most platforms deployed.

Concerning asynchronous and synchronous interactions, Sakai, Moodle, Blackboard, and ATutor offer such requirements. Mainly, most LMS application significantly provides the opportunity for ease interactions for academic activities once integrated successfully. The LMS application has the capabilities to provide a learning environment for on- and off-campus experiences for students. García-Peñalvo (2008) and Coates et al. (2005) argued that universal application of Information and Communication Technology (ICT) and IS had changed the focus of LMS by many HEI to transform the physical learning environment into a virtual learning environment. This has facilitated a paradigm in the structure of lecturer–student engagement (Watson & Watson, 2007).

Consequently, students can submit coursework online, check grades, post discussion for class interactions, and download course materials on- and off-campus. Some LMS platforms have also allowed students to write quiz and test online and immediately access their performance from the system (Jurubescu, 2008). From their review, Kasim and Khalid (2016) identified learning skills tool, communication tool, and productivity tool as the supporting tools LMS offers for academic engagement.

Learning Management System is mostly a focus for most institutions to improve information sharing, ease of access to information, paperless distribution of course materials, peer-to-peer collaborations, and students–lecturer engagement (Jakchaikul, 2015; Courtney & Wilhoite-Mathews, 2015). Clearly, for most HEI, the shift to adopt LMS application is due to accessibility, quality, and cost in the learning process (Coates et al., 2005). In a nutshell, LMS gives equal access to students irrespective of time and location.

Effect of LMS on Students' Academic Engagement

Undeniably, the use of LMS in academic learning engagement in HEI has been suggested to improve student's attitude toward learning (Waluyo, 2019). According to Rubin et al. (2010), "an effective LMS must support active engagement, meaningful connections between segments of the course, easy communication, and formative feedback on work that is presented in class discussions or through other venues" (p. 1). This has led to distinct types of LMS applications developed or deployed by HEI toward the learning process. Examples of common LMS applications include Blackboard, Moodle, SAKAI, Canvas, WebCT, and e-College. Although LMS application comes in diverse types, synchronizing their features with pedagogical factors without much difficulties (Cavus, 2013). It is perceived that students easily familiarize themselves with these applications quickly (Smet et al., 2016) and provide more considerable improvement in their learning process (Emelyanova & Voronina, 2014).

Other studies have posited that applying different LMS for academic learning and administrative engagement improves both the instructor and the students (Rana & Rana, 2020; Islam et al., 2019). For example, Rubin et al. (2010) posited that communication and sharing of information, student–student, and instructors–students response rate improved through an LMS platform. Islam et al. (2019) noted that teachers' perceived ease of usage and usefulness to ICT is essential to support academic research, teaching, and student engagements. Interestingly, Horvat et al. (2015) revealed that Gender was also critical to the level of students' attributes to LMS success. They further reiterated that female students are more inclined to system flexibility, features, and ease using the system.

According to Kasim and Khalid (2016), the success of LMS application depends on selecting the appropriate LMS that meet the HEI context for academic work. From their view, Venugopal and Jain (2015) observed that adopting LMS for a blended learning environment support student online engagements. Specifically, participation and performance in academic learning are improved (Fernández-Gutiérrez et al., 2020). Williams and Whiting (2016) also suggested that LMS usage has a positive influence on academic engagements. Other LMS platforms users at the university level have also indicated positive views on the learning process through LMS use (Adzharuddin & Ling, 2013; Islam & Azad, 2015).

Evaluating the impact of LMS on student academic activities is determined by relevant factors enabling student readiness to accept such a system. Primarily, the success of an information system applications is determined by several factors based on the context of deployment and the level of investment in IT and IS infrastructure.

Additionally, users mainly rate the success of a system with specific benchmarks based on a significant level of expectations. A cursory review of literature has shown various rating instruments and proposal to support the assessments of the impact information system plays on users' level of satisfaction and eventually, the net benefit to an organization in general. These are mostly driven by factors related to human, environment, culture, customer, and organizations inertia and politics (Nguyen et al., 2015; Dwivedi et al., 2015). Because of this, determining an appropriate measurement for IT and IS success is perceived to be complex and elusive (Petter et al., 2008). However, implementers of innovative technologies should derive an approach or models for measuring the benefits of applying these technologies (Hassanzadeh et al., 2012). Key among them include return on investment (Rubin, 2004), the use of balanced scorecards (Kaplan & Norton, 1996), benchmarking (Seddon et al., 2002), and models such as the D&M model (Hsu et al., 2015; Petter et al., 2008; DeLone & McLean, 2003).

Debatably, although all these measurement approaches and models have been highlighted in extant studies, the D&M model for IS success has been a key measurement metrics used in most IS deliberations. In Essence, the D&M model provides components for reviewing IS success for both empirical and conceptual review studies and found to be a suitable framework. Since it was proposed in 1992, several attempts have been made to examine its relationship on post-implementation on IS. Consequently, in 2003, DeLone and McLean proposed an updated model for the reliable degree of IS success. Therefore, the application of this model provides an investigation into the success or failure of an information system created to support an operation process.

Considerably, IS platforms reveal various features characterized with various degree of content and system quality. Therefore, users must use the features provided to indicate the level of satisfaction or dissatisfaction with the system deployed. Therefore, the degree of satisfaction shows the level of acceptance and the conduct of users to the system. The overarching effect reflects on the impact of the operational process of the organization. Hence, the need to optimally identify the system's success or failure is measured through the D&M model. In their review, a modification of the earlier dimensions promulgated was provided to include service quality (Delone & Mclean, 2003). The constructs to evaluate the impact of IS, particularly for LMS, are discussed in the following.

System Quality

The quality of an IS system has been described as essential features to include aesthetics, system flexibility, ease of use, reliability, response to time, and structured design (DeLone & McLean, 2003; Petter et al., 2008; Ho & Dzeng, 2010; Ozkan & Koseler, 2009). The essential characteristics of the LMS platform are the software and the accompanying peripherals. Thus, the quality of the software must be reliable, stable, secure, responsive, easy to use, well-organized design, and user-friendliness (Ozkan & Koseler, 2009). The higher the reliability and stability of the LMS platform, the higher effect on academic activities.

Information Quality

Information quality is the essential characteristics of relevant content and information from the system output. The required content and information received from the system must be complete, understandable, timely, and accurate (DeLone & McLean, 2003; Ho & Dzeng, 2010; Hsu et al., 2015). Content and information provided on the LMS platform must always be relevant and understandable to the user.

Service Quality

Essential support system users receive from technical personnel and the ICT department. Specifically, users expect a quick response to challenges with the systems, empathy of personnel, guidance to the use of the system, and technical competence solving related problems during usage (DeLone & McLean, 2003; Petter et al., 2008; Oztekin et al., 2010; Wang & Wang, 2009). Users must be given the needed support and help in using the LMS platforms from the ICT personnel.

System Usage

This describes the extent to which users apply system capabilities or features and for intended tasks (Burton-Jones & Straub, 2006; DeLone & McLean, 2003; Kember et al., 2010). System usage also defines the frequency of usage, the nature of usage, and the purpose as posited by Petter et al. (2008).

User Satisfaction

The level to which users are significantly pleased with the overall performance of the system. It also addresses the level of confidence users have toward the system (Oztekin et al., 2010; Petter et al., 2008; Chen & Jang, 2010). Using LMS platforms must provide the level of satisfaction that users expect.

Net Benefits

The extent of measuring the benefits or engagements derived from using a system for its intended purpose over a period (Petter et al., 2008; DeLone & McLean, 2003).

Digital Literacy

DL refers to the extent to which a user can demonstrate relevant ICT skills to the medium or system provided (Appel, 2012). Burton et al. (2015) underscore that the level of DL will aid the extent to which users can perform the task effectively. Burton et al. (2015) further suggested that DL should not just focus on the users' technological skills in using the computer. The users must also use relevant DL skills for web and Internet portals for learning. In this digital world, a user must use a different range of skills and literacies than technical abilities. Hence, users must be able to communicate and understand digital technologies at their disposal effectively. DL is acquired through comprehensive computerized pursuits such as researching the web, homework, social media, and entertainment purposes (Appel, 2012). For academic activities purposes, it is essential to identify the level of DL among students toward learning platforms to improve academic engagements.

Accordingly, Ismailova and Muhametjanova (2016) advocated that a higher-level student computer literate rate helps navigate digital technologies. In their study, a student computer literacy ability provides more knowledge for possible web activities. Greene et al. (2014) also argued that students' effective DL level helps navigate digital sources like the Internet to acquire digital information. Tang and Chaw (2016) constructively opined the significance of DL among students in a computer-simulated and physical learning environment. Hence, a student DL level promotes the effective use of technology for learning. Four DL constructs such as underpinning, background knowledge, central competencies and attitudes and perspectives are proposed to be critical in the digital learning environment (Bawden, 2008). Using these constructs as DL dimensions, Tang and Chaw (2016) empirically observed that DL has a significant relationship in a technological learning environment. This further suggests that the more literate students are with technology, the level of usage and satisfaction with a learning management system increases. As such, DL indicates a relationship to system usage and satisfaction levels. This study, therefore, proposes the introduction of DL to assess its impact on student's usage of LMS, more importantly, students from developing country perspective.

Conceptual Model

To provide an in-depth assessment of students' engagement with the use of SAKAI LMS, the D&M model (DeLone & McLean, 2003) was used as a premise for measuring the IS adoption from literature. As exhibited in Figure 22.1, the quality of LMS platforms are categorized into system quality (SQ), service quality (SEVQ), and information quality (IQ) constructs.

Significantly, these three combined influences system usage (SU) and user satisfaction (US) with Sakai LMS. As a result, the causal effect of user satisfaction and usage reflects the level of benefit with the Sakai LMS. In addition, the study introduced DL as the fourth construct to assess its significant

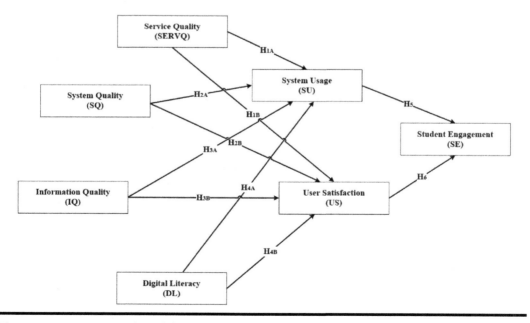

Figure 22.1   Conceptual model.

contribution to system usage and user satisfaction with the Sakai LMS platform. DL, therefore, shows the student's ability to explore the Sakai LMS platform without significant challenges. To ensure the adequacy of the proposed model, all constructs were significantly accessed using key indicators and their appropriateness in the model. Finally, the extent of the relationship between SAKAI "usage and satisfaction" on the level of student academic engagement was measured with the D&M model. This is to determine the extent to which students' attitude toward academic engagement on campus and off-campus activities are affected. The model proposed the following research hypothesis.

The following hypotheses were developed to address the aforementioned research objectives.

1. H_1: *SEVQ significantly affects System Usage and User Satisfaction.*
2. H_2: *SQ significantly affect System Usage and User Satisfaction*
3. H_3: *IQ significantly affect System Usage and User Satisfaction*
4. H_4: *DL significantly affect System Usage and User Satisfaction*
5. H_5: *SU of Sakai LMS significantly affect Student Academic Engagement (SE)*
6. H_6: *US with Sakai LMS significantly affect Student Academic Engagement (SE)*

Methodology

The study adopted a quantitative approach to assess students' satisfaction, user experience, and benefits with Sakai LMS. In this regard, the survey approach was applied using questionnaires to solicit responses from individual respondents. This approach was helpful because the students were on different campuses and at different halls and hostels of affiliations. Mainly, students from the Main campus and Accra City campus were used, respectively.

Specifically, undergraduate students from the Faculty of Humanity, University of Ghana Business School were used for this study. The categories of students used were offering courses such as Accounting Department, Finance Department, Marketing and E-Commerce Department, Human Resource Department, and Public and Health Administration Department. Again, the undergraduate students were appropriate for this study because such are the most active users of the Sakai LMS platform compared to graduate students from the university. Their experiences and objective opinions with Sakai LMS usage for academic activities include accessing content material, submitting assignments, receiving notifications, taking online quizzes, online class discussions, interactions with lecturers, downloading audio and video lecture notes, and others were deemed necessary for this study. The study used the convenient nonprobability sampling method was to select undergraduate student and data collection. The convenient sampling technique was preferred due to its usefulness in supporting large sample collection for generalization.

The survey questionnaire used closed-ended questions for the first part and five-point Likert scale questions for the second part, respectively. The first part of the questionnaire was to collect attributes of the respondents, the medium by which they accessed Sakai LMS and mainly the academic activities most student engages with the SAKAI LMS platform. The second part further assessed the level of satisfaction with Sakai LMS through a Likert scale measurement. The Likert scale questions were developed to aid the IS factors proposed by D&M model metrics and relevant literature (Delone & Mclean, 2003). The factors or construct proposed by the D&M model include system quality (SQ), information quality (IQ), and SEVQ used as independent variables and system usage (SU) and user satisfaction (US) as mediating variables for this study. Net benefits representing benefits from students' academic engagement through Sakai LMS were considered as the dependent variable.

The study further introduced DL as an independent variable recommended by Tang and Chaw (2016). The respondents evaluated their level of agreement based on the constructs provided through the D&M metrics of IS measurement and DL measurement (Tang & Chaw, 2016; Petter et al., 2008). The Likert scale criteria used a measurement scale between 1 and 5, where 1 represents strongly disagree and 5 strongly agrees for the student to rate the level of agreement toward system quality, service quality, information quality, DL, user satisfaction, and system usage and net benefits with SAKAI LMS platform appropriately. The questionnaire was collected in phases, that is, during lecture time in the classroom from the two campuses and online with Google survey forms. In all, 828 questionnaires from students were deemed fully completed and used for the analysis.

Data collected were analyzed using Structural Equation Model (SEM) with the aid of the PLS 3 analytical tool. SEM is a technique that can model latent variables and statistically test the entire model to account for any measurement errors accompanying a "plethora" of research hypothesis (Henseler et al., 2015). Essentially, all the constructs adopted were measured to observe their causal relationship with the use of the IS and IT (SAKAI LMS) mediated through system usage and user satisfaction. Each construct was measured through indicator variables to ensure reliability and validity. Therefore, using the SEM was to determine how student academic engagements were influenced or impacted through the SAKAI LMS platform.

Also, demography responses from students were presented and alongside the various academic activities engage with SAKAI LMS.

Analysis of Results

This section presents results from responses from the questionnaire administered and cohort group discussions. The analysis of results is provided in three (3) parts, first visualization of demographic responses from the students, frequency of assessing SAKAI LMS, and various devices used and the various activities on SAKAI LMS. The second part presents outer loadings and path coefficient analysis of conceptual model development, reliability and validity measurement and extent of relationships and the effect of SAKAI LMS Student Engagement (SE). Finally, the challenges of SAKAI LMS usage are also presented.

Demography and Frequency of SAKAI Usage

From a total of 828 respondents of SAKAI LMS usage, 39% represent Female students, and 61% represent Male students, as shown in Table 22.1. Regarding the specialization program, most students offer Accounting courses representing 43.7%, and the least of students are studying Insurance and Risk Management constituting 3.7%. Table 22.1 also illustrates the frequency of assessing SAKAI, average time spent, and the various types of devices student use to access SAKAI. More than half of the students, 474, accesses SAKAI between a day to two weeks regularly, and the remaining 354 students use the SAKA platform monthly, as depicted in Table 22.1. The result further revealed the devices student uses to access various activities on SAKAI LMS platform. The responses show that 64% of students use Mobile phones to access the SAKAI LMS platform, and 27.2% access SAKAI through laptops. The remaining 8.9% use either desktop computers, tablets, or iPad to access SAKAI.

Table 22.1 Demography and Frequency of SAKAI Usage

Measure	Item	Frequency	Percentage %
Gender	Male	505	61.0
	Female	323	39.0
Program of specialization	Banking and Finance	173	20.9
	Accounting	362	43.7
	Marketing and E-commerce	111	13.4
	Human Resource Management	44	5.3
	Public Administration	107	12.9
	Insurance and Risk Management	31	3.7
Frequency of assessing SAKAI	Daily	17	2.1
	Between 2 and 4 days	63	7.6
	Weekly	239	28.9
	Every two weeks	155	18.7
	Monthly	354	42.8
Average time spent on SAKAI	30 minutes — 1 hour	790	95.4
	2–3 hours	38	4.6
Types of devices often used to access SAKAI	Desktop PC	41	5.0
	Laptop	225	27.2
	Tablet	32	3.9
	Smart Mobile Phones	530	64.0

The average time spent on SAKAI is between thirty (30) and sixty (60) minutes for various academic activities. Additionally, the study revealed the various academic activities students engage with the SAKAI platform. Academic activities were classified into six, mainly downloading lecture notes or slides, submitting assignments, submitting term papers, writing a quiz, online lectures, and reading announcements. The responses show a mix of academic activities SAKAI is being used for my students. As demonstrated in Figure 22.2, 36.1% of students use the SAKAI platform to download lecture notes, 22.6% use SAKAI for announcement notification, submit assignments, and write class and midterm quiz. Respectively, 18.1% and 12.8% of the students use SAKAI to submit assignments, write quizzes only, download lecture notes, and submit an assignment. Finally, the results revealed that 4.5%, 3.1%, and 2.2% of SAKAI usage are for downloading lectures, reading the announcement, downloading lecture notes, submitting assignments, submitting term papers and reading announcements, and submitting assignments, respectively.

Assessment of Validity and Reliability Test

To further ensure internal consistency of the research instrument applied, Cronbach Alpha (CA) coefficient (Hair et al., 2012), Composite Reliability (CR) (Werts et al., 1974), and Average Variance Extracted (AVE) (Fornell & Larcker, 1981) were computed as the standard for all measurements. The composite reliability has been suggested to be ≥0.70 as the confirmatory feature for all construct indicators (Bagozzi & Yi, 1988; Vinzi et al., 2010). AVE scores for all the constructs, as shown in Table 22.2, were above 0.50. This demonstrates an acceptable explanation of variance from the indicators (Vinzi et al., 2010). The factor loadings for each indicator variable is argued to be valid at 0.6 and above (Nunally, 1978; Hair et al., 2012). Additionally, Cho and Cheon (2004) and Hanafizadeh et al. (2014) observed that a final acceptance for indicators should be 0.55. Thus,

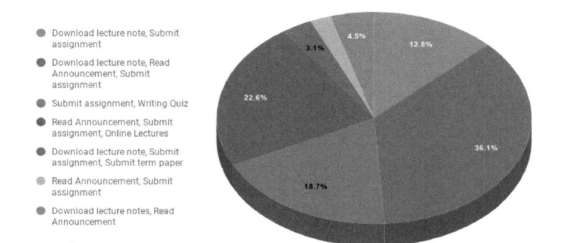

Figure 22.2 SAKAI usage for academic activities.

Table 22.2 Validity and Reliability Test

Variables	Indicators	Factor Loadings	CA	CR	AVE
Information quality (IQ)	IQ1	0.779	0.863	0.900	0.646
	IQ2	0.826			
	IQ3	0.797			
	IQ4	0.799			
	IQ5	0.816			
System quality (SU)	SQ1	0.842	0.837	0.899	0.672
	SQ2	0.835			
	SQ3	0.806			
	SQ4	0.796			

Variables	Indicators	Factor Loadings	CA	CR	AVE
Service quality (SEVQ)	SERV1	0.788	0.849	0.892	0.623
	SERV2	0.790			
	SERV3	0.809			
	SERV4	0.821			
	SERV5	0.737			
Digital literacy (DL)	DL2	0.761	0.884	0.900	0.645
	DL3	0.897			
	DL4	0.842			
	DL5	0.743			
	DL6	0.761			
User satisfaction (US)	US1	0.822	0.860	0.899	0.641
	US2	0.823			
	US3	0.750			
	US4	0.844			
	US5	0.760			
System usage (SU)	SU1	0.682	0.865	0.899	0.599
	SU2	0.819			
	SU3	0.821			
	SU4	0.748			
	SU5	0.771			
	SU6	0.795			
Student engagement (SEG)	SE1	0.840	0.930	0.93	0.689
	SE2	0.862			
	SE3	0.847			
	SE4	0.802			
	SE5	0.833			
	SE6	0.797			

all indicators below this threshold should be dropped from a model. Accordingly, the acceptable level for each indicator is within the acceptable threshold, as illustrated in Table 22.2.

Also, the discriminant validity assessment was tested to ensure validity between two reflective constructs using the Heterotrait–Monotrait (HTMT) ratio of correlation recommended by

Henseler et al. (2015). From Table 22.3, all the HTMT values are below 0.9, which underscores no negative correlation between two reflective constructs.

Measurement of Model Fit

The SEM adopted tested the overall fit of the proposed model and its relevance to the study. Consistency with PLS-SEM model estimation, the model fit indices considered include the standardized root mean square residual for covariance matrix (SRMR), normed fit index (NFI), Chisquare (χ^2), and RMS-theta (Hair et al., 2017). Accordingly, the acceptable threshold for each fit index and the results for this study were within the scale, as illustrated in Table 22.4. The values for fit indices result indicate that the model proposed is satisfactorily good for this study.

Path Analysis and Test of the Structural Model

The path analysis results demonstrate the relationship between constructs and the test of hypothesis for the model. As such, the unique feature of SAKAI and student's ability to use it predict academic engagement. As displayed in Table 22.5, SEVQ from SAKAI LMS was a significant predictor of system usage (*t-statistics* =10.957, *p*<0.00) and user satisfaction (*t-statistics* =12.237, *p*<0.00). Similarly, the results indicate that information quality (IQ) was a good predictor of system usage (*t-statistics* =6.137, *p*<0.00) and user satisfaction (*t-statistics* =5.893, *p*<0.00). Figure 22.3

Table 22.3   Heterotrait–Monotrait Ratio

	DL	IQ	SEG	SEVQ	SQ	SU
DL						
IQ	0.04					
SEG	0.05	0.63				
SEVQ	0.05	0.68	0.73			
SQ	0.05	0.73	0.63	0.68		
SU	0.04	0.63	0.76	0.71	0.55	
US	0.06	0.74	0.85	0.82	0.79	0.81

Table 22.4   Model Fit

Indices	Threshold	Estimated model
SRMS	< 0.08	0.060
NFI	Closer to 1	0.829
Rms-theta	<0.12	0.114
χ^2 /df (3169.89/827)	>1.96	3.833

Table 22.5   Hypothesis Testing

Path Coefficient	Original Sample (O)	Sample Mean (M)	Standard Deviation (STDEV)	T Statistics (|O/STDEV|)	P Values	Decision
IQ → SU	0.258	0.260	0.042	6.137	0.000**	H_{3A} -Supported
IQ → US	0.208	0.211	0.035	5.893	0.000**	H_{3B} -Supported
SEVQ → SU	0.410	0.411	0.037	10.957	0.000**	H_{1A} -Supported
SEVQ → US	0.391	0.389	0.032	12.237	0.000**	H_{1B} -Supported
SQ → SU	0.076	0.072	0.042	1.806	0.036**	H_{2A} -Supported
SQ → US	0.321	0.320	0.033	9.716	0.000**	H_{2B} -Supported
DL → SU	0.014	0.003	0.049	0.290	0.386	H_{4A} -Not Supported
DL → US	0.051	0.042	0.035	1.445	0.075	H_{4B} -Not Supported
SU → SEG	0.302	0.301	0.032	9.330	0.000**	H_5 -Supported
US → SEG	0.543	0.544	0.033	16.559	0.000**	H_6 -Supported

Note: Significance level @ 0.05**.

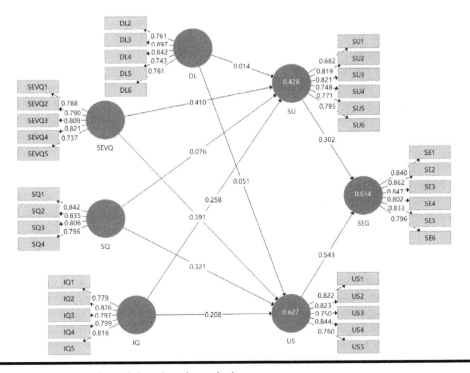

Figure 22.3   Structural model and path analysis.

also shows that DL is fairly positive with system usage (0.014) and user satisfaction (0.051). System quality (SQ) was also a good predictor of system usage and user satisfaction. In contrast, DL is identified as a weak predictor for both system usage and user satisfaction. Hence, the hypotheses were both rejected (DL-SU, *t-statistics* =02.90, *p*<0.386 and DL-US, *t-statistics* =1.445, *p*<0.075).

Further to estimating the level of relationship, Figure 22.3 revealed that service quality, information quality, DL, and system quality account for 42.8% and 62.7% of Variance explain for system usage and user system usage, respectively.

The overall impact of SAKAI LMS usage for students' academic engagement also revealed that system usage and user satisfaction were good predictors (SU-SEG, *t-statistics* =9.330, *p*<0.00 and US-SEG, *t-statistics* =16.599, *p*<0.00). Additionally, both system usage and user satisfaction of SAKAI LMS contribute to 61.4% of various student academic activities (R^2 =0.614).

Discussion of Results

The study sought to explore the IS-related dimensions that promote SAKAI LMS for students' academic engagement and the extent to which these factors affect student engagement through the D&M model. Findings from the study identified seven dimensions to measure the impact of SAKAI LMS. The findings provided essential information on the impact of LMS inclusions for academic engagements, and students perceived assessment of the LMS usage outside conventional classroom engagements and the various academic activities LMS can be used to offer.

With regards to academic activities SAKAI LMS is currently being used for, students offering various programs such as accounting, banking, and finance, and others indicated to activities such as online live lectures, downloading lecture notes, submitting term paper and assignments, course announcement, and writing midterm quizzes within a defined time. As illustrated in Figure 22.2, the dominant academic activities suggest that students use SAKAI LMS tools to download lecture notes, read announcements, and submit assignments together. The next mixed academic activities SAKAI tools are used for reading announcements, participating in online lectures, and submitting assignments. The findings also show that other students only use SAKAI platform to submit assignment and write midterm quiz or test. The least mix of academic activities assess through SAKAI are reading announcements and submitting assignments. The indication from these findings suggests that more students have access to lecture contents and are readily informed with notifications about course-related activities, as corroborated by Jakchaikul (2015). Rhode et al. (2017) also suggested that the most commonly used tools with LMS platforms were announcements, assignment submissions, and writing tests, supporting the findings from this study.

The findings also show that most students access SAKAI LMS via smart mobile phones for academic activities more often. Indeed, the use of smart mobile phones has, in recent times, proven to support learning engagements and provided new ways for students to actively interact with off classroom activities (Fernández-Gutiérrez et al., 2020; Yang et al., 2015). Additionally, most students spent an average of an hour on SAKAI through mobile devices, laptops, and tablets weekly. Overall, students' attitudes toward SAKAI LMS for academic activities such as access to course contents, communication between lecturers and students were positive. This further supports earlier studies that postulated LMS support students' academic activities (Smet et al., 2016; Vandeyar, 2020).

The results from the hypothesis test revealed that all the constructs measured were significant, except the relationship between DL and system usage and user satisfaction. Service quality was found to be the most influencing factor affecting system usage and user satisfaction. Information quality was also identified as the next influencing factor affecting system usage, while system quality has a low impact on system usage. System quality was also found to be influencing user satisfaction more than the frequency of using the system. Although the frequency of using SAKAI LMS is shorter, students were ultimately satisfied with the quality of service from the SAKAI platform. Accordingly, Jafari et al. (2015) also indicated that service quality and system quality are vital components to user satisfaction which eventually drive an overall benefit of the system.

The results further supported the assertion that user satisfaction was more critical to influencing the benefits users derives from a system than the longevity of usage (Chen & Jang, 2010). Therefore, the study's outcome shows that students have positive attitudes toward SAKAI LMS because of the quality of information and the perceived benefits derived from academic activities with SAKAI LMS. Users' appreciation or benefit derived from using LMS largely depend on quality information or content received from the LMS platform (Kyzy et al., 2018). Thus, the degree to which users utilize the capabilities is critical to its success or failure. User satisfaction was, therefore, found to be significant toward the level of using it for academic activities such as online lectures, access to course contents, writing quizzes or tests, and submitting assignments and term papers. The extent of system usage was also significant, mostly through the use of mobile phones and laptops. This indicates that once users understand the use of IS systems, attitudes toward its usage are high. Thus, the degree to which users utilize the capabilities is critical to its success or failure. The findings from the study also indicate that, once academic sessions are in place, almost all students use SAKAI LMS on-campus or off-campus for academic activities. In addition, the findings also revealed that students have acknowledged that services quality is of greater importance for using SAKAI LMS. For some, service quality in terms of the support received from the ICT department, especially empathy from ICT personnel, is relevant.

Overall, all the D&M dimensions used to assess LMS platforms for student academic engagements were identified to be positive with LMS success. Although relevant ICT skills (DL) were identified to be relevant to system usage and user satisfaction in using the LMS platforms (Greene et al., 2014), this study found otherwise. The remaining hypotheses were found to be significant on Student engagements with the application of SAKAI LMS. As posited by Rubin et al. (2010), Emelyanova and Voronina (2014), Jakchaikul (2015), and Courtney and Wilhoite-Mathews (2015), effective management of LMS applications affect students' learning engagements. Ultimately, the use of LMS applications like the SAKAI platform has proved functional and helpful. Lecturers and students can interact using the chat room, and announcements are given out and received for academic purposes regularly. Again, students can download lecture notes and submit assignments through the SAKAI platform. As part of the advantages, SAKAI can be accessed in any part of the world, and it is unlimited.

In summary, the findings from this study reveal a paradigm shift for students' adaptability to the use of educational technologies to support learning activities. Key factors identified to improve user's satisfaction and system usage includes service quality, system quality, information quality and DL. The findings also support the assertion that user satisfaction was more critical to influencing the benefits users derives from a system than the longevity of its usage.

Implications of the Study

Theoretical Implications

Findings from this study have significant theoretical implications. The use of the D&M model to measure IS success reveals new perspectives on utilizing and evaluating the effect of emerging technologies and application. The model further reveals identifiable factors to measure the success of IS applications, including SAKAI LMS for institutional benefits. Conditions under which IS applications may be useful may vary, and researchers need to identify distinct factors that support users' experience within implementation and usage. Therefore, the factors considered from the D&M model in this study highlight a contribution toward evaluating the success of present and emerging ICT usefulness.

Beyond ICT adoption, this study suggests that the success of system usage and user satisfaction is significantly influenced by service quality, system quality, information quality, and DL. In addition, our classification to key success to LMS highlights service quality, system quality, information quality, and DL. Furthermore, theoretically, benefits derived from technology must be examined according to what drives users because not all users are motivated by the same concerns irrespective of cultural peculiarities. Finally, our study contributes to the perspectives of evaluating the benefits to IS and IT applications literature.

Practical Implications

This study sought to provide value to HEIs regarding the exigencies of identifying ICT applications to enable educational reforms and improvements. Also, in the wake of COVID-19, HEIs must deploy specific LMS applications to support student academic engagements. More importantly, this study reinforces the for HEI institutions to identify relevant resources to improve features of LMS applications to support student engagement. In the context of SAKAI LMS, the university administration must address student academic activities with all the relevant features on the learning platform. From the findings, critical consideration should be carefully directed toward systems quality and service quality for ultimate reward during implementation and maintenance of the system to support system usage and user's satisfaction.

The burgeoning issues with COVID-19 also provide the necessities for university administrations to organize training programs for lecturers to improve their DL to improve deliveries using the SAKAI LMS platform. Furthermore, because the SAKAI LMS platform often experiences software and hardware challenges, the school administration must place a team of experts and relevant technical resources for continuous supervision and evaluation of the LMS platform. Overall, this study broadens the discussions for educators and policymakers to critically consider the transition from traditional means of engaging students to the usage of LMS applications in the post-COVID-19 pandemic.

Policy Implications

For policymakers, evidence from this study should enable the government, the ministry of education, other relevant policymakers in higher education and students to engage more on deliberate strategies for deploying resources and educational technologies for academic engagement in Ghana. For example, critical consideration should be carefully directed toward systems quality and service quality for ultimate reward during implementation and maintenance of the system to support system usage and user satisfaction.

Conclusion and Limitations of the Study

This study has further highlighted an effort by HEIs within developing countries to improve student academic engagement through educational technology. Although other studies have been driven toward developed countries (Smet et al., 2016; Horvat et al., 2015), the contribution of this study is unique with SAKAI LMS application in a sub-Saharan country like Ghana. Also, this study argues that acceptance of an information system is not equivalent to success at the adoption and implementation stage. Evaluating the services that a system offers at the usage stage is more critical, hence the need to engage users of SAKAI LMS to measure its success and failures since little research has been contributed in such directions. Finally, this study has also demonstrated that DL also plays a role in system usage and the level of satisfaction derived from learning management systems (Ismailova & Muhametjanova, 2016).

Despite the contributions, this study has few limitations. First, applying the D&M model over the period has been viewed to be a good measure of IS success. However, the debate from other extant studies advocates a more standardized measurement or modification of the model to determine other relationships yet to be uncovered. Therefore, the study proposes future research directions to consider other relevant factors such as facilitating conditions and other factors to evaluate the success of ICT deployment. Second, the sample was mainly from University of Ghana Business School students and that the generalization of the findings may not relate to all students from the University of Ghana. Future study may consider including more students from other faculties or departments to represent students toward SAKAI LMS usage and benefits. Given that there are many universities in Ghana, future research directions should be focused on a cross-university investigation to understand the similarities, challenges, and benefits with different LMS applications.

Acknowledgment

The author wishes to express their sincere appreciation to all respondents for their voluntary participation in this study. The University of Ghana Business School supported this study under a faculty grant.

Declaration of Interests

The author declares that they have no known competing interests or personal relationships that could have influenced the work reported in this research.

References

Adarkwah, M. A. (2021). "I'm Not against Online Teaching, but What about us?": ICT in Ghana Post Covid-19. *Education and Information Technologies*, 26(2), 1665–1685. https://doi.org/10.1007/s10639-020-10331-z

Adzharuddin, N. A., & Ling, L. H. (2013). Learning Management System (LMS) among University Students: Does It Work? *International Journal of E-Education, e-Business, e-Management and e-Learning*, 3(3), 248–252. https://doi.org/10.7763/IJEEEE.2013.V3.233

Appel, M. (2012). Are Heavy Users of Computer Games and Social Media More Computer Literate? *Computers & Education*, 59(4), 1339–1349.

Asongu, S. A., Anyanwu, J. C., & Tchamyou, V. S. (2019). Technology-driven Information Sharing and Conditional Financial Development in Africa. *Technology for Development*, 25(4), 630–659. https://doi.org/10.1080/02681102.2017.1311833

Bagozzi, R. R., & Yi, Y. (1988). On the Evaluation of Structural Equation Models. *Academy of Marketing Science, 16*(1), 74–94.

Bawden, D. (2008). *Origins and Concepts of Digital Literacy*. In C. Lankshear & M. Knobel (Eds.), *Digital Literacies: Concepts, Policies and Practices*. New York: Peter Lang Publishing.

Burton, L. J., Summers, J., Lawrence, J., Noble, K., & Gibbings, P. (2015). Digital Literacy in Higher Education: The Rhetoric and the Reality. In *Myths in Education, Learning and Teaching*. Palgrave Macmillan. https://doi.org/10.1057/9781137476982.0019

Burton-Jones, A., & Straub, D. (2006). Reconceptualizing System Usage: An Approach and Empirical Test. *Information System Research*, 1–52. https://doi.org/10.1287/isre.1060.0096

Cavus, N. (2013). *Selecting a Learning Management System (LMS) in Developing Countries: Instructors' Evaluation. 4820*. https://doi.org/10.1080/10494820.2011.584321

Chen, K. C., & Jang, S. J. (2010). Motivation in Online Learning: Testing a Model of Self-determination Theory. *Computers in Human Behavior, 26*, 741–752. https://doi.org/10.1016/j.chb.2010.01.011

Cho, C., & Cheon, H. J. (2004). Why Do People Avoid Advertising on The Internet? *Journal of Advertising, 3367*(33), 4. https://doi.org/10.1080/00913367.2004.10639175

Coates, H., James, R., & Baldwin, G. (2005). A Critical Examination of the Effects of Learning Management Systems on University Teaching and Learning. *Tertiary Education & Management, 11*(1), 19–39.

Conde, M. Á., García-peñalvo, F. J., Rodríguez-conde, M. J., Alier, M., Casany, M. J., & Piguillem, J. (2014). An evolving Learning Management System for New Educational Environments Using 2.0 Tools. *Interactive Learning Environments, 188–204*(22), 2. https://doi.org/10.1080/10494820.2012.745433

Courtney, M., & Wilhoite-Mathews, S. (2015). From Distance Education to Online Learning: Practical Approaches to Information Literacy Instruction and Collaborative Learning in Online Environments. *Journal of Library Administration, 55*(4), 261–277. https://doi.org/10.1080/01930826.2015.1038924

Dacin, M., Goodstein, J., & Scott, W. (2002). Institutional Theory and Institutional Change: Introduction to the Special Research Forum. *Academy of Management Journal, 45*(1), 45–56. https://doi.org/10.2307/3069284

Davis, F. D. (1989). Perceived Usefulness, Perceived Ease of Use, and User Acceptance of Information Technology. *MIS Quarterly: Management Information Systems, 13*(3), 319–339. https://doi.org/10.2307/249008

Davis, F. D., Bagozzi, R. P., & Warshaw, P. R. (1989). User Acceptance of Computer Technology: A Comparison of Two Theoretical Models. *Management Science, 35*(8), 982–1003. https://doi.org/10.1287/mnsc.35.8.982

Delone, W. H., & Mclean, E. R. (2003). The DeLone and McLean Model of Information Systems Success: A Ten-Year Update. *Journal of Management Information Systems, 19*(4), 9–30. https://doi.org/10.1080/07421222.2003.11045748

Despotovic-Zrakic, M., Markovic, A., Bogdanovic, Z., Barac, D., & Kroc, S. (2012). Providing Adaptivity in Moodle LMS Courses. *Educational Technology and Society, 15*(1), 326–338.

Domingo, M. G., & Garganté, A. B. (2016). Exploring the Use of Educational Technology in Primary Education: Teachers' Perception of Mobile Technology Learning Impacts and Applications' Use in the Classroom. *Computers and Human Behaviour, 56*, 21–28. https://doi.org/10.1016/j.chb.2015.11.023

Dwivedi, Y. K., Wastell, D., Laumer, S., & Henriksen, H. Z. (2015). Research on Information Systems Failures and Successes: Status Update and Future Directions. *Information System Front, 17*, 143–157. https://doi.org/10.1007/s10796-014-9500-y

Emelyanova, N., & Voronina, E. (2014). Introducing a Learning Management System at a Russian University: Students' and Teachers' Perceptions. *The International Review of Research in Open and Social Distance Learning, 15*(1), 272–289.

Engelbrecht, E. (2005). Adapting to Changing Expectations: Post-graduate Students Ó Experience of an e-learning Tax Program. *45*, 217–229. https://doi.org/10.1016/j.compedu.2004.08.001

Eom, S. B. (2014). Understanding eLearners' Satisfaction with Learning Management Systems. *Bulletin of the IEEE Technical Committee on Learning Technology, 16*(2), 3–6.

Fernández-Gutiérrez, M., Gimenez, G., & Calero, J. (2020, May). Is the Use of ICT in Education Leading to Higher Student Outcomes? Analysis from the Spanish Autonomous Communities. *Computers and Education, 157*. https://doi.org/10.1016/j.compedu.2020.103969

Fornell, C., & Larcker, D. F. (1981). Evaluating Structural Equation Models with Unobservable Variables and Measurement Error. *Journal of Marketing Research*, 18(1), 39–50. https://doi.org/10.1177/002224378101800104

García-Peñalvo, F. J. (2008). *Advances in e-learning: Experiences and Methodologies* (Informatio). https://doi.org/10.4018/978-1-59904-756-0

Greene, J. A., Yu, S. B., & Copeland, D. Z. (2014). Measuring Critical Components of Digital Literacy and their Relationships with Learning. *Computers & Education, 76*, 55–69. https://doi.org/10.1016/j.compedu.2014.03.008

Hair, J. F., Hollingsworth, C. L., Randolph, A. B., & Chong, A. Y. L. (2017). An Updated and Expanded Assessment of PLS-SEM in Information Systems Research. *Industrial Management and Data Systems, 117*(3), 442–458. https://doi.org/10.1108/IMDS-04-2016-0130

Hair, J. F., Sarstedt, M., Ringle, C. M., & Mena, J. A. (2012). An Assessment of the Use of Partial Least Squares Structural Equation Modelling in Marketing Research. *Journal of the Academy Marketing Science, 40*, 414–433. https://doi.org/10.1007/s11747-011-0261-6

Hanafizadeh, P., Behboudi, M., Abedini, A., Jalilvand, M., & Tabar, S. (2014). Telematics and Informatics Mobile-banking Adoption by Iranian Bank Clients. *Telematics and Informatics, 31*(1), 62–78. https://doi.org/10.1016/j.tele.2012.11.001

Hassanzadeh, A., Kanaani, F., & Elahi, S. (2012). A Model for Measuring e-learning Systems Success in Universities. *Expert Systems With Applications, 39*(12), 10959–10966. https://doi.org/10.1016/j.eswa.2012.03.028

Henseler, J., Ringle, C. M., & Sarstedt, M. (2015). A New Criterion for Assessing Discriminant Validity in Variance-based Structural Equation Modelling. *Journal of the Academy of Marketing Science, 43*(1), 115–135. https://doi.org/10.1007/s11747-014-0403-8

Ho, C., & Dzeng, R. (2010). Construction Safety Training via e-Learning: Learning Effectiveness and User Satisfaction. *Computers & Education, 55*, 858–867. https://doi.org/10.1016/j.compedu.2010.03.017

Horvat, A., Dobrota, M., Krsmanovic, M., & Cudanov, M. (2015). Student Perception of Moodle Learning Management System: A Satisfaction and Significance Analysis. *Interactive Learning Environments, 23*(4), 515–527. https://doi.org/10.1080/10494820.2013.788033

Hsu, P., Yen, R. H., & Chung, J. (2015). Assessing ERP Post-implementation Success at the Individual Level: Revisiting the Role of Service Quality. *Information & Management, 52*(8), 925–942. https://doi.org/10.1016/j.im.2015.06.009

Hung, S. Y., Huang, Y. W., Lin, C. C., Chen, K. C., & Tarn, J. M. (2016). Factors Influencing Business Intelligence Systems Implementation Success in the Enterprises. *Pacific Asia Conference on Information Systems, PACIS 2016 — Proceedings.*

Islam, A., & Azad, N. (2015). Satisfaction and Continuance with a Learning Management System: Comparing Perceptions of Educators and Students. *International Journal of Information and Learning Technology, 32*(2), 109–123. https://doi.org/10.1108/IJILT-09-2014-0020

Islam, A. Y. M. A., Mo, M., Mok, C., Gu, X., Spector, J. M., & Hai-leng, C. (2019). ICT in Higher Education: An Exploration of Practices in Malaysian Universities. *IEEE Access, 7*, 16892–16908. https://doi.org/10.1109/ACCESS.2019.2895879

Ismailova, R., & Muhametjanova, G. (2016). Cybercrime Risk Awareness in Kyrgyz Republic Cybercrime Risk Awareness in the Kyrgyz Republic. *Information Security Journal: A Global Perspective, 25*(1–3), 32–38. https://doi.org/10.1080/19393555.2015.1132800

Jafari, S. M., Salem, S. F., Moaddab, M. S., & Salem, S. O. (2015). Learning Management System (LMS) Success: An Investigation among the University Students. *2015 IEEE Conference on E-Learning, e-Management and e-Services*, 64–69. https://doi.org/10.1109/IC3e.2015.7403488

Jakchaikul, V. (2015). Application of Learning Management System for Online Learning Modules. *Applied Mechanics and Materials, 804*, 347–350. https://doi.org/10.4028/www.scientific.net/AMM.804.347

Jurubescu, T. (2008). Learning Content Management Systems. *Informatica Economica, 12*(4), 91–94.

Kaplan, R. S., & Norton., D. P. (1996). *The Balanced Scorecard: Translating Strategy into Action.* Boston, MA: Harvard Business School Press.

Kasim, N. N. M., & Khalid, F. (2016). Choosing the Right Learning Management System (LMS) for the Higher Education Institution Context: A Systematic Review. *International Journal of Emerging Technologies in Learning (iJET), 11*(6), 55–61.

Kassem, R., Ajmal, M., Gunasekaran, A., & Helo, P. (2019). Assessing the Impact of Organizational Culture on Achieving Business Excellence with a Moderating Role of ICT: An SEM Approach. *Benchmarking, 26*(1), 117–146. https://doi.org/10.1108/BIJ-03-2018-0068

Kember, D., McNaught, C., Chong, F. C., Lam, P., & Cheng, K. F. (2010). Understanding the ways in which design features of educational websites impact upon student learning outcomes in blended learning environments. *Computers & Education*, *55*, 1183–1192.

Kyzy, Z. N., Ismailova, R., & Dündar, H. (2018). Learning management system implementation: A Case Study in the Kyrgyz Republic. *Interactive Learning Environments*, 1–13. https://doi.org/10.1080/1049 4820.2018.1427115

Laudon, K. C., & Laudon, J. P. (2012). *Management Information Systems: Managing the Digital Firm* (12th ed.). London: Prentice Hall International.

Liaw, S. S., Huang, H. M., & Chen, G. D. (2007). Surveying Instructor and Learner Attitudes toward e-learning. *Computers & Education*, *49*(4), 1066–1080.

Lonn, S., & Teasley, S. D. (2009). Saving Time or Innovating Practice: Investigating Perceptions and Uses of Learning Management Systems. *Computers & Education*, *53*(3), 686–694. https://doi.org/10.1016/j. compedu.2009.04.008

Melo, E., Llopis, J., Gascó, J., & González, R. (2020). Integration of ICT into the Higher Education Process: The Case of Colombia. *Journal of Small Business Strategy*, *30*(1), 58–67.

Nguyen, T. H., Newby, M., & Macaulay, M. J. (2015). Information Technology Adoption in Small Business: Confirmation of a Proposed Framework. *Journal of Small Business Management*, *53*(1), 207–227. https://doi.org/10.1111/jsbm.12058

Nunally, J. C. (1978). *Psychometric Theory* (2nd ed.). New York: McGraw-Hill.

Ozkan, S., & Koseler, R. (2009). Multi-dimensional Students' Evaluation of e-learning Systems in the Higher Education Context: An Empirical Investigation. *Computers & Education*, *53*, 1285–1296. https://doi. org/10.1016/j.compedu.2009.06.011

Oztekin, A., Kong, Z. J., & Uysal, O. (2010). UseLearn: A Novel Checklist and Usability Evaluation Method for eLearning Systems by Criticality Metric Analysis. *International Journal of Industrial Ergonomics*, *40*(4), 455–469. https://doi.org/10.1016/j.ergon.2010.04.001

Petrovic, N., Drakulic, M., Isljamovic, S., Jeremic, V., & Drakulic, R. (2011). Towards a Framework for Higher Environment Education. *Journal of Management Theory and Practice*, *16*(60), 11–18.

Petter, S., Delone, W., & Mclean, E. (2008). Measuring Information Systems Success: Models, Dimensions, Measures, and Interrelationships. *European Journal of Information Systems*, *17*, 236–263. https://doi. org/10.1057/ejis.2008.15

Rana, K., & Rana, K. (2020). ICT Integration in Teaching and Learning Activities in Higher Education: A Case Study of Nepal's Teacher Education. *Malaysian Online Journal of Educational Technology*, *8*(1), 36–47. https://doi.org/10.17220/mojet.2020.01.003

Rhode, J., Richter, S., Gowen, P., Miller, T., & Wills, C. (2017). Understanding Faculty Use Of the Learning Management System. *Online Learning Journal*, *21*(3), 68–86. https://doi.org/10.24059/ olj.v%vi%i.1217

Rogers, E. (2003). *Diffusions of Innovations*. New York: Free Press.

Rubin, B., Fernandes, R., Avgerinou, M. D., & Moore, J. (2010). Internet and Higher Education. The Effect of Learning Management Systems on Student and Faculty Outcomes. *The Internet and Higher Education*, *13*(1–2), 82–83. https://doi.org/10.1016/j.iheduc.2009.10.008

Rubin, H. (2004). Into the light. *In CIO Magazine*.

Seddon, P., Graeser, V., & Wilcocks, L. P. (2002). Measuring Organizational IS Effectiveness: An Overview and Update of Senior Management Perspectives. *The DATA BASE for Advances in Information Systems*, *33*(2), 11–28.

Smet, C. De, Valcke, M., Schellens, T., Wever, B. De, & Venderlinde, R. (2016). A Qualitative Study on Learning and Teaching with Learning Paths in a Learning Management System. *Journal of Social Science Education*, *15*(1), 27–37. https://doi.org/10.4119/UNIBI/jsse-v15-i1-1460

Tang, C. M., & Chaw, L. Y. (2016). Digital Literacy: A Prerequisite for Effective Learning in a Blended Learning Environment? *The Electronic Journal of E-Learning*, *14*(1), 54–65.

Tokareva, E. A., Smirnova, Y. V., & Orchakova, L. G. (2019). Innovation and Communication Technologies: Analysis of the Effectiveness of their Use and Implementation in Higher Education. *Education and Information Technologies*, *24*(5), 3219–3234. https://doi.org/10.1007/s10639-019-09922-2

Tornatzky, L., & Fleischer, M. (1990). *The Processes of Technological Innovation*. Lexington, MA: Lexington Books.

Vandeyar, T. (2020). The Academic Turn: Social Media in Higher Education. *Education and Information Technologies, 25*(6), 5617–5635. https://doi.org/10.1007/s10639-020-10240-1

Venugopal, G., & Jain, R. (2015). Influence of Learning Management System on Student Engagement. *3rd International Conference on MOOCs, Innovation and Technology in Education (MITE),* 427–432.

Vinzi, V. E., Chin, W. W., Henseler, J., & Wang, H. (2010). *Handbooks of Partial Least Squares: Concepts, Methods and Application.* Heidelberg, Germany: Springer Berlin Heidelberg.

Waluyo, B. (2019). The Effects of ICT on Achievement: Criticizing the Exclusion of ICT from World Bank's Education Sector Strategy 2020. *Malaysian Online Journal of Educational Technology, 7*(2), 71–87. https://doi.org/10.17220/mojet.2019.02.005

Wang, W. T., & Wang, C. C. (2009). An Empirical Study of Instructor Adoption of Web-based Learning Systems. *Computers & Education, 53*(3), 761–774. https://doi.org/10.1016/j.compedu.2009.02.021

Watson, B. W. R., & Watson, S. L. (2007). An Argument for Clarity: What are Learning Management Systems, What are They Not, and What Should They Become? *TechTrends, 51*(2), 28–34.

Werts, C. E., Linn, R. L., & Joreskog, Q. (1974). Intraclass Reliability Estimates: Testing Structural Assumptions. *Educational and Psychological Measurement, 33*(509), 25–33.

Williams, D., & Whiting, A. (2016). Exploring the Relationship Between Student Engagement, Twitter, and a Learning Management System: A Study of Undergraduate Marketing Students. *International Journal of Teaching and Learning in Higher Education, 28*(3), 302–313.

Woyo, E., Rukanda, G. D., & Nyamapanda, Z. (2020). ICT Policy Implementation in Higher Education Institutions in Namibia: A Survey of Students' Perceptions. *Education and Information Technologies, 25,* 3705–3722. https://doi.org/10.1007/s10639-020-10118-2

Yang, X., Li, X., & Lu, T. (2015). Using Mobile Phones in College Classroom Settings: Effects of Presentation Mode and Interest on Concentration and Achievement. *Computers and Education, 88,* 292–302. https://doi.org/10.1016/j.compedu.2015.06.007

Author's Profile

Sampson A. Edu is a final year doctoral candidate in Management Information Systems at Cyprus International University in Lefkosa, North Cyprus. He has a background in Big Data, Cloud, and IOT systems security. His research interest is consistent with his knowledge background. He is also an adjunct faculty with the department of Management information Systems at Cyprus International University.

Chapter 23

Toward Building Organizational Resilience to Social Engineering among Higher Educational Institution Professionals

Divine Quase Agozie, Abeeku S. Edu, and Muesser Nat

Contents

DOI: 10.4324/9781003152217-29

347

Introduction

The fast evolution of digital technologies has increased organizational dependency on technology by way of increased connectivity and convenience (Krombholz et al., 2015). A consequence of this increased dependence on digital technologies has been the growth in frequency and complexity of cybercrimes (Aldawood & Skinner, 2020). Cybercrimes are committed behind the vails of computers and have rapidly grown in magnitude to present substantial threats to organizations and even governments (Stiawan et al., 2017; Schatz et al., 2017). As such, many organizations commit substantial financial resources to ensure information security and protect their information assets (Aldawood & Skinner, 2020; Biancotti, 2017). Unfortunately, even the most sophisticated technological solutions available are unable to guarantee the security of information systems from all modes of cyber-attacks because information security is only as strong as its weakest link—humans (Aldawood & Skinner, 2018).

Cybercrimes that seek to exploit the human element in an information system or network through techniques that seek to take induce human beings into divulging information or allowing access are known as social engineering (Salahdine et al., 2019; Gallegos-Segovia et al., 2017). Experts suggest that human weaknesses are the prioritized mode of attack for cyber criminals in recent, as it offers a higher likelihood of success of any cyberattack (Aldawood & Skinner, 2020; Breda et al., 2017).

Despite this known fact, many organizations still relegate the human element in their fight against security risks (Salahdine et al., 2019). The human element contributes significantly to security breaches (Mouton et al., 2016), because it is considered the weak link in any information security chain (Aldawood & Skinner, 2018). Thus, cyber criminals now focus less on the technical modes to breaching a system and seek to target the humans who interact with the system (Aldawood & Skinner, 2020). Many high-profile cyber-attacks over the decade such as RSA, JP Morgan, AT&T were successful through the exploitation of the human element (Aldawood & Skinner, 2020).

The higher educational service sector has relied much on ITs to offer quality education (Daniel, 2020). However, recent developments like the global pandemic (COVID-19) have motivated the increased reliance of higher education institutions on ITs to deliver virtual education (Daniel, 2020; Chick et al., 2020). As a result, it makes the higher educational setting new potential targets for social engineering schemes (Ghazi-Tehrani & Pontell, 2021; Aldawood & Skinner, 2020; Parthy & Rajendran, 2019) because social engineering is determined as an emerging threat to virtual communities (Ghazi-Tehrani & Pontell, 2021). The source of this assertion stems from the fact that the higher education sector, even in highly developed contexts largely remains labour intensive (Fatima & Naima, 2019) making it susceptible to social engineering. This makes need for discussions on building resilience in the educational institutions sector an imperative one.

Reports on the notion of cyber-security assurance for social engineering reveal a lack of consensus on a common resilience framework (Fatima & Naima, 2019; von Solms & von Solms, 2018; Rocha Flores et al., 2015b). Thus, there is a drought of relevant investigations on validating the effectiveness of concepts and frameworks on social engineering (Fatima & Naima, 2019; Rocha & Ekstedt, 2016). For instance, how certain human elements can be leveraged to insulate organizational networks against social engineering remain scant (van Niekerk, 2017). Thus, many of the reports have largely established relationships between concepts and not necessary develop practical implementation modes (Krombholz et al., 2015; Kritzinger, 2017). To contribute to this gap, this chapter empirically prioritizes which human and organizational elements can be precipitates for successful social engineering attacks to develop an implementation framework for resilience against social engineering threats in an Higher Education Institution (HEI) context.

Literature Review

This section provides a review of existing reports and literature to understand the main concepts that underpin this chapter. It provides insights from prior works on concepts such as information security, social engineering, and behavioral elements.

Information Security and Social Engineering (SE)

Information security assurance has attracted different viewpoints from practitioners over the years likewise its meaning from different domains. From a generic standpoint, information security is compasses actions and approaches associated with a cyber threat used to ensure the confidentiality, and integrity of data (Schatz et al., 2017). Scholars like von Solms and von Solms (2018) agree that information security largely seeks to protect integrity, confidentiality, and all available information. The reason being that there are constant variations in the attack vectors that information security mechanisms seek to prevent. Scholars identify six commonly employed attack vectors known to organizations thus, the denial-of-service attacks (DOS), password breaking, web implants, SQL injections, phishing, and malware attacks (Stiawan et al., 2017). Giving these vectors, social engineering emerges as a completely different vector, hence may be easily overlooked. Humans within an information system standout as the weakest elements in a cybercrime (Heartfield & Loukas, 2015), and are often the first point of attack into the system (Mouton et al., 2016). In this regard, social engineering schemes are immensely powerful and difficult to prevent using technical means often employed by organizations (Fatima & Naima, 2019).

Social engineering as an attack vector centers on targeting people (Parthy & Rajendran, 2019). It exploits the psychological weaknesses of the victims to gain access into a network (Pozo et al., 2018) making it the easiest attack vector to execute compared with the existing technical attack vectors. It does not require much technical expertise, time, and effort. In the virtual community, social engineering comes across as a serious security threat to actors there (Parthy & Rajendran, 2019; Krombholz et al., 2015). Beyond the virtual communities, social engineering schemes make any kind of organization susceptible to its modes.

Information Security Awareness

Recent years have seen sufficient growth in efforts to endorse information security awareness campaigns and practice (van Niekerk, 2017). Information security traditionally emphasizes a structured and technical procedure to achieve security assurance. As such, most investigations have largely considered the formal controls enshrined by policy and industry practice (Davidson, 2016).

Developments on information security awareness date back to the late 1990s. Most of the efforts sought to understand how information security can be improved and enhanced using awareness programs; however, these efforts were mainly conceptual (Tsohou et al., 2015). For example, Straub and Welke (1998) showed that information security awareness and efforts then were mainly designed to be deterrent countermeasures and structured to be systematic or plan driven. In actual sense, users of these programs achieved a temporary state of mind, and required periodic reviews (David et al., 2016). The fast-changing nature of information security risks flaws such as structured or systematic approaches (Ding et al., 2015). Emerging technologies come with new sophistication likewise the risks. Thus, security awareness must be approached cautiously with a continuous objective which focuses to help users remain aware and ready to resist security risks always (WEF, 2019; Szczepaniuk et al., 2020).

Despite these thoughts, there are organizations that are still reliant on the formal methods, because they are less resource demanding compared with the user-centered information security awareness programs (WEF, 2019). Contemporary security practice and programs require a more balanced and all-inclusive procedure to ensure improved information security compliance and assurance (Tsohou et al., 2015). Although the importance of information security awareness and compliance is well established, the concept is still unclear direction toward its actualization (Szczepaniuk et al., 2020).

Examinations that have offered insights into information security awareness frameworks have also reported mixed results on their success and effectiveness (Kirton, 2017; Susanto et al., 2011). By effectiveness, Siponen et al. (2014) suggest it is the extent to which an information security awareness program increases a person's security risk awareness and compliance. However, it is argued that this assertion of effectiveness is not likely to hold, as every organization is likely to have a different information security practice and as such there will be design diversity (Abawajy, 2014).

The importance of information security awareness and the neglect of compliance by users presents a paradox worth discerning (Lebek et al., 2014; Kajzer et al., 2014). There are several explanations for this occurrence. For example, Posey et al. (2014) attribute it to the perception of information security risk held by users. In that, the perception of users significantly influences role acting and compliance. Others like Parthy and Rajendran (2019), Johnston et al. (2015), and Clarke et al. (2012) highlight knowledge inadequacy for recognizing information security risks. More recent views also argue along personality traits of users as a cause of this paradox (Karjalainen et al., 2020; Christopher et al., 2017). Thus, the new revelations have driven the recommendations for more user-centered approaches to information security awareness strategies (Karjalainen et al., 2020).

3.0 Method

Design and Framework Development

Social engineering emerges is a significant threat to many labor-intensive organizations (van Niekerk, 2017; Kritzinger, 2017). Thus, settings with many humans integrated into an information system possess high susceptibility to social engineering schemes (Karjalainen et al., 2020). This is because humans (like administrators) in these systems have access to sensitive information and other information assets (Furnell & Vasileiou, 2017), thus making them prime targets. Thus, the need to build resilient and social engineering-proof environments is principal particularly among organizations like HEIs. This chapter investigates the phenomenon of information security awareness and develops a practical resilience framework for social engineering in HEIs. A two-stage analysis procedure is employed: first an exploratory phase which included a computerized content analysis of transcribed industry discussions on relevant behavioral and organizational elements for defending against social engineering schemes.

The second stage validates the factors identified from the exploratory phase to develop the framework. Systems administrators from ten universities in Cyprus were consulted for the confirmatory stage analysis. An Analytical Hierarchy Process (AHP) technique is employed to perform the validation of the factors drawn from the exploratory analysis. This approach is effective for empirical evaluations as it ensures sufficient reliability and generalizability of results (Creswell & Plano Clark, 2011). Data collected for the examination was done using an online AHP questionnaire sent to each systems administrator via the head of information technology in the universities. This process spanned over a period of 4 months.

Exploratory Phase

This stage mainly consists of collecting and content-analyzing of web seminar (Webinar) event recordings on social engineering behavior and preventive approaches. The events were carefully selected because they entailed discussions and expert opinions as well as contributions of other experts who also possess knowledge on the issue of cybersecurity and social engineering. Soujanya et al. (2016) believe this data source to be rich for analysis because offers a broad range of subjects. They also propose the use of information from multiple modalities (audio, visual and textual modalities) for other forms of text analysis. In deciding on the choice of webinars, a sampling criterion is developed with the following conditions.

- The webinar should be organized by a globally recognized cybersecurity organization with cyber security solutions as a core part of its service offerings or should be a global body of professional security experts.
- The event date should be no more than three years ago.
- The title of the webinar event must at least contain keywords as social engineering, prevention, detection, information security, among others.
- The panel or guest speaker should also be an active professional in the cyber security industry with active attachment to an organization and at least 3 years of experience in delivering cyber security solutions.

Five events were sampled and downloaded from the websites of the organizing companies. A summary of the event details is provided in Table 23.1.

Table 23.1 Summary of Details of Selected Webinar Events

Name of Organization	Title and Year of Webinar	Profile of Speakers
BetterCloud	Do Not Be Another Statistic— How to Recognize and Prevent Social Engineering Attacks (2016)	Professional social engineers Managing security assoc. Sr. Application security Eng.
CSIAC: Cyber Security and Information Systems Information Analysis Center	Webinar—Social Engineering (2019)	Cybersecurity expert and professor (Utica College)
CSO Australia and Mimecast	A Malware is Easy to Make, and Social Engineering Makes It Easy to Distribute. Can You Stop It? (2019)	Sr. Technical consultant Head of Info. Security, Auckland Ports CEO Cybersecurity network (UK& Australia) Chief Influencing Agent
Cybrary	Phishing and Social Engineering Trends in 2020: Is the Worst Yet to Come?	CEO of KnowBe4
CISCO	Dismantling Social Engineering in Supply Chain Attacks	Security researcher of Cisco Talos team EMEAR

Recordings from the events ranged between 64 minutes and 102 minutes. These recordings were transcribed using "Google voice typing" Artificial Intelligence software. It must be noted that this tool may not transcribe with absolute accuracy, as such for each recording, the entire transcription process was strictly observed to ensure the correctness of the transcribed text.

Owing to the fact that the exploratory stage mainly focused on identifying themes and elements that will form the factors or behavioral elements relevant to building resilience for social engineering schemes, a keyword generator analysis was performed with the Rapid Miner text analysis software (Stupans et al., 2015). Important keywords were extracted to represent contextual themes relative to social engineering schemes and their prevention. These keywords were considered as themes to build the framework for validation at the confirmatory phase of the analysis. The themes identified were also compared with findings from prior works to ensure a good conceptualization of the factors to reduce construct validity problems such as biasing effect (Susanto et al., 2011). Further, to ensure adequate reliability of an instrument, Susanto et al. (2011) propose the use of expert opinion at the formulation stage of the factors. Thus, this informs the choice of systems administrators to validate the themes drawn from the content analysis, as well as the use of industry experts at the exploratory stage to derive the themes. This approach is believed to guarantee a higher chance of reliability of the results.

Confirmatory Phase

The study prioritizes the relevant factors using the Analytic Hierarchy Process (AHP) technique. Mainly, the AHP helps assigns importance weights to the themes. The AHP as originally proposed by Saaty (1980) is a technique for analyzing complex decisions and has been widely applied in several contexts as healthcare, governance, logistics management, education. The AHP basically uses subjective expert judgments in a well-defined mathematical structure of matrices and their associated eigenvectors to generate a true or approximate weight (Saaty, 1980, 1994). It is founded on three basic principles: (a) problem decomposition, (b) comparative analysis, and (c) synthesis of priorities and consistency. The problem of decomposition involves setting up the problem into a hierarchy of clusters. The objective here is to set the highest hierarchy followed by the sub-criteria. The decision alternatives are then laid at the bottom of the problem. For example, the problem of this analysis is to determine which factors are important at the strategic level, tactical, and operational levels of implementation to minimize the success of social engineering schemes.

Next, the AHP allows pairwise comparison of each parameter using a relative importance scale presented in Table 23.2. Basically, the systems administrators or experts are asked to judge which parameter (i or j) is more important and by how much.

In conducting the pairwise comparison, the rate by which parameter i is more important compared to j (a_{ij}) is the reciprocal of the rate by which j is more important than i. The relative importance scoring will result in a matrix where the score between a parameter i and parameter j is positive, whiles the rating between parameter i and itself is equal to 1.

$$A = \left(a_{ij} \right), \ a_{ij} > 0 \text{ and } a_{ii} = 1$$

This matrix produces a square and reciprocal matrix from the pairwise comparison represented as:

$$A = \begin{bmatrix} a_{11} & \cdots & a_{1n} \\ \vdots & \ddots & \vdots \\ a_{n1} & \cdots & a_{nn} \end{bmatrix}$$

Table 23.2   AHP Rating Score

Score (a)	Meaning
1	Parameter *i* is equally important as parameter *j*
3	Parameter *i* is weakly more important than parameter *j*
5	Parameter *i* is strongly more important than parameter *j*
7	Parameter *i* is very strongly more important than parameter *j*
9	Parameter *i* is absolutely more important than parameter *j*
2,4,6,8	Intermediate values

where

$$a_{1n} = \frac{1}{a_{n1}}$$

Note that the score a_{ij} can be defined as the importance (weight) of parameter *i* to the importance (weight) of parameter *j*, such that $a_{ij} = w_i / w_j$. Based on this matrix the weight (*w*) of the criteria (and any sub-criteria) can be calculated from the pairwise comparison matrices (*A*) using the eigenvalue method (Islam & Abdullah, 2006). This leads to the final step of the AHP process. The eigenvalue approach requires that a successive power of the matrix be generated. The sums of the rows are then normalized to the extent when the difference between successive row sums is infinitesimal. The weight can be estimated for a parameter *i* by solving the equation:

$$w_i = \frac{1}{\lambda_{max}} \sum_{j=1}^{n} a_{ij} w_j$$

where λ_{max} is the largest eigenvalue of the pairwise comparison matrix *A*. Note also that $\Sigma_{j=1}^{n} w_i = 1$.

After this, the credit score of each obligor can be estimated as a product of the matrix *A* and the weight vector *w* such that:

$$\text{Behaviour Element Score} = Aw$$

In the final step, there is the need to compute a CI to measure consistency in the experts' judgment. Saaty (2003) uses the largest eigenvalue (λ_{max}) to define a CI such that:

$$\text{Consistency Index} \left(\text{CI} \right) = \frac{\lambda_{max-n}}{n-1}$$

Finally, the CR is computed as a ratio of the CI to a RI which is estimated from a Saaty's (1977) statistical table.

$$\text{Consistency Ratio} \left(\text{CR} \right) = \frac{\text{Consistency Index} \left(\text{CI} \right)}{\text{Random Index} \left(\text{RI} \right)}$$

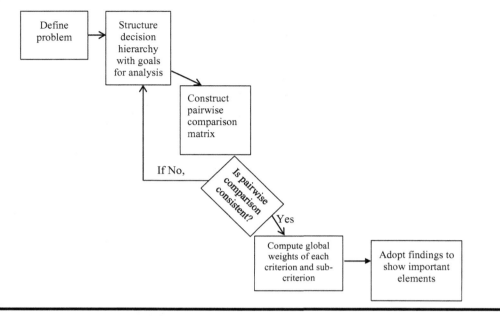

Figure 23.1   Flow chart to conduct AHP.

Source: Talib et al. (2011) and Saaty (2008).

The RI is a randomly generated pairwise comparison matrix that depends on the number of items (*n*) being compared. Generally, it is expected that the CR will be less than 0.10 to ensure high reliability of the ranking system. A CR greater than 1 signifies that the judgment may not be reliable since there are inconsistencies in the views of the expert (Anderson et al., 2018). The procedure discussed earlier is modeled in the flow chart shown in Figure 23.1.

Analysis and Results

Results from the exploratory analysis revealed 9523-word tokens. Further text processing was done to filter stop words, generate n-grams, and filter token length, with minimum characters of 4 and a maximum of 25. Words that had total occurrence less than 0.05% across the entire corpus were discarded (Jelodar et al., 2019). This process was well based on an ideological analysis model to generate a sizeable number list of relevant keywords. The keyword analysis output from the analysis is presented in Table 23.3. The word tokens presented in Table 23.3 were among the top 35 most frequently used terms in the expert discussions during the webinar sessions. In addition, the relative relevance score of each word token is also shown in Table 23.3.

The first thirty-five (35) keywords are presented from the keyword generation analysis with their total occurrence and relevance score, respectively. Notably recurring keywords were "systems" and "password". These words were often used in relation to the targets of social engineering attacks. For instance, statements such as *social engineers identify weaker systems* or *creating an awareness of the need to create strong passwords*. Other keywords like social, information, cyber, and attach were also prevalent. These keywords were subjectively grouped into themes that were used to develop a hierarchical model in Figure 23.2.

Table 23.3 Summary of Keywords

Keywords	Frequency	Relevance
social	38	0.077
behaviour	12	0.024
negligence	5	0.010
hack	12	0.024
attache	23	0.047
social_media	18	0.037
privacy	22	0.045
report	12	00024
attitude	9	0.018
system	48	0.096
information	33	0.067
data	15	0.030
document	4	0.008
manage	14	0.028
leadership	5	0.010
email	13	0.026
mobile	17	0.034
Internet	16	0.032
wireless	5	0.010
password	43	0.087
physical	4	0.008
awareness	4	0.008
culture	15	0.030
computers	11	0.022
device	7	0.014
knowledge	8	0.016
crime	24	0.051
network	8	0.016
organization	14	0.028
cyber	26	0.053
technical	4	0.008
information_systems	18	0.037
hardware	14	0.028
personal	14	0.028
conscious	14	0.028

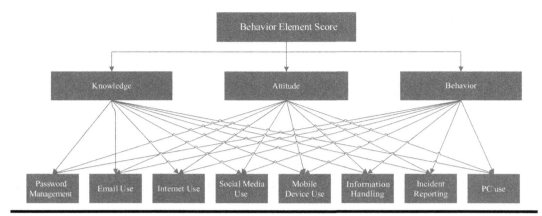

Figure 23.2   General framework for achieving resistance to social engineering schemes.

The framework in Figure 23.2 depicts the hierarchical relationship between top-level factors, and implementation factors. There are three top-level factors (knowledge, attitude, and behavior) to be considered for strategic management direction and eight implementation factors at the tactical level. By implication, the framework proposes a top-to-down approach involving top management strategy and tactical implementation practices. Strategically, HEI must consider building knowledge base, attitude, or behavior of personnel as the strategic focus. This is then broken down into eight policy directions to be implemented at the tactical level. These include password management policy, policy on ensuring safety in email and Internet use, social media use and management policy, mobile device and personal computer use within the organization, and policy on information handling and security incident handling.

Results

Top Level Factors

Results of the relevant factors for the framework are shown in Tables 23.4 and 23.5.

The analysis first assessed the three strategic factors that should be prioritized to allow for top management implementation. The results reveal significant differences in the importance weights attained for each factor. However, "knowledge" emerged the most important factor determined to be considered as the strategic focus by management of HEIs. Thus, focus on this factor will ensure users acquire sufficient knowledge on social engineering schemes. Subsequently, attitude and behavior gained the second and third highest importance weights, respectively. In essence, HEIs should focus on the implementation of strategies that seek to offer knowledge to personnel and other users of the system on cyber security threats and social engineering. Parthy and Rajendran (2019) suggest that knowledge of the common modes, attack variants, and common errors of commission or omission among users that can be exploited should be clear to users of the system to increase their awareness and reduce vulnerability to social engineering. This is mostly achieved through conscious education, training programs, and exercises.

Table 23.4 Priority Weights Relative to Strategic Level Factors

Factors	R1	R2	R3	R4	R5	R6	R7	R8	R9	Ave Weight	Rank
Knowledge	0.413	0.413	0.705	0.26	0.717	0.727	0.74	0.073	0.055	0.456	1
Attitude	0.26	0.327	0.084	0.327	0.217	0.073	0.094	0.727	0.655	0.307	2
Behavior	0.327	0.26	0.211	0.413	0.066	0.2	0.167	0.2	0.29	0.237	3
CR	0.056	0.056	0.034	0.056	0.039	0.001	0.015	0.01	0.084	0.039	
Eigen value	3.054	3.054	3.032	3.054	3.037	3.009	3.014	3.009	3.08	3.038	

Implementation Factors

Regarding the specific policy and practices to be implemented for building resilience or protective behavior, the experts judged the elements according to the order in which they would drive resilience. First, *password management* showed the greatest weight among the eight factors at this second stage of the hierarchy. The practical implication herein lies in the fact that active education and management support on the need to understand how to secure and manage personal and institutional passwords will lead to improved resilience. von Solms and von Solms (2018) attest to the fact that adequate knowledge on managing personal passwords increases user awareness for managing organizational ones too. Thus, this factor is a crucial driver of the successful implementation of information security mechanisms in an organization.

Shown in Table 23.5, *information handling* factor gained the second highest importance weight. An implication that HEIs require a clear procedure and practices that determine how personnel must treat institutional information. This is because information handling could be seen as subjective construct when left to be determined individuals (Kritzinger, 2017). Therefore, procedure on how, for instance, organizational information may be exchanged, shared, or released into the public must be clearly determined. Next, *social media use* attained the third highest importance weight. In the opinion of this examination, it is believed social media generally creates an impression on the user and also allows users to put much information about themselves and their institution of work into the public domain. This information may prove useful for cyber criminals who profile personnel of an organization of interest to them. Therefore, personnel must be knowledgeable about what information about themselves and their institution of work they disclose to the public to minimize the tendency of becoming targets of social engineering schemes. Among the eight factors considered, *personal computer use* (*PC use*) was the least ranked important factor. This suggests an emphasis on the fact that most organizations are making efforts to ensure to discourage the bring-your-own-device (BYOD) phenomenon that is common among many resource-constrained organizations. However, the current global development that encourages virtual workstations gives room for new considerations to this phenomenon.

Operational Practices for Routine Performance

Regarding password management, expert judgments emphasized the "use of *strong passwords*" (Table 23.6). In practice, providing personnel with adequate knowledge about the principles and standard practices of setting and managing passwords as well as equipping personnel with the

Table 23.5 Priority Weights Relative to the Eight Themes Identified for Implementation Factors

Factors	R1	R2	R3	R4	R5	R6	R7	R8	R9	Ave Weight	Rank
Password Mgt.	0.388	0.161	0.355	0.462	0.359	0.218	0.382	0.141	0.366	0.315	1
Info. Handling	0.309	0.127	0.042	0.168	0.287	0.129	0.168	0.408	0.154	0.199	2
Incident handling	0.037	0.116	0.069	0.047	0.153	0.237	0.155	0.125	0.102	0.116	4
Email use	0.018	0.111	0.151	0.034	0.106	0.034	0.103	0.08	0.042	0.075	5
Mob. Devices	0.05	0.14	0.092	0.09	0.027	0.057	0.019	0.057	0.15	0.076	6
Social media use	0.066	0.106	0.228	0.139	0.027	0.229	0.072	0.144	0.089	0.122	3
Internet use	0.045	0.103	0.031	0.027	0.022	0.07	0.063	0.022	0.056	0.049	7
PC use	0.086	0.136	0.033	0.033	0.019	0.025	0.038	0.023	0.041	0.048	8
CR	**0.073**	**0.06**	**0.07**	**0.079**	**0.093**	**0.092**	**0.078**	**0.087**	**0.158**	**0.087778**	
Eigen value	**8.715**	**8.586**	**8.755**	**8.777**	**8.911**	**8.902**	**8.761**	**8.849**	**9.548**	**8.867111**	

Table 23.6 Priority Weights Relative to the Practices under the Eight Implementation Factors

Factors	RES1	RES2	RES3	RES4	RES5	RES6	RES7	RES8	RES9	Ave Weight	Rank
Password Management											
Using same password	0.163	0.333	0.217	0.231	0.217	0.55	0.655	0.086	0.333	0.309444	3
Sharing password	0.297	0.333	0.066	0.708	0.066	0.24	0.29	0.414	0.528	0.326889	2
Using strong password	0.54	0.333	0.717	0.06	0.717	0.21	0.055	0.5	0.14	0.363556	1
CR	0.01	0	0.039	0.074	0.039	0.019	0.084	0.036	0.056	0.039667	
Eigen value	3.009	3	3.037	3.071	3.037	3.018	3.08	3.035	3.054	3.037889	
Email use											
Click link of unknown sender	0.077	0.558	0.066	0.717	0.743	0.082	0.174	0.738	0.333	0.38756	1
Click link of known sender	0.692	0.32	0.217	0.217	0.194	0.682	0.634	0.116	0.333	0.37833	2
Open any attachment	0.231	0.122	0.717	0.066	0.063	0.236	0.192	0.146	0.333	0.234	3
CR	0	0.019	0.039	0.039	0.074	0.002	0.01	0.056	0	0.026556	
Eigen value	3	3.018	3.012	3.037	3.071	3.002	3.009	3.054	3	3.022556	
Internet use											
Downloading files	0.333	0.25	0.066	0.066	0.708	0.637	0.055	0.416	0.168	0.299889	3
Visiting risky sites	0.333	0.5	0.217	0.717	0.06	0.258	0.655	0.458	0.484	0.409111	1
Entering personal info online	0.333	0.25	0.717	0.217	0.231	0.105	0.29	0.126	0.349	0.290889	2

(Continued)

Table 23.6 (Continued)

Factors	RES1	RES2	RES3	RES4	RES5	RES6	RES7	RES8	RES9	Ave Weight	Rank
CR	**0**	**0**	**0.039**	**0.039**	**0.074**	**0.04**	**0.084**	**0.01**	**0.141**	**0.047444**	
Eigen value	**3**	**3**	**3.037**	**3.037**	**3.071**	**3.039**	**3.08**	**3.009**	**3.136**	**3.045444**	
Social media use											
Posting about work	0.333	0.4	0.717	0.717	0.717	0.263	0.07	0.169	0.709	0.455	1
Consider consequences	0.333	0.2	0.217	0.217	0.066	0.079	0.751	0.443	0.113	0.268778	3
SM privacy settings	0.333	0.4	0.066	0.066	0.217	0.659	0.178	0.387	0.179	0.276111	2
CR	**0**	**0**	**0.039**	**0.039**	**0.039**	**0.034**	**0.03**	**0.019**	**0.056**	**0.028444**	
Eigen value	**3**	**3**	**3.037**	**3.037**	**3.037**	**3.032**	**3.029**	**3.018**	**3.054**	**3.027111**	
Mobile devices											
Physically secure mobile device	0.435	0.14	0.06	0.26	0.707	0.691	0.149	0.276	0.208	0.325111	2
Log into work network with mobile device	0.078	0.333	0.231	0.327	0.223	0.091	0.376	0.595	0.131	0.265	3
Send sensitive work info with mobile device	0.487	0.528	0.708	0.413	0.07	0.218	0.474	0.128	0.661	0.409667	1
CR	**0.013**	**0.056**	**0.074**	**0.056**	**0.056**	**0.056**	**0.056**	**0.06**	**0.056**	**0.053667**	
Eigen value	**3.013**	**3.054**	**3.071**	**3.054**	**3.054**	**3.054**	**3.054**	**3.006**	**3.054**	**3.046**	
Information handling											
Disposing work document	0.467	0.178	0.223	0.217	0.185	0.659	0.6	0.095	0.236	0.317778	2
Accepting USB	0.067	0.07	0.07	0.066	0.659	0.263	0.1	0.655	0.082	0.225778	3
leaving sensitive material on desk	0.467	0.751	0.707	0.717	0.156	0.079	0.3	0.25	0.682	0.456556	1

CR	0	0.03	0.056	0.039	0.03	0.034	0	0.019	0.002	0.023333	
Eigen value	3	3.029	3.054	3.037	3.029	3.032	3	3.018	3.002	3.022333	
Incident handling											
Report all incidents	0.727	0.727	0.0158	0.708	0.217	0.25	0.122	0.705	0.069	0.393422	1
Not ignore bad security behavior	0.2	0.073	0.761	0.231	0.06	0.095	0.648	0.09	0.681	0.315444	2
Report suspicious behavior	0.073	0.2	0.082	0.06	0.717	0.655	0.23	0.205	0.25	0.274667	3
CR	**0.01**	**0.01**	**0.001**	**0.074**	**0.039**	**0.019**	**0.004**	**0.019**	**0.01**	**0.020667**	
Eigen value	**3.009**	**3.009**	**3.001**	**3.071**	**3.037**	**3.018**	**3.004**	**3.018**	**3.009**	**3.019556**	
PC use											
Avoid pc use at work	0.462	0.073	0.066	0.111	0.708	0.117	0.243	0.667	0.117	0.284889	2
Avoid backing up of work info on pc	0.462	0.256	0.217	0.111	0.231	0.614	0.088	0.167	0.614	0.306667	3
Installing unverified software on pc	0.77	0.671	0.717	0.778	0.06	0.268	0.669	0.167	0.268	0.485333	1
CR	**0**	**0.019**	**0.039**	**0**	**0.074**	**0.077**	**0.07**	**0**	**0.077**	**0.039556**	
Eigen value	**3**	**3.018**	**3.037**	**3**	**3.071**	**3.074**	**3.007**	**3**	**3.074**	**3.031222**	

necessary technical help drives resilience among personnel toward information security risks including social engineering schemes. This objective can also be achieved through training and education programs to drive security consciousness among personnel.

Second, pertaining to information handling (second greatest ranked implementation factor), *leaving sensitive information* was ranked greatest, and disposing work documents being the second most important practice for consideration. An implication of this to HEIs is that to ensure sufficient security consciousness among personnel, the culture of managing organizational information in physical form also contributes to how personnel will manage electronic forms of information. This practice is vital to shape the orientation of personnel on how they organize, protect, and even dispose of documents containing all sorts of information effectively.

Regarding social media use, knowledge about *posting about work* or disclosing work information is judged the most important practice. Thus, an indication that knowledge of the information disclosure about work roles, engagements, or meetings shared on personal social media accounts is important to avoid social engineering attacks. The final hierarchical interpretation of these results is depicted in Figure 23.3 to form the resilience framework for HEIs.

Results of the expert judgments using the AHP analysis are synthesized to form the model shown in Figure 23.3. Figure 23.3 shows the most important top-level factor, top three implementation factors, and their respective practices to form the hierarchy of factors to be considered for building resilience toward social engineering schemes among HEIs.

Summarizing the framework in Figure 23.3, building the knowledge base of users should be the strategic focus. The most important knowledge aspects determined in this case are knowledge on password management, information handling, and social media use. Specific operational practices are also suggested under each implementation factor. On the whole, these recommendations are achieved through periodic education and training activities. For instance, these implementations

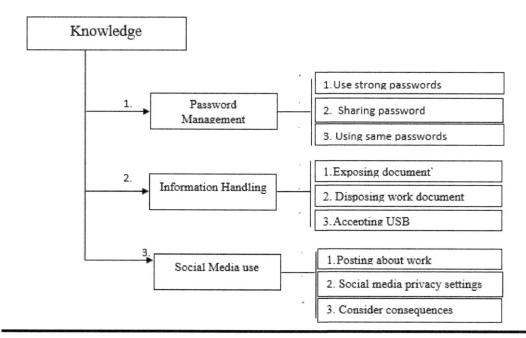

Figure 23.3 Resilience framework for social engineering schemes in HEIs.

can be incorporated into the orientation programs of newly appointed personnel, frequent email communications, updates, and circulars on developments on social engineering schemes. Alhassan and Adjei-Quaye (2017) support that knowledgeable employees show compliance with information security practices and policies than less knowledgeable ones. Similarly, knowledgeable personnel possess higher awareness and consciousness of information security risks compared with less knowledgeable ones (Karjalainen et al., 2020). Parsons et al. (2013) also perceive that awareness of information security and knowledge creation exposes users to their own weaknesses for personal remedial action. Thus, policy and practices depicted in the framework seek to increase user understanding and awareness of social engineering schemes. Thus, HEIs in their design for resilience against social engineering must focus on these factors or areas to build understanding and awareness of users. For instance, knowledge creation under social media use should focus on shaping personnel knowledge on their information disclosure behavior about their work and work environment. Similarly, under password management, strong password creation and the risks of sharing password or using the same password across multiple accounts are relevant knowledge required by personnel to reinforce their resilience toward social engineering schemes.

Conclusion

The growth in the use of information technologies in the organizational setting has also driven the likelihood of cyberattacks such as social engineering remarkably high. To this end, this examination aims to develop a resilience framework for social engineering schemes in the higher education (HEI) setting. First, it explored factors by content analyzing industry discussions on identifying and preventing social engineering schemes in the organization. Then, systems administrators were sampled from ten universities in Cyprus, and their expert judgments were obtained to prioritize which factors should be considered as the strategic and tactical focus of the organization.

Three resilience factors were identified for the strategic focus, and seven sub-factors with specific implementation were identified for actual implementation. First, knowledge acquisition is judged the most important top-level factor for strategic focus. Then password management, organizational information handling, and social media use emerged three most important tactical level factors considered for implementation. The implementation of these practices will increase user knowledge and increase their awareness and consciousness toward social engineering schemes. To this end, the goal of building resilience toward social engineering schemes becomes an all-encompassing approach within the organization to build a culture that resists the forms of social engineering schemes and other information security risks.

Practical Implications

This investigation provides insights into guidelines that allow for building professional and work environments prepared to resist information security risks; thus, this would be of immense importance to managements, institutional heads, and IT professionals who seek to insulate their systems against information security risks, particularly social engineering. Effective implementation of the findings from the proposed framework is likely to introduce some significant changes to the information security culture in the organization. However, they possess the potential of protecting organizational information assets and personnel as well. Therefore, just like the framework highlights the top three factors at each level of the hierarchies, decision-makers can implement the framework in a similar pattern and later address the other least prioritized factors. This would afford the changes to seem gradual and not too many. Thus, we believe will reduce the extent of change management required to accomplish this implementation process,

Further, the application of the AHP technique and questionnaire used for this investigation provides a standard guideline for investigating the effectiveness of phenomena and implementing specific information security practices. To this end, the proposed analysis procedure employed herein could be adopted as a self-assessment procedure for practitioners and decision-makers to assess the effectiveness of policy and organizational practices implemented for various organizational objectives. This examination identifies and empirically validates resilience factors for social engineering from interactions of experts in the information security field. Therefore, these factors offer practical insights that are applicable in another organizational context beyond HEIs. Thus, decision-makers in other service organizations, including banks, hospitals, hotels, retail outlets, can implement these factors to build resilient work environments to resist social engineering schemes.

Limitations

Like any other examination, there are some limitations that could serve as opportunities for future investigations. Foremost, the applicability of the findings is limited to the judgments of nine professionals in the field of information security administration within the HEI domain. In addition, all the expert judgments were sought from one location. Therefore, future examinations can broaden the scope of experts in terms of number and multiple locations to acquire judgments influenced by different experiences, insights, and perspectives.

References

Abawajy, J. (2014). User Preference of Cyber Security Awareness Delivery Methods. *Behaviour & Information Technology, 33*(3), 237–248.

Aldawood, H., & Skinner, G. (2018). Educating and Raising Awareness on Cyber Security Social Engineering: A Literature Review. In *International Conference on Teaching, Assessment, and Learning for Engineering (TALE)*, organized by Wollongong, NSW, Australia: IEEE. p. 62

Aldawood, H., & Skinner, G. (2020). Contemporary Cyber Security Social Engineering Solutions, Measures, Policies, Tools and Applications: A Critical Appraisal. *International Journal of Security (IJS), 10*(1), 1–15.

Alhassan, M. M., & Adjei-Quaye, A. (2017). Information Security in an Organization. *International Journal of Computing, 24*(1), 100–116. Retrieved April 11, 2019, from www.researchgate.net/publication/314086143_Information_Security_in_an_Organization

Anderson, D. R., Sweeney, D. J., Williams, T. A., Camm, J. D., & Cochran, J. J. (2018). *An Introduction to Management Science: Quantitative Approach* (15th ed.). Boston, MA: Cengage Learning.

Biancotti, C. (2017). The Price of Cyber (in) Security: Evidence from the Italian Private Sector. *Bank of Italy Occasional Paper,* (407)

Breda, F., Barbosa, H., & Morais, T. (2017). Social Engineering and Cyber Security. *Proceedings of the International Conference on Technology, Education and Development*, Valencia, 6–8 March 2017, 4204–4211. Valencia, Spain: International Academy of Technology, Education and Development. http://dx.doi.org/10.21125/inted.2017.1008

Chick, R. C., Clifton, G. T., Kaitlin, M. P., Propper, B. W., Hale, D. F., Alseidi, A. A., & Vreeland, T. J. (2020). Using Technology to Maintain the Education of Residents During the COVID-19 Pandemic. *Journal of Surgical Education, 77*(4).

Christopher, L., Choo, K. K. R., & Dehghantanha, A. (2017). Honeypots for Employee Information Security Awareness and Education Training: A Conceptual EASY Training Model. In K.-K. R. Choo & A. Dehghantanha (Eds.), *Contemporary Digital Forensic Investigations of Cloud and Mobile Applications* (pp. 110–128). Cambridge: Elsevier.

Clarke, N., Stewart, G., & Lacey, D. (2012). Death by a Thousand Facts. *Information Management & Computer Security, 20*(1), 29–38s

Creswell, J. W., & Plano Clark, V. L. (2011). *Designing and Conducting Mixed Methods Research* (2nd ed.). Los Angeles: Sage Publications.

CSO. (2019). *CSO Live Webinar: Malware is Easy to Make and Social Engineering Makes It Easy to Distribute. Can You Stop It?* Needham, MA: IDG Communications.

Daniel, S. J. (2020). Education and the COVID-19 Pandemic. *Prospects, 49*, 91–96. https://doi.org/10.1007/s11125-020-09464-3

David, J. Y., Shin, H. C., Pérez, I., Anderies, J. M., & Janssen, M. A. (2016). Learning for Resilience-based Management: Generating Hypotheses from a Behavioral Study. *Global Environment Change, 37*, 69–78.

Davidson, J. (2016). FDIC Reports five "Major Incidents" of Cybersecurity Breaches since Fall. *The Washington Post.*

Ding, Y., Meso, P., & Xu, S. (2015). *A Theoretical Model for Customizable Learning/Training to Enhance Individuals' Systems Security Behavior.* Paper presented at the 21st Americas Conference on Information Systems (AMCIS), Puerto Rico, USA.

Fatima, S., & Naima, K. (2019). Social Engineering Attacks: A Survey. *Future Internet,* (4), 89.

Furnell, S., & Vasileiou, I. (2017). Security Education and Awareness: Just Let them Burn? *Network Security, 2017*(12), 5–9.

Gallegos-Segovia, P. L., Bravo-Torres, J. F., Larios-Rosillo, V. M., Vintimilla-Tapia, P. E., Yuquilima-Albarado, I. F., & JaraSaltos, J. D. (2017). Social Engineering as an Attack Vector for Ransomware. In *2017 CHILEAN Conference on Electrical, Electronics Engineering, Information and Communication Technologies (CHILECON)* (pp. 1–6). Piscataway, NJ: IEEE.

Ghazi-Tehrani, A. K., & Pontell, H. N. (2021). Phishing Evolves: Analyzing the Enduring Cybercrime. *Victims & Offenders, 16*(3), 316–342. https://doi.org/10.1080/15564886.2020.1829224

Heartfield, R., & Loukas, G. (2015). A Taxonomy of Attacks and a Survey of Defense Mechanisms for Semantic Social Engineering Attacks. *ACM Computing Surveys, 48*(3), 1–37. https://doi.org/10.1145/2835375.

Islam, R., & Abdullah, N. A. (2006). Management Decision-Making by the Analytic Hierarchy Process: A Proposed Modification for Large-Scale Problems. *Journal for International Business and Entrepreneurship Development, 3*(1–2), 18–40.

Jelodar, H., Wang, Y., Yuan, C., Feng, X., Jiang, X., Li, Y., & Zhao, L. (2019). Latent Dirichlet allocation (LDA) and Topic Modeling: Models, Applications, a Survey. *Multimedia Tools and Applications, 78*(11), 15169–15211.

Johnston, A. C., Warkentin, M., & Siponen, M. (2015). An Enhanced Fear Appeal Rhetorical Framework: Leveraging Threats to the Human Asset through Sanctioning Rhetoric. *MIS Quarterly, 39*(1), 113–134.

Kajzer, M., D'Arcy, J., Crowell, C. R., Striegel, A., & Van Bruggen, D. (2014). An Exploratory Investigation of Message-person Congruence in Information Security Awareness Campaigns. *Computers & Security, 43*, 64–76.

Karjalainen, M., Siponen, M., & Sarker, S. (2020). Toward a Stage Theory of the Development of Employees' Information Security Behavior. *Computers & Security, 93*, 101782. https://doi.org/10.1016/j.cose.2020.101782.

Kirton, H. (2017). Cyber Security is too Important to be Left to the IT Department: As Hackers Increasingly Exploit Human Vulnerability, HR has a Vital Role to Play—Not Least in Ensuring Businesses Have the Technical Talent to Fight Back. *People Management, 42*

Kritzinger, E. (2017). Growing a Cyber-safety Culture Amongst School Learners in South Africa through Gaming. *South African Computer Journal,* (2), 16.

Krombholz, K., Hobel, H., Huber, M., & Weippl, E. (2015). Advanced Social Engineering Attacks. *Journal of Information Security and Applications, 22*, 113–122.

Lebek, B., Uffen, J., Neumann, M., Hohler, B., & Breitner, M. H. (2014). Information Security Awareness and Behavior: A Theory-based Literature Review. *Management Research Review, 37*(12), 1049–1092

Mouton, F., Leenen, L., & Venter, H. (2016). Social Engineering Attack Examples, Templates and Scenarios. *Computers & Security, 59*, 186–209

Parsons, K., McCormac, A., Pattinson, M., Butavicius, M., & Jerram, C. (2013). Phishing for the Truth: A-based Experiment of Users' Behavioural Response to Emails. In L. Janczewski, H. Wolfe, & S. Shenoi (Ed.), *Security and Privacy Protection in Information Processing Systems. IFIP Advances in Information and Communication Technology* (Vol. 405, p. 366e78). Heidelberg, Germany: Springer Berlin Heidelberg.

Parthy, P. P., & Rajendran, G. (2019). Identification and Prevention of Social Engineering Attacks on an Enterprise. In *2019 International Carnahan Conference on Security Technology (ICCST)*, pp. 1–5.

Posey, C., Roberts, T. L., Lowry, P. B., & Hightower, R. T. (2014). Bridging the Divide: A Qualitative Comparison of Information Security thought Patterns between Information Security Professionals and Ordinary Organizational Insiders. *Informtion Management, 51*(5), 551–567.

Pozo, I. D., Iturralde, M., & Restrepo, F. (2018). Social Engineering: Application of Psychology to Information Security. In *2018 6th International Conference on Future Internet of Things and Cloud Workshops*, pp. 108–114.

Rocha, F. W., & Ekstedt, M. (2016). Shaping Intention to Resist Social Engineering through Transformational Leadership, Information Security Culture and Awareness. *Computers & Security. 59*, 26–44

Rocha, F. W., Holm, H., Nohlberg, M., & Ekstedt, M. (2015b). Investigating the Correlation between Intention and Action in the Context of Social Engineering in Two Different National Cultures. In *The Hawaii International Conference on System Sciences (HICSS)* (pp. 3508–3517). Kauai, Hawaii.

Saaty, T. L. (1977). A Scaling Method for Priorities in Hierarchical Structures. *Journal of Mathematical Psychology, 15*, 234–281.

Saaty, T. L. (1980). *The Analytical Hierarchical Process*. New York: J. Wiley.

Saaty, T. L. (1994). *Fundamentals of Decision Making and Priority Theory with the Analytic Hierarchy Process*. Pittsburgh: RWS Publications.

Saaty, T. L. (2003). Decision-Making with the AHP: Why is the Principal Eigenvector Necessary. *European Journal of Operational Research, 145*(1), 85–91.

Saaty, T. L. (2008). Decision Making with the Analytic Hierarchy Process. *International Journal of Services Sciences, 1*, 83–98.

Salahdine, F., & Kaabouch, N. (2019). Social Engineering Attacks: A Survey. *Future Internet, 11*(4), 89.

Schatz, D., Bashroush, R., & Wall, J. (2017). Towards a More Representative Definition of Cyber Security. *Journal of Digital Forensics, Security and Law, 12*(2), 8

Siponen, M., Mahmood, M. A., & Pahnila, S. (2014). Employees' Adherence to Information Security Policies: An Exploratory Field Study. *Information Management, 51*, 217–224.

Solomon, S. (2016). *Do Not Be Another Statistic—How to Recognize and Prevent Social Engineering Attacks*. Atlanta, GA: BetterCloud. https://www.bettercloud.com/monitor/how-to-recognize-and-prevent-social-engineering-attacks/

Soujanya, P., Cambria, E., Howard, N., Huang, G., & Hussain, A. (2016). Fusing Audio, Visual and Textual Clues for Sentiment Analysis from Multimodal Content. *Journal of Neurocomputing, 174*, Part A. https://doi.org/10.1016/j.neucom.2015.01.095

Stiawan, D., Idris, M. Y., Abdullah, A. H., Aljaber, F., & Budiarto, R. (2017). Cyber-attack Penetration Test and Vulnerability Analysis. *International Journal of Online Engineering, 13*(1), 125–132.

Straub, D., & Welke, R. (1998). Coping with Systems Risk: Security Planning Models for Management Decision Making. *MIS Quarterly, 22*, 441–469.

Stupans, I., McGuren, T., & Babey, A. (2015). Student Evaluation of Teaching: A Study Exploring Student Rating Instrument Free-form Text Comments. *Innovative Higher Education, 41*(1), 33–42.

Susanto, H., Almunawar, M. N., & Tuan, Y. (2011). Information Security Management System Standards: A Comparative Study of the Big Five. *IJECS: International Journal of Electrical and Computer Sciences, 11*(5). www.researchgate.net/publication/228444915_Information_Security_Management_System_Standards_ A Comparative Study of the Big Five. Accessed 20 April 2019.

Szczepaniuk, E. K., Szczepaniuk, H., Rokicki, T., & Klepacki, B. (2020). Information Security Assessment in Public Administration. *Computers & Security, 90*, 101709. https://doi.org/10.1016/j.cose.2019.101709.

Talib, F., Rahman, Z., Qureshi, M. N., & Siddiqui, J. (2011). Total Quality Management and Service Quality: An Exploratory Study of Quality Management Practices and Barriers in Service Industry. *International Journal of Services and Operations Management, 10*(1), 94–118.

Tsohou, A., Karyda, M., & Kokolakis, S. (2015). Analyzing the Role of Cognitive and Cultural Biases in the Internalization of Information Security Policies: Recommendations for Information Security Awareness Programs. *Computers & Security, 52*, 128–141. https://doi.org/10.1016/j.cose.2015.04.006.

van Niekerk, B. (2017). An Analysis of Cyber-incidents in South Africa. *African Journal of Information and Communication, 20*, 113–132.

von Solms, B., & von Solms, R. (2018). Cybersecurity and Information Security: What Goes Where? *Information & Computer Security, 26*(1), 2–9.

WEF. (2019). *The Global Risks Report 2019* (14th ed.). World economic forum. Geneva. Retrieved April 13, 2020, from http://www3.weforum.org/docs/WEF_Global_Risks_Report_2019.pdf.

Authors' Profile

Divine Quase Agozie is an assistant lecturer in operations and management information systems department at the University of Ghana Business School and a final year PhD student in information systems at the Cyprus International University. Agozie's research interest concentrates on natural language processing (text mining), online privacy, and sustainable development. He has authored some scholarly articles on privacy fatigue and online engagement on social media. He also has some publications coming up on applications of text mining approaches to data from the advocacy domain for organizational communication.

Muesser Nat is an associate professor and the director of the school of applied sciences in Cyprus International University. She is also the head of department at the department of management information systems of Cyprus International University. She has conducted research in the areas of social media technology for student engagement, social media engagement, and message classification. She also has several publications in the field of educational technology and learning from different domains.

Sampson A. Edu is a final year doctoral candidate in Management Information Systems at Cyprus International University in Lefkosa, North Cyprus. He has a background in Big Data, Cloud, and IOT systems security. His research interest is consistent with his knowledge background. He is also an adjunct faculty with the department of Management information Systems at Cyprus International University.

Chapter 24

Professional Accounting Students' Intention to Continuously Use E-Learning in COVID-19 Era

Edem Emerald Sabah Welbeck, John Amoah
Kusi, and Godlove Asirifi Lartey

Contents

Introduction

Teaching and learning are experiencing rapid change and adaption due to technological advancement. The use of technological applications in distance education programs has become relevant as this mode of education takes on a global dimension. Hence, students must quickly adapt to new teaching and learning methods and environment to continue the teaching and learning process. E-learning has been seen in the literature as one significant way of continuing teaching and learning globally, without physical presence, but with the flexibility of time and access to teaching materials at any time (Raaij & Schepers, 2008).

The literature acknowledges the rapid evolution of e-learning or virtual learning in developed countries through distance learning programs (Raaij & Schepers, 2008). Students' acceptance and continuous use of the system are key determinants of the system's success. However, the same intensity of progress in education using e-learning systems cannot be said about developing countries, including Ghana, as the intention to use e-learning application is still low (Lee, 2010), in the context of the relatively low level of Internet availability and accessibility and inaccessible facilities and equipment that aid in virtual learning. Consequently, Bretz and Johnson (2000) posit that "the success of an e-learning service depends on both its initial adoption (acceptance) and its continued usage" (p. 515).

The sudden emergence of COVID-19 and its subsequent declaration as a pandemic by WHO (World Health Organization, 2020)[1] questioned the readiness of educational institutions, especially in Ghana, to continue teaching and learning via e-learning in periods of crisis when physical movement and presence was restricted. Based on this, academic institutions had to determine innovative ways of continuing the teaching and learning process without interrupting academic calendars and programs. A key option during this pandemic period was to explore e-learning as an alternative. E-learning allows for flexibility in learning at any time, access to teaching materials, and participation in class from any location (Venkatesh et al., 2000; Boateng et al., 2016). While these advantages are tangible, Chang et al. (2017) reckon that accessibility to the Internet and motivation on learners and staff are major challenges to adopting and using e-learning. On the other hand, Boateng et al. (2018) suggest that users' attitude to e-learning are dissimilar based on their experience and may change over time despite the advantages enumerated in the literature.

With trading on the financial markets opening up globally, there is an increasing need for accountants to assist in providing and interpreting accounting information that meets and reflects global standards to enable users to make informed investment decisions. Ghana is an emerging economy, and as such, the relevance of professional accounting training in the country cannot be overemphasized. There is a need to have more professionally qualified accountants to provide credible financial information to assist existing and potential investors. Therefore, the professional accounting school ran by the Institute of Chartered Accountants, Ghana (ICAG) has long been known for training students to attain professional status.

The ICAG regulates the accounting profession in Ghana. ICAG also runs a professional accounting training institution with the mandate of training professional accounting students who register and sit for the professional examination conducted by ICAG. The ICAG tuition center has been and remains the main tuition service provider for professional accounting students training in Ghana, with key players within the profession appointed to assist the students with their preparations for the professional examination. In the periods before the emergence of COVID-19, teaching and learning accounting for professional accountancy training in Ghana were mainly conducted through in-person sessions. Although there are no reported challenges in the literature (to the authors' knowledge), the emergence of the COVID-19 pandemic negatively impacted the teaching and learning process due to the restrictions on movements imposed by the Government of Ghana. To address this challenge, management of the professional accounting body in Ghana quickly registered students and teachers on the Google applications amidst some training to continue teaching and learning the professional courses. Whether these students accepted the Google technology due to the circumstances and intended to use it if offered another opportunity continually is the study's objective. The study, therefore, sought to determine if professional accounting students intend to continuously use e-learning system and which factors influence this behavior.

In the literature, studies on behavioral intentions and the use of e-learning systems have been explained using the technology acceptance models (Lee, 2010). However, empirical studies report various findings on continuous usage of e-learning systems and the factors that allow students' continuous intention to use a system with varying results (see Raaij & Schepers, 2008; Chang et al., 2017; Lee, 2010). Raaij and Schepers (2008) surveyed 45 Chinese students, analyzing their acceptance of virtual learning and determinants of their continuous usage. They situated their study in the technology acceptance models. They concluded that perceived usefulness is directly associated with virtual learning usage, while perceived ease of use and subjective norms are associated indirectly with usage. Chang et al. (2017) also surveyed students to determine the factors that determine their behavioral intention to use e-learning. Using the extended model, they posit that subjective norms associate with students' behavioral intention. These empirical studies have espoused the following factors as largely influencing behavioral intention: perceived ease of use, perceived usefulness, subjective norms, facilitating conditions, and technology. Therefore, the study sought to ascertain which factors influence professional accounting students' behavioral intention to continually use e-learning systems post COVID-19 pandemic. The study contributes to the literate by determining the key drivers of continuous usage of an e-learning system among professional accounting students in the Ghanaian context. Additionally, it is among the few studies (to the authors' knowledge) to analyze drivers of e-learning in the COVID-19 era.

The second section reviews existing literature and outlines the hypothesis, with section three focusing on measurement methods. The fourth section presents and analyzes the results, with conclusions and recommendations discussed in section five.

Theoretical Framework, Literature Review, and Hypothesis

The twenty-first century has seen much development in the level of education, with technology occupying its pivot. The literature supports the claim that the inclusion of e-learning offers users and beneficiaries the opportunity to study anytime, anywhere with few (if any) restrictions through digital resources. According to Felea et al. (2018), e-learning is a system of learning based on formalized teaching but with the aid of electronic resources. A number of studies have concluded that e-learning implementation is not simply a technological solution but a combination of many factors, be it social or behavioral (Ojwang, 2012; Salloum & Al-Emran, 2018). In developing countries, access to Internet, availability of developed content, lack of skills and infrastructure among others may hinder the acceptance of e-learning.

Studies have suggested a number of factors that influence intention to accept e-learning. These factors, according to Tarhini et al. (2013a), include social, institutional, and individual factors which have been largely explained using the technology acceptance model proposed by Venkatesh et al. (2003). These factors include perceived ease of use, perceive usefulness, facilitating conditions, computer knowledge, attitude, and social norms among others. These factors have been established in the literature as providing an adequate source of measures for students' acceptance of e-learning.

The technology acceptance model has been largely used in the literature to explain technology acceptance at the individual level, based on underpinnings from the theory of reasoned action by Fishbein and Ajzen in 1975 (Venkatesh et al., 2000, 2003). The technology acceptance model explains how two key beliefs—perceived usefulness and perceived ease of use—can affect an individual's attitude toward a system, ultimately influencing behavioral intention and actual use by the individual (Lee, 2010). Although, other models have been used to explain user acceptance of technology in the literature, technology acceptance model remains the pivot underpinning studies on technological acceptance (Van Raaij & Schepers, 2008). This study examines the applicability of the technology acceptance model for e-learning amongst professional accounting students in Ghana in the wake of the COVID-19 pandemic.

To validate empirically the technology acceptance model, Tarhini et al. (2013b) investigated students' willingness to adopt and use e-learning systems in British universities. Data were collected using a cross-sectional survey from 604 British university students who utilize web-based learning systems at Brunel University in England. The study found that perceived ease of use, perceived usefulness, social norms, quality of work life, computer self-efficacy, and facilitating conditions have significant positive influence on the adoption and usage of the Blackboard system. Their study demonstrates that e-learning implementation is not simply a technological solution but should also address individual differences by considering a set of critical success factors such as social, institutional, and individual factors.

In a different jurisdiction, Tarhini et al. (2013c) collected data from 569 undergraduate and postgraduate students in Lebanon. Using the extended technology acceptance model, the study revealed that perceived usefulness, perceived ease of use, social norms and quality of work life are significant determinants of students' behavioral intention. This study employed a multigroup analysis with a structural equation model technique based on AMOS methods.

In a related study by Alkandari (2015) that investigated the factors affecting students' acceptance and intentions to use e-learning systems in higher education in Kuwait using a cross sectional survey and interview of 336 Kuwait university students, it was reported that perceived ease of use and perceived usefulness were observed to be key factors in explaining students' attitudes toward e-learning. Perceived usefulness was found to be a more important factor than perceived ease of use in terms of attitudes of students and also a higher predictor of attitudes towards e-learning. Indeed, the study found support for relations among the constructs of the technology acceptance model through the qualitative and quantitative approaches used. The research suggested that perceived usefulness and attitudes of the students had a substantial influence on the desire to use e-learning in the future with the students' attitude exhibiting a stronger influence on the intention to use e-learning. Furthermore, the results showed that the students' intentions to use e-learning were positively correlated with their overall attitude toward e-learning.

Chen and Tseng (2012) also studied the factors that influence acceptance of web-based e-learning systems for the in-service education of junior high-school teachers in Taiwan. The study collected data from 402 junior high-school teachers in central Taiwan using a well-structure questionnaire. Using the technology acceptance model as the theoretical foundation, the results showed that motivation to use web-based e-learning and Internet self-efficacy tools were significantly positively associated with behavioral intentions regarding the use of web-based e-learning for in-service training through the factors of perceived usefulness and perceived ease of use. The factor of computer anxiety had a significantly negative effect on behavioral intentions toward web-based e-learning in-service training through the factor of perceived ease of use. Perceived usefulness and motivation to use were the primary reasons for the acceptance by junior high school teachers of web-based e-learning systems for in-service training.

In their study to assess the attitudes of lecturers in Jordanian universities toward the adoption of e-learning, Al-alak and Alnawas (2011) posited that computer anxiety is a key determinant of the intention of educators to adopt and use an e-learning system. The study questionnaires were distributed to a sample of 1000 university lecturers with an 83% response rate. Based on the findings, the study concluded that there is a negative relationship between computer anxiety and the behavioral intention to adopt an e-learning system. On the other hand, perceived ease of use, perceived usefulness, normative pressure, experience, computer knowledge, and management support were found to be positive predictors of the behavioral intention to adopt an e-learning system, with experience and computer knowledge being the strongest constructs that predict the behavioral intention to adopt an e-learning system (Figure 24.1).

Indeed, the technology acceptance model has been applied largely in perception studies on technology. However, its use in a developing country context is largely limited in the literature (to the authors' knowledge). More importantly, it has become imperative to understand the perception of professional accounting students in Ghana who for the first time are undertaking their studies through e-learning as a result of the COVID-19 pandemic. Based on the application of the technology acceptance model and prior literature, the study tested the following hypothesis:

H$_1$—*Perceived usefulness positively influences professional students' continuous usage of e-learning system*
H$_2$—*Perceived ease of use positively affects professional students' continuous usage of e-learning system*
H$_3$—*Facilitating conditions positively influences professional students' continuous usage of e-learning system*
H$_{4a}$—*Anxiety affects professional students' perceived usefulness of e-learning system*
H$_{4b}$—*Anxiety affects professional students' perceived ease of use of e-learning system*
H$_{5a}$—*Technology affects professional students' continuous usage of e-learning system*
H$_{5b}$—*Technology affects professional students' perceived usefulness of e-learning system*
H$_{5c}$—*Technology affects professional students' perceived ease of use of e-learning system*
H$_{5d}$—*Professional students' knowledge of technology influences facilitating conditions for e-learning systems*

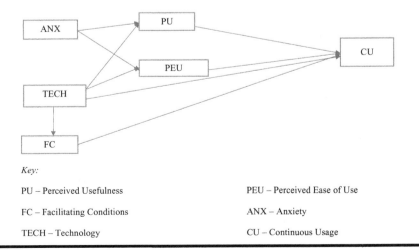

Key:

PU – Perceived Usefulness   PEU – Perceived Ease of Use

FC – Facilitating Conditions   ANX – Anxiety

TECH – Technology   CU – Continuous Usage

Figure 24.1   Conceptual model.

Methodology

Data Collection

The study sampled students enrolled in the professional accounting study program run by the Institute of Chartered Accountants, Ghana (ICAG), who were preparing for the May 2020 professional examinations. As a result of COVID-19, the government issued directives banning public gatherings for almost three months (March to May 2020). This created anxiety among the general student body who had a month to complete their physical teaching contact hours. There was, therefore, the need to use e-learning application to complete the module for the professional examinations that had been postponed from May to July 2020 as a result of the outbreak of COVID-19.

The professional students were chosen because this is the first time their teaching was to be completed using e-learning. Moreover, the students have been used to physical contact with lecturers and solving questions on the white board for easy understanding. Moreover, the focus on the students at the professional training school of ICAG is because this training institute is the oldest accountancy training institution with the highest student population.

The e-learning application used was Google suite (https://gsuite.google.com/). This application is relatively new to the students as before the outbreak of COVID-19, all teaching and learning was via physical interaction. All the respondents were students preparing to take the next accounting professional examination and had at least one more examination to write after the July examinations. All the students were taken through a training session on the usage of Google suite applications. Subsequently, the entire lectures and teaching were delivered through Google meet and teaching materials as well as assignments shared through Google classroom.

The questionnaire was administered through Google forms and the link sent to the students at the end of the online teaching period via a WhatsApp platform. The questionnaire had two parts. The first part was on the demographics (i.e., gender, age, professional level of examination, and computer knowledge of the respondents). The second part had questions on the constructs measuring the perceptions of students to continuously use Google meet and Google classroom as e-learning application after the examinations they were preparing for.

The Measures

The constructs were measured using a seven-point Likert scale with one (1) being strongly disagree and seven (7) being strongly agree. For the latent variables, the study modified various existing scales as deemed suitable. The outbreak of COVID-19 pandemic was unexpected and an unforeseen issue. It generated a lot of fear and panic among the students who were feverishly preparing for the examination through physical contact with their lecturers. The anxiety was about how learning especially accounting subjects could be done via applications on computers. The study therefore adopted the four-item scale by Raaij and Schepers (2008) to measure ANXIETY.

For perceived usefulness, the study used six-point scale by Venkatesh et al. (2003), while the four-point scale of Mohammadyari and Singh (2015) was adopted for perceived ease of use. The study also considered the perceived knowledge of technology of students that may enhance the e-learning technology and assessed six items from the scale of Selim (2007) to measure knowledge of technology. Five-point scale by Venkatesh et al. (2003) was used to measure facilitating conditions. For the dependent variable, the continuous intention to use, the study used the scale of Mohammadyari and Singh (2015) and Bhattacherjee (2001) and added a question bordering on usage beyond the end of the pandemic.

Descriptive Analysis

In all, 121 students responded to the questionnaire. Of the 121 respondents, five (5) question-naires were excluded from the analysis because the questions were largely incomplete. Of the 116 remaining respondents, the majority were male representing 59% (68) while females constituted 41% (48) of the sample. The majority of the respondents had first degree and were between the ages of 18 and 35 years. 54% were in level two of the professional examinations and 78% had fair (intermediate) expertise in technology. The responses to the questionnaire were analyzed using the partial least square (PLS) structural equation modelling technique. The PLS model was used in the analysis of the data because it helps in explaining both direct and indirect relationships between dependent and independent variables (Kwakye et al., 2018). Also, the PLS model does not require a large sample size and as such better handles data that are not normally distributed (Kwakye et al., 2018). Given the sample selected for the study, it was more appropriate to use the PLS technique for the analysis of the data collected.

The demographic profile of respondents has been presented in Table 24.1.

Table 24.1   Demographic Profile of Respondents

	Summary	*Frequency*	*Percentage (%)*
Gender	Male	68	59%
	Female	48	41%
Highest Qualification	Senior High	21	18%
	HND	6	5%
	Undergraduate	58	50%
	Postgraduate	31	27%
Age	18–25	49	42%
	26–35	52	45%
	36–45	10	9%
	46–60	5	4%
	Above 60	0	0%
Professional Exam level	Level 1	14	12%
	Level 2	63	54%
	Level 3	39	34%
Level of IT expertise	Novice	11	9%
	Intermediate	90	78%
	Expert	15	13%
(N=116)			

Data Analysis

Measurement

The constructs were reflective in nature, allowing for reliability, convergence and discriminant validity tests suggested by Hair et al. (2019) to be undertaken. Initially, indicator loadings were examined as a first step in the measurement process with most of the constructs loading above 0.70 as recommended by Hair et al. (2019). Although Hair et al. (2019) recommends 0.7, studies by Lee (2010), Al-alak and Alnawas (2011) suggest acceptable factor loadings above 0.50. The highest factor loading was 0.956 (anxiety), with the least loading being 0.661 (facilitating conditions). This suggests that the indicators explain more than fifty percent (50%) of the constructs and therefore reliably explain the constructs. Subsequently, the study tests for composite reliability of the constructs. Hair et al. (2019) suggest values ranging from 0.70 to 0.90 as "satisfactory to good" (p. 8) benchmarks to test construct composite reliability, while values above 0.95 represent redundant constructs. From the analysis, all the constructs were good per Hair et al.'s (2019) description except that of PU which had a composite reliability score of 0.954, slightly above the benchmark. According to Diamantopoulos et al. (2012), values from 0.95 suggest reduced construct validity. However, Chang et al. (2017) suggest values above 0.7 are appropriate with no upper limit.

In assessing for Average Variance Extracted (AVE), acceptable benchmark is 0.5 and above for each construct (Fornell & Larcker, 1981; Hair et al., 2006, 2019). All the constructs had values above the recommended threshold of 0.50 and above.

The Fornell and Larcker's (1981) test has been used to test the discriminant validity of the constructs. This test examines the extent to which indicators and their constructs differ from other indicators and constructs. This study tested the discriminant validity of the constructs using the Heterotrait–Monotrait (HTMT) ratio test suggested by Henseler et al. (2015). Hair et al. (2019) describe HTMT as the "mean value of the item correlations across constructs relative to the (geometric) mean of the average correlations for the items measuring the same construct" (p. 9). The HTMT test confirms the questionnaire has construct validity as all the values are below the 0.90 threshold. These measurement tests are reported in Tables 24.2 and 24.3 and are within acceptable standards espoused in the literature.

Model Fitness Test

The study reports both the saturated and estimated model, with the estimated model suggested as the "most reasonable choice". Hair et al. (2017) caution researchers to be careful in reporting and using model fit suggesting more studies are required to substantiate the benchmark values. For the current study, a number of diagnostic checks were conducted to assess the models' goodness of fit.

Standardized root mean square residual (SRMR), which is the difference between the observed correlation and the model implied correlation matrix, was calculated for both models. The SRMR was 0.08 for the saturated model and 0.10 for the estimated model. The model had a normed fix index (NFI) of 0.818 and 0.806 for the saturated model and estimated model respectively. Based on the results of the diagnostic checks, the continuous intention to use model is fit (see Cuganesan et al., 2018; Wibowo, 2017; Henseler et al., 2015; Hu & Bentler, 1999; Lohmöller, 1989).

Structural Model

The study examined the causal relationship between perceived ease of use, perceived usefulness, technology, anxiety, facilitating conditions and professional accounting students' intention to

Table 24.2 Measurement Model

Construct	Scale Item	Factor Loading	Composite Reliability	Average Variance Explained (AVE)
Anxiety	ANX1	0.956	0.894	0.810
	ANX4	0.840		
Continuous intention to use (CU)	CU1	0.933	0.934	0.779
	CU2	0.924		
	CU3	0.854		
	CU4	0.815		
Facilitating conditions (FC)	FC2	0.661	0.783	0.650
	FC4	0.929		
Perceived ease of use (PEU)	PEU1	0.798	0.922	0.747
	PEU2	0.888		
	PEU3	0.901		
	PEU4	0.865		
Perceived usefulness (PU)	PU1	0.916	0.954	0.874
	PU5	0.949		
	PU6	0.939		
Technology (TECH)	TECH3	0.900	0.890	0.669
	TECH4	0.775		
	TECH5	0.786		
	TECH6	0.805		

Table 24.3 Heterotrait–Monotrait (HTMT) Ratio

	ANX	CU	FC	PEU	PU
ANX					
CU	**0.227**				
FC	0.363	**0.636**			
PEU	0.367	0.624	**0.560**		
PU	0.321	0.816	0.686	**0.685**	
TECH	0.405	0.544	0.705	0.666	**0.697**

continuously engage in e-learning post COVID-19. Table 24.4 shows the standardized path coefficients and significance. Of the nine hypotheses tested, five were supported with p-values <0.05. The R^2 explains the explanatory power of the independent constructs to the dependent construct. Henseler et al. (2009) and Hair et al. (2011) document benchmarks as substantial (>0.75), moderate (>0.50), and weak (>0.25) although Cohen (2013) and Hair et al. (2011) suggest lower values may be acceptable depending on variables. All the constructs explain 59% of the construct continuous use (R^2 =0.59), while PU explains 40% of professional students' intention to continuously use e-learning, with perceived ease of use explaining 36% explanatory powers and technology having an R^2 of 0.25. From the benchmark by Hair et al. (2011), continuous intention of the professional accounting students to use e-learning systems has moderate explanatory power while perceived usefulness, perceived ease of use and knowledge in technology have weak predictive value. These are all within acceptable benchmarks found in earlier literature (see Cohen, 2013; Martins & Kellermanns, 2004).

Next, the study assessed the model's predictive accuracy (Q_2) using the blindfolding procedure. Hair et al. (2019) outline benchmarks for assessing the predictive relevance of the model's path, i.e., values higher than 0, 0.25, and 0.50 suggest small, medium, and large predictive values respectively. From the data analyzed, Q_2 for continuous intention to use, perceived ease of use and perceived usefulness have medium predictive values with knowledge in technology having a low predictive relevance. Anxiety and facilitating conditions have no predictive relevance based on the data analyzed (Figure 24.2).

VIF values for the constructs are all below the ideal value of 3 suggested by Hair et al. (2019). For the structural path, the path PU–CU shows a positive and significant p-value (p=0.000). This has been previously affirmed by Lee (2010). Students' perceived ease of use of an e-learning system also significantly and positively affects their intention to continuously use the e-learning system (p=0.037). Similarly, the paths TECH–PEU and TECH–PU show a positive and significant relation at 1% (p=0.000). This demonstrates that users' ability to use the technology applicable in any e-learning application positively influences their perceived ease of use and perceived usefulness of the e-learning system. Despite this positive relationship, knowledge in technology does not directly influence students' intention to continuously use e-learning application system. Rather, students' knowledge in technology positively and significantly influences facilitating conditions for e-learning system (p=0.000).

Table 24.4 Predictive Relevance

	SSO	*SSE*	*Q^2 (=1-SSE/SSO)*
ANX	232.000	232.000	
CU	464.000	259.046	0.442
FC	232.000	232.000	
PEU	464.000	346.494	0.253
PU	348.000	228.022	0.345
TECH	464.000	392.894	0.153

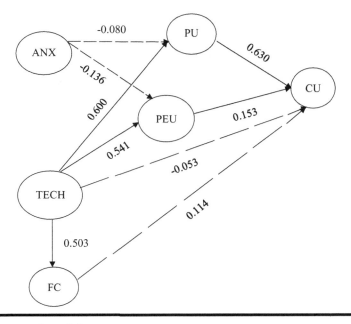

Figure 24.2 Structural model.

Discussion

This study partially validates the technology acceptance model for e-learning amongst professional accounting students in Ghana. It finds that perceived ease of use, perceived usefulness and knowledge in technology directly influence students' intention to continuously use e-learning applications in Ghana.

The results from the bootstrapping analysis are presented in Table 24.5. The results reveal that perceived usefulness is the strongest predictor of professional accounting students' intention to continuously use an e-learning system, followed by perceived ease of use of the system. The results support earlier studies by Alkandari (2015), Taylor and Todd (1995a, 1995b) who found the relation between perceived usefulness and continuous intention to use an e-learning system more prominent than the PEU-CU link. This suggests that professional accounting students in Ghana have a strong belief in the Google suite application to meet their teaching requirements and thus are willing to continuously use it in the event of continuous lockdown. Consequently, it is likely that the professional students realized most academic institutions had begun to consider and use e-learning for the continuation of teaching and learning. Again, it is likely the Google suite application is perceived easy to navigate for purposes of completing teaching and learning schedules. Indeed, the Google suite was recommended by management of the school for the purpose, supporting Lee's (2010) position that these two constructs are "cognitive beliefs" usually obtained from external sources and by reference. Based on the technology acceptance model concept, professional accounting students seem to be highly willing to continuously use the e-learning tool, suggesting a likely preference for e-learning perhaps more than the physical experience. This is possible as most students are working and have to travel long hours through traffic to get to the school for lectures. This may be a better option as lectures may be recorded for future reference by these students.

Table 24.5 Results from Bootstrapping Analysis

Hypotheses	Path Coefficient	P-values
H1: PU → CU	0.630	**0.000**
H2: PEU → CU	0.153	**0.037**
H3: FC → CU	0.114	0.173
H4a: ANX → PU	-0.080	0.261
H4b: ANX → PEU	-0.136	0.120
H5a: TECH → CU	-0.053	0.434
H5b: TECH → PU	0.600	**0.000**
H5c: TECH → PEU	0.541	**0.000**
H5d: TECH → FC	0.503	**0.000**

The study did not find a positive and significant relationship between the other two constructs—facilitating conditions and knowledge in technology and continuous intention to use. Primarily, perhaps, the inadequate technological infrastructure at the school seems to inform their opinion. Aside from this, the knowledge of technology was not a significant factor in informing their continuous use of the e-learning application. Indeed, knowledge of a technological tool or implementing an e-learning application may not be adequate for effective e-learning experience. As suggested by Tarhini et al. (2013b), e-learning implementation should also address individual differences by considering a set of critical success factors such as social, institutional, and individual factors within the learning environment.

As indicated in Table 24.5, the study found TECH-PEU and TECH-PU link to be positive and significant, suggesting that professional students perceive that their knowledge of technology influenced their perception and cognitive belief about the e-learning application. Their knowledge of technology may have assisted them in adapting to and using the e-learning application and resources easily despite the infrastructure deficit. Again, it seems their focus was on access to the requisite study material and on understanding for the purpose of writing the examination for that period. The study could not find support for anxiety as a predictor of perceived usefulness and perceived ease of use, suggesting that despite the fact that COVID-19 pandemic abruptly curtailed physical teaching and learning and in spite of the inadequate infrastructure, skill and unreliable Internet connectivity, the professional accounting students were not anxious about the challenges of virtual learning and the e-learning application. This result is contrary to Chen and Tseng (2012), which found a negative and significant relation through perceived ease of use. Perhaps anxiety did not impact negatively because of the professional students' knowledge of technology and the noncomplex nature of the e-learning application used.

Conclusion

The objective of this study was to determine which factors influence professional accounting students' intention to continuously use e-learning application in the wake of the COVID-19 pandemic. The study found that two key constructs—perceived usefulness and perceived ease of use—were significant and directly influenced professional accounting students' intention to continuously use e-learning applications in Ghana. Again, the study found that knowledge in technology positively impacted perceived usefulness and perceived ease of use but not directly on continuous intention to use. The direct effect of perceived usefulness on continuous usage suggests that students' likely acceptance of the e-learning application and their willingness to use it for learning are perhaps based on the belief that it serves their learning purpose. For perceived usefulness, students perhaps believe they can easily navigate the e-learning application. This is probably due to their knowledge of technology, which positively and significantly affects perceived usefulness and ease of use.

Implications and Recommendations for Future Studies

The study contributes to the literature for being among the few to determine the drivers of continuous intention to use e-learning systems among professional accountancy students as the COVID-19 pandemic disrupted physical teaching. In the era of COVID-19, when the government-imposed restrictions on social interactions to control the spread of the virus, the adoption of e-learning to ensure students were able to learn without borders is imperative. For the management of institutions of higher learning, including professional training institutions, this study will enable them to pay attention to students' requirements for the e-learning application to be user friendly and meet their learning needs if the virtual learning is to be sustained. The results of the study point out that the professional accounting students' intention to continue to use e-learning is influenced by how they perceive the e-learning system to be easy to use. Since the results of the study also suggest knowledge in technology drives students' perceived ease of use and perceived usefulness of e-learning systems, it is imperative for management of institutions of higher learning to organize continuous training targeted at improving the digital literacy of students to enhance technological literacy of these students over time. Aside from training, the e-learning infrastructure should be interactive and meet all user needs.

Aside from this, educators may also have to consider innovating creative ways of teaching online, incorporating curriculum and quizzes suitable for e-learning. Policymakers at the national level may consider investing in the needed e-learning infrastructure required for effective teaching and learning aside from providing the required training for students to navigate the e-learning application easily. For system designers, the study would enable them to improve on e-learning applications to make it user friendly for enhanced learning and make teaching more fun. Finally, this study may drive a national policy that allows more students to be enrolled in e-learning programs in institutions of higher learning given the limited physical facilities available in Ghana's institutions of higher learning. It may assist the government in achieving its Millennium Development Goal for education as the objective of "education anytime anywhere" is achieved through e-learning platforms. The use of e-learning systems will afford people, ho, hitherto, could not enroll for any further education because of the need to be physically present in classrooms, the opportunity to be educated. Given the relevance of e-learning, management of higher institutions should consider permanently introducing programs that will be run mainly via e-learning even in periods after the COVID-19 pandemic to afford students across the country access to higher education without necessarily being physically present in these institutions.

The study was conducted during the COVID-19 pandemic lockdown period in Ghana. Thus, other studies can focus on other constructs such as social and environmental factors that possibly could influence continuance intention. A longitudinal study looking at changes in behavioral intention over time can establish the most prevalent construct in ensuring continual usage. Again, future studies may consider university students for a larger sample size. System designers should evaluate how easy it is for users to use e-learning applications and make updates where required. Such systems could also be segmented based on the level of technological knowledge of users.

Note

1. www.who.int/director-general/speeches/detail/who-director-general-s-opening-remarks-at-the-media-briefing-on-covid-19---11-march-2020

References

Al-alak, B. A., & Alnawas, I. A. (2011). Measuring the Acceptance and Adoption of E-Learning by Academic Staff. *Knowledge Management & E-Learning: An International Journal*, *3*(2), 201–221.

Alkandari, B. (2015). *An Investigation of the Factors Affecting Students' Acceptance and Intention to Use E-Learning Systems at Kuwait University: Developing a Technology Acceptance Model in E-Learning Environments*. Doctoral dissertation. Cardiff Metropolitan University.

Bhattacherjee, A. (2001). Understanding Information Systems Continuance: An Expectation Confirmation Model. *MIS Quarterly*, 351–370.

Boateng, R., Heeks, R., Molla, A., & Hinson, R. (2008). E-Commerce and Socio-Economic Development: Conceptualizing the Link. *Internet Research*, *18*(5), 562–92.

Bretz, R., & Johnson, L. (2000). An Innovative Pedagogy for Teaching and Evaluating Computer Literacy. *Information Technology and Management*, *1*(4), 283–292.

Chang, C. T., Hajiyev, J., & Su, C. R. (2017). Examining the Students' Behavioral Intention to Use E-Learning in Azerbaijan? The General Extended Technology Acceptance Model for E-Learning Approach. *Computers & Education*, *111*, 128–143.

Chen, H. R., & Tseng, H. F. (2012). Factors That Influence Acceptance of Web-Based E-Learning Systems for the in-Service Education of Junior High School Teachers in Taiwan. *Evaluation and Program Planning*, *35*(3), 398–406.

Cohen, J. (2013). *Statistical Power Analysis for the Behavioral Sciences*. Burlington: Elsevier Science.

Cuganesan, S., Steele, C., & Hart, A. (2018). How Senior Management and Workplace Norms Influence Information Security Attitudes and Self-Efficacy. *Behaviour & Information Technology*, *37*(1), 50–65.

Diamantopoulos, A., Sarstedt, M., Fuchs, C., Wilczynski, P., & Kaiser, S. (2012). Guidelines for Choosing between Multi-Item and Single-Item Scales for Construct Measurement: A Predictive Validity Perspective. *Journal of the Academy of Marketing Science*, *40*(3), 434–449.

Felea, M., Albăstroiu, I., Vasiliu, C., & Georgescu, B. (2018). E-Learning in Higher Education: Exploratory Survey Among Romanian Students. In *The International Scientific Conference eLearning and Software for Education* (Vol. 4, pp. 157–162). " Carol I" National Defence University. Bucharest, Romania: Advanced Distributed Learning Romania Association under the patronage of Carol I National Defence University and European Security and Defence College (ESDC).

Fornell, C., & Larcker, D. F. (1981). Structural Equation Models with Unobservable Variables and Measurement Error: Algebra and Statistics. *Journal of Marketing Research*, *18*(3), 382–388.

Hair, J. F., Black, W. C., Babin, B. J., Anderson, R. E., & Tatham, R. (2006). *Multivariate Data Analysis* (6th ed.). Upper Saddle River, NJ: Pearson University Press.

Hair Jr, J. F., Hult, G. T. M., Ringle, C., & Sarstedt, M. (2017). *A Primer on Partial Least Squares Structural Equation Modeling (PLS-SEM)* (2nd ed.). Thousand Oaks, CA: Sage Publications.

Hair, J. F., Ringle, C. M., & Sarstedt, M. (2011). PLSSEM: Indeed a Silver Bullet. *Journal of Marketing Theory and Practice*, *19*(2), 139–152. https://doi.org/10.2753/MTP1069-6679190202

Hair, J. F., Risher, J. J., Sarstedt, M., & Ringle, C. M. (2019). When to Use and How to Report the Results of PLS-SEM. *European Business Review*, *31*(1), 2–24.

Henseler, J., Ringle, C. M., & Sarstedt, M. (2015). A New Criterion for Assessing Discriminant Validity in Variance-Based Structural Equation Modeling. *Journal of the Academy of Marketing Science*, *43*(1), 115–135.

Henseler, J., Ringle, C. M., & Sinkovics, R. R. (2009). The Use of Partial Least Squares Path Modeling in International Marketing. In R. R. Sinkovics & P. N. Ghauri (Eds.), *New Challenges to International Marketing* (Advances in International Marketing, Vol. 20) (pp. 277–319). Bingley: Emerald Group Publishing Limited. https://doi.org/10.1108/S1474-7979(2009)0000020014

Hu, L. T., & Bentler, P. M. (1999). Cutoff Criteria for Fit Indexes in Covariance Structure Analysis: Conventional Criteria Versus New Alternatives. *Structural Equation Modeling: A Multidisciplinary Journal*, *6*(1), 1–55.

Kwakye, T. O., Welbeck, E. E., Owusu, G. M. Y., & Anokye, F. K. (2018). Determinants of Intention to Engage in Sustainability Accounting & Reporting (SAR): The Perspective of Professional Accountants. *International Journal of Corporate Social Responsibility*, *3*(1), 1–13.

Lee, M. C. (2010). Explaining and Predicting Users' Continuance Intention Toward E-Learning: An Extension of the Expectation—Confirmation Model. *Computers & Education*, *54*(2), 506–516.

Lohmöller, J. B. (1989). *Latent Variable Path Modeling with Partial Least Squares*. Heidelberg: Physica-Verlag.

Martins, L. L., & Kellermanns, F. W. (2004). A Model of Business School Students' Acceptance of a Web-Based Course Management System. *Academy of Management Learning & Education*, *3*(1), 7–26.

Mohammadyari, S., & Singh, H. (2015). Understanding the Effect of E-Learning on Individual Performance: The Role of Digital Literacy. *Computers & Education*, *82*, 11–25.

Ojwang, C. O. (2012). *E-Learning Readiness and E-Learning Adoption Among Public Secondary Schools in Kisumu County, Kenya*. Doctoral dissertation.

Salloum, S. A., & Al-Emran, M. (2018). Factors Affecting the Adoption of E-Payment Systems by University Students: Extending the TAM with Trust. *International Journal of Electronic Business*, *14*(4), 371–390.

Selim, H. M. (2007). E-Learning Critical Success Factors: An Exploratory Investigation of Student Perceptions. *International Journal of Technology Marketing*, *2*(2), 157–182.

Tarhini, A., Hone, K. S., & Liu, X. (2013a). Factors Affecting Students' Acceptance of E-Learning Environments in Developing Countries: A Structural Equation Modeling Approach. *International Journal of Information and Education Technology*, *3*(1), 54–59.

Tarhini, A., Hone, K. S., & Liu, X. (2013b). User Acceptance Towards Web-Based Learning Systems: Investigating the Role of Social, Organizational and Individual Factors in European Higher Education. *Procedia Computer Science*, *17*, 189–197.

Tarhini, A., Hone, K. S., & Liu, X. (2013c). Extending the TAM Model to Empirically Investigate the Students' Behavioral Intention to Use E-Learning in Developing Countries. In *2013 Science and Information Conference* (pp. 732–737). Piscataway, NJ: IEEE.

Taylor, S., & Todd, P. A. (1995a). Assessing IT Usage: The Role of Prior Experience. *MIS Quarterly*, 561–570.

Taylor, S., & Todd, P. A. (1995b). Understanding Information Technology Usage: A Test of Competing Models. *Information Systems Research*, *6*(2), 144–176.

Van Raaij, E. M., & Schepers, J. J. (2008). The Acceptance and Use of a Virtual Learning Environment in China. *Computers & Education*, *50*(3), 838–852.

Venkatesh, V., Morris, M. G., & Ackerman, P. L. (2000). A Longitudinal Field Investigation of Gender Differences in Individual Technology Adoption Decision-Making Processes. *Organizational Behavior and Human Decision Processes*, *83*(1), 33–60.

Venkatesh, V., Morris, M. G., Davis, G. B., & Davis, F. D. (2003). User Acceptance of Information Technology: Toward a Unified View. *MIS Quarterly*, 425–478.

Wibowo, M. A. (2017). Model of Construction Waste Management Using AMOS-SEM for Indonesian Infrastructure Projects. In *MATEC Web of Conferences* (Vol. 138, p. 05005). Les Ulis, France: EDP Sciences.

World Health Organization. (2020, March 11). *WHO Director-General's Opening Remarks at the Media Briefing on COVID-19–11 March 2020*. World Health Organization. www.who.int/director-general/speeches/detail/who-director-general-s-opening- remarks-at-the-media-briefing-on-COVID-19-11-march-2020

Authors' Profile

Edem Emerald Sabah Welbeck is a chartered accountant by profession. She is also a lecturer and researcher. She lectures at the University of Ghana Business School and Wisconsin International University College on Auditing and Assurance, Corporate Reporting, and Accounting for Managerial Decision-Making at the undergraduate, graduate and professional levels. She previously worked with the biggest indigenous bank in Ghana—Ghana Commercial Bank—in various capacities. Her research interest is in sustainability performance and reporting, accounting education, corporate governance, and auditing.

John Amoah Kusi is a chartered accountant and a professional tax consultant. He holds a master of philosophy degree in accounting from University of Ghana. His research interests are corporate governance, corporate social responsibility reporting, and accounting education.

Godlove Lartey Asirifi holds a Bachelor's degree in business administration (accounting option) and master of philosophy degree in finance from the University of Ghana. He is a researcher, tutor and professional accountant. He contributed immensely to social and community health development in Ghana (Penyi, Kibi, Navrongo, Gomoa Dego) during his days as Country Director of Proffer Aid International Foundation. He is a result-oriented individual committed to continuous self-development.

Index

Note: Page locators in *italics* indicate a figure and page numbers in **bold** indicate a table on the corresponding page.

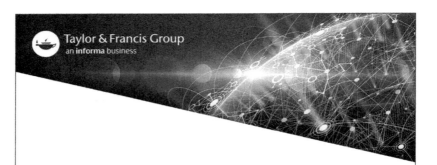

Printed in the United States
by Baker & Taylor Publisher Services